ADDITIONAL PRAISE FOR *ALL THE GREAT PRIZES*

"Utterly fantastic . . . the definitive portrait of a man whose life spanned a crucial era in American history—and whose work helped to define that era. A genius of animation works on every page. It's the author's best book."

—*Open Letters Monthly*

"Given that John Hay's public career was bookended by his service to Lincoln and Roosevelt, it seems surprising that this is the first biography written about him in 80 years. Thanks to Taliaferro's skillful work, it seems unlikely that another will be needed for a while."

—*The Dallas Morning News*

"A valuable reassessment of an underestimated politician and diplomat."

—*The Economist*

"Hay is lucky to have such an accomplished biographer. *All the Great Prizes* is a pleasure—well-written, well-researched, the worthy story of a worthy man who served two of the most interesting of U.S. presidents."

—*The Concord Monitor*

"This is a great biography of a great American."

—*Washington Independent Review of Books*

"This book . . . brings a fascinating historical figure to greater prominence. *All the Great Prizes* shows how central John Hay—often thought of as peripheral—was in preparing America for its 20th-century emergence as a great world power."

—*Pittsburgh Tribune*

"Taliaferro's textured portrait exemplifies the better productions of the biographical craft."

—*Booklist*

"Taliaferro's skillful, admiring biography (the first since 1934) brings Hay vividly to life by setting him among family, friends (many of them well-known figures in their own right), and the well-heeled political circles in Washington, D.C., and elsewhere, in which Hay moved with ease."

—*Publishers Weekly*

"The best life of Hay that we have and a persuasive argument for taking another look at the life of a career public servant"

—*Kirkus Reviews*

"Taliaferro takes the reader on an intimate historical journey through the public and personal lives of Hay. . . . Worthy as the most comprehensive biography of Hay to date."

—*Library Journal*

"John Hay has long been one of those remarkable American figures who hide in plain historical sight—until now. With insight and eloquence, John Taliaferro has brought Hay into the foreground, telling a remarkable story remarkably well."

—Jon Meacham, author of *Thomas Jefferson: The Art of Power*

"John Hay began his career as private secretary to Abraham Lincoln, writing many of Lincoln's letters, and ended it as secretary of state in the administrations of William McKinley and Theodore Roosevelt, responsible for many of their foreign-policy achievements. He was at the bedside of Lincoln and of McKinley as each president lay dying of an assassin's bullet. John Taliaferro's absorbing biography of this notable author, diplomat, and *bon vivant* who knew most of the important people of his time fully measures up to the significance of its subject."

—James M. McPherson, author of *Battle Cry of Freedom*

"John Hay is one of the seminal statesmen in American history. *All the Great Prizes* is the grand book he so richly deserves."

—Douglas G. Brinkley, author of *Cronkite*

ALSO BY JOHN TALIAFERRO

In a Far Country: The True Story of a Mission, a Marriage,
a Murder, and the Remarkable Reindeer Rescue of 1898

Great White Fathers: The Story of the Obsessive Quest
to Create Mount Rushmore

Tarzan Forever: The Life of Edgar Rice Burroughs

Charles M. Russell: The Life and Legend
of America's Cowboy Artist

The Life of
JOHN HAY,

from

LINCOLN *to* ROOSEVELT

ALL

– the –

GREAT

PRIZES

JOHN TALIAFERRO

SIMON & SCHUSTER PAPERBACKS

New York London Toronto Sydney New Delhi

In Memory of

John Christopher Taliaferro III (1916–2008)

and

Audrey Wilson Taliaferro (1920–2010)

Simon & Schuster Paperbacks
A Division of Simon & Schuster, Inc.
1230 Avenue of the Americas
New York, NY 10020

First Simon & Schuster paperback edition May 2014

SIMON & SCHUSTER PAPERBACKS and colophon are registered trademarks
of Simon & Schuster, Inc.

For information about special discounts for bulk purchases,
please contact Simon & Schuster Special Sales at
1-866-506-1949 or business@simonandschuster.com.

The Simon & Schuster Speakers Bureau can bring authors
to your live event. For more information or to book an event,
contact the Simon & Schuster Speakers Bureau at
1-866-248-3049 or visit our website at www.simonspeakers.com.

Designed by Joy O'Meara

Manufactured in the United States of America

10   9   8   7   6   5   4   3   2   1

The Library of Congress has cataloged the hardcover edition as follows:

Taliaferro, John, 1952–
    All the great prizes : the life of John Hay, from Lincoln to Roosevelt /
John Taliaferro. — 1st Simon & Schuster hardcover ed.
        p.   cm.
    Includes bibliographical references and index.
    1. Hay, John, 1838–1905.   2. United States—Politics and government—
1861–1865.   3. United States—Foreign relations—1865–1921.   4. Lincoln,
Abraham, 1809–1865—Friends and associates.   5.   Statesmen—United States—
Biography.   I. Title.
        E664.H41T35 2013
        973.7092—dc23
        [B]   2012032847

ISBN 978-1-4165-9730-8
ISBN 978-1-4165-9734-6 (pbk)
ISBN 978-1-4165-9741-4 (ebook)

Contents

I know death is the common lot, and what is universal ought not to be deemed a misfortune; and yet—instead of confronting it with dignity and philosophy, I cling instinctively to life and the things of life, as eagerly as if I had not had my chance at happiness & gained nearly all the great prizes.

—JOHN MILTON HAY, 1905

CHAPTER I

Oughtnottobiography

The White House would never be the same.

To those who worked there, it was an "ill-kept, inconvenient, and dirty old rickety concern," made even shabbier by the heavy footfalls and hard use of civil war. But for all its disarray, it had been John Hay's home. For four years he and his fellow private secretary, John George Nicolay, had shared a bedroom across the hall from the president's office, and throughout the war no one had lived more intimately with the Lincolns; no one had witnessed more closely the toll of work and worry and death—of a son and of three quarters of a million of the nation's sons— upon Abraham Lincoln.

To be sure, not every day had been dark, and Lincoln's spirit had not always been so somber. On the occasions, spontaneous and evanescent, when Lincoln's native humor had shown forth, it radiated most directly on the two secretaries—Nicolay an earnest twenty-nine and Hay a callow twenty-two when they first accompanied the president from Springfield in 1861. With unconditional devotion and respect, Hay and Nicolay had taken to calling their Zeus-like employer "the Tycoon" or "the Ancient."

But now in May of 1865 they too were a good deal more ancient. And

Lincoln was dead. A month after the assassination, the White House seemed like a corpse itself, laid out in the clothes of a stranger.

Of the two secretaries, Hay had been struck more bluntly by the murder. Nicolay was away from Washington on April 14, when the president and Mrs. Lincoln went to Ford's Theatre. Hay had remained at the White House with Robert Lincoln, the president's eldest son. Over the past five years, Robert had spent little time with his father—off at boarding school in 1859 as Lincoln prepared to run for the presidency; away at college in 1860 when Lincoln won his party's nomination and then the national election; gone for nearly the entire Civil War. After Robert's graduation in 1864, his father found him a place, out of harm's way, on the staff of Ulysses S. Grant, and Robert had been with Grant at Appomattox when Robert E. Lee gave up his sword. Robert and John Hay had known each other for quite a while, and there could easily have been cause for awkwardness between them. Hay in many respects was closer to the president, knew him better than did the twenty-one-year-old captain home from the war. But to the credit of both, there was no uneasiness at all.

On that fateful Good Friday, the two young men were upstairs in the White House, catching up, when a doorman burst in with the news, "[S]omething happened to the President." Robert and Hay hurried by carriage to the boardinghouse where Lincoln lay unconscious with a bullet through his brain. There they remained throughout the night, as doctors probed and Mrs. Lincoln sobbed. They were at the president's bedside at seven the following morning, when he stopped breathing. Indelibly, Hay remembered Secretary of War Edwin Stanton uttering, "Now he belongs to the ages."

The corpse was taken to the White House, where, in an upstairs bedroom, embalmers drained its blood and doctors autopsied the skull. In the hours that followed, Stanton and the other cabinet members (except Secretary of State William Seward, who had been quite nearly slain by one of John Wilkes Booth's accomplices) rallied to take charge of the federal government and to arrange for Lincoln's funeral. The job of handling the president's personal affairs fell jointly to Robert Lincoln and John Hay. Hay suggested to newly sworn President Andrew Johnson that, under the circumstances, Mrs. Lincoln and the family ought to be allowed to remain in the White House for as long as they wished, and when Johnson's emissary appeared later in the morning, he found Robert in the presidential office, standing amid his father's papers. Abraham Lincoln might belong to the ages, but much of the contents of his office now belonged to his family.

Hay stood beside Robert in those first numbed days after the assassination, and when Nicolay at last arrived, he pitched in as well. Hay and Nicolay had been in charge of most aspects of Lincoln's workday. They had handled nearly every military order, every letter and telegram, every request for appointment, promotion, and pardon that crossed Lincoln's desk. They had transcribed his letters and speeches. Nicolay, German-born, was the more organized of the two private secretaries and much stiffer in manner and expression. Hay was the stylish one, dapper and erudite, with the pen of a poet. Mastering Lincoln's signature had been easy for him; what now seems likely is that he also wrote a good many of the letters that went out above Lincoln's signature, including at least one letter regarded today as a gem of Lincolniana.

Indeed, Hay and Nicolay had a vested interest in the papers of Abraham Lincoln, for, with the consent of the president, they had filed away Lincoln's correspondence and other writings with the aim of eventually writing a book about him. Though the assassination had been jarring in the extreme, they never lost sight of their objective. While undertakers dressed Lincoln's body for public viewing in the East Room of the White House, Hay and Nicolay made a careful appraisal of the president's effects. Once Lincoln's widow and sons left the White House, Robert Lincoln would become the new custodian of the presidential papers, with the understanding that he would make them available to the two secretaries—to them and nobody else. They signed no agreement; Hay's friendship with Robert was assurance enough.

Hay and Nicolay's own eviction from the White House was scarcely a surprise. They were both leaving anyway. As strong as the bond had been between Lincoln and his private secretaries, Mary Lincoln, vengeful and devious, had made life difficult for them from the start, and she had made it quite obvious that she did not want them around for her husband's second term of office. Hay and Nicolay did not protest. They were thoroughly drained from four years of relentless, at times crushing, toil and stress, and only too ready to move on. The week after the inauguration, Nicolay had been appointed consul to Paris. Hay, too, was going to Paris, as secretary of legation. The jobs had been promised before Lincoln's death.

Yet neither bright prospects abroad nor an understanding with Robert Lincoln on the presidential papers made the final days in Washington any less dreary. On April 24, five days after Lincoln's funeral, Nicolay wrote to his fiancée: "Words seem so inadequate to express my own personal sorrow. . . . I think that I do not yet, and probably shall not yet for a long while, realize what a change his death has wrought in . . . the personal relations of almost every one connected with the government in this city who stood near to him." Nicolay added, "Hay and I are still here arranging the papers of the office, which has kept us very busy."

Meanwhile, Lincoln's body wended its way, first northward, then westward, taking more than two weeks to reach Springfield, giving millions of Americans a chance to view the darkening face of the martyr. Hay and Nicolay traveled on their own to Springfield, arriving in time for one last memorial service in the Illinois State House. On May 4, the coffin was closed and the president was placed in a receiving vault in Oak Ridge Cemetery, awaiting the erection of a permanent monument to his greatness.

Hay and Nicolay returned to Washington to finish crating the contents of Lincoln's office. By the end of the month, they were through and able to make more leisurely visits back to Illinois—Nicolay to be married in Pittsfield, with Hay as his best man; and Hay to see his family in the Mississippi River town of Warsaw.

Once more Hay returned to Washington, this time to receive his instructions for Paris. Throughout the war years, he had become accustomed to the capital's mood careening from one quarter of the emotional compass to another, depending on the latest news from the war's many fronts: military, civil, political, and diplomatic. Nevertheless, he was not ready for the scene that greeted him in Washington after an absence of only a few weeks.

Andrew Johnson had begun his dubious tenure by setting up temporary shop in the Treasury Building until Mary Lincoln was ready to decamp, which she finally did on May 22, accompanied by some twenty trunks filled with a great many White House furnishings. When Hay paid a visit to the mansion in June, it felt at once haunted and unfamiliar. "I found the shadow of recent experiences resting on everything," he wrote Robert Lincoln later. "The White House was full of new faces, a swarm of orderlies at doors and windows—the offices filled with new clerks, the anterooms crowded with hungry visitors. It was worse than a nightmare. I got away as soon as I could from the place. I think it will never be again anything less than the evil days in which we left it." He sailed for Europe on June 24, along with Nicolay and his bride.

Over the next four decades, John Hay would cross the threshold of the White House hundreds more times, as a friend of presidents, as assistant secretary of state, as ambassador, and finally as secretary of state. But there would always be a before and an after: before the assassination and all that came next. Lincoln was the line of demarcation, by far the deepest tree ring, of Hay's sixty-six years of personal history and public service. He had lived with Lincoln; he had witnessed the infancy of the Republican Party; he had served and survived the republic's trial by fire; and while many of his contemporaries would proudly wave the bloody shirt of Republicanism into the next century, Hay bore the distinction of having been bathed, or nearly enough, in the Great Emancipator's actual blood, not to mention his intelligence, humor, and love.

For the rest of America, Lincoln would represent a bundle of ideals: patience, perseverance, wisdom, humility, kindness, charity—a full panoply of biblical virtues. To Hay, he was the sum of all these, "the greatest man of his time." Yet to Hay, Lincoln was also corporeal. Hay knew firsthand how Lincoln ate his breakfast, sat a horse, cracked a joke. He had been with Lincoln at Gettysburg. On summer evenings he had rocked with him on the veranda of the Soldiers' Home. Lincoln would wake Hay in the middle of the night and read aloud to him. When he finished, Hay recalled, "the tall gaunt figure would rise from the edge of my bed and start for the door and on down the dark corridor. The candle carried high in his hand would light the disheveled hair as the President in flapping night-shirt, his feet padding along in carpet slippers, would disappear into the darkness."

Lincoln had four sons: one died very young; Willie died in the

White House at age eleven; Tad, though his father's pet, was unruly and learning-disabled. Robert was bright, but he and his father for some reason never hit it off. More than with anyone else in the immediate family, Lincoln had a rapport with John Hay. Neither of them ever acknowledged that Hay was the son Lincoln wished he'd had, not in so many words. But by default, Hay became Lincoln's fair-haired boy. Lincoln sanctioned Hay (and Nicolay) to write his biography. Beyond that, he awarded Hay the most precious gift of his patrimony: the spark to forge ahead, first as writer, next as statesman, then both together.

Lincoln did not give his young protégé a specific target so much as the sheer confidence to take aim and fire, and to make his life count for something. The underlying purpose was manifest, the same one Lincoln himself had striven to achieve as president and commander in chief— namely, the protection, preservation, and prosperity of the Union.

Hay was not nearly as single-minded as Lincoln; he was not a man of far-encompassing vision but more a man of successive vantage points, one guiding him toward the next, sometimes by leaps and bounds, at other times rather fitfully, but forward and upward always. He insisted humbly that the opportunities and accomplishments in his life were little more than a series of fortunate accidents, discounting what others recognized as his unfailing perspicacity and sound judgment. Whichever the case, he consistently did his best to repay Lincoln's largesse—by championing Lincoln personally and by furthering the Republican cause in whatever ways he could. These loyalties in turn brought credit and glory to his own name.

And no matter what, Lincoln was the example that Hay always came back to. Lincoln's standards were the standards against which he measured everyone in the world, starting with himself.

HAY'S RISE WAS RAPID and enviable. After Paris, he served in two more legations, Vienna and Madrid, returning to the United States a polished diplomat, conversant in four languages, precociously cosmopolitan in his manners and appetites. In New York he joined the staff of Horace Greeley's *New York Tribune* and quickly won respect as its most able editorialist. He never gave up poetry, and his verses brought him unexpected and extraordinary fame. He wrote a provocative and widely read novel, and with Nicolay he completed the ten-volume *Abraham Lincoln: A History*, which, at a million and a half words, was the heftiest historical exposition since Gibbon's *Decline and Fall of the Roman Empire* and a benchmark for all Lincoln books to follow.

His marriage to Clara Stone, daughter of a Cleveland railroad, steel, and banking baron, ensured he would never again have to worry about money, and his appreciation for fine living bloomed accordingly. His manses on Cleveland's Millionaires' Row and on Washington's Lafayette Square were filigreed to Gilded Age paragon. He built a summer retreat in New Hampshire, and he traveled lavishly in Europe, amassing a magnificent art collection and cultivating distinguished friends, especially in England, which he came to love nearly as much as his own country.

All the while, he never let go of politics. In the years after Appomattox, he looked on with increasing chagrin and frustration as Lincoln's legacy was blasphemed by the chicanery of his party and the venalities of the Johnson and Grant White Houses. "I'm keeper of the President's conscience," Hay had joked in 1861, shortly after first arriving in Washington. Going forward, he never shirked this responsibility. As the age of spoils and graft escalated, he came to be counted on not merely as a steadfast Lincoln man but as a trustworthy guide who helped lead the Grand Old Party back onto the path of righteousness. That he gave generously and regularly to the candidates he considered of the truest mettle further established him as one of the party's most influential lamplighters.

He served briefly in the administration of Rutherford B. Hayes but turned down the invitation of Hayes's successor, James Garfield, to stay on. Instead, he returned to New York to guest-edit the *Tribune* and wound up covering Garfield's assassination and long slide toward death with a sense of alarm that was as much personal as partisan.

Nudged by Republican high priest Mark Hanna, whom, like Garfield, he had come to know in Cleveland, Hay pitched in to help rescue candidate (and fellow Ohioan) William McKinley from personal insolvency, thereby securing the one job he ever truly coveted, the ambassadorship to the Court of St. James's. President McKinley quickly recognized that Hay's extraordinary diplomatic aplomb could be put to higher use, and so, at the close of the Spanish-American War, McKinley brought him home to be secretary of state. In September 1901, for the second time, John Hay hurried to the bedside of a president mortally wounded by an assassin's bullet. When McKinley expired a week later, the new president was Theodore Roosevelt, whom Hay had known since Teddy was a child. At first Hay was not convinced that Roosevelt was not still a child—so impetuous, so rambunctious, "more fun than a goat," Hay quipped.

Much could be made of the differences between Roosevelt and Hay. Hay was genteel, soft-spoken, tailored by London's best, his Van Dyke beard groomed fastidiously. Hay's word for fun was "gay"; for Roosevelt, "bully" was better. Roosevelt was looking for the next war; Hay had his fill with the last one. (While it was Hay who famously described the 1898 conflict between the United States and Spain as a "splendid little war," lost in translation is his relief that it was splendid because it had been so mercifully little.) Roosevelt was an unabashed campaigner, a gate-crasher by temperament; Hay was the one whom everyone begged to be on their ticket and in their cabinet, and he gave in only under a heavy barrage of supplication and flattery. Roosevelt dominated his relations with other men as much by physical force as by the acuity of his ideas. Hay was a sublime conversationalist; great men—and women, too—leaned forward to listen to him and the next day repeated his bon mots.

On the other hand, Hay and Roosevelt did have a great deal in common. Roosevelt had two sides—he was both dog and cat, as the newspaperman William Allen White observed—and Hay, while never entirely able to leash the canine in his president, found the feline aspect winsome.

As ardent Republicans, they had mutual aggravations: anyone who was less than one hundred percent convinced that republicanism was the boon and salvation of "civilization," a list of antagonists that included "jack rabbit" Latin American officials, smug sultans, Filipino insurgents, brigands of any hue, "anti-imps," labor agitators, not to mention Democrats and their waffling poll mates, the Mugwumps. And to the surprise of each, Hay and Roosevelt formed a superb partnership, navigating tricky waters at home and abroad, where the effective strategy was to tread softly (Hay's job) and brandish a big stick (Roosevelt, naturally). Together they jockeyed with the so-called Great Powers—England, France,

Germany, Italy, Russia, and Japan—a stubborn and testy lot of empires, some too long in the tooth, others too sharp. This family of nations was on the road to dysfunction even before they began competing aggressively in the global grab for "spheres of influence," a guileful euphemism if ever there was one. The United States and Britain were hardly chaste, not after ugly campaigns in the Philippines and South Africa, but at least the Americans and English had forged a lasting rapprochement, thanks in no small part to the bridge-building that Hay had done while ambassador. The other powers were unapologetically on the make, inferring and avoiding alliances in a jittery choreography of chauvinism and distrust. For the most part, they left the Western Hemisphere alone—once Hay and Roosevelt dissuaded Britain from remapping Canada's boundary with Alaska, bluffed the Germans from the Caribbean, and, last but not least, pried Panama loose from Colombia in order to build, control, and fortify a long-anticipated "American canal" between the Caribbean and the Pacific.

At the close of the nineteenth century and the start of the twentieth, the biggest canvas of all was China, and here is where John Hay painted his masterpiece, the Open Door. It wasn't a treaty by any stretch but simply a double dare to play fair in China, consented to by various world powers, one by one, with Hay's coaxing. If Lincoln had saved the Union, John Hay deserves a nod of credit for saving China from "spoliation" at the hands of the other powers. How he accomplished this is a wonder, an act of feather-light finesse that shaped not just the future of Asia but also the long-term relations of every nation involved.

HAY HAD ONLY FRIENDS, it seems. The closest was Henry Adams, and arguably theirs was one of the most remarkable friendships of any era. They lived side-by-side in Washington (future site of the Hay-Adams Hotel), and for a quarter century they were inseparable, which is not to say they were always together. Yet when they were apart, they wrote to each other faithfully—long, gossipy, joshing, but always affectionate epistles. They wrote to each other knowing that they would see each other before the letter arrived, and they wrote to each other not knowing whether the letter would ever arrive.

From his parlor, Hay could see across to the window of the bedroom where he lived during the Lincoln years. He and Adams took to walking together every afternoon at four o'clock, followed by five o'clock tea with Hay's wife, Clara, and Adams's wife, Clover, until the latter's death; and on rare and cherished occasions, they were graced by the company of Clarence King, the enchanting and far-roving geologist explorer whose follies of love and speculation gave them all fits. On a whim, they named their nucleus "the Five of Hearts."

Hay and Adams did not see eye-to-eye on a lot of things. For starters, Adams was more of an iconoclast and twice the snob that Hay was. As a grandson and great-grandson of presidents, he looked down his nose on the parade of White House occupants, post-Lincoln, as misfits all. Besides being a keen historian, he also postured himself as a futurist, and the future he foresaw was not pretty. The world order was on the verge of a colossal economic, political, and social comeuppance. Adams poured a steady dose of dourness into Hay's teacup, but, if anything, it worked as a tonic. Hay, meanwhile, discovered a trustworthy sounding board in Adams. He could go on in detail about the affairs of state, knowing that Adams wouldn't think of betraying their confidences. When each published novels anonymously—first came Adams's *Democracy*, a wry send-up of Washington vanity and corruption, followed by Hay's *The Bread-Winners*, a cautionary tale of labor unrest in a city similar to Cleveland—they were tickled when the public suspected that the same author wrote both.

But there were also betrayals within Hay's circle and deeper secrets kept from one another. It has been conjectured that Hay had a romance with Nannie Lodge, the wife of Massachusetts senator Henry Cabot Lodge. Clara Hay evidently never learned of her husband's dalliance, nor did Cabot Lodge, though one wonders if the chronic friction between the senator and the secretary of state, ostensibly over treaties and the direction of foreign policy, was not exacerbated by the subtext of cuckoldry.

Clarence King possessed an even bigger secret—now common knowledge but at the time unspeakable. The reason the Hays and Adamses never succeeded in finding a bride for the fifth Heart was because he already had one. Without telling any of his friends, he was leading a life of a completely different sort in New York.

The dance card gets more intricate still, with Elizabeth "Lizzie" Cameron the center of attention. She was from Cleveland also, the daughter of a judge and the niece of two of Ohio's most illustrious figures, General William Tecumseh Sherman and Senator John Sherman. She arrived in Washington at the age of twenty and within the year was married to Pennsylvania senator Donald Cameron, twenty-four years her senior. Tall, wasp-waisted, and fetching, she quickly became the Madame X of Washington society. After Clover Adams died unexpectedly, Henry Adams was overwhelmed first by grief and then by the charms of young Lizzie Cameron.

The pas de deux between Henry Adams and Lizzie Cameron might otherwise be a sidebar to the life of John Hay if it were not for a trove of titillating revelations: several dozen letters, ignored or misinterpreted for the past hundred years, that now cast the character of John Hay in an immensely more intriguing light. Unbeknownst to Clara Hay, Henry Adams, and Nannie Lodge, Hay too was in love with Lizzie Cameron.

Their romance flamed in London and Paris in 1891, while their spouses were at home in the United States and Henry Adams was half a world away in the South Seas. "You do things so easily," Hay gushed in one of his tributes to her. "You write as you walk. There seems no muscular effort in your *démarche*. You go over the ground like a goddess. . . . Don't you see, you darling, why I love to grovel before you? It is such a pleasure to worship one so absolutely adorable. There is no one in sight of you in beauty, or grace, or cleverness, or substance of character. . . . You are all precious and divine: one to worship *en gros et en detail*."

Caution cooled passion when he was in the company of family and friends, and by all outward measures he appeared devoted to Clara, mother of their four children, font of his substantial wealth. But while Lizzie was lithesome and clever, Clara was quiet, matronly, and, as one society column politely described her full proportions, "*embonpoint*." During the final fifteen years of his life, Hay repeatedly circled back to Lizzie, never retiring from the field.

"I AM INCLINED TO think that my life is an oughtnottobiography," Hay wrote in 1902. Unlike Henry Adams, he had no desire to write a memoir. Throughout his life he urged his friends to destroy his letters after reading them (most did not), but despite Hay's repeated plaints of privacy and self-abnegation, he clearly did not wish to be swallowed by obscurity or diminished to a footnote in the lives of others. He himself kept many thousands of pages of his own writing—diaries, correspondence, poems, speeches—along with letters received over half a century, and he conscientiously kept scrapbooks of newspaper clippings about himself and the events of his day. And to glance at even one of the volumes of his Lincoln oeuvre is to appreciate his high esteem for biography as literature and as one of humanity's vital measurements. Hay was a low-key man in many respects, but he was not without a sense of his own worth. He was aware of the imprint of his career, the momentous passages of history of which he had been witness and, in many cases, author. He knew he had put his signature on the world.

Even so, few twenty-first-century Americans recognize John Hay as more than a Zelig in the corner of someone else's portrait. And the hard reckonings of two world wars and the absolutism of the nuclear age have led historians to look upon Hay's brand of statesmanship as lacking in firmness and forcefulness. Gentleman's agreements like the Open Door have been dismissed as ineffectual and passé.

But to most of Hay's contemporaries, his manners, his mind, and his conduct as spokesman for a nation finding its voice on the world stage were nonpareil and pitch-perfect, and their praise for him was profuse. "He so far overshadows all the other 'statesmen' in Washington and is so far superior to any and all Republicans who have held high office in Washington in the last decade," the *Evening Sun* of New York editorialized in 1903. "That John Hay has been the main wheel of the Roosevelt administration . . . has long been made manifest to everybody who has observed the numerous instances wherein Mr. Roosevelt's strenuous, headstrong actions have been deftly smoothed over by the quiet, notoriety-hating secretary of state. There have been a score of instances . . . where the president in his happy, devil-may-care, we-can-lick-the-world style has overstepped the bounds of diplomacy and the presidential prerogative only to be rescued from a difficult predicament by John Hay." "In sum," the *Sun* declared, "John Hay has performed greater and more substantial service to his country than any Republican since Abraham Lincoln." This from an otherwise unfriendly paper.

His partisans were even more appreciative. "If a man [were to] look over the changes in the world during the last decade to decide what is the most hopeful measure of human progress," the highbrow journal *World's Work* eulogized in 1905, "he might well say that it is the lifting of diplomacy from the level of sharp practice to the level of frank and fair dealing; and this change is the measure of the work of John Hay. For he was a great man [and] if we had not such a man . . . [d]iplomacy might have gone on as the art of low cunning applied to great problems—the good weak and the strong tricky. He made frankness and uprightness strong, and he made trickiness weak by forcing it to confess its character or to retire."

Hay's successor as secretary of state, Elihu Root, was at once a student, observer, and beneficiary of Hay's superb tact and politesse—his "extreme refinement," as Root reminisced at the dedication of the John Hay Library at Brown University in 1910. "He was the most delightful of companions. One found in him breadth of interest, shrewd observation, profound philosophy, wit, humor, the revelations of tender and loyal friendship and an undertone of strong convictions—and now and then," Root went on, "expression of a thought that in substance and perfection of form left in the mind the sense of having seen a perfectly cut stone."

And yet, Root continued in his encomium, "His life was his own and he shared it only with those he loved. The proud modesty of his self-respect made it impossible for him to testify in his own behalf or to allege his own merits."

The pages that follow aim not so much to speak for John Hay as to allow him to speak for himself, in order that the brilliance of his life, the example of his life, and, what is more, the sheer poignancy of his life might at last be considered in full.

CHAPTER 2

Spunky Point

Hays were Scots originally. The first to set foot in America arrived by a roundabout route. John Hay's great-great-grandfather, also named John, hired out as a soldier in the Rhineland of what was not yet Germany before immigrating to the Atlantic colonies in the mid-eighteenth century. One of his sons, Adam, settled in Virginia and served bravely in the Revolution. Adam's son, another John, remembers receiving a pat on the head from George Washington.

This John Hay—our John Hay's grandfather—was of a restless family who came of age in a restless nation. Like so many young men, he rankled at the "harsh and arbitrary ideas" of his father and, at the age of eighteen, launched himself westward, alighting in the bluegrass of Fayette County, Kentucky, where he became an ardent Whig (along with neighbor Henry Clay), a manufacturer of cotton goods, and the husband of Jemima Coulter, with whom he had fourteen children. The John Hay who is the subject of this biography recorded that his grandfather met with "gratifying success" in Kentucky. "But he always had his doubts of the advantages of the system of negro-slavery," and so after thirty years sought "a new home in a region which was, at least, free of this objection"—across the Ohio River in Illinois, where slavery had been proscribed by the original state constitution of 1818.

The Hays relocated to Sangamon County in 1830, the same year, co-incidentally, that Abraham Lincoln arrived in Illinois and with his father built a cabin on the Sangamon River. Hay's cotton business did not thrive in its new location, nor did a brick mill, although he had better luck in land speculation. He and his family lived not in a log cabin but in a solid house in Springfield, where Hay became a pillar of the Baptist Church and, reportedly, the first man to sign the promissory note securing the building of the State House, once Springfield was declared the capital in 1839. The boy who had felt the touch of George Washington lived until he was ninety, lasting just long enough to watch the funeral cortège of his friend Abraham Lincoln pass by his parlor window.

In the 1830 exodus from Kentucky, the one member of the Hay family who did not come along was son Charles, perhaps the most scholarly. Lexington, Kentucky, where Charles was raised, had a reputation as the Athens of the West, a prosperous hub of aristocratic refinement, where Mary Todd, future wife of Abraham Lincoln, learned to speak French with a southern accent. Charles Hay attended a "classical" school, where he made easy progress in Latin and Greek. His son later boasted that his father never lost his command of Virgil and Homer.

Charles received a medical degree from Transylvania University in Lexington and, instead of joining his parents and siblings in Illinois, chose to set up a practice in the town of Salem, Indiana, thirty-five miles from Louisville. Here he married Helen Leonard.

Charles was a man of broad curiosity, and he was by all reckoning a capable physician. But when it came to sheer, demonstrable intellect, the Leonards were of even finer weave. The family of John Hay's maternal grandfather, David Leonard, had founded Bridgewater, Massachusetts. David graduated from Brown University, in Providence, where he delivered the class poem in 1792. While in college he was welcomed into the Baptist Church in "the rigorous fashion of those days," John Hay recounted, "by immersion in the Seekonk River, a hole having been cut in the ice for the purpose." He went on to a distinguished career in various Baptist pulpits in New York and New England; a number of his sermons were published and enjoyed wide circulation. He settled with his family in Bristol, Rhode Island, where he became postmaster, newspaper editor, and insurance agent. Eventually he shed the starched polity of the

Baptists for the roomier doctrine of Unitarianism, undertaking his own translation of the New Testament, only to lose the manuscript in the great gale of 1815.

Undaunted, in 1817 he answered the call of the West and set out for Indiana, buying a tract of land on the Ohio River. Two years later, he was dead, leaving a widow and eleven children, the fourth of whom was Helen, age fifteen. She was taken in by a sister married to a lawyer in Salem, named, apparently by pure chance, John Hay Farnham. The Farnhams chaperoned Helen's courtship to the town's bright young doctor, Charles Hay. They were married in October 1831.

Charles did not exactly flourish in Salem—not at first, and only modestly during the decade that followed, despite the steady passage of immigrants through the Ohio Valley. "[Y]ou are no doubt anxious to know whether I am likely to make enough here to keep my masticators going," he wrote his family in Illinois. In order to establish himself, he assured his relatives, he simply needed more time, "'the nurse and breeder of all good,' as Shakespeare expresses it."

Helen and Charles received a nest egg, perhaps as much as $1,000, from the estate of her father, and in November 1832, their first child, Edward Leonard Hay, was born. The following summer, an epidemic of cholera struck. "It has made our town look like a place besieged by Indians more than anything that I can compare it to," Charles wrote to his brother Milton. "I am sure that Black Hawk with all his forces could [not] carry more terror and dismay into any place than the inhabitants of Salem have shown during this epidemic." Try as he might, there was little Dr. Hay could do to stanch the suffering. His own family was spared, but sixty or seventy of his neighbors died within a few weeks.

The doctor's tireless service won him the admiration and loyalty of Salem, yet even then he pursued other interests besides medicine. He involved himself in Whig politics, needling the "ultra Jacksonians" in a Fourth of July speech and decrying the migration of pro-slavery Kentuckians to Indiana. He became part owner of a local printing office and assumed the editorship of the newspaper, changing its banner from Democratic to Whig. As the region continued to boom, he began speculating in real estate. Three more children were born: a son, Augustus Leonard (known first as Gus, then as Leonard); a daughter, Mary; and on October 8, 1838, a third son, named for Charles's father John and his brother Milton. That an esteemed poet also bore the name was perhaps an added inducement.

For all his engagement with the affairs of Salem, Dr. Hay still felt unsettled. More than anything, he craved a life of the mind, of literature— "the le[a]ven of a better character," he called it. "He cared very little for light reading," his son John recalled. "He barely tolerated the novelists later than Scott; from modern essayists he always went back with pleasure to Addison and Steele; the stately measures of Pope and Dryden were far more to his taste than the ingenious melodies of contemporary poets. But his favorite reading was in the departments of history and natural science."

Charles could be stuffy in his own literary tastes, but he was the first to acknowledge that education, by any means, was the key to advancement and well-being. In a letter to Milton Hay, he declared, "There are quite as many distinguished orators, writers, lawyers, and doctors amongst those who have never been to college as are to be found amongst those who have. . . . But there must still be opportunity, there must be books, there must be society, there must be congenial minds."

How surprising, then, that when Charles at last decided to leave Indiana for Illinois, instead of choosing Springfield, the burgeoning state capital, he picked Warsaw, a Mississippi River town no bigger than Salem.

Warsaw is situated on a high, wooded bluff on the Illinois shore of the Mississippi, opposite the mouth of the Des Moines River, one hundred miles west of Springfield. First it had been Fort Johnson, which quickly burned, then Fort Edwards, both constructed by the army to discourage downstream incursion by the British during the War of 1812. After the war, John Jacob Astor made it a fur-trading post. Speculators arrived in the 1830s, optimistically platting a town they named Warsaw, after the popular historical novel, *Thaddeus of Warsaw*, written by Jane Porter, an Englishwoman. In the heyday of Mississippi steamboats, the location was promising. Rapids immediately upstream prevented bigger boats from navigating farther north in certain months, and many of their goods and passengers wound up on the wharf at Warsaw.

John Hay, who was roughly the same age as his fictional neighbors, Huckleberry Finn and Tom Sawyer, soaked up the sights and sounds of river life. "[H]e had an inexhaustible repertoire of 'river slang,'" recalled one school chum. On the map his hometown may have been called Warsaw, but he preferred the more colorful nickname used by pilots and river men: Spunky Point. "[S]ome idiots . . . who had read Miss Porter thought Warsaw would be much more genteel," Hay griped to an eastern acquaintance, "and so we are Nicodemussed into nothing for the rest of time."

But it wasn't the name that aborted Warsaw's destiny. Sandbars, the blockades of the Civil War, and the eventual decline of steamboats had much more to do with stunting the town's growth. As Henry Adams later remarked, Warsaw was "one of the many western towns which then aspired to the rank of future western metropolis, and which the course of time has not carried perceptibly toward its object."

John Hay's memories of Warsaw cut two ways. In a short story he published in 1871, he reflected on the Mississippi "reposing from its plunge over the rapids" and the rolling hills "patched with the immortal green of cedars and gay with clambering columbines." In a poem, "On the Bluff," his nostalgia was even more mawkish:

> O grandly flowing River!
>   O silver-gliding River!
> Thy springing willows shiver
>   In the sunset as of old;
> They shiver in the silence
> Of the willow-whitened islands,
> While the sun-bars and the sand-bars
>   Fill air and wave with gold.

On the other hand, he was ever so eager to be shut of his roots. When he left Warsaw as a teenager, he would dismiss western Illinois as "a region whose moral atmosphere was never remarkable for purity." And on visits home, he would lament to eastern friends that he was in "exile"—that is, exile from the East. He likewise spilled his disdain for the "barbaric" Illinois frontier in the early pages of the Lincoln biography: "The ruling motive which led most [settlers] to the wilds was that Anglo-Saxon lust of land. . . . Accompanying this flood of emigrants of good faith was the usual froth and scum of shiftless idlers and adventurers, who were either drifting with a current they were too worthless to withstand, or in pursuit of dishonest gains in fresher and simpler regions."

Like two of his lifelong literary friends, William Dean Howells, born in small-town Ohio in 1837, and Samuel Clemens, born in Hannibal, Missouri, just downriver from Warsaw, in 1835, Hay did not regard the West as the Holy Grail. Their forefathers had wandered in the wilderness long enough. The rosier horizon lay in the direction of the sunrise: New England, New York, Europe. While absence tended to soften John Hay's heart toward home, absence is what it took, for over the years he made it plain that he was glad to have Warsaw in his past and doubly glad that he had made for himself a more cosmopolitan future, as a son who did not so much follow his father's example as his father's vision of a wider world rich with higher ideas.

Hay was not yet three when his family settled in Warsaw. His eldest brother, Edward, had died the previous fall, at the age of seven, perhaps one more reason Salem had lost its appeal to his parents. Charles Hay built a handsome two-story brick house upon the bluff and set about re-establishing himself as a physician. His wife bore him two more children, Charles and Helen.

In Warsaw, Dr. Hay was a solid citizen, but he did not make much from either his medical practice or several farms he had bought in the county. "They were not especially profitable," his son recollected. "[H]e treated his tenants somewhat as if they were his children or his wards." But, Hay added, "[T]he hours he spent among them were at least wholesome and agreeable. They gave him a beneficial contact with reality, and a reason for being in the open air and on horseback."

Dr. Hay much preferred to devote his time to books—he was a founder of the Warsaw library—and to the education of his children. He sent them to a schoolhouse in town, and he and his wife, who had received an uncommonly good education from her own father, administered an even more rigorous curriculum at home. "The rule of the household was never lax," John Hay recalls. "Obedience was very much a matter of course."

Young John demonstrated an early facility with languages, beginning with Latin and Greek, followed by German, taught at night by a German immigrant. "John was a student with the others, who were all grown men," his brother Charles remembered. "John was so small that he would occasionally fall asleep during the evening, but he surprised them all by showing he had learned his lesson and could recite easily well with the best of them when awakened."

IN HAY'S EARLY CHILDHOOD, two events stand out vividly. Both involved acts of violence against outsiders seeking freedom. In each case, Hay was only vaguely aware of what had transpired at first, although in later years, once he was able to place these disturbing instances in the context of his own and the nation's history, their import struck a deeper nerve.

In 1839, just as Warsaw was getting its footing, a rival town sprang up twenty miles upstream. Expelled from Missouri, Joseph Smith and his Mormon followers founded Nauvoo; by 1844 its population had swelled to more than twelve thousand, making it the second largest city in Illinois, after Chicago, with more church members pouring in every day from as far away as England. Anti-Mormon hatred was fanned by the *Warsaw Signal*; its editor accused Joseph Smith and his elders of every form of turpitude: perjury, robbery, counterfeiting, and fleecing of their own flock. The most inflammatory offense by far was polygamy and the sexual predation said to go with it. "It can be proven," the *Signal* charged, "that Smith's principal supporters and confidential friends are among the basest seducers and violators of female virtue—that Smith himself has aided villains to accomplish their unholy designs; and . . . that he acted from the impulse of Heaven's dictation, while endeavoring to rob virtuous females of their chastity."

Yet the threat to Warsaw went beyond outrages of morality or religious doctrine. By sheer number of Mormon voters, Joseph Smith, "sitting on his throne," the *Signal* warned, could control the government of Hancock County, which included both Nauvoo and Warsaw, and "without molestation hold over us an iron rod." (Mormons voted solidly Democratic.) Such was Smith's vision of grandeur that he declared his candidacy for president. Another cause of contention was economic: Mormons had nearly succeeded in buying a section of land immediately downstream from Warsaw, which, if the deal had been completed, would have effectively surrounded Warsaw and quite possibly rendered the town obsolete as a viable port.

The crisis came to a head at the end of June 1844, when anti-Mormon militias from Warsaw and nearby Carthage converged on the Carthage jail, where Joseph Smith and his brother Hyrum were being held on a flimsy charge of treason. The vigilantes forced their way into the jail and murdered both men. The succession of Brigham Young and the great Mormon trek to Utah were the direct result of this extralegal aggression.

The only account of Charles Hay's role in the Mormon "war" comes from his son John, who was five years old at the time. "[H]e was everywhere known to be a strong and determined opponent of the Mormons," Hay acknowledged after his father's death. Yet he quickly clarified that his father's "voice and influence" had always been firmly on the side of law and order. "[H]e protested vigorously, but ineffectually, against the march to Nauvoo," Hay insisted. Even so, Dr. Hay did join the Warsaw militia as its surgeon. It was only after the governor of Illinois ordered the regiment disbanded that he and several dozen others decided to turn back.

Twenty-five years later, in an effort to give shape to the wisps of memory of the Mormon unpleasantness and Warsaw's part in it, Hay submitted an article to the *Atlantic Monthly*, which, while denouncing Smith and his leaders as "blackguards" and Mormons in general as "bad neighbors," also castigated the anti-Mormon mob of Warsaw as loutish and craven. "The moment the work was done," Hay wrote, "the calmness of horror succeeded the fever of fanatical rage. The assassins hurried away from the jail, and took the road to Warsaw in silence and haste. They went home at a killing pace over the wide dusty prairie. Warsaw is eighteen miles from Carthage; the Smiths were killed at half past five: at a quarter before eight the returning crowd began to drag their weary limbs through the main street of Warsaw,—at such an astounding rate of speed had the lash of their own thoughts driven them."

In expectation of Mormon vengeance, the women and children of Warsaw—no mention of whether John Hay, his mother, and siblings were among them—fled to safety across the Mississippi while the men "kept guard in the hazel thickets around the town." The reprisal never came, and when the state eventually endeavored to bring the murderers of the Smiths to justice, it took ninety-six men, Hay chided, "before twelve were found ignorant enough and indifferent enough to act as jurors." Every citizen of Warsaw knew who had done the deed. None talked; none was convicted. "And you cannot find in this generation an original inhabitant of Hancock County who will not stoutly sustain that verdict," Hay concluded snidely.

The second violent incident of Hay's childhood was slighter but in many ways more terrifying and far-reaching. He himself left no written record of it; the following account is from his brother Charles:

"When we were both quite young [John] told me he was in the basement of our house, and he heard a ghost. [The ghost] spoke to him and said, 'Little Master, for the love of God bring me a drink of water.' [John] said he was so frightened he hurried upstairs and went to his room. The next day my father told at the table that a party of three runaway slaves had been overtaken by a party of officers from Missouri and the slaves had resisted arrest, and one was captured and taken back, one of the other two was fired upon and killed, and the third had been badly wounded but escaped leaving blood tracks in the wood. I saw my brother John staring at me across the supper table, but saying nothing. After the meal, he told his father about the voice he heard in the basement, and my father, John and I went down to investigate and on a pile of kindling wood was the appearance of some one having used this for a bed, but there was a stain of blood shed there nearly eighteen inches in diameter. This was probably the blood shed by the runaway slave who had escaped capture. What became of the slave afterward, I never heard. Fully forty years afterward I asked John if he remembered this occurrence, and he replied, 'I will never forget it, and that incident has given me a greater horror than anything I have ever read about slavery.'"

This same brother, who went on to serve in the army and later became mayor of Springfield, offered one final glimpse of John's formative years. "[H]e was spoken of as 'Honest and Efficient,'" recalled the younger Hay. "He repeated this remark to me and said, 'I feel my character has been established,—honest and efficient,—this is my pride for my after life.' These words were spoken by a boy not ten years of age."

BY THE AGE OF thirteen, Hay had exhausted the educational possibilities of Warsaw. In 1851 he moved to Pittsfield, in nearby Pike County, to live with his uncle Milton in order to attend a private classical school that would better prepare him for college. A fellow student remembers him as a "red-cheeked, black-eyed, sunshiny boy, chock full of fun and humor and devilment that hurt nobody." Hay instantly won over his schoolmaster, an Irishman named Thomson, with the ease and fluency of his Virgil translation, and he spoke German "like a native." His knowledge of natural history was equally impressive. "[T]he boy could talk of the Eocene period and the old red sandstones like a professor," the classmate attested.

It was in Pittsfield that Hay first made the acquaintance of John George Nicolay. Nicolay was born in Bavaria in 1832, and his family immigrated to the United States when he was six; by the age of fourteen he was an orphan. When Hay arrived to attend school, Nicolay was nineteen, self-educated, and employed in the printing office of the Whig weekly, the *Pike County Free Press*. Within three years he would be the paper's editor and sole proprietor. Gaunt and earnest, he was in many respects the opposite of the younger, more winsome Hay. Still, Pittsfield was a small town and they were two of its brightest residents. They took each other's measure and evidently took a liking as well. Ten years hence they would be roommates in the White House.

After a year of schooling in Pittsfield, Hay moved from his uncle Milton's house to Springfield, this time accompanied by his older brother Leonard, to attend Lutheran-run Illinois State University, which was barely a university at all but, in Hay's case, a stepping stone to one. He and Leonard lived with their grandfather, their bachelor uncle, Nathaniel, and several aunts.

To the eye of John Hay, Springfield was a grand, if muddy, entrepôt. With a population of five thousand, it was ten times the size of Warsaw. "There had been very little of what might be called pioneer life in Springfield," he would write in the Lincoln biography. "Civilization came in with a reasonably full equipment at the beginning." Hay liked his new surroundings immediately. "[A]ll the sentimental talk we hear from the poet and the novelist, about the simplicity and quiet ease of village life, is all humbug," he lectured to one of his sisters. "The city is the only place to gain a knowledge of the world, which will fit a man for entering upon the duties of life."

His coursework included Latin (the *Odes* of Horace), Greek (Homer's

Iliad), rhetoric, and algebra. He also joined a literary society that gathered to debate and share members' essays. Potentially more absorbing were the activities of the Illinois legislature, which convened in the red-topped State House on the city square. At least once Hay attended a session to hear a debate on the extension of slavery to the territories west of the Mississippi.

But even Springfield and the education it had to offer were not enough for the family scholar. All agreed that he had the makings to go much further. His father and mother set their sights on Brown University, the alma mater of Helen Hay's father. Alas, they could not afford the expense, which, including tuition, room, and sundries, came to about $100 a year. Milton Hay, whom Charles Hay had encouraged to pursue a career in law, stepped forward and offered to pay his nephew's way.

JOHN HAY, NOT YET seventeen, boarded a train for Providence in September 1855. "I had a whirling, bustling time on the way here," he wrote his family upon arrival, assuring them he was "safe & sound in every thing except my eyes, mouth & ears were full of cinders & dust." He was the farthest from home he had ever been but adapted quickly. "I don't know whether I will come back to Illinois next summer or not," he announced. "That is too far ahead to look at present." He passed his entrance exams and, despite his age, was admitted to the junior class.

Brown was founded by Baptists in 1764; by the time John Hay matriculated, the curriculum was both classical and practical. Hay's first courses were in chemistry, trigonometry, and rhetoric, for which he received high marks. "He at once took rank among the brightest boys in the college, and maintained it with a degree of ease that was the envy of his classmates," his friend Billy Norris remembered. "In those days, all text was memorized, and it was the general opinion that Hay put his books under his pillow and had the contents thereof absorbed and digested by morning, for he was never seen 'digging,' or doing any other act or thing that could be construed into hard study."

Hay took to life at Brown so readily that in November he persuaded his parents and uncle to let him fall back to the sophomore class. Not that he doubted he could graduate in two years; but, he reasoned, "[I]f I go through so hurriedly I will have little or no time to avail myself of the literary treasures of the libraries. This is one of the greatest advantages of an eastern college over a western one."

He waxed further on the charms of campus life: "The professors are all men of the greatest ability, & what is more, perfect gentlemen. . . . I heard Oliver W. Holmes deliver a poem here last week which was a splendid thing. . . . Thackeray will be here before long & I expect to hear him lecture." Such expressions of enlightenment were surely music to the ears of Dr. Hay.

Brown was beginning a period of refreshing change just as Hay arrived. Incoming President Barnas Sears was loved and respected by the two hundred or so undergraduates for relaxing the restrictions on campus life. Student rooms were no longer subject to daily inspection; for the first time, fraternities and literary societies were allowed to meet in the evening. Hay joined Theta Delta Chi, enduring the customary hazing and the nickname "Thaddeus of Warsaw." At an early banquet, his fraternity brothers prodded him to make an impromptu address—and be sure to make it lively. To which Hay retorted waggishly, "Hay that is green can never be dry."

In a debate, he argued the affirmative to "Resolved—that a prohibition liquor law is an unjustifiable violation of individual rights." For a college man, albeit seventeen and still baby-faced, the cause was just, but he lost nonetheless. Later as a member of the Philermenian literary society, he took on more sober topics: "Resolved—that the course of the President on the Kansas [territorial slavery] question has been unconstitutional" and "Resolved—that prose writers have done more for the English language than poets." In the former, the boy who had heard the bloody ghost in the basement took the affirmative and won; in the latter, the budding bard took the negative and won again.

Hay's cleverness won over his school chums and teachers as well. To a roommate, he was "a young Dr. Johnson without his boorishness, a young Dr. Goldsmith without his frivolity." James B. Angell, professor of modern languages and eventually president of the University of Michigan, remembered Hay a half-century later as "the most felicitous translator I ever met in my classes." He won top honors in rhetoric for a paper entitled "The Saxon Conquest and the Norman Contrasted in Respect of Their Influence on the Language and the Literature of the Conquered Race." Other papers not only reveal his maturing talent as a writer but also hint of the gracious statesman he would become. On the possibility of war with England—hypothetical, one assumes—the future ambassador to the Court of St. James's made the case for comity:

"They are our brothers, speaking the same noble tongue, of which we are all so proud, the tongue which heard in a foreign land makes the warm blood leap gladly to the flushing cheek; the tongue in which Alfred prayed and Chaucer sung, in which Milton embodied the grand tale of a lost Eden & the bard of Avon wrote his deep lore of the soul of man. . . . Our history is the same with theirs, & we claim an equal share in all the story that a thousand years have shed upon the Saxon name."

And the youngster from the Mississippi, who would one day tour the grand hotels, galleries, salons, palaces, plazas, and ruins of the Old World, cast a wistful eye to the horizon in "Foreign Travel Beneficial to the Man of Letters":

"The first who undertook an extensive journey for purposes purely literary was Herodotus the Ionic historian, who travelled over the greater part of inhabited Europe, Asia & Africa, gathering from actual observations, from the testimony of eye-witnesses, and from the traditions of the priests, materials for the construction of his immortal work. . . . A marked difference is presented by our times. By the mighty agency of steam, time & distance are almost annihilated; regions which in other days were considered by each other as the Ultima Thule of earth, are brought by iron chains to within a few days journey."

Yet he did not confine himself to campus life by any means. For instance, in the spring of 1856, in a letter to his uncle Milton, thanking him for his financial support, Hay mentioned that "Political feeling is running very high in Providence at present. . . . I went to a Republican meeting a few nights ago."

And for all his intellectual gravity, he was not above a little mischief. He and his fraternity brothers often repaired to an off-campus location known as the What Cheer. Professor Angell recalled the night that Hay and several others, having fallen under the influence of Fitz Hugh

Ludlow's 1857 memoir, *The Hasheesh Eater*, determined to partake of the potion themselves—to excess, apparently. Hay and a roommate were the only ones in the group able to make their way to Dr. Angell's door at 1 am and lead him back to their room to care for their disabled friends.

Increasingly over his three years at Brown, Hay assumed the pose of the poet, precociously world-wise and prematurely world-weary. For his muses he reached out to Sarah Helen Whitman and Nora Perry, the leading ladies of Providence's small yet vibrant literary salon. Whitman was a widow the same age as Hay's mother. A Transcendentalist-turned-Spiritualist, séance participant, and an occasional poet herself, she draped herself in scarves and veils, and wore a coffin-shaped charm around her neck. Her coterie of friends included Margaret Fuller and Emerson. Perhaps her most noteworthy bona fide was that she had once been engaged to Edgar Allan Poe.

Nora Perry was one of the brightest talents in Whitman's circle. Seven years older than Hay, she had already gained enviable renown; her first poem appeared in *Harper's* when she was eighteen. With deep blue eyes and golden hair, she quickly won Hay's thorough admiration and unrequited adoration.

Like his grandfather sixty-six years earlier, Hay was chosen to deliver the poem for his graduating class. His contribution, "Erato," named for the Greek muse of song, is a 436-line testimonial to the enduring power of verse, of poetry. Its rhymed exhortation is saccharine, but it satisfied the genre and the occasion ably. "To say it was a class poem is sufficiently to characterize it," William Dean Howells later remarked, "and to add that it was easily better than most class poems is not to praise it overmuch."

> *In every age the poet's lyre has rung,*
> *In every land the God-sent bard has sung.*
> *Old memories wedded to the minstrel's rhyme,*
> *Stray ever down the rippled shores of time.*

IT WAS ONE THING to sing the glory and resilience of poetry, quite another to find honest work as a poet. Upon graduation from Brown in the summer of 1858, Hay had no choice but to return to Warsaw, loath as he was to make the journey. "When I look around me and see my trunk packed . . . I begin to realize that I have completed my self-immolation," he sighed to Hannah Angell, daughter of Professor Angell, whose company on picnics he would miss. "A life, not new, but strange from long absence, calls upon me now." Once home, his spirits flagged further. "I am unhappy in my morbid delicacy of spiritual perception," he wrote again to Hannah.

Such brooding was plainly the affectation of a swain bent on winning feminine sympathy. And in Hay's case it was a pose that mimicked the masters. In one of his papers at Brown he had written of the poet whose name he shared: "The prevailing tendency of Milton's mind was to a pensive melancholy. . . . [T]hrough all his writings reigns a saddened sublimity which imparts additional beauty to the creations of his genius. Even in the bright period of his youth, when the sky knew as yet no cloud . . . his writings were pervaded with the same thoughtful pensiveness that adorns the grand music of Paradise Lost."

Hay reckoned that to be a poet one had to act like one, and in Warsaw he clutched the cloak of melancholy with an even more histrionic flourish. "[N]ow that my journey is finished," he wrote to Nora Perry, "I am willing to turn away from the familiar faces I meet in the streets of Warsaw and go to my room to converse with shadows." As fall became winter, he turned the lamp even dimmer. "I have been very near to the valley of the shadow," he told Sarah Whitman. "A few months of exile has [*sic*] worn the lustre from my dreams."

His depression may in fact have been clinical. "I alternate between weeks of sickness & months of my normal condition of chronic worthlessness. . . . I have carried with me this winter in my own heart a portable Hell," he divulged to Hannah Angell. Over the course of his life, he would fall into similar sloughs of "darkness." Yet his distemper also bore the stamp of another tendency that was similarly chronic: affected snobbery. "If you want to see beauty & stupidity united, just go to a party in Warsaw," he confided to a schoolmate. And to Hannah he groused at length: "How like a fool I once dreamed of raising the mental standard of this place. The one cannot raise the many. . . . The average Westerner always spells badly & rides well. Believes in himself & in [Stephen] Douglas [who in 1858 defeated Abraham Lincoln in the race for U.S. Senate], has a profound contempt for goodness & grammar, puts on his gloves & religion only Sundays . . . & is bored when he dies because he thinks heaven will be quiet."

He took a similar posture toward Nora Perry, claiming that "I prefer, for my friends, men who can read," adding, "There is, as yet, no room in the West for a genius"—by which he meant, only half-facetiously, himself.

In Warsaw he continued composing poetry, forwarding his efforts to Providence for suggestion and encouragement. One poem, "In the Mist," was an unapologetic ode to gloom: "Drearily sweeping above the dim plain,/Wanders the rain. . . . Through the murk air/Wails the faint voice of a sullen despair. . . . Dreary the sky!/Dreary the heath! . . . Weary the strife/Of our wintry life!"

Yet aestheticism was not a profession; nobody, not in Warsaw anyway, was hiring sensualists. His parents wanted the best for him, and his father especially hated to see his son's education squandered, even by taking a job as a schoolteacher. Hay briefly tried public lecturing, delivering a talk on, of all topics, the "History of the Jesuits" to an enthusiastic crowd in Warsaw. But he saw no future in this line of work, either. "I believe in the maxim of old Horace, *Poeta noscitur orator fit*," his father remarked. "[T]he Poet is born but the orator is made by cultivation." Hay next weighed the ministry then rejected it as well. "I would not do for a Methodist preacher for I am a poor horseman," he joked to his uncle Milton, who remained very much invested in the graduate's future. "I would not suit the Baptists for I dislike cold water. I would fail as an Episcopalian for I am no ladies' man."

Finally, after months of deliberation, it was agreed that he would move to Springfield and read the law with Milton Hay, who recently had opened a practice there with Stephen Logan, Abraham Lincoln's former partner. "In a short while I shall begin the study of the law," Hay wrote a friend of Sarah Whitman's, "not on account of any love that I bear for the science, but because I do not clearly see what other path of life is open to me. . . . I am aware that I could not depend upon my pen for my life-labor, yet if I have any talent for writing, I should be sorry to let it entirely die. . . . The only numbers which are respected in this country are those preceded by the magical sign '$.' In a year or two, if I live so long, I shall probably fall (or rise, if you will) to the lure of the money-getting masses around me. When I have made my moderate 'pile,' I hope there will be enough soul left within me to draw me back to the beaches & the bays of the blessed Atlantic."

To this letter Hay attached several verses, including:

> Blindly to the grave we go
>   Life to-day is death tomorrow;
> God has kindly willed it so—
>   Shorter life is shorter sorrow.

He arrived in Springfield in May 1859, boarding with his grandfather and maiden aunts once again. Located halfway between the pro-slavery southern tier of the state and the abolitionist-leaning north, Springfield was very much in the throes of the great debate, waged so recently by Abraham Lincoln and Stephen Douglas, on whether slavery ought to be allowed to expand into the territories west of the Mississippi. Lincoln had scored well in his face-to-face exchanges with Douglas, and though he lost his bid for a seat in the U.S. Senate, he was now a political figure of national clout.

As fate would have it, the office of Milton Hay and Stephen Logan adjoined that of Lincoln and his partner, William Herndon, on Fifth Street, across from the Illinois State House. Lincoln, despite his growing renown, still very much depended on the income from his law practice. He continued to work in the courts of the Eighth Judicial Circuit, settled estates, and untangled the affairs of merchants, railroads, and the local gaslight company. In August, he took on the defense and won the acquittal of one Peachy Quinn Harrison, accused of stabbing to death a Sangamon County attorney named Greek Crafton. The other attorneys of record in the case were Herndon, Logan, and Milton Hay. All the while, John Hay fidgeted in the office of Logan & Hay, reading *Blackstone's Commentaries* and whatever other arid texts his uncle prescribed.

Social, rather than legal or political, diversion seemed to be his primary focus, and at first the prospects did not look promising. "I am stranded at last, like a weather-beaten hulk, on the dreary wastes of Springfield," Hay wrote a college roommate. Gradually, though, he was welcomed into a circle of young people, squiring the girls to church, lectures, and socials. He took French lessons, impressing his fellow students with his knack for language. His punning won him favor as well. "One of his original conundrums was this: 'Why is a dog fight like a flirtation?'" recalled the daughter of the town's leading banker, Mary Ridgley, who later married Hay's younger brother Charles. "An[swer]—Because it is an '*affaire du coeur*.'"

Another of the Springfield girls noted merrily that he had "a tongue that could have talked the traditional bird off of the bush." And there was something about those "bright, dark eyes that wrought havoc in the hearts of susceptible maidens."

Hay was now twenty-one, still smooth-faced but with an urbane affect. He gave his height as five foot eight, which was the average for an American man in 1860. Though somewhat slight of build, he carried himself with a jaunty self-confidence. "He was, for those days, elegantly dressed—better than any of us," a Springfield friend observed. Mary Ridgley was another who was taken with his "dark, lustrous" eyes. She remembered, too, his "red cheeks and clear dark complexion; small, well-shaped hands which he had a habit of locking together, interlacing the fingers, and carrying at arm's length, which the girls thought particularly fetching. He wore a long, loose overcoat, flying open, his hands thrust into his pockets, which was also thought very graceful and attractive as he swung himself along the street, for he had a rocking walk in those days."

WHAT FINALLY DREW JOHN Hay into the affairs of Abraham Lincoln, other than his ambivalence for the law, was his renewed friendship with John George Nicolay. If Hay had kept to the periphery of public debate, Nicolay had jumped in with both feet. He and Lincoln had first met in 1856, when Nicolay was editor of the *Pike County Free Press* and Lincoln needed someone to print campaign literature. That same year, Nicolay attended the Republican Convention as a Free-Soiler. After the election, in which the Republicans' first presidential candidate, John C. Frémont, lost to James Buchanan, Nicolay sold the *Press* and moved to Springfield, going to work for Lincoln's close friend Illinois secretary of state Ozias Hatch. Nicolay studied law under Hatch's supervision and was admitted to the bar in 1859, a few months before Hay arrived in Springfield. By then Nicolay had been under the sway of Lincoln for three years.

Nicolay and Hay mixed in the same society, which centered on the Ridgley household. Nicolay was neither as handsome nor as outgoing as Hay. He had "the close, methodical, silent German way about him," commented John Russell Young, who later got to know Nicolay in the White House. "[He was] scrupulous, polite, calm, obliging, with the gift of hearing other people talk . . . [and] with the soft, sad smile that seemed to come only from the eyes." Nicolay compensated for his reserve with a sweet tenor voice and by playing the flute. And unlike Hay, who in those days was sometimes too quick to please, Nicolay was admired for his quiet industriousness; already he had several patents in his name. "[I]f ever there was a man who worked, John Nicolay was that man," Mary Ridgley attested.

Nicolay was in the colossal Wigwam in Chicago on May 18, 1860, when an invigorated Republican Party nominated Abraham Lincoln, everybody's second choice, as its candidate for president. Lincoln had remained in Springfield; the news reached him by noon, and the rest of the capital was soon notified by the ringing of church bells and the firing of a cannon, one round for each state of the beleaguered Union. Crowds packed the State House, then moved to Lincoln's house, where "the Rail-Splitter," as he was now known, made a few modest remarks.

Hay, it must be said, was slow to join the Lincoln bandwagon. He had returned to Illinois from Providence in plenty of time for Lincoln's titanic debates with Douglas. But, while he likely read transcripts in the local papers and could hardly have ignored the enormous hoopla surrounding the seven encounters between the race-baiting Democrat and his unshakeable, anti-slavery nemesis, he never mentioned attending one of them. (The nearest debate to Warsaw took place on October 13, 1858, at Quincy, some forty miles away; none was held in Springfield.) And despite Lincoln's ever-growing stature as a leader of the national Republican movement, nevertheless the ungainly, unkempt lawyer who came and went to and from the adjoining office on Fifth Street may at first have struck Hay as another of the backwoods strivers whom he thought he had escaped when he had gone east to college. Then, too, Lincoln would have been far too preoccupied to pay more than cursory attention to the sharp but slightly glib young man with the clean cuffs and tidy cravat who was making a halfhearted stab at learning laws that Lincoln had absorbed by a far dimmer light more than twenty years earlier.

At best, Lincoln was a long shot. Few men, not even in Springfield, honestly believed he had a chance to be president. (While Lincoln did win Springfield, barely, in the fall election, a majority of Sangamon County voted against him.) For the moment, Lincoln was merely a dark-horse politician—after which, it was assumed, he would be a lawyer again.

Hay still regarded himself as a poet, lukewarm at best about joining the profession of his uncle and the other occupants of the musty, cluttered office on Fifth Street. And so, for the sake of his literary cohort back in Providence at least, he adopted a condescending antipathy. "My insanity has not yet changed its form from rhyme to politics," he told Hannah Angell in early May 1860, two weeks before the Republican Convention. "I occupy myself very pleasantly in thoroughly hating both sides, and abusing the peculiar tenets of the company I happen to be in. . . . This position of dignified neutrality I expect to hold for a very long time unless Lincoln is nominated at Chicago."

With the surprising outcome of May 18, the view from Logan & Hay was transformed dramatically. Lincoln's horse was no longer so dark, and the moody young dilettante could suddenly see the heroic possibilities of the drama taking shape in his midst. "Dignified neutrality" was abandoned. To borrow a term from the forthcoming presidential campaign, he was now Wide Awake.

At the urging of his Brown professor James Angell, Hay submitted an eyewitness account of the Lincoln victory celebration in Springfield to the *Providence Journal* under the pen name Ecarte. Clearly the author of the following item was no fence-sitter: "When the lightning came down from Chicago . . . to tell us that the nation had honored the honest man whom we have so long delighted to honor, the deep and earnest enthusiasm of the hearty western populace burst forth in the wildest manifestations of joy." Suddenly the skies were bright. "No more of the martyr-spirit of four years ago; no more of the forlorn-hope appeals; no more of that feeling of contention against overwhelming odds. . . . [E]very heart seemed filled with the dauntless energy which comes from a premonition of success. . . . The Republicans of the Prairie State feel large-hearted and jubilant."

Hay loved seeing his words in print—and if he could not gain attention as a poet, he would carry on as a propagandist. Anything was better than the programmatic prose of the law. After his first item appeared in the Providence paper, he was invited to submit articles to the *Missouri Democrat* of St. Louis (which, despite its name, was sympathetic to the Republican cause). Lincoln, however self-effacing, had never eschewed publicity, and he and his fellow Republicans understood all too well that to improve the chance of victory in November, they must put a face and personality to the rail-splitting debater from Springfield and create an aura of enthusiasm that, they hoped, would become contagious.

Hay was only too eager to oblige. After another rally in Springfield in August, Ecarte wrote breathlessly: "The deluge of enthusiasm that has swept over us has left no soul unsubmerged by the swelling waters. Lincoln men are too jolly to give any particular reason for the faith that is in them. . . . It was certainly the greatest political demonstration that our State has ever seen. Veteran stumpers, who have mingled in every fight since Jackson's time, fail of comparisons to describe it. Editors and reporters who have haunted for years the mass meetings of the nation, say they have seen nothing to be compared to it. Grey-haired Whigs"—another of Hay's puns—"who shouted and drank hard cider on the Tippecanoe battle field, at the monster meeting of twenty years ago and have lived ever since in the confident belief that no other meeting ever would be like it, shake their heads since yesterday, and mourn over a broken idol, an ideal eclipsed. . . . It was worth many years of ordinary life to see the wild rush and impetuous enthusiasm of the crowd when Mr. Lincoln appeared upon the grounds, to see for a moment, and be seen by the eager thousands who had come so many miles with that one purpose and hope; and to hear when he had been forced onto the stand by their loving violence, the friendly, yet dignified words by which he stilled their clamorous plaudits."

A month later, he wrote, again as Ecarte, "It is one of the truest evidences of the innate nobility of Abraham Lincoln, that he impresses all with whom he is brought in contact, lofty or lowly, with the irresistible magnetism of a large and catholic nature."

One of the magnetized was John Hay, and for the next four years he would make the most of his conversion, sharing his views anonymously or pseudonymously with the press and observing the Lincoln presidency like no other. His bombast was born of artistic ego, but, as time passed, it was even more a measure of his appreciation and admiration for his subject.

NOT LONG AFTER THE nomination, it became obvious that Lincoln could not run a presidential campaign out of a cramped law office. In early June, he moved into the more commodious governor's office on the second floor of the State House, unoccupied when the legislature was not in session. It had room for ten or twelve people, at least before it became cluttered with the miscellany sent by supporters: axes, split rails, surveying tools, and a twelve-foot chain, its links carved from a single piece of wood "to symbolize the indissoluble union of the states." Mail arrived by the bushel. "I wish I could find some young man to help me with my correspondence," Lincoln asked Ozias Hatch. "I can't afford to pay much, but the practice is worth something." Hatch recommended Nicolay, who had initially hoped for the assignment of writing Lincoln's campaign biography. When the job went to a young William Dean Howells, Nicolay readily took the secretary position for $75 a month.

Throughout the summer and into the fall, Nicolay was Lincoln's only secretary; his job was to greet prominent Republicans and manage the mail. Ever more swamped, Nicolay suggested to Lincoln that they enlist John Hay to turn his gifted hand to answering letters. Hay had already proven himself in the articles for the Providence and St. Louis newspapers, and Milton Hay further vouched for his nephew's "great literary talent and great tact."

Hay, needless to say, was all too willing to set aside his legal education. Always a quick study and now a Lincoln believer, he stepped in nimbly,

writing letters for the nominee's signature and continuing to beat the
Republican drum in his Ecarte submissions. When Milton Hay offered
to underwrite his nephew for the first six months, Lincoln declined the
offer, pledging to pay the salary out of his own pocket, if it came to that.
For the time being, Hay worked for nothing.

With the astonishing victory of November—in which Democrats
splintered their ticket, allowing Lincoln to win every northern state but
one, while earning only 40 percent of the popular vote—the office in the
Illinois State House was deluged with exponentially more letters, some
seeking autographs, interviews, and jobs in the new administration; others offering congratulations, advice, and, from more than a few southerners, condemnation. Yet as capable and indispensable as Hay was proving
to be, Lincoln wasn't sure whether he would be able to keep his new aide
on the presidential staff. Officially the White House payroll allowed for
only one private secretary, Nicolay. "We can't take all Illinois with us
down to Washington," Lincoln supposedly said. And then, after a moment's reflection, he gave in: "Well, let Hay come."

A QUARTER CENTURY LATER, when Nicolay and Hay at last divided up
the job of writing Lincoln's biography, Hay would assume responsibility
for the chapters dealing with Lincoln's years in Indiana and Illinois and
his emergence as a lawyer and political figure. Like Hay, Lincoln had endured bouts of melancholy—"a sea of perplexities and sufferings beyond
the reach of the common run of souls"—most famously after the death
of a girl he had loved, Ann Rutledge, and after his fitful engagement to
Mary Todd. By the time Hay sat down to chronicle this period of Lincoln's life, he had spent four years in intimate contact with the president
and understood him much more thoroughly than he did in November
1860. Yet Hay had not been acquainted with the young Lincoln at all,
and when he gave himself to the task of explaining the travails of Lincoln's early life, he brought to bear two frames of reference, both of them
sentimental and entirely subjective: one was his appreciation of the Lincoln he had come to know; the second, perhaps more insightful, was his
own poetic passage from self-absorbed adolescence to more enlightened
manhood.

"In many respects he was doomed to a certain loneliness of excellence," Hay was to observe of Lincoln. "[T]he whole course of his development and the tendency of his nature made it inevitable that his suffering should be of the keenest and his final triumph over himself should be of the most complete and signal character. In that struggle his youth of reveries and day-dreams passed away. Such furnace-blasts of proof, such pangs of transformation, seem necessary for exceptional natures. The bread eaten in tears, of which Goethe speaks, the sleepless nights of sorrow, are required for a clear vision of the celestial powers. Fortunately the same qualities that occasion the conflict insure the victory also. From days of gloom and depression . . . no doubt came precious results in the way of sympathy, self-restraint, and that sober reliance on the final triumph of good over evil peculiar to those who have been greatly tried but not destroyed."

Through his own experience, Hay came to know Lincoln. Through Lincoln, he began to find himself.

CHAPTER 3

Potomac Fever

Abraham Lincoln, who had served a single previous term as a congressman and had traveled beyond the prairie of Illinois only on rare occasions, could have chosen any number of private secretaries more worldly than John George Nicolay and John Milton Hay. Doubtless there were many in the Republican Party who advised him to cast a wider net for men of greater experience and sophistication. But out of loyalty and surely because of the competence and compatibility that his two young aides had demonstrated thus far, he stuck by them. These were two of the easiest decisions he would make over the next four years.

For Hay, the invitation to join the White House staff came as an enormous reprieve from a profession he had chosen by default. "It is cowardly in me to cling so persistently to a life which is past," he had written to Nora Perry before Lincoln had won the party nomination. "It is my duty, and in truth it is my ultimate intention to qualify myself for a Western Lawyer, *et praeterea nihil,* 'only that and nothing more.'" Lincoln's coattails spared him, and he gave no further thought to being a lawyer, although on February 4, 1861, one week before the presidential train left for Washington, he was admitted to the Illinois bar. "I never practiced law myself," he would tell his son Del almost forty years later, "but I have never considered the time wasted I spent studying it." Perhaps not, but in 1861 he was glad to apply himself otherwise.

But now that he was at last getting to escape what so recently he had regarded as the coarse, stunting climate of the West, he found himself unexpectedly wistful for Warsaw. "I shall never enjoy myself more thoroughly than I did that short little winter [1858–59] I spent at home," he wrote a friend in Springfield. "It was so quiet and still so free."

In the four months between the election and inauguration, the mail kept everyone busy. Hay noticed letters overflowing from Lincoln's coat pockets. He spotted Lincoln reading letters as he trod down the street with his distinctive mule's gait. "I believe he is strongly tempted [to read] in church," Hay chuckled.

Lincoln had prudently decided to say as little as possible about his intended positions and appointments until after he was in office. Yet despite campaign assurances that he would not interfere with slavery in states where it already existed, the South declined to give the new administration the benefit of the doubt. Between December and February, seven states seceded from the Union to form their own confederacy. Departing President James Buchanan, eager to keep the peace—and pass the buck—weighed whether to abandon one or more forts in South Carolina.

Hay, in the role of Lincoln's press agent, exhorted the public not to jump to conclusions. "Mr. Lincoln will not be scared or coaxed into any expression of what everybody knows are his opinions until the will of the people and the established institutions of the Government are vindicated by his inauguration," he wrote as Ecarte in the *Missouri Democrat.* "Then if anybody doubts his integrity, his liberality, his large-hearted forbearance and his conservatism, their doubts will be removed. Until then let them possess their souls in patience."

Lincoln left Springfield on February 11, accompanied by Hay, Nicolay, twenty or so friends, colleagues, military escorts, and seventeen-year-old Robert Lincoln. Hay and Robert had first met during Hay's pre-college days in Springfield, and the two had become better friends during Robert's recent visits home. Lincoln, too, was just now getting reacquainted with his eldest son. Thus far they had never been close for the simple reason that they had been too often apart. Lincoln was frequently absent from home as a circuit lawyer when Robert was a boy. Then it was Robert's turn to go away, graduating from Phillips Exeter Academy in New Hampshire and entering Harvard College in the fall of 1860.

Mrs. Lincoln and Robert's younger brothers, Tad and Willie, joined the train in Indianapolis, and over the next ten days and two thousand miles, Lincoln would deliver more than a hundred speeches to crowds totaling nearly a million. Yet the journey had only just begun. For better or worse, this small nucleus, consisting of the Lincolns and the presidential secretaries, would continue as fellow travelers for four more years, living in close quarters, baring every seam of their natures, as war and the affairs of the nation enveloped them, and they in turn endeavored to steer the nation's course.

Hay took advantage of the shared captivity to sketch his employer. "If the reader could see him, as the writer hereof sees him," Ecarte wrote as they passed through Buffalo, "sitting upon yonder seat, deep-eyed, bending forward, his face channeled with deep wrinkles, which hold a shadowy significance of the man within—large-browed, thoughtful, an aspect generally expressive of rugged strength in repose, and of resolute decision in action—the reader would probably arrive at the conclusion that he was the man, of all others, to see that he was right, and then to go ahead. If he be not such a man, why, then physiognomy is a delusion and a snare." Hay's message, above all, was that Abraham Lincoln was in possession of a singular greatness.

Equally evident was Lincoln's unusual, unaffected humanness. After a speech in Trenton, Hay described Lincoln's voice as being "as soft and sympathetic as a girl's." Although he never raised it "above the tone of average conversation, it was distinctly audible throughout the entire hall." After pledging his devotion to "peace and conciliation," Lincoln had added emphatically, " '[B]ut yet I fear we shall have to put the foot down firmly.' " And with "a subdued intensity of tone," Hay observed, Lincoln "lifted his foot lightly and pressed it with a quick, but not violent, gesture upon the floor." Hay noticed that "[t]here was a peculiar naiveté in [Lincoln's] manner and voice, which produced a strange effect upon the audience. It was hushed for a moment to a silence which was like that of the dead. I have never seen an assemblage more thoroughly captivated and entranced."

Lincoln's manifest calm and confidence helped to allay Hay's fear that something bad might happen before they arrived in the capital. After bodyguards spirited Lincoln through Baltimore under the cover of darkness, Hay scoffed at various rumors of "an organized plan to throw the train off an embankment," "sharpshooting desperadoes," "torpedoes . . . thrown beneath the carriage," and "so many desperate and murderous things . . . done that if the President elect had all the lives of a cat he would lose them all." Arriving in Washington on a later train with the rest of the Lincoln party, he denied that Lincoln had altered his itinerary in order to avoid violence, explaining that Lincoln had not made a public appearance in Baltimore, which lately had earned the nickname "Mobtown," simply because he had not been invited to do so.

But even while Hay outwardly doubted the existence of a plot against the president-elect's life, he nevertheless jotted a hasty note to a cousin on the night before he was to leave Harrisburg: "Tomorrow we enter slave territory. . . . If all is well, this letter will do no harm. If anything happens, you will remember that I was, at the present date, very affectionately, your friend, John Hay."

HE FOUND WASHINGTON AT once august and disgusting. Marble for the Capitol's new wings lay stacked about the grounds; the statue of *Freedom*, intended for the dome, stood ominously earthbound. Below Capitol Hill, the Washington Monument was an unfinished stub of marble and granite, with cows grazing about its base. Streets throughout the city were unpaved, alternately rutted or choked with vile mud; garbage lay everywhere; the Potomac estuary was a swill of waste and fever.

The young secretary had never been in the American capital before, but he was familiar enough with the great cities of civilization—by way of the classics he had absorbed as a student. From afar, Washington appeared to him "in broad avenues, which converge upon the capitol as all roads of the Roman empire converged upon that golden milestone by the Pincian gate." Pennsylvania Avenue took on "the stately air of a grand Appian Way."

But on closer inspection he found Washington "a congerie of hovels, inharmoniously sewn with temples," and he wondered, "Why did they attempt to build a city where no city was ever intended to be reared?"

Within two weeks of his arrival, his young eyes could see into the future: "It will never be a capital, except only in name; never a metropolis, like Rome, or London, or Paris. . . . Yet it will sometime, of course, be clustered about with historic memories. Caesar will be slain in the capitol, and Brutus harangue the roughs from the terrace."

Officially Hay was not a secretary at all. Lincoln had found a way around the restriction on the size of his personal staff by appointing him to a clerkship in the Department of the Interior at the modest salary of $1,600 a year, later increased to $1,800. His workplace, however, would always be the White House. John George Nicolay held the position of Lincoln's private secretary; Hay's title, to everyone but the federal paymaster, was designated as assistant private secretary.

He and Nicolay moved into the White House along with the Lincolns immediately after the inauguration on March 4. Hay was on hand when James Buchanan welcomed his successor. "I waited with boyish wonder and credulity to see what momentous counsels were to come from that gray and weather-beaten head," Hay wrote. "Every word must have its value at such an instant." To his surprise and disappointment, Buchanan said merely: "'I think you will find the water of the right-hand well at the White House better than that at the left,' and went on with many intimate details of the kitchen and pantry. Lincoln listened with that weary, introverted look of his, not answering, and the next day, when I recalled the conversation, admitted he had not heard a word of it."

Ever since John Adams, American presidents had lived where they worked, a point of pride for the American republic but, by the time the Lincolns moved in, a challenge to both practicality and privacy. The Lincoln family occupied just seven rooms on the west end of the second floor. The president's office, which was also the cabinet room, was down a central hallway, buffered from the importunate public by only a small vestibule and waiting room. The president had no private entrance. Nor, for that matter, were the first floor and grounds of the White House off limits to the general populace most of the time. Hay and Nicolay shared a bedroom on the other side of the waiting room from the president's office. Each had their own office—Nicolay's immediately next to Lincoln's in the southeast corner, Hay's in the northeast corner, looking out to Lafayette Square.

The White House, like the country, had seen better days. Some visitors found the private and public rooms "seedy," "shabby," and "dilapidated"—an "ordinary country house wanting in either taste or splendor." To another it had all the charm of "an old and unsuccessful hotel." When Mrs. Lincoln counted the good china, she discovered there were not a dozen place settings that matched.

Her husband's secretaries were too busy to complain much. "We have very pleasant offices and a nice large bedroom, though all of them sadly need new furniture and carpets," Nicolay wrote to his fiancée, Therena Bates.

As they settled in, Hay and Nicolay assumed somewhat different duties. Nicolay tended to be more in charge of the office proper, including cabinet meetings, and Hay, the better writer, took greater responsibility for the correspondence. From the very first day, they were both astounded by "the intolerable press of business about the President's office," Hay wrote. "I have positively not had a moment's leisure since we arrived in this city. The throng of office-seekers is something almost fearful. They come at daybreak and still are coming at midnight."

Hay and Nicolay did their best to shield Lincoln from interruption, and their steadfastness elicited hard feelings. "The President is affable and kind, but his immediate subordinates are snobby and unpopular," reported one visitor. Nicolay took the brunt of the ill will, earning a reputation as a "grim Cerberus," after the multi-headed hound that guarded the gates of the ancient underworld. But where Nicolay was "sour and crusty," Hay's nimble humor bought him leniency. "[John Hay] might have drawn to himself more criticism in Washington had he not been born with peculiar charm of manner," Nicolay's daughter later explained.

Neither Nicolay's Germanic tenacity nor Hay's affability was enough to insulate Lincoln, however, for the president was reluctant to cooperate. When Massachusetts senator Henry Wilson suggested to the president that he limit interviews, Lincoln purportedly replied, "They don't want much; they get but little, and I must see them."

And yet, Lincoln confided to his secretaries that he felt as if he were "letting lodgings at one end of the house, while the other end was on fire."

•　　•　　•

THE SURRENDER OF FORT Sumter in mid-April, followed by the secession of Virginia and three more states, soon brought the war that Lincoln never wanted but was now his to end. And as the nation split apart, Washington found itself surrounded and vulnerable. Maryland, Delaware, and the District of Columbia allowed slavery, and their allegiance to the Union could not be taken for granted. Confederate campfires were visible across the Potomac, and the White House was within range of rebel mortars. Some of the first northern volunteers who arrived to defend the capital were billeted temporarily in the East Room. "The White House is turned into barracks," Hay wrote in the very first entry of the diary he kept through most of the war.

He did not feel so much endangered by the southern threat as insulted by the low-down gall of the Confederacy. "I have seen rough company in the west and north, but never in the kennels of the great cities or the wild license of flat boating on the Mississippi did I ever hear words that were not purity, compared with the disgusting filtrations of the Chivalric Southern mind," he snorted after sampling the mail addressed to the White House from the rebel states. "The history of the world is leprous with . . . instances of national folly and crime, but it was reserved for the Southern States to exhibit an infamy to which other crimes show white as mother's milk, and a madness to which an actor's phrensy is sane."

When Lincoln mentioned to him privately that he would like one day to go down to Charleston "and pay her the little debt we are owing her," Hay recorded in his diary, "I felt like letting off an Illinois yell."

Yet for Hay the war began not with a yell but a sob. In May, Colonel Elmer Ellsworth, who had studied law in Lincoln's office and accompanied the Lincolns from Springfield, was killed while cutting down a Confederate flag that waved from atop a hotel in nearby Alexandria, Virginia. Hay knew Ellsworth well and mourned him as everything a soldier and a gentleman ought to be. "He always seemed like a Paladin or Cavalier of the dead days of romance and beauty," Hay wrote in the *Atlantic Monthly*, yet another outlet for his pro-Union evangelizing. "He was so generous and loyal, so stainless and brave." After paying his respects to Ellsworth's uniformed body as it lay in state in the East Room, Hay wrote to Hannah Angell (who by now was married): "When Ellsworth was murdered all my sunshine perished. I hope you may never know the dry, barren agony of soul that comes with the utter and hopeless loss of a great love."

With the war now pressing on the White House, there was no such thing as routine. Nevertheless, Hay and Nicolay tried as best they could to make a life of their own. They took their meals at Willard's Hotel, nearby on Pennsylvania Avenue—"[m]iraculous in meanness; contemptible in cuisine," Hay reviewed. They were no strangers to the "blear caravanserai" of the city's barrooms, where Hay catalogued a clientele representing "every stage of official eminence and every grade of inebriety. There are generals, and colonels, and majors, and captains, governors, senators, honorables; all chew tobacco; all spit; a good many swear, and not a few make a merit of being able to keep two cocktails in the air at once."

The society they kept was not always so raucous. Hay was a regular at the Sunday evening "drop-ins" of Mr. and Mrs. Charles Eames, émigrés from Massachusetts whose drawing room was a gathering place for "the brains of society"—politicians, diplomats, authors, and artists speaking a variety of languages. As an eligible bachelor, he was invited to levees and soirées, though he admitted to his deficiency as a dancer: "'Those light at heart tickle the senseless rushes with their heels,' says Romeo, and though I am rarely heavy in the vicinity of that organ, I am saurian in the deliberation of my movements; never dance, in fact."

As much as his busy schedule would allow, he went to the theater, including several trips to Ford's with the president. Somehow, too, he found time for literature, reading, among other books, George Eliot's *Silas Marner*, and Victor Hugo's *Les Misérables* in French. Besides keeping up his diary, letters, and submissions for publication, he also wrote the occasional poem, customarily sentimental but now bathed in patriotism:

> *O strong, free North, so wise and brave!*
> *O South, too lovely for a slave!*

Mostly, though, the days and many nights overflowed with secretarial duties. "I am getting along pretty well," he joked. "I only work about

20 hours a day." The war increased the size and persistence of the crowd that lined up each morning in the waiting room, corridor, and stairway—thousands seeking "the crumbs of official patronage"; "cold-water" temperance committees who blamed the Union's early setbacks on the military's weakness for alcohol; Quakers petitioning for peace; mothers begging pardons for sons; and more than a few callers of uncertain sanity. When a man appeared in the waiting room, claiming to be the son of God, Hay assured him that the president would be delighted to see him—but first would the caller mind providing a letter of introduction from his father?

Letters arrived at the rate of two or three hundred a day. Hay and Nicolay soon realized that they would never be able to manage the volume and asked the president to find them more help. William Stoddard, a newspaperman from Illinois, had wanted Nicolay's or Hay's job but initially had to settle for a menial position in the Department of the Interior. By the early summer of 1861, however, he was brought aboard the White House staff, chiefly to help with the mail. He was given a desk in Hay's office, where he sorted letters by category: requests for jobs, contracts, money, and autographs—intermixed, Stoddard recalled, with "the rant and drivel of insanity, bitter abuse, foul obscenity, [and] slanderous charges."

Hay welcomed Stoddard but never entirely embraced him, calling the third secretary "statuesque," whether for his vanity or his immobility is not clear. Stoddard was more generous in his appraisal of Hay, remembering him as "quick witted," "a born diplomat." Stoddard also noted Hay's "almost boyish complexion" and remarked that he was "quite a favorite among the ladies . . . with a gift for epigram and repartee." And there was no denying Hay's potential. "What he will make of himself remains to be seen," Stoddard commented, "but he is capable of something far better."

Hay's emergence from boyishness to manliness is evident in a photograph he had printed on a *carte de visite*, the calling card of Washington society. Hay wears a smartly tailored double-breasted coat and broad-looped bow tie; on one hand he wears a leather glove; his other hand is bare, gracefully gripping its glove—the casual but decorous pose of a gentleman wishing to appear somewhat rakish but not so young. ("Ah me! whither are gone my adolescent days?" he groused in one of his newspaper columns.) His dark eyes hold the camera, while his mouth with-holds a smile. Like Lincoln, he is now hirsute: draped across his upper lip is a wispy but promising mustache that he would tend for the rest of his life. "I think the mug is absurd," he said of the photo self-consciously. "The expression of the features reminds me of the desperate attempts of a tipsy man to look sober."

THE WAR NEWS WAS sobering enough. On July 21, the Confederates routed the federal army at Bull Run, near Manassas, Virginia, stamped-ing the troops across the Potomac, briefly sparking alarm that the capital would be overrun. The fighting came so close to the city that the thunder of artillery rumbled through the open windows of the White House. Hay rode out to the battle, returning at dawn the following morning amid the ongoing rout. "With the ushering in of daylight there came pouring into the city crowds of soldiers, some with muskets, some without muskets, some with knapsacks, and some without knapsack, or canteen, or belt, or anything but their soiled and dirty uniform, burned faces and eyes . . . to indicate that they were soldiers," he reported to the *New York World*. "The bodies of the dead were piled on top of one another; the pallid faces and blood-stained garments telling a fearfully mute but sad story of the horrors of the war. And the appearance of the wounded, bereft of arms, of legs, eyes put out, flesh wounds in the face and body, and uniforms crimsoned with blood, proclaimed with equal force the savage horrors of humans battling with weapons of war."

In the *New York Tribune*, Horace Greeley had described Bull Run as the "shipwreck of our grand and heroic army." In his role as White House propagandist, Hay begged to differ, insisting that "the defeat was not a defeat—only a victory of vastly superior numbers over a few segmentary regiments." Lincoln, who had stayed awake all night absorbing the first major reversal of the war, offered Hay a more honest and self-reproachful assessment: "There is nothing in this except the lives lost and the lives which must be lost to make it good."

Lincoln's first step after Bull Run was to relieve General Irvin McDowell as commander of the Army of Northeastern Virginia (soon reformed as the Army of the Potomac) and replace him with General

George McClellan, whose credentials were both impressive and worrisome. As a veteran of the Mexican War and an observer of the Crimean War, he was one of the country's foremost experts on military science. A West Point engineer who became a railroad president, he was superbly qualified to manage men and matériel. But he was also a conservative Democrat who had actively supported Stephen Douglas. He had witnessed at least one of Douglas's debates with Lincoln, whom he regarded as "not a man of very strong character." McClellan's opinion of his own character was considerably greater. Upon accepting the promotion from Lincoln, the general confided to his wife, "I almost think that if I were to win some small success now I could become Dictator or anything else that might please me." "Little Mac," as his troops called him, was an avid student of Napoleon.

Hay, too, received a new assignment. At the end of August, the president sent him to Long Branch, New Jersey, with Mrs. Lincoln and the children, ostensibly as their caretaker but also to give him a needed respite from the White House. Returning to Washington somewhat refreshed, he promptly came down with bilious fever, known not so endearingly in Washington as "Potomac fever." The cause was usually pinned on the fetid summer air. "The ghosts of twenty thousand drowned cats come in nights through the South Windows" is how Hay described the toxic atmosphere.

By September 1 he was better, in time to make another trip at Lincoln's request. He traveled to St. Louis, carrying a letter from the president to General John C. Frémont, commander of the Department of the West. The venerable Frémont—explorer, conqueror of California, and the Republican Party's first presidential candidate—had committed one egotistical blunder after another in Missouri, leading indirectly to the debacle at Wilson's Creek on August 10, which caused the Union to surrender control of nearly half the state. Lincoln was already losing faith in his less than obedient general, when on August 30 Frémont declared martial law in Missouri and freed slaves belonging to anyone considered disloyal to the Union. His reckless initiative threatened to undermine the adherence of border states. Moreover, emancipation was a decision that the president would make in due time and not on a piecemeal or temporary basis.

Lincoln was highly irritated and began the delicate process of removing the popular Frémont.

Whether or not Hay knew the content of the message he delivered to Frémont, he concurred with the president's opinion that Frémont had grown too big for his breeches. In his diary he called the general "imperious." Meanwhile, writing for the *New York World*, anonymously as usual, he endeavored to quell attacks on Frémont—and attacks on Lincoln by abolitionists who approved of the general's initiative—by calling the general a "born leader . . . always equal to himself and the occasion."

Regardless of the outcome, for Lincoln to send his young secretary on a mission of such enormous political and military delicacy was testament to the growing trust he had in Hay's discretion and diplomacy. More such assignments would follow. For Hay, by far the best part of the trip west was the chance to stop in Warsaw for a visit with his family.

In WASHINGTON, LINCOLN WAS already having trouble with General McClellan. On October 21, the Union was again routed, this time at Ball's Bluff, where hundreds of soldiers were presumed drowned as they attempted to retreat across the Potomac. The following night, Lincoln summoned McClellan to the White House for a talk. Hay listened in. Despite the latest loss, the commander of the Army of the Potomac "seemed very hopeful and confident," Hay noted in his diary. But as the conversation continued, Hay commented, "it became painfully evident that [McClellan] had *no plan.*"

Ten days later, Lincoln and McClellan met again; this time Lincoln, accompanied by Hay, called on McClellan at his house on Lafayette Square. The purpose of the visit was to inform McClellan of the resignation of General Winfield Scott as general in chief and to promote McClellan to the supreme command of the entire army. McClellan was honored but hardly humbled. "I can do it all," he told the president.

The honeymoon lasted scarcely two weeks. "I wish to record what I consider a portent of evil to come," Hay recorded in his diary on November 13. "The President, [Secretary of State] Seward and I went over to McClellan's house tonight. The Servant at the door said the General was at the wedding of Col. Wheaton at General Buell's, and would soon return. We went in, and after we had waited about an hour McC[lellan] came in and without paying any particular attention to the porter who told him the President was waiting to see him, went up stairs, passing the door of the room where the President and Secretary of State were seated. They waited about half-an-hour and sent once more a servant to tell the General they were there, and the answer came that the General had gone to bed."

Lincoln appeared not to be offended, but Hay was incensed, as evidenced by his diary and by more subtle criticism published, without byline, in the *Missouri Republican* a month later. "[I]t is ill for a Republic when the military arm begins to rival the civil power," he admonished, adding more pointedly: "Gen. McClellan has always recognized this. . . . He is a soldier, and knows that his duties in that capacity will occupy all the time he has."

Hay's resentment of McClellan began but did not end there. He would wait twenty years to settle his grudge against the general afflicted with the "slows"—who was too cautious to fight or follow orders; who committed repeated acts of near treason; who called Lincoln an "idiot" and a "baboon" behind his back; and who strategized to bring about, if not the defeat of the Union, then certainly of the president. In reviewing a book on McClellan's military career for the *New York Tribune*, Hay would call McClellan "weak, vacillating, insubordinate." And in a long screed in the Lincoln biography, Hay would lambaste McClellan for his "long mismanagement of a great, brave, and devoted army, backed by a Government which strained every nerve to support him, and by a people whose fiery zeal would have made him the idol of the nation if he had given them the successes which their sacrifices deserved, and which was a dozen times within his grasp."

Hay's low regard for the president's enemies, doubters, and detractors—which did not stop at the Confederacy but also included the Democratic Party and the Radical wing of his own party—was an accurate, if inverse, gauge of his increasing affection for his employer. The nicknames that he and Nicolay gave to Lincoln—"the Ancient," "the Tycoon"—while never used within earshot of the president, were an acknowledgment of his Olympian stature and of their wholehearted and steadfast commitment to him.

Although Lincoln, for the most part, treated the two secretaries equally, he did not treat them the same. Not that he gave Nicolay short shrift, but Hay filled a space that only he could occupy. He was so quick-witted, precociously canny in the ways of men, savvy in the customs of both East and West. Perhaps for these reasons, Hay was more often at Lincoln's side when he ventured away from the White House—say, to McClellan's house or to the theater. In summers, when the Lincolns escaped the close air of the White House by sleeping at the Soldiers' Home on the northern fringe of the city, Hay would often ride out with the president and spend the night. Of one such evening, he mentioned, "I went with him to the Soldiers' Home & he read Shakespeare to me, the end of Henry VI and the beginning of Richard III till my heavy eye-lids caught his considerate notice & he sent me to bed."

Lincoln, though, was a poor sleeper, and insomnia frequently drew him to pace the White House—whence comes one of the oft-told stories of the president in his nightshirt. One evening after midnight, as Hay and Nicolay readied for bed, the president appeared at their door, laughing at a caricature he had come across in a book by the humorist Thomas Hood. Lincoln, as Hay recorded in his diary, was entirely unconscious of his "short shirt hanging about his long legs & setting out behind like the tail feathers on an enormous ostrich." The president, Hay wrote, "was infinitely funnier than anything in the book he was laughing at."

Rather than laugh at Lincoln, Hay could only admire him the more: "What a man it is! Occupied all day with matters of vast moment, deeply anxious about the fate of the greatest army of the world, with his own fame & future hanging on the events of the passing hour, he yet has such a simple wealth of simple bonhomie & good fellowship that he gets out of bed & perambulates the house in his shirt to find us."

The contrast between the president's lofty station and his austere habits was a source of constant wonder to the young secretary, whose own proclivities were hardly so reserved. "He was one of the most abstemious of men; the pleasures of the table had few attractions for him," Hay would write of Lincoln in *Century Magazine*. "His breakfast was an egg and a cup of coffee; at luncheon he rarely took more than a biscuit and a glass of milk, a plate of fruit in its season; at dinner he ate sparingly of one or two courses. He drank little or no wine; not that he remained always on principle a total abstainer, as he was during a part of his early life in the fervor of the 'Washingtonian' reform; but he never cared for wine or liquors of any sort, and never used tobacco."

Beyond serving merely as a sidekick on rides to the Soldiers' Home or as audience to Lincoln's recitations of Shakespeare and lesser literature, Hay also gave as good as he got. Recognizing that Lincoln relied on humor to distract him from the pain of war, Hay did his best to divert the president's attention whenever he could—although not even he could soothe the mood for long.

One quiet Sunday, Hay returned to the White House "all one bubble," William Stoddard recalled. "Generally he could tell a story better than most, but this time he broke down with a laugh before he was well started. Through the open door Nicolay heard the peal of laughter and came over from his room, pen in hand, and sat down to listen. Hay began at the beginning and went on very well until the first good point was reached . . . and all three of us exploded as one." Suddenly, there stood Lincoln at the door, drawn by the uproar, and demanded, " 'Now, John, just tell that again' . . . and he sank into Andrew Jackson's chair . . . with Nicolay seated by him and Hay still standing by the mantel. The story was as fresh and was even better told that third time up to its first explosive place. Down came the President's foot from across his knee with a heavy stamp on the floor, and out through the hall went an uproarious peal of laughter."

"It was dying away," Stoddard continued, "and Hay was about to go ahead when we heard, 'Mr. President, if you please, sir, [Secretary of War] Stanton is in your room.' . . . There was something all but ghastly in the manner of the death of that story. Through all the sunny, laughter-filled chamber of the Executive Office poured thick and fast the gloom of death in life. The shadow came back to Mr. Lincoln's face, and he arose, slowly, painfully. . . . [T]he worst news of the war [came] on Sundays, such as brought Stanton in person. . . . What was the point of [Hay's] story, the thing so irresistibly funny? Nobody can tell."

Anecdotes like this have led those with only secondhand knowledge of the war years to suggest that Hay "laughed through his term." But while his levity was welcome in the White House, he was hardly the White

House's court jester. Like Lincoln, he frequently sagged under the gloom of war, especially in the early going when the fortunes of the North appeared not so favorable. On days when the Telegraph Office brought word of yet another setback for the Army of the Potomac, Stoddard remembers Hay "mourning around . . . as he always did after bad news, for his patriotism was fairly a burden to him."

Other burdens were even harder to shake. Friday was the usual day for Lincoln to review court-martial cases in which convicted soldiers, at the president's signature, could be executed for crimes that included desertion and sleeping on guard duty. Lincoln called it "butcher's day." As the war continued, the volume of cases grew astronomically. Hay recalled one six-hour session during which the president slogged through a hundred of them. Lincoln, though, was no butcher. "I was amused at the eagerness with which the President caught at any fact which would justify him in saving the life of a condemned soldier," Hay wrote in his diary. (In at least one instance, Hay himself played a direct role in a pardon: that of a Theta Delta Chi fraternity brother.) The president was "only merciless in cases where meanness or cruelty were shown," Hay observed. "Cases of cowardice he was specially averse to punishing with death. He said it would frighten the poor devils too terribly, to shoot them." Lincoln, after all, had been a soldier, too, during the Black Hawk War of 1832.

And he understood too well the pain of losing a loved one. A son, Eddie, had died in 1850 at the age of three. Then in February 1862 the two younger Lincoln sons, eleven-year-old Willie and eight-year-old Tad, fell ill with fever. Willie was by most accounts Lincoln's favorite—smart and good-hearted. Tad was sweet-tempered in his own way, but more unruly, hampered by a speech impediment and learning disabilities. The two boys had the run of the White House, interrupting their father at will, playing pranks on visitors and the staff, and frequently pulling the spring bell that connected the president's office to the secretaries'.

On February 20, Willie, the golden boy, died. Hay's diary and correspondence are silent on the tragedy that brought the White House to a standstill, but Nicolay wrote in his journal: "At about 5 o'clock this afternoon"—minutes after Willie's death—"I was lying half asleep on the sofa in my office, when [Lincoln's] entrance aroused me. 'Well, Nicolay,' said he choking with emotion, 'my boy is gone—he is actually gone!' and bursting into tears, turned and went into his own office."

Tad Lincoln survived and was loved even more dearly by his parents, sleeping many nights in his father's bed. But Tad, who could not, or at least did not, dress himself while he lived in the White House, was not capable of filling the void. Robert Lincoln, never entirely at ease at home, came down from Harvard when he could, but over the next three years, from the death of Willie to Lincoln's assassination, it was Hay who became, if not a surrogate son, then a young man who stirred a higher form of paternal nurturing that Lincoln, despite his best intentions, did not successfully bestow on either of his surviving children.

And Hay, who held his own father in high regard, found something more, and surely more immediate, in the example and attentions of Lincoln. Lincoln was every bit as high-minded as Charles Hay, but unlike Hay's father, Lincoln was also quintessentially reasonable and pragmatic. "With the fire of a reformer and a martyr in his heart he yet proceeded by the ways of caution and practical statecraft," Hay was to write of Lincoln in the biography. "He always worked with the things as they were, while never relinquishing the desire to make them better."

When the time came to embark on his own career as a statesman, Hay would take almost precisely the same approach.

THE GREATEST DEMONSTRATION OF Lincoln's philosophy of achieving lofty goals through practical means was the Emancipation Proclamation. Lincoln's views on slavery, if not abolition, had been well known for some time. As an Illinois legislator in 1837, he stated that "the institution of slavery is founded on both injustice and bad policy." Twenty-one years later, at the Republican state convention in Springfield, he said in his famous "house divided" speech that the government could not endure "half slave and half free. . . . It will become all one thing, or all the other." He left little doubt which outcome he preferred.

Yet Lincoln was no rabidly abolitionist Radical; he felt that the gradual decline and ultimate demise of slavery could be achieved through gradual measures such as proscription of slavery in territories, compensation to states that agreed to free slaves, and voluntary colonization. His goal, above all others, was not abolition but the restoration and preservation of the Union.

By the spring of 1862, the slavery, or rather the anti-slavery, issue was threatening to get ahead of him. Congress had already passed a Confiscation Act, the first of two bills authorizing the government to seize and free slaves of southerners actively supporting rebellion. Slavery was abolished in the District of Columbia and prohibited in United States territories. Following Frémont's example, two more generals issued orders without first consulting the president, one of them freeing slaves outright, the other holding them as contraband of war. Lincoln's reservations and, in some instances, resistance toward all these measures had to do with their constitutionality, their feasibility, and the effect they would have on border states and millions of constituents in the North, Democrats mostly, who perceived only mayhem and little advantage in emancipation, compensated or otherwise. What Lincoln wanted was more time to sell the border states on some form of gradual emancipation, believing that if the border states could be persuaded to end slavery, the rest of the South would soon fold.

On the other hand, if the border states bolted under the goad of abolitionist impatience, the consequences for the Union might be disastrous. Doubtless speaking for Lincoln in one of his anonymous newspaper columns, Hay urged the public to stay the course on slavery at least for the time being and to maintain faith in the president's strategy. He assured his readers that Lincoln had good reasons for continuing "to conserve and protect an interest which he would rejoice to see equitably blotted forever from the face of the earth." Hay beseeched the border states in particular to believe that Lincoln had their interests at heart. "It is to them," he explained, "that the President chiefly looks for effectual strength and co-operation in his great work of pacificating the storm-rent republic."

Lincoln hoped that Union successes in the spring of 1862 would bring the border states around, but none was forthcoming. In early April, General Ulysses S. Grant, who believed that one great battle could decide the entire war, fought to a bloody draw at Shiloh, Tennessee, suffering more than thirteen thousand casualties. Wrote Hay: "There was onset and repulse, yell of assault and cheer of defiance, screeching of shells and sputtering of volleys, advance and retreat. . . . It was like the flux and reflux of ocean breakers, dashing themselves with tireless repetition against a yielding, crumbling shore."

Meanwhile, Lincoln's recalcitrant general, George McClellan, was botching his grand thrust toward Richmond, squandering the initiative (despite Lincoln's exhortation that *you must act*), and losing the Peninsula campaign—sixteen thousand Union killed and wounded—and along with it the confidence of Congress, the cabinet, and his commander in chief. "[T]he little Napoleon sits trembling . . . afraid either to run or fight," Hay complained during the timid siege of Yorktown.

So willfully craven was McClellan's performance throughout the campaign that many Republicans close to Lincoln suspected that the general was actually conspiring against the president. Clearly the general was not making Lincoln's job any easier, his resistance made evident in a letter that McClellan delivered to Lincoln personally, criticizing the president's desire to free slaves. The commander in chief, McClellan asserted, "should not be allowed to interfere with the relations of servitude, either by supporting or impairing the authority of the master." The letter also carried a warning that verged on threat: Unless Lincoln heeded McClellan's suggestion to forgo emancipation, the effort to recruit fresh troops, which the army sorely needed, would be "almost hopeless."

With good reason, Lincoln soon removed McClellan as general in chief, replacing him with General Henry Halleck, nicknamed "Old Brains" for his heady leadership in the recent campaigns of the Department of the Mississippi. (Grant took Halleck's place out west.) Rebuked and embarrassed, McClellan cursed the administration: "God will yet foil their abominable designs & mete out to them the punishment they deserve."

But even without momentum on the battlefield or the blessing of his best-known general, Lincoln's scheme for emancipation took shape. On July 13—one week after talking to McClellan, one day after Congress passed its second Confiscation Act, and after failing to sell twenty-nine border state senators and representatives on his plan for gradual emancipation—Lincoln took a carriage ride with two of his more moderate cabinet members, Navy Secretary Gideon Welles and Secretary of State William Seward, and for the first time openly broached the subject of issuing a proclamation of emancipation on a national, rather than state-by-state, basis. Welles and Seward offered encouragement.

Hay, too, was privy to Lincoln's intentions early on. Writing to Mary Jay, the daughter of a New York abolitionist, on July 20, he let slip that the president "will not conserve slavery much longer. When next he speaks in relation to this defiant and ungrateful villainy it will be with no uncertain sound. Even now he speaks more boldly and sternly to slave holders than to the world." It is entirely possible that Hay had already seen a draft of the president's proclamation, which Lincoln might have begun as early as mid-June.

HAY HAD BEEN OFFENDED by slavery for as long as he could remember, his sense of outrage inherited from his parents and intensified by incidents such as the runaway slave in the cellar when he was a boy and further politicized by his association with Lincoln in Springfield and now in Washington. Yet like most northerners, including Lincoln, he was not a Radical abolitionist. "Abolition," as a term, was synonymous with extremism and, in its own way, just as much to blame for the Civil War as the stubborn pro-slavery stance of the South. "Both [extremes are] equally mad and equally criminal," Hay wrote in the summer of 1862, as Lincoln was preparing to introduce the proclamation on emancipation. "They have brought all our troubles, and if a hundred of the leaders on each side could be hung in pairs over oak limbs, the tumult would subside and the peace of the country be restored." But since the government had been "dragged into this bloody strife by traitors North and South," he reasoned, "and now that the life of the nation, and the condition of the nigger, is at stake, we must fight it through."

Hay shared Lincoln's fundamental wish "that all men could be free." Complete equality of races, however—citizenship for Negroes, say, or granting Negroes the right to vote—was a topic that Hay and Lincoln rarely discussed, much less contemplated. Later in the summer Lincoln would tell a delegation of black leaders that "even when you cease to be slaves, you are yet far removed from being placed on an equality with the white race." This blunt assessment, it must be said, was not so divergent from the momentous and, to abolitionists, loathsome pronouncement of the Supreme Court's *Dred Scott* decision of 1857, which asserted that Negroes were not intended to be included in the "all men are created equal" phrasing of the Declaration of Independence.

Hay, who before arriving in Washington had never been in the presence of blacks in any number, except perhaps those he encountered on the wharves of Warsaw, received a graphic glimpse of this inequality—and the very otherness—of southern Negroes in June, during a brief tour of Union lines at Yorktown, Virginia, as the Peninsula campaign was coming to an unpleasant end. Most of the white families had already evacuated the invaded town, leaving a "general impression," Hay wrote bluntly, "of old houses and old darkies—big guns and little niggers—dull skies and bright mulattos—complex uniforms and complexions not uniform—piccaninnies and *Enfan[t]s Perdus*—and a general flavor of Colored Persons."

His shading of this tableau of "seedy gentility"—and his casual usage of "darkies" and "niggers"—presents a frank measure of his ingrained racial prejudice, although one that would not have shocked his midcentury readers. But even more, Lincoln's secretary (and editorialist) was conveying a deep revulsion for the degradation of a race by the peculiar institution of slavery. Under such pitiable circumstances, with little precedent and few role models, it was hard to imagine blacks and whites as peers—not soon, anyway. The reason that Lincoln, and, by association, Hay as well, advocated colonization for blacks was not to banish them but to give them a chance to stand on their own, safely beyond the lash, and yardstick, of white culture; the gulf between the races was that immense.

ON JULY 22, 1862, Lincoln convened his cabinet and, after rehashing the terms of the most recent Confiscation Act and his proposal for compensated emancipation, he took dead aim, reading the first draft of what thereafter would be known as the Emancipation Proclamation. Beginning on January 1, 1863, he decreed, "all persons held as slaves within any state or states, wherein the constitutional authority of the United States shall not then be practically recognized, submitted to, and maintained, shall then, thenceforward, and forever, be free."

Though not an actual order, it was a military decision nonetheless, drawing upon the war powers vested in him as commander in chief. The proclamation made no mention of justice, equality, or the rights of man.

Yet in a single sentence, Lincoln turned confiscation into liberation for 3 million enslaved Negroes in eleven southern states. He could do nothing about the slaves in border states, and he did not want to. As it was, these states would be agitated enough by the prospect of freed slaves pouring northward; besides, Lincoln knew that the Constitution did not accord him war powers against states that were not at war. Still, it was the mightiest possible blow he could have struck under the circumstances. Winning the war was the goal. All other ramifications went unstated.

Lincoln invited discussion of the draft proclamation but informed his cabinet that he had already made up his mind. Secretary of War Stanton immediately grasped the military advantage of so many blacks quitting their masters and laboring for the Union cause. Others worried that the South would be inflamed to fight more fiercely or that owners would murder their slaves en masse, and vice versa. Secretary of State Seward warned that a racial war in the South might provoke England and France to intervene, recognizing Confederate sovereignty for the sake of stabilizing cotton exports. Seward also made the point that, because the proclamation was a military decision necessitated in part by recent reversals on the Peninsula, to issue it just now "may be viewed as the last measure of an exhausted government." It might be better, he suggested, to wait until Union forces scored a military victory. Lincoln saw the wisdom in Seward's counsel and tucked the message away in his desk.

Victory, however, was slow in coming. After the Peninsula debacle, McClellan's Army of the Potomac was reconfigured, many of its men and officers joining the newly formed Army of Virginia under General John Pope, who had proven himself a fighter in the West. McClellan, meanwhile, was essentially without portfolio, although still commander of the diminished Army of the Potomac.

But Pope, for all his aggressiveness, performed no better in the field than had Little Mac. On August 30, the Confederate Army—led by Robert E. Lee, Stonewall Jackson, James Longstreet, and J. E. B. Stuart—turned Pope's flank and for the second time thrashed the Union forces at Bull Run, a defeat that McClellan had predicted and, by his spiteful, intentional tardiness in lending reinforcement, had abetted.

"[A]bout Eight o'clock [on September 1]," Hay noted in his diary, "the

President came to my room as I was dressing and calling me out said, 'Well John we are whipped again, I am afraid.'" But rather than acting despondent, Lincoln appeared "in a singularly defiant tone of mind." Earlier he had told Hay, "We must hurt this enemy before it gets away," and when Hay continued moping over the second defeat at Bull Run and the Union's dim prospects, Lincoln countered sharply, "No, Mr. Hay, we must whip these people now."

But Lincoln, in his urgency and desire for one decisive victory, was short on options. In a move that stunned his cabinet, instead of reprimanding McClellan for his latest display of hesitation—or relieving him of duty entirely, as the secretary of war desired—the president placed him in charge of the defense of the capital. Staying put, after all, was McClellan's proven forte, and withal, he remained immensely popular with his troops. Lincoln acidly dubbed the reconstituted Army of the Potomac "McClellan's bodyguard."

Two days after McClellan's reassignment, Lee and nearly forty thousand Confederates crossed the Potomac within a one-day ride of Washington and pushed into western Maryland. Lincoln and General Halleck had little choice but to send McClellan and the Army of the Potomac, merged with the remainder of the Army of Virginia, to meet the invasion. "Again I have been called upon to save the country," McClellan crowed.

Lee's and McClellan's armies converged on hilly farm ground near Sharpsburg, and on September 17 the two sides poured their blood into Antietam Creek. With his far superior numbers and despite a customary overestimation of his opponent's strength, McClellan was able to hurt Lee badly, as Lincoln had wished, although he did not succeed in crushing him. Total casualties, North and South, exceeded twenty-two thousand, the greatest loss of American life and limb in a single day, a mournful record that still stands. The next day, Lee's army limped back across the Potomac, and McClellan, though he had held a third of his force from the fray, elected not to give chase.

Lincoln was hugely peeved at McClellan's failure to pursue Lee and destroy him more thoroughly, but he chose to regard the repulse of the Confederate Army from northern soil as sufficient victory; the time had come to present the Emancipation Proclamation. Over the summer he had refined and expanded the document, providing one early version to William Stoddard for transcription and safekeeping. "Mr. Lincoln says that he has promised God that he would issue that paper if God would give us the victory over Lee's army," Stoddard recalled.

Up to the very last minute, Lincoln was careful not to show his hand. "If anyone tried to dissuade him [from the idea of emancipation], he gave the argument in its favor," Hay observed. "If others urged it upon him, he exhausted the reasoning against it." At the end of August, when Horace Greeley of the *New York Tribune* had accused the president of not doing enough to end slavery, Lincoln had responded cagily: "If I could save the Union without freeing any slave, I would do it; and if I could save it by freeing all the slaves, I would do it; and if I could do it by freeing some and leaving others alone, I would also do that."

Two weeks after Antietam, in a response to several Christian leaders who had pressed him to issue a proclamation, Lincoln wondered, "What *good* would a proclamation of emancipation from me do, especially as we are now situated? I do not want to issue a document that the whole world will see must necessarily be inoperative, like the Pope's bull against the comet!" Little did the clergymen realize that only one day earlier, John Hay had witnessed the president carefully writing out the proclamation, four pages, straight through.

On September 22, Lincoln convened his cabinet and broke the ice. As he had done frequently, and at least once in his nightshirt for the amusement of Hay and Nicolay, Lincoln began by reading aloud an item that tickled him—in this instance a colloquial yarn by the humorist Artemus Ward about a dim-witted yokel who drags a wax figure of Judas Iscariot from a display of The Last Supper and then "commenced fur to pound him as hard as he cood." Lincoln, who grasped that he himself might be in for a pounding, then read aloud the Emancipation Proclamation, the centerpiece of which was the decree that, on January 1, 1863, "all persons held as slaves within any state . . . in rebellion against the United States shall be then, thenceforward, and forever free."

The cabinet, for the most part, voiced approval. Navy Secretary Gideon Welles, War Secretary Stanton, and Treasury Secretary Salmon

Chase were gratifyingly earnest in their support, as was Seward, who offered some minor improvements in the wording. Attorney General Edward Bates and Postmaster General Montgomery Blair, both from border states, were the only skeptics, Blair warning that Democrats would seize the proclamation as "a club to be used against us."

And indeed they soon did, calling the proclamation an act of national suicide. General McClellan, a Democrat whose designs on Lincoln's job were already well formed and well known, vowed that he would refuse to fight for the "accursed doctrine." For this indiscretion, along with failure to pursue Lee after Antietam and yet more displays of military paralysis soon afterward, Lincoln at last relieved McClellan of duty altogether in early November.

From the other side, many Radicals complained that the proclamation was an empty gesture; nothing short of total manumission would do. The Negro leader Frederick Douglass initially lamented that Lincoln's decision "touched neither justice nor mercy."

Generally, though, the announcement of the Emancipation Proclamation met with resounding jubilation. Two nights after news of the proclamation galloped across the telegraph, a large crowd gathered on the White House grounds to serenade and cheer the president. "There was no doubt about the feeling that animated the floating population of Washington last night," Hay wrote. "They collected in large numbers at Brown's Hotel and moved up the Avenue, keeping time to the music of the Marine Band, and halted before the white columns of the portico of the Executive Mansion, standing lucid and diaphanous . . . like the architecture of a dream. The crowd flowed in and filled every nook and corner of the grand entrance as instantly and quietly as molten metal fills a mold." With considerable reluctance, Lincoln finally appeared at the upstairs window and offered a few cautious remarks: "I shall make no attempt on this occasion to sustain what I have done. . . . It is now for the country and the world to pass judgment on it."

Unlike Lincoln, Hay did not mince words. The Emancipation Proclamation, he had averred immediately after the September 22 cabinet meeting, was nothing less than a warning that "the Government [was] done with leniency or paltering with murderous traitors, and had given them but one more opportunity for repentance and safety. If they reject this, let their ruin rest upon their heads."

After the serenade, he joined a group of cabinet members at the home of Secretary Chase. "They all seemed to feel a new and exhilarated life," he observed. "[T]hey breathed freer; the [proclamation] had freed them as well as the slaves. They gleefully and merrily called each other and themselves abolitionists, and seemed to enjoy the novel sensation of appropriating that horrible name."

As promised, Lincoln signed the Emancipation Proclamation on January 1, 1863, after a sleepless night and a long day of greeting visitors at the White House New Year's reception. His strong right arm, which when raised straight from the shoulder once was able to hold a heavy ax parallel to the ground, was played out. "I have been shaking hands since nine o'clock this morning," he reportedly said. "If my name ever goes into history it will be for this act, and my whole soul is in it. If my hand trembles when I sign the Proclamation, all who examine the document hereafter will say, 'He hesitated.'" But sign it he did, remarking with a smile, "That will do."

CHAPTER 4

Bolts of War

The Emancipation Proclamation produced no overnight miracles—not for the nation nor for the White House. Lincoln, meanwhile, continued to be whipsawed by Democrats and members of his own party, many of them demanding that he withdraw the proclamation before wholesale slave insurrection shook the South and stampeded northward; before northern soldiers who had joined the army to rescue their beloved Union but decidedly *not* to free the Negro refused to fight or, worse, rebelled themselves; and before the proclamation was declared unconstitutional and the president was driven from office in disgrace.

None of these scenarios came to pass, but in the beginning of 1863, Lincoln was a lightning rod needing badly to reverse the current of dissatisfaction and demoralization that threatened to cripple his administration. The proclamation was not negotiable—"a fixed thing," he reiterated. What would quell his doubters and recharge the republic's resolve, he well knew, was success, a string of successes, on the battlefield.

The year was not off to a good start. Fredericksburg, at the end of December, was a lopsided loss. General William Tecumseh Sherman had his nose badly bloodied as he approached Vicksburg. The retaking of Galveston by Confederates a few days later was a strategic embarrassment. After relieving McClellan of command of the Army of the Potomac, Lincoln had put General Ambrose Burnside in charge. But after Burnside was humiliated at Fredericksburg, the president felt obliged to cast about yet again for a general who could fight and win. Joseph Hooker stirred cautious hope for the accomplishment of at least one of those criteria; his nickname was "Fighting Joe." For the moment, though, the Army of the Potomac was still "stuck in the mud," John George Nicolay wrote to Therena Bates back in Illinois. In a separate letter to her, he offered an equally frank appraisal: "Our military condition, I am sorry to say, does not appear as yet to improve. Little disasters still tread on each others' heels." With what optimism he could muster, he added, "Nevertheless every point is being strained by the government, and we must continue to hope in patience."

John Hay, however, was running short of patience. It was hard not to feel frustrated and disconsolate, given the grind and disappointment of a war now nearly two years old. Perhaps one indication of the depth of his doldrums is the complete absence of diary entries and letters over the last two months of 1862. When he finally resumed in January, he wrote to his friend Adam Badeau, an aide to General Thomas Sherman, serving in New Orleans: "The war seems to have paralyzed all pens except professional ones. . . . I am far from ranking myself among men of letters, yet when I remember that I used to scribble to my own intense delight and by the kind sufferance of friends who read, I can hardly admit that the used up machine who sits at my desk is the same person still. I can't write any longer. I need a plunge into respectable society and an exile from Washington to save me from absolute inanity."

Once again, Lincoln, who was every bit as harried but could not afford a respite of his own, let his young secretary go. Nominally, Hay's assignment was to carry dispatches to Admiral Samuel Du Pont, who was then preparing a naval assault on the blockaded port of Charleston, South Carolina. Lincoln was especially keen on this campaign. To retake Fort Sumter and Fort Moultrie, to avenge the insult of April 1861, would boost federal spirits immensely.

Hay had his own reasons for going. With several hundred thousand young men in uniform, he was anxious not to be counted among the shirkers. "I want my abolition record clearly defined and that will do it better than anything else, in my own mind and the minds of a few dozen people we know," he told Nicolay. Without actually enlisting, however, the best he could do was serve as a volunteer aide-de-camp to General David Hunter, commander of the Department of the South, headquartered at Hilton Head. He was well satisfied, for his younger brother, Lieutenant Charles Hay, was on Hunter's staff as well.

The trip lasted more than two months, during most of which Hay had little to do except see the sights and occasionally brief the president on the war as it simmered along the southeastern coast. Why he chose to do so, and was permitted to do so, for so long in the midst of what was perhaps the most dismal season of the war and with so much work always to be done in the White House, defies easy explanation. It wasn't a case of Lincoln playing favorites, either. In the four years of his presidency, he sent Nicolay west on three occasions, always on government business but with ample time for stopovers with his fiancée, who waited out the war at home. The Tycoon, it seems, was simply being nice—and fatherly.

Hay arrived, seasick, at Hilton Head, forty miles south of Charleston, on the morning of April 7, just hours before the naval assault was to commence. The attack was an utter failure. In barely an hour, Confederate guns at Sumter and Moultrie fired more than two thousand shells; the federal ironclads answered with fewer than two hundred rounds before turning tail. Hay was too far away to witness the debacle firsthand, but later he wrote a long letter to Lincoln, asking him not to condemn Admiral Du Pont's decision to withdraw. Lincoln had feared the worst, Hay reminded him, and something a little less than that had come true. "I hope," he urged, "that due honor may be given to those who fought with such bravery and discretion the losing fight." Hay's tone with the president was not the least bit forward, but it did reveal an intimacy nurtured by a great many hours of easy chatter in the White House, not to mention scores of military pardons.

When Hay finally caught up with his brother Charles a day or so later, he found him gravely sick with pneumonia. For the next two weeks, while General Hunter's army and Admiral Du Pont's navy deliberated the feasibility of launching a new attack on Fort Sumter, Hay looked to his brother's convalescence. "I shall never cease to be thankful that I came as I did," he wrote to their mother, "for it would have been an even chance, that in another week he would have had his lungs damaged for life." Despite the navy's recent setback, he was full of optimism. "All we have to do, is stand firm and have faith in the Republic, and no temporary repulses, no blunders even can prevent our having the victory." In the meantime, he assured his mother, "I never felt better in my life than I do now."

He was able to make several excursions with members of Hunter's staff to inspect the network of Union fortifications that girded the myriad bays, rivers, and sea islands of the South Carolina and Georgia coast. On one occasion he sailed within range of the Confederate batteries at Savannah. When not on board ship, he rode horseback through the sandy lowlands and strolled the gardens of the old plantations. "The air is like June at noon & like May at morning," he wrote Nicolay. "The sun goes down over the pines through a sky like ashes-of-roses and hangs for an instant on the horizon like a bubble of blood."

This was his second contact with southern Negroes, and this time he was taken with their dialect. At a prayer meeting at Hilton Head, a young Negro, upon learning that Hay worked for the president, announced that he would like to see "Linkum." Hay would embellish on this anecdote in a speech he gave to northern audiences several years later. He remembered that a "gray-haired patriarch" interrupted the youngster who wished to meet Lincoln. "'No man see Linkum,' the older Negro said. 'Linkum walk as Jesus walk. No man see Linkum.'"

When Charles's doctor recommended that sea air might help clear his lungs, the brothers took a boat down the coast as far as St. Augustine. Hay liked Florida even more than South Carolina. "It is the only thing that smells of the Original Eden on the Continent," he told Nicolay. "I wish I could buy the State for taxes & keep it for a Castle of Indolence."

In fact, during his weeklong stay he arranged to buy an orange grove in St. Augustine for $500. The previous owner was away, fighting for the Confederacy; under the Confiscation Act, his land had been auctioned by federally appointed tax commissioners. Hay was told that he would earn back his investment fivefold in the first year's harvest. "The soil is almost as rich as our prairie land," he exclaimed to his grandfather. "All sorts of fruit and grain grow with very little cultivation, and fish and game of every kind abound."

Like his father and grandfathers, whose land speculations had spared them callused hands, he could already picture life as a gentleman planter after the war: "As we sat in the shade at St. Augustine . . . I felt as useless and irresponsible as the lizards in the grass or the porpoises that leaped in the liquid basin of the bay," he wrote Nicolay. "The memory of a land where people worked, was as dim and distant as the dream of home to the enchanted mariners sleeping beneath the whispering pines of the Lotos Islands." So enthralled was he by the prospect of agrarian idyll that on the way home with Charles he committed to buy several more lots in Fernandina, Florida. To the victor maybe would go the spoils.

Back in Hilton Head, he grew restive. Admiral Du Pont, having failed once to penetrate Charleston Harbor, was reluctant to run the gauntlet a second time. "There is positively nothing to hope for from the Navy at present," Hay griped to Nicolay. "The Admiral so dreads failure he cannot think of success. . . . Now is our time to strike them & where they are weak." But the Confederate defenses at Charleston were far from weak, and despite repeated bombardments and land assaults, Fort Sumter would not fall for another two years, abandoned only when Sherman's army swept through the South in the final weeks of the war.

Hay had intended to start north in early May, but his brother's health was not sufficiently improved, and he resolved to take him along; it took another week to secure a medical leave. They did not reach Washington until after June 1; there Charles at last regained his strength. Hay eventually succeeded in getting him assigned as a recruiting officer in Springfield. (Their other brother, Leonard, had enlisted in the infantry and would remain in the army throughout his life, rising to the rank of captain and serving almost entirely in the West.)

At the White House, Hay found the president more beleaguered than when he left. Lincoln had high hopes for Fighting Joe Hooker when in late April he had marched the Army of the Potomac into northern Virginia, crossing the Rappahannock River with the fierce ambition of drawing Lee's army away from Fredericksburg and into the open. But it was Lee who had made the bolder thrust, dividing his army and flanking Hooker near the town of Chancellorsville. Suddenly Hooker looked a lot like McClellan—taking the defensive too hastily, withholding troops, overestimating the size of the enemy. Hay would later criticize Hooker's generalship as "vacillating and purposeless."

News of the army's defeat and retreat reached Lincoln on May 6. "Had a thunderbolt fallen upon the President he could not have been more overwhelmed," wrote the journalist Noah Brooks, who was in the White House at the time. "One newly risen from the dead could not have been more ghostlike." Secretary of War Stanton allowed to Hay that this was "the darkest day of the war. It seems as if the bottom had dropped out."

But Lincoln soon composed himself, lifted by Grant's conquest of Port Gibson on the Mississippi and the tightening of the noose around Vicksburg. The Army of the Potomac might have been whipped at Chancellorsville, but the Confederacy had lost a greater portion of its army, including one of its most revered generals, Stonewall Jackson. Lincoln looked into the faces of the federal soldiers retreating from Virginia and found their spirits surprisingly resilient. "All accounts agree," the *New York Times* reported, "that the troops on the Rappahannock came out of their late bloody fight game to the backbone . . . undaunted and erect, composed and ready to turn on the instant and follow their leaders back into the fray."

But the Army of the Potomac would have to carry on without Hooker, who resigned on June 27. "We need not recapitulate the fatal errors . . . to show that Hooker's reputation as a great commander could not possibly survive his defeat at Chancellorsville," Hay was to write in the Lincoln biography. "He threw away his chances one by one."

A week after Hooker's departure, his army got another shot at Lee, who had seized the momentum of Chancellorsville and once again was taking the fight northward onto Union soil, through Maryland into Pennsylvania, angling toward Harrisburg and, God willing, perhaps even Philadelphia.

Lee's new opponent was General George Meade, whom Hay described as a "tall, thin, reserved man, very near-sighted, with the air of a student rather than of the sabreur." Meade had spent the years before the war building lighthouses and thus far in battle had acquitted himself well, even while his fellow generals were stumbling, from Second Bull Run to Chancellorsville. As a Pennsylvanian, he had the added incentive of defending his home state from invasion.

And so Meade's Army of the Potomac and Lee's Army of Northern Virginia converged on Gettysburg. "[T]hese two formidable armies were approaching each other at their utmost speed," Hay was to recount, "driven by the irresistible laws of human action—or, let us reverently say, by the hand of Providence—as unconscious of their point of meeting as two great thunderclouds, big with incalculable lightnings, lashed across the skies by tempestuous winds."

THE BATTLE RAGED FOR three days, until July 3, when Pickett's Charge upon Cemetery Ridge ended in thorough slaughter, destroying likewise the Confederacy's dream of northern conquest.

News from the front dribbled into Washington on a patchy telegraph line. Years later, Hay succeeded in splicing the pieces together in one of the longest chapters of the Lincoln volumes. Of the great rebel charge, he wrote, summoning the rhapsody of Thucydides or Tennyson, "No sight so beautiful in a soldier's eyes, so full of the pomp and circumstance of glorious war, had ever before been seen upon this continent, as when Pickett led forth his troops from behind the ridge, where they had lain concealed, and formed them in column for attack. There was nothing like it possible in the swamps of the Chickahominy, or the tangled thickets of the Rappahannock, or on the wooded shores of the Rapidan. There no enemy was visible half a musket-shot away; but here, at a distance of nearly a mile across a cultivated valley, part of which was covered with waving grain and part smooth in stubble fields, the whole irradiated with the unclouded beams of the July sun, an army formed itself in line of battle under the eyes of an appreciative adversary. It came on across the valley in the form of a wedge, of which Pickett's own division about 5000 strong formed the finely tempered point."

Hay had not witnessed any phase of the fighting, but he was aided by a visit to the battlefield later in the year when Lincoln made his memorable remarks in recognition of the soldiers who "gave the last full measure of devotion" to the nation. The North and South each suffered twenty-three thousand killed and wounded at Gettysburg, but it was the rebels who paid the bigger price, for their army never regained the strength or esprit that Lee had carried forward from Chancellorsville.

Vicksburg's surrender to Grant on July 4 dimmed Confederate prospects even more. "There were still two years of labor, and toil, and bloodshed before the end came," Hay would write, "but the war reached its crisis and the fate of the rebellion was no longer doubtful from that hour," when Grant sat "beneath the oak tree on the hillside of Vicksburg, and Pickett's veterans were reeling back, baffled and broken by the guns of Meade at Gettysburg."

For a fleeting moment the residents of the White House allowed themselves to believe that the war might be over —provided Meade pursued the mangled Army of Northern Virginia and destroyed it before it could get away. "The President seemed in a specially good humor today," Hay wrote in his diary on July 11, "as he had pretty good evidence that the enemy were still on the North side of the Potomac and Meade had announced his intention of attacking them in the morning."

But the Union troops had their own wounds to lick and no lust for the chase. By the fourteenth, Lee had slipped across the river to relative safety, and Lincoln was beside himself with frustration. "'Our Army held the war in the hollow of their hand & they would not close it,'" Lincoln lamented to Hay. "'We had gone through all the labor of tilling & planting an enormous crop & when it was ripe we did not harvest it.'"

As always, the president maintained his equilibrium, and, over all, Hay's letters and diary began to reflect a resurgence of vitality and optimism, some of which was Lincoln's, some his own. To be sure, many obstacles remained: the South still had plenty of fight left in it; the so-called Peace Democrats were escalating their corrosive demonstrations against the administration; and draft riots had ravaged New York. All the while, the cabinet continued to feud, and Treasury Secretary Salmon Chase had set his sights on Lincoln's job. Even so, the president's mood was noticeably improved. "The Tycoon is in fine whack," Hay wrote Nicolay, who was away on one of his western junkets. "He is managing this war, the draft, foreign relations, and planning a reconstruction of the Union, all at once. I never knew with what tyrannous authority he rules the Cabinet, till now. The most important things he decides & there is no cavil. I am growing more and more firmly convinced that the good of the country absolutely demands that he should be kept where he is till the thing is over. There is no man in the country, so wise so gentle and so firm. I believe the hand of God placed him where he is."

In particular, Hay recognized the singular brilliance and strength of Lincoln's military leadership. In March 1862, when the naval duel between the ironclads *Monitor* and *Merrimac* hung in the balance, Hay had observed: "Lincoln was, as usual in trying moments, composed but eagerly inquisitive, critically scanning the dispatches, interrogating the officers, joining scrap to scrap of information, applying his searching analysis and clear logic to read the danger and find the remedy." And after Meade balked in the aftermath of Gettysburg, Lincoln had declared to Hay, "If I had gone up there I could have whipped them myself." Hay had no doubt that Lincoln could have done so.

When it came to specific orders, Hay noticed that Lincoln's "were always clearer and more definite than any he received from [his generals]." And to those who wished that Lincoln would "keep his fingers out of the military pie," Hay protested: "The truth is, if he did, the pie would be a sorry mess. The old man sits here and wields like a backwoods Jupiter the bolts of war and the machinery of government with a hand equally steady & equally firm."

If Hay had any last, lingering reservations about Lincoln's infallibility, they now evaporated like the morning haze on the Potomac. "I have to a great extent stopped questioning where I don't agree with him, content with trusting to his instinct of the necessities of the time and the wants of the people," he wrote to Charles Halpine, a friend on General Hunter's staff. "I hardly ever speak of him to others than you, because people generally would say 'Yes! of course: that's how he gets his daily bread!' I believe he will fill a bigger place in history than he ever dreams of himself."

Hay's ever-deepening faith in the president, and the president's evident resilience, helped explain why he seemed so much more relaxed after returning from South Carolina and Florida. A week after Lee's escape from Meade, Hay mentioned that he and Robert Lincoln, who was on vacation from Harvard, "had a fearful orgie here last night on whiskey and cheese." Over the remainder of the summer Hay made frequent visits to the Soldiers' Home, rocking on the porch in the sultry air, discussing philology and reading Shakespeare with the president and swapping yarns from back home, many of which were "unfit for family reading," Hay disclosed to Charles Halpine.

He also shared his recent poems with Lincoln, prompting the president to try one himself, a snippet of doggerel written shortly after Gettysburg in the voice of Robert E. Lee. ("Jeff" of course is Confederate president Jefferson Davis.)

> In eighteen hundred sixty-three,
>   With pomp and mighty swell,
> Me and Jeff's confederacie
>   Went forth to sack Phil-del.
> The Yankees they got arter us,
>   And gin us particilar h_ll,
> And we skedaddled back again,
>   And didn't sack Phil-del.

SUCH LIGHTHEARTEDNESS DID NOT permeate the entire White House, however. Hay and Nicolay were crosswise with Mary Todd Lincoln from the start. Her husband was the Tycoon, but she was "the Hell-Cat." When one of the secretaries was away, the other would report on the first lady's latest demonstrations of distemper, dishonesty, and general contrariness. "Madame has mounted me to pay her the Steward's salary. I told her to kiss mine," Hay snarled in one letter to Nicolay. After Nicolay clashed with "the powers at the other end of the hall" over a slight matter of protocol concerning invitations to a White House dinner, "there soon arose such a rampage as the House hasn't seen for a year," he told Hay, "and I am again taboo."

In hindsight, it is a testament to Hay's and Nicolay's devotion to Lincoln that they were not more openly antagonistic toward his wife. She was in many ways Lincoln's opposite—short, vain, devious. In her diamonds, décolletage, and queenly airs, she modeled herself after the empress Eugénie of France. Hay and Nicolay viewed firsthand the string of scandals and near scandals that Mrs. Lincoln hatched seemingly without compunction or concern for the president's reputation. The secretaries were supposed to be the gatekeepers to the president's office, yet Mrs. Lincoln met with office-seekers and lobbyists on her own, promising them jobs and influence and on more than one occasion accepting bribes for these indulgences. They resented the way she leaked secrets and waylaid members of the cabinet and Congress to press on them her own political or patronage demands. The secretaries surely were aware of the séances she held in the presidential quarters after Willie died. What appalled them more than her profligacy—eighty-four pairs of gloves in one month, thousands of dollars in jewelry, and the horrendous overrun in redecorating the White House—was the way she went about hiding her exorbitant expenses in false or padded bills that she attempted to charge to the federal government.

Above all, the thing Hay and Nicolay resented most about Mary Lincoln was the strain she quite evidently put on the president, who on more than a few occasions let slip doleful references to his "domestic troubles." They watched, exchanged worried looks, and, for the most part, chewed on their tongues. They knew, too, that she had it in for them and would scheme to get rid of them if she could. "The devil is abroad, having great wrath," Hay confided to Nicolay early in the war. "The Hellcat is getting more Hellcatical by the day."

ON SUNDAY, NOVEMBER 8, 1863, Hay, Nicolay, and Lincoln took a carriage to the photography studio run by the Gardner brothers, Alexander and James. Alexander had until recently worked for Mathew Brady, taking haunting postmortem pictures of Antietam, Gettysburg, and other battlefields. On this day his main subject was Lincoln, who looked squarely into the lens, firm of jaw, dour and determined. Hay called the images of the president "some of the best I have seen." Next it was his and Nicolay's turn. "Nico & I immortalized ourselves by having ourselves done in group with the Presdt.," he wrote in his diary.

Lincoln sits between them, hands in his lap, looking away; Nicolay is also seated, gazing wanly into the camera, his chin strengthened somewhat by a goatee. Hay stands on Lincoln's other side in light trousers, matching charcoal coat and vest, with watch chain. He can't resist a little jauntiness: one hip is cocked, and his left arm is akimbo, holding a broad-brimmed hat; his right is placed familiarly on the back of Lincoln's chair. His cheeks are smooth but no longer adolescent, and his mustache now looks as if it belongs. He is a month past his twenty-fifth birthday. Altogether, it is a stiff portrait, due more to the chemistry of the camera than of the subjects. They had done it just for themselves, and if Hay and Nicolay had known that it would be the only photograph ever taken of them with Lincoln, they might have striven for better.

The next evening, the two secretaries joined the president and Mrs. Lincoln at Ford's Theatre. "J. Wilkes Booth was doing the 'Marble Heart,'" Hay mentioned in his diary. "Rather tame than otherwise."

Two nights later, Hay returned to the theater to see Booth as Romeo, though he was far more taken with the character of the witty, gregarious Mercutio, who is slain while standing up for his star-crossed chum. After the play, Hay and several of his own chums repaired to Willard's Hotel "and drank a good deal." Indeed, if his diary is any measure, he was drinking more now. This was certainly the case when he and Nicolay accompanied the president on a trip to Gettysburg on November 18 to consecrate the cemetery to the soldiers who had perished there four months earlier.

OF ALL THE EVENTS of the Lincoln presidency witnessed by John Hay, from surprise election to sudden death, the Gettysburg Address is notable not for Hay's immediate observance of its magnitude but for his benign disinclination to do so. Hay got drunk the night he got to Gettysburg, and he was likely hungover the next day when Lincoln gave the most famous speech in American history.

They arrived from Washington late in the afternoon aboard a special train provided by the B & O Railroad; the passenger list included Secretary of State Seward, Interior Secretary John Usher, several foreign ministers, and a few military men. They found Gettysburg packed with thousands of out-of-towners, many of them relatives of the soldiers who had fought and fallen in July. The mood, however, was far from fune-real. While Lincoln, Seward, and the elder statesmen in the party were escorted to their lodgings, Hay joined a group of revelers that included the young chairman of Pennsylvania's Republican Committee, Wayne MacVeagh; Edwin Stanton, son of the secretary of war; and John Forney, owner of the *Philadelphia Press* and Washington *Daily Chronicle*, two of the newspapers most loyal to Lincoln, the latter occasionally publishing Hay's anonymous White House commentary.

The whiskey began and then the serenading. They joined the cel-ebrants and military band that interrupted the president's supper with singing and cheers for "Father Abraham." Finally Lincoln appeared at the door, "said half a dozen words meaning nothing & went in," Hay remarked blithely. "We went back to Forney's room having picked up Nicolay and drank more whiskey." They sang "John Brown's body lies a-mouldering in the grave," and soon a "large and clamorous" throng gathered outside. More singing. Forney and MacVeagh made short speeches. More drinking. Another round of "John Brown." And finally to bed, though no one got much rest.

The following morning, Hay did not join Lincoln and Seward on their tour of the battlefield. But shortly before noon, he reported, "I got a beast and rode out with the President's suite to the Cemetery"—a procession that included nine governors, three members of the cabinet, foreign min-isters, dignitaries of every rank and rung, a Marine band, and an escort of cavalry and artillery.

Hay did not mention whether he sat on the platform or stood in the crowd of nine thousand during the memorials that followed. Edward Everett, nationally renowned for his tribute to "The Character of George Washington," spoke for two hours in the autumn air. He compared Get-tysburg with the Peloponnesian War and lyrically, reverently, painstak-ingly iterated every thrust and parry of the northern "martyr-heroes," some of whose corpses still lay within view, unburied and a-mouldering. Hay said Everett spoke "perfectly," but even Lincoln was fidgety by the end. Everett was the country's greatest orator, but he could enrapture an audience for only so long.

Nor when time finally came for Lincoln to make a few "remarks" could he hold the crowd in the palm of his broad hands, for his address was over almost as soon as it began—"Four score and seven years" lasting barely four minutes. His auditors were foot- and, for some, head-sore, and they hardly had time to take in the 260 or so words delivered in Lincoln's high-pitched, prairie cadence. Hay heard him clearly, but as Lincoln's secretary and after-hours companion, he had listened to the president read aloud many times, from *Richard III* to Robert Burns. Hay was attentive, but he could be forgiven for not being entirely transfixed. The same could be said for most everyone present, for the momentousness and resonance of the Gettysburg Address would only begin to be recognized once it was transcribed and printed in hundreds of newspapers, and read and reflected upon by the greater populace.

Throughout the rest of his life, in conversation with poets and plenipotentiaries and in service to three of Lincoln's successors, Hay could recreate with dignified detail that sunny, somber afternoon when Lincoln, with signature self-effacement, suggested, "The world will little note, nor long remember, what we say here; but it can never forget what *they* did here." But on November 19, 1863, Hay recorded in his diary, almost in homage to Lincoln's own lapidary concision: "[T]he President in a firm free way, with more grace than is wont, said his half dozen lines of consecration and the music wailed and we went home."

THREE WEEKS LATER, LINCOLN issued another proclamation, this one nowhere near as eloquent as his address at Gettysburg or the Emancipation Proclamation of the previous year. He attached the Proclamation of Amnesty and Reconstruction to his annual address to Congress. As Hay reported, the plan was a reflection of the president's increasing optimism that "the rebel power is at last beginning to disintegrate." Yet even as the momentum shifted, Lincoln felt a sense of urgency, pressed as he was on one side by the Peace Democrats, who wanted to negotiate a truce, even if it meant legitimizing the Confederacy and perpetuating slavery, and on the other by Radical Republicans, who wanted to crush and punish the Confederacy and remake the South according to their abolitionist designs. Lincoln, who did not recognize the Confederacy, or rather, did not acknowledge the legality of secession, sought a middle road that would permit states to "reconstruct" on their own, without reprisal. Toward this end, his proclamation of December 8 delineated the so-called Ten Percent Plan, whereby a state would be welcomed back into the Union once 10 percent of its citizens (based on 1860 voter rolls) swore an oath of allegiance to the Union and agreed to accept emancipation. The first place he proposed driving this wedge was Florida, to which he dispatched Hay at the first of the year. To succeed he would need only fourteen hundred signatures.

No longer was Hay merely the president's private secretary. To invest him with the authority commensurate to the task ahead, Lincoln commissioned Hay as a major in the army and assigned him to the position of assistant adjutant general. He sailed, in uniform, from Washington on January 15, arriving in Hilton Head four days later, where he reported to General Quincy Adams Gillmore, commander of the Army of the South.

A year earlier, Gillmore had welcomed the addition of the 54th Massachusetts Infantry to his command, a regiment comprised entirely of black enlistees and led by the Boston abolitionist Robert Gould Shaw. Two weeks after Gettysburg, Gillmore had chosen the 54th to spearhead the assault against Fort Wagner, near Fort Sumter. The charge was repulsed, but the black troops fought bravely, and their showing went a long way toward validating Lincoln's Emancipation Proclamation and encouraging further enlistment of black troops.

When Hay reported to Gillmore, the commander was preparing to launch a fresh offensive, this one in northeastern Florida. His goals, in addition to cutting off Confederate access to cattle and other desperately needed supplies, were to recruit former slaves into his black regiment and now, with Hay's arrival, "to inaugurate measures for the speedy restoration of Florida to her allegiance."

Hay lingered several days in South Carolina, waiting for the Florida campaign to concentrate. Since his visit the previous year, the siege of Charleston had escalated, with gargantuan Parrot guns pounding the battlements of the guardian forts, Sumter, Moultrie, and Wagner. The enemy's fire got "pretty warm" as well, he wrote in his diary after an excursion to within range of Fort Wagner's batteries. The incoming shells had a "regular musical note like Chu-chu-wachu-wachu-*brrr* and each of the fragments a wicked little whistle of its own. Many struck in the black marshy mud behind us burying themselves & casting a malodorous shower. . . . I often saw in the air a shell bursting—fierce jagged white lines darting out first, like javelins—then the flowering of the awful bud into full bloom." He saw men torn apart by shrapnel, and when a shell exploded close by, "I made a bad dodge," he confessed. Yet for a brief moment he had come under fire while wearing the uniform of the Union.

FROM THE INSTANT HAY arrived in Fernandina, Florida, on February 5, 1864, the motives for issuing the amnesty proclamation came under suspicion. The president's opponents saw the Ten Percent Plan as a ploy to bring Florida back into the Union merely to provide pro-Lincoln delegates to the Republican Convention in June. Hay, too, had much to win—and lose—personally. If Florida rejoined the Union, the orange groves he had purchased a year earlier would increase in value immensely and he might not need to worry about money for a long while. If, on the other hand, the Confederacy were to prevail, keeping Florida in its fold, his groves would likely revert to the previous owners and his ambition of a life of languid leisure would be nullified.

It was no coincidence that the biggest promoter of the amnesty plan was Lyman Stickney, the federal tax commissioner who had facilitated Hay's land speculation. Stickney himself had everything to gain politically and financially by returning Florida back to the Union. He was a well-connected scoundrel and a confidant of Treasury Secretary and presidential hopeful Salmon Chase, and he knew just how to sweeten the pot for Lincoln's young secretary. He suggested that, once Florida was reconstructed, Hay would be the right man to serve as its representative in Congress.

Hay's presence in Florida, meanwhile, made General Gillmore's job more complicated. From the start, the army's objective was to occupy Jacksonville and, only if opportunity presented itself, to drive westward as far as the Suwanee River. Before leaving Hilton Head, Hay had tried to explain to Gillmore that "it was not the President's intention to do anything to embarrass the military operations—that all I wished from him was an order directing me to go to Florida & open my book of records for the oaths." Nevertheless, the general recognized the added political dimension of the operation, believing that the president would not have sent his own secretary if he did not regard the mission as vital.

Hay's project got off to a less than rousing start. "Opened my book [of loyalty pledges] in an office over Robinson's Store, sent out my posters [of the proclamation] & sat like a spider," he wrote on his first day in Fernandina. "A few straggled in and swore [allegiance]. One hesitating cuss who evidently feared he was going to be tricked into the army swore, but dallied so on the signing that I shut the book & told him to make up his mind before calling again."

The next day, he was with the first troops, led by the all-black 54th Massachusetts, to land in Jacksonville, which they found undefended by the rebels. He immediately renewed his effort to gather signatures, writing optimistically to Lincoln, "I have the best assurances that we will get the tenth [ten percent]." But he also acknowledged that the state was "well-nigh depopulated," and those citizens whom he did encounter were "ignorant and apathetic." With the pickings so slim, he was not choosy about who took the oath of loyalty. Some of his early successes were deserters and prisoners of war, hardly the most promising material for reviving the state. One Union officer described Hay's prospects as "a lot of stragglers, poor, white-livered, fever-stricken, scrawny, ignorant creatures."

His experience in Jacksonville was marred further by a ghastly exhibition of military justice—the hanging of a black man convicted of rape. "In [the] middle of the square a gallows was erected," Hay recounted. "A cart drove in & after pulling & hauling & swearing was backed under the gallows: the poor devil stood upright. . . . His sentence was read, the noose adjusted, [and with] the cart beginning to move he jumped up & tried to break his neck but failed & gasped & jerked & struggled dreadfully. His stertorous breathing could have been heard over the square. A man jumped up to his shoulders & hung on him swinging—No Effect: Another man got on: he still gasped. At last they raised him up & jerked him down hard: & he ceased struggling & after a while the crowd dispersed."

Hay moved on to St. Augustine, now accompanied by Stickney, the opportunistic tax commissioner and land shark. Evidently Hay was confident enough in the amnesty campaign that he committed to buy several more orange groves, again with Stickney's encouragement, and attended a lecture on orange horticulture. All was going well enough until February 20.

General Gillmore had returned to his headquarters, leaving the Florida expedition under the command of General Truman Seymour, who, for reasons still not entirely comprehensible, ignored Gillmore's firm instructions to consolidate his forces around Jacksonville and avoid overextending his lines. Instead, Seymour grossly underestimated the size and resolve of the Confederate Army in Florida and impetuously marched into a fight at Olustee, fifty miles west of Jacksonville. Five thousand entrenched rebels shredded a federal advance of equal size. "The fighting on both sides was very fine," wrote Hay, who was well removed from the action. He singled out the bravery of the Negro regiments, who stood "like rocks in a fire that decimated their ranks."

Finally, the Union Army retreated to Jacksonville, leaving all but the blockaded coast in rebel hands. In the course of an afternoon, the federal army had suffered eighteen hundred dead and wounded, or 40 percent of its force, one of the worst casualty rates of the entire war. Hay blamed the defeat on General Seymour, who had been "unsteady and queer since the beginning of the campaign . . . subject to violent alternations of timidity & rashness."

Seymour was not the only one whose behavior came under criticism for the debacle at Olustee. Three days after the battle, the *New York Herald* charged Hay and Lincoln with "Executive intermeddling" with the military campaign in Florida. "[I]t is rumored that the expedition was intended simply for the occupation of Florida for the purpose of securing the election of three Lincoln delegates to the National Nominating Convention, and that of John Hay to Congress. The cost of the operation to the government is estimated at about one million of dollars." Unrelentingly, the *Herald* excoriated Lincoln and Hay for sending "brigades of our brave armies . . . into rebellious states to water with their precious blood the soil that may produce Presidential votes. . . . [T]he President and his secretary are the only ones to blame in the business."

After Olustee, Hay tried not to be discouraged, although the portion of the state under federal control was now reduced and even more sparsely inhabited. "I can't think of leaving the field till it is ours," he wrote Nicolay immediately after the battle. "I don't believe I could take my daily tramp down [Pennsylvania] Avenue, if I skedaddled just now." Four days later, though, he saw that his efforts were futile. The few citizens who remained in Florida, even if they did represent 10 percent of the state's population, "would not give us the moral force we want," he acknowledged. "The people of the interior would be indignant against such a snap-judgment taken by incomers & would be jealous & sullen." Still he followed through on his orders, traveling as far as Key West, where he found the civilian population either disinterested or "unscrupulous scamps."

By March 10, he was headed home. Passing through Fernandina, he read for the first time the press allegations of his and Lincoln's ulterior scheming in Florida. He could only wonder what recriminations awaited his arrival in Washington. As his ship bucked northward through a raw headwind, he fought seasickness by writing verse and reading Charles Dickens's *American Notes*.

His folly was complete and undeniable. The Ten Percent Plan was a bust, first in Florida and thus nationally. And thanks to Stickney, his life savings were invested in Florida real estate, a venture that now seemed speculative in the extreme.

Hay got back to the White House at daybreak on March 24 and went in to see Lincoln, prepared to take his medicine. To his relief, the president brushed the matter aside. "[T]he Tycoon never minded it in the least," Hay wrote bluffly to Charles Halpine once he was sure he had weathered the worst, "and as for me, at my age, the more abuse I get in the newspapers, the better for me. I shall run for Constable some day on the strength of my gory exploits in Florida."

LINCOLN HAD FAR MORE important things on his mind. At a White House ceremony two weeks earlier, he had made Ulysses S. Grant a lieutenant general, the first to hold that rank since George Washington. The no-nonsense hero of Vicksburg and Chattanooga was now in charge of all the Union armies. (Halleck became chief of staff; Sherman assumed command of the armies of the West.) By the time Hay returned to work, Grant was already preparing a spring campaign so massive and violent that, if successful, it would render the Confederate Army helpless to defend its capital at Richmond. Hay, too, was impressed by Grant when he was introduced for the first time on March 27—"a quiet, self-possessed and strong sense looking man," he noted in his diary.

In early May, leading an army of more than one hundred thousand, Grant crossed the Rapidan River near Fredericksburg and Chancellorsville—sites of past Union humiliations—and pitched into Lee's Army of Northern Virginia without remorse or respite. The battles of the Wilderness and then of Spotsylvania, which followed immediately after, were an unprecedented nightmare of desperately close combat. "The primeval forest had been cut away in former years," Hay was to write in the Lincoln biography, "and now the whole region, left to itself, had been covered with a wild and shaggy growth of scrub oak, dwarf pines, and hazel thicket woven together by trailing vines and briers. Into this dense jungle the troops . . . plunged."

At the infamous "Bloody Angle" of Spotsylvania, "Men were killed by bayonet thrusts over the logs. . . . The thickets were withered by the fire; large trees were cut down by the missiles; the dead lay piled upon each other. . . . [T]here was no especial advantage of position; no skill of tactics brought into play; they both fought to kill, with undaunted spirit, from the first flush of dawn, through the misty morning, the dull, rainy day, to the black night."

Unlike McClellan or Hooker before him, Grant never winced. What Hay called "mutual slaughter" was for Grant a Union victory by virtue of the fact that it was not a loss; and though he did not succeed in prying Lee from Spotsylvania, clearing the path to Richmond, he chose to view his work there as a success as well. Both armies had bled profusely—in ten days of fighting, the Union casualties exceeded thirty-five thousand; the Confederacy twenty-four thousand—but Grant was convinced, mercilessly so, that Lee would bleed out sooner than he.

During the savage days of May, Hay and Nicolay watched Lincoln pace endlessly in the White House. As the dispatches came in from the front, Lincoln expressed approval of his commander's conduct. "The President thinks very highly of what Grant has done," Hay observed on May 9. "He was talking about it today with me and said 'How near we have been to this thing before and failed. I believe if any other General had been at the Head of that army it would have now been on this [north] side of the Rapidan [in retreat]. It is the dogged pertinacity of Grant that wins.' It is said that Meade observed to Grant that the enemy seemed inclined to make a Kilkenny cat fight of the affair, & Grant answered, 'Our cat has the longest tail.'"

Six days later, as Grant's heavy blow against Lee became apparent, Nicolay wrote to his fiancée, "The President is cheerful and hopeful—not unduly elated, but seeming confident."

Convinced that he had Lee whipped, Grant kept driving toward Richmond. He was beaten badly at Cold Harbor, ten miles northeast of the Confederate capital, where Union losses were three times those of the Confederacy. Still he continued to tighten the clamp, besieging Petersburg, twenty miles to the south of Richmond, in early June. Despite enormous casualties—in a single month Grant had shed more blood on Virginia soil than spilled by all the armies of the previous three years—the president's confidence in his general in chief was unwavering. Speaking at a banquet in Philadelphia on June 16, Lincoln said, "I have never been in the habit of making predictions in regard to the war, but I am almost tempted to make one. . . . If I were to hazard it, it is this: That Grant is this evening . . . in a position from whence he will never be dislodged until Richmond is taken."

LINCOLN HAD OTHER REASONS to feel encouraged. In Baltimore on June 8, the Republican Party nominated him for reelection on a platform calling for preservation of the Union, no compromise with the rebels, and a constitutional amendment to prohibit slavery. To replace Hannibal Hamlin as vice president, the convention nominated Andrew Johnson, who was serving as military governor of Tennessee.

But even while Grant was closing in on Richmond, Lee had his eye on Washington. On July 5, he sent General Jubal Early across the Potomac with a column of fifteen thousand. Four days later, the Confederates sliced through Union resistance at the Monocacy River, near Frederick, Maryland, and bore down on the capital. At Silver Spring, they ransacked the estate of Postmaster General Montgomery Blair. After telegraphing Grant for reinforcements, Lincoln actually seemed to welcome the effrontery. Only at the insistence of Secretary of War Stanton did he consent to give up his nighttime residence at the Soldiers' Home.

At the White House, Hay and Nicolay could hear the batteries announcing the rebels' approach to the capital. On the morning of the eleventh, the president and Mrs. Lincoln drove out to witness the attack on Fort Stevens, which guarded the Seventh Street entrance to the city. "He was in the Fort when it was first attacked, standing upon the parapet," Hay wrote in his diary. "A soldier"—Captain Oliver Wendell Holmes, Jr., as it turned out—"roughly ordered him to get down or he would have his head knocked off."

The day turned into somewhat of a lark. "The President is in very good feather this evening," Hay noticed. "He seems not in the least concerned about the safety of Washington. With him the only concern seems to be whether we can bag or destroy this force out in front." Two days later, Early gave up on his gambit, more a taunt than an earnest invasion, and withdrew back across the Potomac. Lincoln was predictably annoyed that the federal army had let him escape. By the fourteenth, the president and Mrs. Lincoln were back sleeping at the Soldiers' Home.

On July 8, while Early's army was marching on Washington, Lincoln received a letter from Horace Greeley, editor of the *New York Tribune*, informing him that he had been approached by rebel agents in Canada, claiming that they possessed the full authority of Confederate president Jefferson Davis to negotiate peace between the North and South. Greeley asked Lincoln to arrange for safe passage for the Confederate negotiators between Niagara Falls and the capital, reminding the president that "our bleeding, bankrupt, almost dying country also longs for peace [and] shudders at the prospect of fresh conscriptions, of further wholesale devastations, and of new rivers of human blood." Not to pursue peace talks, Greeley warned, could cause Lincoln the November election—with the mutual understanding that a Democratic victory would likely lead to armistice and, ultimately, the continuation of slavery in the southern states.

One week later, John Hay left Washington on the most delicate mission he would undertake for his president by far.

Hay had met Greeley once before, in February 1861, when the editor had boarded the train carrying Lincoln from Springfield to Washington. At the time, Hay had remarked on Greeley's vanity—his white coat and "yellow hand bag, labeled with his name and address, in characters which might have been read across Lake Erie."

Above all, Greeley was an idealist. As a younger man, he had dabbled in Universalism, utopianism, socialism, and Transcendentalism; he had published the first draft of Thoreau's *Walden*. He advocated land reform, labor reform, and, more than anything, the end of slavery. He founded the *Tribune*—"the Great Moral Organ"—in 1841, and, with the founding of the Republican Party in 1854, he made the paper its mouthpiece.

Greeley welcomed stories fed to the paper by the White House, yet he also reserved the right to hold Lincoln's feet to the fire on slavery, most famously in his "Prayer of Twenty Millions" of August 1862, in which he demanded that the president issue an emancipation proclamation.

By the summer of 1864, Greeley, like most Americans, was sick of war. The recent carnage in Virginia had not bought Richmond, and now the president was calling for five hundred thousand more volunteers. Greeley was convinced that the time had come to consider a negotiated peace. Even if it could not be achieved right away, he told Lincoln, "I do say that a frank offer by you to the insurgents, of terms which the impartial will say ought to be accepted, will, at the worst, prove an immense and sorely needed advantage to the national cause."

Lincoln saw the rub immediately. He doubted that the agents in Canada spoke for Jefferson Davis, but he agreed with Greeley that if he refused out of hand to talk to the men, he would pay an enormous price politically. On July 9, the day after receiving Greeley's letter, he responded cagily, "If you can find any person, anywhere, professing to have any proposition of Jefferson Davis in writing, for peace, embracing the restoration of the Union, and the abandonment of slavery, whatever else it embraces, say to him he may come to me with you, and that if he really brings such proposition he shall at the least have safe conduct." Greeley answered several days later that peace commissioners were waiting at Niagara Falls.

Hay traveled all night by boat and rail, arriving at the *Tribune* office on the morning of July 16. At first Greeley balked when Hay relayed Lincoln's message requesting that Greeley be the one to meet with the agents and accompany them to Washington; he worried that he would be too easily recognized by newspapermen in Niagara Falls and "abused & blackguarded." He was also upset that Lincoln had spelled out his terms—restoration of the Union, end to slavery—in advance. Greeley would have preferred that the other side "propose terms which we could not accept," Hay reported. When Hay stood firm, Greeley agreed to make the trip to Niagara Falls. Hay wrote out the safe-conduct passes himself, leaving the names blank, and handed them to Greeley. He left for Washington the next day.

He barely had time to report to Lincoln before a dispatch arrived from Greeley. As Lincoln had suspected, the peace commissioners revealed that they were not accredited by Jefferson Davis after all, but insisted that if Lincoln would grant them safe passage to Richmond, they would surely gain Davis's ear.

That evening, Hay was again aboard a train, heading this time to Niagara Falls. With him he now carried a letter from Lincoln, an expansion of his July 9 offer, known today as the Niagara Manifesto. "To whom it may concern," the president began, addressing the peace commissioners. "Any proposition which embraces the restoration of peace, the integrity of the whole Union, and the abandonment of slavery, and which comes by and with an authority that can control the armies now at war against the United States will be received and considered by the Executive Government of the United States, and will be met by liberal terms on other substantial and collateral points, and the bearer or bearers thereof shall have safe conduct both ways."

Arriving in Niagara Falls, Hay found Greeley at the International Hotel, and together they rode across the suspension bridge to the Clifton House on the Canadian side, where they found two of the Confederate agents "tea & toasting," as Hay noted sarcastically. George Sanders was a Kentuckian who had supported Stephen Douglas, advocated the overthrow of European monarchies, and befriended John Wilkes Booth. To Hay he appeared "a seedy looking rebel with grizzled whiskers." The other man, James Holcombe, was a law professor from Virginia and a former member of the Confederate Congress, whom Hay described as a "spare false looking man with false teeth, false eyes & false hair." One of their associates, Clement Clay, a former Alabama senator, was absent. Also hovering somewhere nearby was William "Colorado" Jewett, a Peace Democrat from Maine who had earned his fortune in western gold mines and a reputation as a "half-witted adventurer." It was Jewett who had first alerted Greeley to the purported peace commissioners, and as soon became evident, neither Jewett nor Greeley proved to be trustworthy emissaries—not for Lincoln, anyway.

The meeting was brief. Hay delivered Lincoln's "To whom it may concern" letter spelling out the terms on which he was willing to discuss peace. Sanders and Holcombe said they would talk over the proposal with their associates. Hay and Greeley rode back across the bridge to Niagara Falls.

The Confederates at the Clifton House were shocked by the terms of the Niagara Manifesto. Greeley had never shown them Lincoln's original letter of July 9 stipulating "the restoration of the Union, and the abandonment of slavery." Now they regarded the July 18 letter as a low-handed betrayal.

Hay spent two days cooling his heels, awaiting an answer from the Confederates in Canada; finally he was informed by Jewett that a response had already been sent—not to Lincoln, but to Greeley, who by then had returned to New York. Copies had also been circulated to the press. The Confederates' letter accused Lincoln of a "rude withdrawal of a courteous overture." The South desired peace, the letter declared, but Lincoln's implacable terms were tantamount to "fresh blasts of war to the bitter end." The commissioners, who were anything but, beseeched the South to strip from its eyes "the last film of such delusion" that peace by negotiation was possible, and implored "any patriots or Christians" in the North "to recall the abused authority and vindicate the outraged civilization of the country."

This last point—the recall of "abused authority"—was perhaps the blow the southerners had wished to strike all along. If peace was their goal, they had gone about it clumsily. If unseating Lincoln was the objective, they had advanced the cause cleverly. By the Niagara Manifesto, Lincoln had implied that he was willing to undergo more Antietams, more Gettysburgs, more Shilohs, more Cold Harbors, the killing and maiming of tens of thousands more soldiers, all in order to free slaves. The majority of northern Democrats wanted peace at any cost, with no thought to emancipation.

Abolitionist Republicans naturally applauded the president's resolute stand, but a good many moderate Republicans were convinced that Lincoln had destroyed the party. One of the most vocal, Joseph Medill, editor of the *Chicago Tribune*, complained to Hay that the Niagara Manifesto had enabled "Copperheads [pro-slavery northern Democrats] to get an enfilading fire on us. Heretofore we have argued that the war was conducted to save the Union, that the *object* of the war was national integrity, that freeing slaves was a measure of policy, a military necessity to strengthen ourselves and to weaken the enemy. But the President by a stroke of his pen overthrew all this and proclaimed in effect that the war was waged for the object of freeing negroes. The Copperheads will shell us on this point . . . and I assure you our political prospects do not look bright. Unless we have *decided* military success [before the November election] you will be not a private sec[retary] but a private citizen and Mr. L also, while the Cops will have the Govt."

Hay was livid. "The damned scoundrel needs a day's hanging," he said of Medill. Indeed, the entire Niagara experience had been extremely trying. It had been a great honor to be entrusted with such a fragile responsibility, and he had acquitted himself ably. But once again he had been burned. Greeley, though well intentioned, had behaved shabbily, fending off his critics with "half statements," Hay complained, and blaming Lincoln for the whole misunderstanding with the peace commission.

Nonetheless, Hay had learned a thing or two about the chess game of negotiation: how to read an opponent, when to go first, when to demur, and when to take the offensive. One day he would be not merely a messenger but an ambassador in his own right.

Then, too, he certainly had sized up Horace Greeley, agreeing with Lincoln's assessment that "in some respects Mr. Greeley is a great man, but in many others he is wanting in common sense." Seven years later, when Hay was to go to work for Greeley at the *Tribune*, his opinion of the man would improve, but only slightly. Writing in the Lincoln biography after Greeley's death, Hay still could not forgive the "peculiarities of caprice and impulse which formed the special weakness of that remarkable character."

By mid-August, even Lincoln believed he might not be reelected. He went so far as to tuck away in his desk a "blind" memorandum pledging to support the next administration in prosecuting the war to save the Union. He also wrote a letter to Henry Raymond, editor of the *New York Times* and chairman of the Republican Party, proposing that Raymond travel to Richmond and discuss with Jefferson Davis "what terms of peace would be accepted"—with no mention of slavery or emancipation. He pigeonholed this letter, too, but such gestures, though they never saw the light of day, were a fair indication of how soberly he viewed his prospects. Friends from nearly every state warned him that if the election were held immediately, he would lose badly. At the end of the month, Nicolay wrote that the Republican Party had reached "almost the condition of a disastrous panic—a sort of political Bull Run."

Hay, still irritated by the Niagara fiasco, would not abide such pessimism. "I lose my temper sometimes talking with growling Republicans," he wrote Nicolay. "There is a diseased restlessness about men in these times that unfits them for the steady support of the administration. . . . If the dumb cattle are not worthy of another term of Lincoln then let the will of God be done & the [pestilence] of McClellan fall on them."

On August 31, McClellan did fall on them, although at long last he proved to be not a curse but a political blessing. At the Democratic National Convention in Chicago, the general whom Lincoln had admired then fired was nominated as the party's candidate to run against Lincoln and bring an end to "four years of failure." The party platform stipulated that "immediate efforts be made for a cessation of hostilities." Whereas the Republican platform promised union and emancipation, the Democrats pledged peace based only on "the Federal Union of the States." In his acceptance letter, McClellan attempted to downplay the so-called peace plank, and he ignored the issue of slavery entirely.

Nicolay and Hay, who had only scorn for Little Mac, preferred to call the peace plank "the surrender platform." "The Lord preserve this country [from] the kind of peace they would give us," Nicolay wrote. "It will be a dark day for this nation if they should elect the Chicago ticket, and purchase *peace* at the cost of Disunion, Secession, Bankruptcy and National Dishonor, and an 'ultimate' Slave Empire. I cannot think that Providence has this humiliation or disgrace and disaster in store for us."

Providence did not. The day after McClellan's nomination, the Confederates evacuated Atlanta one step ahead of Sherman's army, and the Democrats' charge of "failure" seemed suddenly empty. "From the moment the Democratic Convention named its candidates the stars in their courses seemed to fight against them," Hay was to write in the Lincoln biography. "During the very hours when the streets of Chicago were blazing with torches, and the air was filled with the perfervid rhetoric of the peace men, rejoicing over their work, [Confederate general John] Hood was preparing for the evacuation of Atlanta; and the same newspapers which laid before their readers the craven utterances of the [surrender] platform announced the entry of Sherman into the great manufacturing metropolis of Georgia—so close together came bane and antidote."

In the weeks that followed, discord among Republicans subsided as they weighed the greater peril of a McClellan victory. Even those who had once wished to dump Lincoln from the ticket, a list that included the Gettysburg orator Edward Everett and Horace Greeley, now pulled for the president. "I shall fight like a savage in the campaign," Greeley told Nicolay. "I hate McClellan." One of Lincoln's old irritants, General John C. Frémont, who had entered the race as a third-party candidate, dropped out. Lincoln was especially heartened by the resounding support expressed by the officers and soldiers who might have been expected to embrace their former general but now smelled victory and resolved to stay the course, guided by "Father Abraham."

And while victory was not assured, it was coming. Admiral David Farragut had captured Mobile Bay. By strangling Petersburg, Grant was shortening Richmond's breath. General Philip Sheridan was spurring his cavalry the length of the Shenandoah Valley, thrashing Jubal Early when he could, harassing him no matter what. Sherman was uncoiling his supply lines, preparing to march from Atlanta to Savannah, then to Columbia, gouging upward along every rib of the Confederacy "with the steady pace and irresistible progress of a tragic fate," Hay was to write.

The political signs were favorable as well. On the evening of October 11, Hay accompanied Lincoln to the Telegraph Office in the War Department to follow the congressional, gubernatorial, and legislative elections in Pennsylvania, Ohio, and Indiana. During the wait, Lincoln read aloud from a volume by the humorist Petroleum V. Nasby. His audience, which included Secretary of War Stanton, was amused, but not nearly as much as the president, who read on "*con amore*," Hay noted cheerfully. Meanwhile the telegraph tapped out the returns that would foretell how the Union as a whole would behave in the presidential election one month hence. In Indiana and Ohio, the Republican gains were resounding. In the end, Pennsylvania went solidly Republican as well, thanks largely to the votes of absentee soldiers. More good news was not long in coming: on November 1, Maryland adopted a new constitution abolishing slavery.

On the night of November 8, Hay again joined Lincoln in the Telegraph Office to await the outcome of the national election, making special note of the evening in his diary. In many instances, his diary entries served merely as memoranda to be salted away for the Lincoln history that he, in partnership with Nicolay, would one day write. On other occasions, he extended himself, writing impressionistically, for no one knew better than he—the voracious reader of Charles Dickens, George Eliot, and Victor Hugo—that these novelistic entries would wind up being historically resonant. Granted, there were times, such as at Gettysburg, when he missed the moment almost entirely. But on others, such as election night of 1864, he was hyper-aware, recognizing that he was surrounded by posterity in the making.

"The night was rainy steamy and dark," he began his sketch of the scene. "We splashed through the grounds to the side door of the War Department where a soaked and smoking sentinel was standing in his own vapor with his huddled up frame covered with a rubber cloak. Inside a half-dozen idle orderlies: upstairs the clerks of the telegraph."

Hay seemed less attuned to the actual returns as they arrived from the states than he was to Lincoln's every word and sentiment. When Thomas Eckert, chief of the Telegraph Office, came in, soaked and muddy from a fall in the street, the Tycoon was reminded of one of his country homilies. "For such an awkward fellow, I am pretty sure-footed," Lincoln said, with Hay transcribing. "It used to take a pretty dextrous man to throw me. I remember, the evening of the day in 1858, that decided the contest for the Senate between Mr. Douglas and myself, was something like this, dark, rainy & gloomy. I had been reading the returns, and had ascertained that we had lost the Legislature and started to go home. The path had been worn hog-backed & was slippering. My foot slipped from under me, knocking the other one out of the way, but I recovered myself & lit square: and I said to myself, '*It's a slip and not a fall.*'"

As the evening wore on and the dispatches brought good news from around the country, Lincoln relaxed into a mood of magnanimity. Of Henry Winter Davis, a Radical Republican who had fought bitterly with the president over plans for reconstruction, he said, "A man has not time to spend half his time in quarrels. If any man ceases to attack me, I never remember the past against him." Lincoln may as well have been addressing a different Davis, the one in Richmond.

At midnight, they ate fried oysters, the president shoveling his down "awkwardly and hospitably." More good news arrived from Missouri and Michigan. At half past two, a party of serenaders appeared outside the War Department with a band playing "The Battle Cry of Freedom." Lincoln obliged them with a short speech. Finally, he and Hay walked, as they had so many times during the war, the short distance across the grounds to the White House, weary but replete. Upstairs they found Ward Hill Lamon, Lincoln's old friend from Illinois who now acted as the president's bodyguard. Once Lincoln had gone to bed, Lamon accepted a glass of whiskey from Hay and, "rolling himself up in his cloak lay down at the President's door; passing the night in that attitude of touching and dumb fidelity with a small arsenal of pistols & bowie knives around him. In the morning he went away leaving my blankets at my door, before I or the President were awake."

Lincoln had predicted that he would be lucky to beat McClellan by 3 electoral votes; he beat him by 191. The popular vote was much closer, but still commanding: 55 percent for Lincoln. Most gratifying was the military vote: McClellan, who had once professed, "I can do it all," and modeled himself on Napoleon, received only one in five votes cast by soldiers.

ON THE NIGHT OF the tenth, two days after the election, Lincoln spoke to a second crowd of serenaders, this time from a window of the White House beneath the north portico. The president declared that his victory was proof that "he who is most devoted to the Union and most opposed to treason can receive most of the people's votes." Calling for "common interest [to] unite in a common effort to save our common country," he declared, "So long as I have been here, I have not willingly planted a thorn in any man's bosom."

Lincoln wrote this speech in haste, admitting to Hay that it was "[n]ot very graceful . . . but I am growing old enough not to care much for the manner of doing things." Hay also mentioned that both serenade speeches were "very highly spoken of" and that he had written down the first of the two "after the fact"—one of the few times that Hay acknowledged casting, or recasting, any of Lincoln's words. In retrospect, it is apparent that he did so quite often.

A year after Lincoln's death, Hay told Lincoln's old law partner, William Herndon, that the president wrote very few letters and did not read one in fifty that he received. "At first we tried to bring them to his notice, but at last he gave the whole thing over to me, and signed without reading them the letters I wrote in his name," Hay admitted. In fairness to William Stoddard, this was not always the case; Stoddard did most of the opening, passing the letters on to Hay. But even Stoddard acknowledged that "Colonel Hay imitated the signature of his Excellency very well."

Hay made no record of the letters he drafted and signed—as Lincoln—but one that seems most likely is the now immortal Bixby letter. Sometime not long after the election, John A. Andrew, governor of Massachusetts and a loyal Lincoln man, asked a favor of the president. It had recently been brought to the governor's notice that one of his constituents, Lydia Bixby of Boston, had lost five sons in the war. Andrew hoped that the president would write a letter to "the best specimen of a true-hearted Union woman . . . yet seen." In late November 1864, the

White House was flooded with an inordinate quantity of congratulations and solicitations of patronage, in addition to the constant cataract of war-related correspondence. Andrew's request most probably came across Hay's desk, and it fell to him, as the in-house eulogist, author of heroic verse, and deft conveyor of countless condolences during the previous three and a half years of wartime fatalities, to draft a response.

"I have been shown in the files of the War Department a statement . . . that you are the mother of five sons who have died gloriously on the field of battle," the letter began. "I feel how weak and fruitless must be any words of mine which should attempt to beguile you from the grief of a loss so overwhelming. But I cannot refrain from tendering to you the consolation that may be found in the thanks of the Republic they died to save." And in closing: "I pray that our Heavenly Father may assuage the anguish of your bereavement, and leave you only the cherished memory of the loved and lost, and the solemn pride that must be yours, to have laid so costly a sacrifice on the altar of Freedom."

The letter was signed "A. Lincoln"—whether in the president's handwriting or in that of his clever secretary will never be known, since the original letter was apparently destroyed by Mrs. Bixby, who, it turned out, was not a "true-hearted Union woman" but a southern sympathizer with only two dead sons, not the five she first claimed. The depth and validity of the woman's grief is now beside the point, but the text of the Bixby letter, as reprinted in newspapers, endures as part of the Lincoln canon. Admirers place it in a peerage with two other jewels of Lincoln prose, the Gettysburg Address and the Second Inaugural, both of which are inscribed in the marble of the Lincoln Memorial. Carl Sandburg, a Lincoln biographer and a poet himself, vouched the Bixby letter "a piece of the American Bible."

The argument that Lincoln did *not* write the Bixby letter and that Hay did is persuasive. For one thing, Hay never denied writing it, and he pasted newspaper clippings of the letter in two of his scrapbooks, alongside poems he published anonymously during the Civil War. Over the years, several people close to Hay testified that he had alluded to being the author.

And he was certainly capable of imitation. By the time the Bixby letter was written, Hay had read thousands of pages of Lincoln's words. The sleepy boy who had mastered German by mimicking his teacher, the college man who could recite entire verses of Horace and Poe from memory, the son of the soil who could replicate the patois of Mississippi rivermen and South Carolina slaves—for him, imitating or, better said, honoring the prose style of Lincoln would not have been difficult.

In the end it is his own prose that gives him away. While the cadence and tone, majesty and tenderness of the Bixby letter are thoroughly Lincolnesque, words and phrases such as "beguile" and "cherished," "I cannot refrain from tendering," and "I pray that our Heavenly Father" are more characteristic of Hay, appearing over and over in his own letters and seldom in Lincoln's.

Hay harbored no desire to upstage Lincoln; he was only doing his job, and if he did it well, who would be the wiser? "The more [Lincoln's] writings are studied in connection with the important transactions of his age," Hay would write in the conclusion of the Lincoln biography, "the higher his reputation will stand in the opinion of the lettered class." For Lincoln's loyal secretary, to bask in a patch of reflected light was flattery enough.

"FROM THE HOUR OF Mr. Lincoln's reelection the Confederate cause was doomed," Hay was to write of the war's final act. "A slow paralysis was benumbing the limbs of the insurrection, and even at the heart its vitality was plainly declining." It was easy to write with such bravura two decades after the fact, but at the end of 1864, Hay seemed no less certain that the war would soon end.

Four days after the election, he—that is, Major John Hay, Assistant Adjutant General—accompanied Admiral David Porter on a trip to City Point, Virginia, to confer with General Grant, whose army now invested Richmond. What impressed Hay about Grant was what impressed him about Lincoln: the fact that a man of such little pretense could radiate such thorough trust and confidence. Hay reported that when Porter knocked on the door of Grant's "common little wall tent," the general answered the door himself, looking "neater & more careful in his dress than usual; his hair was combed his coat on & his shirt clean, his long boots blackened till they shone." At dinner, Grant further impressed his audience with his iteration of how the war would end, telling Porter, Hay, and the other assembled officers that "he does not think [the rebels] can recover from the blow he hopes to give them this winter."

And Grant was entirely correct. Before Christmas, federal armies pressed down upon the Confederates at Nashville and Savannah, and Admiral Porter commenced the bombardment of Fort Fisher, the last rebel port open on the Atlantic. "The Anaconda is beginning to squeeze," Nicolay wrote to Therena Bates. "There remains but the army of Lee to be caught and overcome, and the military strength of the rebellion is at an end. I think this result will almost certainly come within the next year, and I hope that we may even gladden our next fourth of July with the rejoicing over the great event."

LINCOLN LIKEWISE SAW HIS chance to bear down. All along he had worried that the Emancipation Proclamation was a constitutionally shaky wartime exigency that might not survive once the rebellion ended. Lincoln had initially wished that abolition would be accomplished on a state-by-state basis, but in the spring of 1864, a group of senators and congressmen, led by Charles Sumner, Lyman Trumbull, and Isaac Newton Arnold, had drafted a constitutional amendment to end slavery entirely and forever. In April, the Senate had approved the Thirteenth Amendment by a wide margin, but the vote in the House had fallen short of a two-thirds majority. But then in June, Lincoln had been nominated on a Republican platform calling for a permanent prohibition of slavery, and the November elections had boosted the ranks of Republicans in the House. With the mandate he had received at the polls and with momentum building on all battlefronts, the president threw his weight behind the amendment, arguing that its passage would further dishearten the South and shorten the war. Still, even he had his doubts. Hay and Nicolay overheard him admitting to Senator Edwin Morgan of New York: "We are like whalers who have been long on a chase: we have at last got the harpoon in the monster, but we must now look how we steer, or with one 'flop' of his tail will send us all into eternity."

The abolition amendment was reintroduced in the House on January 6, 1865. To win a two-thirds majority, more than a dozen Democrats would have to be pried from the grasp of the Copperheads, led by men like minority leader George Pendleton, who had been McClellan's running mate, and Representative Fernando Wood, who, when mayor of New York, had wanted the city to secede from the Union.

Lincoln, with the help of stalwart allies, cajoled Congress by every method possible. For some members, a moral argument was enough, now that the outcome of the war appeared inevitable. For others, the time-honored approach of dangling favors and patronage did the trick. Up until the last minute, the pro-slavery forces were confident they could block the bill. But on January 31, the Thirteenth Amendment abolishing slavery passed the House by a vote of 119 to 56—more than a dozen of the ayes coming from border slave states. Even then the bill would not have passed if eight Democrats had not been absent.

When the vote was announced, the floor and gallery of the House erupted in unison. The cheering lasted a good ten minutes. Men clapped one another on the back and threw their hats in the air; women waved handkerchiefs. There were many blacks in the crowd that day whose tears of joy were unstanchable.

Hay and Nicolay were in the White House with the president when the vote was taken. Where once they had listened to the batteries firing from Bull Run and Fort Stevens, now they felt the very walls of the White House shudder as artillery on Capitol Hill bruited the end of slavery with a hundred-gun salute. On the following night, a raucous crowd of serenaders drew Lincoln again to the upstairs window. This time it was Nicolay who scribbled down the gist of the president's remarks as he spoke. The Thirteenth Amendment was "a king's cure-all" for the shortcomings of the Emancipation Proclamation, Lincoln said, and it was "the fitting, if not indispensable, adjunct to the consummation of the great game we are playing." Before stepping away from the window, Lincoln congratulated all present—"himself, the country, and the whole world."

Yet the Thirteenth Amendment was not yet law, for it still had to be ratified by the states. By mid-April, only twenty had voted in its favor; the necessary vote of three quarters of the states would not be accomplished until December. Nonetheless, Lincoln knew that he had already achieved a "great moral victory." He had come a long way since his days in Illinois when he had suggested that simply limiting the growth of slavery in western territories would cause the institution to wither and die; and only two and a half years earlier he had told Horace Greeley that he would be willing to keep slavery if he could save the Union by doing so. Now, having expanded and stiffened the Emancipation Proclamation into the permanency of the Thirteenth Amendment, he had abolished slavery *and* saved the Union. Perhaps it was also true that he had saved the Union *by* abolishing slavery. "The great job is ended," he was heard to say. Not quite, but nearly so.

John Hay and John George Nicolay were almost through as well. They had shared a room together in the White House for four years, except for their assignments outside Washington. Once the outcome of the war appeared certain, neither had a compelling desire to stay on for a second term. Nicolay turned thirty-three in February 1865 and had delayed his marriage to Therena Bates for long enough. He had in mind returning to the newspaper business; one idea was to buy an interest in the *Baltimore Sun.* Hay, now twenty-six, was likewise keen to broaden his horizons, and there was little holding him back. His status as a bachelor was well burnished, like the buttons on his military tunic. And yet he had no idea in which direction he might point himself. Returning to Warsaw or Springfield was a last resort, and Florida was even more remote. Shortly after the election, he quit writing in his diary altogether, another sign of his growing detachment.

Even if he and Nicolay had wanted to stay on, they might not have been able to do so. Mrs. Lincoln was determined to replace Nicolay with Noah Brooks, the journalist who had curried favor with her for years. In the meantime, every encounter with the first lady was a test of will. "About three days of the week have been taken up with a row with my particular feminine friend," Nicolay wrote before Christmas. As went Nicolay, soon would follow Hay. With Lincoln's second inauguration near, there were no bridges left to burn with the Hellcat.

HAY AND NICOLAY WERE in the audience on March 4, 1865, to witness Lincoln's inauguration and hear his Second Inaugural Address. As at Gettysburg, neither had much to say at the time about the president's now immortal speech. For one thing, they had read it beforehand; unlike the Gettysburg Address, the Second Inaugural was typeset and printed, likely with the assistance of the secretaries.

The day began with rain, but by noon the clouds surrendered to sunshine as Lincoln stepped to the podium on the east portico of the Capitol, with the statue of *Freedom* now at her post atop the completed dome. A crowd of perhaps fifty thousand pressed around the platform, cheering and waving flags at first, then quieting as the president put on his spectacles and began to read. Many of the faces in the audience were black, though not all listeners were friendly, such as John Wilkes Booth, who stood near the front with a loaded pistol in his pocket.

Lincoln's speech was short, seven hundred words, and over in six or seven minutes—as succinct as it was solemn. The message throughout was one of shared blame and assumed responsibility: "God . . . gives to both North and South this terrible war, as the woe due to those by whom the offense [of slavery] came." Together, North and South must "bind up the nation's wounds." Those who listened for the slightest undertone of vainglory were disappointed, for Lincoln was, if anything, contrite that the war had been waged at such a magnitude for so long. The true measure of accomplishment would be the "just and lasting peace" yet to be forged. "Fondly do we hope—fervently do we pray—that this mighty scourge of war may speedily pass away," he said.

The Lincoln who took the oath of office that afternoon and then bowed to kiss the Bible had not been hardened by war but made more conciliatory, more penitent. In this he endeavored to set an example for the nation. "Men are not flattered by being shown that there has been a difference of purpose between the Almighty and them," he wrote a few days after the inauguration. "To deny it, however, in this case, is to deny that there is a God governing the world. It is a truth which I thought needed to be told, and, as whatever of humiliation there is in it falls most directly on myself, I thought others might afford for me to tell it."

John Hay discerned the effect of the war upon Lincoln more clearly than almost anyone. "He bore the sorrows of the nation in his own heart; he suffered deeply, not only from disappointments, from treachery, from hope deferred, from the open assaults of enemies and from the sincere anger of discontented friends," Hay was to write. "One of the most tender and compassionate of men, he was forced to give orders which cost thousands of lives; by nature a man of order and thrift, he saw the daily spectacle of unutterable waste and destruction which he could not prevent. The cry of the widow and the orphan was always in his ears. . . . [H]e was in mind, body and nerves a very different man at the second inauguration from the one who had taken the oath in 1861. He continued always the same kindly, genial and cordial spirit he had been at first; but the boisterous laughter became less frequent year by year; the eye grew veiled by constant meditation on momentous subjects. . . . He aged with great rapidity."

ONE WEEK AFTER THE inauguration, Nicolay had a new job. With the help of Secretary of State William Seward, he had been confirmed as consul to Paris. A few days later, Seward was able to offer Hay a job in Paris, too, as secretary of legation, serving the new minister, John Bigelow. The two positions were not closely related, but Nicolay and Hay would be able to see a great deal of each other, and doubtless they would have time to discuss their plans to write a book on Lincoln. Nicolay and Therena would marry and sail to Europe together.

For Hay, the post abroad was "entirely unsolicited and unexpected," he told his brother Charles. Perhaps so, but he had hardly needed to sell himself to Seward. During the previous four years, Hay had spent hundreds of hours with the secretary of state, in the White House and as a guest, whether for a meal or a game of whist, at the Seward house on Lafayette Square. Hay's gift for languages, his polish as a secretary, and, above all, his profession of Republican principles more than qualified him for the Paris position. What was more, he had made no secret of his admiration for Seward and his appreciation of Seward's own service to Lincoln. The secretary of state and president had started out as rivals for the presidential nomination but set aside their differences to form a dynamic team, shrewd and dedicated, balancing the shifting factions of conservatism and radicalism within their party and within the cabinet itself. "Mr. Seward, while doing everything possible to serve the national cause," Hay would later testify, "was, so far as can be discerned, absolutely free of any ambition or afterthought personal to himself."

In later years, Hay would come to appreciate Seward's deft handling of foreign affairs that much more. Seward favored American expansion, but not through force. "The sword is not the most winning messenger that can be sent abroad," Seward averred. When time came for Hay to serve first as an ambassador and then as secretary of state, he would not find a better role model to draw upon.

Yet in the spring of 1865, Hay had yet to map out a career as a diplomat. "I think [Paris] will be a pleasant place for study and observation," he wrote to a cousin. "I shall no doubt enjoy it for a year or so—not very long, as I do not wish to exile myself in these important and interesting times. . . . I go away only to fit myself for more serious work when I return."

THE NIGHT AFTER WRITING this letter, Hay was in the White House with Robert Lincoln while the president and first lady attended *Our American Cousin* at Ford's Theatre. In the five weeks since the inauguration, the news had been nothing but good, culminating with the federal occupation of Richmond on April 3, the surrender of Lee's Army of Northern Virginia at Appomattox on the ninth, and the surrender of Mobile on the twelfth. Nicolay was even now on his way to Fort Sumter to attend the raising of the Union flag, four years to the day after its rude removal. Robert Lincoln had come to the capital with Grant and had spent part of the morning regaling his father with his eyewitness account of Appomattox.

Of the events of that evening and the next few days Hay wrote nothing at all in his diary, and no letters from that period have turned up, either. His memory, however, was stamped profoundly, and eventually it would serve his pen reliably in the last volume of the Lincoln biography, which concludes abruptly and necessarily on April 15, 1865.

The assassination of Abraham Lincoln has been chronicled any number of times. Most Americans know that the actor John Wilkes Booth entered the Lincolns' theater box after ten o'clock on Good Friday, April 14, and shot the president in the back of the head with a derringer.

Hay's account, written twenty years afterward, is a thorough rendering of the long night, reconstructed from testimony of eyewitnesses and the statements of the doctors who attended the stricken president. Yet his narrative is more literary than most. For him, first and last, the context of life was classical. Upon his arrival in Washington four years earlier, he had written frivolously, "Caesar will be slain in the capitol, and Brutus harangue the roughs from the terrace." Not surprisingly, when the time came to present his version of Lincoln's murder, he chose to tell it as a play within a play, comedy exploding into tragedy, Brutus played by a fiend who knew the part by heart.

"No one, not even the comedian on the stage, could ever remember the last words of the piece that were uttered that night—the last Abraham Lincoln heard upon earth," Hay wrote. "The whole performance remains in the memory of those who heard it a vague phantasmagoria. . . . Here were five human beings [Lincoln, Mrs. Lincoln, and their guests, Major Henry Rathbone and his fiancée, Clara Harris, plus Booth] in a narrow space—the greatest man of his time, in the glory of the most stupendous success of our history, the idolized chief of a nation already mighty, with illimitable vistas of grandeur to come; his beloved wife, proud and happy; a pair of betrothed lovers, with all the promise of felicity that youth, social position, and wealth could give them; and this young actor, handsome as Endymion upon Latmos, the pet of his little world. The glitter of fame, happiness, and ease was upon the entire group, but in an instant everything was to be changed with the blinding swiftness of enchantment. Quick death was to come on the central figure of that company—the central figure, we believe, of the great and good men of the century."

Hay's theatrical reportage continues: "The murderer seemed to himself to be taking part in a play. Partisan hate and the fumes of brandy had for weeks kept his brain in a morbid state. He felt as if he were playing Brutus off the boards; he posed, expecting applause. Holding a pistol in one hand and knife in the other, he opened the box door, put the pistol to the President's head, and fired; dropping the weapon, he took the knife in his right hand, and when Major Rathbone sprang to seize him he struck savagely at him. Major Rathbone received the blow on his left arm, suffering a wide and deep wound. Booth, rushing forward, then placed his left hand on the railing of the box and vaulted lightly over to the stage. It was a high leap, but nothing to such a trained athlete. He was in the habit of introducing what actors call sensational leaps in his plays. In 'Macbeth,' where he met the weird sisters, he leaped from a rock twelve feet high. He would have got safely away but for his spur catching in the folds of the Union flag with which the front of the box was draped. He fell on the stage, the torn flag trailing on his spur, but instantly rose as if he had received no hurt, though in fact the fall had broken his leg; he turned to the audience, brandishing his dripping knife, and shouting the State motto of Virginia, 'Sic Semper Tyrannis,' fled rapidly across the stage and out of sight. Major Rathbone had shouted, 'Stop him!' The cry went out, 'He has shot the President.' From the audience, at first stupid with surprise, and afterwards wild with excitement and horror, two or three men jumped upon the stage in pursuit of the flying assassin; but he ran through the familiar passages, leaped upon his horse, which was in waiting in the alley behind, rewarded with a kick and a curse the call-boy who had held him, and rode rapidly away in the light of the just risen moon."

The rest of the tragedy Hay was able to recount firsthand. While the president was removed from the theater to a boardinghouse across the street, a messenger hurried to the White House. As Hay and Robert Lincoln sprang into a waiting carriage, they were informed that Seward and the rest of the cabinet had been murdered. In fact, only Seward had been attacked. One of Booth's accomplices had assaulted the secretary of state as he lay in bed, slashing him several times with a knife, but not fatally. Hay and Robert knew none of this as they raced to Tenth Street, where the president was dying.

Hay's published description of the final scene is accompanied by a floor plan of the boardinghouse, detailing who was present and where they positioned themselves in the cramped bedroom. He lists more than twenty people, including four doctors, two generals, one minister, and six cabinet members. Hay stood at the head of the bed, just behind Navy Secretary Gideon Welles, Senator Charles Sumner, and Robert Lincoln. Mrs. Lincoln passed most of the night in the adjacent parlor, attended by friends.

"[The president] was, of course, unconscious from the first moment; but he breathed with slow and regular respiration throughout the night," Hay recalled. "As the dawn came, and the lamplight grew pale in the fresher beams, his pulse began to fail; but his face even then was scarcely more haggard than those of the sorrowing group of statesmen and generals around him. His automatic moaning, which had continued throughout the night, ceased; a look of unspeakable peace came upon his worn features. At twenty-two minutes after seven he died. [Secretary of War] Stanton broke the silence by saying, 'Now he belongs to the ages.' Dr. Gurley [of New York Avenue Presbyterian Church] kneeled by the bedside and prayed fervently. The widow came in from the adjoining room supported by her son and cast herself with loud outcry on the dead body."

In the years to come, this scene would be sanctified as a latter-day Calvary. One of Lincoln's cuff buttons, retrieved from the theater box, would be cherished as a splinter from the true Cross. Locks of hair, removed immediately after Lincoln's death and during the postmortem examination, were even more sacred. And despite Hay's published diagram, bickering inevitably broke out over the roster of disciples who were actually at the bedside at the moment the Martyr died.

Hay would spend the rest of his life mourning Lincoln. In eulogizing the man who had been a second father, he would devote most of his words to extolling the president's greatness as a leader of the "common people." But beneath Hay's characterizations of Lincoln as "a great and powerful lover of mankind" and "the greatest character since Christ," there lay an implicit acknowledgment of his tenderness toward Hay personally. "He never asked perfection of any one; he did not even insist, for others, upon the high standards he set up for himself," Hay wrote, speaking as a primary beneficiary. "[He possessed] a charity which embraced in its deep bosom all the good and the bad, all the virtues and infirmities of men, and a patience like that of nature, which in its vast and fruitful activity knows neither haste nor rest."

Lincoln belonged to the nation, to the people, and to the ages. But always there would be a part of Lincoln that belonged to John Hay alone. A year after the assassination, on February 12, 1866, Lincoln's birthday, one of the country's most venerated historians, George Bancroft, would deliver a memorial to Lincoln before the House of Representatives. Hay was in Paris when he read a transcript of the speech. "Bancroft's address was a disgraceful exhibition of ignorance," he wrote scornfully and possessively to William Herndon, who, like Hay and Nicolay, was contemplating a book on Lincoln. "Bancroft & the rest of that patent leather kid glove set know no more of him than an owl does of a comet, blazing into his blinking eyes."

CHAPTER 5

Progress of Democracy

John Hay sailed for Europe at the end of June, accompanied by newly wedded John George and Therena Nicolay. No longer was he the dreamy college boy who had arrived in Washington four years earlier. Tempered by the war and matured by the example of Lincoln, he had become a confident man of affairs. He now wore the uniform of a colonel, the rank brevetted him by Secretary of War Stanton a month earlier.

On one hand, it was a relief to get away—from Springfield, where he had gone to bid his final respects to the president, and from Washington, where a pall lingered over the White House and a government at odds over Reconstruction. On the other hand, he missed his familiar vantage point, inside looking out. "I envy you that you are at home," he wrote Robert Lincoln, "preparing to do your part manfully in the work that will rest seriously on every American of our age."

His life was very much his own, but now it had more gravity, and perhaps even a compass. "While most of the men I meet are throwing up their hats and getting drunk to the glory & long life of the American Eagle," he continued to Lincoln, "the thinking man [realizes] that the times before us are more serious than the times behind. We shall be fortunate if all our honest industry and courage can supply, in the moral fight that is to come, the place of the high heart and unfailing wisdom of him who is now watching us from heaven." From now on, wherever Hay went and whatever he did, Lincoln would *always* be watching.

On his way to France, he passed through London, where he introduced himself to Charles Francis Adams, the distinguished American minister who had been so instrumental in stemming British interference in the Civil War. It was in London also that he met the minister's son Henry, a Harvard graduate Hay's own age, who was serving as his father's personal secretary.

When Charles Adams's counterpart in Paris during the war, William Dayton, had died the previous December, Seward had promoted Consul John Bigelow, a former editor of the *New York Evening Post*, to minister, opening Bigelow's job to Nicolay and then appointing Hay as Bigelow's secretary. He had come well recommended by both Seward and Seward's friend Thurlow Weed, the New York political boss who had recently aligned himself with President Andrew Johnson. "Hay is a bright, gifted young man, with agreeable manners and refined tastes," Weed vouched to Bigelow. "I don't believe that he has been spoiled, though he has been exposed. If he remains the modest young man he was, I am *sure* you will like him." Hay in turn found Bigelow a "genial gentleman."

He was thrilled to be abroad for the first time. "In my boyhood & early youth," he told his father, "I regarded this place [Paris] as the brightest object of legitimate ambition." He had learned French at Brown and kept it up afterward by reading French literature. The Paris of 1865, however, opened his eyes in an unexpected way. Fourteen years earlier, Louis Napoleon, nephew of Napoleon Bonaparte, had staged a coup, crowning himself Emperor Napoleon III and supplanting the Second Republic with a despotic regime known as the Second Empire. As emperor he saw himself as a visionary; to his detractors he was "the Sphinx," for his adamant and enigmatic nature.

Hay was predisposed not to like the parvenu French king. Coming from a country that had sacrificed hundreds of thousands of lives to remain a functioning, unified republic, he had little tolerance for a dictator who would usurp one. That Napoleon had wanted to recognize the Confederacy—deterred only by dogged American diplomacy and the reluctance of England to join the alliance—was another mark against the Second Empire. Then, too, France's opportunistic invasion of Mexico in 1863, in the middle of the American Civil War, insulted the Monroe Doctrine, not to mention the Mexicans under French hegemony.

To his credit, Napoleon III modernized France, especially Paris, building new railroads, sewers, parks, and monuments. By the time Hay and the Nicolays arrived, the emperor's master planner, Baron Georges-Eugène Haussmann, had razed many of Paris's medieval neighborhoods to make way for a disciplined geometry of broad, shaded boulevards and clean, homogenous facades, which upgraded the quality of life for the city's nearly 2 million residents—a grand transformation, to be sure, but one that also consolidated Napoleonic authority.

Hay was taken aback at first. Instead of the farrago of Victor Hugo's *Les Misérables* or Henri Murger's *Scènes de la Vie Bohème*, he was greeted by a "bright new spick and span city with stretches a mile long of drab-colored stone palaces, all new and glistening, with avenues and boulevards with pavements like a bathroom floor," as he remarked to one of his brothers. "I wish you could be here to see the old city before the rest of it is gone. There is still enough to deeply interest you in the Faubourg St. Antoine, where they grow revolutions, and in the Latin Quarter, where the students live & young France dreams of things it must not talk about. But demolition has its teeth fastened there, and the great Boulevard St. Germain is steadily marching on, ripping, and crushing, and grinding to powder the oldest and most storied quarter, and evicting the wild and uncombed savagery of the Old City. . . . There is the deepest interest in its squalor and blackness to me. I leave to English snobs and American tourists the beauty of the new dispensation and pay my homage to the town that has seen better days."

Homage was one thing, housing another for the debonair young colonel. Instead of living among the "swarming hives of humanity that toil and fight and breed in the Paris of history and romance," he took more genteel rooms in the "new West End," on a quiet street near the Arc de Triomphe. From there it was a pleasant walk to the American legation on rue de Chaillot.

Compared to the White House, work at the legation was not demanding. During the first summer in Paris, Bigelow took his family on vacation to the seashore, leaving Hay in charge. He was just busy enough to "keep from stagnating," he reported cavalierly. He saw Nicolay on occasion—the consulate was several blocks from the legation. But they seldom socialized after hours. Nicolay and Therena were homebodies, and soon after their arrival in Paris, they announced that they were expecting a child.

Hay, meanwhile, did not hesitate to partake of the pleasures of Paris, often in the company of Americans bearing letters of introduction from home. After a succession of evenings at the opera and theater with a Miss Wright, he confessed to her that "[Paris] is so tyrannical in its seductive powers that it is less fatiguing to surrender at discretion than to keep up the hopeless fight against temptation." Hay's reputation as a ladies' man was soon well enough established that he was called upon to deliver a toast to "Our Countrywomen" at a dinner for three hundred Americans at the Grand Hotel.

One of the many American visitors to Paris was Andros Stone, president of the Cleveland Rolling Mill Company, accompanied by his wife and daughters, "in pursuit of health and pleasure." Hay recorded nothing in his diary of the Stones' visit, but later that summer he submitted a short story to *Harper's New Monthly Magazine* about a young American diplomat who falls in love with the daughter of "what the newspapers call a Merchant Prince"—a man "enriched by sagacious trade" whom "no country on earth but America could send out." The fictional love affair ends most grimly, with the young diplomat hurling himself off the top of the Arc de Triomphe.

Not that Hay gave even the remotest indication of being suicidal or even downcast while in Paris; on the contrary, his letters are uniformly cheerful. Yet merchant princes and their daughters did leave a lasting impression. Six years later in New York, Andros Stone would introduce Hay to his niece, Clara Stone, daughter of Amasa Stone, also of Cleveland and a merchant prince in his own right.

In Paris, Hay also composed poetry. The bard of Providence was now a *belletrist*, and his muse was Paris itself. One August morning he was moved to write:

I stand at the break of day
In the Champs Élysées
The tremulous shafts of dawning
As they shoot o'er the Tuileries early

It truly was a gay life, and he found the openness of the French charming and infectious. "It never seems to occur to these people that there is any objection to eating, drinking, sleeping and even courting in public," he wrote to his family in Warsaw. "Wherever you go, in the splendid public gardens, in the great picture galleries, which are free to all the world, you see them, singly, or in pairs, or in whole families, amusing themselves in their quiet, simple way, without any modesty, or bashfulness or false pride."

But if everyday living was refreshingly uninhibited, Old World diplomacy was a study in pomp and fustiness. The "season" began on New Year's Day with a reception for the diplomatic corps at the Palace of the Tuileries. Hay attended with Bigelow, wearing a dress uniform that was "more gold than broadcloth." Here he was introduced to Napoleon III for the first time, and his assessment was not favorable. "He is a short stubby looking man, not nearly so tall as I," Hay told his family. "His face is just as you see it in the pictures, only older and more lifeless."

Hay bowed and smiled, expecting no recognition from the emperor. "But he stopped, took a good look, and said, in English, 'Are you arrived from Washington?' 'Have you been previously engaged in Diplomacy?' 'Were you present at the death of President Lincoln?' . . . I answered his questions, everybody looking with all their eyes to see what the great potentate had to occupy him talking to a light-weight Republican."

Several weeks later he attended a ball at the palace, dressed in "small clothes with knee-buckles and silk stockings, with coat and waistcoat, all black and cocked hat." On this occasion he met the empress Eugénie, who was adorned with "a blaze of diamonds." "She is still very handsome," he noted, but her "full face is not as fine as her profile."

Familiarity bred further contempt, and for Hay the contrast between the French emperor and Lincoln—physically and with respect to the ideals they embodied—was all too stark. "I consider Lincoln Republicanism incarnate—with all its faults and all its virtues," he declared after sizing up the Second Empire. "[I]n spite of some rudenesses, Republicanism is the sole hope of a sick world." Lincoln's straightforwardness and high-mindedness, his humility and humanity shone ever more brightly the nearer Hay got to the court of the French king. "[L]et us look at him," Hay wrote in his diary after another audience with Napoleon III. "Short and stocky, he moves with a queer sidelong gait like a gouty crab: a man so wooden looking that you would expect his voice to come rasping out like a watchman's rattle. A complexion like crude tallow. . . . Eyes sleepily watchful—furtive, stealthy, rather ignoble: like servants looking out of dirty windows & saying 'nobody at home' and lying, as they said it."

AFTER A YEAR IN Paris, Hay began to think about going home, and the home he yearned for was Warsaw. With his Florida land purchases unresolved, he sent whatever money he could to his father to invest in vineyards in Illinois. "[One] of these days my history will belong to the past," he wrote to his brother Leonard. "I don't mean that I am going to heaven immediately but I am going to Warsaw, if I can make sure of the means of living without too much work."

The resignation of John Bigelow in the summer of 1866 made Hay's decision to leave much easier. As Bigelow's replacement, Andrew Johnson chose General John Adams Dix as a reward for Dix's support of the president's policies on Reconstruction, which were decidedly lenient toward the South. Johnson's—and Dix's—opposition to the Freedmen's Bureau and the proposed Fourteenth Amendment, providing equal rights for blacks, had enraged the hard-liners of the Republican Party, and Hay, too. Unlike many Radicals, Hay stopped short of advocating impeachment of Johnson (a Democrat), but he regarded the president's "obstinate and angry partisanship" as an insult to the legacy of Lincoln. Accordingly, he wanted as little as possible to do with Johnson's man Dix (although a Republican), and the antipathy was evidently mutual. Hay left Paris at the end of January 1867.

His hankering for home was always of the mistiest sort. Anticipating a new and languid life on the banks of the Mississippi, he wrote to his brother Charles, now a grocer in Springfield: "I will be comfortable and brown, sleeping sound at night, & hoeing my vines by day. . . . We have been so separated that we need about a century together on the hills of Warsaw." Yet his vision of bucolic contentment was never very realistic. "I have money enough to buy bread & cheese for a year or two & old clothes enough for the rest of an ordinary life time," he insisted to his father.

At the same time, a greater ambition spoke more volubly. First, he wanted a comfortable and "uncmbarrassed" income. Second, he still yearned to be a man of letters. Before leaving Nicolay, who was staying on in Paris as consul, the two friends had renewed their commitment to write "the History of Lincoln." More than ever the world needed to be reminded what Abraham Lincoln and the Republican Party stood for.

Upon docking in New York, Hay took an overnight train to Washington and went to see Secretary of State Seward. He was impressed by Seward's calm in the midst of the escalating fractiousness between Radical Republicans and President Johnson's coterie of Copperhead Democrats. The Copperheads accused Republicans of vindictiveness toward the South; the Radicals charged Democrats with squandering the Union victory; each side was determined to remove the other's allies from office. Hay commended Seward's capacity for holding the middle ground—"the same placid philosophic optimist as ever."

There was more to the meeting than simply catching up, however. Hay was angling for another job. But because he had witnessed with disgust the endless parade of patronage-seekers through the Lincoln White House, he was hesitant to broach the subject—and relieved when Seward brought it up first.

Seward promised to do what he could for Hay, though he emphasized just how fierce the infighting had become over all appointments. Radical Republicans were already calling for the withdrawal of General Dix from Paris. Democrats, meanwhile, had pressed for dismissal of the historian John Lothrop Motley as minister to the Austrian Empire for his alleged disloyalty to President Johnson. Motley resigned indignantly, and Dix's fate awaited judgment by the Senate. Even Nicolay, conscientious in the extreme, had been accused of "habitual disrespect" toward the administration.

Seward also lectured Hay on the dangers of "dessication and fossilizing" that resulted from holding public office for too long. Having said all this, the next evening over dinner, he offered Hay the job of minister to Sweden. Hay hesitated.

For the next three weeks, he knocked about Washington, renewing old acquaintances. He had cordial talks with Navy Secretary Welles, who had remained in the Johnson administration, and Salmon Chase, who was now chief justice of the Supreme Court. He visited the Senate and House of Representatives, and dropped by the Eames house. This being the season, he attended several balls. He went twice to the White House, which he found "more richly and carefully furnished than in my time."

Two more things kept him in the capital. Because he still had hopes that he might yet gain possession of his Florida real estate, he spent some time working connections in the Interior Department. There also remained the possibility that, if General Dix were recalled from Paris, Seward might submit Hay's name as chargé d'affaires, the number two position, which would make him the acting minister until Dix's replacement was chosen.

While these matters hung fire, Seward offered him a temporary job as his private secretary. Hay was honored but remained reluctant, reasoning in his diary, "[I]f he had done this out of his usual kindness for me, [then] I ought best to decline [and] go home & see my parents for the present." On March 3, he learned that Dix was to stay after all. Three days later, he left Washington. "I bid farewell to diplomacy," he wrote Nicolay.

By way of adieu, he wrote an obsequious letter to Seward, expressing his gratitude for the secretary's years of mentorship and steadfast service to the Republican cause. "To own the knowledge that I have been thought worthy of high trust by you is worth more than any office," Hay fawned. "I shall go into private life prouder that you proposed my name for a mission than if I had received it by the direction of any other man. . . . I have come to regard you as . . . the Ideal of the Republican workingman—calm without apathy, bold without rashness, firm without obstinacy, & with a patriotism permeated with religious faith."

He made one more stop before heading west. On February 23, he went back to New York to meet with Alfred Guernsey, editor of *Harper's*, who had published "Shelby Cabell," Hay's short story set in Paris. Guernsey told him he would welcome other stories, although he and the other editors whom Hay saw expressed no enthusiasm for a Lincoln biography.

Hay and Nicolay had been beaten to the punch. The previous year, Isaac Newton Arnold, one of Lincoln's ardent congressional supporters, had come out with *The History of Abraham Lincoln and the Overthrow of Slavery*, hasty and hagiographic but substantial enough that "[n]obody is keen for our book," Hay told Nicolay after knocking on doors in New York. Worse still, he had heard a rumor that Robert Lincoln had given Arnold permission to publish the papers of Lincoln previously promised to Hay and Nicolay.

Leaving New York, Hay hastened to Chicago and met with Lincoln, who had opened a law practice there and was looking after his mother and brother. Lincoln reassured Hay that he would not give Arnold "the key to the boxes" and that "he still hopes for our assistance in classifying them," Hay told Nicolay. Even so, "We will have to write [our book] on our own hook some day, when we can afford." He advised Nicolay to "stay where you are. . . . You had better not come home till you are kicked out."

Finally he reached Warsaw on March 12 and was pleased to find his mother "better than usual and full of her good spirits" and his father "at 66 with not a gray hair, with the ruddy cheek and ravenous appetite of a growing boy." He passed the next three months tending his vineyard and orchards. "I am doing work," he declared in his diary, "substantial real work which will have its result doubtless some day & so I plod on & watch the sun, glad after all when my day is done & I can ramble home through the magnificent hills and valleys that surround this town." To John Bigelow he wrote, "I suspect I am at last in my place. If not, if I grow discontented, the world is just around the corner & I can try my luck again. But I think I can endure a good deal of starving before I go on another tour of asking for employment."

If he was trying to convince himself, he did not succeed. As summer approached, he grew predictably restive. Throughout John Hay's life, the world had a way of opening itself to him just as he was ready to take the next step. For the moment, though, he was having difficulty seeing beyond Warsaw. "I have scarcely any plans," he admitted in his diary.

In April, he was officially mustered out of the army. Offers he had explored when he was last in the East—to join a business venture in New York, a law practice in Washington—all were withdrawn "as if they had suddenly discovered I was a leper." And, he confessed, "I long ago made up my mind not to lose any sleep over my ill-starred Florida speculation." (He never did take possession.) With no other immediate prospects, he estimated that with a few pieces for magazines, a lecture or two, and the income from his Illinois land, he possibly could make $1,000 a year. He told himself that it would suffice, that life in Warsaw had its own reward of "a more tranquil mind than anywhere else."

Thanks to William Seward, he did not have to find out. In early June, he received word that he had been commissioned as secretary of legation in Vienna, to act as chargé d'affaires. Although Dix had managed to keep his job as minister to Paris, John Lothrop Motley was coming home from Austria. Hay would take charge of the legation until Motley's replacement was chosen and then approved by the Senate. The salary was $6,000. He steamed for Europe on June 29, six months after leaving Paris.

He landed in Liverpool ten days later. His first visit to England in 1865, en route to Paris, had been all too brief. Now with no apparent urgency to get to Vienna, he gave the country his full attention. He dined with Minister Charles Francis Adams. In the House of Commons, he was impressed by the "directness and simplicity" of Disraeli's and Gladstone's oratory. After a visit to the House of Lords, he could recite from memory a roll call of lords and earls and marquises and viscounts and dukes, with colorful descriptions of each. "It is hard to imagine anything finer," he said of Westminster Abbey. Taking a river omnibus on the Thames, he was smitten by the "exquisite harmony" of mist and sunlight. When he beheld J.M.W. Turner's Luminist paintings of the same river scenes in the National Gallery, he wrote in his diary: "I would go to him very often if I lived in London." During a trip to Stonehenge at the end of his two-week stay, he happened upon an agricultural fair, where "I could not help remarking what a different crowd that would have been in America. Here they were clean, decent, stolid fellows." By the time he left England, he was a thorough Anglophile.

VIENNA WAS A DIFFERENT story. From the start, knowing that his posting was only temporary, he didn't take the city or his job seriously. "It is a pleasant, happy-go-lucky, old-fashioned, good-natured and rather stupid town," he wrote in a sketch he submitted to *Putnam's*. From a diplomatic standpoint, the country as a whole did not command his respect, either. A year earlier, Prussia, under its king, Wilhelm, and prime minister, Otto von Bismarck, had prodded Austria into war and trounced it soundly. The once mighty Hapsburg Empire, under Emperor Franz Joseph, was now regarded as hapless, anachronistic, and marginalized. "Austria is perhaps next to Turkey in passivity and hopelessness," Hay wrote dismissively.

Vienna did have its diversions, however. "The great luxury is music," Hay told Nicolay. He heard Strauss waltzes in the public gardens and saw the opera *Faust* from the box he inherited from Motley. One festival followed another throughout the summer, on which occasions, he noted, "the whole town shuts up shop and goes to the country" to eat, drink, and "lie on the grass . . . and let the world roll on."

His diary and letters make only passing reference to the work at hand, and evidently there was little. His fluency in German emboldened him to wander in directions he might have not gone otherwise—tramps in the mountains of the Tyrol and into the back streets of Vienna's working-class neighborhoods, the most squalid of which, he judged, was the Jewish quarter.

Thirty-six years later, in 1903, when Hay was secretary of state, he would take a public stand against the persecution of Jews abroad, his advocacy garnering him the widespread gratitude and respect of American Jewry. His posture at the time was somewhat unexpected, especially since so many of his friends were openly anti-Semitic—Henry Adams among the worst. Perhaps Hay merely suppressed his own bigotry, or, as seems more likely, he had outgrown it. Yet in Vienna in September 1867 there was no mistaking the revulsion he expressed toward life in the cul-de-sacs surrounding the Judenplatz.

"I have never seen a decent person in those alleys or on those slippery stairs," he wrote. "[E]verywhere [there are] stooping, dirty figures in long, patched and oily black gabardines of every conceivable material . . . covering the crouching creeping form from the round shoulders, to the splay shuffling feet. A battered soft felt hat crowns the oblique indolent crafty face, and what is most offensive of all, a pair of greasy curls dangle[s] in front of the pendulous ears. . . . In America we always say rich as a Jew, because even if a Jew is poor he is so brisk so sharp and enterprising that he is sure to make money eventually. But these slouching rascals are as idle as they are ugly."

His first impressions of Jews as a culture were not unlike the generalizations he had made of the enslaved Negroes he had observed in the South: a race apart, retrograde, removed from grace, and a dismally long way from assimilation into the mainstream.

In the fall, Nicolay visited from Paris for several days. Afterward, Hay left Vienna on his own trip—to Krakow and Warsaw in Poland, then down the Danube to Budapest, and as far as Constantinople, returning by way of Trieste. At the first of the year, he went south to Italy, with stays in Rome and Venice. By the spring of 1868, he knew his interim as chargé d'affaires was nearing an end. "I have had a pleasant year of it," he wrote to John Bigelow. "There is very little work to do at the Legation. I have sinned grievously against certain ten-day [leave] regulations. . . . I have drawn my salary with startling punctuality. I have not wearied the Home office with much despatches. My sleep is infantine & my appetite wolfish."

Yet he had not been entirely irresponsible, and his commentary on the declining authority of the Austrian aristocracy and the rise of liberalism was surely welcomed by Secretary Seward. His reports on the gestation of the new Austro-Hungarian Empire were likewise trenchant, and a letter he wrote to Seward in February 1868 was quite prescient on the shape of things to come. "The great calamity and danger of Europe today are those enormous armaments," he observed. "No honest statesman can say that he sees in the present attitude of politics the necessity of war. No great Power is threatened. . . . Why then is the awful waste of youth and treasure continued? I believe from no other motive than to sustain the waning prestige of Kings."

His experience, first in Paris and now in Vienna, was paying off. Not only had he mastered the protocol of diplomacy; he was also drawing his own map of the world and developing his own sense of how foreign relations ought to be conducted. Already he observed the desperation of monarchies and foresaw the volatility of rampant nationalism when backed by modern weaponry—a dangerous combination that would vex the world into the next century.

In Vienna, as in Paris, the more he saw of the Old World's way of governance, the more he appreciated his own country's methods. "It is curious and instructive to see these people starting off on the awkward walk of political babyhood," he told John Bigelow. "Two years ago it was another Europe. . . . If ever, in my green and salad days, I sometimes vaguely doubted, I am safe now. I am a Republican till I die. When we get to Heaven, we can try a monarchy, perhaps."

Due to the bitter political turmoil in Washington, the appointment of Hay's replacement was slow in coming. In February, the House of Representatives had voted to impeach President Johnson—nominally for the rude manner in which he had attempted to fire Secretary of War Stanton—only to have the Senate acquit Johnson in May. In the meantime, the Vienna job was offered to a half-dozen men, including Horace Greeley, who turned it down. Finally in July, Henry Watts of Pennsylvania accepted the commission. Hay, who dubbed his successor "Watt-shisname," turned in his resignation and spent the rest of the summer at his leisure in the Tyrol and the Swiss Alps. Passing through London on the way home in October, he had little opportunity to see the sights, although he did chance to attend a lecture by one of his favorite authors, Charles Dickens.

ONCE AGAIN HE RETURNED to Warsaw, and once again he did not stay long. By November he was back in Washington, "in peaceful pursuit of a fat office." Ulysses S. Grant was the new president, but Hay's patron, Seward, was leaving the State Department after the inauguration in March. Seward had nothing immediate to promise Hay. "I go back tonight to the West a broken down politician," Hay joked mournfully to Nicolay in early December. Nicolay, too, was out of work and headed back to the United States with his wife and infant daughter.

Hay was now thirty years old, with no dependents, few burdens, and time on his hands. He had friends in every city, it seemed, and he was well received wherever he went. A newspaper clipping in one of his scrapbooks chimed a typical welcome: "John Hay . . . invariably a good fellow, and always an immense favorite of the ladies, is in town, having returned from somewhere, and is looking as bright as a basket of chips, evidently being of that sort of hay which is made when the sun shines. . . . We do not know what he is doing, or what he wants; but the heart of power must be indeed obdurate which would refuse him anything he asked."

Left to his own devices, he tried his hand at lecturing. In late January 1869, he spoke to a large audience in Buffalo and then to a smaller one in Warsaw on "The Progress of Democracy in Europe," tracing the movement, from the French Revolution through the reversals of the Second Empire to the aftermath of the Austro-Prussian War. "He is severe upon Louis Napoleon; he doesn't like Bismarck," wrote one reviewer. On sum, though, "Mr. Hay is hopeful for Democracy in Europe." The review lavished equal praise on his delivery—"a good voice, a fine elocution"—and on his intellect—"versatile, polished, brilliant."

By spring, he was in Washington once again, courting the Grant administration and Secretary of State Hamilton Fish. He knew the drill by heart, and he was somewhat chagrined to be joining the very throng of favor-seekers he had once deprecated. "You will find Washington intolerable," he warned Nicolay in mid-May. "I have been here one day. I am quite sure that by hanging around and eating dirt I could get some office. But my stomach revolts. It is almost too great a strain of a man's self-respect to ask for an office: still worse to beg for it."

Instead, he found a job as editor of the *Illinois State Journal*, a Republican paper in Springfield. "He is a bright, handsome young fellow, full of talent and possessed of a vast deal of tact," a rival newspaper commented. "If he makes as much impression upon Western readers as he did upon Washington ladies he will make himself felt as a journalist."

His plan was to edit the newspaper and write for magazines on the side. The *Atlantic Monthly* had recently bought his in-depth account of the attack and murder of Joseph Smith by the Warsaw militia. But $100 every now and again for his freelance work was not enough; nor did it compensate for the drudgery and meager pay of the *Illinois State Journal.* He lasted there only a month.

In mid-June, he was offered the position of secretary of legation in Madrid. After the White House, Paris, and Vienna, to accept another commission as secretary of legation, at such a modest salary, was an admission, if not of defeat, then of desperation. Seward had warned him about the pitfalls of low-level patronage. The salary was his smallest so far: $1,800 a year. But Hay had no better plan.

All the same, there were intriguing reasons for going to Madrid. One was the minister under whom he would serve: General Daniel Sickles, one of the most renowned swashbucklers of his day. Another was the political situation in Spain: a year earlier a democratic revolt had dethroned Queen Isabella II, and in June, just as Hay was offered his job, the Spanish Cortes, or parliament, enacted a constitution providing universal suffrage (for men) and greater civil rights. "I have determined, *malgré* my better judgment, to go to Spain for a little while," he wrote John Bigelow. "I have read and thought a good deal about revolutions, and I cannot resist an opportunity so favorable of lifting the very pot lid and seeing the 'hellbroth seeth and bubble.'" The Progress of Democracy in Europe was opening a brand new chapter.

Hay knew Daniel Sickles, as did nearly everybody in America. He had served as a secretary to the U.S. legation in London and in the U.S. Congress. He had been censured for escorting a prostitute into the chambers of the New York assembly and, on a trip to London, was said to have introduced her to Queen Victoria. Then in 1859, he killed Philip Barton Key, son of the composer of "The Star-Spangled Banner." Key, the district attorney of Washington, was having an affair with Sickles's wife when Sickles shot him down in broad daylight in Lafayette Square, across from the White House. He won acquittal on grounds of temporary insanity. In the Civil War, he quickly rose from colonel to general, thanks mainly to his friendship with General Joseph Hooker.

Sickles's performance at Gettysburg renewed his notoriety. At Cemetery Ridge he defied the order of General Meade to hold his troops in a defensive position, instead ordering it forward and unduly exposing it to a devastating fire that hacked its ranks from ten thousand to six thousand before it could get into the fight. Had he not lost his leg to a Confederate cannonball, he might well have been court-martialed. After the war, he made himself useful by commanding Reconstruction efforts in the South and by displeasing Andrew Johnson. For these last services, Grant sent him to Spain.

Sickles, in many ways, was just the man for the post. He was battle-tested, as his uniform and crutches made plain; he was an inveterate intriguer; and at forty-nine, despite his missing leg, he was yet dashing and virile. He would need all of his talents to fulfill the instructions he carried from President Grant by way of Secretary of State Fish: to broker a deal for Cuba.

For the past year, Cuba had been in revolt, seeking to shake free of the dictatorial grip of the Spanish Empire. The United States proposed that Cuba be allowed to buy its independence, with the United States guaranteeing the payments. The American goal, of course, was to gain possession of the country that produced one third of the world's sugar. With the Spanish government virtually bankrupt, the time seemed opportune. But to achieve his delicate mission, Sickles first had to navigate the confounding chaos of four or more political parties plotting and rioting to seize control of a newly forged but scarcely tempered constitutional monarchy, which, at the moment, was without a monarch.

John Hay's time in Spain was not unlike his years in Paris and Vienna. He was at once engaged and aloof—part envoy, part journalist. On the strength of the Mormon article, *Atlantic Monthly* assistant editor William Dean Howells told him he would welcome pieces from Spain. The first appeared before Hay left the country in the summer of 1870, and they would soon be collected in *Castilian Days*, his first book.

As much as he denounced Madrid as "cheerless and bare," it was nonetheless an ideal subject for portraiture. As secretary of legation, he had a box seat on the grand drama of a nation in the throes of shedding "the twin despotism" of church and crown and claiming "its rightful inheritance of modern freedom and progress." His commentary was characteristically mordant, more so as his Spanish improved.

He was aided by his friendship with Emilio Castelar, a history professor who had fled to France after a failed revolt in 1866 and then returned in 1868 as the most outspoken champion of republicanism. Castelar, like Hay, spoke French and took the American secretary into his confidence, educating him on the nuances of Spanish society and the inflections of national debate. Hay regularly attended sessions of the Cortes and was mesmerized by Castelar's oratory, even if he could not understand all he heard. "I have never imagined such fluency of speech," Hay wrote in his diary. "He never says a foolish or careless word. All history is at his fingers' ends."

Hay shared Castelar's vision of a government progressing steadily, if fitfully, toward full democracy. What held Spain back, Hay came to recognize, was "blind reverence for things that have been." He ridiculed the Catholic Church and its fixation on "knuckle-bones of apostles and splinters of true crosses." He decried dueling as "the lack of modern civilization." He attended bullfights but was not amused. He was charmed by the "tender melody" of the Castilian tongue but remarked to John Bigelow that the Spaniards "retain the speech of Don Quixote, but the heart and stomach of Sancho's."

He made exception for the grand tradition of Spanish fine arts, as represented in the galleries of the Prado. He was entirely enchanted by Diego Velásquez's masterpiece *Las Meninas*, a seventeenth-century portrait of the daughter of King Philip IV and her attendants. "The longer you look upon this marvellous painting, the less possible does it seem that it is merely the placing of color on canvas," he observed. "If art consists in making a fleeting moment immortal, if the True is a higher ideal than the Beautiful, then it will be hard to find a greater painting than this."

After only a few months in Madrid, it became obvious to Hay, as well as to Sickles, that General Juan Prim, president of the latest Spanish government, dared not consummate the cession of Cuba for fear of incurring the wrath of rival factions within Spain and other monarchies throughout Europe. "The Spanish people are too ignorant to see their empire in America is really at an end," Hay told his father. Writing to Bigelow, he declared, "If we want the Island we must go there and take it." Twenty-eight years later, when Hay was serving as ambassador to England, the United States would do precisely as he had suggested.

But as frustrated as he was by the Cuba impasse, he did not flag in his optimism for the future of the Spanish republic. "[A] new and beneficent spirit has begun to influence the political life of Spain," he prophesied. "Its voice rings out in the Cortes in strains of lyric beauty that are only heard in the fresh and dewy dawn of democracies. The day that is coming is not to be tranquil and cloudless. . . . There will be bloodshed and treasons and failures enough to discourage and appall the faint-hearted. But . . . the shadow will go forward on the dial. . . . Spain, the latest call of the nations of Europe, is not condemned to everlasting punishment for the crimes of her kings and priesthood."

Hay did not stay long at the legation. The failure of the Cuba negotiations, and the Grant administration's unhappiness with Spain's treatment of Cubans and of the American filibusterers who were aiding them, made relations with the Spanish authority increasingly testy. And while he developed a dour appreciation of "Españolismo," he confessed that he "never felt so thoroughly out of the world before."

Another reason to leave was the lack of suitable female companionship. He complained that few Americans, especially American women, came through Madrid. And not all those who did met with his approval. To one female visitor from New York, whose name is unrecorded, he wrote: "You have beauty enough to be a first rate belle, if you had less wit. . . . You are witty, but you are not hearty and cordial. Your wit is as cold as an icicle." As for Spanish women, he found them "built on the old-fashioned generous plan." What they offered in form they lacked in substance: "They know a little music and a little French, but they have never crossed, even in a school-day excursion, the border line of the ologies."

The one lasting friendship he did forge was with Sickles's personal secretary, Alvey Adee, who would prove to be one of the most remarkable men in Hay's lifetime circle of colleagues. Alvey Augustus Adee was four years Hay's junior, trim, sandy-haired, and "chipper as a mudlark." The son of a naval surgeon, he was tutored at home and then trained as a civil engineer. He had an abiding curiosity for the workings of the world and had spent a year touring Europe. Like Hay, he had a knack for languages, an aptitude made more remarkable by the fact that Adee was quite nearly deaf—although, as a reporter noted some years later, "It seems to be a peculiar sort of deafness that enables him to hear what he cares to hear and to remain oblivious to things that annoy or bore him."

While in Madrid, Hay and Adee collaborated on a tale of a mad German scientist who transfers the soul of an American tourist into the body of a local drunkard, using a "life-magnet." Adee took credit for writing the story, but it had been Hay's idea, and they sold it to *Putnam's*. It would not be their last joint effort. In 1879, when Hay rejoined the State Department as assistant secretary of state, after a nine-year absence, he found Adee ensconced as chief of the Diplomatic Bureau, ably overseeing department correspondence. Two decades later, when Hay returned to diplomatic service once again, Adee had risen to assistant secretary of state. They would work together, hand-in-glove, for the remainder of Hay's life, having no difficulty understanding each other in any of four languages.

Hay resigned from the Madrid legation on August 1, 1870, allowing Adee to take the official position of secretary of legation. The reason he gave for quitting was the low salary, but clearly he had gotten what he could out of Madrid. "Hopes of a Spanish Republic," the first installment of what would become *Castilian Days*, appeared in the March 1870 *Atlantic Monthly*, and in July he received a flattering offer from Nicolay, who was back home in America, endeavoring to regain the health that had failed him in Paris. Nicolay had taken a job as editor of the *Republican*, a Chicago daily in need of its own revival. He wanted Hay to join him. The offer was tempting; for one thing it would bring Hay closer to his family in Illinois; for another, "I could get along with Nicolay more easily than with almost anyone I know," he wrote to his parents.

WHILE SPAIN REMAINED HOBBLED by its past, France was colliding head-on with the future. Since 1866, when Hay had last appeared in the French court, Louis Napoleon III had begun to lose his grip. Corpulent and slouching, wracked by gout and gallstones and drugged with opiates, he suffered one insult after another. In 1867, the insurgency of Benito Juárez had forced French troops to withdraw from Mexico; that same year, Napoleon had failed in his attempt to annex Luxembourg and Belgium. Meanwhile, within his own borders, radicalism was on the rise, centered in the king's once orderly cities. Riots in the streets of Paris and angry opposition at the polls signaled that decadent monarchy could not withstand the forces of liberal republicanism for much longer. A coup d'état seemed imminent. To keep the country intact and to preserve imperial authority, the king and his ministers endeavored to redirect French passions outward, toward a foreign enemy. In the summer of 1870, that enemy was Prussia.

After the Austro-Prussian War of 1866, King Wilhelm and Prime Minister Bismarck had bundled a succession of German states, duchies, and cities into the North German Confederation, the ascendant forerunner of the modern German state, its capital the Prussian city of Berlin. The population of the North German Confederation was nearly that of France, and its army was now one third larger than France's and growing—yet another reason why Napoleon III felt diminished and threatened. Bismarck seemed almost to be taunting the French emperor by refusing to cede lands on the west bank of the Rhine, which, under Napoleon Bonaparte, had buffered the French homeland. War with the upstart Prussians seemed to Napoleon III, and to most of his otherwise discordant countrymen, the solution to a multiple of ills. It would restore French territory and pride and drive an enemy from its doorstep.

Bismarck saw the logic in war as well. His own circumstances, while not so precarious as Napoleon's, were nevertheless troubling. In his zeal to stitch together a German confederacy—small states and large, north and south, Protestant and Catholic—the total did not yet equal the sum of the parts. To solidify the "fatherland," he persuaded Wilhelm to assume the title of emperor of the North German Confederation. Then he set out to nudge France into a fight that would galvanize German spirit once and for all.

Napoleon took the bait like the glutton he was. He resented the presence of another emperor in the European pantheon. And he was even more annoyed over the emperor who had been chosen, through Prussian meddling, to succeed Isabella II in Spain. At Bismarck's urging, in early July 1870 the Spanish crown was offered to Prince Leopold von Hohenzollern-Sigmaringen, who, not by coincidence, was of the same noble family as Wilhelm.

When the announcement reached France, Napoleon and his ministers were incensed by the prospect of having their empire hemmed in by not one but now two arms of the Hohenzollern dynasty This reaction was just what Bismarck had hoped for. The French foreign minister, Duke Antoine Agénor of Gramont, demanded that Leopold's name be withdrawn. And even after Leopold complied, Gramont would not back down until Prussia expressed its contrition formally and publicly. Gramont sent a telegram to Wilhelm, who was vacationing at the spa of Bad Ems, demanding that Prussia pledge never again to suggest a candidate for the Spanish throne. Bismarck, ever manipulative, twisted the now-infamous Ems Dispatch into a colossal slur on German virtue, at once inflaming his own generals and, by refusing to renounce Prussia's designs on Spain, goading Napoleon into mobilizing his own vaunted armies.

France declared war on Prussia on July 19, just as John Hay was preparing to depart for home. "I leave Europe in a grand and imposing time," he wrote his family in early August. "The greatest historical drama of our time is now being played. I hope the war will not last much longer."

His remark was on target in both respects. Although the war did not last long, it changed the world forever. The French army, led by the king, failed miserably—most significantly in its estimation of the size, discipline, and nimbleness of its opponent. In a rapid succession of clashes, the Prussian army, with its fearsome Krupp artillery, rolled over the French lines. On September 2, Prussian General Helmuth von Moltke captured Napoleon and his entire army of one hundred thousand at Sedan, an embarrassment that France has never lived down. When word of this mammoth defeat reached Paris, an angry mob converged on the royal palace and government buildings, vandalizing and chanting "Death to the Bonapartes!" Empress Eugénie, without her diamonds, fled through the Louvre and eventually to England, where she was later joined by her freed husband. With that, the Second Empire was no more, supplanted by a provisional Government of National Defense.

The war was for all intents and purposes over, although fighting continued for another four months. The Prussian army laid siege to Paris, bombarding and starving it into submission. France—the nascent Third Republic—finally capitulated in January 1871, giving up all of the frontier province of Alsace, part of Lorraine, and an indemnity of 5 billion francs. Bismarck achieved all he wanted and more. Even before Paris had fallen, he gathered together the leaders of the confederate German states and their allies in the Hall of Mirrors at Versailles and formed the German Empire, with Wilhelm as its kaiser (a titled derived from "Caesar") and himself as chancellor. As one empire was swept away forever, a far more expansionist and more militaristic state lifted its proud head in Europe.

John Hay had traveled through Paris in late August, before the siege and before Napoleon was defeated, deposed, and disgraced. The city was frantically fortifying itself; Baron Haussmann's boulevards were now patrolled by an undisciplined civilian militia. Foreigners were abandoning the city by every available conveyance. Regrettably, any accounts of his short stay in Paris are lost, if they existed at all. But later he bid farewell to the Bonaparte dynasty in an article for *Harper's*. He began by describing Paris as it had appeared in 1869, while he was on his way to Madrid: "The Empire attained its most resplendent bloom the year before its fall. . . . The grand sweep of the avenue to the Place de l'Étoile was one sea of glimmering radiance, and the Arch of Triumph at the crest of the hill was transfigured by the magic of lime light into a vast dome of porcelain and mother-of-pearl, a temple standing in the midst of the opulence and art of new Paris, dedicated to the worship of the material splendor of Napoleonism."

But exactly one year later, in the throes of war, he observed a vastly different tableau: "A few servants of the [municipality] were tearing down the pipes and gas-fixtures which had been planned to celebrate the entry of the French army into Berlin. At every corner panic-stricken groups were reading the bulletins, in which a false coloring was given to terrible defeats. A beaten army was rolling back toward Paris, shouting as beaten armies always shout, 'Treason,' and the Emperor, stunned and helpless, abandoning the command to others, was muttering with the iteration of idiocy: 'I have been deceived!' "

During his three tours of Europe—in Paris, Vienna, and Madrid—Hay had watched while governments came together, fell apart, and re-formed. He had followed firsthand the evolution of states into nations, monarchies into republics. He had been presented in the courts of moribund regimes and in the assemblies of democracies striving to define themselves. After his years in the White House during the Civil War, the rivalry and tumult that he observed abroad perhaps seemed tame in comparison, but by the time he stepped ashore in New York in September 1870, there were few men in America, certainly few his age—a month shy of thirty-two—who could match his understanding of foreign affairs or, for that matter, politics of any provenance.

CHAPTER 6

Plain Language

Hay landed in New York in the first week of September 1870, ten years after volunteering to open mail for presidential candidate Abraham Lincoln. He was now thoroughly cosmopolitan, dressed by London tailors, conversant in the finest opera and art, and polished in the etiquette of the haute monde. He was headed for Chicago to see John George Nicolay about the job on the *Republican*; but first he wanted to have a talk with Whitelaw Reid, the acting managing editor of the *New York Tribune*. Hay had a proposal to make.

The *Tribune* was still very much Horace Greeley's paper, although he was absent much of the time, giving lectures and bending ears in Albany and Washington. If Hay bore any hard feelings after the Niagara Falls fiasco of 1864, he kept them to himself. Nor did he hold a grudge against Reid, whom he had come to know during the war as well, when Reid was Washington correspondent for the *Cincinnati Gazette*. Reid had criticized Grant's poor generalship at Shiloh, and he had been no less harsh on Lincoln, working to block the president's renomination in 1864 while promoting the campaign of fellow Ohioan Salmon Chase. At one point, Hay had even tried to have Reid fired—to no avail. Arriving at the *Tribune* after the war, Reid was given the official title of first writing editor, or head editorial writer, though it was now quite apparent that he was Greeley's right hand and heir.

Hay and Reid had too much in common not to get along. Reid was only one year older, and like Hay, he had grown up west of the Appalachians, in his case, Xenia, Ohio. He was an exemplary scholar, enlightened by reading Rousseau and Keats at Miami University. And he too had cultivated a buoyant urbanity. Long, lean, with a Van Dyke beard similar to the one Hay would soon grow, he was a hale bachelor well met in the clubs and drawing rooms of postwar New York.

The *Tribune* was not the biggest daily in New York. The *Herald, Times*, and *Sun* all claimed daily readership greater than the *Tribune's* forty-five thousand, but the *Tribune* also printed weekly and semi-weekly editions that had more subscribers than the other three competitors combined, making it the most widely read newspaper in the country.

Reform was the journalistic byword of the day. The Union had been preserved, Andrew Johnson had been purged, and time had come for a fresh start. Newspapers, in their hunger for readership, vied to expose corruption and tout their own virtuosity. The enemy was fraud, graft, quid pro quo, and the spoils system. Rings came in various sizes, all of them unscrupulous: the Whiskey Ring, the Gold Ring, the Tweed Ring. Railroads were crooked, machines rapacious. "Boss" was a bad name, and an honest politician was someone who, when bought, stayed bought. It was said that Mark Twain and Charles Dudley Warner dubbed the era—and their 1873 novel—the Gilded Age because to them "gild" sounded an awful lot like "guilt."

Horace Greeley's Great Moral Organ was in its element. Its city reporters exposed corruption in the New York Customs House and cruelty in the city's mental asylum. The paper also boasted some of the very best writing of its time. Twain's *Innocents Abroad* was first serialized in the *Tribune*. William Winter, writing for the *Tribune*, set the standard for drama criticism. Henry Villard, John Russell Young, Noah Brooks, and George Smalley—to name four of the worthiest reporters of the Civil War—all filed to the *Tribune*. Yet what separated the *Tribune* from its rivals on Newspaper Row—and the reason Hay came to see Whitelaw Reid—was coverage of overseas news.

Foreign reporting was revolutionized in 1866 with the completion of the transatlantic telegraph cable. That same year, George Smalley was sent to London to supervise a foreign bureau that would take advantage of the new technology. The Austro-Prussian War ended before he could set up shop, but in 1870, when the Franco-Prussian War erupted, Smalley's reporters were well deployed at the front. The *Tribune*'s blow-by-blow coverage, funneled first to Smalley in London and then transmitted to New York at the rate of six words a minute, scooped most other papers by days.

The *Tribune*'s triumph, not to mention its editorial harangues of Napoleon III, got Hay's attention and gave him an idea, which he spelled out to Reid over dinner at the Union League Club. Rather than going to Chicago to work for Nicolay, he proposed that he return to Paris to cover the siege and its aftermath for the *Tribune*. Reid informed Hay that he already had a man in Paris writing a weekly letter. Instead, Reid countered, "I would rather . . . have you come to New York, and if you were not a fellow of such diplomatically extravagant habits as to be beyond the reach of our modest salaries, I should try to tempt you."

After seeing Nicolay in Chicago a few days later, Hay was more than tempted. "I do not find the elements of stability [at the *Republican*] I expected," he wrote Reid. "N[icolay] is fighting a good battle but the figures will beat him." Indeed, Nicolay cut his losses after three months and took his family to Florida for the winter. Hay spent the next few weeks in Warsaw and promised to come back to New York sometime later in the fall—that is, if Reid's offer still stood. Any coolness that had lingered from the war years had already melted away.

Hay found Warsaw as welcoming as ever. The grapes from his "shy little vineyard" had produced 200 gallons of wine, and autumn flattered the landscape. "The great River is wrapped at daybreak in a morning-gown of fog," he wrote Nicolay, "and the light has a regular spree on the many colored foliage of the hills and the islands. I am doing nothing and find it easy to take."

He had too many irons in the fire to linger for long. *Castilian Days* was to be published by James R. Osgood, who was also a part owner of the *Atlantic Monthly*. Meanwhile, William Dean Howells was preparing several more of the book's chapters for the magazine. And the *Tribune* looked promising, although Reid had yet to make a firm offer. At the end of October, Hay headed east to talk "*au grand sérieux*" with his editors.

In New York, Reid persuaded him to accept a job writing "breviers," the *Tribune*'s term for editorials, for $50 a week, a handsome salary for those days. For convenience, Hay took a room in the nearby Astor House, where he also ate his meals. "I cannot regard it as a successful experiment as yet," he wrote Nicolay after a few weeks on the job, "though Reid & the rest seem satisfied." "The rest" included Horace Greeley, who initially was displeased to learn that Reid had hired his old Niagara Falls companion. But once Greeley began reading Hay's editorials, he changed his tune and declared Hay the most brilliant editorial writer ever to darken the door of the *New York Tribune*.

Others were singing his praises as well. Hay went up to Boston to meet Howells and James T. Fields, the venerable editor of the *Atlantic*, whose circle of friends included Hawthorne, Emerson, Longfellow, Whittier, Bronson Alcott, James Russell Lowell, and the James brothers, William and Henry. For Hay, who had once worshipped at the feet of Edgar Allan Poe's mistress, entrée to Fields's universe was intoxicating, though he was not so stage-struck that he was unable to comport himself impressively, as he always managed to do in the presence of royalty. "Come as often as you please to Boston," Fields wrote after Hay's visit. "Chaps the likes of you don't often stray this way." Fields urged Hay to return for a meeting of the legendary Saturday Club, consisting of Hawthorne, Emerson, et al. "[Y]ou shall be my guest whenever you choose to give me that pleasure."

Hay hit it off well with Howells, too. It was the first time they had met in person, though they had known about each other for years. Howells had grown up in southern Ohio (not far from Reid), making ends meet as a newspaper reporter and yearning to succeed as a poet and author. In 1860, he was chosen—over John George Nicolay—to write a campaign biography of Abraham Lincoln. For his service, Howells was awarded the consulship to Venice, where he wrote a series of sketches eventually bound together as *Venetian Life*. Hay's articles from Spain may well have been inspired by Howells's from Italy. Howells's novels,

A Hazard of New Fortunes and *The Rise of Silas Lapham*, would one day be American classics.

Howells and Hay were a year apart in age, and their small-town roots, their dedication to Lincoln, their tours of Europe, their devotion to literature, and their attraction to the cultural offerings of the East made them kindred spirits even before they shook hands in the *Atlantic Monthly* offices. A year earlier, when James Fields had sailed for Europe, leaving his assistant in charge, one of the articles Howells had picked out was "The Mormon Prophet's Tragedy," recognizing not just the author's name but also a fresh voice from a region not unlike the one where he was raised.

In December 1870, after his trip to Boston, one of Hay's first editorials for the *Tribune*, entitled "The Western School," saluted their common ground: "[T]here are many good and honest literary workmen who have grown up in the great West, not unmindful of its strange and striking lessons," Hay pronounced, putting aside his earlier disdain for the "savagery" of his homeland. "Some of them, Howells among the best, have already given some earnest of the promising future. Others are just rising into notice."

Like James Fields's Saturday pride of literary lions, western writers were now a force to be reckoned with. One of the strongest, of course, was Mark Twain, whose acquaintance Hay and Howells had made the previous year—Howells when Twain had walked into the *Atlantic* office to thank the man who had written such a glowing review of *Innocents Abroad*; Hay at the *Tribune* office when the tall, shaggy-locked author with drooping mustache brought in a letter he wished printed in the paper. (Hay naturally obliged.) Twain, or Samuel Clemens, was about the same age as Hay (and Howells and Whitelaw Reid), and he was another who had gone through the war wielding a pen instead of a rifle.

One member of the Western School cut a wider swath than all the rest, and that was Bret Harte. Born in Albany, New York, in 1836, Harte had moved to California as a young man. In 1868, he became the founding editor of *Overland Monthly*, the Pacific's first great literary journal. Harte's short stories, "The Luck of Roaring Camp" and "Outcasts of Poker Flat," brought him overnight acclaim, but it was his poem "Plain

Language from Truthful James," first published in the September 1870 issue of *Overland Monthly*, that made Harte's name a household word.

He composed the poem in the vernacular of the western camps and outposts that he knew so well. He had meant it as a lampoon of the profane prejudice shown toward immigrants, particularly the Chinese in California. Low-handed and low-browed, "Truthful James" and his partner set out to cheat Ah Sin, a "heathen Chinee," at cards, except that it is Ah Sin—"his smile it was pensive and childlike"—who winds up euchring the cheaters.

> *In his sleeves, which were long,*
> *He had twenty-four jacks,—*
> *Which was coming it strong,*
> *Yet I state but the facts;*
> *And we found on his nails, which were taper,*
> *What is frequent in tapers, —that's wax.*

Most readers did not dwell upon Harte's intended irony, in which native savvy is embarrassed by a new breed of newcomer, choosing instead to appreciate the poet's stereotyping of Ah Sin and his drolly realistic depiction of yokels familiar to nearly all Americans but, heretofore, rarely given such mannered treatment in verse. It was the same respectful condescension, or condescending respect, that Twain would display so effectively in his novels, from *Huckleberry Finn* to *Pudd'nhead Wilson*. "Truthful James," better known as "The Heathen Chinee," was reprinted in hundreds of newspapers, memorized by thousands of its admirers, and illustrated endlessly. James Fields would soon offer Bret Harte an annual salary of $10,000 to write for his magazine, making Harte the highest paid author in the country.

John Hay, who himself spoke a word or two of vernacular, took a special interest in "Truthful James" and Harte's other "dialect" poems. Along the Mississippi there proliferated characters known derisively as "Pikes," named for their home counties—Pike County, Illinois, immediately south of Hay's home county of Hancock, and Pike County, Missouri, just south of Twain's Hannibal. The typical Pike, or Piker, was described as an

"Anglo-Saxon relapsed into semi-barbarism . . . long, lathy, and sallow; he expectorates vehemently; he takes naturally to whiskey." As the century progressed, Pike County men had wandered westward, joining the rush for gold and land and carrying with them their coarse reputations. In California, Bret Harte tapped the taxonomy for "Truthful James" and for many of his other poems and stories. Hay recognized the genus every bit as well and reckoned that if Harte could dash off a poem in "Plain Language," he supposed he could, too.

"Little Breeches" appeared in the *Tribune* on November 19, 1870, shortly after Hay joined the paper and two months after "Truthful James" ran in *Overland Monthly*. In lilting couplets, it tells the story of a child lost in a blizzard after his father's wagon bolts with the boy aboard. The poem, narrated by the father of Little Breeches, strikes the same half-earnest, instructional tone as Harte's poems, and the pitch of the Pike dialect is dead true.

> *I come into town with some turnips,*
> *   And my little Gabe come along,—*
> *No four-year-old in the county*
> *   Could beat him for pretty and strong,*
> *Peart and chipper and sassy,*
> *   Always ready to swear and fight,—*
> *And I'd larnt him to chaw terbacker*
> *   Just to keep his milk-teeth white.*

When the search for the boy grows cold, his father "flopped down on my marrow-bones,/Crotch-deep in the snow and prayed." Finally, with divine guidance, the child is found in a sheep shed, huddled safely among the lambs.

> *How did he git thar? Angels.*
> *   He could never have walked in that storm.*
> *They jest scooped down and toted him*
> *   To whar it was safe and warm.*

And I think that saving a little child,
  And bringing him to his own,
Is a derned sight better business
  Than loafing around The Throne.

"Little Breeches" was signed simply "J.H.," but the poet's identity spread quickly. "[L]et me thank you heartily for your Pike County view of special Providence," James Fields wrote in early December. "The Lord smile on you for those verses; they are good and will do good."

Within days the poem was reprinted in hundreds of newspapers. "That ridiculous rhyme of mine has had a ridiculous run," Hay told Nicolay. He claimed not to be proud of it, yet he was pleased enough by its reception to try another piece of dialect. "Jim Bludso" appeared in the semi-weekly edition of the *Tribune* on January 6, 1871, again attributed to "J.H." The voice is the same, breezy yet preachy, and the hero, Jim Bludso of the Mississippi steamboat *Prairie Belle*, is rough but right-minded.

He were n't no saint,—them engineers
  Is all pretty much alike,—
One wife in Natchez-under-the-Hill
  And another one here, in Pike;
A keerless man in his talk was Jim,
  And an awkward hand in a row,
But he never flunked, and he never lied,—
  I reckon he never knowed how.

One night the *Prairie Belle* makes the mistake of racing a newer boat, pouring on steam—"With a nigger squat on her safety-valve,/And her furnace crammed, rosin and pine." Disaster results, and Jim Bludso stands tall:

The fire bust out as she clared the bar,
  And burnt a hole in the night,
And quick as a flash she turned, and made
  For that willer-bank on the right.

There was runnin' and cursin', but Jim yelled out,
    Over all the infernal roar,
"I'll hold her nozzle agin the bank
    Till the last galoot's ashore."

True to his word, Jim Bludso puts the boat on the bank, saves the passengers, and only he burns up with the *Prairie Belle*. As with "Little Breeches," the ballad ends with a populist sermon:

He were n't no saint,—but at jedgment
    I'd run my chance with Jim,
'Longside of some pious gentlemen
    That wouldn't shook hands with him.
He seen his duty, a dead-sure thing,—
    And went for it thar and then;
And Christ ain't a going to be too hard
    On a man that died for men.

One of the first to compliment Hay on "Jim Bludso" was Mark Twain. Though Twain's letter is now lost, Hay's reply makes clear that its praise came with a slight quibble from the former Mississippi River pilot. Twain pointed out, teasingly no doubt, that Jim Bludso ought to have been a pilot, not an engineer, to steer the ship to shore. Hay insisted that the poem was based on a true story and that the saviour of the *Prairie Belle* had indeed been an engineer. Still, he promised Twain he would revise Bludso's job description, and he even proposed to Twain a change for his approval; but by then the poem was too popular to tinker with.

Most critics overlooked Hay's gaffes of navigation and nomenclature and welcomed the poem as worthy and inspirational. The *Courier-Journal* of Louisville saw "a dash of Browning's marrow and backbone" in Hay's verse. "It has been many a day since our literature produced anything nearly so good as 'Jim Bludso' and 'Little Breeches.' . . . The vulgate is not strained. The sentiment is not stilted." Hay's own paper, the *Tribune*, was high-minded in its approbation: "These specimens of Western dialect . . . though couched in the boldest forms of the sylvan vernacular, have no expression of coarseness. . . . They are to be taken as the spontaneous expression of the spirit of the age, which, in its yeasty effervescence, is throwing off all falsities in order to fill the cup of refreshment with the pure elixir of life."

Readers made the connection between Hay and Harte right off, and most believed there was ample room in the firmament for both stars. "Bret Harte and Col. John Hay sit at the very head of the list of dialect poetry makers," proclaimed an unnamed devotee. "Their style, at once quaint and peculiar, has developed a new thought and awakened something more potent than mere evanescent popularity. A chord of the heart has been touched, and the most indifferent, imperturbed reader lays down the poems he has been reading in a frame of mind new to him. A sort of 'gushing' feeling passes over him, and he feels very much in the humour to grasp the first man he meets by the hand and vow eternal friendship for him forever, simply because he is human."

Inevitably a few prudes chose to read Hay's verse as blasphemy. "It is poor poetry, foolish argument, wretched logic, and shameful theology," the *Hartford Post* said of "Little Breeches." Little lost Gabe was deemed filthy and depraved, and his father a drunkard. As for Jim Bludso, he was nothing but a foul-mouthed bigamist. One pious reviewer declared Hay's description of "loafing around the throne" a "prostitution of the mission of poetry. It is vulgar doggerel."

Hay did not protest this appraisal and was astonished and slightly embarrassed by the continued attention the poems were receiving. "I am no poet—I make no claim whatever that way," he confessed to Richard Henry Stoddard, whose own reputation as a poet was well established. "[P]eople who wouldn't read you or Tennyson to save their lives read this and guffawed over it." To John Bigelow, he dismissed the Pike County ballads as "a temporary disease of taste" and fretted good-naturedly that he would be "nothing but the 'author of' them henceforth, until people forget them."

But they did not forget them quickly. The poems were printed over and over, read and read again, and the name of the author was no longer a secret. "After Bret Harte," one critic declared, "John Hay has become more popular more suddenly than any writer of recent years."

Reluctantly he squeezed out two more Pike County ballads, "Banty Tim" and "The Mystery of Gilgal," which, while not nearly so clever, helped to appease his hungry readership. Magazines wanted anything else of his they could get their hands on. *Harper's Weekly* had previously rejected "Kane and Abel," a pat and predictable short story about twin brothers who live gaily in Paris until a can-can dancer comes between them. Before *Harper's* could make another bid, *Frank Leslie's Illustrated* grabbed up the tale, publishing it under the byline "John Hay, Author of 'Little Breeches,' 'Jim Bludso,' 'Banty Tim,' Etc."

"Reputation is very convenient for a man doomed to write," quipped one of Hay's newfound admirers. "Having that, he has the passport to success."

James R. Osgood, the Boston publisher, wrote Hay that he wanted his poems even more than *Castilian Days*, which he was then preparing for publication. He pulled together some of Hay's more traditional verse, including "Sunrise in the Place de la Concorde," his best Paris effort; "Northward," written aboard ship returning from Florida during the war; and "On the Bluff," set in Warsaw. Osgood hurried *Pike County Ballads and Other Pieces* into print in May 1871, shortly after publishing Bret Harte's first book of poetry. The two were frequently reviewed in tandem, to the advantage of both. *Castilian Days*, meanwhile, was postponed until the fall.

Lecture bureaus wanted him, too. The esteemed Boston Lyceum Bureau, which represented the likes of Harte, Twain, Emerson, Harriet Beecher Stowe, Susan B. Anthony, Horace Greeley, and Petroleum V. Nasby, contracted with Hay to reminisce on his years with Lincoln and to freshen up his talk on "The Progress of Democracy in Europe." Audiences who came to hear the author of the famous dialect poems were pleasantly surprised that someone so young-looking could hold forth so intelligently on subjects so meaty. "His countenance is fresh and his cheeks are full, the youthfulness of his expression relieved only by a moustache," a reporter in Rochester observed. "He is very fastidious in his dress, but not flashy. The impression he leaves upon hearers after talking to them for an hour is that they have been listening to a sensible, manly gentleman of superior ability and culture."

On another evening, Hay delivered a "prose epic . . . illuminated by such vivid lights and deepened by such broad shadows as only a true artist can use in a masterpiece of word-painting." After presenting "The Progress of Democracy in Europe" at Lincoln Hall in New York, he relented and recited "Banty Tim" for his audience, which responded with "vociferous and prolonged applause."

WORD PAINTING FOR THE *Tribune* presented an entirely different challenge. The "Old Rookery" on Park Row, facing City Hall (and Boss Tweed's bloated, yet-to-be-completed city courthouse), was a gritty calliope of chugging steam presses and clattering type forms, its five floors connected by a crude system of dumb waiters and speaking tubes. The editorial office was beyond disheveled. There were not enough places for the thirty or so writers and reporters, and as one veteran recalled, "There was scarcely a desk . . . that had not been for many years in a state of well-nigh hopeless decrepitude, and scarcely a chair with its full complement of original legs." One of Hay's colleagues, Isaac Bromley, is said to have implored of art critic Clarence Cook, "[A]re you through with that desk? If you are, scrape off the blood and feathers and let me come." The room was thick with cigar smoke. Those who didn't smoke chewed and spat on the floor.

Hay and the others on the editorial staff typically straggled into the office around midday and spent the afternoon reading newspapers, sorting through the wires, and gathering their thoughts. They would write into the evening, often not turning in their final copy until after midnight. "I manufacture public opinion until 2 in the morning," Hay told John Bigelow, "and then I calm my agitated mind with a piece of pumpkin pie and go to bed. This is my daily life."

Editorials in the *Tribune* were never signed, but Hay's can be traced by way of his scrapbooks. His forte, naturally enough, was foreign affairs, and Reid encouraged him to become the paper's voice on matters relating to England, France, Germany, Russia, and especially Spain and its ongoing difficulties in Cuba. Often Hay expressed some variation on his favorite theme, "The Progress of Democracy."

Monarchies were in the midst of rapid, if stubborn, evolution, he maintained, and despite the corruption corroding American politics—sins that were laid bare in nearly every edition of the *Tribune*—the United States was still a sterling role model. "The leading liberal minds of the Old World clearly recognize that the American system of government is the nearest to perfection of all that have ever been evolved from the intelligence of man and the force of circumstance," he averred. "We do not mean that they think of adopting our constitution and our organization in a lump, nor do we have the presumption to say that such action is desirable. But . . . [by] observing the nature, the method, and the result of our Democratic system, it may be possible [for other countries] to settle upon some analogous form which may meet the requirements of those people of Europe who may desire to better their condition." The message was idealistic, optimistic, and realistic—and within it grew the germ of a Hay philosophy on foreign relations.

For the most part, he steered clear of local politics. He took whacks at the Tweed Ring, but plenty of more experienced *Tribune* writers had their pens pointed at Tammany Hall full time. He contributed the occasional art review and obituary, and with increasing frequency, he expressed his frustration with Grant's presidency. One especially sore point was the arbitration between the United States and Britain over violations of British neutrality during the Civil War—the so-called *Alabama* claims, named for one of the Confederate ships built in England that had destroyed or disrupted many millions of dollars in American shipping. Secretary of State Seward had wanted Britain to hand over Canada as indemnity—the greater design being to link the continental United States with Alaska, which Seward had bought from Russia in 1867. Grant and his secretary of state, Hamilton Fish, were not nearly so strident and saw the *Alabama* negotiations as a means to settle a number of other rankling issues, such as fishing rights and a disputed boundary. Hay took a stand closer to the middle but nonetheless cautioned the administration against forsaking "not only the interests but the dignity of the country, at the dictation of the English Ministry, and in obedience to a cowardly spirit of political expediency."

Such criticism of the Grant administration was stout brimstone for a historically Republican paper. But by 1871, quite a few formerly staunch

Republicans had grown dismayed with Grant and, in Hay's words, "the corrupt cabal which has gained control of him." During the past year, shady dealings by some of Grant's cronies had doomed his bid to annex Santo Domingo. Worse, the president's brother-in-law and wife had been implicated as accessories and beneficiaries in a brazen gambit to corner the country's gold market—a scheme foiled by Grant at the eleventh hour but which nevertheless triggered a panic on Wall Street.

Horace Greeley and Whitelaw Reid had no deep reserve of affection for the president, nor had Hay been very intimate with him during the war years, though he had learned to respect him. When a group of disgruntled fire-eaters that included Senator Carl Schurz of Missouri and Henry Adams's brother, Charles Francis Adams, Jr., proposed forming a new, Liberal Republican party, they found open ears at the *Tribune*.

Within a year, the newspaper would be a Liberal Republican clarion and Greeley its candidate. Hay had long-standing differences with Greeley, and he would have even more in the campaign to come, but his dedication to the cause of Republican reform was steadfast and would eventually fill hundreds of column inches. He held Grant to the highest of standards: the general had won the war for Lincoln, but regrettably, he was proving that he could not fill Lincoln's shoes.

ALTHOUGH HAY WAS DILIGENT and earnest when he had to be, "[H]e never made the mistake of taking the journalistic work too seriously," recalled Joseph Bucklin Bishop, who joined the paper fresh out of Hay's alma mater, Brown. "A more conscientious man never lived, but his saving sense of humor forbade his conscientiousness should ever become a disease." Bishop remembered an evening when Hay, after putting the finishing touches on yet another editorial prodding one of Europe's monarchs, waved his manuscript and laughed with mock self-importance: "I've been going for them kings again, and *if they only knew it*, they'd be shaking in their boots at this moment."

If he could be hard on kings and cabinets, he was invariably kind to his colleagues. Years later, Isaac Bromley wrote to Hay: "I was always fond of you since that lovely morning when you came to my desk pulling off your gloves and looking more like an angel than any human being ever looked to me before, saying, 'Mr. Bromley, that was one of the best articles I ever saw in print.' I grew into a sort of bathos of fondness and, I think, cried."

Not long after Hay's arrival, Reid raised his salary to $65 a week. "Your work thus far has been exceedingly valuable," the editor complimented, "and I have seen now enough of your capacity in sudden emergencies and in a wide scope to be ready to repeat the assurance which I gave you at the beginning, that journalism is sure to prove your true field. . . . I hope that, so long as I remain on the *Tribune* at least, you will add to my comfort as well as my strength by feeling it to be your home also."

Hay did feel at home, as evidenced by the force and clarity of his work. He did not, however, compose his editorials quickly. "I waste two-thirds of my time trying to think of something to write about," he told John Bigelow. "[Literary critic John] Hassard writes his column while I sit staring . . . in blank imbecility. Reid writes very little, but when it is necessary he beats me two to one."

HAY HAD ONE OTHER shortcoming: for all his erudition on a worldly range of subjects, he had no real experience as a reporter. How surprising it was, then, that when Chicago burst into flames on October 8, 1871, Reid sent Hay to cover the story. He arrived on the twelfth, after thirty-eight hours on trains, joining another *Tribune* man, Henry Keenan. The first problem they faced was overloaded telegraph lines; operators claimed to be several thousand messages behind and, to Hay's greater frustration, they were giving preferential treatment to the *Tribune*'s rival, the *New York Herald*. He was finally able to file his first dispatch on the thirteenth.

He approached the assignment as if he were writing in his diary about Paris, Vienna, or Florida. In Chicago, at least, he knew his way around, and he did have connections. Upon arrival he tracked down Robert Lincoln and straightaway asked about the presidential papers, which Hay and Nicolay had helped remove from the White House after the assassination six years earlier. Thankfully most of them were in Bloomington, Illinois, in the care of David Davis, President Lincoln's trusted friend, now a justice on the U.S. Supreme Court. The papers that were in

Robert's possession in Chicago were safe as well, but only barely. "[Robert Lincoln] entered his law office," Hay wrote, "about daylight on Monday morning, after the flames had attacked the building, opened the vault and had piled upon a table-cloth the most valuable papers, then swung the pack over his shoulder, and escaped amid a shower of falling fire-brands." On his way to safety, Lincoln stopped to eat breakfast at the house of a friend, the financier and philanthropist J. Young Scammon, Hay reported that afterwards "Lincoln went home with his papers, and before noon the house of Scammon was in ruins."

The following day, the fourteenth, Hay headed to DeKoven Street, where the fire had begun. "I have here before me six miles, more or less, of the finest conflagration ever seen," he recounted. "I have smoking ruins and ruins which have broken themselves of smoking; churches as romantic in their dilapidation as Melrose by moonlight [a reference to a poem by Sir Walter Scott]; mountains of brick and mortar and forests of springing chimneys; but I turned from them all this morning . . . to see the first footprint of the monster who had trampled a great city out of existence in a day."

At last he reached the address of Mr. and Mrs. O'Leary, where it was said but never proven—and ultimately disproven—that their cow had kicked a lamp into the straw. Hay may not have had much practice as a reporter, but he had a gift for getting to the heart of the matter: "I went around to the rear, and there found the Man of the House, sitting with two of his friends. His wife, Our Lady of the Lamp—freighted with heavier disaster than that which Psyche carried to the bedside of Eros— sat at the window, knitting. I approached the Man of the House and gave him a good-day. He glanced up with sleepy, furtive eyes. I asked him what he knew about the origin of the fire. He glanced at his friends and said, civilly, he knew very little; he was waked up about 9 o'clock by the alarm, and fought from that time to save his house. . . . He seemed fearful that all Chicago was coming down on him for prompt and integral payment of that $200,000,000 his cow had kicked over. His neighbors say this story is an invention dating from the second day of the fire. There was something unutterably grotesque in this ultimate atom feeling a sense of responsibility for a catastrophe so stupendous, and striving by a fiction, which must have heavily taxed his highest powers of imagination, to escape a reckoning he was already free from."

Hay spent three days in Chicago, gathering images randomly but with the pieces adding to a grim and graphic whole:

"I passed one modest grave, near the scene of a night-camp. A heart was carved upon the wooden tombstone by pious hands, and into this touching emblem a steel fork had been driven by some brutal fist. Above the outraged blazon were the tender words, *Ruhe Sauft* ('Sleep Softly'). . . .

"Delicate women came as they had escaped from death in thin fluttering night clothes blown about by the surly Autumn wind. . . .

"Many little children were thrown into the crowd too young to speak their parents' names. . . .

"I heard of one company of German singers from a low concert saloon, who flew out into the night in nothing but their tawdry evening dresses. . . . They talked little, but sometimes they cheated their misery with songs. . . . Nearby the fragments of a Methodist congregation had improvised a prayer-meeting, and the sounds of song and supplication went up mingled with that worldly music to the deep and tolerant heavens."

He left Chicago, exhausted but satisfied. "I have done all I could," he wrote to Reid on October 15. "I have a clean conscience. Your condemnation will not gall my withers."

Reid's reply has not been preserved, but he surely appreciated how hard Hay had worked under such enormous disadvantage. At least one other paper noticed as well. "John Hay has, within a brief period, become widely recognized as a brilliant essayist, a genuine poet, and an accomplished editor," the *Syracuse Standard* commented. "His reputation, however, in one of the most difficult departments of journalistic work—that of reporting—was yet to be made. . . . We hazard little in saying that it is now splendidly attained. . . . The dispatches he has sent to the *Tribune* concerning the Chicago fire have something of the qualities of the poet and the essayist; but they also bear the unmistakable evidences of the true reportorial instinct. . . . Here is [Daniel] De Foe pencil in hand amid ruins greater than those of the London fire of two centuries agone, with all the olden power and all the olden accuracy."

• • •

HE RETURNED TO NEW York and a lifestyle that was neither as one-dimensional nor as ascetic as he purported. There were many days and evenings when his presence was not required at the *Tribune*. A society column pasted in his scrapbook placed "the handsome and popular John Hay" at a party in the company of the African explorer and gorilla stalker Paul du Chaillu; Cyrus Field, whose company had laid the transatlantic cable; and his friend Albert Bierstadt, whose magnificently romantic landscapes of the American West had established him as one of the country's most treasured painters. Other letters and newspapers had him, "finical and fine, exquisitely gloved," dining at Delmonico's and other fashionable restaurants and quenching his thirst at the Lotos Club, a cheerful sanctuary for writers and artists, including Mark Twain, one of its founders. Soon he was elected to the smart and genteel Knickerbocker Club and Century Association, where he mingled with leading men of business, science, politics, and the arts.

Along the way, he formed a number of lasting friendships. After Reid and Twain, he finally met Bret Harte, who had moved to New York in order to cash in on his meteoric fame. "He is a delightful fellow," Hay mentioned, "and I would be happy to 'drop in and take dinner' as he and Mrs. Harte kindly suggest; but he lives in 49th Street, just an hour by rail from me"—this a gibe at Manhattan's expansion northward. The two authors were thrown together often, usually in the clubs or homes of mutual friends. Harte lived well in those days, certainly more comfortably than Hay, and neither ever would have imagined that nine years later Hay would be the one on top, with Harte begging him for a job.

Sometime during that first year in New York, Hay also made the acquaintance of Clarence King, whose fortunes would prove even more erratic than Bret Harte's. Over the next three decades, King would by turns inspire and frustrate Hay like no other friend.

King acquired manners in Newport, geology at Yale; straitened by the early death of his father and then of his stepfather, he was obliged to support his mother and sister by applying his considerable athleticism and intellect to a series of ventures that exposed him to great risk, promised lifelong riches and acclaim, and too often fell short of expectations for reasons that never seemed to be his fault.

For a while, though, everything did go his way. In 1867, at the age of twenty-five, King was named head geologist of the Fortieth Parallel Survey, a daring scientific expedition to map some of the least traveled terrain in the American West. Over the next four years, he trekked across the deserts of California and Nevada and scaled the peaks of the Sierras, dodging bandits, enduring thirst and blizzards, and surveying meticulously all the while. In the summer of 1870, he discovered active glaciers on the summit of Mount Shasta, the only ones believed to exist in the continental United States. Working from his field notes, King wrote an account of his mountaineering exploits for Bret Harte's *Overland Monthly*. On Harte's endorsement, William Dean Howells accepted several of King's pieces for the *Atlantic Monthly*, and James R. Osgood agreed to collect them in a book, as he had done for Hay and Harte.

Fit and youthful, his whiskers sun-bleached from months in the wild, King came east in the fall, passing through New York en route to Boston—a "brilliant and beaming creature," recalled Howells. Here was a man for all seasons: King had crawled into a cave to shoot a grizzly bear; around a campfire in the evening he was known to wear silk stockings and clean linen. When he came east, he brought along his pith helmet.

The first of King's *Atlantic Monthly* articles appeared in May 1871, coinciding with the final installment of Hay's *Castilian Days* sketches. A coincidence of another sort occurred in the fall: King's article in the November *Atlantic* describes an encounter with a filthy, degraded family who had driven their prized hogs from Pike County, Missouri, all the way to the foothills of the Sierras. As a scientist, King noted the devolution of the Pike stock "in all its deformity of outline, all its poverty of detail, all its darkness of future." And as a raconteur, he recorded the Pike dialect as faithfully and comically as Harte or Hay had done in their stories and poems.

The circle of association was cozy indeed. The same issue of the *Atlantic Monthly* that carried King's piece on the Pikes also ran Howells's review of Hay's *Castilian Days*—anonymously, as was the magazine's custom, but also to make the log-rolling seem less obvious. "Every page sparkles with witty comment," Howells commended unsparingly. "No other book in English about Spain can compare with it."

Other notices were equally generous. One reviewer called the prose of

Castilian Days "so alive that it affects the reader with that slight running tingle of surprise." When the book arrived in London, it was welcomed as "one of the brightest, most piquant and withal instructive publications of the year." Some of the kindest compliments came from reviewers who previously had dismissed Hay as merely the "author of" the Pike County poems. "If any one has indulged in the fear that Mr. Hay was so irretrievably entangled in the quagmire and bog of modern 'Dialect'-ics," stated one of his redeemers, "this volume will help very sensibly to remove that impression. For *Castilian Days* . . . is really a strong and masculine performance."

ALL TOLD, IT HAD been a heady year. Since joining the *Tribune* in November 1870, Hay had made a name for himself as an editorialist, poet, lecturer, reporter, and *belletrist.* He was meeting the most influential people in New York; moreover, he was now regarded as one of them. "Hay is doing admirably and even growing corpulent," John Bigelow remarked.

The bachelor life seemed to suit him—and Reid, too. They had become bosom chums, professionally and socially, and they were often on the town together. "We *ought* to see the Black Rook before it stops," Hay prodded Reid on one occasion. "Send the boy for two tickets (good ones) and we will dine together chez le Frenchy and go." The publisher Henry Holt told of leaving the Century one Saturday at two in the morning in the company of Hay, Reid, and several others. Encountering a line of ash cans on the sidewalk, the cohort of top-hatted revelers decided the moment was ripe for leapfrog.

The subject of marriage came up from time to time. Hay's and Reid's imminent captures were rumored every time they were observed in anything more than casual conversation with one of New York's eligible ladies. Hay was now thirty-three; Reid a year older. It was not so much a question of whether they would succumb as of which one would succumb first. "I cannot get Reid to marry," Hay joked to Bigelow. "I shall take my own medicine as soon as I own two or three shares of Tribune stock"—an impossibility, at least for the foreseeable future, since only one hundred shares existed, each valued at $10,000. In the meantime the two bachelors continued to partake of the pleasures of the Gilded Age.

Marital medicine was forthcoming, however, and of a far richer dosage than he expected. In the winter of 1872, Hay was introduced to twenty-three-year-old Clara Stone, who was visiting New York from Cleveland. In the months that followed, he fell for her, head over heels. "I have been brought down," he told a friend, announcing the closure of his career as a blade about town. "Mourn for me. *La femme* has ceased to exist for me. There is only one—and one is enough. . . . I part from the old life without regret save for the dear old reprobates whom I shall hereafter love in secret and remorselessly cut in public. . . . Believe me, I am not the thing I was."

CHAPTER 7

Millionaires' Row

Of their many differences, most did not seem to matter, or perhaps they were what drew them together. Clara Louise Stone was ten years younger than John Hay, and whereas he had been precocious as a young man, she, according to the custom of her class and era, had enjoyed a protected upbringing. She was reserved; he was gregarious. He was classically educated, had seen the world, and spoke several of its languages. She had graduated from the Cleveland Academy and had been abroad once with her parents. But her life thus far had been a chaperoned affair.

In the spring of 1872, Clara and her sister, Flora, were visiting their aunt and uncle, Mr. and Mrs. Andros Stone, whom Hay had first met when the Stones had passed through Paris in 1866. Stone had made his fortune in iron in Chicago and Cleveland, and like many industrialists from the West, he had moved to New York to enroll in the burgeoning society of first-generation affluents. How Hay had become reacquainted with the Stones is not clear, but his manners, his résumé, and his acclaim as a writer put him high on the list of bachelors suitable for introduction to a visiting niece.

Hay met Clara for the first time in the Stones' parlor on 37th Street. The encounter went well enough—nothing close to love at first sight, as

Hay later confessed—but afterward he realized he wanted to see more of this demure, bright-faced visitor.

She was not girlish, at least not in her appearance. For one thing, she was stout, not in the way of women who never lose their baby fat, but like a nurse—like a mother. Her eyes were dark and warm beneath full brows and an even fuller head of hair, which she wore braided in a generous bun. She would never bowl anyone over, not with her looks or her dynamism; she was not a woman who threw off sparks. Her appeal was an innate serenity and constancy of mind and metabolism—the essential qualities that suited the "finical" Hay, even if he did not realize it at first.

Yet she was far from complacent. In a school essay, "Literature versus Housekeeping," she expressed higher expectations for her sex. "Housekeeping appears to be the particular end of woman," she acknowledged. "But is there any real reason to think that a woman with a well-balanced mind and ideas concerning the economy of her hours may not find time for other affairs beside those of housekeeping?"

She then made a case for a "literary woman," who is "able to make better plans for her house, knows how to control her servants, has better developed talents, and most of all has her understanding enlarged as to the relations she bears to her fellow beings and has wider ideas of the manner in which to make her home pleasant and enjoyable." Her intention was not to rock the boat; she was merely suggesting that she could steer it one-handed, if she chose—with plenty of maids, cooks, and nurses helping out, of course.

Hay, once he was done chasing petticoats around New York, could ask for nothing more in a mate. When the time came to tell John George Nicolay about her, he chose words that were less than exuberant but, in a nobler context, more flattering: "She is a very estimable young person," he said, "large, handsome and good."

He admired her, then, before he loved her. They saw each other once or twice more after the introduction on 37th Street. They discovered how close they had come to meeting four years earlier, when Clara and her parents were in Vienna. ("Would the music of Strauss's orchestra have introduced our souls to each other at the Volksgarten?" he asked her once they were engaged.) He was also pleased to learn that Clara had a healthy appetite for literature, and when time came for her to return to Cleveland, he gave her a present to read on the train. "Dear Miss Stone," he wrote. "As you are going West, I know of no more charming book for you to take with you than that of my friend Mr. Clarence King." *Mountaineering in the Sierra Nevada* had been published in February. "Its descriptions of our mountain life and scenery are to me so satisfying and so evidently truthful that it consoles me for my ignorance of them." He closed: "Yours faithfully, John Hay."

THREE BUSY MONTHS WENT by before he saw her again. In May, just before Clara left New York, the newly formed Liberal Republican Party had convened in Cincinnati and nominated Horace Greeley as its candidate for president. Hay climbed aboard the bandwagon, although in many respects it was an awkward fit for him, especially after the Democratic Party met in July and gave Greeley its nomination as well.

Simply put, the Liberal Republicans had had enough of Grant and Reconstruction. They were convinced that the administration was rotten at the core and that the South had been punished enough under federal misrule. But for Hay, Greeley was not someone he could embrace wholeheartedly. Eight years earlier, Greeley had disappointed Lincoln and embarrassed Hay at Niagara Falls. Though the editor had rallied behind Lincoln against McClellan in the 1864 election, after the war he turned around and posted the bond that freed Jefferson Davis. It was hard to love Lincoln to the degree that Hay loved him and still swear fealty to Greeley.

In the pages of the *Tribune*, Hay mostly ignored his employer and took aim at Grant. All the qualities that had made Grant an effective general—his snap decisions, his willingness to ride roughshod over his enemy—now made him a dangerous executive, or so Hay charged. Emboldened by anonymity, he got on Grant for backing legislation to suspend habeas corpus and deploy federal troops in areas of the South in which the Ku Klux Klan was terrorizing freedmen. Overlooking the fact that Lincoln had also been criticized for suspending habeas corpus, Hay objected to the Ku Klux Klan law as overbearing, warning that Grant was aggravating old wounds while establishing himself as a "soldier Dictator." Grant "makes no effort to conciliate," Hay complained, "but uses all means to crush the other faction." To hear the *Tribune* tell it, Grant was snuffing out the very beacon of democracy: "The world's history furnishes no parallel for the absolute power of one man and the abject humiliation of a whole people as exhibited to-day in this country."

The opposition was every bit as fierce. Greeley's high-principled independence made him a bundle of contradictions in the eyes of voters and a subject of ridicule to rival newspapers and the Republican establishment he rebuked. He had striven mightily to end slavery but then preached reconciliation just as fervidly. Southern Democrats remembered the kindness he had shown Jefferson Davis, but they also remembered it was Greeley who had quipped that, while not all Democrats were horse thieves, all horse thieves were Democrats. African-Americans knew him as an abolitionist; but Greeley, the *Tribune*, and most Liberal Republicans were against the recent Ku Klux Klan law. Greeley, who had raised himself from the humblest roots, was now cast as a moralizing, meddlesome demagogue, removed from the farmers and workingmen whose interests he had so steadfastly championed in the pages of the *Tribune*. While it was difficult to question his honesty, many tried, accusing him and "Whitelie" Reid of secret ties to the Tweed Ring. His vows to end "Grantism," to right the wrongs of Republicanism, and to reunite the country were viewed as traitorous. Cartoonist Thomas Nast drew him leaning across Lincoln's grave to grip the hand of John Wilkes Booth.

Throughout the mud-slinging, Greeley campaigned relentlessly, whistle-stopping across the country in his wattle of whiskers and white linen coat, like the one he wore when he boarded the train carrying Lincoln from Springfield to Washington in 1861.

Meanwhile, the veteran of the bloody Wilderness neither budged nor flinched. Grant, not Greeley, was the man of the soil, the soldier who had ended the war and now ensured that order would prevail. If he was surrounded by a "discreditable throng of flatterers," as Hay asserted, he appeared above flattery. Hay himself acknowledged that Grant was unaware of the corruption all about him—an immunity that was dramatically challenged in September when a number of Grant Republicans, including Vice President Schuyler Colfax, Speaker of the House James G. Blaine, and Congressman James Garfield, were entangled in the Crédit Mobilier scandal, an octopus of bribes and railroad stock sufficiently monstrous to upset every voter in America if only they could decipher what exactly was supposed to have transpired. The story broke in the *New York Sun* and was vigorously amplified in the *Tribune.* In the upshot, "Smiler" Colfax was obliged to resign, but Grant once again was untarred. He remained a hero still, while Greeley, the patriotic oracle of the Great Moral Organ, was marginalized as a blackguard, a heretic, a buffoon.

The stakes were high not only for Greeley and the *Tribune* but also for its leading editorial writer. So far, Hay's credentials as a Republican had been immaculate; his Lincoln connection had opened every door. He seems to have given little thought to what recriminations might be in store for him if Greeley were to lose. His confidence politically and professionally was such that, no matter what happened, he believed he would come out all right.

ROMANTICALLY, HE WAS NOT so sure. At the first of August he made a trip to Warsaw, and on the way back he stopped off in Cleveland to "present my homage" to the Stone sisters. He found Flora at home, but, to his dismay, Clara was away. He stayed only a night, then continued east. At Painesville, Ohio, one of the stations between Cleveland and Buffalo, he stepped off the train for a moment and saw Clara—whether by prearrangement or purely by kismet he did not specify in the letters that followed. "Has Miss Clara told you of the fleeting glimpse of her that was granted me at Painesville?" he wrote Flora, who was now his co-conspirator. "I thought I had never seen any finer picture of fresh and beautiful life." Looking back a year later, in the same letter in which he confessed to Clara that he had not loved her at first sight, he described the next stage of his heart's awakening: "I saw you for that short interval at Painesville. I could not help asking myself, 'What is the young lady to me that I should be so delighted to see her?' and then I thought she is very lovely and I like lovely girls—*voilà tout.*"

He carried away other strong impressions. On his stopover in Cleveland he had visited the Stone residence on Euclid Avenue and met Clara and Flora's parents, Amasa and Julia Stone. Further enhancing the picture, he had arrived at Cleveland's Union Depot, built by Stone, and when he departed, he rode on the Lake Shore & Michigan Southern Railway, the newly consolidated line between Buffalo and Chicago, of which Stone was a major stockholder.

Like many of the tycoons of his generation, Amasa Stone started out in skilled but lowly jobs. Andrew Carnegie of Pittsburgh, for example, had been a telegraph operator. Two of Stone's fellow Clevelanders—John D. Rockefeller, founder of Standard Oil, and Jeptha Wade, founder of Western Union—had worked as bookkeeper and portrait painter, respectively. Stone had apprenticed as a carpenter in Massachusetts, and by the time he was a teenager, he was building houses and churches. At the age of twenty-one, he and a brother-in-law, William Howe, contracted to build a railroad bridge across the Connecticut River, using a truss system patented by Howe and improved by Stone. Afterward, Stone, with new partners, bought the patent and commenced building not just bridges but entire railroads. In 1848, at the age of thirty, his firm contracted to complete the line between Cleveland and Columbus.

In 1850, he moved to Cleveland with his wife, six-year-old son Adelbert, and one-year-old daughter Clara, and became superintendent of the Cleveland, Cincinnati & Columbus Railroad. Stone and his partners next took on the more challenging task of linking Cleveland to the Pennsylvania state line at Erie—a railroad that became the Cleveland, Painesville & Ashtabula and later consolidated with the Cleveland & Toledo as the Lake Shore & Michigan Southern, with Stone as president. The Lake Shore soon connected to the Jamestown & Franklin, reaching deep into the heart of the booming oil regions.

He owned a piece and usually was a director of everything he built. With his brother Andros and several others, he formed the Cleveland Rolling Mill Company. He invested in more iron mills, a woolen mill, a bridge-manufacturing company, and still more railroads. He designed and built railroad cars and Cleveland's much-admired Union Depot. He held an interest in several banks. As the wealthiest man in Cleveland, he was assured a look at nearly every deal in town. When Jeptha Wade bundled together several smaller telegraph companies, Stone took a flier and bought a hefty chunk of Western Union. When John D. Rockefeller executed a similar consolidation of refineries, creating Standard Oil,

Stone acquired five hundred shares—5 percent of the stock—and became a director. Standard's refined oil soon flowed eastward on the Lake Shore railroad at sweetheart rates. Even as the millions piled up, he continued to work like the carpenter he had once been. A stern, abstemious Presbyterian, his only personal indulgence was his wife and children—and them he indulged lavishly.

The *Cleveland Leader* described the house he built on Euclid Avenue, Cleveland's "Millionaires' Row," as the "finest, most complete and convenient residence west of the Hudson." The architecture of the two-story mansion was "nearly, although not strictly, that of the 'Italian Villa.'" Gothic windows, gargoylish rooftop corbels, and a crownlike clerestory lent the exterior the look of an ornate chess piece. Inside, the mantels were of the finest statuary marble, the woodwork of rosewood, the balustrades of carved mahogany—all solidly constructed under Stone's gimlet eye. Seven hundred thousand bricks and 8,000 square feet assured the comfort of the Stone family and testified immodestly to the worth of its owner.

This was the house that Hay visited in the summer of 1872, and surely he had never been in anything quite like it. Nowhere else in the United States was there a street comparable to Euclid Avenue. Robber barons had yet to erect their palaces in New York. Chicago was just beginning to boom when the great fire struck. Even the most prosperous Bostonians lived rather puritanically, cheek-by-jowl on Beacon Hill. Buffalo, thanks to the Erie Canal's umbilical to the Great Lakes, was Cleveland's closest rival for ostentation; but Cleveland, its population approaching one hundred thousand, was the showplace of the moment, with Euclid Avenue the new Champs-Elysées. It ran extravagantly eastward from the Public Square beneath a bower of elms, lined with sandstone curbs, flagstone sidewalks, and filigreed fencework. The lawns were groomed and bedded, and the houses, "which wealth [had] spared no pains in perfecting," rose from deep in their lots. The Stones' neighbors were Cleveland's wealthiest: the Rockefellers, Wades, and the rest of the nouveaux riches of rail, steel, oil, and banking. Most of them had been raised austerely. Few had made the Grand Tour. Now all lived like royalty. If proof of this were needed, the previous winter Grand Duke Alexis of Russia, passing through Cleveland, had danced a quadrille in the Stones' drawing room.

GRANT BEAT GREELEY BADLY in November, taking every northern state and eight of the eleven states of the former Confederacy. It was the widest margin of victory since Andrew Jackson's in 1828. Republicans surged in the Senate and House and now controlled both chambers by comfortable margins. For Greeley, the loss was compounded by the death of his wife four days before the election. "My house is desolate, my future dark, my heart a stone," he grieved. He made a brief and brave attempt to resume the editorship of the *Tribune*, but the double blow had shattered him physically and mentally. Two weeks later he was taken, stooped and delirious, to an asylum near his farm in Chappaqua, New York, where he died on November 29.

Hay was in Warsaw when Greeley collapsed and relieved to be removed from the tragedy. He lectured on Lincoln at the Warsaw public library, where he was received warmly by a "house crowded by the intellect, wealth and beauty of his home." Besides a leisurely few days with his family, he also stopped in Cleveland on both his outbound trip and return. He made no mention of seeing Clara or any others of the Stone family, but he had. After giving his Lincoln lecture again at Case Hall, he reported to his mother, "I think I will stay here until tomorrow evening and then go through to New York."

Back at the *Tribune*, Reid was in trouble. During the presidential race, the paper had lost many of its Republican readers, and the stock was slumping. A play was afoot, led by the largest stockholder, Samuel Sinclair, to replace Reid with, of all people, Schuyler Colfax, Grant's defrocked vice president. As a gesture of loyalty to his friend, Hay submitted a letter of resignation, effective upon Reid's exit.

Reid, however, was not ready to relinquish control of the paper, and perhaps if he had had more time to find a financial knight, he might have settled for one less dark. Jay Gould was precisely the sort of scoundrel Horace Greeley had devoted his life to demonizing. With the help of President Grant's brother-in-law, Gould had schemed to corner the gold market, and with his partner, Jim Fisk, he had made a killing in a series of wickedly brazen manipulations of Erie Railroad stock. In that caper, one of their accomplices was New York's king crook, Boss Tweed. In October 1871, while Greeley, Reid, and the rest of the *Tribune* were celebrating the arrest of Tweed, it was Gould who stepped forward to post Tweed's million-dollar bail.

Not surprisingly, Reid went to great lengths to conceal the identity of the man who put up the money to buy or otherwise tie up a majority of *Tribune* stock, vanquish Colfax, and secure the editor's desk for himself. Precisely what sympathies Gould expected from Reid in return seems never to have been spelled out, but those with unkind suspicions could not resist referring to Reid as Gould's hireling.

Hay's correspondence sheds almost no light on the events of December 1872, and his role in Reid's triumph seems to have been peripheral at best, although he did write to his mother that "Reid has managed the paper so admirably during the last month that no reasonable objection can be made to him. If there is any attempt made to oust him I shall oppose it with all the means in my power."

This endorsement was made before he learned of Reid's pact with Gould. Whether or not he regarded it as Faustian, and whether or not he spoke his mind to Reid, their friendship bore up. On Christmas Eve, Reid took a moment to thank Hay: "I didn't try to answer your letter of resignation for I couldn't. Neither can I try to pay you for the admirable work you have done. . . . But it is at any rate a great pleasure to me to be able to connect with the Christmas time an advance of your salary to $100 per week. It is inadequate & late; but it may serve at least to mark the admiration every editor and owner feels for your writing and for you." Along about this time, Hay also came into possession of one of the *Tribune*'s hundred shares of stock.

WITH THE DEATH OF Greeley and the ascendance of Reid, Hay continued to anchor the editorial pages with his able commentary on foreign affairs. He spoke out against the brutalities of hanging as a form of execution—recalling no doubt the horrid scene he had witnessed in the South during the war. When it was his turn to jab at Tweed and Tammany Hall, he pulled no punches. His tone with the Grant administration remained cynical, if somewhat less sharp. He deemed Grant's inaugural address "the utterance of a man of the best intentions profoundly desirous to govern wisely and justly. . . . He promises little but what we heartily approve. . . . But what warrant have we that the President can do anything more for the accomplishment of these beneficent ends during the coming term than during the last?"

Nevertheless, these posturings were starting to seem old hat, as if he had worn them once too often. Hay had been at the *Tribune* two years, longer than he had lasted at any of his diplomatic posts. He was not thinking of resigning, but his thoughts were drifting. After the election, he had written to John George Nicolay, suggesting that at long last they turn their attention to the Lincoln biography. He was glad to learn that Nicolay was moving to Washington to accept an appointment as marshal of the U.S. Supreme Court, a sinecure that provided a comfortable salary of $3,500 and would allow Nicolay time and opportunity to begin gathering the materials and interviews they would need to flesh out their narrative.

Then, too, Hay was preoccupied with Clara Stone. Something had happened on his stopovers in Cleveland, and after the New Year, Clara came to New York to stay with her uncle and aunt for the winter.

For three months, she and Hay saw each other nearly every day, and Hay's coyness gave way to romantic abandon. "I have sometimes gazed at you until your eyes and mouth seemed radiant and glorified with some divine beauty and promise," he told her, "until it seems to me that I could not live without falling at your feet and pouring out my full heart in worship." For all his ardor, he hastened to assure her that his suit was built upon proper premise. "If there is any one reason why I loved you at first, it is because I respected you more than any other woman," he pledged. He complimented her on her "firm and inflexible Christian character."

His sincerity, good intentions, and the sheer volume of his adoration finally prevailed. One evening after attending a concert of Mendelssohn music, the dam burst, and she consented to marry him, although they agreed not to announce their engagement for several months.

In April, when Clara returned to Cleveland, they promised to write each other every other Sunday. But by May his letters to her were so frequent, so lengthy, and so passionate, that it is no wonder that his contributions to the *Tribune* occasionally fell on the perfunctory side of diligent. (Clara's letters to Hay from this period have never surfaced.)

He now addressed her as *Clärchen*, German for "dear wife," uttering it repeatedly as if too good to be true. He was the dashing, brilliant, insouciant one; she was taciturn, sensible, less than prepossessing. But once he was sure he had won her and had convinced her of his absolute devotion, he humbled himself before her. By his estimation, he was getting everything and she nothing. "Ah, think what you give," he wrote her. "Beauty and goodness and youth, a rich and noble nature, candor and honor and affection, and in return you get only the worship of a soul which has no existence but in you."

Setting aside his past, his career, and his public persona, he made it clear that, within their relationship, she was the guiding force and the ideal to which he would defer and adhere. He wanted her to believe, because he believed it himself, that he loved her so deeply that she could not possibly love him as much. By this inequality an equilibrium was struck, although by setting the terms, even without saying so, Hay retained the upper hand. Which, by all evidences, was fine by Clara.

On May 8, Hay wrote to her submissively: "I love you Clärchen —but I worship you also; you have come so strongly and bountifully to me that I can scarcely yet be at ease and contented in my happiness. How could it ever have happened? I continually ask myself. It cannot be merely because I loved you, for others have loved you before. You have always been petted and courted, and still retained your sweet and serene self-control. But all at once you come down to the least worthy of all your lovers, and give him your heart and lips and now your hand. . . . I would not care if all my interests and affections were submitted this moment to your will. You have captured me. I am the spoil of your bow and spear, and I am at your mercy."

He was the ancient mariner, she the safe harbor: "You are much younger than I am, darling, and have lived in an atmosphere of love and confidence. If, like me, you had passed many years in the troubled current of the world, and met everywhere deceit and folly and sin, treachery and malice, then you would know how infinitely comforting it would be to meet one heart which is true and noble and kind, one which you could trust for time and for eternity. You lovely girl, if you had not cared for me, I should still have been grateful that I had known you. But to think that you love me, that you are to be mine forever! how can I be anything but humbly grateful?"

The formality of asking Amasa Stone for his daughter's hand went more smoothly than Hay anticipated. The letter he received from Stone in return was of the "kindest and nicest character," he told Clara. "[I]t seems too good to be true." They set a date in February 1874, and once the wedding was fixed and sanctioned, his elation took a more solemn tone. "I do devote and consecrate my life to you," he wrote her. "I give thanks to God for you and I pray that He will make me worthy of you." He swore to her that he was a new man. "I was never a happy character," he admitted. "It has been a rough and somewhat cheerless life I have led, notwithstanding its variety and interest and apparent pleasure. I never had known real happiness before. But you have given me happiness. . . . It was knowing you and loving you that changed the world for me."

His world changed in other ways, too. With Reid now in control, the *Tribune* moved to temporary quarters to make way for construction of a new, grander headquarters designed by Richard Morris Hunt.

Two months later, Hay received a telegram that his sister Helen had died during childbirth in Warsaw. He hurried home to console his parents. As he mourned "the dear young saint," the tragedy only reinforced his conviction to begin a family of his own.

In his letters to Clara that summer, he pledged that he would take responsibility for her welfare but again confessed that he looked forward to putting himself in her care. "I do need somebody to look after me," he wrote in early August, "and when she comes to assume that office, I shall exaggerate every little flicker of a headache, to be petty and spoiled by her."

Here was yet another of his sweet surrenders, but it was more prophetic than either of them realized. After their marriage, Hay's health would become chronically fickle. In another of the letters he wrote at the time of their engagement, he told Clara about his other sister, Mary, who had given her whole life to taking care of a husband who was "not very strong." On one hand, Hay found this inequity exasperating; on the other hand, he said, "I must admit that those are the happiest families where the husband is all selfishness and the wife all devotion. Shall we try to cultivate those talents, you and I?"

Rumors of their engagement spread widely. The end of bachelorhood for John Hay was too delicious not to be broadcast in the newsrooms and clubs where his reputation was the object of envy and reverence. That he was betrothed to one of Amasa Stone's daughters only made the story richer, literally. When Robert Lincoln heard the news, he wrote jocularly to John George Nicolay, "I have a letter from New York today which says that J. Hay is about to marry a Miss Stone of Cleveland, whose [father] will one day [be] obliged to leave to . . . J.H. and one other fellow [Flora's eventual husband] from $6000000 to $8000000—which will make John to write with a first class gold pen."

Suddenly, however, the numbers were not so big. At the end of September 1873, Jay Cooke, a banker who had grown immensely wealthy financing the Civil War, was unable to sell millions of dollars in Northern Pacific Railroad bonds, triggering a run on his bank and a panic on Wall Street. The New York Stock Exchange closed for ten days, and in the weeks and months that followed, more banks, dozens of railroads, and thousands of businesses failed; tens of thousands of Americans lost their jobs.

Hay, who earlier might have treated the grim news with a certain detachment, now had a personal reason to be alarmed. Financial speculation and consolidation depended on the total being stronger than the sum of its parts, when in fact the latticework of investment in banks and railroads was mostly flimsy, with only a few stout pillars holding up the whole. One of those pillars was Amasa Stone. Through conversation with the wife of Stone's brother, Andros, Hay learned that Stone had lost many hundreds of thousands of dollars, perhaps well over a million, in honoring his obligations and propping up those of others. And these losses did not take into account the immense amount of stock in Western Union and Lake Shore he was forced to sell at panic prices to keep up his margins at various banks.

As the markets sank, Hay could only watch and hope. "He is a man of great courage and energy and may be able still to retrieve himself,"

Hay wrote of Stone in late October. "He will not do any whining in the mean time." So stolid was Amasa Stone that Clara apparently had no idea how dangerously close her dowry was to disappearing. Hay, who had not imagined he would have to support Clara solely on his *Tribune* salary, tried not to dwell on the downside either. "I am making an active campaign to have my marriage earlier," he wrote bluffly to Reid. "If the Herr Papa is really dead-broke my chances ought to improve."

NEWSPAPERS IN THE 1870S were not in the habit of splashing wedding announcements across their pages, and the marriage of John Hay to Clara Stone was no exception. The ceremony took place in Cleveland on February 4, 1874, after which the newlyweds returned to New York and settled into the apartment Hay had been renting on East 25th Street. "We have more room and more comforts here than we could have at any hotel for three times the expense," he wrote contentedly to Flora.

Amasa Stone was pleased that the couple had chosen to "begin life without pretensions." He had not gone under in the Panic of 1873 after all, but the scare had served to remind the sensible New Englander that there were no substitutes for hard work and self-sufficiency. His goal had always been simple: to be better off at the end of the year than at the beginning. One bad year had made him grateful for so many good ones.

In many ways, he was the opposite of Hay's father. As a small-town doctor and small-time speculator, Charles Hay was a man of lofty principles, content simply with making ends meet. By these measurements, John Hay had already exceeded his father's expectations, although he had yet to prove himself fully to Amasa Stone. Hay's accomplishments and renown were impressive, to be sure, but his career thus far had been more whimsical than deliberate. He was now thirty-five; by the time Amasa Stone was that age, he was running entire railroads.

Hay attempted to allay any paternal anxieties Stone might have by assuring him that he was fully capable of providing for Clara. Stone applauded Hay's independence and resolve, but knowing something of Hay's history, he also felt it his duty to remind his son-in-law to stick to the strait and narrow. "Your life and habits have been such," Stone offered with Presbyterian firmness, "that it would have been quite easy for you to have fallen into idle habits. I presume experience has taught you that such habits would only lead you to ruin. I doubt whether any one can enjoy true happiness who is not reasonably industrious and feels that he is doing something for himself and his fellow beings."

Stone's interest in Hay's character and well-being was not merely that of a future father-in-law. He had never gotten over the death of his only son, Adelbert, who had drowned in the Connecticut River on a geology field trip from Yale in 1865, and he sincerely wished for Hay all that had been taken so cruelly from his own boy. As a token of "affection and esteem" for the newest member of the family, and as a way to reel him into the fold, Stone presented Hay with two Lake Shore Railway bonds valued at $10,000.

Which was not to say that Hay's devotion to Clara required any external encouragement. "[T]he best of all good luck that could possibly happen to a man I have found," he told his friend Alvey Adee, who was still in Madrid. "We were not much known to each other when we were married. But I know her now and I never could have imagined so desirable a wife."

All indications were that marriage suited Clara, too. "O you two are the greatest pair of spoons I ever saw," Flora chirped to Hay from Cleveland. "I don't believe she will get homesick, & what is more, I don't believe she will be spoiled; it will only bring out her best qualities. As a little girl she was always (Don't show this letter to her) shy and diffident, never thought she could be or do anything, & the general public, not having as much faith as we, did not encourage her much. Now, however, I can fairly see her blossom out in the sunshine of her happy life."

The spoons were inseparable for the first four months, and when Clara went to Cleveland for a visit in June, her absence stirred Hay's ardor to new heights. As the day of her return neared, he gushed: "It does not seem to me that I shall ever want to let you a minute out of my arms again . . . I would give a good deal to have you here. . . . I would kiss your sweet face till nothing was left unkissed. You grow dearer to me and more precious day by day. . . . The only thing that reconciles me to my youth and early years, passed away from you, is that I was learning the world, forming my own character, and getting such knowledge of life as fitted me to appreciate you. . . . You satisfy my whole heart and mind and soul because I have learned enough to know what a perfectly lovely and dear woman you are. It is that which makes me afraid. I am like a miser in a hovel with a chest full of treasure."

Hay changed his schedule at the *Tribune* so that he could be home with Clara in the evening. By midsummer, she knew she was pregnant. Perhaps it was coincidental, but just then Hay's health faltered. He complained of an intermittent "dazzling of the eyes," which brought on dizziness and prevented him from reading. As with so many of the maladies that were to come over him during the next thirty years, the cause, other than stress, was difficult to determine. In August, he and Clara took their respective conditions to the curative springs at Saratoga. "I am living a merely vegetable life," Hay wrote Reid. "We listen to music, drink water, and in the afternoon my wife reads Dickens to me."

That fall, in anticipation of the baby's arrival, they took a house on 42nd Street, just off Fifth Avenue. There Helen Julia Hay, named for Hay and Clara's mothers, and also for Hay's deceased sister, was born on March 11, 1875. A week later, an elated Hay reported to Flora: "She looked like me for a day or two but rapidly recovered from it and now she is not at all ugly. . . . Clara is prettier than you ever saw. Here I know what I am talking about and can speak impartially."

HAD HE NOT MARRIED and started a family, Hay might have remained a journalist the rest of his working life. Few editorial writers made more than he. The *Tribune*'s magnificent new office building, with its distinctive Italianate campanile, was nearing completion. Hay's reputation and circle of friends were all any man could wish for.

Yet he had many reasons to leave New York. He had burned the candle at both ends until his health began to sputter. While he and Clara were comfortable enough at their new address and had nurses to help out, she missed Cleveland. And there was one more incentive for moving, Hay explained to Alvey Adee: "[M]y father-in-law wishes me to go into another line of business, which will bring me immediate wealth."

Amasa Stone's offer was generous but also vague. He proposed that Hay come to Cleveland and become familiar with his myriad investments and enterprises and eventually take on greater responsibility for their management. For a while he would be Stone's protégé, a job that he expected would allow him to continue submitting occasional editorials to the *Tribune*. And at last he could bear down on the Lincoln biography.

With a few pangs for his days as a boulevardier, Hay made one last round of his clubs and bid farewell to his colleagues at the paper. By the first week of June, he had installed his family in the capacious house of his in-laws. Next door, construction began on a comparably grand house of their own.

In designing the house, the architect, Joseph Ireland, borrowed from the angular, late-Victorian style known as Eastlake, turning a cottage into a castle of finely carved sandstone. The house was not as huge as the Stone mansion, but it was every bit as sumptuous. Much of the wood-work, including the staircase, was carved by the gifted German craftsman John Herkomer. The furnishings were chosen by the Herter Brothers, the New York decorators who redid the Red Room of the White House and soon would take on the Fifth Avenue mansions of William Vanderbilt and Jay Gould. Although Hay pretended to be annoyed by the noise and dust of "some half hundred workmen," he took great interest in the con-struction. The house was a wedding present from his father-in-law, but he made sure he got just what he wanted.

As expected, the demands that Amasa Stone made on him were not great. "I do nothing but read and yawn," he told Adee. "My work is merely the care of investments which are so safe that they require no care." He had ample time to go to Springfield and meet with Nicolay, who had begun interviewing friends and associates of Lincoln. Upon his return, he took an office on Cleveland's Public Square and pronounced himself ready to begin the biography. He wrote little, if at all, for the *Tri-bune*, but he made up for his absence by arranging for one of America's most brilliant writers to contribute to the paper.

If it is true that Hay knew every important figure of his day, then it was only a matter of time before he and Henry James made each other's acquaintance. In the fall of 1874, James was back in the United States after two years abroad. His travel writings had been appearing in *The Na-*

tion, and William Dean Howells was about to begin serializing James's first important novel, *Roderick Hudson*, in the *Atlantic Monthly*. Howells deserves credit for introducing James to Hay, but there were many others who would have gladly done the honor. James was four years younger than Hay, and in 1875 he was well respected in literary circles, although not yet a major literary light—certainly not as well known as the author of "Little Breeches" and "Jim Bludso."

Having lived in Europe, James was never quite at home anywhere else. His visits to America were precisely that—visits—and after a few months he was always restless to get away. Though the Jameses came from money, Henry's father was a prodigal dreamer; in order to make ends meet, Henry wrote for magazines and newspapers while pursuing his primary passion, which was, as the world soon would recognize, fiction.

At the end of July 1875, James wrote to Hay with a proposal that was not so different from one Hay had made to Whitelaw Reid five years earlier. "There is apparently in the American public an essential appetite, & a standing demand, for information about all Parisian things," James suggested. "It is a general thing flimsily and vulgarly supplied, & my notion would be to undertake to supply it in a more intelligent and cultivated fashion—to write in other words for the American (or it doesn't seem presumptuous to say so, as far as might be from the *cosmopolitan*) point of view a sort of *chronique* of the events and interests of the day." The *Tribune* was the only paper he considered worthy of "these brilliant gifts."

He was wise to choose Hay as his broker. For years the *Tribune* had been publishing regular letters from Paris by the author and critic Arsène Houssaye, with Hay serving as translator. With Hay gone, Reid was eager to replace Houssaye. Hay vouched for James's "wonderful style and keen observation of life and character." Reid acquiesced, Hay offered James $20 a letter, and James accepted.

The letters, which commenced in November, would not be what immortalized Henry James, but the friendship he formed with John Hay in 1875 was everlasting. "I feel as if my sails had caught a very liberal capful of wind . . . from your good wishes," James wrote after the *Tribune* arrangement was assured. They would meet again many more times, mostly in Europe, two cosmopolitans of a similar point of view.

• • •

HAY'S RELATIONSHIP WITH JOHN George Nicolay was evolving as well. In the White House, Nicolay had been the primary private secretary, Hay officially the assistant. But with Hay's success as an author and newspaperman, and now with his sudden affluence, the tables turned. Henceforth Nicolay would be the engineer stoking the Lincoln work, and Hay would remain abovedecks. Nicolay would continue to do the interviews, dig through archives, delivering his yield to Hay. Nicolay's income from the Supreme Court was adequate to support his family, but when he needed money to sustain the Lincoln work, Hay was always ready with a check—$200 here, $100 there.

In the fall, Nicolay sent his first box of material to Cleveland—notes from his interviews and a selection of recent books on Lincoln and the war. "The work is a heavy one, continually growing on our hands," Hay confessed. "I have many misgivings about it, [but] we shall put in it all we can." He promised Nicolay, "I shall go seriously to work upon it. I hope to make considerable progress by next spring."

But once again his eyesight gave out; he described the symptoms as "partial blindness." The glare from the snow on Euclid Avenue was so irritating that he wore a special pair of blue goggles whenever he went outdoors. He was well enough to keep tabs on the construction of the house next door but unable to get very far on the Lincoln material. In March 1876, he told Whitelaw Reid that his mind was "enfeebled with illness." It wasn't until June that he began to feel better, and even then he advised Nicolay that, to be on the safe side, he would take it easy throughout the summer and then try to buckle down in the fall, by which time the house ought to be done. Clara, he might have added, was pregnant again.

They moved into the new house in October and were thrilled by every opulent detail, from the "gilding and black dado" to the *H* and *S* carved into the newel posts of the black-walnut staircase. "If other people don't like it, something is the matter with their eyes," proclaimed Hay, whose eyesight was evidently improved.

A SON, ADELBERT STONE Hay, named for Clara's drowned brother, was born on November 1. "He is a fine little manchild, ugly and strong, lean and bigboned," Hay wrote proudly to Reid. "[H]e looks already like a railroad maker and statesman."

Six days later, the nation went to the polls to elect a successor to Ulysses S. Grant. As Hay had feared, Grant had not exonerated himself in his second term. Two major scandals had sullied his administration, although, as usual, the president had been blinded by loyalty and shielded by ignorance while those around him broke the law. First came exposure of the Whiskey Ring, a conspiracy between whiskey distillers and federal revenue collectors to defraud the government of millions of dollars in taxes. Among those arrested was Grant's private secretary Orville Babcock. Not long afterward, Grant's secretary of war William Belknap was impeached for taking kickbacks from operators of supply posts on Indian reservations.

In such a climate of shame, the best Hay could hope for was "a man on one ticket or the other for whom I can vote without nausea." He would have liked Speaker of the House James G. Blaine to win the party's nomination, even though Blaine had been dirtied by two different scandals himself. Instead, Hay had to settle for thrice-elected Ohio governor Rutherford B. Hayes. The Democrats chose as their worthy New York governor Samuel Tilden, whose dismantling of the Tweed Ring had burnished his reputation as a reformer.

The election of 1876 was not decided until the following March. Tilden won the popular vote, and at first it appeared that he had won the electoral vote as well. But Republicans disputed returns in Florida, South Carolina, and Louisiana, and only after lengthy and delicate debate by a congressionally appointed commission and backroom promises involving the removal of federal troops from the three states still up for grabs was it officially determined that Hayes, who, until the last minute, expected to lose, had won the election by 185 electoral votes to 184.

As the suspense finally came to a close, Hay wrote to Adee, "I shall never . . . run for any office. . . . The depredation is beyond computing." Two years later, he would be sorely tempted to change his mind.

In the meantime, he had reservations about Rutherford Hayes. A brainy lawyer, brave soldier (wounded four times), and long-laboring party man, Hayes nonetheless lacked the magnetism of Hay's first choice,

Blaine. Yet Whitelaw Reid had thrown the weight of the *Tribune* behind Hayes, and William Dean Howells had written Hayes's campaign biography. And so Hay finally paid his respects to his fellow Ohioan. He sent Hayes a gold ring into which he had cast a strand of hair from the head of George Washington, a relic he had obtained from the son of Alexander Hamilton. Hayes was extremely touched by this talismanic link to the nation's first president. "It will be difficult to wear it at all times," the president-elect told Hay, "but I shall prize it, and will wear it on special occasions if not constantly."

For the past twelve years—four of Andrew Johnson and eight of Grant—Hay had wanted nothing to do with the White House and its residents. Now, by giving Rutherford Hayes his blessing, he was hinting none too subtly that he would not mind being invited back.

CHRISTMAS THAT YEAR WAS especially cheery. The new baby was thriving, with lungs "like Stentor" and an appetite "like Gargantua," and Clara had come through her confinement as well as ever. They loved being in their own house, with their own cook and nurses for the children. Hay had begun collecting art, a passion that would continue the rest of his life. One of the first pieces he acquired was a sketch from Albert Bierstadt, and on December 19 he sent a telegram to Whitelaw Reid, asking his friend to bid as much as $500 on an oil by Winslow Homer that was up for auction in New York. They were as secure and satisfied as any family could hope to be.

Then, on December 29, fortune turned upside down. At seven thirty that night, the Pacific Express from New York crawled westward along the Lake Shore Railway into the teeth of one of northeast Ohio's infamously ferocious snowstorms. The train—two engines pulling eleven cars—was two hours behind schedule as it approached the bridge over Ashtabula Creek. The first engine was nearly across when the bridge gave way at the center, spilling the second engine and all of the cars seventy feet into the creek bed. Of the nearly two hundred passengers and crew, ninety-two died—most from the direct impact, others from the fires ignited by the stoves in each car. All told, it was the worst rail disaster in U.S. history.

The following day, even before all the bodies had been recovered, a coroner's jury began investigating the cause of the tragedy. A few facts were known already. The iron I-beams that buckled had been cast by the Stones' Cleveland Rolling Mill Company. The bridge was constructed using the Howe truss system, developed from a patent purchased more than twenty years earlier by carpenter Amasa Stone, now the principal owner of the Lake Shore & Michigan Southern Railway. Soon enough the jury and the public learned that the stoves that had overturned, burning many passengers alive, were not the self-extinguishing model required by state law.

CHAPTER 8

Roses in a Glue-Factory

When John Hay left New York for Cleveland, he anticipated a life as husband, father, and gentleman of letters, comfortably removed from the hurly-burly of politics and deadlines. While it was never his intention to detach entirely from the affairs of the world, he surely did not expect the world to disturb his peace so soon.

In mid-January 1877, Amasa Stone and the Lake Shore Railway's chief engineer, Charles Collins, were called before the Ohio legislature to testify on the Ashtabula bridge's construction and the cause of the collapse. Stone defended the bridge as "very perfect" and insisted that the disaster was caused by the derailment of the second engine and not by any flaws in the design or the manufacture of the iron. He also scoffed at the notion that stoves on Lake Shore trains were any less safe than the so-called self-extinguishing models stipulated by law.

Charles Collins was not so self-assured in his defense. The night after answering the questions of the legislative committee, he went to bed and put a bullet through his brain.

Two months later, a jury impaneled by the Ashtabula coroner concluded its inquiry. "Mr. Stone had great confidence in his own abilities," the jury prefaced, "and believed he could build and had built a structure which would prove the crowning glory of an active life and an enduring monument to his name." However, Stone's method, employing cast iron in place of stone and wood, as called for in the original Howe truss design, was condemned in the report as "an experiment that ought never to have been tried or trusted to span so broad and so deep a chasm." For this recklessness the jury blamed the railway—"which, by its executive officer, planned and erected this bridge."

The Lake Shore eventually paid more than $500,000 in damages, a hefty penalty in those days, but the price incurred by its founder and chief stockholder was in some respects more staggering. Long before the Ashtabula disaster, a cynical American public had come to assume that the railroads that crisscrossed the continent had been built to line the pockets of crooked men; now came proof that these men were not just robbers but killers as well. This, anyway, was the hue and cry of the preachers and pamphleteers who moralized on the horror of December 29. It mattered little that a subsequent study discovered flaws in one of the bridge's bearing blocks and exonerated Stone's use of iron trusses. By then his vilification was complete.

To distance him from public attention and to restore his battered spirits, Stone's wife and daughter Flora took him to Europe. In his absence, Hay gamely pledged to look after Stone's business affairs, a responsibility that proved to be more nerve-wracking than either man could have anticipated.

During the four years that followed the Panic of 1873, railroads had slashed the wages of employees, even while continuing to pay healthy dividends to stockholders. Finally, on July 16, 1877, a group of workers on the Baltimore & Ohio Railroad went on strike to protest a 10 percent pay cut. Their action sparked the first widespread labor uprising in the nation's history. Over the next two weeks, strikes shut down dozens of railroads across the eastern half of the country. Militias reinforced by federal troops met the rocks and clubs of strikers with bullets and bayonets, killing and wounding hundreds in Baltimore, Pittsburgh, and Chicago. Millions of dollars in engines, rolling stock, and buildings were destroyed.

Workers in the Lake Shore shop in Cleveland joined the strike on July 23, seeking a 20 percent wage increase. Like most men of his class and income, Hay blamed international conspiracies and demagoguing labor organizers for putting "the very devil . . . into the lower class of working men." He also was frustrated by the fecklessness of the army and local militias. "There is nowhere any firm nucleus of authority," he wrote to Amasa Stone, keeping his father-in-law abreast of the trouble in Cleveland. For the time being, the situation was calm, he advised, but "[t]he town is full of thieves and tramps waiting and hoping for a riot, but not daring to begin it themselves. If there was any attempt to enforce the law, I believe the town would be in ashes in six hours. . . . A few shots fired by our militia company would ensure their own destruction and that of the city." If the situation worsened, he told Stone, "I shall send Clara and the babies away out of danger . . . and keep house myself."

But in Cleveland no spark ever ignited. In an extraordinary display of moderation, striking Lake Shore workers agreed to respect and protect all railroad property and to abstain from intoxicating liquors during the trouble. By August 3, they returned to work, with no loss of property and no blood shed. (And later that fall they received a wage increase.)

Hay breathed a sigh of relief, although he remained shaken and disappointed by the country's apparent polarization. "The prospects of labor and capital both seem gloomy," he wrote to his father-in-law. "I am thankful you did not *see* and *hear* what took place during the strikes. You were saved a very painful experience of human folly and weakness." Soon he would have much more to say on this subject in his novel, *The Bread-Winners*, set in a fictitious city that was Cleveland in all but name.

In the meantime, he hastened to assure Stone, "All your investments look reasonably safe and snug. I make no new ones except with ample margins."

AFTER WEATHERING THE ASHTABULA disaster, the strike, and two years in Cleveland, Hay itched to get away. Not that he hadn't made good and lasting friends in Cleveland—his round table, the Vampires Club, became his version of the Century or the Lotos—but he nonetheless felt the urge to mingle with eastern men, whom he regarded as the true arbiters of American civilization. To be sure, in the late nineteenth century, great wealth and great men were made in Cleveland, but it was also disappointingly true that too few great men from elsewhere came to visit. For stimulating social, political, and intellectual intercourse, Clevelanders of Hay's refinement, a stratum he regarded as sparse, felt compelled to venture afield, to New York, Washington, or Europe.

In late January 1878, Hay and Clara went to Washington for several weeks. The primary purpose of the trip was to meet with Nicolay and go through the trove of papers that Robert Lincoln had entrusted to their care. For Hay, some of the material was so redolent and revealing that it gave him pause about his own trail of correspondence. "Burn all my letters as soon as read," he commanded Nicolay, only half-facetiously. "My observations show this is the only safe way. I want my biographer to be restricted to official documents."

It was the right time to be in the capital. January and February, the period between New Year's and Lent, were "the season," and with Grant gone at last, Hay looked forward to rubbing shoulders with the new Republican establishment. On February 2, he and Clara attended a reception at the White House, a sober affair, like all recent White House events; Mrs. Hayes, nicknamed "Lemonade Lucy," forbade alcohol on the premises. That same night, the Hays made the rounds of several other receptions, dropping by the houses of James Blaine, now a senator, and Assistant Secretary of State Frederick Seward, son of Hay's mentor, William Seward, who had died in 1872. Later he and Clara were invited to dinner at the house of Henry and Clover Adams. Whether he realized as much, a new chapter in his life had just begun.

EXCEPT FOR ABRAHAM LINCOLN, no other person—certainly not John George Nicolay or Whitelaw Reid, nor Theodore Roosevelt, perhaps not even Clara—played so important a role in Hay's life as did Henry Adams. Once they made each other's acquaintance, it was as if they had been friends forever. Theirs would not be a case of one person finishing the other's sentences—they disagreed too often for that ever to occur—or of one completing the other in any way whatsoever. They were both very independent; they respected each other's privacy and withheld many secrets. Yet when one was in the presence of the other, he gave him his full attention, a form of recognition afforded to no one else, to the point that the two men seemed almost to fill the space around each other, an atmosphere infused when they occupied the same room or when they exchanged letters, which they did by the score. For reasons that no one but they fully understood, and not even they articulated, Adams was the person in whose company Hay felt most himself. And Adams, the more irascible and phlegmatic of the two, recognized in Hay an admirable peer who consented to put up with him just as he was.

They were the same age, though Adams, prematurely bald and gray, looked older. He was slightly shorter, too, but, contrary to his persona as a drawing-room prig, he was athletic of build, with "an air of self-contained strength." They had met earlier in London and perhaps also in Paris. Since then, Adams, like Hay, had made a name for himself as a writer. In 1870, the same year Hay joined the *Tribune*, Adams accepted a position as professor of history at Harvard and assumed the editorship of the *North American Review*. Their list of mutual friends was lengthy and impressive: Clarence King, William Dean Howells, Henry James, and a great many statesmen. Moreover, they each possessed extraordinary insight into the American presidency: Hay through his time with Lincoln, Adams as the great-grandson of John Adams and grandson of John Quincy Adams.

They both were giving Washington another chance. Adams had spent years abroad, mostly in London, and as a Brahmin and a congenital snob in nearly all respects, he had declared the capital "outside the social pale"—a city with "no *monde*, no *demi-monde*, no drives, no splendor." As best he could tell, "[n]o literary or scientific man, no artist, no gentleman . . . had ever lived there." Anyone who was attracted to the place was either "an adventurer," "an office-seeker," or "a person of deplorably bad judgment."

Now, however, Adams had a good reason to be in Washington. He had undertaken to write the biography of Albert Gallatin, secretary of the Treasury under Thomas Jefferson and James Madison, after which he would begin on what he expected to be his *grand oeuvre*, thorough histories of the Madison and Jefferson administrations. For all of these, he would require access to papers archived in the capital.

To their surprise, Adams and his wife, Marian, better known as

Clover, found the capital quite livable. The activity they enjoyed most was looking down their noses at the world, and in Washington the opportunities for dour spectatorship were never-ending. And whatever *monde* they found lacking, they created for themselves. Clover instituted five-o'clock tea in the handsome house on H Street they rented from the philanthropist and art collector William Corcoran, at which she and Adams suffered as few fools as was possible in a town perpetually rife with them. "We have had a very cheerful winter in Washington," Adams admitted to an English friend. "We have had all the society we wished. . . . Our little dinners of six and eight were as pleasant as any I ever was at even in London. And Washington has an advantage over other capitals that a single house counts for more than half a dozen elsewhere; there are so few of them." Continuing with his stuffy praise, he observed, "Washington is not very unlike the north of Italy in its climate, malaria included, so that I expect it to become one day or another a favorite winter watering-place."

For Hay, the renewal of his acquaintance with Adams was as fortuitous as it was enjoyable. He too was embarking on his magnum opus, and doubtless Adams bolstered his belief that Americans were capable of writing history on the scale of Gibbon's *Decline and Fall of the Roman Empire*, which both he and Adams revered. After their February dinner together, Hay returned to Cleveland, eager to bear down on Lincoln "with some force." He had a new desk made, "so big that it will not go upstairs," he told Nicolay.

He was not able to work for long. Once more his eyes acted up; the complaint this time was double vision. He was nearly forty and soon would wear glasses, but this latest problem was not so simply solved. Reluctantly, he alerted Nicolay that he intended to lay off until at least the end of the summer. In early May he went to Philadelphia to consult with Dr. S. Weir Mitchell, the unrivaled authority on "nervous exhaustion."

Mitchell had earned a reputation for his study of gunshot wounds in Civil War soldiers. His expertise in neurology led him to write a series of popular books—*Wear and Tear, Fat and Blood, Nurse and Patient*—which described for the layman the nervous disabilities brought on by the unnatural strain of the age. "Our city life has become perplexing and trying by its intricacy," Mitchell pronounced. "[S]o many wheels must be kept moving in order to [carry out] social, domestic, civil and professional duties that in the hurry of well-filled lives we are hardly at rest." Symptoms included anxiety, dizziness, depression, and dyspepsia. Bundled together, they were often called neurasthenia. Common treatments included massage and mild electric shock. Dr. Mitchell went further, prescribing the Rest Cure, which for women called for several weeks of absolute bed rest and for men the opposite: robust diet, moderate exercise, and time out of doors. Regardless of the patient's gender, Mitchell advised altering the "moral atmosphere" created by the smothering attentions of "the self-sacrificing love and over-careful sympathy of a mother, a sister, or some other devoted relative."

In Philadelphia, Mitchell put Hay through a battery of tests and had him examined by an oculist. Patient and physician got along famously, for Mitchell, besides possessing impressive medical acumen, was also a man of letters and philosophy. His circle of friends included the poet Oliver Wendell Holmes, the historian George Bancroft, and the minister Phillips Brooks. An author in his spare time, he would eventually become as well known for his historical novels as for his scientific prowess.

Mitchell did not put a name to Hay's affliction—no mention of neurasthenia, for instance, nor, for that matter, of hypochondria. Nevertheless, he prescribed a version of the Rest Cure, tailored to Hay's cosmopolitan appetites: he and his brother Leonard would spend the summer touring Europe. "I have been under the weather a good while & hope this may pick me up," Hay wrote Robert Lincoln. "I expect to be back in October & shall probably see you on my way to Warsaw if we are both still extant." For the first time since his wedding, he would be apart from the "self-sacrificing love" of Clara.

Hay and Leonard enjoyed several leisurely weeks at the Hessian spas of Schlangenbad and Schwalbach, amid "[s]erene and tranquil dullness, the finest air and the loveliest scenery." He assured Clara that the vacation was worthwhile. "I am feeling very well, and looking better, I believe, than you ever saw me," he reported, adding, however, that he had "not got rid of that little buzz yet."

The trip entailed immersion of another sort as well. He and Leonard spent the first month in England, dining in London with Henry James and shopping for art—"scarcely anything tolerably good for less than one hundred guineas," Hay grumbled. They next wended their way through Belgium and Holland. They stopped in Frankfurt, Munich, Innsbruck, Verona, Venice, Milan, and Turin, finishing up with a swing through Scotland and the Lake District—a lively march that surely stretched the limits of Dr. Mitchell's definition of rest. To Flora Stone, Hay wrote: "I think a man needs about ten lives to get through all he would like to do—one to pass in great cities, and to learn them thoroughly, with their art, their history, and their social life . . . one for country and provincial life . . . one for public life and for doing good . . . one for literature etc. etc. Because we have only one we go blundering along in nervous haste."

The cure seemed to take; by the time he arrived in Cleveland, his double vision and whatever other woes were nagging him had disappeared. Throughout the fall and early part of the winter, he applied himself to writing. By agreement with Nicolay, he would tackle the first forty years of Lincoln's life, up through his term in Congress. Nicolay, working simultaneously and chronologically, would carry on as far as Lincoln's election to the presidency and the opening of the Civil War. They would decide the remainder of the schedule later.

By 1878, THIRTEEN YEARS after Lincoln's death, the biographical landscape had filled in somewhat, although Hay and Nicolay regarded the recent crop of books as historical weeds—unnourishing or, worse, downright noxious. Their own commitment to tell the Lincoln story in full was now fanned by a resolve to set the record straight.

The thorn that irritated them most was Ward Hill Lamon's *The Life of Abraham Lincoln*, published in 1872. Following the election of 1860, Lamon had taken upon himself the role of bodyguard and had spirited Lincoln into Washington to avoid kidnap or assassination. After the inauguration, Lincoln found a job for his friend as marshal of the District of Columbia, and Lamon was a frequent visitor to the White House; it was Lamon who had slept on the floor outside Lincoln's bedroom on election night in 1864.

Several years after the assassination, Lamon undertook a biography of Lincoln, only to discover that another of Lincoln's former law partners,

William Herndon, had already interviewed scores of Lincoln's neighbors and kin with the aim of writing a book of his own. But before he could complete his project, Herndon ran out of steam and, facing foreclosure on his farm, sold his material to Lamon (and Chauncy Black, a ghost-writer recruited by Lamon).

Herndon's, and then Lamon's, intention was to humanize Lincoln before he was rendered unrecognizable by hagiographers. If this meant calling attention to Lincoln's blemishes, then so be it. For instance, Lamon's book was the first to question whether Lincoln's parents were married at the time of his birth. It documented young Abe's strength, popularity, honesty, and intellect, but also detailed his vulgarity and his denial of the Bible as "the authority of divine revelation." It was also the first biography to chronicle Lincoln's early love for Ann Rutledge, whose death sent him into such deep depression that he "lost all self-control, even the consciousness of identity, and every friend he had in New Salem pronounced him insane, mad, crazy." When Lincoln broke off his engagement with Mary Todd (temporarily), again he went "crazy as a loon," and his friends took the precaution of removing razors and knives from his rooms to keep him from attempting suicide.

Having painted Lincoln as a bastard and infidel who had "walked that narrow line that divides sanity from insanity," Lamon finished his portrait with a flurry of less than flattering brush strokes: "Mr. Lincoln was a man apart from the rest of his kind, unsocial, cold, impassive. . . . It was said that 'he had no heart'; that is no personal attachments warm and strong. . . . It was seldom that he praised anybody. . . . His encomiums were most likely to be satirical than sincere. . . . No one knew better how to 'damn with faint praise.' . . . He had no reverence for great men. . . . He felt that he was as great as anybody. . . . Intensely secretive and cautious, he shared his secrets with no man. . . . Feeling himself perfectly competent to manage his own affairs, he listened with deceptive patience to the views of others, and then dismissed their advice with the adviser."

And one last swipe for good measure: "Notwithstanding his overweening ambition, and the breathless eagerness with which he pursued the objects of it, [Lincoln] had not a particle of sympathy with the great mass of his fellow-citizens."

The only person more offended than Hay and Nicolay by Lamon's book—and the rummagings of Herndon on which it was based—was Robert Lincoln. Now more than ever, he was the guardian of his father's, and his family's, legacy. His third and last brother, Tad, had died in 1871; his mother's mental state had deteriorated since the assassination, and in 1875 Robert undertook the painful steps of having her committed to a mental hospital. After her release, they remained estranged. (She would die in 1882.)

Robert had done his best to dissuade Herndon from completing his book and was enormously displeased when Lamon brought the project to bittersweet fruition. "It is absolutely horrible to think of such men as Herndon and Lamon being considered in the light they claim," Lincoln griped to Hay. He had confidence that Hay and Nicolay would write a "respectable book," and, to be doubly sure, he renewed his pledge giving them exclusive access to his father's papers—on the condition that he be able to review the manuscript before publication.

It would take Hay and Nicolay fifteen years to rebut Lamon, and even then they could not entirely dismiss him. Because Hay had not known Lincoln until 1860, he found, reluctantly, that he was obliged to draw upon Lamon's account of Lincoln's early life. Only when it came to summarizing Lincoln's character, a task that naturally fell to Hay, the more lyrical of the co-authors, was he able to counter Lamon's blasphemy with his own personal insight. "His heart was so tender," Hay eventually was to write of Lincoln, "that he would dismount from his horse in a forest to replace the young birds which had fallen by the roadside; he could not sleep at night if he knew a soldier-boy was under sentence of death. . . . Children instinctively loved him; they never found his rugged features ugly. . . . He was absolutely without prejudice of class or condition. . . . He was tolerant even of evil: though no man can ever have lived with a loftier scorn of meanness and selfishness."

This was the truer Lincoln, the Lincoln whom Hay and Nicolay knew and loved, and they put their credentials above Lamon's and everyone else's. "We knew Mr. Lincoln intimately," Hay asserted in the first pages of the biography, which he began in earnest in 1878. "We were the daily and nightly witnesses of the incidents, the anxieties, the fears, and the hopes which pervaded the Executive Mansion."

By March 1879, he was able to report to Nicolay that he had written 50,000 words. "If I could get three months of good quiet work without worry I would be up to where you began."

The quiet did not last. Hay spent three weeks in Warsaw at the bedside of his seventy-five-year-old mother, who had broken her hip. Then in midsummer, he allowed himself to be drawn into local politics. One of the Republican planks that year was "sound money," a movement to stabilize the economy by backing paper currency—"greenbacks"—with gold. Hay joined the Honest Money League and stumped for his local candidates.

Mostly he enjoyed being back in the hustings. "We are having a red hot canvass here . . . I am invited to make four speeches a week," he enthused to Whitelaw Reid. At the end of August, he spoke to a crowd of ten thousand at the annual picnic of the Western Reserve Pioneer Association, saluting the heritage of Ohio's founding fathers: "They believed in order, decency, sobriety; in reverence for all things reverend, for religion, for law," he said of the pioneers. "[T]hey claimed their own, while they allowed each man his own."

In October, he gave a speech to five thousand in Cleveland's Public Square. Upon reading a transcript of yet another of Hay's addresses that fall, Reid complimented his former editorial star: "I wish you would do more such things, so that the general public may come by and by to think of you as the national spokesman for Cleveland."

Hay was thinking along the same lines. His hard work for the ticket had won him the favor of incoming Governor Charles Foster, Ohio congressman James Garfield, and President Hayes; the latter two men were guests at Hay's house that fall. They and other Republican friends were suggesting he run for the U.S. House in 1880.

He gave it some consideration, if only to get away from Cleveland, which—as was now quite apparent—tended to make him uneasy or, worse, unwell. His recent visit to Washington had him yearning to spend more time there. He had sworn he would never run for office, but even in his adamance, he gave hints that he was wavering. "The Congress matter is not so simple as my high-toned friends think," he told Reid. "All Euclid

Avenue says with one accord that I am the man, but E.A. with all its millions and its tone does not influence a single primary."

In the end, he did not have to decide. In late October, Frederick Seward submitted his resignation as assistant secretary of state, and Secretary of State William Evarts asked Hay to take the job.

Evarts was a brilliant and well-traveled attorney from New York. He had managed William Seward's campaign for the Republican nomination for president in 1860. During the war, Seward had sent him abroad to halt the construction and supplying of Confederate ships in England and France. Afterward he represented America in the *Alabama* indemnity tribunal. He served briefly as attorney general under Andrew Johnson and as Johnson's private counsel in the president's impeachment trial, winning acquittal. He grew disgusted with Grant, supported the reform ticket of Rutherford Hayes, and, during the disputed election of 1876, served as lead counsel for the Republicans, helping gain the White House for his party.

Hay did not know Evarts personally but had many reasons to respect him. Evarts was a link to Seward and an exemplar of the better sort of Republican. He openly bucked the power-hoarding party bosses in New York and backed sound money and civil service reform. Quick-humored and debonair, he possessed all the social graces required of a diplomat. "He had the rare faculty," Hay told Joseph Bucklin Bishop, "of saying at the dinner-table the best things that were said there, invariably something that was quoted everywhere for days and even years afterward—and giving the impression while saying it that he had better things in reserve if he really cared to produce them." Very much the same would eventually be remarked about Hay.

At first he turned down the State Department offer. "Interests which I cannot disregard make it impossible for me to be away from Cleveland this winter," he wrote Evarts. What he was too discreet to mention was that Clara was seven months pregnant. Evarts would not give up, however, and pressured their mutual friend Whitelaw Reid to lobby Hay. The tactic worked; Hay informed Evarts on November 11 that he would report for duty in ten days. But even then he had his doubts. "I stand like a hydrophobical on the edge of a bathtub," he told William Dean Howells.

Leaving Clara and the children behind in Cleveland, he moved to Washington and took a room at Wormley's Hotel on H Street, one block off Lafayette Square. The State Department was located in the south wing of the still unfinished State, War, and Navy Building, immediately west of the White House. Its architecture borrowed heavily—rather too heavily—from the ornamental extravagance of Napoleon III's Second Empire. Told that the exaggerated edifice was fireproof, General William Tecumseh Sherman, the man who had torched the South, supposedly remarked, "What a pity."

In 1879, the department had only eighty employees in Washington and fewer than a thousand serving in diplomatic legations and as trade consuls worldwide. (The term "ambassador" would not come into usage until 1893.) When Hay arrived for work on November 22, the first to greet him was his old friend Alvey Adee, who had transferred from Madrid two years earlier and was now chief of the Diplomatic Bureau, overseeing departmental clerks and correspondence.

One of the principal responsibilities of the assistant secretary was to stand in for the secretary during the latter's absences from Washington. Hay was on the job only four days when Evarts went to New York. "Today was an important one in our history," he wrote soberly to Clara. "I sat for the first time in Cabinet meeting, and took the place of highest rank in the room, at the President's right." The last time he had attended such a meeting had been fourteen years earlier, as a lowly, silent presidential secretary. Now, taking the chair once occupied by William Seward, he experienced a confusion of emotions. "I felt very odd and very modest, sitting there among the grey-haired elders of the land, entitled to speak first on matters of national importance," he told Clara. "You may imagine I did not avail myself of the privilege. . . . It seems a much more important matter to me now, to be so near the source of authority than it did when I was younger. I did not appreciate it in Lincoln's time."

Evarts ran a low-key department. Explaining his executive philosophy to Rutherford Hayes, he quipped, "You don't sufficiently realize, Mr. President, the great truth that almost any question will settle itself if you only let it alone long enough." Most of the issues before the State Department involved matters affecting commerce—fisheries, foreign markets, tariffs. Hay had little to say about his duties, except that he found them "more exacting in the matter of time, and less exacting in the matter of brains." He clearly liked the honor and authority that came with his position but seemed not to have contemplated making a career out of it. "I can hold on until the end of Hayes' administration and then quit public life without a sigh or a tear," he assured Clara, who remained in Cleveland. "I do not want or need any office in the world."

He did not make it home for Christmas, and his correspondence does not mention whether he was present for the birth of Alice Evelyn Hay on January 6. Perhaps he was able to dash to Cleveland at New Year's, or perhaps not. Train travel that time of year, particularly along the Lake Shore route, could be unreliable, as everyone in the Hay-Stone households knew far too well. Quite possibly he did not see his new daughter until the end of March, when the weather improved enough for Clara, Flora, three-month-old Alice, and the baby's nurse to visit Washington for a few days. (Helen and Adelbert stayed behind with their own nurse.)

In the meantime, he found plenty of diversion in Washington. He was a welcome guest in the homes of Alvey Adee, who lived with a married niece, and the Nicolays, who lived on Capitol Hill, conveniently close to the Library of Congress. The Adamses had left for Europe before Hay arrived, but Clarence King was in Washington. Through a combination of scientific expertise, influential contacts, and scintillating personality, he had been appointed the founding director of the U.S. Geological Survey. He was staying at Wormley's, too, and he and Hay resumed their kinetic friendship. Later on, they briefly shared a house together.

During the winter of 1879–80, no two men were in greater demand in Washington society. "[H]e and I are such belles that they can't have a dinner party without us," Hay joked to Clara about his ad hoc partnership with King. Each was charming, but in tandem they were a performance. Their New York friend Henry Holt described a typical volley of Hay-King repartee. "I had a rather large dinner party one night," Holt recalled, "when I sat at the middle of one side of the table and put those two fellows . . . at the ends, thinking that each of them would keep his end going. All the evening they fired at each other, the whole length of the table, and hardly anybody else said a word."

•   •   •

FROM JANUARY ONWARD, THE season was a whirl of balls and diplomatic receptions. Hay made the rounds and continued to attend smaller gatherings, such as the two dinner parties he attended at the house of Pennsylvania senator Donald Cameron and his wife, Elizabeth. Donald Cameron's father, Simon, had made a fortune in railroads and banking before taking a seat in the Senate. Lincoln had made Cameron *père* his first secretary of war, but soon dismissed him for corruption and incompetence. After the war and a stint as minister to Russia, Cameron reclaimed his Senate seat, from which he controlled the patronage and politics of his state. When Rutherford Hayes declined to retain Cameron's son Donald as his secretary of war—a job he had held for the last year of Grant's presidency—Simon Cameron relinquished his Senate seat and directed the Pennsylvania legislature to give it to Donald.

Cameron was forty-three when he came to the Senate, a millionaire, an alcoholic, and a widower with five daughters and a son. Like his father, he was more powerful than clever, strong of will but lacking in imagination. "The iron crown which Don Cameron inherited from his old Highland father seem[s] too heavy for his tender temple and weaker brain," observed one capital columnist. He owned a mansion in Harrisburg; a fifty-room summer estate on the Susquehanna River; and a large tobacco farm in Lancaster County. In Washington, he had a house on K Street. What he lacked was a wife.

Lizzie Sherman was from one of Ohio's most illustrious families. Her father, Charles Taylor Sherman, was a judge in Cleveland; General William Tecumseh Sherman and former senator, now Secretary of the Treasury John Sherman were her uncles. She was just turning twenty in 1878, when she came to Washington to stay with her uncle John and aunt Cecilia. She was tall and slim, with bright blue eyes and a luxuriant head of light brown hair. She was delicate without being frail, thoroughly feminine but not in the least demure. She was better read than most women. She kept up with the affairs of the day as well as most men. She loved art and music; she danced well; and she put her good manners to good use. All of these qualities—her beauty and her vivacity—made her extraordinarily irresistible to men, and she played them as a coachman would drive a four-in-hand. "With perfection of grace and manner," recalled one of Lizzie's friends, "she seemed to me a picture of accomplished seductiveness, of which her able and ambitious mind was in no way unconscious." After one particularly successful evening in Washington, Lizzie merrily mimicked the solicitude of one of her pursuers, an Austrian count: " 'Mein Gott! One must walk over corpses to see you!' "

With men, she was always in charge, and it was she who chose Don Cameron from the long parade of suitors who fell over themselves to win her favor. Love apparently had nothing to do with her decision. Of four sisters, she was the last to wed. Her father, whom she adored, was elderly and failing; her mother was eager to launch her. In the end, her marriage to Cameron was said to be arranged, but Lizzie was the one who arranged it. She appraised the pluses and minuses and assured herself that she could make the terms work to her advantage.

He was twenty-four years older than she. His children were old enough—the eldest was Lizzie's age—and well enough off that she would not be responsible for their upbringing. Don Cameron was, on one hand, so obviously smitten by her and, on the other, so consumed by politics and his backroom habits of bourbon and poker that he was not likely to be an overbearing husband. In place of affection, and not necessarily in exchange for it, she would enjoy the benefits of great wealth and a commanding place in a society where being a Sherman and a Cameron was tantamount to royalty. For a canny twenty-year-old, this seemed a fair bargain. In breaking the news of her engagement to her mother, she wrote rather tellingly, "He is very nice about it all and keeps away from me except when I tell him he can come."

While Hay knew and respected the Sherman family, he cared little for the Cameron clan, beginning with Simon Cameron, whose sins he had observed firsthand in the Lincoln White House. Don Cameron was a hard-shelled Republican, but he was also a Grant man, one of the leaders of a growing movement to reelect the general to a third term in 1880. Still, Hay could not avoid the senator, who frequently prevailed upon the State Department with requests for patronage. And Cameron and his new wife were very much at the center of the social life of the capital.

Hay called at the Cameron house shortly after arriving in Washington and reported to Flora Stone that Lizzie "was looking far more beautiful than ever." This was the first mention of her in his letters—nothing more than an observation to a mutual friend. To be charmed by Lizzie was not surprising. Just the same, he had made a point of noting her beauty—a beauty that would grow on him each time he saw her.

His first dinner at the Camerons' did not go so well; he found himself monopolized by his host, whose "boundless ambition and passion for intrigue" tested his table manners. But the next party, in mid February, was different. "The table was absolutely covered with roses and violets. I should think there were a thousand," he reported to Clara so that she would not feel left out of his Washington activities. On this occasion, he talked very little to his host, who was seated at the far end of the table. Instead, he enjoyed the company of Lizzie, who honored him with a seat next to hers. The evening was "most exquisite," he wrote Clara, innocently enough.

He did not pass along any of their dinner conversation and indeed made a point of assuring his wife that he was not so caught up in the gossip and gaiety of Washington that he had lost his bearings. The day after their sixth wedding anniversary, he reminded her how much she meant to him: "[E]very year my darling I have loved you with a deeper and happier and more peaceful love. More than ever you fill my life with joy. You are the home of my heart."

But in light of his growing infatuation with Lizzie Cameron, another of his observations proved to be far more telling. He was writing to Clara not about Lizzie but about Kate Sprague, daughter of Salmon Chase and wife of the governor of Rhode Island, who, as all the world had come to learn, was having an affair with Senator Roscoe Conkling, the rascal boss of New York's political machine. "I cannot believe the foul stories," Hay remarked with evident sympathy for a woman of great charm and (formerly) good station whom he had known and on occasion courted during his days in the Lincoln White House, "but the fact is that married people cannot have an intimate friendship outside of their own families without danger of trouble and suffering."

THE DAY-TO-DAY WORK AT the State Department provided its share of satisfactions. For instance, Hay was able to help out Bret Harte, who, after his rapid ascent in the literary universe, had squandered most of his money and was now making ends meet as U.S. consul in the German city of Crefeld. The State Department had a long tradition of honoring authors with overseas assignments—Washington Irving to Madrid, Nathaniel Hawthorne to Liverpool, William Dean Howells to Venice—and Harte believed he deserved something more commensurate with his reputation than a damp factory town on the Rhine. He complained to Hay of neuralgia; what he feared was obscurity. Hay succeeded in transferring Harte to Glasgow, hardly more temperate but at least a city where a facsimile of English was spoken. Hay was also gratified to renew his acquaintance with James Angell, his favorite professor from Brown, whom President Hayes was sending off as the new minister to China. How far Hay had come: both Harte and Dr. Angell now worked for him.

Those who worked for, or with, Hay—whether in the Lincoln White House, at the *New York Tribune*, or at the State Department—invariably found him genial and reliable. "He was loyal to his associates and subordinates," the journalist Walter Wellman remembered. "His was one of those rare natures that win, without conscious effort, the deep and abiding affection of all who draw near." And if at first there were skeptics who assumed that Hay was yet another "favorite of fortune" who had won appointment more through cronyism than merit, he quickly proved them wrong. His only mistake was that he did his job so well that it appeared effortless. "Hay seemed to me to possess in a high degree a silent power of work, doing a great deal and saying little about it," recalled another newspaperman. After his death *The Nation* would remark, "Everything he undertook was done with a kind of divine ease."

His affability and unflappability were ideal qualities for a diplomat. So too was his facility with languages. Hay's fluency in French was put to valuable use in early March 1880 with the arrival in Washington of Ferdinand de Lesseps, the celebrated builder of the Suez Canal. In 1879, de Lesseps had formed a new company to construct a canal across the Isthmus of Panama, and he had come to the United States in search of investors and the blessing of the government. Secretary Evarts asked Hay to serve as translator during the delicate discussions with the administration, an experience that gave him a thorough grounding in American policy on the isthmian canal.

Thus far the State Department had maintained a stance of cautious indifference toward French ambitions in Panama. Like most Americans, Evarts believed that Nicaragua offered the only sensible route for a canal; he doubted that a Panama canal was feasible or that de Lesseps could raise the necessary capital. Still, the graying French visionary was hard to resist. "He is a very agreeable old gentleman," Hay told Clara after a morning in the White House, translating for President Hayes and de Lesseps. He stuck by de Lesseps's side at receptions and dinners throughout his stay, which, while an enjoyable assignment for the assistant secretary, was less than a triumph for de Lesseps. The president allowed de Lesseps to make his case and then issued a message to Congress on March 8, objecting to the Panama enterprise. "The policy of this country is a canal under American control," Hayes declared, emphatically invoking the Monroe Doctrine. "Our merely commercial interest in it is greater than that of all other countries, while its relation to our power and prosperity as a nation, to our means of defense, our unity, peace, and safety are matters of paramount concern to the people of the United States."

De Lesseps did not let Hayes's admonishment deter him. Returning home, he raised 300 million francs, asserting that he could complete a canal across Panama in eight years. Construction would begin in 1882. "I work not for selfish motives, but for the interests of humanity," the Frenchman insisted, in translation, of course.

THROUGHOUT THE SPRING, AS the campaign season began to heat up, influential friends continued to press Hay to run for Congress. When Mark Twain heard that Hay might get in the race, he quipped to William Dean Howells, "The presence of such a man in politics is like a vase of attar of roses in a glue-factory—it can't extinguish the stink, but it modifies it."

Hay was reasonably confident that he could win his party's nomination, but he shared Twain's opinion on the pungency of politics; politely he told his Republican allies that he was not interested. As much as he enjoyed life in the capital, he disliked being away from his family and recognized how impractical it would be to uproot a wife and three small children from Cleveland. As a compromise, he suggested to Clara that she bring the children to Washington for the remaining months of the Hayes administration. There was ample room for the entire family in the house he leased on Massachusetts Avenue.

Yet his decision not to seek a job for himself in the glue works of Congress did not mean that he lacked the stomach for the larger, only slightly less acrid, chore of getting good Republicans on the ticket and into higher office. President Hayes had declared early on that he did not wish a second term. At the top of the Republican field to succeed him were Treasury Secretary John Sherman, Senator James Blaine, and the man they all wanted to beat, former President Grant, who had recently returned from a two-year world tour and was ambling toward the White House under the escort of party spoilsmen calling themselves "Stalwarts." Hay and Whitelaw Reid were violently opposed to another Grant presidency and bore comparable disdain for the Stalwart ringleaders, Senators Roscoe Conkling and Don Cameron. Hay at first backed Blaine over Sherman, his fellow Ohioan. Awkwardly, his friend James Garfield headed the Sherman movement at the convention in Chicago.

To the shock and chagrin of nearly everyone, the nomination went to none of the three front-runners but to the darkest of horses, Sherman's canny understudy, Garfield, on the thirty-sixth ballot. As a sop to the stunned and bitter Stalwarts, the convention awarded the vice-presidential nomination to one of Conkling's protégés, the former collector of customs for the port of New York, Chester Arthur. As soon as the news reached Washington, Hay hurried a letter of congratulations to Garfield and promised his cooperation for the rest of the campaign. When the Republican Central Committee of Ohio asked him to give a speech in Cleveland, he readily assented. "I am doing this because I did not run for Congress & want to help a little," he confided to Clara.

THE SPEECH HE GAVE on July 31 helped more than a little. The committee had wanted him to speak on the Public Square, but after his previous experience there he worried that his voice had not been big enough to command such a large space. Instead, he addressed his audience in the exquisite Euclid Avenue Opera House, a centerpiece of Cleveland opulence owned by one of the Republicans' up-and-comers, the coal and iron merchant Mark Hanna. As Hay stepped to the stage, he was greeted by the applause of a standing-room crowd of more than two thousand, including a good many women. He had written out his speech in advance, both to calm his stage nerves and to ensure that his words would attain the widest possible circulation. Summoning all of his experience on the lyceum circuit and as an editorial writer, he waited till the audience settled, then delivered a tour de force.

"The Balance Sheet of the Two Parties," as he titled his address, presented a stark and strident audit of the differences between North and South, Republicans and Democrats. "'By their fruits you shall know them,'" he began. "[T]he fruits of the one"—Republicans—"are freedom, peace, and prosperity; of the other"—Democrats—"the Dead Sea apples of dust and ashes, of partisan rage and bitterness."

He had dipped his pen in sulfur and donned his bloodiest shirt. "Which party elected Abraham Lincoln? Which party opposed, vilified and finally killed him?" he asked his listeners. "On the one side is a record of glory and good repute which sheds something of lustre on the declining days of every man who fought that desperate battle against slavery and treason. On the other it is a shameful story of half-hearted loyalty or open rebellion, of ignorant and malicious opposition to light and knowledge, of blind and futile defiance to the stars in their courses."

Hay's balance sheet took no account of the deep rifts or chronic corruption within his own party. James Garfield, who had been implicated but never quite incriminated in the Crédit Mobilier scandal, was, in Hay's view, "an able, patriotic and honest man, of great capacity, unsullied character and blameless life." The Democratic candidate, General Winfield Scott Hancock, who had been a hero at Gettysburg but humdrum ever since, was merely "a mask behind which the treasons, defeats and hostilities" of his party were hiding. He was, in short, another McClellan.

Hay's speech was widely reviewed. "The Bombardment Has Opened Up, and the Battle Has Begun," bruited the following morning's *Cleveland Leader*. Whitelaw Reid's *Tribune* also invoked military metaphor, asserting that Hay had "made havoc of the Democratic ranks." Yet another paper called it "The Great Speech of the Campaign." Published as a pamphlet, it was distributed throughout the country and drew congratulations from rank-and-file Republicans and party leaders alike. Even Hay allowed himself to brag just the slightest bit to Reid: "We had an excellent meeting at Cleveland. . . . My speech was lengthened to an hour and three quarters by the kind participation of the audience."

Not everyone in Cleveland was so adoring, however. The Democratic *Plain Dealer* could not resist calling the darling of the Opera House "'Little Breeches' Hay."

He gave several more speeches after that, though none so grand as "The Balance Sheet." In September, he returned to Cleveland and spoke at a few ward meetings and smaller assemblies. Continuing on to Illinois, he took great pleasure in addressing the townspeople of Warsaw, with his father alongside him on the platform and his brittle-boned mother listening from a nearby window. "There was a slight breeze against me," he told Howells, whom he knew would appreciate the emotion of such a homecoming, "but I spoke nearly two hours, with no distress . . . and was fresh as paint at the end."

As Hay began to look ahead to the end of his stint at the State Department, his and Clara's life in Washington took an agreeable turn. The Adamses had returned after a year and a half in Europe, and the two couples became a foursome, anchored by the bond between the men but with the wives holding up their ends, each in her own way.

When Adams had first met Clover, he threw himself "head over heels" in her pursuit. "I found her so far superior to any woman I had ever met," he confessed to a friend, "that I did not think it worth while to resist." She knew German, Latin, and was studying Greek. She read *Middlemarch* on their honeymoon and breezed through the twenty-volume autobiography of George Sand in French. The daughter of a doctor raised in a proper Boston household, she commanded excellent etiquette and an independent income. She was not a beauty, but she was trim and active and loved morning rides through Rock Creek Park every bit as much as her husband did. Her powers of observation and the piquancy of her humor were, if anything, sharper. Henry James, whom the Adamses had come to know in England, called her "a perfect Voltaire in petticoats." In sum, her husband declared with frank tenderness, "I should say that we two were a perfectly matched pair." If there was any deficiency in their marriage, it was the inability to have children.

Clara Hay's place in the picture is more difficult to discern, simply because none of her letters from this period survives and only occasionally is she mentioned in the letters of the Adamses. "Mrs. Hay is a handsome woman—very—but never speaks," Clover remarked when they first met, adding that Clara's husband "chats for two." The two wives were in many respects opposites. Clara had provided her husband with three healthy and delightful children; but, as one of her friends in Cleveland confided, she was not an abundant source of "mental stimulus." She remained a devout Presbyterian, steadfastly observant of the Sabbath, while the Adamses and Hay took little interest in church. Since the birth of Clara's children, the author of "Literature versus Housekeeping" had inclined toward the latter, and, while she still retained "a serene and classic beauty," motherhood improved neither her figure nor her "versatility and gayety of manner," acknowledged another friend. When asked what sort of atmosphere Clara created, Clarence King was said to have remarked, "She is not an atmosphere; she is a climate"— albeit a climate calm, sweet, and temperate.

As for King, he had left Washington before the 1880 election, returning the following February just long enough to resign from the U.S. Geological Survey. Although he, the Hays, and the Adamses would see one another many times thereafter in smaller combinations, the four short weeks that they mingled in Washington was the longest the five of them were ever together in one place.

THE TALK OF THE town was a new novel, *Democracy*, a lampoon of Washington courtship and corruption. The book had been published anonymously, and the identity of the author became the object of delicious speculation—and a source of great amusement to Henry Adams, from whose desk the story had sprung.

The leading character of *Democracy*, Madeleine Lee, moves to Washington "to learn how the machinery of government worked, and what was the quality of men that controlled it." She is quickly attracted to the "Prairie Giant," Illinois senator Silas P. Ratcliffe, leader of his party (unnamed, but plainly Republican). The scales fall from Madeleine's eyes when she learns that Ratcliffe has received a $100,000 bribe from a steamship company. Beneath his senatorial grandeur, she perceives a "moral lunatic" who "talked about virtue and vice as a man who is colour-blind talks about red and green."

Readers of *Democracy*, of which there were many thousands in both the United States and Europe, easily recognized the resemblance between Ratcliffe and "the Plumed Knight," Senator James Blaine of Maine, who had been exposed in the Crédit Mobilier scandal and was later accused of receiving $64,000 from the Union Pacific Railroad, a charge he never entirely disproved but somehow talked his way out of on the floor of the Senate.

Adams's antipathy for the senator was long-standing. In the presidential campaign of 1876, he and a band of reformers had favored almost anyone as an alternative to Blaine. When the Republican nomination was won by neither Adams nor Blaine, but by "a third-rate nonentity," Rutherford Hayes, Adams drew some consolation from at least having succeeded in "barring the road to our opponents." Yet, he groused, "If any storm of popular disgust"—toward Blaine in particular—"is impending, no sign of it yet darkens the air. We shall keep at it, and good will come in time."

His scorn carried forward to *Democracy*, although he revealed his authorship to no one besides Clover and his publisher, Henry Holt. When the book first appeared on April Fool's Day 1880, Adams was in Europe, which helped remove him from suspicion for the time being. His brother Charles sent him a copy, pronouncing it "coarse" but reckoning Henry might be interested in it, anyway. Clover's father thought he saw something of his daughter's mordancy in its pages; she took the compliment but did not divulge the secret. Clarence King and John Hay, eminent wits of Washington society, also came under scrutiny, to the point that Hay told Clover that he had "given up denying it" and King found himself shunned by Blaine. That Hay would be a suspect did not make much sense since he remained a Blaine believer, convinced that the earlier charges of corruption against Blaine had been the absurd and malicious fabrication of Democratic scoundrels eager to derail the senator's bid for the White House. Nevertheless, when Hay and King at last learned the author's identity, they took great merriment in perpetuating the mystery.

Returning to Washington in October, Adams was at once gratified and appalled by the trenchancy of his satire, for not only had he taken to task malefactors of the recent past, but he had also foreseen with uncanny accuracy the next sordid chapter of partisan intrigue about to grip the country. In *Democracy*, Senator Ratcliffe holds a grudge against the president-elect, who has beaten him out of the nomination by three votes. Ratcliffe then brings to bear all of his guile to gain appointment as secretary of the Treasury—this scenario spelled out and published well before Blaine lost the nomination to Garfield and then maneuvered to become secretary of state. Next Ratcliffe becomes locked in a war with the president-elect over patronage that he, as "chief" of "Clan Ratcliffe," feels is his to control: "At the thought that [the Clan's] harvest of foreign missions and consulates, department-bureaus, custom-house and revenue offices, postmasterships, Indian agencies and army and navy contracts, might now be wrung from their grasp by the selfish greed of a mere accidental intruder—a man whom nobody wanted and everybody ridiculed"—this too published before Garfield's dark horse nomination—"their natures rebelled, and they felt that such things must not be."

In the end, Ratcliffe gets his comeuppance, but Adams, hardly a romantic, makes clear that American democracy is intrinsically venal. Expose a Ratcliffe, or a Blaine, and a new scoundrel will always step to the fore—someone, as would soon be seen, like New York's powerful senator, Roscoe Conkling.

In November, Garfield prevailed easily in the Electoral College but won the popular count by the merest margin of 2,000 votes. The big-state bosses, most notably Roscoe Conkling, had come through for him—which, by the rules of the game, meant they expected a say in the next cycle of presidential appointments. The worry now among those who supported Garfield but loathed Conkling's brand of cronyism was that the president-elect would not be tough enough to resist the persuasions that would soon be brought to bear on him. Before the election, Hay had written to Garfield, exhorting him to stand tall. "Beware of your own generosity! On the 2nd of November, *you* . . . are to be made our President. I believe it is to be an administration full of glory and benefit to the country—and it will be glorious and fruitful just in the proportion that it is your own."

To Reid, Hay was more blunt and unusually feisty: "[A]s you will see Garfield before I do, I hope you will inoculate him with the gall which I fear he lacks. . . . The time has come to be vindictive. We do well to be angry. I am through, for one, with being goodnatured with those coarse grained blackguards. They are a bad lot through and through."

When Hay had first accepted his job at the State Department, he anticipated remaining until the end of Hayes's term, then returning to Cleveland to work on the Lincoln biography. He felt comfortable advising Garfield on his appointments, yet harbored no ambition for himself. Much to his surprise and discomfort, on December 10 Garfield made him a rather unusual offer. He invited Hay to join the administration as his private secretary, but not in the capacity in which Nicolay and he had served under Lincoln. Garfield wanted to redefine the position to make Hay more of a private counsel. He proposed, rather vaguely, to raise his rank "at least to that of the Asst Secs of the Departments."

As was his habit, Hay looked for reasons to say no. And this time he did so. "To do a thing well," he wrote Garfield on Christmas Day, "a man must take some pleasure in it, and while the prospect of spending a year or so in intimate relations with you and Mrs. Garfield affords a temptation which is almost more than I can resist, the other half of the work, the contact with the greed and selfishness of office seekers and bulldozing Congressmen is unspeakably repulsive to me. . . . The constant contact with envy, meanness, ignorance, and the swinish selfishness which ignorance breeds, needs a stronger heart and a more obedient nervous system than I can boast. I am not going back on Democracy. It is a good thing— the hope and salvation of the world. I mean simply that I am not fit for public office."

He and Clara remained in Washington until after Garfield's inauguration in March 1881. Though he had bowed out of the running for a spot in the administration, he continued to make suggestions to Garfield on whom he should appoint and, more crucially, on how to play Roscoe

Conkling, who was demanding outright control of all New York patronage. Despite the scoldings of Henry Adams, Hay lobbied, successfully, for James Blaine as secretary of state. And he was every bit as delighted when Garfield tapped Robert Lincoln to be secretary of war.

Roscoe Conkling was accustomed to getting his way. Women tended to melt before his seductions, and men knew better than to cross the six-foot-three senator who worked out daily at a punching bag. Even so, when it came to appeasing Conkling, the professorial but war-tested Garfield would go only so far. In February, the New York boss told Garfield in no uncertain terms that he wanted the New York congressman and banker Levi Morton as secretary of the Treasury. Instead, Garfield offered Morton secretary of the navy and finally, after Morton's demurral, minister to France. Conkling was livid.

Garfield was indeed showing more gall than expected. By far the biggest patronage job in New York was that of customs collector for the port, a position that controlled fifteen hundred jobs and handled—usually crookedly—millions of dollars in tariffs and duties. In 1878, President Hayes had removed Chester Arthur as collector for his lax oversight; but with Arthur now redeemed as vice president, Conkling regarded the customshouse as his diadem to dispense as he wished. Garfield felt otherwise, giving it, without consulting Conkling, to William Robertson, a New York state senator who had worked to derail Conkling's juggernaut to nominate Grant at the Republican Convention. When Conkling learned of Garfield's choice, he vowed then and there to block the appointment. He would show the "trifling" Ohioan who was boss.

But not if Whitelaw Reid and the *Tribune* had anything to say about it. Reid's disdain for Ulysses S. Grant now became his campaign to thwart Roscoe Conkling, a crusade in which he had capable allies. One was Secretary of State Blaine. Another was Hay, who instead of going back to Cleveland, unexpectedly agreed to return to the bare-knuckled precincts of partisan journalism.

Reid, at the ripe age of forty-three, had decided to put bachelorhood behind him. In April, he married Elisabeth Mills, the twenty-two-year-old daughter of Darius Odgen Mills, a wealthy California banker and financier who now lived on Fifth Avenue in New York. Reid, whose salary and shrewd acquisition of *Tribune* stock already ensured him a comfortable standard of living, was suddenly, like Hay, a millionaire. Reid and his bride intended to embark on a long honeymoon through Europe in May. In his absence, he wanted his most trusted friend to steer the newspaper.

This time Hay could not beg off, though of course he tried. "I find myself low in nerves, irritable, excitable, reduced. . . . I must go home and take things easily," he pleaded. Reid assured him that the workload would be minimal and that Hay would hardly need to come into the office. And besides, "light employment . . . will keep you from brooding, keep you alert without burdening or tiring you. . . . To come here is the best thing for your health." Reid made the job sound like the Rest Cure.

By the first week of May, with Clara and the children reestablished in Cleveland, Hay had moved into Reid's house on Lexington Avenue and into his office in the Tribune building. The war against Conkling escalated immediately. "I write only to say I am with you to the end in this matter," Hay assured Garfield on his first day at the *Tribune*.

For Garfield, the end would come all too soon.

CHAPTER 9

Scorpions

The pending appointment of William Robertson as collector of customs for the port of New York was seen as nothing less than a toe-to-toe duel between Senator Conkling and President Garfield, with well-armed seconds lobbing taunts and huzzahs at the two combatants. At stake was control of the Republican Party. "I wish to say to the President that in my judgment this is the turning point of his whole Administration," Whitelaw Reid wrote to Hay before the latter left Washington. "If he surrenders now, Conkling is President for the rest of his term and Garfield becomes a laughing stock. . . . [T]here is no safe or honorable way out now but to go straight on. . . . The least wavering would be fatal."

Conkling was playing for keeps as well. Since the election, he had not let Chester Arthur out of his sight, rooming with him in Washington, paying for his meals, and plotting with him over patronage. Arthur's loyalty was hardly a secret; he might be Garfield's vice president, but he was Roscoe Conkling's lackey. Also under Conkling's sway was New York's newly elected junior senator, Thomas Platt, who would soon wear the spiteful nickname "Me-Too." Together they figured to exert plenty of influence in the Senate to block Robertson and humiliate the president.

Garfield had his own guardian in Secretary of State Blaine, who made a point to be at the president's side on the occasions the vice president was permitted in the White House. A majority of the newspapers in the country were rooting for Garfield, too, though none more vociferously than the *Tribune*.

If Conkling thought that the *Tribune* would modulate its attack during Reid's absence, he was sorely mistaken. Hay took up the cudgel against the bully senator with righteous ferocity. "Well, which did the Republican voters decide to trust, and pledge themselves to uphold, Roscoe Conkling or James A. Garfield?" he asked on May 4. "Is it not the business of Republican voters to see that their Senators, in their chronic hunger for patronage and power which has become the curse of political life, do not rob a President of his chances of usefulness? It seems that the issue is joined. If the people want government by Senatorial bosses, let them countenance by their silence the attempt of Senators to usurp a power which does not belong to them."

The editorial was unsigned, but anyone who knew Hay's "Balance Sheet" speech recognized the rhetoric: "Have the people lost all that they shouted for, has the Republican party found its fruits of victory turn to Dead sea apples . . . ?"

From then on, the salvos were unrelenting. In an exchange of letters that Hay later tried to have expunged from official files, he and Garfield shared their thoughts on the most effective way to vanquish Conkling. "Give me a line when you can and it shall be my marching orders," Hay beseeched the president, to which Garfield responded, "You are handling the work with admirable force & discretion. . . . Shall be glad to hear from you at any time."

All the while, Reid followed the *Tribune*'s coverage from Europe and encouraged Hay to keep the heat on Conkling. Hay dutifully obliged. On May 14, the *Tribune* was downright brutal: Conkling was no better than "a patriot of the flesh-pots." His statesmanship was that of "the feed-trough." And there was not the slightest evidence that "his soul has ever risen above pap and patronage."

Around this time, John Russell Young and Henry Watterson, two newspapermen who had known Hay since the Civil War, paid a visit to the *Tribune* office and were surprised by the transformation that had come over their easygoing friend. "We found little joyousness about him," Young recalled. "It was a time of political sensitiveness, Republicans at war, the battle fought as the English fight in the Soudan—no prisoners, no quarter. Hay entered into the business with Highland gravity and courage. . . . [He] actually believed in the sincerity of the conflict, and that there were real issues, that it was something more than the mere politicians' brawl. The *Tribune* was never so fierce even in Mr. Greeley's masterful days. The rule of the paper under Reid was that of whips, with Mr. Hay it was that of scorpions."

Throughout the spring, Conkling, Arthur, and Platt continued their efforts to stymie the appointment of William Robertson. When their schemes fell short and it became apparent that Robertson would be approved, Conkling resorted to the most desperate of acts: on May 16 he gave up his seat in the Senate, and Me-Too Platt did the same. Their tactic, extreme as it seemed, was to withdraw just long enough for the New York legislature to reelect them; emboldened by a fresh grip on the New York machine, they figured to return to Washington and settle the score with Garfield. Immediately upon resigning, Conkling and Platt decamped for Albany to set the scheme in motion.

Conkling's adversaries were shocked, elated—and cynical. "There is certainly not a statesman in America who excels our Senator in getting into quarrels without cause and out of them without dignity," clucked the *Tribune*'s lead editorial of May 17. Bearing the telltale erudition of Hay, the column compared Conkling and Platt to Don Quixote and Sancho Panza and their resignation to a French farce in which a man leaves his mistress in a rage but makes sure to leave behind his umbrella "as a pretext for return and a means of reconciliation."

Two days after the senators' exit, their erstwhile colleagues approved Robertson as New York customs collector. The reinstatement of Conkling and Platt was not so readily accomplished. For the rest of the month and throughout June, the New York legislature voted time and again without achieving the requisite majority to affirm Conkling, Platt, or any of the other contenders who dared to crowd the ballot. With each round, in fact, Conkling and Platt's popularity sank lower.

"Roscoe is finished," Hay wrote to Reid. "That Olympian brow will never again garner up the thunders of yore." Reid was thrilled by the turn of events and Hay's role in them. "You've made a splendid paper of it— strong, wise, aggressive, a leader & an inspiration," he wrote from Paris. "If Conk is ruined—as I firmly believe—it is largely your tomahawk that has let out the worthless life."

The ax fell not in a way anyone expected, and Conkling's head was not the first to fall. On June 30, a group of Platt's more dastardly detractors followed him to an Albany hotel room and observed him having sex with a woman not his wife. The next day he officially withdrew his candidacy for the Senate.

MEANWHILE, A DIFFERENT SORT of stalker was afoot in Washington. Charles Guiteau, a thirty-nine-year-old former lawyer, debt collector, and peddler of religious tracts, had spent the past year hanging around Republican offices, first hoping to help out in the campaign, next angling for a place in the administration. He was a Grant Stalwart early on, but after Garfield won the nomination, he shifted his attention, if not his wholehearted allegiance, to the party's new standard-bearer. As a calling card, Guiteau brandished a copy of a speech he had initially written (but never given) on behalf of Grant but then had edited to advocate Garfield. By incessant loitering and pestering, in New York and Washington, he managed to introduce himself to Conkling and Arthur and even achieved a brief interview with Garfield in the White House.

Guiteau followed the nasty fracas between Garfield and Conkling fanatically, and, ever a Stalwart, objected to many of Garfield's choices, from Blaine as secretary of state to Robertson as customs collector. His disapproval, though, did not keep him from continuing to pursue a slice of patronage for himself. He would prefer a consulship in Vienna—better yet, Paris. Such was his obsession, such was his delusion, that he believed he was a presentable candidate, despite his shabby dress and even shabbier portfolio. He took to hounding Blaine, and it is quite possible that on one or more of his many visits to the State Department in March and April he encountered Assistant Secretary Hay, who remained on the job after the inauguration until his successor was approved.

Finally Blaine had stood enough, and on May 14 he snapped at

Guiteau, "Never speak to me again on the subject of the Paris consulship!" This occurred two days before Conkling and Platt resigned, and shortly thereafter a bruised, vengeful, and clearly deranged Guiteau reached the conclusion that the only way he was ever going to right the party's and the nation's political wrongs and gain the attention he had been so desperately seeking would be to shoot the president.

On Saturday morning, July 2, Garfield and Blaine took a carriage from the White House to the Baltimore & Potomac Depot, from which the president was to embark on a two-week vacation. Waiting at the station were several of his cabinet members, including Secretary of War Robert Lincoln. None seemed to notice as Guiteau approached, raised a .44-caliber English Bulldog revolver, and shot the president from behind, hitting him once in the upper arm and once in the lower back. Garfield cried out and fell to the floor. Collared immediately, Guiteau blurted: "I did it. I will go to jail for it. I am a Stalwart and Arthur will be President."

THE NEXT DAY'S *TRIBUNE* gave a full account of the shooting and reported that the president was resting comfortably in the White House with a good chance of recovery. The lead editorial, perhaps not written by Hay but surely an accurate reflection of his thoughts, drew the obvious connections to Lincoln, by name, and to Conkling, by inference: "A second President lies stricken down by assassination. President Lincoln was murdered, not by the rebellion, but by the spirit which gave rebellion life and force. President Garfield has been shot down, not by a political faction, but by the spirit which political faction has begotten and nursed."

Acknowledging that Guiteau might be considered insane, the *Tribune* asked, "Yet did not men call Booth a madman? Both were sane enough in all the ordinary walks of life . . . and both were sane enough to prepare . . . for a deed toward which they were moved by a spirit shared by many others."

Now came the *Tribune*'s indictment: "Do the leaders of faction ever intend all the mischief which grows from the wild and desperate spirit which they create, feed and stimulate, week after week? Is it not their constant crime against self-government that, by kindling such a spirit, they send weak or restless men beyond the bounds of right or reason? The assassin, it seems, was not ignorant that he was trying to kill one President and to make another. . . . As 'a Stalwart of the Stalwarts,' his passion was intense enough to do the thing which other reckless men had wished were done. So the assassin Booth put into a bloody deed the malignant spite of thousands of beaten rebels. His deed stands in history as the cap-sheaf of the rebellion: So the spirit of faction which fired the shots of yesterday gave in that act the most complete revelation of its real character."

The newspaper's vehemence was to be expected, although in this instance the *Tribune* stopped short of naming Roscoe Conkling and Chester Arthur outright. "It is almost impossible to keep from being savage," Hay confessed to Reid. "I have put the muzzle on editorial writers [William] Grosvenor and [Joseph Bucklin] Bishop and myself and I think we are pretty decent. I *know*, and everybody *thinks*, that Conkling is fighting for time . . . solely in the hope that Garfield may die. . . . I *know* this, and yet it is too vile to print and I will not print it."

On July 4, however, Hay wrote an editorial that gave little quarter. It began with a tribute to the fallen Garfield, "the people's President," whose "good-natured firmness" had won the respect of the public and stirred "the dread of what may come after him if the 'Stalwart' bullet proves to have done its work effectively."

Hay no longer resisted pinning a proper name to this dread: "Arthur is a gentleman of many accomplishments and many amiable and engaging qualities. He is represented to us by those who know him well as one of the most upright of citizens, one of the most loyal and devoted friends. It is precisely here that the public mind finds its cause of doubt and apprehension. It is feared that he is more devoted to his friends than to the public welfare; that he can see nothing but good in them, and nothing but evil in their opponents. If this be true, and if the grief of misfortune is in store for us of losing the noble, enlightened, placable and generous ruler whom we chose in joy and hope last year, then the bitterness of the present sorrow and the weight of the present anxiety will be as nothing to what we shall have to endure in the four troubled years which are to come."

Nor did the *Tribune* spare Conkling, who, after the assassination, sequestered himself in the Fifth Avenue Hotel. The New York legislature had yet to elect new senators, and the thought of Conkling returning to Washington, with or without Arthur as president, was unthinkable to those who had toiled so doggedly to keep him at bay. "It can do no good, but will do great harm, to represent that nobody has been to blame, and that one fanatical Stalwart is the only person in all this land who has done anything wrong," the *Tribune* advised. "[T]he world knows that Mr. Conkling has done everything in his power to destroy the character of the brave and true statesman who lies at the door of death . . . and has spared no pains to make the people believe that the Republican party was being ruined, and the Republic itself was being endangered, solely by the bad conduct and bad faith of the President."

Sympathy for Garfield and the merciless excoriation of Conkling by the *Tribune* and numerous other papers, including the *New York Times*, had their effect on New York legislators, who, on July 22, on the fifty-sixth ballot, awarded Conkling's former seat to a mild-mannered congressman from Canandaigua, Elbridge Lapham. Conkling at last had been routed. Three weeks later, Hay wrote to Reid, "It is perfectly amazing to see how utterly Conkling is forgotten for the moment. Of course he will come up again, but for the present, he simply is not."

President Garfield, meanwhile, hung on, and each day's *Tribune* reported faithfully on his condition, which was alternately hopeful and grievous throughout the summer.

During the vigil, Hay's thoughts naturally turned to Robert Lincoln, with whom he had shared the long evening of April 14, 1865. Two days after the attack on Garfield, he had wired his friend: "Please send me what you can. We are living on telegrams." Hay was playing the diligent newspaperman, but he was also acting on a more intimate impulse: the shooting of a president in Washington had struck a common nerve. In the weeks that followed, he and Lincoln kept in touch, as Garfield gained and then worsened. "I wish I felt better about the President," Lincoln wrote Hay in late July. "He is an awfully wounded man."

Doctors never succeeded in finding the bullet in Garfield's back, and their unsanitary probing of the wound assured only lethal infection. On September 5, Garfield was moved from the White House to a cottage on the New Jersey shore, where it was believed the sea air might be more salubrious. On the nineteenth, exhausted by a long season on the ramparts of the *Tribune*, Hay set out for Cleveland to spend a few days with Clara and the children. "I go West tonight," he wrote Garfield's private secretary. "I hope and pray good news will follow me."

It did not: shortly after ten o'clock, as Hay's train rolled across New York State, joining the Lake Shore line west of Buffalo, Garfield fell back on his pillow and died, eighty days after Charles Guiteau had kept him from boarding the train that would have taken him on his own justly deserved vacation.

Upon learning of Garfield's death, Hay hurried back to New York, then returned to Cleveland a week later to join the assembly of dignitaries at Garfield's burial in Lake View Cemetery. Secretary of State Blaine and his wife stayed with Hay and Clara, while Robert Lincoln and his wife were next door with the Stones.

When the last guest had left, Hay took to his bed, physically and emotionally drained. On Garfield he had already said his piece in a letter to Reid: "[S]o brave and good and generous—how much eloquence, good cheer, poetry and kindness, how much capacity for work and enjoyment, extinguished by a hound too vile for anger to regard. . . . [T]he dismal prospect of Garfield's death and Arthur's accession takes all the heart for political work out of me."

For the rest of the fall Hay kept watch over the *Tribune*, counting the days of his "interim-ity," until Reid's homecoming, now anticipated for November.

CLARENCE KING WAS IN New York that fall, and he and Hay dined together regularly at the Union League Club. After leaving the Geological Survey, King had thrust himself into a series of mining ventures in Mexico, Arizona, and California, vouching for their potential, managing their erratic production, and drumming up investors; Hay invested in at least one. King's proven expertise and contagious energy left little doubt that he would soon be a very wealthy man. For the time being, at least, he was able to pay most of his bills.

Clara came to New York at the end of October, coinciding with Henry and Clover Adams, who were en route to Washington after a summer at Beverly Farms, Massachusetts. The reunion was all very gay. The Adamses stayed four days at the Brevoort House, which was also King's hotel. Two nights in a row they all dined at Delmonico's, the ephemerally flush King picking up the tab for one of the meals. Afterward, they went to the theater, an opéra bouffe, *Les noces d'Olivette*, and *Patience*, Gilbert and Sullivan's latest.

At some point, perhaps at one of the bibulous dinners at Delmonico's, Hay and King pressed Adams on his authorship of *Democracy*. By now they were already fairly sure that he had written it, although Adams continued to wink his denial. After holding his feet to the fire, the others knew for certain. To seal the conspiracy and to toast their incomparable friendship, they made up a name for their merry band: "the Five of Hearts."

A few days later, Hay ordered stationery printed with a simple monogram of a five-of-hearts playing card in the upper left corner. He sent several sheets to Adams for use as "the official correspondence of The Club." King later had a tea service made with a five-of-hearts motif; on the pot was painted a clockface with the hands set at five, the hour that Clover served tea. The service was seldom used, never so much as the stationery, and rarely were all the cups filled at once. Indeed, their collective correspondence indicates that, after their rendezvous in New York, all five Hearts were assembled in the same room perhaps no more than a half-dozen times—a poverty of attendance that did nothing to diminish the value of their relationship.

In some ways, actually, it was easier for them to be apart. As the friendship between Hay and Adams grew, a little distance allowed them to express feelings that were only implied when they were in each other's company; and for the peripatetic King, his absences allowed him to indulge his exotic appetites, not just for wild places but, as Hay and Adams only remotely understood, for women whom King was not anxious to introduce to his fellow Hearts. Their correspondence became a tender, slightly lopsided triangle of reinforcement and empathy: in their letters, Hay and Adams talked about King; when they wrote to King, they talked to him about each other. It was an oblique form of intimacy, but it was honest and unequivocal, and it worked.

Of the three, King was the most magnetic, although he was in no way the charge that fused the Hearts. He did precious little to bring them together and for months at a time was lost to them entirely. Yet he was not the odd man out, either. It was his desire for closeness and unity, separate from his ability to achieve it, which bound the five together. The other four were forever urging him to marry, settle down, and live more as they did. But he bridled always. For him, the point was for the others to be as they were so that he didn't have to. Through the Hays and Adamses, he achieved a vicarious, intermittent, unclaustrophobic normalcy. Meanwhile, the two married men found something between escape and fulfillment in their appreciation of their elusive Proteus. "[T]he men worshipped not so much their friend," Adams explained, "as the ideal American they all wanted to be."

Adams had first met King a decade earlier in Colorado and had been instantly taken with his virtuosity. "He knew more than Adams did," Adams wrote in his quirky autobiography, in which he always referred to himself in the third person. "[King] knew more . . . of art and poetry; he knew America, especially west of the hundredth meridian, better than anyone; he knew the professor by heart, and he knew the Congressman better than he did the professor. He knew even women; even the American woman; even the New York woman, which is saying much."

Hay was similarly dazzled. "It was hard to remember," he was to write after King's death, "that this polished trifler, this exquisite wit, who diffused over every conversation in which he was engaged an iridescent mist of epigram and persiflage, was one of the greatest savants of his time."

No one recognized the effect that King had on Adams and Hay better than Clover. In one of her frequent letters to her father, she observed, "I never knew such fanatic adoration could exist in this practical age."

HAY DID NOT NEGLECT his other friends during his final weeks at the *Tribune.* In September, William Dean Howells volunteered to review Mark Twain's *The Prince and the Pauper*, a novel Howells had edited. Twain's history with the paper was checkered at best. After *Roughing It* and *The Gilded Age* had received less than worshipful attention, he damned Whitelaw Reid as a "contemptible cur" and threatened to write a vengeful, "dynamitic" biography of him. Twain and Howells decided to take advantage of Reid's absence when they proposed the review to Hay, three months before the book's publication. Hay didn't mind obliging two authors he greatly admired, but he was politic enough to alert Reid of his intention. "I took into account your disapproval of Mark in general and your friendship for Howells—and decided for the benefit of The Tribune," he advised the honeymooning editor. "If it does not please you—wait for his next book and get Bret Harte to review it. *That* will be a masterpiece of the skinner's art."

Reid was grouchily acquiescent. "As to Twain," he wrote Hay from Vienna, "it isn't good journalism to let a warm personal friend [Howells] . . . write a critical review of him in a paper wh[ich] has good reason to think little of his delicacy & highly of his greed. So, if you haven't printed it yet, I w[ou]ld think of this point before doing so. If you have, there's no harm done."

The review, which ran on October 25, was long, laudatory, and unsigned. Howells praised Twain's "Cervantean" humor and "poetic delicacy." *The Prince and the Pauper* was both a "satire on monarchy" and "a manual of republicanism . . . airy and flawless . . . so solidly good and wholesome in effect that one wishes it might have happened." In return for the *Tribune's* kindness, Twain abandoned the biographical bomb he had intended for Reid.

HAY USED THE *TRIBUNE* to help out one more writer that fall. Thirty-eight-year-old Henry James was by then thoroughly established; his previous novels, *The Bostonians, The Europeans, Washington Square*, and especially the short story "Daisy Miller," had won widespread public favor, if not yet resounding critical or financial success. He had high hopes for his new novel, *The Portrait of a Lady*, the story of Isabel Archer, an American woman who moves to Europe to establish her independence, only to be tricked into a loveless marriage. To James's consternation, however, the early reviews, particularly those from England, were lukewarm. *The Portrait of a Lady*, they averred, had no faith, "no heart," no proper ending.

The book was published in the United States on November 16, a week before Hay was to be released from a "summer" of stewardship that had lasted more than seven months. He was back in Cleveland by the first of December, but he did not forsake Henry James. Ignoring Whitelaw Reid's admonishment against reviewing the work of friends, he composed a thorough and thoughtful defense of *Portrait.* "It is a remarkable book . . . perfectly done," he wrote Reid, enclosing his review.

Hay applauded James's manner of drawing his characters "entirely from the outside." Any "vagueness of our acquaintance with Miss Archer," he declared, was in fact what made the novel so engaging. "[A]fter all, when we lay the book down, we cannot deny, if we are candid, that we know as much of the motives which induced her to refuse two gallant gentlemen and to marry a selfish and soulless scoundrel as we do of the impulses which lead our sisters and cousins to similar results."

With *The Portrait of a Lady,* Hay attested, James had matured to his full potential. "Of the importance of this volume there can be no question," he wrote in conclusion. "It will certainly remain one of the notable books of the time. It is properly to be compared, not with the light and ephemeral literature of amusement, but with the gravest and most serious works of imagination which have been devoted to the study of the social conditions of the age and the moral aspects of our civilization."

Reid made no protest, and Hay's review was published in the *Tribune* on Christmas Day. It was not the first nor by any means the only appreciative notice to appear in the American press. Most likely the book would have done well had Hay never given it his blessing; in the first month, it sold a respectable three thousand copies. Yet Hay's recognition of the momentousness of *The Portrait of a Lady* meant a great deal. Henry James, post-*Portrait,* would join a pantheon of American fiction writers that included Nathaniel Hawthorne and Herman Melville, and Hay's announcement helped make it so. The novel is not simply "one of the notable books of the time," but stands today as one of the most brilliant literary achievements of any time or country. That Hay recognized this and had the confidence to say so is a testimony to his own literary acuity and his appreciation of a new group of writers who were at work refining the art form—Howells, Twain, Adams with *Democracy,* and the new master, Henry James. Within a year, Hay would submit his own contribution to the canon, *The Bread-Winners*, an anonymous novel he subtitled "A Social Study."

FIRST, THOUGH, HE PLEDGED to Nicolay that he would bear down on Lincoln. He wrote diligently until March 1882, when, inevitably, his health gave out. This time it was diphtheria, and this time he planned a convalescence even lengthier than his Rest Cure of 1878. The previous fall, Clara's sister, Flora, had married Samuel Mather, heir to an iron-mining fortune, and a man with a good head for business, and Clara at last felt comfortable leaving her aging parents for an extended vacation. They booked passage to Europe in July. The plan was to deposit the children with their nurse "at some warm sand" on the Mediterranean while Hay and Clara wandered afield, after which the whole family would pass the winter in the South of France. "I never promised myself that much of a spree in my life," Hay told Howells, who, he was delighted to learn, was to be in Europe for the summer as well. They also hoped to see Clarence King, who was somewhere in England or on the Continent, ostensibly to drum up investors for his mines.

In the meantime, Hay consulted a variety of doctors who "pounded and sampled" him. His newest complaint was heart palpitations, for which he was prescribed digitalis. Finally he was able to finish the seventeen chapters he had agreed to write on Lincoln's early years. He promised Nicolay that he would continue writing in Europe, but to Howells he confessed that the notes he was taking in his trunk would more likely serve as "ballast."

There was another reason that his work on Lincoln slowed. Sometime that winter or spring he started writing *The Bread-Winners*, and, once he began, he could not let go. He finished the manuscript in June and sent it to Richard Watson Gilder, editor of *Century Magazine*, who pronounced it "a powerful book." It is not clear whether Hay was offering the manuscript to Gilder for publication at this point or merely seeking criticism. In his response to Hay, Gilder made no formal bid, but he had good reason to curry favor. He knew that Hay and Nicolay were at work on the Lincoln biography, and he very much wanted to excerpt it in the *Century*.

Besides Gilder and members of the Hay family, the only other person who possibly knew about *The Bread-Winners* was Adams; that, anyway, is the inference of a letter Hay wrote to his fellow Heart in early June. Hay attached a newspaper clipping that declared him, Hay, the author of *Democracy*, and, feigning injury at the misplaced attribution, complained to Adams, "First, if people get into their heads that I wrote 'Democracy,' they will require of me a glitter of style and lofty tone of philosophical satire far beyond me . . . or else they will say of me, 'Did it once, can't do it twice.'"

THE HAY FAMILY LANDED at Liverpool on July 24. "The children have stood the trip beautifully," reported Clara, who was no great veteran of sea travel herself. The nurse, whose name was Reade, was English and the happiest of all to be ashore. Leaving the children with her at St. Leonards-on-the-Sea, in Sussex, Hay and Clara went up to London. At a dinner at the house of the American minister, the poet James Russell Lowell, Hay was seated between Henry James and Robert Browning. Next they were off to Scotland as the guests of Adams's dear friends Sir John and Lady Clark, whose estate, Tillypronie, commanded a magnificent view of the rolling hills and lush moors of Aberdeenshire. Both Hay and Clara were so smitten by the "purple glory of the heather" that after three weeks in Scotland, "the beauty and verdure of the Lowlands seemed commonplace."

Back in London, Hay found the atmosphere no less heady. "I assisted last night at the most remarkable gathering of vagrant poets I ever saw collected at one table," he told Samuel Mather. Henry James was on hand. Bret Harte came down from Glasgow. Clarence King arrived mercurially. Howells was also in town, as were Edwin Booth, the venerated Shakespearean actor and brother of Lincoln's assassin; the American abolitionist Moncure D. Conway; and Charles Dudley Warner, the Hartford newspaper editor who co-wrote *The Gilded Age* with Mark Twain. The dinner was hosted by yet another American sojourner, James Osgood, the book publisher and owner of the *Atlantic Monthly*. Hay called the gathering "so improbable that a bet of a million to one against it ever happening would be a good bet."

As for bets, guessing the authorship of *Democracy* was one of the liveliest games in London that summer. Hay sent Adams a sixpenny edition he had bought at a train station. The book was selling "by the thousands," he told its clandestine author. "I think of writing a novel in a hurry and printing it as by the author of 'Democracy.' Have you any objection?" Adams responded with equal facetiousness, encouraging Hay to "repudiate for me and my wife all share or parcel in the authorship" and to take credit for himself. "I expect to see you a lion in British society , , , and your portrait by [Edward] Burnes-Jones at Grosvenor Gallery, with 'Democracy' under your arm." (The prank was too droll to resist; later Clover Adams took a formal photograph of Hay holding a copy of the French edition of the book, *Démocratie*.)

At some point that summer, Hay showed the completed manuscript of *The Bread-Winners* to Howells, who in turn recommended it to Thomas Aldrich, the new editor of the *Atlantic Monthly*. Aldrich offered to serialize the book "unsight and unseen," Howells informed Hay, but only on the condition that it bear Hay's name. This Hay would not do. He wrote again to Richard Watson Gilder at *Century*, who cheerfully agreed to honor Hay's anonymity and offered $2,500 for the serial rights.

Before leaving England, Hay and Clara paid a visit to two more of Adams's friends, Sir Robert and Lady Cunliffe, at their country estate in Wales. Like the Clarks in Scotland, the Cunliffes would become lifelong favorites. Sir Robert, in addition to being a baronet, was a member of the House of Commons, and he generously provided Hay entree to the inner circles of British politics. For Clara, the hospitality shown by the Clarks and Cunliffes provided an invaluable primer in English customs. Her letters to Flora and her mother chronicled the smallest details of table and service: "The breads & muffins were at the four corners, the butter on each side. In the centre of the table was a revolving porcelain tray with jams of two kinds and two cream jugs"—and so on.

The family passed the rest of the fall in Paris, where they were again pleased to have the company of King, who had taken to Europe, and the Europeans to him, as if he had lived there all his life, when in fact this was his first trip outside North America. "Do you think you know the aforesaid King," Hay wrote Adams. "The revised edition bears little likeness— though it is equally loveable. . . . He is run after by princes, dukes and millionaires, whom he treats with amiable disdain. He never answers a letter and never keeps an engagement, and nobody resents it."

In Paris they were glad to meet up with a fellow Clevelander, Constance Fenimore Woolson, who was an aunt of Samuel Mather and a distant relative of James Fenimore Cooper. She was also a somewhat frustrated friend of Henry James and an accomplished author in her own right. Her short stories appeared frequently in *Harper's*; her first novel, *Anne*, a mystery set in the Great Lakes, had been published earlier in the year.

Hay and Clara introduced Woolson to King, who scarcely gave her the time of day. She, on the other hand, adored King at first sight. She promptly ordered a copy of his *Mountaineering* and was charmed all the more. After her time with Hay and King, she became convinced that they were the authors of *Democracy*. "They wrote it together," Woolson proclaimed to Clara. "In this way they escape direct falsehood. They wrote it during that first winter of Col. Hay's residence in Washington when you were not with him. *Voilà*."

While in France, Hay also had the good fortune to meet one of the greatest writers of the age. Bearing a letter of introduction from Henry James, he pressed a call upon the ailing Ivan Turgenev, who was living out the final year of his life in Bougival, just outside Paris. "I never saw a great man so kind and simple," Hay reported to James. "It fills one with a brute rage to see the mighty and gentle soul crippled by disease when thousands of people need his work."

Hay was still quite anxious about his own health. His complaints included "dizziness, deep depression towards evening, a sense of uncertainty in my gait, irregular pulse after any muscular effort—over all the invincible sense of something worse waiting just around the corner." In Paris, he put himself in the care of Jean-Martin Charcot, the preeminent neurologist in Europe—"the Napoleon of neuroses." Charcot diagnosed "Neurasthenia Céphalique"—nervousness of the head—and prescribed the customary treatment for most ailments, a regimen of douche baths. When the treatment brought no improvement, Hay consulted another doctor, who suggested he might just as well continue the baths somewhere sunnier. By Christmas the entire family was installed at the Hôtel Beau Site in Cannes.

The three children adapted well to hotel life and the periodic absences of their parents. Helen, nearly eight, was petite and pretty and already an avid reader and writer of rhymes—"quite reasonable and thoughtful for her years," according to her proud father, whom she took after most closely. Six-year-old Adelbert, or Del, as he was called, was another story. Big-boned and dark-browed, he looked more like his mother and seemed always a trial to his father. "Del is more heedless but I hope he will profit by the course of his years," Hay wrote to his mother-in-law. This was how he would forever tend to see his son—endowed with great potential but somehow always on the brink of falling short. Meanwhile, the baby, Alice, was healthy, jolly and the joy of the family.

AFTER THE FIRST OF the year, Hay heard from Gilder, informing him that serialization of *The Bread-Winners* in the *Century* was to be delayed from May until August 1883. Gilder also presented a list of editorial quibbles, though he assured Hay that he was even more enthusiastic than ever about the book and the sensation it was bound to stir.

Hay may have insisted on anonymity, but he nonetheless left clues lying about on almost every page. Arthur Farnham, the central figure of *The Bread-Winners*, bears a flattering likeness to its author. His face, Hay wrote, "suited the hands—it had the refinement and gentleness of one delicately bred, and the vigorous lines and color of one equally at home in field and court. . . . His clothes were of the fashion seen in the front windows of the Knickerbocker Club [where Hay was a member]. . . . He seemed, in short, one of those fortunate natures, who, however born, are always bred well, and come by prescription to most of the good things the world can give." (In a paragraph deleted from the manuscript, he also wrote: "His shoes might have come from distant Piccadilly—they were so strong and sensible and ugly—the sort a cad envies but never dares to put on.")

After the Civil War, Farnham served in the army on the frontier, as had Hay's brother Leonard. Farnham is chairman of his local library board, as was Hay's father. Farnham keeps a greenhouse of exotic flowers; Hay's other brother Charles was a flower fancier. Hay's Farnham is, for the sake of the novel, a widower, whose principal occupation is to look after the "Farnham millions," which have exercised upon him "a sobering and educating wisdom." With a group of friends similarly heeled and enlightened, Farnham endeavors, unsuccessfully, to "rescue the city" from corrupt ward bosses; Hay's own high-minded and deep-pocketed efforts to reform Cleveland's government had likewise fallen short.

The setting of *The Bread-Winners* is the biggest giveaway. Farnham lives in a large stone house on Algonquin Avenue in Buffland, "a young and thriving city on Lake Erie." Readers are handed the following directions: Algonquin Avenue "is three miles long and has hardly a shabby house in it, while for a mile or two the houses upon one side, locally called 'the Ridge,' are unusually fine, large, and costly. They are all surrounded with well-kept gardens and separated from the street by velvet lawns."

As the story begins, Farnham sits in a room "marked, like himself, with a kind of serious elegance. . . . All around the walls ran dwarf bookcases of carved oak, filled with volumes bound in every soft shade of brown and tawny leather. . . . The whole expression of the room was one of warmth and good manners." Hay's own stamped-leather wall covering, the palm-leaf frieze, and even his collection of bronze and porcelain bricà-brac are described in detail.

The "social study" of the novel is one of class. Maud Matchin, a "hearty, blowsy" girl of humble home and upward ambition, asks Farnham for help in getting a job at the library. Inflamed by the "unhealthy sentiment found in the cheap weeklies," her greater dream is to marry a rich man, and she sets her cap on Farnham. Seeking romantic counsel at a séance, she is advised that the way to win love is to "tell your love," which she does during a visit to Farnham's greenhouse. Farnham, who has practiced flattery "in several capitals with some success," is not immune to Maud's home-sewn dress that "held her like a scabbard." "[I]t was a pity she was so vulgar," he thinks, "for she looked like the huntress Diana." He gives her roses and succumbs to her "breathless eagerness," stooping to kiss her "with hearty good-will."

Two other women vie with Maud for Farnham's attentions: his next-door neighbors, Mrs. Belding, genteel widow of a "famous bridge-builder," and her daughter, Alice, of "bonny face" and "pure and noble" lineament. Meanwhile, in pursuit of Maud, not counting Farnham, are the two extremes of American labor. Representing goodness is the blond, blue-eyed carpenter Sam Sleeny, whose sense of "contented industry" serves as "a practical argument against the doctrines of socialism." His nemesis is the dark-skinned, "oleaginous" Andrew Jackson Offitt, ringleader of the Brotherhood of Bread-winners. The Bread-winners are not a proper union, but made up of "the laziest and most incapable workmen in the town . . . a roll-call of shirks," who preach "what they called socialism, but was merely riot and plunder." To Offitt and his motley cohort, "wealth and erristocracy is a kind of dropsy," Algonquin Avenue a "robbers' cave," and Arthur Farnham a "vampire"—this last a nod to Hay's Vampires Club. Offitt organizes a general strike in Buffland, calling for "downfall of the money power," although his more sinister goal is to rob Farnham's safe and make away with Maud, fooling her into believing that he has made a fortune—shades of Clarence King—in a Mexican silver mine.

The story gallops to a melodramatic finale: Farnham's genteel composure saves him from further forwardness with Maud; he musters a militia of army veterans, who gallantly repel Offitt's strikers; Offitt brains Farnham with a hammer, framing Sleeny for the crime; Sleeny escapes jail and breaks Offitt's neck; Farnham is nursed back to health by proper Alice; Sleeny is acquitted on all charges and at last wins the heart of Maud; and Buffland forges onward, its sky "reddened by night with the glare of its furnaces, rising like the hot breath of some prostrate Titan, conquered and bowed down by the pitiless cunning of men."

In his only published commentary on *The Bread-Winners*, Hay explained, anonymously still, that his account of the labor unrest that rattles Buffland was drawn from the strikes and riots that tore through the East in the summer of 1877. What he did not mention was that in June 1882, workers at the Cleveland Rolling Mills—of which the Stone brothers, Andros and Amasa, were major stockholders and whose president, William Chisholm, was one of Hay's Euclid Avenue neighbors—staged a virulent strike which on several occasions turned violent, as union members fought to keep scabs from entering the mills. Hay's June 30 letter to Gilder of the *Century* suggests that he was shaping his harsh depiction of the Bread-winners right when the Rolling Mills unrest took place.

•   •   •

Yet he might not have written *The Bread-Winners* at all if he had been able to foresee the tragedy about to transpire in the real Buffland.

Amasa Stone never got over the Ashtabula bridge collapse and the public shame that followed. He continued to keep a close watch on his investments—railroads, steel mills, banking, Western Union—but he was not the man of strength and confidence he once had been. After Ashtabula, he gave generously to a number of worthy causes—the city's charity hospital, the Children's Aid Society—and was the principal bene-factor of the Cleveland Home for Aged Women. Yet still there were those who whispered that he ought to have followed the example of Charles Collins, the bridge engineer who had taken his own life.

In 1880, Stone bequeathed a half-million dollars to Western Reserve College on the condition that it relocate from Hudson, Ohio, to Cleve-land. At the same time, the philanthropist Leonard Case, Jr., conveyed $1 million to found a polytechnic school in Cleveland to be called the Case School of Applied Science. Adjacent sites were found for the two institutions on Euclid Avenue, three miles east of downtown. In honor of Stone's son who had drowned while a student at Yale, the academic department of the newly minted Western Reserve University was named Adelbert College. The college's first building, Adelbert Hall, was dedi-cated two years later, in October 1882, after Hay and Clara had left for Europe. For Amasa Stone, it was the last great achievement of his life. From then on, everything went drearily downhill.

Stone wrote frequent letters to Hay in Europe, discussing business but dwelling mainly on his health. Insomnia and chronic indigestion in-dicated a deepening depression, and by the first of the year, Stone began suggesting that the Hays consider abbreviating their trip. "[S]hould I be taken away," he told Hay, "you are the one to take the helm."

However flattered Hay may have been by his father-in-law's trust, he was reluctant to interrupt his itinerary or his own rest cure. "I came abroad hoping to get some benefit to my [own] health," he answered Stone, adding even more selfishly, "As this is the last visit we shall make to Europe for many years, perhaps we shall *ever* make, I want to see as much as convenient."

They had accepted invitations to the Clarks in Scotland, the Cunliffes in Wales, and several more country houses. American minister Lowell had promised to present Clara to Queen Victoria at one of the first drawing rooms of the season. Both she and Hay were thoroughly in love with England, but for Hay the communion was especially profound, and thus his disgruntlement at being pulled away prematurely was more pronounced. "If I am able to spend a month or two of the early summer in London," he reasoned with his father-in-law, "I can meet and make the acquaintance of a considerable number of the leading men of letters and science in London, whose acquaintance and perhaps occasional correspondence will be a pleasure and advantage to me the rest of my life."

Throughout the winter, Stone's letters grew more pitiful and his hints more plaintive. "I seem to have lost vigour," he wrote in early March 1883. "You should not be asked to come home until you are fully ready, but it may be for your interest to come home at an early day." It was hard to believe he was near death; then again, he honestly seemed on the verge of losing his grip. Finally Hay and Clara could stand no more mewling, and they booked passage for May 10, cutting their trip short by four months.

They were not deprived of all diversion. At the end of January they enjoyed a short jaunt through Provence, and in February they made their way to Florence and Siena, catching up with Howells and Constance Woolson. By the third week of March, they were in Paris, tarrying not as long as they would have wished but allowing plenty of time for Clara to be fitted by Worth and several other couturiers. They crossed the Channel on April 2, with a full month remaining before they had to sail home.

In London they found hardly a moment's rest. King was in town, still tearing about, trying to round up buyers for his Mexican mines. They also saw a good deal of the Clarks, Cunliffes, and two more friends of Henry Adams, Mr. and Mrs. Charles Milnes Gaskell, all of whom were in London. They were given private tours of Windsor Castle and the galleries of the Royal Academy. At a reception hosted by Lord Granville, the foreign secretary, Hay met "many of the Diplomatic Body and principal nobility of the kingdom," he reported to his father-in-law, whom he knew was decidedly averse to such pomp and circumstance. "As a rule the higher the rank, the uglier and queerer they looked and the worse they were dressed." Regrettably, the queen's drawing room receptions were delayed, due to the death of her personal servant, John Brown, at the end of March. The first was now scheduled for the day the Hays were to depart London.

There was little that either of them could say to cheer up Amasa Stone. His spirits had sunk even further after the failure of the Union Iron & Steel Company of Chicago and three more companies in which he was a major investor. "[E]verything combined to go wrong all at once," he lamented to Hay.

Hay wrote from London a week before his departure, offering one more cup of sympathy and encouragement to his suffering father-in-law: "You have had a hard and distressing winter and spring. It seems very hard that one who like yourself has spent his life in doing good to others should now be placed in a position where nobody can do *you* any good. . . . I rely on your strong constitution, your sober and moral life, the reserve of vitality you have about you, to wear out all your present troubles and to bring you to a healthy and happy condition again. You have so much to live for—to enjoy the results of the good you have done, and to continue your career of usefulness and honor."

These were his last words to Stone, and they might not have reached him in time. On the afternoon of May 11, two weeks after his sixty-fifth birthday, Stone locked himself in an upstairs bathroom of his Euclid Avenue house, climbed into the tub, and shot himself through the heart with a revolver.

Hay, Clara, and the three children were by then aboard the steamship *Germanic*, one day beyond the English coast. They would not receive word of Stone's suicide until they reached New York a week later.

CHAPTER 10

Everlasting Angels

The pilot boat brought the grim news to Hay and Clara as their ship entered New York Harbor. Clearing customs with the bounty of clothing, jewelry, artwork, furniture, and antiques acquired during eleven months of travel was no small chore, but they got through as quickly as they could and hastened to Cleveland. They were too late for Amasa Stone's funeral, but the burial at Lake View Cemetery was postponed until their arrival. The casket was interred alongside that of Adelbert Stone, on the same hilltop as the grave of James Garfield.

Amasa Stone had appointed Hay and Samuel Mather executors of his estate, and his sons-in-law set to work satisfying the will. "I have a long and toilsome task before me to bring some sort of order out of the confusion in which the Chicago [steel mill] enterprise is fallen," Hay wrote Henry Adams two days after the burial, "but in the end there will be enough for the widow and the daughters."

Indeed, there was more than enough. For all his financial worries and recent setbacks, Stone died a very wealthy man. Estimates of his worth ranged from $6 million to $22 million (equivalent to more than twenty and, by some indices, more than fifty times that today). His daughters each were given $600,000 in securities outright, and Hay and Mather each received $100,000 in securities. After various smaller disbursements were made to other relatives, the rest of the estate was divided between the Hays and the Mathers, share and share alike. By early June, with the debts and bequests sorted out, the two couples knew they were now not merely millionaires but millionaires many times over.

Among the many letters of condolence Hay received was a tender note from Henry James: "I thought of you when your ship came in the other day. . . . You are still in the midst of the wretchedness of the event & perhaps you will be too tired & too shocked to read these lines. Put them aside then—for they are only a handshake." In closing, James mentioned a thought that, even in the days of grief and upheaval, might already have been forming in the mind of John Hay. "It occurs to me," James said, "that Mr. Stone's death may perhaps make Cleveland less your residence."

Hay's aloofness from Cleveland had begun well before the death of his father-in-law. Ever since moving there in 1875, he had found reasons for getting away, and *The Bread-Winners* was certainly no love letter to his hometown. He had hoped to be abroad when serialization began in the *Century*, but with the postponement of publication and his early return from Europe, he now had no choice but to hide in plain sight and hope that the veil of anonymity would not be penetrated.

The first four chapters appeared in August 1883, and sleuthing the identity of the author became a minor national pastime. "It is hoped that in the next census there will be a special table devoted to 'the number of persons' who have claimed or been proclaimed as the author," one columnist joked. "It will stand by the 'number of persons struck by lightning' and 'the number run over by streetcars.'" The journal *Art Interchange* offered a five-dollar reward for "the most keenly appreciative answers" to the question of whether the author was a man or a woman. (Most contestants guessed man. A woman would not allow Alice Belding to "bang and crimp" her hair, one respondent pointed out. "Every average woman of eighteen knows that banging and crimping do not go together.") So lively was the man- (or woman-) hunt that the September number of *Century*, containing the second installment of chapters, sold out and went into an unusual second printing. "Everybody is reading it, everybody is talking about it," exclaimed the *Critic*. "The Sensational Novel of the Year," proclaimed another journal.

Hay, not unexpectedly, was the primary suspect from the start. One newspaper pointed out that the description of Arthur Farnham's library "corresponds almost exactly with the appearance of that cosey room in the residence of Colonel John Hay," including the location of the safe. Another literary Sherlock Holmes called attention to similarities between *The Bread-Winners* and Hay's 1871 short story in *Lippincott's* involving a séance and ending with the wholesome hero murdering the oily interloper who has made advances upon his beloved.

A few fingers pointed elsewhere, however: toward Henry Adams, Clarence King, Constance Woolson, and Hay's editor, Richard Watson Gilder. When William Dean Howells, one of the few people who knew for certain that Hay was the author, came under scrutiny, he deftly deflected his inquisitor, saying, "I *wish* I had written it." Hay and Adams found endless amusement in purporting mutual ignorance of the authorship of their respective novels. "I long ago forgave you for writing 'Democracy,'" Hay wrote Adams in August. "1st because you did not write it and 2nd because you are a Five of Heart. But if you have been guilty of this . . . libel upon Cleveland, there is no condonement possible in this or any subsequent worlds."

Adams replied: "I am glad you did not write 'The Breadwinners.' . . . Should I ever come to Cleveland, I hope you will introduce me to the author. . . . As a work of art, I should not hesitate to put the 'Bread-Winners,' as far as the story has gone, quite at the head of our Howells-and-James epoch. . . . Howells cannot deal with gentlemen or ladies; he always slips up. James knows almost nothing of women but the mere outside; he never had a wife. This new writer not only knows women, but knows *ladies*; the rarest of literary gifts. . . . If I had a criticism to make it would be that he is a little hard on reformers."

Their charade bore hilarious fruit several months later when Adams's brother, Charles, published a carefully reasoned letter in *The Nation*, asserting that the authors of *The Bread-Winners* and *Democracy* were one and the same. Adams's mirth was uncontainable. "I want to roll on the floor," he wrote Hay, "to howl, kick and sneeze; to weep silent tears of thankfulness to a beneficent providence which has permitted me to see this day; and finally I want to drown my joy in oceans of Champagne and lemonade. Never, No, never, since Cain wrote his last newspaper letter about Abel, was there anything so droll."

At least one review saw a qualitative disparity between *The Bread-Winners* and *Democracy*, with the former shining far more brightly, a contrast that must have taken some of the bubbles out of Adams's champagne. "*The Bread-Winners . . .* has what *Democracy* has not—it has depth," the *Saturday Review* discerned, "and its author has what the authors [the *Review* believed there was more than one] of *Democracy* had not. . . . [I]t has both feeling and imagination. The characters of *The Bread-Winners* are rounded; those of *Democracy* are thin and flat. Stick a pin in the best character in *Democracy*—the Senator—and you can see daylight through him. Stick a pin in [Buffland steel baron] Mr. Temple or Maud Matchin, of *The Bread-Winners*, and they bleed."

Reviewers spotted "touches of Fielding or Thackeray" in *The Bread-Winners*. One called it "a novel of action and spirited incident in an age of introspection and analysis." A southern critic found a "largeness, a force, a vitality" in the novel and went so far as to declare it "the most masterly novel of American life that has been published since the days of 'Uncle Tom's Cabin.'"

Yet for all the laudatory clippings that Hay pasted in his scrapbook, there were others far less kind. "How this disagreeable story ever got . . . access to the public through the fastidious pages of the *Century Magazine* we are at a loss to imagine," *Literary World* derided. The *Springfield Republic* accused the author of having "no sympathies beyond the circles of wealth and refinement," from which vantage point "the workingman is either a murderous ruffian, or a senseless dupe, or a stolid, well-meaning drudge, while the man of wealth is, necessarily, a refined, cultivated hero, handsome, stylish, fascinating." Blue-nosed complainants, meanwhile, expressed dismay at Arthur Farnham's ungentlemanly miscue—the kiss in the greenhouse. "A man of his breeding" would have resisted the "boldness" of Maud Matchin, scolded the *Boston Evening Transcript*.

The Cleveland papers were no more welcoming. The *Leader*, normally a Hay ally, advised that "the anonymous author shows more good sense in remaining unknown than anything else connected with his remarkable work. . . . If called upon to guess the writer we should say that he was a callow youth who at some period in his existence had endured the wild Western horrors of life in Cleveland and was now basking in the fellow-ship of like-minded dudes in the East."

Finally, as the serial came to the end of its six-month run in the magazine and was published as a book by Harper & Bros., Hay found it impossible to remain silent. In the March 1884 number of the *Century,* he aired a long, unsigned letter, addressing criticisms that *The Bread-Winners* was "conceived from an aristocratic point of view"; that it was "not well written"; and that it was "a base and craven thing to publish a book anonymously."

His answer to the first charge was less than forthright: "I hardly know what is meant by an aristocratic point of view. I am myself a working man, with a lineage of decent working men; I have been accustomed to earning my own living all my life, with rare and brief holidays." As a fur-ther demonstration of his populist bona fides, he distanced himself from his leading man: "I care little about Farnham. It is true that I gave him a fine house and a lot of money,—which cost me nothing. . . . I wanted him to be a gentleman, and I think he is; but that I can not discuss, for I have never known two people to agree upon a definition of a gentleman."

To the second charge, that the book was poorly written, he pleaded abject humility, again slightly disingenuously: "I have little technical skill in writing, and no experience whatever in writing of this kind. The fact that my purpose and feeling have been so widely misunderstood is itself the condemnation of my style and method. If people think I meant to represent Arthur Farnham as an ideal hero, or that I have any sentiment but profound admiration and respect for the great mass of American working men, I admit that I have expressed myself with singular and la-mentable awkwardness. . . . All this, I admit, is a very inadequate defense against the charge that I have written an inartistic book. No matter how true it is, if the effect is untrue, the book has been badly written; but I, at least, contend that the book *is* true, and written with an honest purpose."

His reason for remaining incognito was more defiant but still short on frankness: "I am engaged in business in which my standing would be seri-ously compromised if it were known that I had written a novel."

Perhaps so, but his reasons for withholding his name were more involved than the one he provided the *Century's* readers. First, of course, he wanted to follow in the enigmatic footsteps of Adams and to feed the confusion over authorship of their respective books. Second, he did not want to bring any further exposure to the Stone family. Then, too, he preferred anonymity because he had written anonymously all his life, beginning with his newspaper contributions during the Lincoln campaign and Civil War. The Pike County ballads had initially appeared with only his initials attached; his editorials in the *Tribune* were unattributed; and his pact with Nicolay called for obscuring which one wrote which sections. There were exceptions to the anonymity rule—*Castilian Days*, several short stories—but, in general, Hay eschewed immediate recognition and the scrutiny and judgment that came with it.

The same circumspection also helps to explain why he did not allow his name to appear on a ballot and why, in later years, he was more comfortable as secretary of state and never wished to be president. Was he simply humble, or was he also wary? A man who can reap glory without fame never has to pay a public price when he falls short or topples from grace. Even after a good many people guessed correctly that Hay wrote *The Bread-Winners*, he steadfastly continued to take "the ascription of its authorship to him in the light of a personal grievance."

Whatever his motives, the ruse reaped rewards. The *Century* reported that the serial brought in twenty thousand new subscribers. When the book came out, a single store, Brentano's in New York, sold five hundred copies in a month. In the first year, the novel sold twenty thousand copies, more than *Democracy* or *The Portrait of a Lady*, and did well overseas, translated into French and German. However discreetly, Hay had achieved membership in a rarefied club that included Howells, Twain, James, Adams, and Constance Woolson—all of whom were at the top of their game in 1883. (A jealous Clarence King swore that he too had a novel in the works, to be entitled *Monarchy*, but like many of his ambitions, it amounted to so much wishful thinking.)

FOR ALL THE SUCCESS of *The Bread-Winners*, Hay also paid an unexpected price. A year after the book's publication by Harper & Bros., another anonymous novel appeared, entitled *The Money-Makers: A Social*

Parable. Hay might have been slightly amused if it had been merely a send-up of his own title, but *The Money-Makers* far exceeded the impudence of parody. It was a downright vicious assault on Hay and the Stone family, with plenty of slashes left over to bloody Whitelaw Reid. The author, Hay soon discovered, was Henry Keenan, a former colleague from the *Tribune*, who had been with him in Chicago in 1871, covering the fire. The novel takes place that same year.

The main character in *The Money-Makers* is Archibald Hilliard, whose resemblance to Hay leaves nothing to guesswork: "He glanced in the mirror . . . and smiled complacently at his rosy cheeks, his clear hazel eyes, and graceful tawny mustache, falling in a golden sweep over the corners of his decisive mouth." Raised in the West, Hilliard serves as an "elegant and refined" secretary to a senator in Washington, learning "to shine in the exclusive drawing-rooms of the capital," followed by postings to several foreign legations. He finally lands a job as an editorial writer for the *Atlas*, a moralizing New York daily edited by Horatio Blackdaw—no mistaking Whitelaw Reid—who is in the midst of "solidifying his relations with the clique that controls the fortunes of this country, and before ten years he will own the 'Atlas' and use the executive chair in Washington as a footstool."

At the *Atlas*, Hilliard becomes a prima donna, writing brilliantly but only on subjects of his choosing, "to keep his hand in." He makes a killing in railroad stock, trading on insider knowledge—an allusion to Crédit Mobilier or perhaps to Reid and Hay's questionable relationship with the shady Jay Gould in New York—and is welcomed into the most exclusive literary and social circles, where he becomes a model of elegance and taste: "If he loved fine things, it was always remarked that he was well and properly placed when surrounded by them. He could put on a glove with such grace that women who saw him would have kissed his hand. He could present a gentleman to a lady with an ease that gave the man a peculiar standing and appreciation in the eyes of the lady." And yet, "He still persisted, to those who rallied him on the waste of his genius, that he was a journalist and nothing else; that he hadn't the imagination for fiction."

Inevitably, Hilliard is introduced to the daughter of Aaron Grimstone, a self-made railway and steel baron from Valedo, a once "slatternly hamlet" in the state of Appalachia now known for "nothing but business, no literary men, no artists, nothing but stocks, iron, corn, and money-making." Grimstone is said to have amassed his fortune, estimated to be as much as $50 million, through "sharp practices"; his overriding ambition is to "round his millions out and make the sum so colossal that he can bear down rivalry by the mere weight of his wealth." The mansion he builds for his family on Geometry (Euclid) Avenue is so garish that it is "a never-exhausted source of mirth" to Valedoans of lesser addresses.

Before Hilliard meets daughter Eleanor, she is described to him as "not pretty," with an "awkward" figure and large feet. Hilliard falls for her just the same, convincing himself that he is attracted by more than her father's millions. "He was in no sense a vulgar fortune-seeker. He had reflected long and deeply on the seriousness of the marriage-contract. He preserved enough of the sentimentality of his boyhood to seek in his wife the companion of his heart, his aspirations, his better impulses. . . . But the more he saw her, the clearer her nature revealed itself, the more certainly he saw that she was not the ideal of his youth."

Eleanor, meanwhile, is thoroughly smitten by Hilliard. She sees him as "the ideal of her girlish dreams . . . a creature of poetic refinement." "'That's just what I like,'" she confides, "'a man whose brains give him rank, and yet who can outshine those who have only money or family to give them precedence.'"

Hilliard finally coaxes his heart to catch up with his material appetites. "'Gad! what beauty there is in her eyes!'" he tells himself. "'She is really lovely, and I could form her. Millions in the scale would justify anything, even love: I could love her—I could love her—I will love her—I do love her—I will risk it!'"

Yet, in *The Money-Makers* at least, the courtship comes to an impasse. Grimstone recognizes Hilliard's dual impulse and tells him that if he marries Eleanor, he will disinherit her: "'Millions may cover deficiencies as your wife; but as your wife, mark my words, she will never have them!'"

To such needling, Hay may have been able to turn the other cheek, but *The Money-Makers*' cruel characterization of Amasa Stone as Aaron Grimstone was beyond toleration. In place of the Ashtabula bridge, the author substitutes the Academy opera house, which collapses, killing three hundred people. Called before a grand jury, Grimstone acknowledges that he is the owner and hears testimony that his greed, parsimony, and alterations of the architectural drawings are to blame for the tragedy. The verdict breaks him: "A robust man of large stature, he was shrunken to mere flesh and bones. . . . [H]e, a Colossus among pygmies, lord of millions . . . was hated, and his humiliation gave the masses more joy than his early popularity." In the final chapter, Grimstone retreats to his bathroom and shoots himself.

Hay did not confront Henry Keenan directly. All he cared about was suppressing the book. He received a copy on February 2, 1885, and immediately wrote to the publisher William Appleton, whose advertisements were billing *The Money-Makers* "as an answer to the much-discussed 'Bread-Winners.'" Hay made no mention of himself as a target of the book's attack—nor did he concede that the depictions of him were in any way credible. Instead, he concentrated on the "savage libel" against Amasa Stone. "What the motive of this brutal vengeance can be I cannot imagine," he told Appleton. "Mr. Keenan, I believe, never saw Mr. Stone in his life. He did know me, at one time, and my relations with him, I thought, were perfectly kindly." Hay's tone was civil but insistent. Something must be done immediately "lest this thing should come to the knowledge of Mrs. Stone and her daughters." He did not threaten legal action, for fear it would draw more attention to the book. But he did request that Appleton cease advertising and offered to pay for any loss that the publisher might incur in letting the book fall into obscurity.

Appleton responded contritely, allowing that the work was indeed "a malicious attack on Mr. Stone" and offering to do "whatever you may desire to repair the wrong we have so innocently committed." He promised to cease advertising the book and to alter the death scene and the name of Geometry Avenue; but he chose *not* to change the name of Grimstone.

Hay pressed the publisher no further but took measures to buy up every copy on sale in New York, Boston, Philadelphia, and other cities. He did not entirely succeed in quashing the first edition, but he kept the damage to a minimum. Still, it must have galled him to read in a Cleveland journal that *The Money-Makers* was "much better in all its parts" than *The Bread-Winners*. Whether Clara or her mother ever saw the ugly portrayal of Amasa Stone, he did not say. One thing is certain, however: never did he imagine when he sat down to write his little "social study" that, before it had run its course, Amasa Stone would fall on his sword and a jealous figure from the past would seize upon both occasions to pile insult upon injury.

Now MORE THAN EVER, he wanted out of Cleveland. "I eat, sleep, and perform all natural functions like the average Homo Americanus," he wrote Dr. Mitchell in Philadelphia, but then complained, "I am ready to do anything, go anywhere, stay any length of time, with a fair chance of getting out of this moral fog I am in." At the end of the summer, he and Nicolay took a trip, just the two of them, to Colorado to look at property in Manitou Springs, near Pike's Peak. "I came away from Cleveland pretty wretched," he wrote William Dean Howells from Colorado, "and am already a good deal better." He and Nicolay did not find any land that suited them, but they vowed to continue looking.

Henry Adams had a better idea: why didn't the Hays move to Washington? In October, Adams alerted his friend that a developer was planning to build a six-story apartment building next door to the house that Adams and Clover rented at 16th and H streets, on Lafayette Square. Adams wanted to prevent the construction that would dwarf his house and disturb his peace; more than that, he wanted the Hays as neighbors.

With Hay remaining in the background, Adams dickered with the developer, and by early December the lot was theirs for $75,000. The plan from the start was to build side-by-side houses. The Adamses, of more modest means, of more austere nature, and childless, did not require as much space as the Hays and so paid one third of the price and took a proportionately smaller lot on H Street facing the square. The Hays, needing and desiring a much bigger house, paid the other two thirds and took the larger, more prominent lot on the corner of H and 16th. Fleetingly they entertained the possibility of finding space for Clarence King, but they knew they were only dreaming.

It was agreed that each would build their own house but employ the same architect. Adams and Clover had in mind "a square brick box" with "no stain glass—no carving—no nothing," small enough that "for extra furniture we shall need only two new corn brooms and a new ice cream freezer," Clover announced. The Hays, accustomed to the extravagance of Euclid Avenue, wished to fit in with the Adamses and with the more staid vernacular of the capital, but they also desired and could afford something more elegant. Hay had Joseph Ireland, the architect of the Cleveland house, make a preliminary sketch. Adams and Clover preferred their dear friend H. H. Richardson.

Richardson was at the zenith of his celebrated career, his beefy, monumental, neo-medieval style expressed in the stone and brick of courthouses, railway stations, libraries, Trinity Church in Boston, the State Capitol in Albany, and, most recently, the handsome house of Nicholas Anderson on K Street, a block from the Adamses' address. In many ways, Richardson was ideally suited to satisfy his two newest clients. He was the antithesis of late Victorian frippery; yet all of his buildings conveyed a formalism that was stately in its understatement. Clover dubbed the Richardsonian aesthetic "Neo-Agnostic," and soon they were all believers. They met with Richardson in Washington in January and again in March, when he presented a set of drawings that pleased everyone.

IT DIDN'T TAKE MUCH to keep Hay away from Cleveland. While in Washington he received a telegram from Clarence King in London, urging him to come to England on a bachelor holiday. Hay sailed from New York on April 19, 1884. As usual, he felt better once he got away, afflicted by nothing more than homesickness for Clara. "God bless you & keep you till I take you to my arms again," he wrote her from aboard the *Britannic.* "My mind and heart, the very pulses in my blood are full of you, my beauty and my love. I wish you were with me. How much gayer and brighter this journey would be with your dear face beside me."

The next two months were a pageant of dinners and teas and visits to galleries and artists' studios. First off, he made appointments at his tailors in New Bond Street and Savile Row to be fitted for shirts, suits, overcoats, and a new top hat. He found King, as usual, on the brink of financial ruin, sustained by credit, bluff, and the kindness of friends. He spent time with Henry James and Constance Woolson, gossiping to Clara that "James tells me he has seen a good deal of Miss Woolson & evidently likes her on further acquaintance." He hosted a breakfast for James, King, Bret Harte, James Russell Lowell, the foreign correspondent George Smalley, and the urbane young secretary of the American legation, Henry White. At a private showing at the Royal Academy, one of the paintings he particularly admired was a portrait of White's wife by John Singer Sargent—a "beautiful, stylish . . . distinguished looking picture, splendidly painted." He fell in with the English landscape painter Alfred Parsons and his American studio mate, Edwin Abbey. He bought several of Parsons's pieces, and in mid-May, Hay, Parsons, Abbey, and King dashed across the Channel to Paris to take in the spring Salon. The spree finally came to an end, and Hay, replenished by the non-stop social excitement, returned to Cleveland in mid-June, where Clara, three months' pregnant, greeted him with her large and grateful heart, as always.

BY THE TIME HE arrived home, the presidential campaign was in full swing. Rather than allow Chester Arthur, the accidental incumbent, to top the ticket, Republicans nominated their tarnished but unbowed knight, James Blaine of Maine. The Democrats chose Grover Cleveland, who was barely known outside his home state of New York, where he had served one year as mayor of Buffalo and two as governor. Hay remained a steadfast Blaine man, although many of his fellow Republicans no longer trusted Blaine to carry the standard; these apostates earned the nickname "Mugwumps," a made-up Indian word for a renegade tribe whose "mugs" were on one side of the fence, their "wumps" on the other.

Hay had little patience with his friends—Adams among them—who favored Cleveland, and he could not bear the thought that, after five successive Republican presidents, a man whom he regarded as an obscure "rural sheriff" might unseat the party of Lincoln. "You know perfectly well that the Republican party contains, on the whole, the majority of the better sort," he ranted to Richard Watson Gilder. "Do you think that if you put Cleveland under the microscope you would find him more faultless than the Maine man? . . . [B]etween Blaine and Cleveland, Blaine is the more civilized."

The campaign was hard-fought and nasty, the low point reached when Republicans publicized that the otherwise spotless Cleveland had fathered an illegitimate child. Still, enough voters forgave Cleveland and enough Mugwumps jumped the fence to tip the vote in his favor. Hay was bitterly disappointed. At the very moment he was ready to shed one Cleveland, he was now preparing to move to the neighborhood of another.

The other blow that autumn was the death of Dr. Charles Hay, of heart disease. "He was 83 years old but so well and alive last spring that I felt sure he would live to be a hundred," Hay told Adams. "He laughed and talked with visitors while he was dying, to avoid giving my mother pain. . . . She is 80 and cannot walk but has the spirit and wit of a young woman. What trick of breeding has made me the son of such people? I feel ashamed of myself, when I think what a poor devil I am."

Yet while losing a father, he gained a second son. Clarence Leonard Hay was born in Cleveland on December 19, 1884. "The Doctor scared the five wits out of me early in the evening," he told Adams, "but subsequently behaved himself like a gentleman and presented me with a fine gaillard of a fellow, eleven pounds of him in the garb of Paradise." The choice of name honored Clara, more so Clarence King.

WITH A DEMOCRAT IN the White House, *The Bread-Winners* behind him, and his Washington house under construction, the time had come to bear down again on the Lincoln biography, which he had barely touched during the past year and a half. Nicolay, too, picked up the pace after his own spate of eye trouble.

In January, Nicolay sent Robert Lincoln the chapters covering the first forty years of Lincoln's life, all of them written by Hay. Although most of Hay's account of this portion of Lincoln's history was based on interviews conducted by Nicolay and on secondary sources, including Ward Hill Lamon's warts-and-all biography, Hay assured Robert that he and Nicolay would still honor the original agreement to allow Robert to review the entire manuscript before publication. "I need not tell you," Hay assured Robert, "that every line has been written in a spirit of reverence and regard. Still you may find here and there words or sentences which do not suit you. I write now to request that you will read with a pencil in your hand and strike out everything to which you object. I will adopt your view in all cases whether I agree with it or not."

Lincoln, once his term as secretary of war ended in March, had time to go over the manuscript with care. He took issue with Hay's depiction of Thomas Lincoln, the president's shiftless father: "It is beyond doubt that my departed grandfather was not an enterprising man & it is likely that your graphic assaults upon him . . . are not undeserved but I could not help feeling better if you would 'let up' on him a little in a final revision. He did not have much chance to prepare & pose in the reflection of his son's fame & I feel sorry for him."

For the most part, though, Robert was delighted with Hay's rendering of his father. Indeed, Hay had treated Lincoln with great sensitivity and adoration. Unlike Lamon (working with William Herndon's material), Hay trod politely, almost apologetically, through the Lincoln genealogy, and of Lincoln's aborted romance with Ann Rutledge, which had driven him to the brink of suicide, Hay mentioned merely that Lincoln was "profoundly affected by her death."

He did give a frank account of Lincoln's engagement and marriage to Mary Todd and of the uncertainty and depression it prompted: "The engagement was not in all respects a happy one, as both parties doubted their compatibility, and a heart so affectionate and a conscience so sensitive as Lincoln's found material for exquisite self-torment in these conditions." But then, after pointing out that "[t]his taint of constitutional sadness was not peculiar to Lincoln; it may be said to have been endemic among the early settlers of the West," Hay discreetly drew the curtain on this sad but formative episode of Lincoln's life: "It is as useless as it would be indelicate to seek to penetrate in detail the incidents and special causes which produced in his mind the darkness as of the valley of the shadow of death. There was probably nothing worth recording in them; we are only concerned with their effect upon a character which was to be hereafter for all time one of the possessions of the nation. It is enough for us to know that a great trouble came upon him, and that he bore it nobly after his kind."

Robert Lincoln, whose mother (now dead) had given him a full measure of torment and whose father's tenderness he had received in small and intermittent doses, allowed this segment of the narrative to stand just as it was.

Nicolay had been even more productive than Hay, carrying forward

Lincoln's life through the debates with Stephen Douglas, his nomination and election as president, to the outbreak of rebellion. After twenty years of preparation and postponement, the co-authors buckled down and wrote much of the remainder of the biography in less than two years, with Hay taking on nearly all the military chapters: Chancellorsville, Second Bull Run, Antietam, Fredericksburg, Vicksburg, Gettysburg, Petersburg, Chattanooga, Chickamauga, the Wilderness, Spotsylvania, Cold Harbor, Jubal Early's assault on Washington, Sherman's March to the Sea, Sheridan in the Shenandoah, Farragut at Mobile Bay, the *Monitor* versus the *Merrimac*, and the campaigns in South Carolina and Florida.

Where once they had worried that their field was becoming crowded, now they sensed that the ground was fertile. Two rather sentimental and less than thorough biographies of Lincoln—one of them by William Stoddard, the third secretary in the White House, whom Hay had considered so ineffectual—appeared in early 1885 and were well received. More encouraging was a series of articles that had begun in the *Century* the previous fall under the rubric "Battles and Leaders of the Civil War." These recollections by key generals and officers on both sides of the conflict were instantly popular. "[T]he market is ready," Hay wrote Nicolay. "I am getting anxious to print a volume or two."

Throughout the spring and summer of 1885, Richard Watson Gilder pursued Hay and Nicolay for the rights to publish the biography, first as a serial in the *Century* and then in book form. In mid-July, Nicolay met Gilder in New Hampshire and presented him with 114 chapters. Gilder read the manuscript straight through. Later that month, he wrote to Hay, congratulating the co-authors for their "comprehension and treatment" of the subject and beseeching them to allow the *Century* to be their publisher: "If the Century can accomplish this I will consider it one of its proudest achievements. . . . As great as Lincoln's . . . hold upon the present and the future, the work of yours and Nicolay will strengthen this hold, will lift him still higher above the group of great men about him, and will widen and deepen the lesson of his pure life and extend its influence upon the character of men and the whole course of history." When Gilder offered $50,000, an extraordinary sum, for the serial and book rights, Hay and Nicolay accepted.

The first excerpt was scheduled for November 1886. They would have to write the remaining chapters—roughly half the biography—at a pace that would keep them ahead of the serial.

With publication now imminent, Hay was more aware than ever that he was writing to render the fullest possible honor to Lincoln. Accordingly, he sent a chapter to Nicolay, asking his opinion: "I want you to say with entire frankness whether you think it is up to the mark, of course I mean up to our mark. I don't compare it with Gibbon or Thucydides. As to style, arrangement, effect, am I, in your opinion, holding my own?"

In fact he *was* thinking of Gibbon and Thucydides, for he knew that the chapter he sent Nicolay was one of the most forceful in the entire biography. It was the one in which he damned George McClellan for his craven conduct during the Second Battle of Bull Run in September 1862. With great care and long-simmering animus, Hay detailed how McClellan's spiteful recalcitrance had left General John Pope's Army of Virginia to face the full fury of Robert E. Lee. He attacked McClellan's assertion that Lincoln had regarded Washington as all but lost after the battle and that McClellan was the only person who could save it. By the end of the chapter, Hay had succeeded in reducing McClellan's self-aggrandizing account of these events to contemptible fiction.

Yet while he had waited more than twenty years to prosecute his case against McClellan, once the moment arrived, he recognized that vengeance was best served cold. "I think I have left the impression of [McClellan's] mutinous infidelity," he told Nicolay, "and I have done it in a perfectly courteous manner. . . . It is of the utmost moment that we should seem fair to him, while we are destroying him."

Nicolay had crossed the line of courtesy at least once in his own chapters, suggesting that Robert E. Lee ought to have faced a firing squad. Hay reminded his colleague that, even while settling old scores, they ought to give the impression that they were above the fray: "We must not show ourselves to the public in the attitude of two old dotards fighting over again the politics of their youth. . . . [W]e ought to write the history of those times like two everlasting angels—who know everything, judge everything, tell the truth about everything and don't care a twang of their harps about one side or the other."

Still, he added, there was one prejudice they need never repress: "We are Lincoln men all the way through."

HAY CAME TO WASHINGTON several times that winter and spring, scheduling meetings with Nicolay and sessions with his architect. He was frustrated by the slow progress and soaring expense of the house, but Richardson assured him that it would be finished by the end of the year.

Hay and Nicolay were too busy to make it back to Colorado that summer. Instead, Hay and Clarence King made a trip to New Hampshire in September to look at property. They were particularly taken with the country surrounding Lake Winnipesaukee and Lake Sunapee. Hay wrote to Adams, proposing that the Five of Hearts "seize a hill or two" for a summer retreat.

But Adams and Clover were having a hard enough time holding on to each other, much less their friends. When Clover's father, Dr. Robert Hooper, died in April, she had fallen into a depression that Adams was helpless to alleviate. The "Voltaire in petticoats" who once had dubbed Chester Arthur "our chuckle-headed sovereign" and said of Henry James, "[H]e chaws more than he bites off," lost both her humor and vigor and shrank from society.

Those who search for clues to Clover's collapse inevitably parse the pages of *Esther*, a novel Adams published a year earlier under the pseudonym Frances Snow Compton. The book sold few copies, and Adams had no difficulty keeping his secret from an indifferent public. Hay and King did not read it until two years later.

Esther Dudley is a free-thinking artist who is given the chance to paint one of the frescoes in a new church (similar to Richardson's Trinity Church in Boston), where she tangles aesthetically with the church's principal artist (inspired by Adams's friend John La Farge, whose work decorates Trinity Church) and theologically with the church's minister (of the same cloth as Phillips Brooks, another Adams friend). Stirring the mix is Esther's cousin, the picaresque paleontologist George Strong, who bears an uncanny likeness to Clarence King.

The story of *Esther*, denser than *Democracy*, is a scaffold from which Adams paints his own philosophical frescoes on religion and science, faith and atheism, intellect and instinct, masculinity and femininity. Esther nurses her ailing father until his death—this written two years before Clover did the same for her father. In her grief, Esther becomes a "wandering soul, lost in infinite space. . . . She said to herself that youth was gone. What was she to do with middle-life?"

There are many more similarities between Clover and Esther. Wharton, the artist, describes Esther's "bad figure" and "imperfect" features. "She is too slight, too thin; she looks fragile, willowy. . . . She gives one the idea of a lightly-sparred yacht in mid-ocean; unexpected; you ask yourself what the devil she is doing there. She sails gayly along, though there is no land in sight and plenty of rough water coming." Esther does her best to stand up to the "impalpable tyranny" of the men who press upon her their notions of God and art and truth. Yet she nonetheless finds herself desiring masculine approval. Strong, the King stand-in, quips, "Once in harness she will be kind and gentle, a little tender-mouthed perhaps, and apt to shy at first, but thorough-bred."

It was almost as if Adams had dug through one of his old letters describing Clover. "She is certainly not handsome," he had written to an English friend in 1872, "nor would she be quite called plain. . . . She is very open to instruction. *We* shall improve her. She dresses badly. She decidedly has humor and will appreciate *our* wit."

If Esther is not Clover precisely, then perhaps a kinder observation is that Clover informs Esther. In this sense it can also be said that neither one was necessarily intended as a deprecation of the other, for in the end Esther passes the test, rejecting the domineering beliefs—and proposals—of her suitors and declaring, "Is it not enough to know myself?"

Clover, too, had triumphed, Adams believed, at least until her depression hit. Like Madeleine Lee in *Democracy*, she overcame "a woman's natural tendency toward asceticism, self-extinction, self-abnegation." He was truly proud of his wife's eccentricity and independence. "How did I ever hit on the only woman in the world who fits my cravings and never sounds hollow anywhere?" he asked.

As for his suggestion that Clover or Esther was in need of "harness" or improvement, in *Esther* Adams acknowledged that men fumbled at playing Pygmalion and needed the guidance of women just as badly: "The business of educating their husbands will take all the rest of their lives." In her droller days, Clover also appreciated that the shortcomings of marriage were not solely the woman's fault. "Lot's wife . . . would have had a sweeter old age and been a pillar of strength to her reprehensible husband," she joked in 1883, as she turned forty, "but I suppose she looked back because with such a mate she had nothing to look forward to."

Yet Clover did have much to look forward to. Beside the new house, in which she had shown great interest until the illness and death of her father, she had mastered photography, taking thoughtful portraits of her parents, her husband, the family dogs, H. H. Richardson, John La Farge, and the historians Francis Parkman and George Bancroft. She also seemed content in her marriage, although it was true that her husband could be prickly and undemonstrative. "As it is now thirteen years since my last letter to you, possibly you have forgotten my name," he had written while she was in Boston caring for her father. "If so, please try and recall it. For a time we were somewhat intimate." Adams was, in this instance, being facetious; until the spring of 1885 they had been virtually inseparable, and after Clover lost her grip, Adams's devotion, by all evidences, was steadfast. "Henry is more patient and loving than words can express," she vouched. "God might envy him— he bears and hopes and despairs hour after hour."

Her decline would be blamed variously on infertility, menopause, and an inherited tendency toward melancholy. Still, no one will ever know which factors carried Clover to the brink and beyond. On November 29, Adams wrote to Robert Cunliffe, "My wife . . . has been, as it were, a good deal off her feed this summer, and shows no fancy for mending as I could wish."

On December 4, Clover was able to pull herself together to bring a bouquet of roses to Lizzie Cameron, who was pregnant and abed with morning sickness. Two days later, a Sunday morning, while Adams had stepped out of the house, she took her life by drinking potassium cyanide, one of her photographic chemicals. In a letter she left for her sister, she despaired: "If I had one single point of character or goodness I would stand on that and grow back to life." Unlike Esther, she no longer believed in herself, or in anything at all.

The funeral on the ninth was for family only. Hay happened to be in New York with King that day and was frustrated to be so far away from their friend at such a sad time. "I can neither talk to you nor keep silent," he wrote Adams. "The darkness in which you walk has its shadow for me also. You and your wife were more to me than any other two. I came to Washington because you were there. And now the goodly fellowship is broken up forever. I cannot force on a man like you the commonplaces of condolence. In the presence of a sorrow like yours, it is little for your friends to say they love you and sympathize with you—but it is all anybody can say. Everything else is mere words. Is it any consolation to remember her as she was? that bright intrepid spirit, that keen fine intellect, that lofty scorn of all that was mean, that social charm which made your house such a one as Washington never knew before, and made hundreds of people love her as much as they admired her. No, that makes it all so much harder to bear."

Adams was devastated but held his chin up. "Nothing you can do," he wrote Hay, "will affect the fact that I am alone in the world at a time in life when too young to die and too old to take up existence afresh; but after the first feeling of desperation is over, there will be much that you can do to make my struggle easier. I am going to keep straight on, just as we planned it together, and unless I break in health, I shall recover strength and courage before long. If you want to help me, hurry on your house, and get into it. With you to fall back on, I shall have one more support."

IN HIS GRIEF, ADAMS also drew closer to the Camerons, especially Lizzie. He and Clover had seen quite a bit of their Washington neighbors in recent years. Adams found he could put up with Cameron because he enjoyed the company of his young wife. In 1883 he had written to Hay: "Don is behaving himself again. . . . We were asked to a charming dinner there the other evening, and I am now tame cat round the house. Don and I stroll round with our arms round each other's necks. I should prefer to accompany Mrs. Don in that attitude, but he insists on my loving him for his own sake."

Yet three months later, when the Camerons were preparing a trip to England, Adams declined to write letters of introduction, as he had done for Hay and King. "I . . . cannot saddle my friends with Don," he confided to Hay. "I adore her [Lizzie] and respect the way she has kept herself out of scandal and mud, and done her duty by the lump of clay she promised to love and respect. . . . [I]f you can tell our friends to show *her* kindness, pray do so."

After the Camerons departed, Adams wrote Lizzie, "The dogs wept all the morning. . . . The town is deserted without you."

Clover may possibly have grown jealous of her husband's attentions to their lively neighbor, fourteen years younger than she and nineteen years younger than Adams. Then, too, she might have felt a twinge of envy in November, when Lizzie returned from California and revealed she was to have a baby. Still, the roses that Clover delivered two days before her suicide were surely a token of sympathy and kindness. Whatever further understanding was reached by the two women, one morbidly depressed, the other nauseous and unhappily married, will never be known. The flowers were still on Lizzie's bedside table when she learned about Clover.

Adams was touched by the letter of condolence he received from Don Cameron, but instead of responding directly to its author, he wrote to Lizzie. He invited her to show his letter to her husband, but plainly she was the one he wanted to reach. "All I can now ask is that you will take care of yourself and get well," he implored. "All Clover's friends have now infinite value for me. I have got to live henceforward on what I can save from the wreck of my life, and it is lucky for me that she has no friends but the best and truest."

Two weeks later, he sent Lizzie a piece of Clover's jewelry. "Will you keep it," he asked, "and sometimes wear it, to remind you of her?" Grieving and alone, he also hoped the present would connect Lizzie more closely to him. Beyond what he had said in his most recent letter, he chose to think of Lizzie as not just Clover's friend, but now very much his own.

ADAMS MOVED INTO THE new house three weeks after burying his wife. The Hays' house, twice as large, was not yet ready, though Richardson tried to persuade them to take occupancy immediately, "even if it does necessitate some little picnicking and even discomfort in the beginning." Had Clover not died, Hay would have preferred to wait until spring. But out of concern for his stricken friend, he arrived in Washington on January 26, 1886, followed by the rest of the family a week later. Clara could not have been thrilled to be uprooted from Cleveland in the dead of winter, and evidently there was no talk of giving up Euclid Avenue any time soon. That was one thing she would not permit. They bought separate furnishings for the new house, and in the coming years they would fill it with an extraordinary collection of art, antiques, rugs, and bric-à-brac.

The two houses were more siblings than twins, each tailored to the personality of its respective owner. Both had three stories and were faced in red brick, with Ohio sandstone at street level. Adams's entranceway, which fronted on Lafayette Square and the White House, was set back from the street beneath a stern archway of carved stone; the first floor had a study and a library, but no parlor—an arrangement that allowed Adams to gaze directly on the affairs of the capital while guarding his privacy.

Hay's house was more of a public monument, commanding the corner of H and 16th with a castlelike turret. Its high-arched entrance was on scale with a train tunnel. The exterior was modestly adorned, like Adams's; not so the interior. The front hall and stairway were even more finely crafted and more splendid than the woodwork of the Cleveland house; the ceiling was coffered in gold leaf. The dining room was exquisite, its crown jewel a fireplace of emerald green marble called Royal Irish of Galway. "It looks like *under* the sea," Lizzie Cameron wrote gaily to Clara, "and we'll all have to dress like mermaids with funny tails."

The parlor had two kinds of stonework: an African marble called Aurora Pompadour and a Mexican onyx. "I have forgotten the name of the hall fireplace," Hay would write many years later to his daughter Helen, as she prepared to build her own house. "[It] is a pink tinge, you remember. In the library the fireplace is yellow, and the hearth is a reddish porphyry. The name they called it, I think, was 'Boisé d'Orient.'" Upstairs were five capacious bedrooms. The servants lived on the third floor; the kitchen, laundry, and furnace were in the basement. Washington could boast a number of houses that were grander, but, at 12,000 square feet, Hay's was the biggest on Lafayette Square, unless one counted the White House.

From his richly appointed parlor and library, he could look across H Street, across the park with its rocking-horse statue of Andrew Jackson, across Pennsylvania Avenue, to the house into which he had moved twenty-five years earlier. From his bedroom he could see the light in the window of the room he had shared with Nicolay.

The nearness made a difference. One of the reasons for moving to Washington this time, besides his friendship with Adams, was to complete his work with Nicolay. They had many chapters yet to write, but they knew what they had done so far was good and reputable, and that the end was within sight. This was the land of their Lincoln, and they were bringing his story home.

FOR NICOLAY, HOWEVER, THE path darkened abruptly. On November 25, eleven days before Clover Adams's suicide, Therena Nicolay—the sweetheart from Illinois who had waited out the war to get married, then accompanied her husband to Paris, where their daughter was born, and afterward worked as his assistant during all the years of research and writing—died at home on B Street after a short illness. "Now I am sundered from the past by a chasm which can never be bridged," Nicolay wrote Hay on the day of Therena's death. "How I may walk in the twin shadows of conscious age and loneliness is more than my oppressed heart can now divine."

Yet even in his misery, Nicolay's mind did not drift far from the Lincoln biography. "[A]n additional and immediate loss will be the absence of her cheer and help in our work," he reflected. "If our volumes ever reach the full dignity of the binder's art, they will be in some degree a monument to her zeal and labor as well as our own."

Early in the new year, Hay decided he had better send a letter to Robert Lincoln to assure him that all suggestions on revision had been heeded and, beyond that, to let their patron know that his and Nicolay's resolve had not flagged. "I do not know that Nicolay has told you what Gilder of the Century Co. thinks of the work," he wrote. "He is enormously struck with the whole thing—says Lincoln was a veiled statue before this and . . . that 'even if we died now, and left the book as it is, it would still be the most historical book of the time,' and etc., etc. I say this not to blow our own trumpet, but I hope it will please you to think the long toil has not been thrown away. We have been making great progress for the last year or two. . . . If we live two years more, we shall get through."

Two on the Terrace

When Henry Adams returned from Europe after the Civil War, he had described Washington as nothing more than a "happy village . . . a mere political camp." Within a few hundred yards of the Jackson monument on Lafayette Square, one could find "all one's acquaintances," and, "in four-and-twenty hours," one could "know everybody." Twenty years on, as Adams and the Hays settled into their handsome new houses, the city possessed considerably greater sophistication and boasted two hundred thousand residents; yet the same sense of intimacy prevailed. Nearly everyone with whom Adams and the Hays mixed lived either on the square or in the surrounding blocks.

History haunted the Federal-style row houses that framed the six-acre park. Dolley Madison, Daniel Webster, sundry Supreme Court justices, various vice presidents, and several of Lincoln's cabinet members had lived on Lafayette Square. Charles Guiteau had stalked President Garfield here. A house once occupied by Henry Clay and then Martin Van Buren became the home of Edward F. Beale, whose daughter, Emily, bore a striking resemblance to one of the characters in *Democracy*. General McClellan had rudely kept President Lincoln waiting in his Lafayette Square parlor. A few doors away had lived Colonel Henry Rathbone, who was stabbed by John Wilkes Booth at Ford's Theatre; on that same night, on the east side of the square, in a house that would eventually be occupied by James Blaine, one of Booth's accomplices tried to murder William Seward. And none of the residents of the square, whether old or recent, would ever forget their notorious neighbor, Daniel Sickles, who in 1859 strode from his house and shot Philip Barton Key for trysting with his wife; mortally wounded, Key was carried into the house of Benjamin Tayloe, and he is said to haunt it still. In 1886, the Tayloe House at 21 Madison Place became the home of Senator Don Cameron, his wife Lizzie, and their new baby.

Just as Lafayette Square was the hub of Washington culture, it also reflected its social hierarchy. Hardly anyone who lived on the square was *from* Washington, and while many made their money in Washington, few made a fortune. Henry James, who had been a guest of Henry and Clover Adams in 1882, observed that "Washington is the place in the world where money—or the absence of it—matters least."

Which was not to say that the city lacked wealth. Hay and Adams's neighbor William Corcoran was as flush as any robber baron. Money meant power in Washington; it always had and always would. It bought legislation, contracts, commissions, and the very souls of public servants. Yet, at the same time, the rungs of Washington society were not automatically measured by rich-versus-richer or old money–versus–new, as they were in, say, New York or Adams's Boston. In Washington, the venerable were often vulnerable; the pecking order was reconfigured with every election. Hay and Adams needed only to look out of their windows to watch this sometimes subtle, often brazen game of succession and survival being played out. The difference between the two friends was that Hay regarded himself as a participant, while Adams insisted, with his customary hauteur, that he wished only to be a spectator.

Perhaps because of the capital's inherent volatility, Hay and Adams chose to live there without actually putting down roots. Now a widower, Adams yearned to take his sorrow abroad as soon as he finished the last volume of his Madison and Jefferson histories. Hay, once he and Nicolay were done with Lincoln, would fall into a migratory pattern that continued for the next eleven years. Until he became secretary of state in 1898, he never spent more than seven months of any given year on Lafayette

Square, which was better than he could say for Cleveland. Although he and Clara would own and maintain the house on Euclid Avenue for the rest of his life, he never again spent more than a few weeks a year there.

He and Nicolay worked diligently throughout the winter, spring, and early summer of 1886, and then in July, he and Clara, with Clarence King in tow, went to New Hampshire to look more closely at farms surrounding Lake Sunapee, a landscape that had charmed Hay so thoroughly the year before. He knew all too well from his years in the White House just how muggy and malarial Washington could be in the summer; government slowed to a crawl, and those who could escape the capital did so with determination. At Nicolay's instigation, Hay had considered Colorado as a possible retreat, and, though his enthusiasm had waned, he had gone in with Nicolay and purchased several acres near Pike's Peak anyway. The deal had come up just as Nicolay's wife was dying, and Hay hadn't the heart to back out.

Sunapee was much closer and, to Hay's eye, every bit as gorgeous as the Rockies. He already had in mind a colony of sorts. The Five of Hearts, who, since their whimsical consecration in New York in 1881 had never again been together in one place at one time, were now four, and Hay, with King's enthusiastic if impecunious encouragement, envisioned sharing summers together in the regenerative air and maple-cloaked hills of New Hampshire. A rail line had recently been completed to the town of Newbury, and the hardscrabble farms along the lake could now be reached from Boston in a morning and from New York in a single day.

Hay, Clara, and King "fell daft over the Lake," Hay wrote Adams. "This time we seriously concluded to buy a farm." He suggested to Adams that he sell his house in Beverly Farms, Massachusetts, and throw in with the remaining Hearts. King pictured three writers' studios, side by side. Hay was so sanguine that he wrote also to William Dean Howells, urging him to join their conclave. "[W]e will give you an acre or two for nothing for the pleasure of your wit and wisdom," he tempted. King, it went without saying, was unable to follow through, and Adams and Howells never committed, either. Hay and Clara would take two more years to settle upon just the right farm, but at Lake Sunapee they knew they had found their sanctuary.

•   •   •

OF MORE IMMEDIATE FOCUS was the start-up of the Lincoln serial in the *Century*. To alert the magazine's quarter-million readers to the cavalcade of chapters that was about to dominate the pages of the magazine for the next three years and more, Gilder prevailed upon Clarence King to write a profile of the co-authors for the October 1886 issue. "As to Lincoln, what the world thirsts for is the truth, the whole truth, and nothing but the truth," King ballyhooed. "From the hands of John George Nicolay and John Hay we shall have *all* that."

Expectations ran high for the first and only authorized biography of the Martyred President, and early reaction was immensely positive. "There is every sign in the first installment [written by Hay] of a noble chapter of American history told man-fashion," *The Nation* complimented. Old and loyal friends were quick to send their salutations. "Lincoln lives again," John Bigelow wrote to Hay, "and, as in prior times, you & Nicolay live with him, never again, however, to be separated in history." Howells thought the early pages "easy, dignified, without solemnity, and extremely interesting; the frankness is just what it should be."

Yet as the serial continued, the nitpickers and sour grape eaters came forward. Lincoln's law partner, William Herndon, who had provided the grist for Ward Hill Lamon's revelatory biography, was "astonished at the length and dullness" of the second installment in the *Century*. "If *that* article is a sample of *what is to come*, I make a prediction that the whole thing will fall still born," he belittled. He was flabbergasted that Hay and Nicolay had suppressed many of the most important episodes of Lincoln's life—"the Ann Rutledge story—L's religion—L's insanity—the facts of L's misery with Mary Todd—L's *break down* on the night that he & Mary Todd were to be married &c &c." To Herndon's biased eye, "N & H handle things with silken gloves & 'a camel hair pencil': they do not write with an iron pen."

Even Gilder, whose praise for the biography had once been unqualified, now saw room for improvement and concision. One day at the Century Association in New York he ran into the sculptor Augustus Saint-Gaudens, a fellow Lincoln worshipper who had carved one of the nation's most superb Lincoln monuments—relying, as it happened, on a cast of Lincoln's face that had been loaned to him by Hay. It stung Gilder to hear Saint-Gaudens, of all people, complain "how damn partisan" the Lincoln biography was getting. Gilder took the criticism to heart and urged the authors to condense or omit passages in forthcoming installments that might rankle any "actors" still alive and, in general, he begged them "to err on the side of calmness of tone & generosity" as they readied the proofs for publication.

At this point, Hay was too frazzled to care. As far as he was concerned, Gilder could cut any parts or entire chapters he wished, "provided we were to do nothing in the way of re-writing." He estimated that he had sufficient energy to finish ten more chapters, taking the narrative up through Sherman's March to the Sea and Sheridan's campaign in the Shenandoah—the end of what would be the ninth volume of the ten-volume biography. In early June, he, Clara, and the children were to sail to England for the celebration of the Golden Jubilee of Queen Victoria. The rest of the book would have to wait till his return.

HAY AND CLARA LOVED England more with each visit. They took a room along the parade route and watched the queen roll past in her gilded landau, accompanied by fifty foreign heads of state and a panoply of princes in their finest plumage. By now the Hays were fluent in the peerage and protocol of the British Empire. They knew which gloves and hat to wear on which occasions, and Clara no longer wrote to her mother, describing how the toast was served at breakfast. They received invitations to Buckingham Palace, the House of Commons, and a series of teas at Wimbledon. They dined with Henry James and visited the studios of Edwin Abbey and another American painter, Francis Millet. Leaving the children with their nurse at Folkestone, on the Channel, they made their customary rounds of the Cunliffes in Wales and the Clarks in Scotland. They also spent two days with the steel tycoon Andrew Carnegie, who was renting a castle in the Scottish Highlands while he looked for one to buy. Hay told Nicolay, "I have been passing the idlest summer of my life," although it scarcely seemed that way.

They sailed for home the first week in September, well refreshed by another amiable tour of the country they enjoyed every bit as much as their own.

Upon landing, they went directly to Cleveland, an autumn routine that Clara insisted upon. Hay established another seasonal tradition, joining the Winous Point Shooting Club, west of Cleveland. The membership comprised two or three dozen of Cleveland's ruling class, who each fall traded the comfort of Euclid Avenue for an austere (though amply staffed) barracks and the infamous inclemency of Lake Erie. Each day local marsh men poled them into the reeds along Sandusky Bay to hunt ducks seduced by their decoys. Hay readily admitted that his aim was erratic, but he tried never to miss a year at Winous Point. When the shooting was good, he proudly sent the harvest of his marksmanship to the kitchens of his friends in Washington and New York.

By mid-November, he was back in Washington. The season did not officially commence until January, but Congress opened its session in December, filling the capital and energizing the table talk. The presidential primaries were only a few months away, and already the handicappers were speculating on who would be given the chance to unseat Grover Cleveland. Hay had at last given up on Blaine and was poised to back Senator John Sherman of Ohio, whom he regarded as "thoroughly fit for power," despite his "lack of magnetism." Sherman, of course, was Lizzie Cameron's uncle.

IF THE ELECTION WAS the main event, a much smaller but no less absorbing side show was taking shape on Lafayette Square: Henry Adams had fallen for Lizzie.

After Clover's death, while Lizzie was pregnant, Adams had put his wife's affairs in order and then gone off to Japan with John La Farge for several months. He was in the middle of the Pacific on June 25, when Lizzie's baby girl was born. She had wanted to name her Marian—Clover's Christian name—but dared not do so without Adams's permission. Instead, she chose Martha.

Before he sailed, Adams had invited Lizzie to spend the summer at his house in Beverly Farms. She accepted—without needing to explain, in writing at least, why she preferred the Adams homestead to one of the fully staffed, palatial Cameron estates in Pennsylvania. (Don Cameron's other children, by his previous marriage, had grown and were living elsewhere.) "I little thought when I said goodbye to you in Washington," Lizzie wrote Adams in August, "that my first letter would be written from your own home. . . . I felt in an hour's time as if we had always been here. . . . The little baby—I present Martha to you, dear Mr. Adams— lives under the pine trees and is growing strong and big and I lie on the piazza and watch the sea." She would return to Beverly Farms for many summers thereafter.

Adams came back to Washington in November and found the three Camerons—Don, Lizzie, and Martha—settled in their newly refurbished house on Lafayette Square. Adams, who loved all children and spoiled his many nieces and nephews, became devoted to Martha. Through her, he found a way to channel his affections for Lizzie. Mother and daughter were often out and about in the square, and it was hardly unseemly for Adams, a balding, avuncular fifty-year-old, to invite them into his library. He began stocking a desk drawer with chocolate drops and ginger snaps and turned a closet into a trove of dolls and picture books. As Martha learned to talk, which she did precociously, she gave Adams the nickname "Dobbitt" and later "Dordy." Soon he took to writing her directly, though she could not yet read—"Mr. Dobbitt has much pleasure in accepting Miss Martha Cameron's very kind invitation for this afternoon, and begs to send flowers for her table"—his words and affections intended for more than one member of the Cameron household.

His conduct was all very chivalrous. Martha was a great balm to his loneliness and childlessness, and his affection for her was genuine. While he was increasingly enchanted by Lizzie, she was, after all, a married woman who cared very much about appearances and the advantages that came with being the wife of a rich and powerful senator. Yet she found comfort in Adams's benevolence and doubtless unloaded upon him the unhappy circumstances of her marriage. Over time, he grew more protective of her and occasionally allowed his jealousy to show. But never did he pry, never was he judgmental, and in this way he won her confidence and gratitude. Always he told her that it was she who lifted his spirits. And if truth be told, he was putty in her hands.

Don Cameron was not exactly an attentive or observant husband; for the most part, he seems to have treated Lizzie as uxorial ornament and granted her extraordinary latitude, so long as she continued to perform her public duties with poise and propriety. Out of indifference or ignorance, he noticed nothing untoward in the attachment of Adams to his wife and daughter. Privately, Adams regarded Cameron as an ineffectual philistine, despite his political rank and heritage. Even so, he was conscientiously respectful and indulgent toward the plodding Pennsylvanian and careful to honor the outward decorum of the marriage. He addressed Lizzie respectfully as "Mrs. Cameron," or, when writing to Hay and other friends, as "Mrs. Don" or "La Dona." She belonged to the senator, just as Adams was still attached to the memory of Clover.

When the Camerons returned to Adams's house at Beverly Farms in the summer of 1887, he did not disturb them, choosing to pass much of the summer at Quincy—which was south of Boston; Beverly was north—working on the last of his histories. The rules seemed awkward, but they prevented injury and embarrassment to all concerned. Still, Adams wrote Lizzie regularly and was not too timid to admit, "I am homesick to see you." When Martha was barely two years old, Dobbitt confessed to her: "I love you very much, and think of you a great deal, and want you all the time. I should have run away from here, and looked for you all over the world, long ago, only I've grown too stout for the beautiful clothes I used to wear when I was a young prince in the fairy-stories, and I've lost the feathers out of my hat. . . . So I can't come after you, and feel very sad about it. If you would only come and see me, as Princess Beauty came to see Prince Beast, we would go down to the beach and dig holes in the sand. . . . I am very dull and stupid without you; and have no one but old people to live with."

John Hay was aware of the growing intimacy between his two neighbors, and certainly Lizzie's charms were not lost on him, either. He and Adams reported on Mrs. Don and her movements like worshippers at the same temple. Hay related to Adams after a dinner party that "Mrs. Cameron . . . was looking prettier than ever." After he and Adams encountered Martha on the street, Adams wrote to Lizzie, "[We] bowed as meekly to her will as we do to that of her mother."

Hay, though, was somewhat more brazen than his neighbor. Once, when Adams was still in Japan and Clara was in Cleveland, he was alone in Washington and thrilled to be asked to dinner by Lizzie. "Your invitation is seductive to a cookless wanderer," he wrote her. "My trouble, however, is not so much one of food as of a sentimental wish to see you again and hear of your welfare." This was all just playful posturing, but there were few women he would have addressed with such bravura.

AT THE SAME TIME that Adams—and now Hay—were falling under the spell of Lizzie Cameron, Clarence King was taking a much more dramatic, and secretive, plunge. Hay and Adams had long since grown accustomed to their friend's long silences and unpredictable appearances. He seemed to have no fixed address, choosing to receive his mail at the Century, the Knickerbocker, or one of several other clubs to which he belonged. He was at best a sporadic correspondent, and on the occasions he did write, his letters gave only sketchy clues to his whereabouts. "I think he must have joined some oath bound order which pledged him, under fearful sanctions, never to tell anybody anything," an exasperated Hay caviled to Adams. Describing a rare and unexpected King encounter, Hay again wrote Adams: "Yesterday morning I went to King's office [in New York] and asked if they had any tidings of him. They said he was in [Nevada] and might be home in a week or a month. I went to the Hotel and there, in the midst of the shrimps, sat King."

Trips to the Sierras or Mexico did not fully explain King's chronic disappearances. Nor did his desire to dodge the debt collectors, of whom there were many, as his mining ventures collapsed one after the other and he continued his princely lifestyle. What none of his friends realized was that King was living a double life.

Over the years, King had disarmed his share of women with his mountaineer's physique, sweet smile, and gift for conversation. But, he confided to Adams, his sexual appetites were particular: "To kiss a woman and feel teeth through her thin lips paralyzes me for a week." By thin lips, he meant those belonging to white women. "If he had a choice," Adams revealed, "it was in favor of Indians and negroes."

Ever the scientist, King had collected a bounty of data on women of diverse race and physiognomy. On his geological expeditions in the West and to Mexico, most of his encounters were with women of darker skin or shadier conduct. On a voyage to Hawaii, he admired the "old-gold" natives, and in London his companions blushed at King's enthusiasm for conducting "studies of the lower strata." During the summer of 1887, King told Hay, "Man in the process of transit from his Archaic state to his very best forms of culture tires me. I like him at the start and at the finish. Woman, I am ashamed to say, I like in the primitive state."

Sometime that year or the next, King met Ada Copeland, a thirty-seven-year-old African-American born into slavery, who was working as a domestic servant in New York. Despite his fair complexion and what William Dean Howells described as his "blithe blue eyes," King convinced her that he too was black—light-skinned, but black. He gave his name as James Todd and told her he was a Pullman porter from Baltimore. And she believed him.

They were secretly married in September 1888. Their first child was born the following year. "Miscegenation is the hope of the white race," King once told a friend. For the rest of his days, his own experiment in interracial living would require long absences and a great deal of lying. When his gentrified friends assumed he was off mining minerals or investors, he may have been no farther away than a working-class precinct of Manhattan in the arms of Ada; and his fictive job as railroad porter put him out of her reach for long stretches, which he apparently regretted as much as she. In one of the only letters between them that survives, he wrote: "I thank God that even if I am forced to travel and labor far away from you [I] have the daily comfort of remembering that far away in the east there is a dear brown woman who loves me and whom I love beyond the power of words to describe."

As Ada's dependency on King increased, so too did King's dependency on Hay, Adams, and others. Beginning in 1888, when King (or James Todd) took Ada as his wife, he began borrowing money from them: first $6,000, then $11,000; no one knows how much more. "[N]ow in middle age I am poor," he lamented to Adams, "and what is worse so absorbed in the hand to mouth struggle for income that I see the effective literary and scientific years drifting by empty and blank."

IN MAY 1888, THE Hays made a hurried trip to New Hampshire and at last bought the farm on Lake Sunapee, the first of several parcels of rocky pasture and woodland they were to acquire. King described it to Adams as "a rough fell land full [of] admirable trees & rough strewn boulders." The geologist knew his terminology: a fell is a high, barren field. And so the farm was named "the Fells."

After New Hampshire, Hay went on to Chicago for the Republican Convention. He and Whitelaw Reid once again joined forces, this time behind Senator John Sherman. Instead, the nomination went to Senator Benjamin Harrison of Indiana, a well-spoken, if uncharismatic Civil War veteran and grandson of President William Henry ("Tippecanoe") Harrison.

Hay would have preferred to be in London that summer, but instead he decided to take the family to Colorado. There was no suitable house on the property he and Nicolay had purchased at the foot of Pike's Peak, so the Hays lodged in a hotel in nearby Manitou Springs. The children had a splendid time. Thirteen-year-old Helen and twelve-year old Del galloped horses at "Buffalo Bill speed," and the younger two—eight-year-old Alice and three-year-old Clarence—rode about in a donkey cart. Hay, however, felt "under par," whether from "air, or water, or age, or total depravity" he could not say. He told Nicolay he would "never again have the courage" to return to Colorado and offered to sell him his share at a bargain rate.

Adding to his discontent that summer was a series of annoying letters from the editors of the *Century*. As the chapters chronicling the battles of the war—the majority written by Hay—were serialized in the magazine, the editors who had overseen the immensely popular series "Battles and Leaders of the Civil War" complained that Hay and Nicolay were plowing old ground "after the wheat had been threshed so exhaustively." They also pronounced Hay and Nicolay's expertise as military historians "inadequate." "I assure you that they are extremely anxious about the matter," Richard Watson Gilder wrote Nicolay. "They feel that it would never do to let [these chapters] go out as now written." He then issued an ultimatum: "cut the military portion down to a smaller scale," or it would be done for them.

Hay offered no resistance. "Leave out anything you like in the Magazine. . . . [C]huck it all over board," he replied to Gilder. To Nicolay he griped, "I am perfectly willing to have him cut out every military chapter I have written. I am sick of the subject." The chapters were trimmed for the magazine but reinstated in the book.

Following the customary stopover in Cleveland and a week of duck shooting, Hay returned to Washington. He arrived just after the election, in which Harrison unseated Grover Cleveland. Hay did not know Harrison well, though he had sent a $1,000 check to the campaign, and on a whim he had invited Harrison to join him at the duck club. (Harrison declined.) Hay disavowed rumors that he was in the running to be minister to England; instead, he met with Harrison and touted Whitelaw Reid for the job. Harrison had his own ideas and dispatched Hay to New York to persuade Reid to accept France instead. Reid said yes, chewing on his disappointment as the London mission went to Robert Lincoln. James Blaine was named secretary of state, for the second time.

For all his disdain for the groveling and pandering that went with office-seeking, Hay loved observing the game and enjoyed even more playing the role of broker. After doing what he could on Reid's behalf, he urged Robert Lincoln to retain his friend Henry White as secretary of the London legation. He also advocated on behalf of William McKinley as the next Speaker of the House. McKinley, a sober, forty-seven-year-old congressman from Canton, Ohio, was the party's leading spokesman for protective tariffs, the wedge issue that had toppled Cleveland. Although Thomas Reed of Maine ultimately beat out McKinley for the speakership, McKinley was now a force to be reckoned with. So, too, was Mark Hanna, the savvy fund-raiser and strategist whose labors on behalf of McKinley would eventually make the latter president and himself successor to John Sherman in the Senate. By lending these two Ohioans his support in 1888, Hay laid the groundwork for his own resurgence as a statesman. In the coming years, the careers of Hay, Hanna, and McKinley would become increasingly intertwined. Hay would outlive them both, but without them he would never have gone as far as he did.

As THE HARRISON ADMINISTRATION took shape, Hay became acquainted with two other up-and-comers: Theodore Roosevelt and Henry Cabot Lodge.

He had met Theodore Roosevelt, Senior, during the Civil War and came to know the rest of the Roosevelt family during his years in New York. Roosevelt's son, Theodore Junior, puny and asthmatic as a lad, was now a fit and formidable thirty (exactly twenty years younger than Hay). He had served in the New York assembly; run (unsuccessfully) for mayor of New York; established his reputation as an author with his naval history of the War of 1812; and earned his spurs as a hunter and rancher in Dakota Territory. He had campaigned vigorously for Harrison with the hope of gaining a place in the new administration: he set his sights on assistant secretary of state, the job Hay had held ten years earlier. But the impatient, pugnacious "Teddy," who had never outgrown the high-pitched voice and pince-nez squint of his youth, would have to bide his time. Secretary of State Blaine accurately appraised Roosevelt's nature when he wrote: "My real trouble in regard to Mr. Roosevelt is that I fear he lacks the repose and patient endurance required in an Assistant Secretary. Mr. Roosevelt is amazingly quick in apprehension. Is there not danger that he might be too quick in execution?"

As a consolation, Harrison offered Roosevelt the office of civil service commissioner, where his righteous aggression might have some reformative effect on the spoils system. Roosevelt jumped at the invitation. On his modest salary of $3,500, he was able to rent a small house at Jefferson Place, a half-dozen blocks from Lafayette Square and only a few strides from the door of his closest friend in the capital, Henry Cabot Lodge, a second-term congressman from Massachusetts.

In many respects, Lodge was to Roosevelt what Hay was to Adams. Lodge and Roosevelt were ambitious young partisans, active ideologues committed to improving American government. Both were Harvard men, members of the same elite undergraduate clubs, Hasty Pudding and Porcellian. Each was the most trusted confidant of the other; their personal correspondence is as prolific and devoted as that of Hay and Adams.

Their most obvious contrast was in stature. Whereas Roosevelt was stocky and bull-necked, Lodge was long and wiry, almost frail-looking, his sharp chin accentuated by a goatee, much like Hay's. But looks were deceiving; Lodge was athletic, every bit the horseman Roosevelt was. Intellectually he gave ground to no man. He had been Henry Adams's star student at Harvard and earned both a law degree and a doctorate in history from that university. Eight years older than Roosevelt, he was the more accomplished historian, having published essays on Anglo-Saxon law and a biography of his great-grandfather Henry Cabot, a patrician friend of George Washington and Alexander Hamilton.

Unlike Roosevelt—and Adams and Hay, for that matter—Lodge was not broad in his appetites and in fact tended to be reflexively, combatively close-minded. Brahmin to the core, he had never wanted for money, and his clipped speech and haughty manner were oft-used weapons. He had "a certain ready-to-fight element" without the offsetting charm that helped restore the comparably pushy Roosevelt to the good graces of his adversaries. Margaret Chanler, who was one of Lodge's loyal friends, had to acknowledge that he was "one of those who care more for downing his adversary than for discovering some common ground for possible agreement." Lodge had little concern for what anyone thought of him. "He considers himself so far superior to the ordinary run of people," the *Saturday Evening Post* observed, "that the mere addition of another enemy to his long string means nothing to him one way or the other."

In 1889, when Benjamin Harrison was inaugurated, neither Hay nor Adams wielded any direct political power, but they were the standard-bearers of Washington gentility, the ideological brain trust in which Lodge and Roosevelt sought membership. Further on, after Lodge ascended to the Senate and Roosevelt rose all the way to the presidency, the two younger men would, between themselves, fault Hay and Adams for being too reserved, indeed too prissy, and, in Hay's case, *too* diplomatic. But at the outset, all four seemed genuinely pleased to be in one another's company. They were not the new Hearts; their age differences prevented that. But they did play similar hands. For instance, each had a book coming out: Hay, with Nicolay, had turned in the final chapters of the Lincoln biography; Adams had finished his nine-volume history of the Jefferson and Madison administrations; Lodge had written a biography of George Washington; and Roosevelt had dashed off *The Winning of the West*.

They had yet another connection, beyond literature or politics. Each of these four had made a study of greatness in American life—although they diverged in their interpretations. If there was one essential difference between the older men and the younger, it was that Hay and Adams gained wisdom and strength—and a measure of humility—as witnesses and heirs to greatness, while Roosevelt and Lodge, who had come of age after the Civil War, aspired to an ideal of greatness and heroism they knew only secondhand.

Still, their distinctions were of style more so than of substance, and socially the group gelled right away. Adams was the only one without children, and he became the uncle to the brood of Hay, Roosevelt, and Lodge offspring. The Camerons, too, were part of the circle; Senator Cameron was older than all of them, but Lizzie fit right in.

Except for Adams, they all dispersed in the summer of 1889, according to the Washington custom: the Lodges to Nahant, on the Massachusetts shore; the Roosevelts to Oyster Bay, Long Island; and the Hays to Europe for their usual rounds, this time with the added entree provided by newly installed ministers Robert Lincoln in London and Whitelaw Reid in Paris. The Camerons also went abroad that summer and saw a good deal of the Hays in London and Scotland, until the death of the senator's father summoned them home prematurely.

Back in Washington in the fall, they picked up where they had left off. Adams, who had never been very outgoing even when Clover was alive, preferred to entertain friends at home, and his "breakfasts"—brunches they would be called today—became an institution, especially among his many women friends, including, it goes without saying, Lizzie Cameron. As the social season came to a close in the spring, Adams wrote a family friend, "Our little set of Hays, Camerons, Lodges, and Roosevelts never was so intimate or friendly as now, and for the first time in my life I find myself among a set of friends so closely connected as to see each other every day, and even two or three times a day, yet surrounded by so many outside influences and pressures that they are never stagnant or dull."

HAY HAD HIS OWN reasons to feel fulfilled. The last installment of Lincoln appeared in the February 1890 issue of the *Century*, and he and Nicolay were already proofing the pages of the ten-volume edition. At a million and a half words, it was 25 percent longer than Gibbon's *Decline and Fall.* Because of its sheer bulk, the publisher decided to offer the set not in shops but through door-to-door canvassers—as Mark Twain and others did with their books. Five thousand sets sold quickly, a good response, given the cost, $50, and the fact that a million or more people had already read excerpts in the magazine.

Hay and Nicolay were by now fairly well inured to the fault-finders: *New York Sun* editor Charles Dana insisted that Hay was not with Lincoln on the night of his reelection (Hay's diary said otherwise); General Fitz-John Porter, who was court-martialed (and later exonerated) for his conduct at Second Bull Run, was incensed by Hay and Nicolay's characterization of his collusion with McClellan. "We shall not have a friend left on earth by next Fall," Hay joked to Nicolay. He admonished Nicolay, but only weakly, to soften his treatment of Jefferson Davis. "Let the facts make him as despicable as he is—*we* do not want to appear to hate and despise him. But we do, and I suppose we can't keep it from sticking out."

Meanwhile, the judgments of the critics who most mattered to them were extremely gratifying. "The labor of a generation and the affection of a lifetime have, indeed, joined in raising to the memory of the greatest American of our days a monument worthy of his fame," William Dean Howells applauded in an unattributed review in the *New York Tribune*. Defending the decision to write a "history" of Lincoln, as opposed to a "life," Howells reasoned that the subject required "elbow-room." Richard Watson Gilder, whose commitment to the book had been steadfast, though stern, was perhaps even more satisfied with the final result than were its authors. "There is no doubt in my mind, and I trust there is none in yours," he wrote Hay and Nicolay, "that the principal desire of our hearts has been gratified:—namely, that not only Lincoln's fame, for all time, has been firmly established by your labors, but that the people now living, so many of whom were also living during his lifetime, have had an opportunity of knowing the man."

Gilder dismissed charges of bias in the biography's condemnation of Lincoln's opponents. "It may be that future historians or critics . . . may be called upon to take into view the 'personal equation';—but when all is said that can possibly be said in criticism, the fact will remain that you have followed your convictions, and by your devotion and industry have presented a picture of the man, and of the times, which will have an indistinguishable value."

Henry Adams, whose quirky modesty prevented him from trumpeting his own accomplishments as a historian, saw no reason to wait for posterity to rule on Hay and Nicolay's achievement. He recommended that Harvard award Hay and Nicolay honorary doctorates for "a work the equal of which I know not in any literature." (Harvard president Charles Eliot politely disagreed. "They were actors in many of the scenes they described," he wrote Adams, "and, therefore, could not be historians.")

The praise that meant the most by far came from Robert Lincoln. By dark coincidence, while Lincoln was looking over the biography's final pages, a chapter written by Hay entitled "Lincoln's Fame," his only son, sixteen-year-old Abraham "Jack" Lincoln II, lay gravely ill. Wracked with worry, Robert was moved to muse on his relationship with his own father, recognizing just how much it had been strengthened, posthumously, by the memories and mediation of John Hay and John George Nicolay. "I have . . . the last sheets of the book," he wrote Hay in January 1890. "Without being the proper critic, I can express my delight with the last part & with the whole of the work & I shall never cease to be glad that my father had two such devoted & exceptionally competent friends as you & Nicolay to make this testimonial."

When Jack Lincoln died three months later, Hay wrote to Robert, "You can never outlive it, but we hope that time may bring you peace, and that memory, which is now nothing but pain, may even become a blessing." Perhaps he had said something quite similar to his friend twenty-five years earlier, after they had rushed from the White House and stood by each other's side at a different deathbed. The moral, anyway, was the same: One ought never attempt to blot out memory; Robert must find a way to savor the lives of his father and son, especially now that there would never be another Abraham Lincoln.

BY THE SPRING OF 1890, Hay had nothing especially pressing to do. The Lincoln odyssey was now complete—"the last kick of my expiring Pegasus," he declared. He had declined an offer to edit the *Tribune* while

Reid served in Paris. He had no role in any administration or campaign, and his business affairs—which included a stout stock portfolio and sizable commercial real estate holdings—were ably managed by a man in Cleveland. His three eldest children were in school, and the latecomer, Clarence, was well cared for by a live-in nurse.

Yet it was too soon to be bored. Adams was right next door, and Hay was surrounded and celebrated by a circle of Republican stallions: Roosevelt, Lodge, Blaine, not to mention Don Cameron. President and Mrs. Harrison welcomed him and Clara at the White House. And with the Lincoln book finished, he had more time to write other things. He turned again to poetry, pulling together an edition of some of his early work—post–"Banty Tim" and "Jim Bludso"—which, as he explained to Henry James, "I have had specially printed for my good friends and lovers." He also composed a new sonnet, "Love's Dawn," whose weary narrator discovers love after a long search:

> *In wandering through waste places of the world,*
> *I met my love and knew not she was mine. . . .*
>
> *And then one blessed day, I saw arise*
> *Love's morning, glorious, in her tranquil eyes.*

He sent the sonnet to the *Century*, though he admitted, "I am rather too old a bird to be singing in this strain."

At fifty-two, however, he was evidently not too old to be beguiled by other women. His fixation on Lizzie Cameron, while still inchoate, was ongoing, and she was not the only woman who turned his head. Sometime in 1889, and certainly by the spring of 1890, he became enamored of Nannie Lodge, the congressman's wife. Soon he and Nannie were finding ways to be together, frequently in the company of Adams and Lizzie. How far their romance progressed can only be conjectured, but for a short while they were drawn to each other, concealing their attraction from their spouses and the rest of capital society. Given the timing and the circumstances, it is hard to believe that "Love's Dawn" was written with Clara in mind.

Anna Cabot Mills was the daughter of the commandant of the Naval Observatory and a cousin of Cabot Lodge, whom she married in 1871, when both were twenty-one. While Lizzie Cameron was seductive and effervescent, Nannie Lodge's beauty was enchanting in its grace and serenity. While men tended to fawn over Lizzie, women were jealous of her, suspicious of the undercurrent of guile implicit in a marriage to a much older man. Nannie, on the other hand, was adored equally by both sexes. Theodore Roosevelt's sister, Corrine, declared that Nannie had a "fascination possessed by no other." Nannie's friend Margaret Chanler proclaimed: "Forget any praises I may have bestowed on others. She was the most charming woman I have ever known. . . . [S]he took delight in all that was delightful, yet never lost her bearings in fogs of enthusiasm."

Nannie was slim and fair; she loved poetry and played the piano well. Friends commended her wit and strength, her sweetness and gentleness. Yet it was her eyes that bewitched all those fortunate to meet their sympathetic gaze. (Were these the "tranquil eyes" of "Love's Dawn"?) Margaret Chanler described them as "the color of the sky when stars begin to twinkle." John Singer Sargent, lamenting that he had never painted Nannie's portrait, remarked, "I had such an unqualified regard for her that the odds were in favor of my succeeding in getting something of that kindness and intelligence of her expression and the unforgettable blue of her eyes."

Hay and Nannie were together often, although they found few occasions to be together alone—surrounded, as they were, by their spouses, children (Nannie had three), and social set. Still, nothing would have prevented them from engaging in pleasant, even subtly flirtatious conversation, an idiom in which Hay excelled. They were in each other's company at Adams's breakfasts, frequent dinners, and a string quartet performance at the Hay house. Hay's renewed interest in romantic verse may have been purely coincidental, but at about the same time that he submitted "Love's Dawn" to the *Century*, he wrote Henry James, "I was drinking tea this afternoon with one of the most charming women in America, Mrs. Cabot Lodge."

While Hay was being charmed by Nannie, Adams was doting on Lizzie. By the spring of 1890, Adams had made plans to sail to the

South Pacific, departing in August, to be gone for as long as a year. In the months leading up to his absence, Adams looked for every possible chance to be with Lizzie, visiting her at Beverly Farms and at Blue Mountain, in western Maryland. In Washington, they were back and forth to each other's houses and on several occasions were able to get away on walks and carriage rides. "[D]o you remember those June nights?" Lizzie wrote after he had gone. "Have you seen anything so beautiful since?"

Hay and Nannie remembered those nights, for on a number of them they, Adams, and Lizzie were a foursome. And on one particular evening the foursome divided into two separate couples. The evidence of this more intimate interlude is a poem written by Hay sometime between June and August, after a moonlit visit to the Capitol. "Two on the Terrace" describes a pair of lovers gazing, suggestively, westward down the Mall toward the Washington Monument:

> *See the white obelisk soaring*
> *To pierce the blue profound.*
> *Beneath the still heavens beaming,*
> *The lighted town lies gleaming . . .*

The narrator sees "the wide pure heaven" reflected in the eyes of his companion and exclaims:

> *Ah love! a thousand aeons*
> *Shall range their trooping years;*
> *The morning stars their paeans*
> *Shall sing to countless ears.*
> *These married states may sever,*
> *Strong Time this dome may shiver,*
> *But love shall last forever*
> *And lovers' hopes and fears.*
>
> *So let us send our greeting,*
> *A wish for trust and bliss,*

> *To future lovers meeting*
> *   On far-off nights like this.*
> *Who, in these walls' undoing*
> *Perforce of Time's rough wooing—*
> *Amid the crumbling ruin*
> *   Shall meet, clasp hands, and kiss.*

Hay showed the poem to Lizzie, and presumably to Nannie, shortly after completing it, but Adams did not read "Two on the Terrace" until it appeared in *Scribner's* a year later. By then, he was on the other side of the world. "Great Kung-fu-tse!" he wrote Lizzie. "[W]hat two? which two? for were we not four? or do I dream it? and the kiss! I can say that the pair to which I belonged, knew nothing of any kiss. If kissing there was, the other two were the sole parties of it! Is the kiss to be regarded as poetic, or is it attributed on trust to me, or was it—oh no! it would be naughty to even think it. I never could have believed that John should so compromise a trusting and lovely female. What must she think? and Mrs. Hay?"

Perhaps Adams was right, and there had been no kiss. His letter at least seems to substantiate that his relationship with Lizzie was platonic, or anyway not consummated sexually. Likewise, it is safe to surmise that Hay never got much farther than a kiss with Nannie, if in fact he got that far. Nevertheless, his admiration was real, persistent, and to a certain yet unknowable degree requited.

As for Clara's reaction, there is nothing to tell. Hay had written numerous romantic poems over the years, assuring his wife that they were merely exercises of imagination. Doubtless the sexual imagery of a white obelisk piercing "the blue profound" was lost on her. Nor would she have given second thought to her husband's phrasing, "These married states may sever," assuming he meant states of the Union and not unions of matrimony. Hay, however, was no naïf; his choice of words may have been wistful, but it was hardly accidental.

Other clues to the affair are provided in Lizzie's letters to Adams. In July, Hay, Clara, and the children went to Lake Sunapee, boarding in the town of Newbury while construction began on their new house. At the end of August, Hay and Clara met Lizzie and Nannie in Boston, followed by visits to Beverly Farms and Nahant. "John and Nannie got a little walk together," Lizzie informed Adams, "but on the whole behaved extremely well." Later in the fall, Lizzie wrote again to Adams: "Nanny and Cabot go to New York on the 10th. It is rather a coincidence that Mr. Hay must start on the same day." And in Washington the following January, Hay got Lizzie aside after a musicale and told her that Clara was going to Cleveland and that, while his wife was away, he hoped he might lunch with her and Nannie at the Washington Country Club and possibly also squire them to Mount Vernon, the theater, and "a few other quiet entertainments."

"So Friday we go to the play," Lizzie told the wayfaring Adams, "and Tuesday next to the [Country Club] and Mt. Vernon depends on the weather. But we cannot decide on the fourth man and Mr. Hay and Nannie seem to think it very stupid of us not to like anyone well enough to want to spend long hours with him."

Several short letters from Hay to Lizzie are similarly suggestive. None is fully dated. "I have asked Mrs. Lodge if she would like to go with you—if you come for her," he wrote Lizzie, arranging a rendezvous. "Would you like to do this & let me try to find somebody"—presumably a "fourth"—"or will you give it up?" On another occasion, he proffered: "Here are two tickets, for you and the mysterious but welcome fourth person. I will meet you at the Theatre."

Lizzie was aware also that Hay had written intimate letters to Nannie. After Hay's death, when Clara began collecting her husband's letters for publication, Lizzie recalled that Nannie "destroyed all hers in a panic of terror . . . in order that she could truly say she possessed no letters at all."

Yet regardless of its degree or depth, Hay and Nannie's romance broke off at the end of April 1891, when he sailed to Europe alone. By chance, Lizzie Cameron sailed two weeks later, without her husband. Before leaving Washington, she wrote Adams, somewhat speculatively and, as it turned out, inaccurately, "[Hay's] love for Nanny does not wane. I am awfully sorry for him."

Little did she anticipate that Hay's ardor was about to be transferred to her. The tryst with Nannie had lasted hardly more than a year. He would be in love with Lizzie Cameron for the rest of his life. As he had written seven years earlier in *The Bread-Winners*, describing Arthur Farnham's maneuverings among the ladies of Buffland: "He then gave himself up to that duplex act to which all unavowed lovers are prone—the simultaneous secret worship of one woman and open devotion to another." John Hay's open devotion would always be to Clara. Henceforth the object of his secret worship would be Lizzie Cameron and none besides.

ON THE BOAT OVER, Hay caught a cold that worsened after he got to London. The doctor prescribed a cocaine spray that made his throat go numb. He wrote mournfully to Clara: "I do not believe it pays, at my time of life, to travel alone and I shall never do it again."

Yet he was hardly by himself. He made the rounds of the galleries and auction houses and looked up old friends, including Robert Lincoln, George Smalley, and Henry James. Lizzie arrived on the fourteenth, accompanied by her daughter, Martha; her stepdaughter Rachel; and Hattie Blaine, daughter of the secretary of state. As she came ashore, Lizzie mailed a letter to Adams: "I shall see John Hay at once. . . . It is so nice to be able to talk of you to some one, and it does me a lot of good. I'll talk of you and he of Nannie!" Hay immediately invited them to dinner at the Bristol Hotel, along with James, Bret Harte, and several others.

On the advice of his doctor, he cut short his time in London and went to Paris, staying with Whitelaw Reid. Again his letters to Clara are forlorn and tender. "I am already looking forward to getting home—& home is not Washington nor Cleveland nor any other town—it is you, my own darling, my dear sweet, good wife." And four days later: "I want to get back to you. I want to hold you in my arms. I want to love you & kiss you. You are the only person in the world I care for or who cares for me."

He also told Clara that he had seen "the Cameron clan," who had crossed to France soon after he did. What he did not bother to mention was that, despite his nagging cold, he was escorting Lizzie Cameron around Paris. "John Hay and I have had a real Parisian spree," Lizzie confessed to Adams on May 26. "I hope that you are jealous. Please don't tell him I told you, but we dined in a *cabinet particulier*, and went in a lover loge to a ballet. I actually felt wicked and improper. He did, too, for he felt obliged to follow up the precedent and to tell me how much he loved me."

By now Lizzie was accustomed to men falling under her spell, and in her letter to Adams she made light of Hay's advances, using one man to play the other—something she did very well. Adams had served as her buffer against the boorishness of her husband, and now Hay was the bait to draw Adams to Paris. Neither she nor Adams was sure what would happen when he arrived, but Adams's heart was hopeful. Writing to Lizzie from Tahiti, he divulged: "Actually I wish I were at sea. My only source of energy is that I am actually starting on a ten-thousand-mile journey to see—you!" In the same letter to Adams in which she recounted her "Parisian spree" with Hay, Lizzie sang a siren song: "I feel sure now that you will come to Europe. . . . Of course you understand that if you come here you come home. I'll use force, if necessary, but home you must come."

After his fling with Lizzie, Hay returned to London and promptly collapsed with what he at first reckoned was a heart attack—and it may well have been, although the doctor dismissed the incident as a bad case of indigestion. Lizzie arrived in London several days later and found Hay looking pitiful. "He told me yesterday that he felt that this was the last year of his life," she wrote Adams.

He was not too frail, however, to take Lizzie to see a collection of old masters at the Dulwich Picture Gallery in South London or to *L'Enfant Prodigue*, performed in pantomime by the sad, white-faced Pierrot. Lizzie cried all through the final act, and afterward wrote to Adams about Hay: "When I think of how freely I am seeing him, and that it might be you—! It *will* be you soon. We are having a desperate affair, so hurry up. Something must break it up before we return to Washington. It was that night in Paris that did the mischief." Her tone was teasing; she was playing the coquette, as ever. But she was telling the truth—in such a way that Adams dared not believe her.

She and Hay saw each other throughout the month of June—at the Royal Enclosure at Ascot, in Burlington Gardens, at lunches, teas, and dinners. In his own correspondence to Adams, Hay was not as forthcoming in his descriptions of *l'affaire* as Lizzie had been, remarking simply, "I sought her genial presence and we took sweet counsel together concerning you and encouraged each other a good deal." To his wife he mentioned his frequent sightings of Lizzie, making sure in his gossipy commentary to surround her with "the Cameron party," "all the Camerons," and "her usual little court."

Several days after returning from Paris, he wrote Clara: "When I think of the seventeen years you have been with me, the happiness and content of the heart you have given me, I am filled with a wondering and grateful sense of my great good fortune. In the whole world there was no other woman who could have made me so happy and I found just the one. If I could only dare to hope you have been happier with me, or as happy as you would have been with anyone else, there would be nothing wanting to my content. But I am so conscious of what I lack, I often feel that it was selfish in me to take you for my own, and appropriate to myself your rich, beautiful nature. But that is done, and no repentance will undo it."

And so he did not repent. Before his ship departed England, he sent a letter to Lizzie: "London is floating way in the Eastern distance like a city of dream. Before I get to New York I will convince myself that all our innocent sprees were too nice to be true, and I will try to seize them again in visions of the night."

When he landed a week later, he found Clara and the two eldest children on the dock to greet him.

CHAPTER 12

Tame Cats

After a short stay in Cleveland and a quick trip to Warsaw to visit his mother, Hay arrived at Lake Sunapee with Clara and the children at the beginning of August. The house at the Fells was not quite finished but far enough along for them to move in. Hay called the place a "pine shanty," but it was considerably more substantial than that. Its bowed gambrel roof was typical of genteel summerhouses of the day. Sunny upstairs bedrooms and a sixty-foot-long piazza afforded panoramic views of the lake and the magnificent mountains beyond. In addition to a servant wing, icehouse, and stable, Hay also installed a dock; the best way to and from Newbury was by hired steam launch. The Fells would never again be a working farm, although sheep continued to graze in the boulder-strewn pastures.

Half in earnest, Hay wrote Lizzie Cameron during the summer to suggest that she buy one of the adjacent properties and "retire from the world you adore and seek real solitude." Lizzie, meanwhile, remained in Paris, awaiting the arrival of Henry Adams, who, when last heard from, was in Australia. "John Hay writes to me now & then," she informed Adams. "He pretends that he likes me since our London season together, but I know better. Nanny is the first." Yet by now even Lizzie had to recognize that this appraisal was out of date.

Hay was slow to recover from whatever had sapped his health in Europe. He complained that he was constantly dizzy and that his heart was "miserably weak." But, as he had hoped, the air at the Fells and the simpler rhythm of daily life had a restorative effect. And it was the only time during the year that he could spend unhurried hours with the children.

Helen was now sixteen and had taken on "a young lady look that startles and depresses me," Hay told Whitelaw Reid. In the fall she would enroll in boarding school at Dobbs Ferry, an hour north of New York, and, like all fathers, he hated to see a daughter he doted on leave the nest. Helen and her younger sister, Alice, would remember their father as an unconditional pushover, sweet-tempered and adoring. "He was so tender-hearted that my mother always had to deal with our youthful injuries, illnesses & discipline," Alice would reminisce. "He couldn't bear to see us hurt or made unhappy even for our own good. He spoiled us shamefully." Helen described him as "the jolliest kind of pal," who sang "old war time songs & plantation melodies" and made up stories about a pixie "who was as real to us as a member of the family."

As the two girls matured into young women, their father was ever more indulgent. "The greatest treat we had was to go 'on a spree,'" Helen recalled. "When I was away at school he used to come out & always arranged a programme ahead which began with 'we will have a nice sandwich for lunch at the Station, we then will go & call on an old lady who wishes to see you & we will finish the day with a delightful & improving lecture on Astronomy'—which of course meant that we lunched at Delmonico's on whatever I wanted to order, be it ever so indigestible, & shopped & 'played' all the afternoon & finished up with a musical comedy." In the same munificent vein, Hay told Alice, "'If you see a thing you *really want*, get it, no matter what it costs; because if you don't, it will haunt you all the rest of your life, & come between you & the later desires of your heart & make them appear less & less desirable by comparison.'"

With his son Del he was not so liberal. To a father quick of wit and slight of build, the boy seemed "fat and dull." Hay complained to Adams that he had bought Del "a carload of fishing tackle, which he will never learn how to use." When Del's uncle Samuel Mather suggested that Hay acquire their own launch for Lake Sunapee, Hay thought it a bad idea:

"I have no knowledge or capacity that way, and Del is too lazy." What he did not recognize was just how rapidly Del was growing into his sturdy bones—a physique he inherited more from his mother. By fourteen, he was taller than his father, and his baby fat was already maturing into brawn. His great desire was to play football, the rage among schoolboys and college men but not exactly his father's game. The most strenuous exercise Hay had undertaken in recent years was to shiver in a duck blind on a raw Lake Erie morning.

HENRY ADAMS HAD NOT seen Lizzie in a year, and now he could not travel fast enough. While he was in the South Pacific, she had written him that she would be in Paris in October, waiting for him. "To think that you are coming, are on your way!" she beckoned. "That I shall see you, shall take you home. I can scarce realize it tho' I walk on air in consequence."

From Sydney he replied: "I am grateful as though I were a ten-year-old boy whom you had smiled at, and put in rapture of joy at being noticed." He was not the least alarmed by her disclosure that she and Hay had been having an "affair." "The more you please others, the more you delight me. . . . Fascinate John Hay by all means," he wrote with merry magnanimity. He arrived in Paris on October 10 and sent a note the next day inquiring "at what hour one may *convenablement* pay one's respects."

Lizzie was delighted that a man would come more than ten thousand miles to pledge his affection. Yet once he was at her door on the rue Bassano, off the Champs-Elysées, the currency of romance depreciated to the small change of anticlimax. It was the pursuit that had appealed to her; she had no intention of being captured, nor of capturing Adams. What either of them imagined might unfold in Paris, or after Paris, seems never to have been fully articulated. Once they stood face to face, the gulf between them was immeasurable, their nearness a dream dissolved. She was as blithe as Adams was stunned.

During the two weeks they were both in Paris, she avoided seeing him alone, using her daughter and stepdaughter as convenient foils. "Mrs. Cameron is no good," Adams finally wrote to a friend. "She has too much to do, and lets everybody make use of her, which pleases no one because of course each person objects to the other persons having rights that deserve respect. As long as she lives it will always be so." Quoting Elizabeth Browning, he told Lizzie he felt as if he'd been hit over the head with "an apocalyptic *Never.*"

Just the same, Adams followed her to London, where she tarried briefly on the way to America. On the day of her departure, as her cab rolled away from Half Moon Street, she told him she was sorry that their "Paris experiment" had not worked out. From the ship she wrote, "Thank you a thousand times for everything."

In reply, he composed a series of lugubrious letters that would follow her to Washington. "[N]o matter how much I may efface myself or how little I may ask," he confessed, "I must always make more demand on you than you can gratify, and you must always have the consciousness that, whatever I may profess, I want more than I can have. Sooner or later the end of such a situation is estrangement, with more or less disappointment and bitterness. I am not old enough to be a tame cat; you are too old to accept me in any other character."

Nevertheless, he was willing to be taken back on any terms, if only he knew what they were: "I would give you gladly as many opal and diamond necklaces as Mr. Cameron would let you wear if I could only for once look clear down to the bottom of your mind and understand the whole of it." Until then, he reconciled, "[Y]ou are Beauty; I am the Beast."

A few days later, Adams wrote a breezier letter to Hay, recapping his recent activities, including his stay in Paris. "I could find nothing new that pleased me either in art or literature," he reported, "and as for society nothing of the satisfactory sort was within the bounds of my imagination; but a fortnight or so passes quickly even if nothing is the result." Of his rendezvous with Lizzie, he mentioned merely that her company served to "beguile my ennui at intervals." Adams and Hay were confidants in many things, but the particulars of their respective relationships with Lizzie Cameron evidently were not among them.

Adams did not return to Washington until the following February. In the meantime, Hay and Lizzie saw each other often. In late November and early December, while Clara was still in Cleveland, Hay hosted at least two dinner parties at which Lizzie was a guest. After one of them, Lizzie wrote to Adams, reciting the guest list, which included the Blaines, the Roosevelts, and the Lodges. "We all talk to each other and dine with each other just as we have done for two years past," she said, noting too that Hay was looking much better than when she had last seen him in London. Hay wrote Adams a few days later, remarking that "the women looked extremely pretty in their new gowns. Mrs. Cameron's Parisian bravery causes all the others to die with envy."

After the New Year, as the season for balls and diplomatic receptions picked up its pace, Hay seemed never to stray far from the women he admired. At one debutante ball he sat with Nannie Lodge, discussing civil service reform with Charles Bonaparte, the Baltimore-born great-nephew of Napoleon I. "Or at least, I think it was Civil Service—we complimented her eyes," he joked. He was not so captivated by Nannie that he did not notice Lizzie in a beautiful black satin gown, dancing with the Turkish minister. "Mrs. Cameron is at her best, which is superlative enough," he reported to Adams. "One never sees her, though, except through a fluttering haze of dagoes and dudes."

In late January, after another evening during which he had been un-able to talk to Lizzie with any satisfaction, he took a walk around the square to gather his thoughts. Returning home, he put pen to paper, pouring out emotions that had been building up since the previous spring. The letter carries no salutation, no signature, and no address—suggesting that it was delivered by hand. "Good night, my tantalizing goddess," he began. "A dozen times this day I have been at the point of believing that you are not really so complicated as you seem, but that last half hour threw me into the wildest confusion again. I give it up. I will not try to comprehend you. Still less can I criticize you. I shall never know you well enough to do either. After you were gone the usual outcry of admiration broke forth. I said, 'She has an absolutely different man-ner in speaking to each man in the room.' . . . Upon my word I believe if you spoke to a thousand men, you would naturally, by some divine gift of sympathy—or else by some benign science of cruelty—assume to each one of them the form, the eyes, and voice of his ideal. And yet it seems to me that you cannot be to others anything different from what you are to me. A form of perfect grace and majesty, a face radiant with a beauty so gloriously vital that it refreshes and stimulates every heart that comes within its influence; a voice, a laughter so pure and so musical that it carries gladness in every vibration of the air. You sweet comrade, you dear and splendid friend, who is worthy to be *your* friend and comrade? I am humbled to the ground before you."

He went on to summon the memory of their time together in England, when he allowed himself to believe he might hold her undivided affection. "What can restore the sweet serenity of that early worship?" he wondered. "My proud goddess, my glorious beauty, my grand, sweet woman, I want to shut my eyes to everything about you here, and adore you as I did at Dulwich, as I did on the terrace by the Thames. Why is it different now? You were surrounded then by adorers *bien autrement formidables* than the people who obscure you here. Yet I did not mind—any more than a devout person objects to a church being full. Now I feel that your altars are in danger of profanation—the worship itself is threatened."

In the end, he could only blame himself. "Perhaps the fault is all in me: the resentment may be purely personal, because I have lost the place I have held dear. You know you appointed me No. 3. I can remember the day and the hour, opposite the Knightsbridge Barracks. As nearly as I can now compute I am No. 13—if indeed I am on the list at all. I do not care what my exact number is—I would as soon be 13 as 4—since I have *dégringolé* [tumbled] from my own place. A true presentiment—which I did not then appreciate—impelled me to worry you to say you would be the same, when we met again. As if promises could avail anything against 'the strong god Circumstance.' But I shall never cease to praise and bless you, dear, for what you were, and what you will always be in those sweet memories of Ultramar which I shall carry with me to my dying day."

Apparently she had given him the same treatment she had given Adams two months earlier—and Hay had responded in a similar fashion. Also like Adams, Hay kept coming back for more. At the end of January, he, Clara, and the Lodges were guests at the Camerons' new house on St. Helena Island, South Carolina. The three couples evidently got along cordially. "I shall remember the week as a bright spot in my life," Hay wrote, thanking the senator. As for Lizzie, she seemed to have added another tame cat to her menagerie. Hay basked in whatever attention she would give him, knowing that he would be demoted further when Adams arrived in mid-February.

Once Adams was home, they all behaved fairly well through the rest of the winter and spring. In June, Lizzie and Martha again took up residence in Adams's house in Beverly Farms—without him. "It is rather funny that your house is the only place I have ever had the home feeling," she wrote him. "If I didn't like you so well the sense of obligation would be intolerable."

They all knew what the rules were. After Hay had bared his soul to her in February, she must have told him not to expose himself in that way again, for that summer, when Adams injured his leg in a riding accident, Hay wrote to Lizzie: "This letter ought not to be charged against me, as I only write to tell you how Mr. Adams is." After a hasty medical report, he signed off, "Just think! I am closing this letter without a single word of Tra-la-la!" When she scolded Adams for not responding quickly enough to her letters of sympathy—and her offer to care for him during his convalescence—he replied, "The first law of tame cats is that under no circumstances must they run the risk of boring their owners by writing more than once a month or so. You never consider that a tame cat's business is to lie still and purr."

Hay, however, would not give up the pursuit. In June, he saw Lizzie briefly at the wedding of Cabot and Nannie Lodge's daughter in Nahant. A few weeks later, he wrote Adams, "I was sorely tempted to run down to Beverly and see Mrs. Cameron, but I had a list of agenda as long as my arm . . . so I came away without visiting that shrine." In August, he tried again to tempt the Camerons to buy property on Lake Sunapee, though he admitted the notion might seem far-fetched to the owners of a winter retreat in South Carolina and vast estates in Pennsylvania. "We like the place more and more," he wrote Lizzie of New Hampshire. "We like the gentle squalor of it, and the incredible idleness. There is absolutely nothing to do from morning till night. I hardly dare to recommend it to princesses and goddesses."

But he did succeed in persuading the Camerons to accept an invitation to the Fells. For the first time in their lives, they were just four—Hay

and Clara, Cameron and Lizzie (plus Martha and the Hay children)—
and somehow the two-day stay went smoothly. Lizzie had always gone
out of her way to compliment the stout, matronly, and habitually reserved Clara. "Mrs. Hay is looking too stunning," she had told Adams
the previous winter. "She is really superb." The senator was an agreeable
enough fellow when he was not drinking heavily. And while he was not
entirely oblivious to his wife's flirtations with other men, for the most
part he too was a tame cat. Once when he had tried to rein her in at a
dinner party, she had put him in his place. "I just intimated that he must
not make me pay for his jealousies," she told Adams, "and I must talk to
whomever I pleased whenever I pleased."

Still, Hay must have had supreme mastery of his emotions for neither
Cameron nor Clara to suspect his true disposition toward Lizzie. Proper
manners went only so far; mere glances, even the avoidance of glances,
would have spoken volumes to a spouse who harbored the slightest doubt
of a partner's faithfulness. Their friend Henry James had written entire
novels that turned on words unspoken between lovers. But if Clara noticed, she held her peace. If Cameron truly cared, he would have done
something about it long before.

After the New Hampshire visit, Lizzie sent a favorable report to
Adams. "Our little trip to the hills was a great success," she wrote. "The
Hays were kindness itself, and if Mrs. is a poor hostess for a gathering of
dip[lomat]s and notables in Washington, she makes up for it in the country to simple folk like ourselves." Lizzie loved everything about the Fells.
"One can scarcely conceive a wilder spot. . . . That lake is exquisite," she
gushed. She also mentioned, "Mr. Hay looks so well that if he tells you
he is dying tomorrow you must believe him even less than usual."

Hay was equally pleased: "Don was grumpily good natured and la
Dona was radiantly lovely. They pretended to like the place and commissioned me to ask the price of farms." In the end, he wrote Lizzie, offering
to lease a portion of his own property—"on reasonable terms, say a nickel
a year, and then you would have all your money to squander on your
house. . . . You could have free range over the whole place and be everywhere welcome as flowers in May."

Living on the same square with her in Washington was challenging—

and frustrating—enough. How they could ever live side by side in the wilds of New Hampshire was something neither of them could fully imagine. Needless to say, nothing came of their summer fancy.

WHILE HAY WAS SAVORING the peace and quiet of the Fells, national politics had broken into its quadrennial lather. Hay had never particularly taken to President Harrison and would have preferred that his friend and neighbor James Blaine vie for the Republican nomination in 1892. Instead, Blaine resigned as secretary of state and retired from politics. In June, the party, with some ambivalence, renominated Harrison; to Hay's delight, the delegates replaced incumbent Vice President Levi Morton with Whitelaw Reid. "It is the general judgment that Harrison is a good, safe candidate," Hay wrote Reid after the Republican Convention, "and you are universally regarded as giving the ticket a great reinforcement." Later in the summer, Hay presented the Reids with a puppy, bred from a collie brought back from Scotland. Reid named the new family member Harrison.

The election of 1892 was a rematch of four years earlier. This time, however, it was Grover Cleveland who was on the outside, knocking to get in. The McKinley Tariff Act had helped many industries, but working-class Americans believed that it made too many imported goods unaffordable. The Sherman Silver Purchase Act, intended to stabilize the currency, was attacked as a "cowardly makeshift." Violent strikes at Andrew Carnegie's steel mills in Pennsylvania; a hoarsening resentment of the wealthy by labor and the mostly agrarian Populists; plus a president who caused "a chattering of teeth among warm-blooded Republicans of the East"—all these factors worked in Cleveland's favor.

Throughout the campaign, Hay enjoyed sparring with Henry Adams, who was more liberal, more Democratic in voice and principle, though it was beneath him to take an active role in politics at any level. "[Y]ou will be so happy and gay over the nomination of your fellow-mugwump Cleveland that there will be no enduring you," Hay teased his friend before the Democratic Convention. "Well, go to! be as happy as you please. You can never take away from me the blessed memory of four years of Harrison." The week before the election, Hay retreated to Winous Point and braced for the bad news. The day after Cleveland's victory, he sent Adams a dozen ducks and a bitter lament: "Woe is me for my unhappy country, which is to struggle under the double affliction of a stuffed prophet and a stuffed ballot box." But with Hay and Adams, friendship trumped partisanship no matter what. "I love you in spite of your politics and your dishonest victory," Hay signed off.

His message of condolence to Whitelaw Reid was not so jocular. "I will not waste words in attempting to expose my deep disgust and grief," he told him. "At present my chief sorrow is that you and Mrs. Reid are not to be our neighbors in Washington." And he asked, "Is it not horrible—that fat and fatuous freak, bellowing his inane self-laudations in the White House for four more years, amid the amens of enraptured Mugwumps? The gorge rises at it."

THE NEW YEAR GOT off to a poor start. On January 27, 1893, James Blaine died of a heart attack; Hay was among his pallbearers. A week later, Hay learned that his mother, who had just reached her ninetieth birthday, was failing. His brother Leonard advised him not to attempt the trip west. For the time being, she was comfortable and well cared for by their sister, Mary. "But you know how it is with old people," Leonard wrote. "The light grows dim then flickers then goes out suddenly." She lasted ten more days. When Hay sent word that he could not possibly arrive in time for the funeral, Leonard hastened to console his brother's regret and sorrow: "[Y]ou must not blame yourself for anything that even the most distorted fancy could picture as a neglect. You have done your whole duty as a son & brother to all of us three & four times over."

Within a week, Hay was called upon to perform another duty—one that would have a direct bearing on his future. While passing through Buffalo en route to New York to give a Washington's Birthday speech, William McKinley, who was now governor of Ohio, was handed a telegram informing him that an old friend, Robert Walker, had gone broke in the tin-can manufacturing business—which, incidentally, was an industry protected and nurtured by the McKinley Tariff. A pandemic of insolvency was on the verge of enfeebling America, caused by overzealous expansion, easy credit, and blind optimism. Over the next three years, dozens of railroads, hundreds of banks, and thousands of businesses would fail. One of the earliest to do so was Robert Walker's in Youngstown, Ohio.

Walker had helped McKinley through law school and his early political campaigns. In gratitude, McKinley had co-signed several bank notes for his friend, and each time that Walker asked him for another signature, McKinley naively assumed that he was signing renewals, when in fact the notes were entirely new. McKinley figured he was accountable for only a few thousand dollars; by the time he received the telegram in Buffalo, the amount exceeded $100,000, more than he could ever hope to reconcile. McKinley, too, would be obliged to declare bankruptcy. Moreover, the embarrassing enormity of his gaffe would surely derail his campaign for reelection as governor in November and snuff any hope he had of running for president in 1896. That is, unless . . .

Immediately a group of McKinley's most powerful supporters stepped in to make him whole again, led and cajoled by the governor's chief political booster, strategist, and fund-raiser, Mark Hanna. One of the people Hanna called upon in Cleveland was John Hay's brother-in-law, Samuel Mather. Mather promised $5,000 to the fund and then wrote Hay, asking if he would help share the load.

Hay needed no prompting. By the time he received Mather's request, he had already sent McKinley $1,000 directly, unsolicited. He now volunteered to pay $2,000 of Mather's commitment and mentioned that he might be good for more. Other big industrialists wound up giving as much or more than Hay—Henry Clay Frick $2,000; George Pullman $5,000; Philip Armour $5,000—but Hay's checks were two of the first, and his touch was more personal, a kindness that McKinley never forgot.

In short order, the money was raised and McKinley was relieved of his debt. Rather than regard McKinley as a scofflaw or beggar or as too inept to manage the affairs of the state, the voters of Ohio expressed resounding sympathy for his plight and in November reelected him by the greatest margin of victory since the Civil War. "I have no words with which to adequately thank you," McKinley wrote Hay from the governor's office. "You must interpret my deep sense of obligation and appreciation. How can I ever repay you & other dear friends?" Hay had no immediate answer, but soon enough he would think of something.

• • •

THE BIG EXCITEMENT IN the spring of 1893 was not the McKinley debt, the second coming of Grover Cleveland, or even the darkening economic picture, but the World's Columbian Exposition: the Chicago World's Fair. Anyone who could afford it, and many who could not, had to see the neoclassical phantasm of the White City that had sprung up, seemingly overnight, on the shore of Lake Michigan. Farmers and small-town shopkeepers who still lived without electricity and heretofore had traveled scarcely farther than the county fair were beguiled by the vast pavilions of inventions, entire villages inhabited by aborigines from every corner of the globe, and a farrago of attractions and confections illuminated by thousands upon thousands of dazzling electric light bulbs. Even cosmopolitan visitors were impressed. Adams, who arrived in May in a private railcar paid for by the Camerons, was overwhelmed by the fair's immensity and pleasantly surprised by its beauty—"something that the Greeks might have delighted to see, and Venice would have envied." The Hays went in June and were similarly smitten. "[I]n architectural beauty . . . it so far transcended anything which the genius and the devotion of man have ever yet achieved," Hay exclaimed to Richard Watson Gilder.

On June 27, a week after the Hays returned from Chicago, the New York Stock Exchange crashed, and America suddenly appeared as flimsy as the facades of the White City. By the time the collapse came, Hay had already purchased passage to Europe for his family, with the intention of staying for a year—except for Del, who in the fall would enroll in the Westminster School in Dobbs Ferry to prepare for Yale.

All of Lafayette Square was abroad that summer, or so it seemed. Adams had sailed a few weeks earlier with the Camerons, the widowed Harriet Blaine, and her children. Another of Adams's fellow passengers was Thomas Bayard, President Cleveland's ambassador to the Court of St. James's—the first time the rank of ambassador was assigned to an American foreign minister. The Hays reached London on July 20 and spent two days with Adams before he headed to Scotland. By then the Camerons had already left for Switzerland.

As the news from America became more dreary, Adams and Cameron both cut their trips short and returned home. "Everyone is in a blue fit of terror," Adams wrote Lizzie after he was back in Washington, "and each individual thinks himself more ruined than his neighbor." The only one of their group who seemed not outwardly affected was Hay. Adams wrote Lizzie that their friend was "calm as the Lake of Lucerne."

For the next eleven months, the Hays lived a life of leisure and luxury, visiting their good friends Sir John and Lady Clark in Scotland and soaking up the sun and the baths in the South of France. They passed much of the fall in Paris, followed by a month-long sojourn in Spain. Hay read of the American economic and political news from afar, clucking at the missteps and misfeasance of the Cleveland administration in letters to Adams and Reid. For the most part, though, he was content being idle and aloof. Writing to Adams from Paris on New Year's Day, 1894, he groused amiably: "I am bored out of my sweet life." To those back home, some of whom were barely hanging on, this sort of grumbling might have sounded a bit like bragging.

ADAMS, BLESSEDLY, WAS NOT hurt by the panic as badly as he initially feared. The same could not be said for Clarence King. Even in the best of times, King had made a botch of business. "Every struggle he makes in his world of finance gets him deeper in the mire [and] costs him something of life as well as of money," Hay had remarked to Adams several years earlier. And to William Dean Howells he had sighed: "A touch of Avarice would have made [King] a Vanderbilt—a touch of plodding industry would have made him anything he chose." When King was flush, he dashed about Europe, eating and entertaining like a lord and buying art and curiosities with abandon. Hay would eventually compose an ode to King's acquisitiveness, entitled "A Dream of Bric-À-Brac." But he and Adams, while admiring King's exquisite taste, could only shake their heads at his profligacy. When the author and taste-setter John Ruskin sold King two paintings by J.M.W. Turner, King was said to have laughed, "One good Turner deserves another." Now the paintings, along with a bundle of unredeemable stock certificates in far-flung mines, were pledged to Hay, who, along with Adams, continued to loan money to King with no intention of ever foreclosing, regardless of how much he admired the Turners or how delinquent King was in making good. "He owes nobody except those who will never bother him," Hay told Adams. "I am in despair about him. I cannot make him do what he ought, even though I offer to stand the racket."

The most painful pinch caused by King's indebtedness was his increasing reluctance to be in their company. "[W]henever I think of you and the splendid work you are carrying through with such solemnity of purpose and conscientiousness of effort," King told Adams, "I feel that you must regard me with despair and be amazed at the barrenness of my poor life. . . . With all the sense of disappointment and the anger at fate there has grown up a sense of shyness about being much with the only friends I care for—you and Hay. . . . But you must be patient with me, and remember the millstone I wear 'round my neck."

King of course had another reason for his shyness, and other undisclosed millstones. In July 1893, three weeks after the stock market crash, his wife, Ada, had given birth to their fourth child. At about that time, King also received word that the National Bank of El Paso, which he had founded and in which he was a principal stockholder, had failed. He lost everything, and yet he was too proud to tell Hay or Adams—and he certainly couldn't tell Ada, who still believed he was a railroad porter. Over the next three months, King fell apart. He let his hair and beard grow shaggy, and his clothes became seedy. On Sunday, October 29, visitors to the Lion House in Central Park noticed a man acting agitated, enraged. When police intervened, he gave his name, Clarence King, and his address, first the Union League Club and then Newport, where his mother lived. No mention of the street where he lived with Ada and their children.

Arrested for disorderly conduct, King was committed to the Bloomingdale Asylum for the Insane in Harlem Heights. The diagnosis was nervous depression, brought on by his recent financial setback and aggravated by an inflammation of the spine. Dr. S. Weir Mitchell was summoned from Philadelphia, but, rather than prescribe his customary Rest Cure of fresh air and a rural setting, he recommended that King stay on at Bloomingdale, where he remained for the next two months, without telling a soul about his bipolar life, and presumably without telling his wife of his whereabouts.

Adams kept Hay informed of King's recovery, and Hay was consoled to learn that the two were planning a trip to the West Indies after King's release, anticipated for early January 1894. Yet Hay was frustrated that he had heard nothing from King directly. "It would seem incredible to anyone but you," Hay complained to Adams from Paris, that "King has not written me a letter for a year and has never given me the least hint of his affairs except that they were desperate. I have sent him money and securities sufficient, I hoped, to clear him, but have never been informed that he received them, much less what he made of them. I am as much worried over him as if he were my child, but I do not know what to do to help him, in face of his obstinate silence." In a subsequent letter, he urged Adams to "jolly" King up in the West Indies and then bring him to Washington. "Now that his affairs have gone to everlasting smash we can set him up in a bijou of a house." Hay had no idea how implausible this proposition would sound to King, aka James Todd.

KING WAS NOT THE only friend to fall by the wayside that winter. After New Year's, Hay, Clara, and Helen made their way to Italy, leaving Alice and Clarence in the care of a tutor outside Paris. They were in Rome at the end of the month when Hay read in a newspaper of the death of Constance Woolson in Venice.

For all her popularity as a short story writer and then as a novelist, Woolson had led a solitary life. One of the few people with whom she gained a modicum of closeness was Henry James. She was an ardent admirer of James's work and had come to Europe to meet him and, to the best of her ability, emulate his Continental lifestyle. She had tracked him down in Florence while James was beginning *The Portrait of a Lady*, and he kindly introduced her to the Renaissance city and its stirring architecture, galleries, and statuary. Thenceforth they were loyal friends and correspondents. James described her to an aunt as "old-maidish" and "intense," but she was grateful for his artistic kinship and clearly would have welcomed something more. While he gently criticized her prose for its preoccupation with "tender sentiment," she encouraged him to create a female character "who can feel a real love." Her wish was never fulfilled. In the fall of 1893, she was living in Venice when her "deadly enemy," depression, took hold. In January 1894, she came down with influenza and perhaps typhoid, and in the early morning of the twenty-fourth she leapt (or fell, as her family chose to believe) to her death from her window to the cobblestones below. She was fifty-three years old.

Because Woolson was a relative of Samuel Mather, the Hays felt a special responsibility to help with her funeral and burial. When Hay read of the tragedy in the paper, he telegrammed the American legation in Venice and offered to pay all expenses for shipment of Woolson's body to Rome, where she would be buried in the Protestant Cemetery, according to her wishes.

In the meantime, he and the rector of St. Paul's, the American church in Rome, went to the cemetery and found a spot near the graves of Shelley and Keats. "She is worthy company for the best and brightest that sleep around here," Hay wrote Mather. "Her grave will be a shrine for the intelligence of the world for many years to come." To Adams, who understood suicide better than most, Hay confided, "We buried poor Constance Woolson . . . a thoroughly good and most unhappy woman with a great talent bedevilled by disordered nerves. She did much good and no harm in her life, and had not as much happiness as a convict."

Henry James, who was in England when he learned of Woolson's death, was stricken with remorse. "Miss Woolson was so valued and close a friend of mine and had been so for so many years," he wrote Hay in Rome, "that I feel an intense nearness in participation in every circumstance of her tragic end." Even so, he elected not to make the long journey to the funeral.

HAY, CLARA, AND HELEN stayed on in Rome until early spring, then began working their way north, first to Florence and next to Venice, where they visited the house that Constance Woolson had rented near the Grand Canal. From there they proceeded to Vienna, Dresden, Berlin, and finally arrived in Paris at the beginning of April to retrieve fourteen-year-old Alice and nine-year-old Clarence, who by now were speaking passable French.

They started for London on May 2 to be in time for Helen's "first great day of grandeur"—her presentation to Queen Victoria. Writing to

Whitelaw Reid, Hay tried to make light of the occasion. "My woman-kind have just driven off to the Buckingham Palace in gowns whose vast-ness and splendor abashed me," he complained lamely. "H[elen] thought she would like to be presented and Mrs. H[ay] and I, who for 20 years have avoided that function, weakly yielded and are swept into the vortex."

Perhaps he had forgotten Clara's great disappointment at having missed her first drawing room in 1883 due to her father's worsening health. Hay, too, rarely passed up a chance to make the acquaintance of great and better Britons. A week after Helen's presentation, he dressed "like an ape of Borneo"—in knee breeches and stockings—and himself bowed to the queen.

As much as he tried to downplay the London season, this was his fa-vorite time of year in a country he had come to regard as almost a second home. He and Clara made another pilgrimage to the Clarks in Scotland, then returned to London for a dizzying round of engagements. They at-tended a ball at Buckingham Palace. Hay was invited to a dinner at the House of Commons with the prime minister's son, Herbert Gladstone, the historian and Scottish secretary George Trevelyan, and Under-Secretary of State for the Colonies Sydney Buxton. At a dinner party at Trevelyan's house, he spent an hour talking to the new foreign secretary, Lord Kimberley. And he and Clara had cards for the Royal Enclosure at Ascot—"the goal of every true Briton's ambition," he wrote Samuel Mather.

By the time they sailed for home at the end of June, Hay was well sated. "I never could have believed that a succession of what used to be pleasures, balls, concerts, shows, and dinner parties could become such a weariness to the flesh," he sighed, but it was clear that he had relished every minute of his latest English immersion. "They are a dear and simple folk, in some ways—these English," he observed cheerily to Adams.

HE COULD NOT HAVE been too worn out by the London carousel, for within a week of getting home he agreed to take a much more grueling journey: this one to Yellowstone National Park with Adams, who sug-gested that they take Del along, too. Del had excelled in his last year in school and had passed the entrance exams for Yale. He was now six feet tall and a beefy two hundred pounds. A summer riding and camping would harden him for football in the fall. Adams also asked King to join the trip—the ideal companion for such an adventure—but he would not commit. Instead, they were accompanied by Hay's friend William Phillips—"Bilfilips," Hay called him—who was an early advocate for the preservation of Yellowstone and, along with Theodore Roosevelt, a founder of the Boone & Crockett Club. The final member of the party was Joseph Iddings, a geologist who knew King and, like Phillips, had spent a number of seasons in Yellowstone.

Initially, they worried that they might not make it past Chicago. While Hay was in Europe, the economic panic had stirred extreme disaffection among the nation's working class. Earlier in the spring, Jacob Coxey, an eccentric rabble-rouser from Massillon, Ohio, had led an "army" of several hundred unemployed men on a cross-country march to Washington, where they intended to present a list of demands to Congress. Before he could deliver his ultimatum, Coxey was arrested for walking on the grass of the Capitol. Ten days later, a different, more volatile sort of army took to the field: three thousand workers at the Pullman Palace Car Company in Illinois went on strike over low wages and demeaning labor conditions. By the end of June, fifty thousand members of the American Railroad Union, led by Eugene Debs, had walked off the job. Angry strikers stopped trains and destroyed rolling stock, switches, and railyards, until U.S. Attorney General Richard Olney obtained an injunction authorizing federal troops under General Nelson Miles (who happened to be married to Lizzie Cameron's sister) to impose order. Debs was taken to jail, and by the time Adams and his companions set out for the West on July 17, most of the strikers had returned to work. Ten days earlier, and the Yellowstone expedition might have had to follow a more roundabout route.

They arrived a week later at Mammoth Hot Springs, the north entrance to the park. Yellowstone had been founded in 1872, but until the completion of the Northern Pacific Railroad in 1880, few tourists had ready access to its 2 million acres of geysers, waterfalls, and wilderness. By 1894, though, the route was well traveled. Hotels, tent camps, and coaches allowed visitors to make a grand tour of "Wonderland," as the railroad brochures advertised, providing plenty of spectacle and just enough hardship to make the trip a true adventure.

For the first week, they took in the sights by coach. To Hay's cosmopolitan eye, nature imitated art, not the other way around. The Grand Canyon of the Yellowstone compared favorably with Thomas Moran's inspirational painting of the same scene, which he had first viewed in the Capitol. He also recognized paintings of the park by his old friend Albert Bierstadt. A waterfall was as high as the Washington Monument; an enormous rock, when seen in the right light, was a Sphinx; and a certain spring was twice as big as Rome's Trevi Fountain.

For a man who purported to have a weak heart and rheumatism, Hay thrived unexpectedly in Yellowstone. An unheated salon in Paris gave him sniffles, but an accidental dunking in frigid Yellowstone Lake seemed only to refresh him. Much of Yellowstone Park is more than eight thousand feet above sea level; yet Hay tramped up hills for better views and slept under frosty skies without complaint.

After touring the park's Grand Canyon, falls, and lake, the party truly began to rough it. For the next month, they rode horseback through the rugged, densely timbered backcountry, nearly to the Grand Tetons. Led by five guides and packers and pulling a pack string of a dozen horses, they covered more than two hundred miles of "absolutely trackless woods and plains and mountains," Hay boasted to Flora Mather. "We lived like fighting cocks."

No one was more impressed by Hay's grit than Adams, who up until then had seen his friend stroll barely more than a few city blocks. "Hay has become a blooming mountaineer," Adams wrote Lizzie. "I am quite proud of having dragged [him] through this extravagant mountain non-sense just to show that he can do that sort of thing as well as anyone. . . . As an invalid with constitutional heart-failure, he [is] an abject fraud. I hope he will never try again that bunco-game on us. If he does, whack him up a mountain!"

In his letters to Clara, Hay fairly exulted in his stamina and spirit: "We had a long ride—the route being unknown to any of us & there being no distinct trails. . . . We got off our horses & began our scramble down the mountainside; slipping in the ashy dust, sinking in the boggy grass, sliding and slipping over great fields of snow, we at last got to the bottom. . . . We are living altogether too well." He fretted that his appetite was so great that he was losing his "sylph-like proportions." On one of the few layover days, he lounged about camp, reading a biography of Cicero and drinking in the glorious view of the Tetons, which, he attested, "are nearly as tall as Mont Blanc."

Del, too, seemed to blossom under the rigors of the trail. He hunted elk with the guides, shot grouse, and learned to fly-fish. "Del was a favorite in the camp . . . very good-natured, bright-tempered, cheery and companionable," Adams reported to one of his nieces, although, "according to his father, [he] will never be fit for doing anything in life."

AFTER FINISHING OUT THE summer in New Hampshire, followed by a month in Cleveland and at the duck club, Hay at last returned to Washington in late November. He had not been in Lafayette Square in sixteen months and had not laid eyes on Lizzie Cameron since early in 1893. In the fall of that year, he had written to her after her mother's death: "It is a savage irony of nature that all that charm of yours which brightens every scene you enter, which is a joy to every heart and every eye you come near, is now in this moment of need, of no use to your self. If you could call in one tithe of the happiness you have radiated on others, you would have a reserve sufficient for any use. . . . Love and sympathy mean nothing in real [times of] trouble, but still I must send my love and sympathy."

Sadly for Hay, Lizzie did not call upon him in her time of need. Yet whatever were the circumstances that kept them apart—their unsynchronous trips to Europe, her sojourns to South Carolina, his to the Fells and Yellowstone, and, what seems more decisive, her gentle but firm request that he not pursue her so intently—he did not stop pining for her company. Though she discouraged him from writing love letters, he found release in verse. In 1893, he published "Love and Music" in *Harper's Monthly*:

> *I gazed upon my love while music smote*
> *The soft night air into glad harmony. . . .*

Her form, white-robed, the jewel at her throat,
Her glimmering hands, her dusky, perfumed hair,
Her low, clear brow, her deep, proud, dreaming eyes,
Bent kindly upon me, her worshiper

There is no record of whether Hay showed this particular poem to Lizzie before he published it, but he sent other poems to her directly, for she later mentioned that "I had a pretty collection of Hay's verses, but he one day asked me for them to revise, and then destroyed them! The only one preserved was the sonnet to me which he published in his last volume of verses."

The sonnet in question is most likely "Obedience," which provides a frank assessment of Hay's ongoing enchantment with Lizzie and the authority she continued to hold over him:

The lady of my love bids me not to love her.
I can but bow obedient to her will;
And so, henceforth, I love her not; but still
I love the lustrous hair that glitters over
Her proud young head; I love the smiles that hover
About her mouth; the lights and shades that fill
Her star-bright eyes; the low, rich tones that thrill
Like thrush-songs gurgling from a vernal cover.
I love the fluttering dimples in her cheek;
Her cheek I love, its soft and tender bloom;
I love her sweet lips and the words they speak,
Words wise or witty, full of joy or doom.
I love her shoes, her gloves, her dainty dress;
And all they clasp, and cling to, and caress.

That Lizzie was indeed the object of "Obedience" is corroborated by a letter Hay wrote her at about the same time, in which he worships her with comparable anatomic specificity: "Never was a body and spirit united on such equal terms. Your mind and character are extraordinary; but not more so than your hair and eyes, your arms, your waist and your dear little feet. How they trot through my dreams, asleep and awake."

From then on, however, Hay became, if not exactly a tame cat, then at least one who kept his distance. He and Lizzie were both in Washington for the Christmas holidays, but not long after the first of the year, she was off to South Carolina for the winter. And so the coals were banked, though hardly extinguished—not so far as Hay was concerned.

CHAPTER 13

The English Mission

In the summer of 1895, Hay was content to retreat to the Fells and leave the affairs of the nation and the world to others. Henry Adams had become an outspoken champion of the insurgency against Spanish oppression of Cuba. Senator Don Cameron had waded clumsily, as was his nature, into the Republican debate on which currency standard the party should advocate in the next election. And in crucial states, party bosses commenced the age-old mating dance of bluff and bluster, warning the next batch of presidential suitors that, no matter what position the party eventually took on currency, tariff, or any other issues of the moment, the favor of allegiance must once again be paid in patronage. Meanwhile, Hay wrote to Whitelaw Reid at the end of July, "I am living in the Place-Where-Nothing-Happens. It would be difficult to imagine a life more stagnant than we lead in this rocky solitude."

For the time being, he made no plans and took on no more writing projects. Nicolay had done most of the work on a two-volume collection of Lincoln's speeches, letters, and other writings—materials they had gathered from Lincoln's office after the assassination and in the course of their research for the biography. Hay would continue to write speeches, poems, and an endless flow of letters, but his days as an active author were behind him. This abstinence may not have been premeditated; but neither was it cause for dismay. The only regret he would feel for the idleness that now enveloped him was that he did not cherish it fully enough while it lasted.

As accessible as Lake Sunapee was to Boston and even New York, the Hays seldom succeeded in luring guests to the Fells. Henry Adams and William Dean Howells received annual invitations that they seemed never quite able to accept; the Camerons never came again. The one distinguished visitor to the Fells that summer was Rudyard Kipling, who was living near Brattleboro, Vermont, with his American wife. At thirty, Kipling was already famous throughout the English-speaking world for stories such as "The Man Who Would Be King" and poems such as "Gunga Din." When he arrived at the Fells, he had just completed the *Second Jungle Book* and was starting on his only American novel, *Captains Courageous.* He and Hay had met previously in London, perhaps introduced by Henry James. "How a man can keep up so intense an intellectual life without going to Bedlam, is amazing," Hay wrote Henry Adams after Kipling had gone back to Vermont. "He rattled off the framework of about forty stories while he was with us. One day I was, as an ignorant layman will, abusing the sun-myths, and happened to say I expected to see 'Mary had a little lamb' become one. He instantly jumped upon it, and as fast as his tongue could wag, he elaborated the myth. . . . He was bright and pleasant: entertained himself and the rest of us." Nobody enjoyed Kipling's company any better than ten-year-old Clarence.

The other three Hay children came and went throughout the summer, dashing off to visit friends in various seaside towns and receiving them at the Fells in "relays," Hay marveled with feigned fatherly fatigue. Helen and Alice had a surfeit of beaux, and Del had collected a good set of companions at Yale. The previous fall, Hay had gone to New Haven to watch his son play football but derived no paternal pride from seeing him "rolled and tumbled and pulverized until he became a sorry spectacle of dirt and misery." The violence of the sport led Hay to compare it to the graver rites of passage of his own generation. "I am sure that you and I were never so young as the boys of today," he reflected to Whitelaw Reid.

"The fellows who came of age in the Lincoln years were forced to look at life in wider aspects."

Hay had always kept in touch with his former *Tribune* colleague, but now, with an election on the horizon, their communication picked up. Although Hay saw less of Reid than he did of Adams, he and Reid had much more in common politically and thus shared more political confidences. In fact, Hay and Reid rarely disagreed on any issue or candidate, and this time around they were both wholeheartedly backing McKinley. Reid, who had already served in Paris and been on the ticket with Benjamin Harrison in 1892, was hoping for something more for himself—if not secretary of state, then perhaps London.

UPON LEAVING THE FELLS at the end of September, Hay and Clara visited Reid and his wife, Elisabeth, at Ophir Farm, their estate in the Hudson River Valley—the splendid grounds of which were designed by Frederick Law Olmsted, the baronial house restored by Stanford White. The two old friends gossiped and strategized, much as they had done over the past quarter century. In one respect, the game had changed very little since 1881, when they had stood behind James Garfield and defied New York senators Roscoe Conkling and Thomas Platt. Conkling had long since retired, but his lieutenant, Platt, had reestablished himself as the state's political boss, much to the disgust of Reid. One of the men now in Platt's pocket was Levi Morton, who, after serving as Garfield's minister to France and Harrison's vice president (later displaced by Reid on the ticket for reelection), was now governor of New York.

Once again, then, Reid and Hay had cast their lot with an Ohioan (McKinley) in the next election, while the head of the New York machine issued loud hints of his own preference: this time he wanted either Morton or Speaker of the House Thomas Reed for the White House. But if momentum were to swing toward McKinley, at the very least Platt expected to control a seat or two in a McKinley cabinet, along with other appointments, in exchange for the votes of New York's delegates at the Republican Convention to be held in St. Louis in June.

Although the battlefield was familiar, Hay's position on it had shifted somewhat. He was as well connected in Republican circles as he had been in 1881, when he had filled in for Reid at the *Tribune*, but he had not been in the thick of a political fight in years and had not held office since the Hayes administration. Now, after the poor showing of Harrison and the heartbreak of Blaine, he considered making one more foray. "The summer wanes, and I have done nothing for McKinley," he wrote his Yellowstone companion Bill Phillips in September. To make up for his omission, he mailed a $500 check to Mark Hanna. Many more would follow.

Reid, all the while, still had the presses of the *Tribune* at his command, although his day-to-day presence at the paper had shrunk and his own voice had weakened, quite literally. Since the defeat of Harrison in 1892, he had spent more than half of his time away from New York, seeking to cure his chronic bronchitis and asthma in drier climates. When Hay saw him in October, Reid insisted he was gaining strength, but a month later his doctors ordered him to Arizona. Optimistically he predicted to Hay that he had "a fair prospect of a comfortable Winter," although Hay confided to Adams, "Arizona has to me a mournful sound."

THERE WAS PLENTY TO like about McKinley, even if there was not that much to love. Hay and McKinley had both grown up in what was still regarded as the West (McKinley was born in Niles, Ohio, in 1843), and both had flourished during the war under leaders whose blessings would accelerate their ascent of the Republican ladder (Hay under Lincoln, McKinley under General, then Governor, Rutherford Hayes). Their personalities and intellects, however, were vastly different. For McKinley, literature was the Bible; poetry he found in a hymnal. He neither danced nor attended the theater. He rarely tasted strong drink and did not try ice cream until he was in law school. He played whist, never poker. His one vice was cigars: he smoked (or chewed) as many as fifty a week. In personal appearance, his sole vanity was tidiness: every day an immaculate boiled white shirt and piqué waistcoat, a black frock coat with a carnation in his lapel. In an era when most men, Hay included, cultivated some form of whiskers, McKinley was bare-faced (and so disciplined in his grooming that he could shave without a mirror). His marble jaw and gray eyes inevitably invited comparison to statuary. As a letter writer he was perfunctory, as a storyteller unmemorable. His public oratory was clear and effective, but never histrionic—rarely more than a clenched fist punched gently into an open palm to drive home a point.

Yet if he was not the smartest man in the room, he was the most trusted. If his was not the strongest voice, he was the best listener. Adjectives used by McKinley's peers to describe his character could fill a Sunday School tract: responsible, industrious, determined, patient, imperturbable, sincere, fair, courteous, and kind. He was devoid of guile, incapable of manipulation. It scarcely mattered that he was often impassive or that he had few close friends. Among Republicans, he had rivals but precious few enemies.

In 1893, when Hay had stepped forward to help bail McKinley out of debt, he hardly knew the man whose honor and career he was rescuing. Surely they had met on more than a few occasions during McKinley's years in Congress and then as governor of Ohio, but McKinley was not someone Hay would have invited to dinner, like James Garfield, James Blaine, Cabot Lodge, Theodore Roosevelt, or even Don Cameron. (The invitation probably would not have been accepted, anyway; due to Ida McKinley's frailty, attributed to epilepsy and the wrenching death of two young daughters, she and her husband rarely went out.) But by now Hay was shrewd enough to appreciate that one did not have to be chummy with a candidate to respect him. He had backed Blaine more steadfastly than any politician since Lincoln, yet Blaine proved not to be electable. McKinley was. With the right Republicans behind McKinley early enough, solidly enough, he could be propelled all the way to the White House. It didn't matter if "the Majah"—as Hay called McKinley, a reference to his brevet rank at the end of the war—was short on sophistication and imagination. His broad shoulders could carry the party standard; moreover, he had earned the right to do so.

Throughout the winter of 1895–96, Hay supported the McKinley campaign by serving as a listening post in Washington, passing along to Hanna and Reid the gist of his conversations with leading Republicans like Don Cameron and Cabot Lodge, who was now a senator. Cameron was particularly useful as a link to Pennsylvania's other senator, Matthew Quay, who, like Thomas Platt in New York, controlled his state's Republican machine. "I think you are as good at the game as either of the Penn[sylvani]a Senators," Hanna wrote to Hay, thanking him for his briefings, "and I am perfectly willing to leave them in your hands."

Hanna knew how to delegate; he also appreciated better than anyone before him the importance of strong central command in a political campaign. In 1895, Hanna turned over responsibility for his business affairs in Cleveland to his brother, which freed him to devote his full attention to the task of getting McKinley nominated and elected. So single-minded was Hanna that the perception grew that he had some devious, Svengaliesque control over his candidate—that because he had saved McKinley from financial ruin, he now owned him. The *New York Journal*, purchased by William Randolph Hearst that same year, hastened to establish its pot-stirring, "yellow" reputation by predicting that Hanna would "play McKinley like a pack of cards." The paper's cartoons depicted Hanna as the bloated Beast of Greed, his suit checked with dollar signs; as a puppet master pulling the strings of McKinley; or as an organ grinder calling the tune for his trained monkey.

The reality was something quite different. Hanna was a millionaire, to be sure, his fortune made in coal, steel, shipping, and banking, and he was indeed full-figured in his profile. But despite his affluence, he lived a relatively conservative, abstemious life. While he was by nature acquisitive and aggrandizing, he had nothing but admiration and respect for McKinley, whom he had first met in 1876, when McKinley had defended a group of coal miners arrested during a strike. Hanna was one of the mine's owners, and he never forgot the poise and humanity McKinley displayed in the courtroom. Here was a horse to bet on.

Though six years older than McKinley, Hanna would always be somewhat obsequious toward him. "His attitude was always that of a big, bashful boy toward a girl he loves," explained H. H. Kohlsaat, publisher of the *Chicago Evening Post* and another early McKinleyite. "It was not the power that it brought Mr. Hanna that made him fight for McKinley's nomination and election; it was the love of a strong man for a friend who was worthy of that affection."

And even if Hanna had wanted to control McKinley, he would not have succeeded; McKinley was not so pliable, and for all the effort Hanna put into McKinley's campaign, it was Hanna who depended upon McKinley more than the other way around. Hanna possessed the blunt ambition of a businessman, but McKinley had the tact and equilibrium of a lifelong statesman. "Hanna was impulsive and intuitive where McKinley was calm and reasonable," the Kansas newspaperman William Allen White remarked. "Hanna would rip out a good red double-distilled God damn where McKinley would stifle a scowl with a smile." Hanna was the more brusque of the two, White added, and yet, "Hanna gave McKinley his heart."

In the first months of the campaign, Hanna insisted on paying all of McKinley's expenses himself, "until I knew more about who his friends were to be," he explained. He thanked Hay for his first check but deposited it in the general account of the Ohio Republican Party. As the national convention drew near, McKinley's chances for nomination looked very strong, and he and Hanna agreed that they would avoid any unnecessary obligations that might come due after the election and inauguration. Rather than give in to the demands of men like Platt and Quay, they played up their resistance by coining a decidedly un-Republican campaign slogan: "The People Against the Bosses."

The Republican bosses, all but Platt, eventually fell in line, and McKinley won the nomination handily on the first ballot. After Morton and Thomas Reed declined to join the ticket, McKinley chose as his running mate Garret Hobart, a wealthy, well-connected, but rather bland businessman from New Jersey.

The whole thrust of the campaign was to restore confidence after the three years of uncertainty and upheaval that had followed the Panic of 1893. Millions of Americans were still out of work; commodity prices continued to sag; and strikes and riots had driven a jagged wedge between the "masses" and the "classes." There was nothing radical or polarizing about McKinley; he was exactly who he said he was: a moderate, modest midwesterner. Scintillating he was not; and yet his steadiness and stoicism were reassuring, even inspiring. He had first come to national attention as an advocate of tariffs, a bundle of incentives and restrictions designed to protect American markets and encourage American industry and agriculture. In tariffs, he and Hanna now reckoned they had the perfect Main Street issue on which to build a presidential campaign. Everyone, regard-

less of the rung or region they occupied, was eager to see the country heal
and grow. While there was no question that tariffs were a boon to big business, they were also touted as good for the little guy. Campaign literature
portrayed McKinley as "the Advance Agent for Prosperity," a trustworthy
and benevolent purveyor of a brighter future for class and mass alike.

Nothing was that simple, however. The issue that wound up dominat-
ing the presidential race in 1896 was not tariffs but money—the debate
over whether to base the currency on silver, gold, or a fixed ratio (16:1)
of the two. Going into the convention in St. Louis, McKinley and most
Republican leaders had miscalculated the virulence of the so-called free-
silver movement, whose proponents, known as "silverites," argued that an
inflated dollar would make it easier for farmers and laborers to settle debts
and pay taxes. In contrast, a currency based on gold tightened the money
supply and was assumed to benefit only big business and foreign (mostly
English) bondholders. After rancorous debate and the tempestuous exit
from the convention by two senators from western silver-producing states,
the Republicans finally adopted an equivocal plank that opposed free coinage of silver, unless it was favored by other nations; until then the gold
standard must be maintained. Republicans called this position "sound
money"; their opponents called them "straddlers."

Nearly drowned out in the uproar over currency were several other
planks in the platform that would soon loom much larger than the rest:
pledges to take control of the Hawaiian Islands; to build a canal across
Nicaragua; to enforce the Monroe Doctrine "in its full effect"; and to "actively use [American] influence and good offices to restore peace and give
independence" to Cuba.

If the currency issue was an unwelcome distraction to Republicans, it
thoroughly disrupted the Democrats. At the Democratic Convention in
Chicago on July 9, William Jennings Bryan, a tall, youthful, messianic,
pro-silver populist from Nebraska, accused the "holders of idle capital"
of attempting to "crucify mankind on a cross of gold." The effect of his
speech was electrifying and metamorphic. The Democratic Party, which
under Grover Cleveland had backed a gold standard, voted overwhelm-
ingly for free coinage of silver and enthusiastically nominated Bryan to
take the fight to McKinley.

Yet Bryan, for all his heat, possessed far less fuel than McKinley. No one ever ran a national campaign as masterfully as Mark Hanna. In previous presidential elections, the task of raising money and winning votes was the job of the party committee in each state. Hanna now insisted that the states take their marching orders from his headquarters in Chicago. Between June and November, he oversaw the distribution of millions of pamphlets, posters, buttons, and newspaper supplements—prompting Theodore Roosevelt to comment that Hanna had "advertised McKinley as if he were a patent medicine." Hundreds of speakers, campaigners, and brass bands were deployed to districts where they were most needed and to many where they were redundant, just to make sure.

Hanna, who had served only briefly in an Ohio regiment at the end of the war, tackled his new endeavor like a West Pointer. "The enemy have begun an assault on our lines . . . so that we are obliged to put our men in the field at all points to hold our position," he wrote Hay as the campaign took shape. Hay, who had taken the measure of many an officer, was genuinely impressed by Hanna's military prowess. "I never knew him intimately until we went into this fight together," he declared, "but my esteem and admiration for him have grown every hour. He is a born general in politics . . . with a *coup d'oeil* for the battle-field and a knowledge of the enemy's weak points which is very remarkable."

To pay for the grand offensive, Hanna was no less diligent. Once the Democrats declared war against sound money, he had little trouble dunning big business. "[Bryan] has succeeded in scaring the goldbugs out of their five wits," Hay reported to Adams, who was a committed silverite (as was Don Cameron at first, under Adams's persuasion). Under Hanna's direction, banks were assessed one quarter of 1 percent of their capital. Standard Oil alone gave $250,000. All told, Hanna collected $3.5 million, more than twice the amount raised in any previous campaign. Hay, who gave early and with minimal prompting, was good for at least $5,000 and soon considerably more. "If Gov. McKinley had a few more friends like you I would have a more comfortable time," Hanna wrote Hay before the convention, thanking him for his latest check, this one for $2,000.

In the months leading up to McKinley's nomination, Hay continued to run errands for Hanna and pass along intelligence. "You can be of great service by picking up what is going on . . . in W[ashington]," Hanna wrote in March 1896. "If you want to try your hand at 'diplomacy,' make that your mission. Use Cameron and get Quay away from Platt and our work is over."

BY MAY, WITH MCKINLEY's nomination all but assured, Hay put in play a strategy of his own, If Indeed that was what it was. With no desire to do any public campaigning on McKinley's behalf and well aware of Hanna's keen nose for any solicitation of support bearing the faintest whiff of quid pro quo, he decided that the wisest thing he could do would be to leave the country until the fall.

He and Henry Adams sailed on May 20, chaperoning Helen and a friend. Clarence King saw them off at the pier in New York. The only other passenger of note aboard the *Teutonic* was the author and theatrical manager Bram Stoker; Adams remarked in a letter to Lizzie Cameron that he "devotes occasional hours to the girls in the intervals of writing a novel." Stoker's *Dracula* would be published the following year.

London was the usual luncheons and dinners, fittings at the tailor, visits to galleries. Hay's dinner guests one evening included Adams, Henry James, Bret Harte, John Singer Sargent, Theodore Roosevelt's sister Anna ("Bamie") Cowles, and her husband, William, who was U.S. naval attaché in London. In conversations with Colonial Secretary Joseph Chamberlain and other public men, Hay discovered how unfamiliar the English were with William McKinley, except as concerned his advocacy of protective tariffs. Hay vouched for his candidate, first in a letter to *The Times* and then in published interviews, stressing McKinley's decency and level-headedness. "It is difficult to describe Mr. McKinley in a picturesque manner," he told the *Daily Chronicle*. "A man like Mr. McKinley is all one side—there is nothing to be said against him. His character is absolutely blameless and spotless. . . . He is distinguished by great moral earnestness." When the *Chronicle* asked if there were any truth to the rumor that Hay was interested in higher office in a McKinley administration, he banished the notion with a shake of his head.

Hay was in Holland with Adams and the girls when he read of McKinley's nomination, and he quickly cabled his congratulations. For the next two months, as he traveled through France and Italy, he followed the campaign avidly and as best he could. In Paris (where they were joined by Del, on summer vacation from Yale), Hay ran into his old friend Wayne MacVeagh, a notorious Mugwump who had served in both the Hayes and Garfield administrations and was now Grover Cleveland's ambassador to Italy. (MacVeagh also happened to be married to Don Cameron's sister.) Hay was pleased to report to Clara that the Democratic Party's pro-silver leanings had made MacVeagh "almost a Republican again." MacVeagh further ingratiated himself by advising Hay "in the most solemn manner not to refuse the office of Secretary of State." Once again Hay acted surprised: "I told him I saw no more chance of being offered it than of being turned to salt, and that I had as little desire as prospect of it."

But on August 3, as he crossed the Atlantic, he composed a letter to McKinley to be posted upon arrival. "I inclose a thousand dollar note to help meet the personal demands which will be made on you during the canvass," he began. "I shall, unless you see some reason to the contrary, send you the same sum each month till November." Lest McKinley jump to the conclusion that he was shopping for a favor, Hay added emphatically: "I want to make one matter perfectly clear. I do not know whether or not I shall ask you for any public employment. It will depend on various considerations—health, domestic or business affairs, &c. But whether I do or not, I want it understood that anything I may have done, or shall do, between now and next March [Inauguration Day], shall have no bearing on the case whatever. I shall feel as free to make known my own wishes, and you must feel as free to grant or refuse them, as if we had never met."

Yet in the same letter, he let McKinley know that he had already been rehearsing for a position in the State Department. Over the past year, diplomatic relations between the United States and England had grown absurdly tense, sparked by a boundary dispute between Venezuela and British Guiana. In July 1895, Cleveland's secretary of state Richard Olney—who in his previous post as U.S. attorney general directed federal troops to break up the Pullman strike—had sent Britain a stern warning that any bullying of Venezuela would be regarded as a direct affront to the vital interests of the United States as expressed in the Monroe Doctrine. In his annual address to Congress in December, President Cleveland reaffirmed Olney's bumptious interpretation of the Monroe Doctrine, declaring that it was the duty of the United States "to resist by every means" any British aggression in Venezuela. Somewhat astonished by such sudden and seemingly uncalled-for belligerence, Great Britain, without acknowledging that it had behaved inappropriately or that the Monroe Doctrine even applied to the Anglo-Venezuelan boundary, agreed to arbitrate the dispute—which is where the matter stood while Hay was in London.

Hay had discussed the issue at length with Sir William Harcourt, leader of the Liberal Party in the House of Commons. When Harcourt hinted that Lord Salisbury, who at the time was both England's Conservative prime minister and its foreign secretary, might be inclined to drag out the Venezuelan negotiations in hopes of getting better terms with the next American administration, Hay cautioned against it. "I disclaimed any authority to speak for you or any knowledge of your plans," he informed McKinley, "but assured him, from my acquaintance with public feeling in America, that the British government would make a great mistake if it fancied [that] the incoming Administration would fall behind the present one in the firm and resolute upholding of the Monroe Doctrine. . . . I have not taken any liberty with your name in this thing, but I felt sure you would be glad of anything your friends might do to facilitate the clearing away of this vexatious dispute before March."

March was still a long way off, but, if nothing else, Hay had provided a flattering glimpse of himself in diplomatic harness. He was loyal, informed, confident, and very well connected. Maybe McKinley had other people in mind and maybe Hay wasn't looking for a job, but, based on his past and recent conduct in London, McKinley would be hard-pressed to find anyone with better qualifications.

WHILE HAY WAS ABROAD, McKinley remained at home in Canton. All summer long, as Hanna's well-funded operatives trumpeted "Patriotism, Protection, and Prosperity" across the land and William Jennings Bryan brandished the Cross of Gold at a dozen whistle-stops a day, McKinley scarcely left the front porch of his tidy, two-story house on North Market

Street. "I might just as well put up a trapeze on my front lawn and compete with some professional athlete as go out speaking against Bryan," he remarked. Instead, he welcomed delegations—veterans, farmers, trade associations, unions, and every fraternal organization under the sun—to call upon him and express their concerns and wishes. When they were finished, the calm, unruffled McKinley would stand on a chair and deliver a set speech, punctuated with platitudes such as "Good money never made times hard" and "Our currency today is good as gold."

He might not have been a trapeze artist, but Canton quickly turned into a circus. The route from the train station was spanned by a gigantic McKinley arch and lined by souvenir vendors; one item that sold by the thousand was a tin dinner pail—tin being an industry fostered by the McKinley tariff, the pail to be filled once the "McKinley Boom" revitalized the economy. (Tin was also the inspiration for one of the characters in L. Frank Baum's popular novel of the day, *The Wizard of Oz*.) Between the Republican Convention in June and election day, seven hundred and fifty thousand people from thirty states made the pilgrimage, turning McKinley's yard to mud and nearly pulling the porch off the house.

Hay did not join the parade of supplicants to Canton. He passed the remainder of the summer at the Fells and watched from afar. "He has asked me to come," Hay told Adams, "but I thought I would not struggle with the millions on his trampled lawn." It tickled him to learn that Cabot Lodge and Theodore Roosevelt, who had not been McKinley men at first, had been to see the nominee, hats in hand.

Not until Hay was back in Cleveland in October did he at last wade into the fray with his old vigor. "What a strange and portentous campaign this is," he had written Reid, who had returned from Arizona and was again stoking the *Tribune*. "The only real issue between the two parties is the tariff—but by the malice of fate and the limber jaws of demagogues the whole country has been set to talking about coinage—a matter utterly unfit for public discussion."

Hay called Bryan a "half-baked glib little briefless jack-leg lawyer," who charged about the country "begging for the Presidency, as a tramp might beg for a pie." Sounding not unlike Arthur Farnham in *The Bread-Winners*, he fumed: "[Bryan] makes only one speech—but he makes it twice a day. There is no fun in it. He simply reiterates the unquestioned truths that every man who has a clean shirt is a thief and ought to be hanged: that there is no goodness and wisdom except among the illiterate & criminal classes."

Finally, two weeks before the election, after giving a speech for McKinley in Cleveland, Hay accepted an invitation to Canton. Few men ever got to know the inner McKinley, even those whom he took into his confidence. William Allen White, the journalist, devoted half his career to looking for "the real man back of that plaster cast" and never succeeded. Hay's meeting with McKinley evidently went well enough, but he too got only so far. "I spent yesterday with the Majah," Hay reported to Adams. "I had been dreading it for a month, thinking it would be like talking in a boiler factory. But he met me at the station, gave me meat & took me upstairs and talked for two hours as calmly & serenely as if we were summer boarders in Bethlehem, at a loss for means to kill time. I was more struck than ever with his mask. It is a genuine Italian ecclesiastical face of the XVth Century."

Hay did not offer any details on what he and McKinley discussed—or whether the subject of appointments came up at all—but he left town assured that "the Majah" was very much in command. "And to think," he told Adams, "there are idiots who think Mark Hanna will run him." As proof of his fealty and admiration, not to mention his own steady aim, a few days later Hay sent McKinley several ducks from Winous Point.

McKinley won the election emphatically, thanks to Hanna's generalship and the alarmism and divisiveness of the Bryan campaign. If McKinley were a patent medicine, as Theodore Roosevelt had suggested, Hanna peddled him in millions of carefully measured doses as one part cure for economic anemia, one part stimulant for a robust national future. Despite covering tens of thousands of miles and delivering more than two hundred speeches, Bryan could not keep pace with the Republican onslaught. His effort to convert currency into class warfare—agricultural interests versus industrial, rural versus urban—gained traction west of the Mississippi and in the South but fell flat everywhere else. In the end, Hanna's propaganda machine, abundantly funded by the baited bulls of capitalism, convinced Americans that they ought to care more about expanded markets (tariffs) than inflated prices (silver). Persuasion in some instances was said to border on coercion: the Bryan camp alleged that many employers went so far as to tell their workers that their jobs depended on a McKinley victory; bankers warned the same about mortgages. Meanwhile, Republican artillery battered the image of the Great Commoner, as Bryan cast himself, stigmatizing him as a radical doomsayer and "Popocrat," since he was also the nominee of the anti–big business Populist Party.

Of 14 million votes cast, McKinley beat Bryan by 600,000; in the electoral count, the margin was more impressive, 271 to 176, the greatest edge since Grant's trouncing of Horace Greeley in 1872. Bryan held the rural vote, but not all of it, and little else besides. He was the younger candidate but in some ways the older, for he purveyed a nostalgic, agrarian, nineteenth-century vision of America. McKinley, for all his front-porch fustiness, emerged as the first twentieth-century candidate, appealing to non-rural, commerce-minded voters—the expanding "middle," whose fates were now tied more closely to those of industry and international markets than to the family farm. A race that initially had hinged on the question of money had come down to precisely that, and in 1896 Mark Hanna made sure that his man had much more of it. Running for president would never be the same.

IN THE CUSTOMARY HANDICAPPING of who would fill which seats in the new administration, John Hay's name came up often. Speculation focused not on whether he was in or out, but on which place would be his. "We are at sea here as to whether you are going to be Secretary of State or Ambassador to England," wrote Theodore Roosevelt, who was angling to trade his job as New York police commissioner for something with more national prominence; his best shot was assistant secretary of the navy.

Hay had not gone looking for a job since 1869, when he had grown bored with life in Warsaw and wangled a place in Madrid from the Grant administration. He never wanted anything so much that he would bow or scrape for it (except perhaps the affection of Lizzie Cameron), and he was never one to call in a debt, political or otherwise. And yet it was now quite plain that he desired a spot in McKinley's State Department. His qualifications and his loyalty to McKinley were manifest, and to friends like Roosevelt, his appointment was inevitable. There was really only one person he worried about: Whitelaw Reid.

Earlier in the year, Hay had hoped that McKinley would choose Reid as his running mate, but Reid's long-standing feud with Thomas Platt ruled this out. Reid now had his sights on secretary of state, but Platt was headed back to the Senate after a sixteen-year hiatus, and McKinley did not relish having to fight Platt over this particular patronage, once they were both in Washington. Nevertheless, Reid believed he had a good chance, and Hay assured his old friend that he would stand clear; he would be content to take the ambassadorship to London.

For two months after the election, Hay and Reid outdid each other in their chivalry, Hay encouraging Reid to take aim at the secretary of state appointment, Reid urging Hay to think twice about his withdrawal from running for the same. "What you say about your own unwillingness to take the Secretaryship of State is in its personal aspect far too generous," Reid wrote Hay. "I cannot think that you would be right in refusing merely to make place for another. At our time of life these baubles are not likely to be offered often. If, on the other hand, you should distinctly prefer the other place [London], that would doubtless be a sufficient reason."

To which Hay replied: "I do not see now anybody of the first rank who could come into competition with you, either in personal merits, or in unquestionable service to McKinley. . . . On the whole I am inclined to think McKinley will find his pleasure and his interest coinciding in calling for you."

Hay was sincere in his wish that Reid gain the secretaryship, but he intentionally overstated his optimism. And it was not an especially great sacrifice to defer to Reid. Hay recognized early on that there was no circumstance under which he himself would get the secretary of state job, with or without Reid in the hunt. Too many other factors worked against him, the most crucial of which was Mark Hanna, the man to whom McKinley owed a favor above all others.

Hanna had his heart set on the Senate, but one of Ohio's seats had already been promised to the former governor and party potentate Joseph Foraker, in exchange for Foraker's pledge not to block McKinley's nomination at the Republican Convention. (Senators were still elected by legislatures and thus more easily controlled by state political machines.) The other seat was occupied by John Sherman, who, at seventy-three, was now a crumbling pillar of Republicanism. Already a plan was taking shape to ease Sherman toward retirement with a brief stopover in the McKinley cabinet—most likely State, since he had already held Treasury in the Hayes administration—thereby opening Sherman's seat to Mark Hanna. No matter what, there wasn't room for a second Ohioan—namely Hay—anywhere in the cabinet.

Throughout the fall and winter, Reid discounted the Sherman scenario and believed that his path to the State Department could be blocked only by Thomas Platt, who was purported to have growled, "I told Hanna to tell McKinley, if he wanted Hell with the lid off, at the very start, to appoint Reid." In fact, as Hay knew but Reid chose to overlook, the far greater impasse remained Mark Hanna's senatorial aspirations and the bond of loyalty and indebtedness Hanna had forged with McKinley.

Hay saw the wreck coming far in advance and chose another route and destination. The plum he wanted more, the one he now believed was within his reach, was the ambassadorship. If Reid became secretary of state, all the better. But if Reid came up short, due to the Sherman-Hanna switch, and then went after the London post, Hay would already have the inside track. The brilliance of Hay's strategy—in which he stood behind Reid and did not betray him but ultimately outmaneuvered him and established even greater cohesion with McKinley and Hanna—is not revealed overtly in his letters, or at least not in any that survive. Only by reading between the lines and only after the deed was accomplished and Hay was installed as the ambassador to the Court of St. James's would it be possible to detect just how subtly and completely he had finessed his ally and friend, Whitelaw Reid.

By the end of December, McKinley and Hanna had quietly agreed that Sherman would get the State Department. Accordingly, they had taken Hay into their confidence and recruited him to help appease Reid. A telegram from Hay to McKinley, filed in McKinley's presidential papers for the year 1897 but clearly marked "Dc 26"—which can only mean December 26, 1896—advised: "How would it answer to say that [Reid's] selection for a place in the cabinet or a foreign embassy . . . had been under consideration, that his friends had thought it would be imprudent for him to risk the confinement of official work until his health was more completely restored, that you then reluctantly gave up the idea of appointing him[?]"

If the date on this telegram is correct, Hay knew a full month before Reid that McKinley did not intend to offer Reid a job. Even if the date is not correct, Hay's conduct in the weeks that followed, while well intentioned, was an exercise in self-promotion unprecedented and unrepeated in his exemplary life. Never did he lie outright; but neither did he reveal the whole truth.

Two days after sending the telegram to McKinley, Hay reached out to the president-elect in a different, more magnanimous way: "I send you a ring today which I hope you will wear on Inauguration day. It contains a few hairs from the head of George Washington." Hay saw no reason to mention that he had presented a similar ring to Rutherford Hayes twenty years earlier. McKinley was touched, and he began wearing the ring immediately.

McKinley, however, was far too canny to make any larger promises to Hay; nor did Hay make any demands, assuring McKinley, "I shall not question either your judgment, or your friendship." Even so, in early January 1897, he drafted a letter to McKinley, laying out the case for his own appointment to London: "I do not think it is altogether selfishness and vanity which has brought me to think that perhaps you might do worse than select me. 1. My appointment would please a good many people & so far as I know would offend nobody. . . . If Reid can't get it, he would rather have me go than any one else. 2. I should not hold the office very long. It would be at your disposal in some critical time when it might serve a useful purpose. 3. As I have no claim on the place, and as it is really above my merits and deservings, I think I would be more grateful than any one else would be, and would do as much to show my gratitude." He then urged McKinley to make up his mind as soon as possible because "[a]lready it is difficult to find a suitable house for an Embassy."

Reid, meanwhile, had not helped his own case by going to Arizona for the winter, distancing himself from the field of play and reinforcing rumors of his questionable health. (Actually, Reid was feeling better than he had in years, riding horseback twenty or more miles a day.) By early January, he was willing to acknowledge that secretary of state was no longer in the cards; yet he still could not bring himself to believe that the job would go to Sherman. Instead, he sketched out a scenario in which Hanna would become secretary of the navy (leaving Sherman in the Senate) and Hay would vie for secretary of state, thus opening England for himself. The only hitch, as usual, was Platt, who wanted New York Central president Chauncey Depew for the English ambassadorship. These and other prognostications Reid sent in cipher to a trusted underling in the *Tribune* office, who decoded and forwarded them to Hay.

Hay, who by now grasped that Reid was not in serious consideration for any position, either in Washington or abroad, nonetheless encouraged his friend to persevere. One of his morale-boosting letters brought tears to the eyes of Mrs. Reid. "She said it made life worth living to have such friends as you & Mrs. Hay," Reid wrote, "whether we get the place or not." Hay gave Reid the impression that his own chances for London were worse than dismal, and even while newspapers continued to mention him as a possibility, he clarified to his friend, "I have so constantly talked for you and refused the use of my own name, that I am considered out of it."

And yet, just to be safe, on January 22 he told Reid about the letter he was about to send to McKinley, spelling out the reasons why London *should* go to John Hay and not Whitelaw Reid: "I think I shall let it be known . . . that while I continue to prefer your appointment to my own, in case the President does not think it expedient, for any reason to appoint you, I know you would prefer me being selected than any New York man identified with the Platt interest."

Even then, Reid would not recognize the inevitable. He diagrammed another chessboard, with himself as secretary of the navy (now that it was clear that Hanna would try for the Senate) and Hay as *assistant* secretary of state, with the understanding that Hay would replace Sherman as secretary in a year or so. (The second part of this picture was of course quite prescient: Hay would succeed Sherman after eighteen months.)

As the days passed and no announcements were forthcoming from

Canton, Reid grew steadily more upset with McKinley for allowing himself to be badgered by Platt. Inevitably, Reid compared 1897 to 1881. "Garfield's fatal mistake was that he gave Platt and Conkling five or six nominations before he had the courage to name the man [Blaine] to whom he owed his own nomination. Naturally they had already 'sized him up' as timid, and acted accordingly, and my own comfort in recalling that sad period is that I had earnestly warned him of this danger before hand." (Once again Reid was partly prescient: in four years Garfield and McKinley would have something more fatal in common than Thomas Platt.)

Hay's correspondence with Hanna and McKinley contains several hints that he knew by the end of January that he was at the top of the list for London, although nothing was locked in yet. Before anything further could transpire, McKinley still had to dispense with Reid. Once Reid was out of the picture, Hay could accept the appointment without bruising the friendship. How carefully this end game was choreographed is not known, but what is evident is that Hay shifted, deftly and discreetly, from brokering the candidacy of Reid to brokering Reid's withdrawal. With McKinley's consent, Hay met with Reid's father-in-law, Ogden Mills, and persuaded him to make the long journey to Arizona to break the news that no job awaited Reid in the new administration. Hay also wrote Reid a letter that he hoped would arrive shortly after Mills. "You will come back well & strong and take your place at the head of the greatest paper on the continent," he comforted, "and everybody will desire [your] friendship & offer theirs." In closing, he added wearily, "I am indifferent as to who gets the Eng. Mission"—a statement which, at this stage, was at best disingenuous.

A week later, Hay got from Reid the response he had hoped for in the form of a telegram: "Repeat in strongest and most unreserved way . . . don't throw your own chance away." And in a follow-up letter, Reid was even more gracious. "I think you have acted with a generosity and self-sacrificing devotion far beyond my desserts. . . . I want to release you from any obligation you may think you have placed yourself under to neglect your own interests in order to promote mine."

It now fell to Hay to find a way for Reid to save face—and to curb

Platt's satisfaction at having stymied his nemesis. This he accomplished by drafting a letter to go out over McKinley's signature, in which McKinley expressed his great disappointment at learning that Reid's fragile health prevented him from accepting appointments to either the cabinet or England. Out of fairness, Hay also gave McKinley an option. He composed a second letter, in which the president-elect offered Reid the ambassadorship to England.

Hay, of course, was betting that Reid would not accept out of concern for the effect of London's damp and coal-clotted air on his lungs—a debility Hay had himself experienced firsthand. "[I]t would be suicide," Hay advised McKinley, "but if he should [accept], he would make an excellent Minister." But then Hay made an uncharacteristically blunt comment that revealed just how much confidence he had in his alignment with McKinley—and just how little genuine sympathy he had for Reid: "If on the other hand, Reid should decline, you would be free to look somewhere else. In all this, I am thinking only of you. I have ceased thinking about Reid; he thinks enough about himself for two."

As Hay expected, McKinley sent the first letter, not the second. Without suspecting that Hay was the true author, Reid saw right through it. "The President's letter is . . . extremely complimentary, charming, and everything else delightful, excepting sincere," he wrote Hay after McKinley's inauguration. There was nothing the matter with his health, Reid insisted. Just the same, the deed was done.

And with that, the tumblers fell into place, and the door swung open. With Reid out of the way, Platt acquiesced, and McKinley was finally free to award Hay the prize he so greatly desired. Reid would blame many people for his rejection, but he never faulted John Hay. Hay had done all he could for Reid, although, in retrospect, he had done a good deal more for himself.

EVEN BEFORE HAY'S APPOINTMENT was made official, his friends in England wrote to express their great hope that he would be the next ambassador. George Smalley, who had worked with Hay at the *Tribune* but was now with *The Times* of London, was the first to publish the news, prematurely it turned out, but correctly. He spoke for a great many in Great Britain when he wrote Hay, "You are the ideal man for the place. . . . We want a man who is a true American yet not anti-English."

Hay, Clara, Helen, and Henry Adams sailed from New York on April 14 aboard the *St. Paul.* Henry Adams, despite his pronounced cynicism for the nascent McKinley regime, was proud to accompany his dear friend and neighbor as he filled the august place once occupied so ably by Adams's father. "Thucydides"—one of Hay's many nicknames for Adams—"was in fine form and gave us the encouragement of his gentle pessimism every day," Hay told Bill Phillips after the crossing.

As they disembarked at Southampton, they were delighted to see the face of Henry James among the greeters. "This is tremendous and delicious," James had told Hay when he first learned he was coming to London. "You make the plot of existence thicken more delightfully—even across the hiatus of the Atlantic—than anything I can manage on paper this morning . . . at least until I have embraced you. I long for the hour when I shall come as near as I dare to laying hands with that intent on your inviolable ambassadorial person."

Four hours later, they were installed at 5 Carlton House Terrace, in a house they had rented from the Earl of Caledon, who also owned a sizable estate in Northern Ireland. Hay had no intention of trying to get by on the $17,000 salary provided by the State Department; not only would he live in the manner to which he was accustomed in the United States, but he would also present himself in a way that would place him on equal footing with those in England who mattered to him most. To do so, he and Clara brought along their own silver, two carriages (a brougham and a landau), and five horses. Before leaving home, Hay had his initials monogrammed on the carriages and harness.

The house was a two-story Georgian, entered from Pall Mall—"very plain on the outside but very nice inside," Clara wrote her mother. The rear windows overlooked St. James's Park and Horse Guards Parade. The rooms were furnished with "many fine pictures and plenty of furniture," Clara observed cheerily. A large, high-ceilinged drawing room was ideal for state occasions. Hay and Clara each had their own bedrooms and morning rooms, and Helen had her own sitting room on the third floor. Upon their arrival, the Hays found the staff already in place: a coachman, two footmen (to whom a third was later added), a butler, three house-maids, a chef, and three kitchen maids.

No foreign minister had ever lived so sumptuously, Hearst's *New York Journal* commented. "The scale of expenditure on which he has estab-lished his household and the gorgeousness of his entourage cause even the English people to gape." Maybe not *all* English people; the Hays' neighbors were lords, dukes, and earls, and William Waldorf Astor, the expatriate heir to one of America's greatest fortunes. To be included in this rarefied peerage at such a prestigious address, Hay reportedly paid $5,000 a month, a sum that probably did not include the salaries of the servants.

Before his tenure as ambassador could begin officially, Hay first had to present his credentials to Queen Victoria. On May 3, a royal coach ap-peared at Carlton House Terrace to carry him and Clara to Paddington Station for the trip by train to Windsor. Clara complained that her bon-net, pink with roses, rubbed on the carriage's low roof, and as they rolled through the streets of London, her husband roughened the soles of her new boots with his pocket knife so she would not slip while descending the carriage's velvet-covered steps.

It can be assumed that Hay, as ever, was perfectly and appropriately dressed for the occasion, though his precise wardrobe was not noted. At the end of the nineteenth century, many foreign diplomats still wore military-style tailcoats with gold embroidery, sashes, even plumed hats and swords. But in recent years, the U.S. State Department had directed its envoys to wear "the simple dress of an American citizen." Court appearances, such as drawing rooms, were evidently a different mat-ter; an invitation Hay received from the Prince and Princess of Wales, for instance, specified: "The ambassador would of course come in his uniform"—the normal court getup of the day being tailcoat, waist-coat, neck cloth, velvet knee breeches, silk stockings, and buckle shoes. (Women wore tiaras and dresses with trains at court.) Hay did not men-tion whether he wore his court dress or one of his meticulous Bond Street suits for his audience with the queen.

They arrived at Windsor Castle in time for lunch with the prime minister and the Duke of Devonshire. Afterward, first Hay and then

Clara were shown to the private apartment of the queen. They had both been "presented" at previous drawing rooms, but this was the first time they conversed directly with Victoria. Each was pleasantly surprised by her kindness. "I had always been told that royalty spoke first," Hay wrote McKinley, "but she evidently waited for me." Clara was astonished when the seventy-seven-year-old queen rose and shook her hand. "[S]he struck me as nothing more than a nice little old lady," Clara recorded. "She seems to have made the same impression on the Ambassador."

After being properly welcomed, Hay looked forward to a pleasant, engaging, but not too taxing term, and unlike previous American envoys, who were not so well acquainted with London, he had little desire to grandstand for his country or himself. "I have determined to appear in public as little as possible, and resolutely to avoid slobbering over the British," he informed McKinley.

In the spring of 1897, relations between the United States and Great Britain were not at the kissing stage, but they had come a fair way since Grover Cleveland and Richard Olney's saber-rattling over Venezuela two years earlier—and an even longer way since the tense days of the Civil War, when the *Alabama* and other British-built vessels were destroying American shipping. There were still plenty of jingoes in America—Henry Cabot Lodge perhaps the most vocal—who held a grudge against England for the colonial boot prints it had left on American soil and for the persistent smugness of the crown toward all colonies, past and potential. America's Irish, most of whom voted Democratic, bore no love for England; nor did American silverites, who resented England's adamant allegiance to the gold standard. But lately the pendulum had begun to swing. Rancor over the *Alabama* and Venezuela had been mollified by arbitration, and with the election of McKinley, the silverites were melting away. Moreover, as the United States and Great Britain surveyed the globe—the American gaze pausing anxiously on Cuba, in its own backyard, and the British on the recalcitrant Boers in South Africa—the two countries recognized that they shared more than laws and language. On the brink of a new century, rapprochement made more sense than at any time in their respective histories.

As George Smalley had noted, Hay was ideally suited to the job of nurturing friendship—a polite, perspicacious American with no hankering to twist the lion's tail. In his first months in London, the only issues that demanded immediate diplomatic attention were a perfunctory pledge by the United States to pursue an international agreement on the currency question and a proposal to regulate fur-seal hunting in the Bering Sea. Hay dutifully broached these subjects with the Foreign Office, but when England demurred on both, he did not press, and the new secretary of state, John Sherman, deep in his dotage, did not remonstrate with his ambassador for his lack of aggression.

Hay's touch was light, borrowed more from the genial William Evarts, under whom he had served in the Rutherford Hayes State Department, than from the confrontational Olney. One of the first things Hay did, once he settled into his offices at 123 Victoria Street, was to order new stationery, changing the heading from "United States Embassy" to "American Embassy"—less muscular, more personal. And the first address he delivered was at the unpompous unveiling of a bust of Sir Walter Scott in Westminster Abbey. "I should have no excuse for appearing," he said with characteristic modesty, "except as representing for the time being a large section of Walter Scott's immense constituency." As a diplomatic overture, it was slight, yet it hit the right notes: American admiration for a cherished British subject, two peoples joined by a common literature. "His ideals are lofty and pure," Hay said of Scott. "[H]is heroes are brave and strong, not exempt from human infirmities, but always devoted to ends more or less noble."

The next event on Hay's calendar was likewise strictly ceremonial but exponentially grander in scale. The Diamond Jubilee, a celebration of the sixtieth anniversary of Queen Victoria's accession to the throne, was scheduled for the end of June. Every country, dominion, and colony was invited to send military and diplomatic delegations for observances that included services at Westminster Abbey and a royal procession from Buckingham Palace, through the heart of London, to St. Paul's Cathedral. President McKinley announced that the United States would send an admiral, a general, and one "eminent citizen" as envoys, with Ambassador Hay heading up the mission.

Seizing the opportunity to patch a recent wound, the president named

Whitelaw Reid to deliver the American message of congratulations and goodwill to the queen, an offer that Reid accepted enthusiastically. There was only one problem: the full delegation was welcome for the jubilee, but the queen announced that she would receive only one envoy from each delegation at Buckingham Palace. Once again it looked as if Reid would lose the position of honor to Hay. This time, however, Hay humbly surrendered the field, cabling McKinley that Reid ought to be made the head of the American mission. McKinley was relieved and grateful to Hay for solving what surely would have caused an even greater awkwardness in relations between the White House and the *Tribune*. "Whitelaw would have gone clean daft, if he had arrived here & found that Her Most Gracious would only receive [me]," Hay wrote Lizzie Cameron.

Lizzie had recently been in London herself, surrounded by her usual courtesans and again at the center of her own drama. Her husband, Don, had decided not to run for reelection; worse, from Lizzie's standpoint, he announced his intention to sell the house on Lafayette Square and withdraw to Pennsylvania. Her already troubled marriage had reached a new low. "The dark days are coming, I fear," Lizzie confided to Adams. "I do not mind being out of politics—on the contrary—but to live in Penn[sylvani]a! Well, I won't. I'll travel." Instead of selling the house, Cameron rented it to Vice President Hobart for four years, beginning May 1.

Before Lizzie could make her getaway, she fell gravely ill with influenza. Doctors feared her heart was damaged, though Adams knew the real problem was nervous collapse. "There is a long history of mental weakness and mental struggle," she admitted to him. "I have always wanted to tell you but I couldn't." When Adams had left Washington with Hay in mid-April, he fretted that he might never see her again. She rallied sufficiently to sail to Europe on May 5 with her daughter, Martha. Adams met her at Southampton and escorted her in a train compartment reserved for invalids to Brown's Hotel in London. When Hay went by to see her, she still looked "poorly," he wrote Reid in New York. "She seems disturbed about the future."

After several days in London, Adams took Lizzie to France and installed her in a house on the outskirts of Paris, where she continued to convalesce. "It almost consoles me for the gloom in which your flight plunged London to know you are growing stronger every day," Hay wrote from Cliveden, where he was a guest, apparently without Clara, at the magnificent country estate of William Astor. "Since you went away there is no news—there never is, after you go." Here was one more example of what Lizzie would later attempt to dismiss as Hay's "habit of gallantry," but he too would have been devastated if she had not survived her latest flight from unhappiness.

Two weeks after Lizzie and Adams departed, Reid with his wife and two teenage children arrived in London. They were met by Elisabeth Reid's parents, Mrs. and Mrs. Ogden Mills, who had rented a house for them just a few doors down from the Hays on Carlton House Terrace. Bearing the title of special ambassador, Reid conducted himself as if the jubilee were for his benefit alone. The Hays, who were invited to any number of dinners and galas and were given favored seats at St. Paul's Cathedral for the service in the queen's honor, were careful not to upstage the Reids and in fact seemed relieved to share some of the wearisome diplomatic responsibilities that bracketed the actual jubilee. "I have succeeded in effacing myself so that I shall have to bring certificates to show I hold a commission," Hay joked to McKinley.

But even in their conscientious deference, he and Clara took considerable pleasure in chronicling the conduct of the special ambassador and his entourage. Clara mentioned to her mother that while she herself had grown bored mingling with so many lords and ladies ("as they always look alike"), the Reids, on the other hand, "have enjoyed themselves hugely. . . . I do not know who they will associate with when they get home they are so set up by their intercourse with Royalties."

Hay commented cattily to Adams: "I have seen my friend Whitelaw Reid sitting between two princesses at supper every night, a week running. . . . His rapture had the *aliquid amare* [bitter flavor] that an end must come, but the memory of it will soothe many an hour of ennui at Ophir Farm. As for Mrs. Oddie [Reid's mother-in-law], her tiaras got heavier and higher hour by hour, till the ceilings were all too low. . . . I naturally run to slanderous gossip—but I suppose one must once in a while abuse one's friends. . . . [D]estroy this promptly and tell me you have done so—that I may sleep."

• • •

AT LAST (AND BELATEDLY) the Reids departed. At the beginning of
August, Clara and Helen left for America also, to be gone until the fall.
Immediately Hay reached out to Lizzie, who had written to invite him to
visit her in France. "You dear sweet woman, what can I say to you?" he
replied. "To hurt those who love you is as natural to you as to breathe.
You know how it breaks my heart to have you ask me to come when I ab
solutely can't. . . . Twenty times I have made up my alleged mind to drop
everything & go—but then comes a lucid interval and I see that 'Desertion' never looks pretty in a court martial. I cannot leave this blessed
island."

Then, recalling their intimacies of six years earlier, he continued: "I
walked through Duke Street again today. My heart ached with the vision
of the beautiful small feet that caressed the pavement on an errand of
mercy so long ago. You are a sweet, sweet woman. There is no other word.
You are beautiful, and clever, and splendid, and charming and fascinating
and lovely. But you are, more than all, sweet. It is a keen, living sweetness
that lifts you up above all others in charm; that makes the sight of you,
the sound of your voice, the touch of you, so full of delight. One can
never have enough of you, never. It is because you are so sweet, because
the memory of you is so entrancing, that I find a dozen spots in this
grimy town like Paradise. The vivid beauty of your face the day we came
back from Kensington shines out even now in the mist & fog and gloom
and makes the whole town throb with pleasure. You sweet Lizzie; the
words are forbidden but I say them over and over. You sweet woman—if I
had twenty pages, I could fill them with saying, You sweet!"

The same day he wrote Lizzie, he also jotted a brief letter to Clara,
whose ship had not yet lost sight of England: "I have a few minutes before breakfast and cannot put them to a better use than writing to you."

Hay's life was now more public than ever. Yet there were secrets he
would never divulge—as much as he would have liked for them to see the
sweet light of day.

CHAPTER 14

Setting the Table

The year that followed was surely one of the best of Hay's life. His work at the embassy was engaging and quite manageable; the society he kept was as elevated and congenial as he could ever have wished for.

If he made the job seem effortless and enjoyed himself a bit too obviously, his contribution to diplomacy was nonetheless crucial. The comity he fostered during his time as ambassador to the Court of St. James's was unprecedented in the history of the United States and England, and the bond he established set both nations on firmer ground everywhere they chose to venture and in doing so altered the balance of world power for the long haul. What is more, Hay's experience in London, abbreviated though it turned out to be, prepared him for the greater task ahead—that of secretary of state for a nation whose horizons were expanding by leaps and bounds.

But while Hay would soon play a pivotal role in international relations, he had little to do with setting the table or choosing the guests. By the time he returned from England in September 1898, the United States had fought a war with Spain, occupied Cuba, Puerto Rico, Guam, and the Philippines, and annexed Hawaii. Through all this, Hay's responsibility was simply to make friends and to pass along the English point of view to Washington. These friends and, moreover, this method of making them—by civil, sociable conversation—would become the cornerstone of his diplomacy, not just with England but with all nations.

Across the Atlantic, the topic that topped all others was the increasing possibility of American military intervention in Cuba. Hay's familiarity with the situation in Cuba went back nearly thirty years to his time in Madrid, when U.S. Minister Daniel Sickles had tried fruitlessly to persuade Spain to sell the Caribbean island. Later, at the *New York Tribune*, Hay had written numerous editorials scolding Spain for its oppression of Cuba. More recently, Henry Adams, who had close ties with the Cuban junta for independence in the United States, had shared disturbing accounts of concentration camps, starvation, and extermination inflicted by Spanish soldiers upon Cuban civilians.

Hay did not need to be convinced that the Old World ought to relinquish its colonial possessions in the new, but unlike Senator Henry Cabot Lodge and new Assistant Secretary of the Navy Theodore Roosevelt, he was not impatient to enforce eviction—and certainly not before his government had a better feel for how continental Europe's powers would respond to this radical invocation of the Monroe Doctrine. To improve his grasp of England's disposition, he met with Lord Salisbury in October. Afterward he was able to inform McKinley that "we need apprehend no interference from England if it became necessary for us to adopt energetic measures for putting an end to the destruction and slaughter now going on [in Cuba]."

Later in the year, Hay had another conversation, which, while perhaps not as meaty as his exchanges with the prime minister, various cabinet ministers, and members of Parliament, was every bit as valuable. He had made such a superb first impression on Queen Victoria that she invited him and Clara again to Windsor Castle, this time to dine and spend the night. Clara's letters home painted a colorful picture of Indian servants in turbans and a table "that did not differ from any other well appointed table only we ate off silver and gold plates for hot things—china for cold." Again Victoria shook Clara's hand, but it was Hay who captured Her Majesty's attentions. "Her custom is to have a member of her family on each side of her at dinner," he wrote proudly to McKinley. "The table was arranged in this way on this occasion; but the Queen sent for the diagram a few minutes before dinner and changed it so that I should sit next to her. She was extremely gracious and talked freely with me for an hour."

The next day, Victoria's daughter Beatrice took tea with Margaret White, wife of embassy secretary Henry White (whose portrait by John Singer Sargent Hay had so admired), with the express purpose, according to Clara, of conveying what a pleasing impression the American ambassador had made on the queen.

HAY'S RAPPORT COUNTED FOR a lot, but for the time being, there was little of substance he could do for his country. And so, anticipating a smoggy winter in London, he booked a trip to Egypt, with McKinley's assent. For the past half-century, Europeans and Americans had been taking to the Nile like latter-day pharaohs, journeying from Alexandria to Memphis, Cairo, Luxor, and the cataracts at Aswan aboard native *dahabiehs*, adaptations of traditional river vessels, refitted with all the luxuries that affluent travelers had come to expect on the Orient Express and the Grand Tour.

Adams, who had spent his honeymoon in Egypt in 1872, agreed to go again. Henry James thought about joining them, then sent his regrets. Hay also invited Lizzie Cameron to play the part of Cleopatra—their " 'Star Eyed Egyptian and glorious Sorceress of the Nile' "—but she had recovered from her collapse and returned to the United States. In the end the party comprised Hay, Clara, Helen and Alice, Adams, and Spencer Eddy, a promising young Harvard graduate whom Hay had brought to London as his personal secretary.

To travel in Egypt, no matter when, is to drop out of time. In Hay's case, he missed most of a chapter in American history. While McKinley continued to believe that Spain could be persuaded to let go of Cuba without the military intervention of the United States, a growing number of Democrats and jingoistic members of his own party were agitating otherwise. The *New York Journal*, jingoistic *and* Democratic, derided McKinley's caution as "lacking in virility." McKinley, who had anonymously donated $5,000 of his own money to a Cuban relief fund, vowed to hold his ground until all options for peaceful resolution were exhausted. "I shall never get into a war until I am sure that God and man approve," the veteran of Antietam declared. "I have been through one war; I have seen the dead piled up; and I do not want to see another." Events would soon make this position untenable.

At the start of February 1898, the Hay family and friends steamed leisurely up the Nile, encountering along the way former Secretary of State Hamilton Fish; James Angell, Hay's former language professor from Brown who was now the American minister to Turkey; and Elizabeth Custer, the widow of the reckless general slain at Little Bighorn. Meanwhile, the U.S. battleship *Maine* lay at anchor in Havana Harbor, not as a show of hostility, but to be on hand in the event that Americans in Cuba needed protection.

A week later, as the Hays continued from Luxor toward Aswan, the *New York Journal* got hold of a private letter written by Enrique Dupuy de Lôme, Spain's minister to Washington, in which he characterized President McKinley as a *politicastro*, translated to mean an ineffectual, would-be politician, but in Spanish literally a castrated politician. To the *Journal*, which itself had publicly doubted the president's manhood, the Spanish minister's gaffe was "The Worst Insult to the United States in Its History."

Arriving at Aswan on the eighteenth, ten days' journey above Cairo, seven hundred miles from the Mediterranean, and surrounded by temples of a civilization three thousand years removed from London, Washington, and Cuba, Hay was handed the news that the USS *Maine* had exploded three days earlier, killing 260 American sailors and wounding ninety. The assumption was that the tragedy had not been accidental. When Adams learned of the hour of the explosion, nine o'clock, he blurted mysteriously, "Then the Spanish did it."

"We have been much shocked and grieved," Hay wrote to Henry White in London. "We feel very much out of the world." To McKinley, he offered perspective and encouragement. "I shall never regret the years I have passed in Europe," he reflected, "[as] they have rooted in my very soul a confidence and trust in our future, which is beyond and above any temporary or personal disappointments. The greatest destiny the world ever knew is ours."

Despite the alarming news from home, Hay did not display any particular urgency. Descending the Nile, he and his fellow travelers stopped for several days in Cairo before continuing north to Athens, while Adams went eastward to Beirut, Jerusalem, Damascus, Constantinople, and eventually overland to Paris. In Athens, Hay had a pleasant visit with the American minister, William Rockhill, whom he had first gotten to know in Washington several years earlier.

Tall, red-haired, and suavely handsome, Rockhill was a character straight out of an H. Rider Haggard novel. Born in Philadelphia but raised in France, he had graduated from the French military academy Saint-Cyr, after which he served two years in the Algerian desert as an officer in the French Foreign Legion. Even while at Saint-Cyr, he had devoted his spare hours to studying Tibetan Buddhism, and after leaving the Foreign Legion, he mastered Tibetan, Sanskrit, and Chinese in order to translate Buddhist scriptures and to publish his own *Life of Buddha*. His extraordinary talents were soon recognized in more than academic circles, and he landed an appointment as a secretary to the American legation in Peking. Insatiably curious and thoroughly intrepid, he undertook two harrowing treks into Tibet, becoming the first Westerner in half a century to penetrate the Himalayan kingdom from China. If State Department appointments had been based purely on merit, Rockhill's ascent would have been meteoric; instead, he took whatever he could, serving briefly as an assistant secretary of state under Richard Olney. The best he could squeeze out of McKinley was Greece, which is where Hay found him, "bored into extinction," in March 1898. Undoubtedly the two men had a great deal to talk about: Cuba of course, the senility of Secretary of State John Sherman, their mutual friends Henry Adams and Theodore Roosevelt, and surely China, the topic always foremost in Rockhill's mind. War against Spain had not yet been declared, and Hawaii and the Philippines were still not annexed, but Rockhill could see more clearly than most the place China ought to fill in America's emergent extracontinental scheme.

Hay arrived back in London the last week in March, after an absence of two months. On the twenty-eighth, McKinley sent to Congress the report of the investigation on the *Maine*, which blamed the explosion on external causes. The president had bought as much time as he could, hoping that Spain would relinquish Cuba peacefully, but the American public would cut the administration no more slack. McKinley finally delivered his war message to Congress on April 11; the blockade of Cuba commenced on April 22; McKinley called for 125,000 volunteers on the twenty-third; Congress declared war two days later; and on May 1, on the far side of the world, Admiral George Dewey sank or captured Spain's entire Pacific squadron and blockaded Manila.

"We are all very happy over Dewey's splendid Sunday's work," Hay wrote a few days later to Theodore Stanton, son of the suffragist Elizabeth Cady Stanton. "I detest war, and had hoped I might not see another, but this was as necessary as it was righteous."

After the navy's easy triumph in the Philippines, the war's outcome was all but inevitable, though the end game was still not clear. The concern in Britain, and among the other "Great Powers"—Germany, France, Italy, Russia, and Japan—was not what would become of Cuba, for it was a foregone conclusion that Spain would resist perfunctorily, then capitulate, allowing the United States either to annex the island or to grant independence outright. The bigger question was the Philippines, which ostensibly had nothing to do with why the United States had gone to war in the first place. None of the powers, including the United States, cared very much about the Filipinos as a sovereign people, but they were keenly interested in who would wind up controlling the archipelago, and how much of it, most particularly its harbors. Manila, like Hawaii, Guam, Samoa, and the Caroline Islands, was a valuable coaling station on the trade route to China, the prize that stirred the greatest jealousy and ambition among the empire builders.

And any play by one power for overseas territory wound up affecting the relationships of all the others. The term "colony" was gradually being replaced by the less possessory euphemism "sphere of influence," yet, as national economies expanded and competition for foreign markets increased, the desire to stake claims, both commercial and strategic, continued unabashed. The United States was not especially worried that another power would side with Spain in the Caribbean, but, even as Admiral Dewey was besieging Manila, the German navy hovered nearby, like buzzards over ripe carrion, its strength quickly exceeding that of the American fleet. Later in the summer, Germany's foreign minister confided to his ambassador in Washington that the kaiser—Wilhelm had been succeeded by his grandson, Wilhelm II—"deems it a principal object of German policy to leave unused no opportunity which may arise from the Spanish-American War to obtain maritime fulcra in East Asia."

Hay had followed the rise of German nationalism since his time in Vienna and had observed the well-drilled aggression of Bismarck during the Franco-Prussian War. Now that Spain had been put in its place, he recognized it was Germany that bore watching above all other powers. "The jealousy and animosity felt toward us in Germany is something which can hardly be exaggerated," he wrote Lodge. "They hate us in France, but French hate is a straw fire compared to German. And France has nothing to fear from us while the Vaterland is all on fire with greed, and terror of us. They want the Philippines, the Carolines, and Samoa— they want to get into our markets and keep us out of theirs. . . . There is to the German mind something monstrous in the thought that a war should take place anywhere that they not profit by it."

Germany's animus, not just toward America but also toward Anglo-American friendliness, had been building for some time. Well before the Spanish-American War began, Wilhelm II had complained about "the American-British Society for International Theft and Warmongering." The kaiser's characterization may have been extreme, but his anxiety was legitimate. The United States remained emphatically opposed to entangling alliances, and Britain's stance during the Spanish-American conflict was officially neutral, yet each nation was increasingly outspoken in its affinity for the other. Addressing the lord mayor of London at an Easter banquet the day before the U.S. Navy commenced its blockade of Cuba, Hay was especially eloquent in his affirmation of the connection. "The reasons of a good understanding between us lie deeper than any considerations of mere expediency," he said. "All of us who think cannot but see that there is a sanction like that of religion which binds us to a sort of partnership in the beneficent work of the world. Whether we will it or not, we are associated in that work by the very nature of things, and no man and no group of men can prevent it."

Three weeks later, after Dewey's victory at Manila, Colonial Secretary

Joseph Chamberlain delivered his now-famous address in Birmingham, in which he expressed Britain's long-term duty to the United States: "It is to establish and to maintain bonds of a permanent amity across the Atlantic. They are a powerful and generous nation. They speak our language, they are bred of our race. . . . I do not know what arrangements may be possible with us, but this I know and feel,—that the closer, the more cordial, the fuller, and the more definite those arrangements are, with the consent of both peoples, the better it will be for both and for the world. And I even go so far as to say that, terrible as war may be, even war itself would be cheaply purchased if in a great and noble cause the Stars and Stripes and the Union Jack should wave together over an Anglo-Saxon Alliance."

Chamberlain's speech was circulated throughout Europe and America, much to the satisfaction of Hay, who claimed that the secretary's remarks were "partly due to a conversation I had with him." Indeed, he had done his work well. Writing to Henry Cabot Lodge, Hay declared, "For the first time in my life I find the 'drawing room' sentiment altogether with us." Some weeks later he elaborated further: "The Royal Family, by habit and tradition, are most careful not to break the rules of strict neutrality, but even among them I find nothing but hearty kindness and, as far as is consistent with propriety—sympathy."

Hay solidified this sympathy throughout the summer. At a Fourth of July banquet for the American Society of London, he reciprocated Chamberlain's espousal of amity. "We are glad to think that this is no passing emotion, born of a troubled hour," he stated. "[I]t has been growing through many quiet years" and "[n]ow that the day of clear and cordial understanding has come . . . may we not hope it to last for ever?" Then, broadcasting his remarks over the heads of his immediate audience, in the direction of Spain, Germany, and as far as Russia, he added: "It threatens no one; it injures no one; its ends are altogether peaceful. . . . We shall still compete with each other and the rest of the world, but the competition will be in the arts and the works of civilization, and all the people of goodwill on the face of the earth shall profit by it."

THE WAR IN CUBA ended in mid-July, shortly after the U.S. Navy destroyed the Spanish fleet as it attempted to escape Santiago and less than four weeks after the first American soldiers waded ashore at Daiquirí. A month later, the United States controlled Puerto Rico, Guam, and Manila. Hay followed the campaigns through the newspapers. He did not question the strategic and moral reasons for the war; nor did he exult in them overly much. He was pleased with the outcome, but if he was less than ebullient, perhaps the reason had to do with being so far removed, in both miles and years. Then, too, Spain had hardly been a formidable adversary.

Hay's modulated enthusiasm is apparent in a letter he wrote to Theodore Roosevelt, acknowledging his contribution to the Cuban campaign. Roosevelt, as the entire world knew, had resigned his position as assistant secretary of the navy and led a regiment of voluntary cavalry known as Rough Riders in an assault on the hilly defenses surrounding Santiago. "I am afraid I am the last of your friends to congratulate you on the brilliant campaign which now seems drawing to a close," Hay began with fitting bonhomie. "When the war began I was like the rest; I deplored [that you left] your place in the Navy where you were so useful and so acceptable. But I knew it was idle to preach to a young man. You obeyed your own daemon, and I imagine we older fellows will all have to confess that you were in the right."

Hay's next paragraph, or the first sentence of it, would be repeated for generations to come, too often ironically, in light of the not so proud events that would ensue in the Philippines. While his words were without a doubt sincere, they were more a reflection of his relief than of his sanguinity or even, as some historians would eventually aver, of his cavalier imperialism.

"It has been a splendid little war," Hay told Roosevelt, "begun with the highest motives, carried on with magnificent intelligence and spirit, favored by that Fortune which loves the brave. It is now to be concluded, I hope"—and here is the phrase that more fairly captures Hay's temperance—"with that fine good nature, which is, after all, the distinguishing trait of the American character."

These were sentiments Abraham Lincoln might well have conveyed: engage in the fight for proper reasons, honor the soldier; then, once victory is achieved, hold the moral high ground. Also embedded in Hay's phrasing was the inference that the United States was not like other countries—brutal Spain or greedy Germany—and that America ought to set a better example, wielding its authority more decently and more wisely.

Little did Hay consider when he wrote to Roosevelt that in two months he would be expected to put his inchoate philosophy into applicable policy as secretary of state; or that in three years Roosevelt would be a president who believed, based on his giddy run to the top of San Juan Hill and his own inflated exceptionalism, that most any war could be splendid.

ON AUGUST 12, 1898, McKinley signed a protocol, already approved by the Spanish Cortes, stipulating that Spain evacuate Cuba immediately and that it cede sovereignty over all its possessions in the West Indies, including Puerto Rico. The fate of the Philippines was purposefully left vague. At the time of Dewey's surprise attack on Manila, the majority of Americans, including many in the administration, perhaps even the president, could not find the Philippines on the map. But once Manila had fallen, the archipelago was recognized as not only a vital interest but a point of national pride as well. "While we are conducting war and until its conclusion we must keep all we get," McKinley observed sensibly, and "when the war is over we must keep what we want."

But what did the United States want? Should it annex all the Philippine Islands, as it had done the Hawaiian Islands a month earlier, or hold on to only one or two as "hitching posts" on the road to China? If McKinley merely took Manila, or perhaps the entire island of Luzon, then Germany would surely gobble up the rest. There was also the matter of the Filipinos themselves, who, like the Cubans, expected the United States to enable their independence. All of these issues required a clearer definition of national interests abroad. Were Americans conquerors or liberators, imperialists or merely "expansionists"? Was it America's duty to enlighten the benighted Filipinos or to let them find their own way? McKinley, a cautious commander in chief who had never seen the Pacific, was in a quandary. "If old Dewey had just sailed away when he smashed that Spanish fleet, what a lot of trouble he would have saved us," he remarked. But Dewey had not sailed away, and so the president chose to defer his decision until the time when a final treaty could be negotiated with Spain later in the year.

The newspapers conjectured that Hay would be appointed one of the peace commissioners, on the assumption that the conference would take place in London. He was not the least interested, however, and Clara dreaded the thought of having to entertain the delegation, whether her husband was a member or not.

Still, there was no escaping the changes that were about to transform the State Department. Secretary of State Sherman had muddled through the spring, forgetful and disgruntled. To make up for Sherman's disabilities, McKinley had appointed Judge William R. Day, a trusted friend from Canton, to serve as Sherman's first assistant secretary, knowing that Day's surrogacy would provide only a temporary fix. In April, with war imminent and after one too many lapses of memory, Sherman had been persuaded to resign, and Day had replaced him as secretary of state. Day served ably enough during the war, supported, as he was, by the department's true mainstay, Second Assistant Alvey Adee, Hay's colleague and fellow traveler from Madrid. Yet Day, while undoubtedly a quick study, had little experience in statecraft beyond the Stark County courthouse, and now that the American portfolio bulged with new acquisitions, McKinley needed a secretary with deeper experience and more lustrous credentials. Hay should not have been surprised to find his name atop the list, especially after his impeccable showing in London during the past year.

IT WAS TOO SOON to think about going home. Hay and Clara were thoroughly comfortable with their life in London. The entire family was in England for the summer; Helen and Alice had stayed on after the trip to Egypt, and Del and Clarence arrived from America once the school year was over. Del had finished Yale, and his father found things for him to do at the embassy, where he seemed to enjoy himself immensely.

There was yet another reason for staying put: the Camerons had rented a country house in Kent near Dover. Lizzie and Don were reconciled, at least to the point of living under the same roof for a few months, and according to their long-standing custom, they invited their "tame cat" to take up residence with them. Adams, after ambling through the Holy Land and Europe, arrived in England in early June.

The estate was named Surrenden Dering—"Surrender Daring," to the Americans—a rambling, thirty-bedroom Elizabethan elephant "filled with handsome, ponderous and uncomfortable furniture and enlivened only by dull family portraits," remembered Adams's niece Abigail, one of many guests that summer. The setting, though, more than made up for the dowdiness of the house, with gardens and grassy terraces overlooking a deer park and the lush Weald of Kent. Abigail described her uncle leading excursions to parish churches and riding the lanes with Martha Cameron on "two chubby brown ponies." Don Cameron was his usual vulgar self; he scorned tea and ordered his favorite foods sent over from the States. The cook acquitted herself with corn on the cob, but she stewed watermelon as if it were squash.

Hay could not get away from his desk until the season was nearly over. From London he wrote Lizzie wistfully, "I am a ghastly wreck and nothing but Surrenden air will bring me round." He also regretted having missed her when she came through London. "I had most dexterously arranged things so as to shake the diplomatic complications and take you to supper. In advance I indulged my vanity by imagining people saying, 'Who is that beautiful woman with old Hay?'"

The Hays finally arrived on August 6, and Abigail observed the differences between Clara and their American hostess: "Mrs. Don Cameron was on the whole the most socially competent woman that I ever met. . . . She was not perhaps strictly beautiful, but she was such a mass of style and had such complete self-assurance that she always gave the appearance of beauty and she gave everyone a good time when she set out to please." Mrs. Hay, meanwhile, "was a most majestic-appearing person with an alarming exterior but a warm heart. She was kind, generous, unpretentious, and completely unselfconscious. . . . Though she made no pretense of being an intellectual, she had a wonderful fund of common sense."

As for Hay, Abigail noticed beneath his "lighthearted wit and conviviality" a certain "nervous tension"—a tension that increased dramatically on August 14, when Henry White arrived from London, bearing a telegram. McKinley had named William Day to head the commission that would hash out a final treaty of peace with Spain, and he wanted Hay to return to Washington as the new secretary of state.

The news that Hay had been offered the highest cabinet post in the administration, a position that ranked beneath only the vice president, was not cause for jubilation at Surrenden Dering. If anything, the opposite was true. Hay was naturally flattered to be asked, and he would have felt bruised if the job had been offered to someone else; yet as much as he had wanted the ambassadorship and had intrigued to get it, he did not relish the prospect of promotion. He was "utterly depressed" by McKinley's invitation, Henry White noted. Hay confided to White that the strain of being secretary of state would likely kill him in six months. And if he decided not to accept the offer, he realized that he would have to resign as ambassador, for, as Adams commented, "No serious statesman could accept a favor and refuse a service."

Hay spent the rest of the day deliberating and finally wrote McKinley a frank but tentative letter of acceptance: "The place is beyond my ambition. I cannot but feel it is beyond my strength and ability." He told the president that he had not been feeling well lately (his kidneys this time) and could not get away from England until the middle of September. "If you conclude after all to order me home," he continued tepidly, "it will be with unfeigned anxiety and diffidence that I shall enter upon the duties of an office I have never aspired to, and which I honestly think too great for me."

Hay's consternation so alarmed Henry White that he sent outgoing Secretary Day a rather bold cable: "I think it is my duty to let the President and you know that it is very doubtful whether the Ambassador's present condition of health is equal to [the] onerous duties of your office. In fact . . . such are his devotion to and desire to be with the President that he will not tell him so."

White told Hay what he had done, assuring him that he had acted purely out of duty and heartfelt concern and with no treachery intended. Hay did not take offense; nor was McKinley deterred. The one upshot was that the president consented to let Hay stay in England for another month to regain his health and to close out his affairs.

He lingered at Surrenden Dering until the end of August, and then, before returning to London, made a short visit to the Isle of Wight for one more audience with Queen Victoria. Again he was invited to sit by the queen's side at dinner, and the next morning she unexpectedly invited him to her apartment for another talk. "That's what you get by being a royal favorite," Hay wrote Clara, who had gone to Paris with the girls to shop. Afterward, Victoria told the British minister to the United States, Julian Paunceforte, that Hay was "the most interesting of all the Ambassadors I have known."

For the next two weeks, the British papers were full of congratulations and regrets: congratulations for Hay's promotion, knowing that Anglo-American relations would improve further with him as secretary of state; regrets over losing such an amiable ambassador. Speculation over Hay's successor focused on Whitelaw Reid, especially after Reid was appointed to the peace commission that was to convene in Paris (not in London, as had first been thought). On the day that Hay left England, he wrote Reid, extending "the old love, the old confidence, the old trust." He was less fulsome about his own prospects. "[Y]ou can imagine with what solemn and anxious feelings I am starting for home," he told his old colleague. "Never, even in war times, did I feel anything like it. But then I was young and now I am old."

To another friend he confessed: "I am full of hurry and full of dread, but perhaps I may pull through."

HAY WAS SWORN IN as secretary of state on September 30, 1898, where-upon he took his seat at McKinley's right hand. The mantle of authority was new, but the milieu was familiar, with a few obvious differences. The first floor of the White House had been spruced up nearly twenty years earlier to suit the Gilded Age appetites of Chester Arthur, but the second floor, where the president worked and lived with Mrs. McKinley, was hardly more opulent and possibly even more hectic than during the Lincoln years. The first telephone had been installed while Hay was serving in the Hayes administration, and electricity had arrived while Benjamin Harrison was president. Light bulbs now festooned the formerly gas-lit chandeliers, and a labyrinth of wires latticed the ceilings. The bedroom in the northeast corner once occupied by Hay and Nicolay and the adjacent office shared by Hay and the third secretary, William Stoddard, were jammed with the desks of more than a dozen secretaries and clerks. Nicolay's office had become the telegraph office—no more journeying across the White House lawn to the War Department, as Lincoln had done with ritual solemnity.

Yet for all the amenities and innovations that had modernized life in the White House over the years—a steam-heating system, bathrooms with running water, and an elevator—privacy and quiet were still in short supply. On the first floor, only the dining room was closed to public gawkers. Upstairs the halls were jammed with the same petitioners, reporters, and pests who had annoyed Hay and Nicolay three decades earlier. McKinley became so distracted by the traffic traipsing in and out of his office—the same south-facing room where Lincoln had worked—that he usually repaired to the cabinet room next door, using the end of the cabinet table as a desk.

Cabinet meetings were held on Tuesdays and Fridays, and Hay needed neither introduction nor initiation. In the years to follow, spanning part or all of four different presidential terms, the responsibility of advising the president and interacting with the other cabinet secretaries would bring forth the best of John Hay's talents as conciliator, problem solver, and sounding board. The greater challenge was the actual management of the State Department.

His forte had never been administration, and suddenly he found himself in charge of nearly ninety employees in Washington and twelve hundred dispersed in embassies, legations, and consulates overseas. For support, Hay tried to bring William Rockhill back from Athens as his first assistant secretary, but McKinley gave the job to David Jayne Hill, president of the University of Rochester, who, while a well-regarded expert on international law, had even less experience in the State Department than did Hay. Fortunately, the capable and nearly indefatigable Alvey Adee continued as second assistant. Hay quickly came to rely on him for almost everything. Adee's hearing was worse than ever; nevertheless, he and Hay would communicate with little difficulty for the next seven years.

But even with Adee guarding the door of the office in the State, War, and Navy Building, Hay could not avoid a certain amount of aggravation.

"I receive twenty or thirty worrying visits a day, all from people wanting something," he wrote Clara. "[T]wo or three chargés d'affaires call; from fifty to a hundred despatches must be read and signed. . . . I get the hour off from one to two & then go back till 4:30." A week later, a few days after turning sixty, he lamented to her again: "I feel so dull and worthless I almost dread to have you come and plunge into this life of dreary drudgery. It is going to be vile—the whole business. . . . All the fun of my life ended on the platform at Euston [Station]. I do not mean . . . that England was so uproariously gay—but this place is so intolerable."

His woebegone mood was decidedly out of step with the rest of the country. The quick and "splendid" victory over Spain had brought the nation together to a degree that had not existed since the onset of the Civil War. America was now the dominant force in its own hemisphere and a formidable presence in the Pacific. "We have never in all our history had the standing in the world we have now," Hay wrote McKinley shortly after the war ended. The American economy was booming again, exports at an all-time high. The discovery of gold (by Americans) in the Canadian Klondike, so near to Alaska, seemed almost providential. " 'We're a gr-reat people,' " one of humorist Finley Peter Dunne's barroom regulars boasted to his Irish-American sage, Mr. Dooley, who in turn replied, " 'We ar-re. . . . We ar-re at that. An' th' best iv it is, we know we ar-re.' "

It was hard for Hay to stay glum, now that he was back in his own house on Lafayette Square, amid his beloved books and art collection. Although Adams was still in Europe and Vice President Hobart continued to occupy the Cameron house, life resumed much of its familiar cycle. Hay's carriage could deliver him to the State Department in ten minutes, to the White House in half that.

And he liked his boss. Hay had always been effusive in his praise of McKinley, but once he was in a position to observe the man more closely, his respect for his leadership grew even greater. "The President rules [the cabinet] with a hand of iron in a mitten of knitted wool," he told Lizzie Cameron. "It is delightful to see the air of gentle deference with which he asks us all our opinions, and then decides as seemeth unto him good." Then he paid McKinley the highest of compliments: "He is awfully like Lincoln in many respects."

McKinley had won election as a promoter of domestic prosperity, not as an international visionary. Foreign affairs, beyond the pocketbook ramifications of tariffs and trade reciprocity, had never aroused him. State dinners, or anything the least bit exotic, made him uncomfortable. Yet during the first critical months of his administration, he had been obliged to act as his own secretary of state, suffering the liability of John Sherman and getting by on the lieutenancy of William Day. After a season of war, he was only too glad to turn responsibility for the country's foreign relations over to the man whom, McKinley acknowledged, ought to have been in charge from the beginning. "He scared me by saying he would not worry any more about the State Department," Hay told Clara, who was still abroad.

THE MOST PONDEROUS ISSUE before him remained the Philippines. While in London, Hay had informed McKinley that it would be a considerable disappointment to the British if the United States did not take control of the entire archipelago; beyond that he had not taken a conspicuous position on the matter—which was not the case with most public men he knew.

The leading advocate for annexation was Henry Cabot Lodge, whose bully pulpit was the Senate Committee on Foreign Relations. Eschewing the term "imperialism," Lodge preferred to call his brand of international aggrandizement a "large policy"—in which he couched America's self-interest abroad in terms of Christian benevolence and divine inevitability. "I do not believe that this nation was an accident," he told his fellow senators. "I do not believe it is the creation of blind choice. I have faith that it has a great mission in the world. . . . I wish to see it master of the Pacific. I would have it fulfill what I think is its manifest destiny."

Theodore Roosevelt was even less varnished in his pronouncements on the subject. America's manifest destiny, he had once asserted, was "to swallow up the land of all adjoining nations who were too weak to withstand us." He was thinking of the American West when he wrote these words, but to him and other large-policy proponents, the Philippines were the new frontier (and the Filipinos another Indian tribe). In November, on the strength of his Rough Rider exploits and contagious patriotism, Roosevelt would win the New York governorship.

McKinley, meanwhile, still had mixed feelings about seizing all or any of the Philippines. Having once deplored "the greed of conquest" and having regarded annexation as "criminal aggression," he now acknowledged the "new duties and responsibilities which we must meet and discharge as becomes a great nation." He exhorted the peace commissioners to exercise "moderation, restraint, and reason" in their negotiations with Spain, and then he embarked on a tour of the Midwest to take the country's pulse. He returned to the White House, convinced that "the American people would not accept it if we did not obtain some advantage from our great victories at Manila" and that "the well-considered opinion of the majority would be that duty requires we should take the archipelago." He did not believe the Philippines were capable of self-rule even as a U.S. protectorate, like Cuba, and he was now quite certain that anything less than full annexation would invite predation by Germany and others. If he did nothing, allowing Spain to retain the Philippines, he feared that America would be the laughingstock of the world.

Finally the pious president got on his knees and prayed for guidance. "[O]ne night late it came to me," he told a group of Methodist ministers, "that there was nothing left for us to do but to take them all, and to educate the Filipinos, and uplift them and civilize and Christianize them [although many were already Roman Catholic], and by God's grace do the very best we could by them, as our fellow-men for whom Christ also died. And then I went to bed, and went to sleep, and slept soundly, and the next morning I sent for the chief engineer of the War Department . . . and I told him to put the Philippines on the map of the United States."

On October 26, at McKinley's request, Hay directed the peace commissioners to insist upon cession of the entire Philippine archipelago. Two days later, to clarify that the administration had not abandoned the path of righteousness, he sent the commissioners another cable. "It is imperative upon us that as victors," he reaffirmed, "we should be governed only by motives which will exalt our nation. Territorial expansion should be our least concern; that we shall not shirk the moral obligations of our victory is . . . the greatest."

Not everyone applauded McKinley's decision or swallowed Hay's avowal of national virtue—not the Filipinos, who had cooperated with the American military with the expectation that their sovereignty would soon be recognized; not Democrats, who had a new brickbat to use against Republicans in upcoming elections; and not the bipartisan coalition of critics who regarded the decision to annex the Philippines as an exercise of tyranny that would lead to proportionate tyranny at home— or so proclaimed Carl Schurz, a friend of Hay's since the Greeley presidential campaign.

Schurz was one of the founders of the Anti-Imperialist League, whose membership grew to include a number of men Hay knew and respected: Henry Adams's brother Charles Francis Adams; Henry James's brother William James; Andrew Carnegie, Mark Twain, and even former Secretary of State John Sherman. The Anti-Imperialists did not dwell on the economic implications of imperialism; rather, their main grievance was that their government would do precisely what McKinley and Hay pledged it would not—that is, inflict irreparable damage on American values and turn the United States into a "vulgar, commonplace empire."

Despite their vociferous efforts to intercede, the Anti-Imperialists had little effect on the outcome of the peace negotiations in Paris. On November 28, Spain capitulated to nearly all the American demands and agreed to renounce all rights to Cuba, to cede Puerto Rico and Guam, and to sell the Philippines for $20 million. But the Anti-Imperialists did not surrender as quickly as the Spaniards, and they now turned their wrath to blocking congressional approval of the peace treaty.

Their opposition put Hay in a particularly awkward spot. Earlier in the summer, for example, he had congratulated Andrew Carnegie on an article the steel baron had written in the *North American Review,* in which he warned that "Triumphant Democracy" was on the brink of "Triumphant Despotism." Carnegie had taken Hay's compliment to mean that their views on the Philippines and American expansion were not so far apart. But once Hay backed McKinley and the peace commissioners on annexation of the Philippines, Carnegie wrote Hay a four-page screed, first accusing the president of plunging the country into an abyss and then condemning Hay for associating with a "military dictator." "You have made a mistake," he told Hay, scrawling at the bottom of the letter, "Bitterly opposed to you yet always your friend."

(From left) John George Nicolay, Abraham Lincoln, and John Hay, photographed by Alexander Gardner, November 8, 1863

2

Hay as New York blade, 1874

3

Robert Todd Lincoln

4

General George B. McClellan

5

Secretary of State William Seward

6

Horace Greeley

7

Whitelaw Reid

8

Bret Harte

9

William Dean Howells

10

Constance Fenimore Woolson

11

Henry James

12

Rutherford B. Hayes

13

James Garfield

14

Roscoe Conkling

15

Henry Adams, photographed by Clover Adams

16

Clarence King

17

Marian "Clover" Adams

18

Anna "Nannie" Lodge

19

Henry Cabot Lodge

20

John Hay with French edition of *Democracy*, photographed by Clover Adams

Elizabeth Sherman Cameron, portrait by Anders Zorn

James Donald Cameron

Clara Stone Hay, portrait by Anders Zorn

24

William McKinley, John Hay, and cabinet

25

26

Alvey Adee

William Rockhill

27

Mark Hanna

Philippe Bunau-Varilla

29

28

William Nelson Cromwell

Hay house, Euclid Avenue, Cleveland

Amasa Stone

32

Hay and Adams houses, Washington, D. C.

33

The Fells

34

Helen Hay

35

Adelbert Hay

36

Alice Hay

37

Clarence Hay

Theodore Roosevelt, portrait by John Singer Sargent

John Hay, portrait by John Singer Sargent

Hay had not been the author of the Philippine doctrine, nor had he been especially outspoken in advocating extracontinental expansion. But now he had to withstand the crossfire as best he could. Moreover, the new world charted by the Treaty of Paris was his to navigate.

HENRY ADAMS WAS TOUCHED when Hay suggested that he would make a worthy successor as ambassador to England. But he recognized that he could be of greater service to his dear friend in the unofficial capacity of counselor and comforter. After settling Lizzie Cameron in an apartment in Paris for the winter, Adams arrived at Lafayette Square in mid-November. "Hay needs an *alter* or *double*," he wrote to Nannie Lodge, "somebody like me, as intimate and as imbecile, but with traces of energy still left."

Thus commenced a new phase of Adams and Hay's relationship. The teas and dinners during the Five of Hearts days had been convivial and the talks lively, but this was something different. The two friends fell into the habit of walking together after Hay finished up at the State Department—the dour historian and beleaguered diplomat in top hats and high-buttoned topcoats, clearing their heads and collecting each other's thoughts. "[W]e tramp to the end of 16th Street discussing the day's work at home and abroad," Adams related to Lizzie.

In his own letter to Lizzie, Hay gave his version of the ritual: "I go to the Department at nine and work till five and then carry home a little portfolio of annoyances. . . . If it were not for that blessed Dor [one of Martha Cameron's nicknames for Adams] my lot would be most pitiable. He takes me for a walk in the gloaming and predicts catastrophes and ruin till my own cares fade away in the light of the coming cataclysm."

Adams would never warm to McKinley, and while not a member of the Anti-Imperialist League, he thought annexation of the Philippines a shameful error. "I turn green in bed at midnight if I think of the horror of a year's warfare," he wrote Lizzie, "[in which] we must slaughter a million or two of foolish Malays in order to give them the comforts of flannel petticoats and electric railways." Yet neither he nor Hay ever argued over politics or found fault with each other. Instead, they "united in trying to help each other to get along the best way they could," Adams wrote in his *Education,* "and all they tried to save was the personal relation." Even then, Adams added, he "would have been beaten, had he not been helped by Mrs. Hay who saw the necessity of distraction, and led her husband to the habit of stopping every day to take his friend off for an hour's walk, followed by a cup of tea with Mrs. Hay afterwards, and a chat with anyone who called."

One of the callers that fall was Cabot Lodge, who lived a few short blocks away on Massachusetts Avenue. In many ways, Hay and Adams's relationship with Lodge was even odder than their relationship with Don Cameron. Cameron was dull, and now that he was retired from the Senate, he was even easier to finesse. Besides, with Don also came La Dona. Cabot Lodge, on the other hand, was hard-nosed and arrogant, as self-serious as Hay and Adams were self-deprecatory. The romance between Hay and Nannie Lodge, such as it was, had long since dimmed, with Cabot and Clara none the wiser—their ignorance evidenced by the fact that the Hay and Lodge families continued to see a great deal of each other. All the same, neither Hay nor Adams could look at Lodge without seeing the hint of horns poking from his patrician brow.

As difficult as Lodge was socially, his political style was what really grated. Hay and Lodge were both Republicans, but Lodge was much less moderate and immensely more intractable. Lodge still regarded McKinley as meek and felt somewhat the same about Hay. As for Lodge's large policy, the larger the better. When it came to asserting America's place in the world, no one was as aggressive and cocksure as Cabot Lodge, unless it was Theodore Roosevelt. And if the world was Lodge's oyster, so too was the State Department. Since gaining a seat on the Foreign Relations Committee, he had come to regard the department as his virtual fiefdom, its secretary and staff on call to do his senatorial bidding.

Hay, though, was not so easily cowed by Lodge's forceful nature, nor did he readily subscribe to the senator's ultra-expansionist rhetoric. Hay had been around his share of egotists and knew that the best way to accommodate them was to let them have their say and to hold one's ground as calmly and politely as possible. Such was his approach when Lodge began dropping by Lafayette Square in December. After one of these sessions, Adams described to Lizzie Cameron the chill he saw growing between the two statesmen: "[T]he Senator, while agreeing in general approval of the Secretary of State's health, expresses an earnest wish that he would not look so exceedingly tired when approached on business at the department; while the Secretary with sobs in his voice assures me that the Senator gives him more trouble, about less matter, than all the governments of Europe, Asia and the Sulu Islands [in the Philippines], and all the Senators from the wild West and the Congressmen from the rebel confederacy. Tell me, does patriotism pay me to act as a buffer-state?"

Adams's snide humor was not lost on Lizzie, for she was one of four people who understood why Hay was willing to put up with Lodge but would never entirely bend to his will. After all, she and Adams had been the other "Two on the Terrace."

THE MATTER THAT HAY and Lodge spent so much time discussing over tea was the Treaty of Paris and its chances for ratification. All treaties, even after they had been agreed upon by the nations of interest, still required a two-thirds vote of the Senate. In the case of the treaty with Spain, the Anti-Imperialists and obstructionist Democrats mounted a formidable front against the annexation of the Philippines, their moral objections strengthened by the legalistic contention that the U.S. Constitution forbade acquisition of territory not intended to become a state. (On the other hand, there was little or no public outcry against the cession of Cuba, Puerto Rico, or Guam.) To block ratification they needed only 28 votes. And they might well have succeeded if a new war had not broken out in the Philippines.

Filipinos, who had cooperated with the Americans in ousting the Spanish, felt bitterly betrayed when the United States proceeded to enforce military rule over the archipelago and scoffed at a newly written Philippines constitution and fledgling government. Filipinos likewise bristled when American soldiers routinely dismissed them as "niggers," "jungle babies," and "gugus," and the leader of their independence movement, Emilio Aguinaldo, as a "halfbreed adventurer." When Aguinaldo and his cohorts were excluded from the peace negotiations with Spain and barred from Manila, the city that they had helped to liberate and hoped would become the capital of an independent Philippines republic, the crisis ignited. On February 4, 1899, a standoff between natives and their occupiers turned violent, killing some sixty Americans and perhaps as many as three thousand Filipinos. The insurrection that ensued was to last four years and would require a force of more than seventy thousand American troops to suppress.

On February 6, one day after news of the outbreak of fighting reached Washington, Vice President Hobart put the Treaty of Paris to a vote of the Senate. The tally was 57 to 27, one more than the required two-thirds majority. Annexation accomplished.

Ten days later, McKinley gave a speech in Boston, reiterating his reasons for taking the Philippines. "Our concern was not for territory or trade or empire, but for the people whose interests and destiny, without our willing it, had been put in our hands," he explained, even as the rebellion escalated. "We were doing our duty by them, as God gave us the light to see our duty, with the consent of our own consciences and with the approval of civilization. . . . Nor can we now ask for their consent. . . . It is not a good time for the liberator to submit important questions concerning liberty and government to the liberated while they are engaged in shooting down their rescuers."

The treaty, he elaborated, committed the Filipinos "to the guiding hand of the liberalizing influences, the generous sympathies, the uplifting education, not of their American masters, but of their American emancipators." And finally McKinley aimed his rhetoric not just at the Anti-Imperialists but also at the nations of the world who wondered at the true nature of America's intent: "No imperial designs lurk in the American mind," the president asserted. "They are alien to American sentiment, thought, and purpose. Our priceless principles undergo no change under a tropical sun."

WHILE THE WAR DEPARTMENT endeavored to smother insurgency in the Philippines, the State Department took up the far more complex task of making the world smaller, or at least more accessible. With America's billowing presence in the Pacific and the enchanting promise of the Far East, the need for a shorter and speedier route to foreign fronts and markets was greater than ever. After the completion of the Suez Canal in

1869, a comparable project across Central America had at last seemed feasible. A French company was the first to try, digging in Panama for seven years, from 1882 to 1889, before going broke. Hay had been assistant secretary of state—and in-house translator—when the director of the French project, Ferdinand de Lesseps, attempted to get the United States involved; but President Hayes and Secretary of State William Evarts wanted nothing to do with a French canal. Any endeavor involving the United States, Evarts declared, would be an American canal under American control. Furthermore, he insisted, the United States would not consent to the surrender of this control to any European power or to any combination of European powers.

This view grew only stronger during the Spanish-American War, when the battleship *Oregon* required ten anxious weeks to steam from Puget Sound to Key West. An American-controlled canal between the Pacific and the Atlantic would have given the U.S. Navy an enormous strategic advantage; a canal controlled by an enemy or blocked by a neutral power could have been disastrous.

In 1887, the Maritime Canal Company, an American firm, had begun to dig in Nicaragua, a much longer route, but one considered by most American engineers to be less problematic. This effort collapsed in the Panic of 1893, but thereafter Nicaragua was regarded as "the American route." In Congress, the greatest champion of Nicaragua was Senator John Tyler Morgan of Alabama, a seventy-five-year-old former Confederate general whose enthusiasm for an interoceanic canal predated the urgency of the Spanish-American War but now benefited from it enormously. In June 1898, as the navy blockaded Manila and Santiago, Morgan introduced a bill calling for the federal government to rehabilitate the Maritime Canal Company's concession and renew work on the canal across Nicaragua—a canal built and owned by Americans. The war ended before the Senate could take up the legislation, but in his annual address to Congress in December, McKinley stressed the indispensability of "a maritime highway" and urged Congress to act without delay. The president expressed optimism for the Nicaragua route—and made no mention whatsoever of Panama.

On January 21, 1899, the Senate passed Morgan's canal bill by an overwhelming majority. "Permit me to congratulate you most heartily," John Hay wrote the senator. "I hope you will not consider it presumptuous in me to express my admiration of your work, and that you may soon see the complete accomplishment of it."

What Hay did not mention to Morgan at the time was that a canal across Central America was in clear violation of a treaty that proscribed precisely what Morgan and the Maritime Company were proposing to do. By the terms of the Clayton-Bulwer Treaty of 1850, Great Britain and the United States pledged that neither country would exclusively control or fortify any prospective isthmian canal and that *both* would guard the safety and neutrality of any canal they might build.

The Clayton-Bulwer Treaty was not put to the test, at least not immediately, for the Morgan bill hit an impasse in the House, where William P. Hepburn, a Republican from Iowa (Morgan was a Democrat), smelled something funny in the Maritime arrangement. Hepburn had come under the sway of a new group of canal advocates who had reasons, both mercenary and patriotic, to believe that Panama, not Nicaragua, ought to be the American way. To Morgan's dismay and frustration, his bill was tabled until a newly created Isthmian Canal Commission could investigate the relative merits of both paths. So began "the battle of the routes," which would drag on for four more years and alter the politics of Latin America for at least the next century. Hay would be in the very thick of it—but first he had to dismantle Clayton-Bulwer.

His task would have been much more straightforward if the British Foreign Office had not insisted on entangling the old canal treaty with more recent and far testier negotiations to resolve the boundary between Canada and Alaska.

The boundary in question was the rugged, jig-sawed coastline of northern British Columbia, delineated rather hazily in an 1825 treaty between Britain and Russia. The ambiguity of the boundary had been of no consequence when the United States purchased Alaska in 1867; the American assumption was that the boundary followed the coastline, including all inlets and harbors. But the Canadians, whose foreign policy was still determined by Great Britain, believed that the boundary cut across the mouths of inlets, making the inlets theirs. Neither side pushed the issue until the gold rush began in 1897—at which point Canada became convinced that there ought to be an all-Canadian route to the gold fields via the Lynn Canal, the longest inlet and the preferred jumping off point to the mountain passes that connected the coast to the Klondike. From distant Washington and London, the controversy appeared rather picayune, but to the Canadians it was regarded as a national affront. Such was their indignation that a joint high commission had been impaneled in 1898, before Hay became secretary of state, to work out an amicable solution.

Bickering continued through the fall and into the winter, proving irksome to the State Department and embarrassing to the British Foreign Office, whose stubborn North American dominion threatened to bruise the newly ripened friendship between the two countries. With resolution nowhere in sight, Prime Minister/Foreign Secretary Salisbury seized on the Clayton-Bulwer Treaty as the lever that could break the Alaskan logjam: If America would give ground in the north, Britain would give ground in the south, consenting to a revised treaty that would allow for an American canal.

Hay had no desire to stir up trouble with Britain, but, on the other hand, he was sure that the Canadian claims were "ridiculous and preposterous," and it galled him that the canal could be held hostage. "The two questions have nothing to do with each other," he vented to Henry White, who was the acting ambassador in London until Hay's replacement was appointed. "Every intelligent Englishman is ready to admit that the canal ought to be built, that the United States alone will build it, that it cannot be built except as a Government enterprise, that nobody else wants to build it, that when built it will be to the advantage of the entire civilized world, and, this being the case, it is hard to see why the settlement of the matter ought to depend on the fish duty or the lumber duty or the Alaska boundary. . . . We shall have to make the best we can of a bad situation."

A week later, the high commission adjourned until the end of the summer, without reaching a settlement and without agreeing on even basic ground rules for arbitration. Hay went into the spring "convinced that the Canadians prefer that nothing shall be settled between the two countries. . . . I cannot at this moment look forward in any hopeful spirit to a renewal of our negotiations." He had accomplished nothing; worse still, he knew that men like John Morgan and Cabot Lodge would not let a fifty-year-old treaty with Britain keep the United States from building a canal. Unless he succeeded in separating Clayton-Bulwer from the Alaskan boundary, a great deal of the goodwill he had worked so hard to establish between the two countries would be dashed.

HE DID NOT HANDLE the strain well. Adams noticed that Hay's temper had turned "quite savage." After a dinner party to celebrate Hay and Clara's twenty-fifth wedding anniversary, attended by Cabot and Nannie Lodge, among others, Adams wrote to Lizzie Cameron: "I am in daily terror lest Hay should bolt the course. I can see, beneath his silence, how he suffers under the imbecility of his colleagues, and the increasing difficulties of his situation. Yesterday, or rather Friday, everything seemed to give way together—The Canada Joint Commission broke down, dragging with it the Clayton-Bulwer negotiation and all Lord Salisbury's honeymoon. . . . [T]he whole work of the winter was in ruins."

(Adams also couldn't resist mentioning that Clara had worn her wedding dress to the dinner. "I did not dare to ask how much alteration it required.")

Hay's letter to Lizzie two days later was no less forlorn: "[I]t is an evil life I am living—hounded by fellow-creatures from dawn till snowy eve, and not one soul of them but wants me to do something difficult or improper." Some weeks later he was able to give an only slightly sunnier report to Henry White. "I am horribly rushed, and not very well," he wrote. "By the time you get this, I shall have been in this place of punishment six months—the limit you and I set last August to my probable endurance. I may have deteriorated somewhat . . . but not fatally, and if I could get rid of a beastly cold which makes my life miserable, I should be pretty fit."

Some of that fitness he owed to two recent appointments. Whitelaw Reid, despite his valuable service on the peace commission, had not been named the next ambassador to England. Instead, McKinley had given the job to New York attorney Joseph Choate, a law partner of William Evarts and a trusted adviser to Wall Street. Besides being one of America's foremost legal minds, he was also a most charming public speaker. Everybody, it seems, had his favorite Choate witticism. (Asked who he would like to be if he could not be himself, he replied: "Mrs. Choate's second husband.") Like Hay, he was worldly and well-to-do—but without the grandiosity of Reid—and in London, where he arrived in March, Choate too could afford a house on Carlton House Terrace. A loyal Republican, with the admirable battle scar of having run for Senate against Thomas Platt, he would serve Hay steadfastly and adroitly for the next five years.

The other valuable addition to Hay's team was William Rockhill. After failing to find a place for Rockhill in the State Department, Hay had tried to secure a sinecure for him as librarian of Congress, only to be blocked by Cabot Lodge, who wanted the job for a defeated Massachusetts politician. Finally in April, he succeeded in having Rockhill appointed director of the Bureau of American Republics, founded in 1890 to promote cooperation between eighteen nations of North, Central, and South America (the forerunner of the Organization of American States). The tacit understanding was that Rockhill would perform his duties for the Americas with an efficiency that would leave plenty of time to advise the State Department on Far Eastern affairs. The salary was meager, but Rockhill leapt at the offer and reported for duty in mid-May.

The placement of Choate and Rockhill enabled Hay to persevere, for even with the canal and the Alaskan boundary at an impasse, he felt encouraged that Choate would carry the administration's brief with tact and determination without twisting the lion's tail unduly. And with Rockhill close by, the State Department was poised to take the next step in American foreign policy. The Philippines, Hawaii, and the canal, whether in Nicaragua or Panama, were all links in the same chain, the jewel of which was China. In John Hay's career as secretary of state, no two issues would loom larger or contribute more indelibly to his legacy than the interoceanic canal and China. The related diplomacy he accomplished with such determination and delicacy in the coming year would not only shrink the globe but also forestall goodly portions of it from falling apart.

MEANTIME, HE DID HIS best to keep his friendships intact as well. Hay had known since October that Reid would not win the English ambassadorship, but had been obliged to remain mum until the president was ready to make his decision public. The most awkward moment came at Christmas, when the peace commissioners arrived in New York and were escorted to Washington, at McKinley's request, by Del Hay to present the signed treaty. At the end of Christmas Day, Reid had come to tea with Hay and Adams, and even then Hay was obliged to keep Reid in the dark. "Poor Hay had to bear the brunt of Whitelaw's insane voracity for plunder," Adams confided to Lizzie Cameron after the tea. Writing that same day to Flora Mather, Hay confessed, "I fear he [Reid] will never forgive me for not having been able to get him the English Embassy."

Hay apologized to his friend for being less than forthcoming and begged Reid's understanding: "I shall continue to hope that no cloud shall ever come between us. Your friendship has been one of the greatest pleasures of my life, and in the short space which remains to me I trust I shall retain it." But the cloud had come just the same, and, without either of them ever saying so, the friendship was thenceforth mentioned mostly in the past tense.

In mid-June 1899, Clara and the children left Lafayette Square to spend the summer at the Fells, leaving Hay to hold down the State Department. In the muggy heat of summer, the government fell into a state of semi-torpor; socially the city was dead. Hay and Adee worked out an arrangement by which Adee would take his vacations in June and early July—most years cycling in France—and, upon his return, Hay would depart for the Fells, remaining through September. "[T]he State Department, always impossible, has been a little Hell," Hay told Adams, who was gone as well, staying in Lizzie Cameron's apartment in Paris. "It was bad enough before you went away; but it has grown constantly worse, and there being nobody to talk to, and call it names, makes the whole thing intolerable."

As usual when Hay was alone, he wrote to Lizzie. With Adams in Paris, she was back in the States, biding her time in New York and avoiding going to the Cameron farm in Pennsylvania. Hay beseeched her to come to Washington. Her house was vacant, Vice President Hobart having taken his failing heart to the New Jersey shore for the summer. "Did you ever spend the hot season in Washington?" he asked her. "I have, several times—but one forgets. Certainly I have no recollection of such steady, dense, unpitying heat. One loses one's mind, heart, and conscience." If she preferred not to trespass in her own house, there was always Adams's. "But come and do not delay," he pleaded five weeks later. "I would fain refresh my worn and weary eyes—bleared with too much diplomacy, by contemplating something more attractive." He was frightfully busy, he told her somewhat mischievously. "I could not dedicate to you more than 24 hours per day."

When she did not accept his invitation, he asked if he might not see her in New York on his way to New Hampshire. When she hesitated even then, he did not relent. "I am afraid you will not take time to think of that scheme I proposed this morning . . . because it does not amuse you," he wrote just before leaving Washington. "But that is the wrong way to look at it: you should think how it will amuse me. And I am the elder & should be considered. And where shall I see you and where shall we have lunch? Is the Metropolitan Museum—near the Rembrandts—too far away? And the Metropolitan Club Annex—how is that? But anywhere you say will suit me."

He closed his letter with a stiff "Regards to J.D.C." (James Donald Cameron), but those regards were perfunctory at best. The only one he ever longed for was Lizzie. "It seems so unreal and impossible that I am to see you again—*if* I am," he mused with ardent anticipation. "Are you as beautiful as ever, and as heartless? I hope so. It would be such a pity if you grew kind. Men are so numerous and unworthy. But be kind enough to say Yes this time and send your letter to my house and not to my shop." Until then, he assured her, "I shall not sleep."

Finally she did consent to have lunch with him, and it was enough to sustain him until the next time.

CHAPTER 15

Spheres of Influence

As much as Hay had complained about the clammy climate and diplomatic frustration of Washington, he fretted obsessively about the business yet unfinished. "I am plagued by the foul fiend fibbertijibbish," he wrote Alvey Adee, who was minding the store in his absence. "I cannot give myself up to rest and be thankful." After only three weeks at Lake Sunapee, he went to Lake Champlain, where President McKinley was vacationing, "to bore him for a few hours about Alaska, and Samoa and China, and Nicaragua and the other outlying nurseries of woe and worry." From there he proceeded to Washington to face "the purgatory I have left," he told Adams.

Prospects of a resolution of the Alaskan boundary dispute had brightened considerably since Joseph Choate's appointment. As Hay had hoped, he and his new ambassador made an effective team: Hay working through British minister Julian Paunceforte in Washington and Choate with Lord Salisbury in London. In early August 1899, Great Britain and the United States at last succeeded in coaxing Canada to accept a provisional boundary, pending final settlement. If nothing else, this modus vivendi now cleared the way for unencumbered discussion of the Clayton-Bulwer canal treaty.

Next he sold Britain on another map. For the past decade the Pacific islands of Samoa had been controlled jointly and rather unsatisfactorily by the United States, Great Britain, and Germany. After a brief civil war earlier in 1899, in which the Americans and the British backed one side and the Germans the other, the three powers concluded that it was in their mutual interest that the islands be divided. The timing made sense, for Britain was already arming for war with the Boers in South Africa and very much needed the sympathy of the United States and, just as crucially, the neutrality of the kaiser, who had made a show of congratulating the Boers for their early resistance.

Hay met with a German envoy on August 31 to draw up a plan of partition and then had Choate present it to the British. The final details took several more months, but in the end the United States gained what it wanted: the superb harbor of Pago Pago, the island of Tutuila, and several smaller islands. Germany got the rest. For its gentlemanly deference, Britain was given rights to islands in the Tonga and Solomon groups, plus sundry concessions in Africa. Hay's style of unruffled, round-robin diplomacy worked just as he had wished, and it would soon reap even greater rewards as he directed his foreign policy even farther afield, to China.

FOREIGN INCURSION IN CHINA had begun in the 1840s with the establishment of the first sanctioned trading port at Canton. After the First Opium War (1839–42), China gave up five more coastal cities, most notably Hong Kong and Shanghai; in 1858, a dozen more "treaty ports" opened, and for the first time foreigners gained access to the Yangtze River. Looking down the barrels of European guns, China had little choice but to allow low tariffs on foreign goods. China's impotence to defend itself was laid bare on a grand and gory scale in a confrontation with Japan in 1894–95. In six months, the Japanese army and navy thoroughly thrashed the Chinese, established a "sphere of influence" in Korea, and seized Taiwan outright.

With that the scramble for larger spheres of influence—territory extending well beyond the original treaty ports—became a virtual stampede. Over a two-year period, from mid-1896 to mid-1898, Germany secured the port of Tsingtao and mining and railroad rights throughout the northern province of Shantung. Russia, whose presence in Manchuria was already well established and who plainly had designs on extending its empire from the Baltic to the ice-free Yellow Sea, tightened its grip on the Liao-tung Peninsula, leasing Talienwan and a naval base at Port Arthur and also securing the right to build a railway connecting these warm-water harbors to the Trans-Siberia Railway. To counterbalance the Russian presence at Port Arthur, Britain carved out a base at Weihaiwei, on the northern tip of Shantung; and to increase its dominance of the central Chinese trade, it leased Kowloon, across from Hong Kong, and gained further commercial guarantees in the Yangtze Valley. France, not to be left out, crept northward from Indochina, leasing Kwangchowan on the Luichow Peninsula.

The United States was a relative latecomer to China. While hundreds of American missionaries had been proselytizing within its borders since midcentury, American businesses had made only slight inroads. At the outbreak of the Spanish-American War, less than 1 percent of American exports went to China (although U.S. ships carried a third of all the Western goods exported to the country). But once the war was over, the Far East beckoned with heightened seductiveness. Indeed, China was one of the main reasons the United States had decided to hang on to the Philippines. Moreover, as Rockhill stressed to Hay, if the United States did not exert its influence, the powers would surely slice the pie into pieces, sundering China perhaps forever—with the imperial Qing government helpless to do anything about it.

American businesses with interests or ambitions in China—textiles, steel, and oil predominantly—were not about to sit by while the feeding frenzy escalated. The American Asiatic Association, formed in New York in June 1898, commenced a well-funded campaign to persuade the administration to secure America's "fair share" of the China trade. The National Association of Manufacturers, numerous chambers of commerce, and jingoes of all stripe joined the chorus exhorting McKinley to become more deeply involved in China.

Even then, McKinley hesitated to take a stand. In his annual address to Congress in December 1898, he acknowledged that the United States was not indifferent to "the extraordinary events transpiring in the Chinese Empire, whereby portions of its maritime provinces are passing under the control of various European powers." But as long as American com-

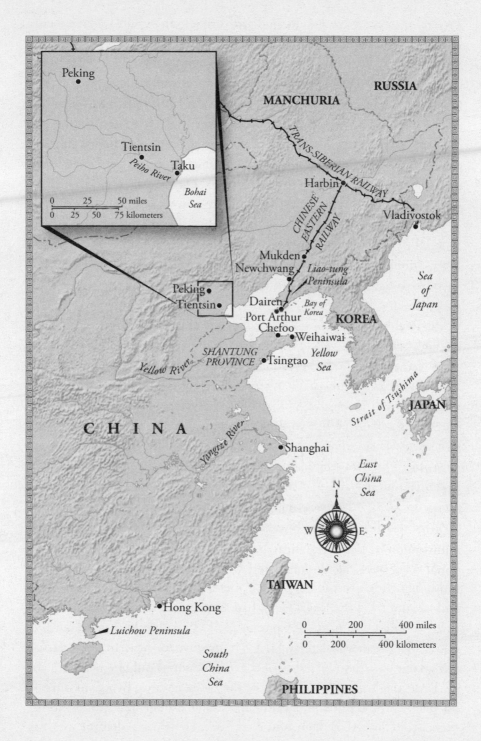

Peking

Tientsin

Taku

Peiho River

Bohai
Sea

0   25   50 miles

0   25   50   75 kilometers

RUSSIA

MANCHURIA

TRANS-SIBERIAN RAILWAY

Harbin

Vladivostok

CHINESE
EASTERN
RAILWAY

Mukden

Newchwang

Liao-tung
Peninsula

Peking

Tientsin

Dairen

Port Arthur

Bay of
Korea

KOREA

Sea
of
Japan

Chefoo

Weihaiwai

SHANTUNG
PROVINCE

Yellow River

Tsingtao

Yellow
Sea

Strait of Tsushima

JAPAN

CHINA

Yangtze River

Shanghai

East
China
Sea

N

W   E

S

TAIWAN

Hong Kong

Luichow Peninsula

South
China
Sea

PHILIPPINES

0   200   400 miles

0   200   400 kilometers

mercial interests were not "prejudiced through any exclusive treatment" by the new occupants, McKinley saw no need for America to become "an actor in the scene."

One reason for McKinley's circumspection, other than his congenitally restrained nature, was his uncertainty over the proper role the United States should play in China. The commercial lobby wanted the United States to establish its own sphere of influence. But to join in the gluttony for territory seemed demeaning and in some respects more baldly colonialistic than annexation of the Philippines. On the other hand, to speak out against the conduct of the powers, after America's own recent burst of acquisitiveness, would appear hypocritical. And what if the powers ignored American demands to curb their appetites? For all its newfound international prestige, the United States possessed neither the might nor the will to fight another war in the Pacific—not against the powers, not over China.

Inevitably the task of cobbling a practicable China policy was Hay's responsibility. Like McKinley, he had never set eyes upon the Pacific. (The farthest west he had ever traveled was Yellowstone.) But he had followed with great interest Henry Adams's account of his trips to Japan and the South Seas, and William Rockhill tutored him frequently on Far Eastern affairs. While in England, he had made the acquaintance of two men whose expertise would elevate and solidify his understanding of China. One was Archibald Colquhoun, who had traveled extensively in India and all parts of Asia. Hay was an avid reader of Colquhoun's *China in Transformation*, published in 1899, in which the author recommended that Britain—and by extension America—adopt a "room-for-all" doctrine.

Another book, *The Break-Up of China*, by Charles Beresford, was even more influential. In the fall of 1898, Beresford, a member of Parliament and an admiral in the Royal Navy, had made a tour of China on behalf of the Associated Chambers of Commerce of Great Britain. From Hankow, on the Yangtze, he wrote Hay, "[I]t is imperative for American interests as well as our own that the policy of the 'open door' should be maintained."

Returning from China by way of the United States, Beresford pitched his book and the principle of the Open Door to business groups in San Francisco, Chicago, Buffalo, and New York. He stressed that the interests of Britain and America in China were "absolutely identical," but because Britain was not acting swiftly enough, it now behooved the United States to take the lead in preventing the breakup of China. To keep this disintegration from occurring, Beresford proposed a policy he entitled "The Open Door, or Equal Opportunity for All," in which Britain, the United States, Germany, and Japan would combine "not for purely selfish motives, but to guarantee the independence of China, and the maintenance of a fair field and no favor for all comers." The strength of such an agreement, he elaborated, "would lie in the fact that it would be too powerful to attack, and that it could maintain the peace while preserving the open door to all. . . . To China herself, the Powers would prove friends in need. By guaranteeing her integrity, they would give a new lease of life to the Chinese Empire."

In Washington, Beresford met with the president and of course Hay, who hosted a banquet in his honor. Hay, however, was still in no hurry to mold the Beresford idea into a concrete doctrine, much less a treaty or even a set of guidelines for his Far Eastern ministers. "It is not very easy to formulate with any exactness the view of the Government in regard to the present condition of things in China," he equivocated three weeks after Beresford's visit. "In brief, we are, of course, opposed to the dismemberment of that Empire, and we do not think that the public opinion of the United States would justify this Government in taking part in the great game of spoliation now going on. . . . [B]ut for the present we think our best policy is one of vigilant protection of our commercial interests without formal alliances."

In the early summer, yet another China hand, Alfred Hippisley, visited the United States, on leave from his post as British inspector of Chinese maritime customs. Hippisley was an old friend of Rockhill, going back to Peking in the early 1880s, and doubtless it was Rockhill who brought Hay and Hippisley together to discuss the situation in China. Hippisley followed up with a letter to Rockhill, offering practical suggestions on how to sustain and stimulate the China trade. Specifically, he recommended that the United States strike an agreement with the other powers, ensuring that Chinese tariffs be applied equally throughout the various spheres of influence—in short, no power would be discriminated against by another in its access to China.

Rockhill forwarded Hippisley's advice to Hay in New Hampshire. He also wrote to Hippisley, proposing that the United States go even further in its posture toward China. "I would like to see [us] make a declaration in some form or other, which should be understood by China as a pledge on our part to assist in maintaining the integrity of the Empire," Rockhill suggested. Still, he doubted that he could win support for any such plan, on either tariffs or the overall integrity of China, for the simple reason that it was likely to cause trouble in the next elections: "[I]t might be interpreted by a large part of the voting population of the United States, especially the Irish and Germans, as an adoption of the policy advocated by England and any leaning toward England on the part of the administration would, at this time and for some time to come, be dangerous, and might lose the President his nomination."

By August, though, the time to act on China appeared more propitious, if not urgent. Jacob Schurman, president of Cornell University, had returned to the United States after touring the Philippines and the Far East at the behest of President McKinley and warned that China was on the verge of being divided and devoured. "[N]ow that Russia has taken Manchuria," Schurman declared, "it will try to encroach gradually on some or all of the other eighteen provinces of China." Accordingly, he continued, it was critical that China "maintain its independent position" and that "its doors should be kept open." China's future, he repeated, was "the one overshadowing question" facing American foreign policy.

On the same day that Schurman spoke out on China and Russian aggression there, the Russian government issued a *ukase*, or proclamation, pledging that Dairen, its trading center on the Liao-tung Peninsula, would operate as a "free port." Hay and Rockhill took this announcement to mean that perhaps the door to China might yet be open. And recognizing the influence that Schurman, a highly respected educator and an avowed anti-imperialist, had on the president and the American public, they agreed that now was as opportune a moment as any to play their hand.

Prompted by Rockhill, Hippisley prepared a memorandum enumerating the points on which the powers might feasibly concur. Rockhill urged that any agreement ought to go beyond concerns of trade to ensure the integrity of China. Hippisley was more realistic. "Of course, if the independence and integrity of China can be safeguarded, too, let that be accomplished," he replied to Rockhill. For the time being, he recommended that they keep their proposals to "the irreducible minimum."

All of the points in Hippisley's memo hinged on the premise that Russia, Germany, France, Britain, and Japan, having already established their separate spheres, tacitly accepted the legitimacy of the others. The challenge, then, was how to respect a country's tangible investments, such as mining and railroad concessions, while keeping the spheres open to trade. Hippisley wanted the powers to agree that all ports within the spheres be declared "free," by which he meant equitable: the proprietary nation of one sphere would not charge higher tariffs, duties, harbor dues, or railway charges to other nations doing business in that sphere. It was a modest proposal, to be sure, but at least it stood a chance. Certainly nothing like it had been tried before.

Hay read Hippisley's memo and liked its commonsense approach. He promptly asked Rockhill to put together his own memorandum, distilling all the current wisdom on the Open Door. Citing Beresford, Colquhoun, but not Hippisley, Rockhill iterated that spheres of influence "must be accepted as existing facts," and he endorsed (still without attribution) Hippisley's proposal on free ports. "Such understandings with the various Powers," Rockhill wrote, "would secure an open market throughout China for our trade on terms of equality with all other foreigners, and would further remove dangerous sources of irritation and possible conflict between the contending powers." He stopped short, however, of making a case for the integrity of China, suggesting simply that the Open Door "has the advantage of insuring to the United States the appreciation of the Chinese Government, who could see in it a strong desire to arrest the disintegration of the Empire and would greatly add to our prestige and influence in Peking."

Although British advice had shaped Rockhill and Hay's thinking, the Americans still did not wish to appear in lockstep with British interests in China. Concern for the Irish and German vote was part of the reason, as Rockhill had underscored. Additionally, the United States did not feel quite so strident toward Russia as did Beresford, Hippisley, and their countrymen. Furthermore, Hay believed that the other powers would be much more receptive to an Open Door if they knew that they were all equals and not up against an Anglo-American alliance. When all was said and done, Hay and Rockhill wanted it to be an American policy in China.

After delivering his memorandum to Hay, Rockhill sent an apologetic note to Hippisley, explaining why he had incorporated Hippisley's ideas without giving him credit: "As the memo will have to be submitted to the President I thought it better that it should seem as if coming from one alone. . . . If coming from you it would require additional explanations. I have, and shall again whenever I can, show that I am but your mouthpiece." In the end, he never quite did give attribution where it was due.

A week later, Rockhill drew up what would forever be known as the first Open Door note, echoing Hippisley's guidelines almost exactly. First, each power was asked to pledge that it would "in no way interfere with any treaty port or any vested interest within any so-called 'sphere of interest' [a term Rockhill preferred to "influence"] or leased territory it may have in China." Second, Chinese tariffs would apply "to all merchandise landed or shipped to all such ports as are within said 'sphere of interest' (unless they be 'free ports'), no matter to what nationality it may belong." And a third leveled the commercial playing field even further: the powers would levy "no higher harbor dues on vessels of another nationality frequenting any other port in such 'sphere' than shall be levied on vessels of its own nationality, and no higher railroad charges over lines built, controlled, or operated within its 'sphere' on merchandise belonging to citizens or subjects of other nationalities transported through such 'sphere' than shall be levied on similar merchandise belonging to its own nationals transported over equal distance."

Nowhere did the note mention an "open door" in so many words. Nor did it pay lip service to the integrity of China. Yet for a document so narrow in focus, so accommodating in tone, the impact of the Open Door note on China and international relations, not to mention the legacy of John Hay, would prove to be colossal.

Alvey Adee sent identical versions to Britain, Germany, and Russia on September 6, and soon thereafter to Japan, France, and Italy. In the meantime, Hay went back to New Hampshire to resume his vacation.

• • •

SURROUNDED ONCE MORE BY the green solitude of the Fells, he took stock of what he had accomplished in recent months. In a letter to Charles Dick, chairman of the Republican Party in Ohio, he shrugged off charges circulated by Democrats that a secret alliance existed between the United States and Great Britain. He proudly acknowledged that "our relations with England are more friendly and more satisfactory than they have ever been," but quickly added, "It is a poor starved heart that has room for only one friend."

He also refuted suggestions that the administration had embraced imperialism. "[W]e took up arms to redress wrongs already too long endured, without a thought in any mind of conquest or aggression," he explained to Dick. "But no one can control the issue of war. Porto Rico and the Philippines are ours, and the destinies of Cuba are for the moment entrusted to our care. It is not permitted us to shirk the vast responsibilities thus imposed upon us, without exhibiting a nerveless pusillanimity which would bring upon us not only the scorn of the world, but what is far worse, our own self-contempt. But as we did not seek these acquisitions— which came to us through the irresistible logic of war—we are not striving anywhere to acquire territory, or extend our power by conquest."

Finally, undoubtedly thinking about the Open Door notes, which were even then being circulated abroad, he declared: "The whole world knows we are not covetous of land; not a chancery in Europe sees in us an interested rival in their schemes of acquisition. What is ours we shall hold; what is not ours we do not seek. But in the field of trade and commerce we shall be the keen competitors of the richest and greatest powers, and they need no warning to be assured that in that struggle, we shall bring the sweat to our brows."

HAY STAYED AT THE Fells until the end of September. "The hills are now wrapped in color like flame," he wrote Henry White. "We have thousands of maples which give the dash of scarlet that makes the picture perfect." With his usual misgivings, he returned to Washington and then went off on a two-week tour of the Midwest with the president. And still there were no firm answers from the powers on the Open Door.

On October 11, war broke out in South Africa, as the British sought to gain control of the gold-rich Boer republics of the Transvaal and Orange Free State. Officially the United States remained neutral, but privately Hay told Henry White, "I hope . . . that England will make quick work of Uncle Paul"—referring to Paul Kruger, president of the Transvaal. "Sooner or later, her influence must be dominant there, and the sooner the better." His wish did not come true; within days the Boers, armed with state-of-the-art German guns, gamely took the offensive, besieging the British garrisons of Kimberley, Mafeking, and Ladysmith. Perhaps there was no secret Anglo-American alliance, as Hay insisted, but there existed plenty of grounds for commiseration. In the Philippines, the United States had its hands full with Aguinaldo's guerrillas, who, like the Boers, were fighting for independence with unexpected tenacity.

At last the powers addressed the Open Door. Japan and Italy assented with no prodding; the other four required considerably more coaxing. None wished to precede the others, and none would come forward if the others refused. Britain finally acquiesced, once the United States made clear that military ports—Weihaiwai and Kowloon for the British, Port Arthur for the Russians—did not count as "leased territory." France quibbled over railroad rates but then came around. Germany was initially worried about being caught between England on one side and Russia and France on the other but then accepted the terms provided "all other powers do so." That left Russia.

Hay well knew that without Russia, by far the most aggressive of the powers in China, the Open Door would dissolve. To make sure this did not happen, he and Rockhill went to work on the Russian ambassador in Washington, Count Arturo Paul Nicolas Cassini. At the same time, the American ambassador in St. Petersburg, a railroad tycoon and amateur archeologist with the storybook name Charlemagne Tower, was given the more prickly task of winning over the recalcitrant foreign minister, Count Nikolai Muraviev. Muraviev, backed by the even more skeptical Russian finance minister Sergei Witte, presented a list of objections: they suspected that the Open Door notes were a conspiracy to block Russian ambitions in Manchuria; they complained that the terms "free ports," "treaty ports," and "spheres of interest" were confusing; and they balked at the stipulation on railroad rates. Mostly, they just wanted to keep the advantages they already had.

Hay expected Cassini would be more amenable. An urbane diplomat who had once lived in China, now spent summers in Newport, and kept a kennel of borzois in Washington, Cassini conversed comfortably with Hay and Rockhill in French, the language of international diplomacy. Nor did it hurt that Cassini lived not far from the Hays, on I Street; Cassini's daughter, Marguerite, and Helen Hay were dear friends.

But for all his cosmopolitan congeniality, Cassini would not budge. "I get profoundly discouraged," Hay told Henry White, "with the infernal cussedness of the little politicians who have the power to tip over the best bucket of milk I can fill with a year's work. Just now it is Cassini who seems likely to spoil all my 'open door' labor."

Finally, it was time to call the Russians' bluff. Hay had Rockhill inform Cassini in no uncertain terms that further delay on Russia's part would be "misinterpreted by the people [of the United States] and would be extremely prejudicial to the friendly relations between the two nations."

Hay also exhorted Charlemagne Tower to keep pressing Muraviev. After several frank conversations, the foreign minister did not actually blink, but he lowered his gaze just enough. Muraviev reckoned there was nothing in the terms of the agreement that warranted risking Russia's friendship with America or isolating Russia from the other powers. Begrudgingly, lukewarmly, he communicated to Tower his general compliance with the Open Door, "upon condition that a similar declaration shall be made by other powers having interests in China." As for its caveats on tariffs and railroad rates, Russia was willing to let these slide, knowing that the Open Door was fundamentally pliable and ultimately unenforceable—and that Washington would settle for anything other than a categorical no.

Hay made the most of it. "We got all that could be screwed out of the Bear," he wrote Adams, "and our cue is to insist that we got everything." Without holding a strong hand himself, he had won every card. When at last all the players had been heard from, he sent a circular to his foreign ministers in London, Berlin, St. Petersburg, Paris, Rome, and Tokyo, directing them to inform their governments that "all the various powers having leased territory or so-called 'spheres of interest' in the Chinese Empire" had accepted the terms of the Open Door and that the United States now regarded their assent as "final and definitive."

• • •

THERE WAS ONE COUNTRY left out of the Open Door negotiations and final entente, however, and that was China. At a time when strict exclusion laws closed the United States to nearly all Chinese, the United States and the other powers gave little or no thought to how China might feel about the proliferation of foreigners in its midst. Wu T'ing-fang, the Chinese minister in Washington, was not aware of the existence of the Open Door note until he read about it in the newspaper. Hay belatedly wrote Wu a letter that offered no apology and asked for only token cooperation. "I sincerely hope that in this effort of ours to secure an equitable share of the commerce of China," he informed the minister politely but emphatically, "that no arrangements will be entered into by the Government of the Emperor which shall be to the disadvantage of American commerce."

In treating the Chinese government as an ineffectual afterthought, Hay revealed the underlying dynamic—and, for that matter, prejudice— of the Open Door. Heretofore the powers had done business with China based on their own separate treaties; their respective spheres of influence had no substantive connection to one another. It was as if all the powers boarded at the same rooming house, eating from a common kitchen, barely speaking to one another, and paying separate checks. The Open Door established a semi-formal diners' club whose members now set the menu, agreed not to eat off one another's plates, and ignored the landlord, so long as the lights stayed on and the meals kept coming. The assumption, of course, was that the landlord would profit by this cooperation and therefore ought to be grateful for the business the powers brought him. How enlightening—civilizing!—for China to have such diverse guests under one roof. And no matter what, the new arrangement surely beat the alternative: a shoving match, with the furniture broken up and the boarders locking themselves in their rooms. If this analogy did not translate perfectly into Chinese, it made enough sense to the powers that they adopted Hay's ground rules.

The consensus—among the powers, anyway—was that the benefits of the Open Door exceeded the limitations, although, in the final accounting, nobody gave up less and gained more than the United States. Following the Spanish-American War, Americans were still trying to come to terms with their new accessions, and they did not necessarily welcome the stigma of international land-grabber. Part of the genius of the Open Door was that it dispelled charges of imperialism, or so the administration averred. The United States had made a point of not demanding its own sphere of influence and, in doing so, secured commercial access to all of China's treaty ports, with very few military or administrative obligations to worry about. The Open Door boosted America's ongoing economic expansion in the Far East—and justified cession of the Philippines. But, on its face, it was an anti-imperialistic doctrine or, at any rate, post-colonialistic. Along the way, John Hay had prevented the dismemberment of China—although this was not one of the aims articulated in the notes he sent to the powers.

Perhaps the greatest benefit of the Open Door had little to do with China directly. Just as the United States possessed no sphere of influence in China, its status as a power was also inchoate. Too often America had followed Britain's example on the world stage. Now, without establishing—indeed, by determinedly avoiding—entangling alliances, the United States commanded a position of preeminence, not so much by military might or even by economic vigor, but by the sheer intelligence and persuasiveness of its diplomacy. And John Hay, who had not coined the term "Open Door," who could not fairly claim authorship of the Open Door note, and who honestly had no grandiose expectations for it, other than as a commercial expedient, emerged after only one year as secretary of state as a deft and forceful fulcrum, an arbiter of world events, independent but coalescent, respected and heeded by all nations.

To be sure, the Open Door policy had its share of critics, beginning with those who found it ironic that the United States had barred its own doors, at home and in the Philippines. Other cynics were quick to point out that the Open Door would splinter the moment one of the powers decided to ignore the rules. "If, for example," posed the *Independent*, "Russia should, when her great eastern railroad is completed, formally annex Manchuria, and apply thereto her present laws of commerce, with free trade on the Russian side and a prohibitive tariff on foreign trade, what would the United States do? Would she resist by force?" (The answer was no, she would not, but Japan soon would, fighting Russia over Manchuria in the Russo-Japanese War of 1904–05.)

By and large, though, public reaction to the Open Door transaction was congratulatory. The *Philadelphia Press* predicted that the Open Door would be for the newly arrived twentieth century what the Monroe Doctrine was in the just-ending nineteenth. *The Times* of London was sure that the Open Door was more than diplomatic confection. The United States, *The Times* vouched, "is the last Power in the world to have gone to the trouble of getting paper assurances and then to allow them to remain paper assurances only. If she has got them she has got them because she means them to be observed."

Hay may have wondered to himself just how effective the notes would prove to be; but even he, modesty aside, could not ignore the wave of adulation that followed the announcement that the Open Door was settled. His scrapbooks hold many pages of clippings with headlines such as "Our Great Diplomatic Victory," "One of the Greatest Triumphs Ever Achieved by This Country," and "Hay Praised by All."

Perhaps the most gratifying salute came not from the *New York Tribune*, though its attentions were plenty kind, but from the *New York Post*, which for the previous fifteen years had been edited by Edwin L. Godkin, an ardent anti-imperialist. Godkin's paper treated Hay's handling of the Open Door as if it were a magic act: "From the diplomatic point of view the negotiation appears simplicity itself. No treaties; just an exchange of official notes. No alliances; no playing off of one Power against another; simply a quiet inclusion of them all in a common policy. This is simple enough, but so is any common feat of skill when you know how to do it. . . . In the end, Mr. Hay appeared smiling with his whole sheaf of acceptances, and the thing was done. It was an exceeding daring and skillful stroke of diplomacy."

As one door opened, the hope was that another would soon do the same. In December 1899, as Hay had waited to hear from the powers on China, Congressman William Hepburn reintroduced his canal bill, despite the fact that the Clayton-Bulwer Treaty with Britain had not yet been revised and the commission charged with weighing the relative merits of a Nicaragua or Panama route was still a year from completing its report. Congress and the American public were eager to start digging, and this time Senator Morgan was vowing that the Senate would work in concert with the House. "Nothing in the nature of the Clayton-Bulwer prohibition will finally prevent the building of the canal," Hay alerted Joseph Choate in London. He immediately went to work on a new treaty "so at least the Administration would have its skirts clear of any complicity" if Congress ran roughshod over the old one.

A number of factors were in his favor. The canal was no longer held captive by Canada, thanks to the provisional boundary settlement earlier in the year. And with the war in South Africa going badly, Britain needed its American friends more than ever. At the start of January 1900, Hay and British ambassador Julian Paunceforte buckled down and worked out a set of terms they figured would make both their governments happy. They agreed that the United States had the exclusive right to build and regulate a canal across the isthmus. Hewing to conventions applied to the Suez Canal, their proposed treaty stipulated that the isthmian canal would be "free and open, in time of war as in time of peace, to the vessels of commerce and of war of all nations," and that, while the United States would have the right to maintain military police along the canal, it could neither blockade nor fortify the route. Like the Open Door note—like every diplomatic transaction Hay ever conducted—the treaty that he and Paunceforte signed on February 5 and sent to the Senate was infused with the expectation that nations, like men, would treat one another fairly if treated fairly.

Given the national juggernaut favoring a canal, Hay was hopeful that he would win over the Senate with little debate. "Hay scored on his treaty," Henry Adams wrote Lizzie Cameron the day after the Hay-Paunceforte Treaty, as it was instantly called, went to the Senate. "He beams with content."

Soon enough, though, content collided head-on with senatorial contempt. Hay ought to have known better than to submit a treaty without first circulating a draft. His hubris was received on both sides of the aisle as gross impudence. When the senators realized the treaty did not call for a fortified canal, the impact was "that of a 13-inch shell," Adams reported to Lizzie. The mood soured further once someone leaked a copy of the treaty to the press. "What shall be said of the value of a diplomatic victory by which we acquire ownership which does not own and a control which does not control?" the *New York Sun* queried scornfully. "It is a diplomacy of the empty phrase."

Hay's reaction was, in turn, nearly as extreme. "He is about as furious as you can imagine," Adams went on to Lizzie, "and threatens to resign if they defeat more of his treaties. . . . He regards the Nicaragua matter" (for this was the presumed route) "as personal, and loathes the Senate with a healthy anarchical energy."

Hay was so annoyed with Cabot Lodge that the two quit talking while the treaty was before the Foreign Relations Committee. He did, however, exchange words with New York governor Theodore Roosevelt, an unapologetic zealot on the subjects of sea power and the necessity of an American-controlled canal. Rather than writing directly to Hay, Roosevelt had issued a statement to the press, in which he insisted that the canal be fortified.

"Et tu!" Hay fired back at the Rough Rider. "Cannot you leave a few things to the President and the Senate?"

Roosevelt, never one to hold his tongue or bide his time, was not inclined to keep out of the administration's affairs. Vice President Garret Hobart had died in November, and Roosevelt, with Lodge's encouragement, was already angling to join McKinley on the next ticket.

Adams, from his front-row seat on Lafayette Square, could only shake his head at the conduct of Hay's fellow Republicans. "Washington is just at the full tide of nervous ill-temper," he gossiped to Lizzie at length. "As usual, the Senate makes the trouble; you know that to me the Senate means practically Cabot; and you know Cabot; [but] you don't know that Cabot is ten times more *cabotin* [showman] than ever. The word was made to describe him, and it fits as though a Sargent portrait. The new Nicaragua treaty makes the pretence. Teddy Roosevelt, I imagine, is the cause. Teddy appears disposed to paddle his canoe and upset the [party] machine. Cabot is in deadly terror, and finds his only resource in going back on everybody. At that trick, he is, as you know, quite incomparable. So he has thrown Hay over; declared against his Treaty; alienated the Major [McKinley], and destroyed all the credit with the administration which he has labored so hard to create; and probably, within a twelve-month, he will go back on Teddy, and help cut his throat as he is helping to cut Hay's.

"Everybody sees now that Hay must go out very soon," Adams continued. "Cabot himself told me, on Saturday, that the Treaty would not be approved by the Senate, and that the German vote [in the upcoming presidential election] was the reason;—he disavowed the Irish, but it counts too. So every day I receive Hay's comments on Cabot, and once a week I receive Cabot's comments on Hay; and, what is more, I know that the brunt of it falls on Sister Anne [Nannie Lodge], and that she is, as usual, at her wits' end to make her husband out not to be what he is. You have seen this show so often and you know it so thoroughly by heart, that you will understand all my embarrassments as well as hers. That Hay should resign and go out, is to me indifferent. If I were he, I would stay in . . . but, if he does not choose to stand kicking, it is his affair, not mine; and it is not my administration Cabot is kicking, or my treaty or my canal. . . . [B]ut it is quite useless for me to play pretend about Cabot. He knows by instinct my contempt. . . . Is it not a pretty mess?"

Hay's own disdain for Lodge ran even deeper than Adams's, for reasons he chose not to express fully in his letters. His distaste for the Senate, on the other hand, was well formed, deep-seated, and hardly a secret. He regarded the system of senatorial ratification of treaties as no less than a flaw in the Constitution. "You may work for months over a treaty," he griped to Henry White, "and at last get everything satisfactorily arranged and send it into the Senate, [where] it is met by every man who wants to get a political advantage or to satisfy a personal grudge, everyone who has asked for an office & not got it, everyone whose wife may think mine has not been attentive enough—and if they can muster one third of the Senate + one, your treaty is lost without any reference to its merits."

There was obvious spite in the Senate's reaction to the Hay-Pauncefote Treaty and, in Lodge's case, perhaps even a measure of personal grudge. Hay had dropped the treaty in the lap of the Foreign Relations Committee, recognizing that if he had allowed Lodge and his committee to tinker with it in advance, they would have added the objectionable fortification clause. Either way, he was damned. On March 9, the committee reported the treaty favorably but added an amendment that would allow the United States to defend its canal. Hay condemned the amendment as "a weak resort of ignorance and cowardice." Lodge, he told Henry White bitterly, "was the first to flop."

Yet the conversation was not over, merely postponed. Since it was an election year, and Lodge and his fellow Republicans were disinclined to expose the administration to the sniping of Democratic critics, the Foreign Relations Committee put off general debate until the following winter. In the meantime, the House went ahead and passed the Hepburn bill, authorizing construction and fortification of an isthmian canal. Once again, though, the Republican-dominated Senate decided to delay consideration until after the election.

HAY DID NOT RELISH being around for the final defacement of his handiwork. And, truth to tell, he had been looking for an excuse to quit almost as soon as he had accepted his appointment as secretary of state. "I have never had yet the evil courage to tell [the president] I shall not stay," he had confided to White back in August. But he had told Adams of his intention to "go out" during their walks and teas throughout the winter. "[M]y natural pessimism works now on Hay's natural pessimism, and his on mine, until we are both half out of our minds," Adams told Lizzie in January.

Adams had never seen his friend so agitated, yet he was mildly relieved to observe that the quarrel with the Senate had brought color to Hay's cheeks. "Curiously enough," Adams reported to Lizzie as the treaty went before the Senate, "Hay was never in better health or spirits, and takes poundings with positive improvement of health—like massage."

However, once the Foreign Relations Committee amended Hay-Pauncefote, Hay hit his limit. On March 13, 1900, he submitted his resignation to the president. "The action of the Senate indicates views so widely divergent from mine in matters affecting, as I think, the national welfare and honor," he wrote McKinley, "that I fear my power to serve you in business requiring the concurrence of that body is at an end. I cannot help fearing also that the newspaper attacks upon the State Department, which have so strongly influenced the Senate, may be an injury to you, if I remain in the Cabinet."

McKinley wrote back immediately, returning Hay's resignation. "Had I known the contents of the letter which you handed me this morning I would have declined to receive or consider it," he replied. "Nothing could be more unfortunate than to have you retire from the Cabinet. The personal loss would be great, but the public loss even greater. . . . Your record constitutes one of the most important and interesting pages of our diplomatic history." The president closed with an exhortation Hay could not dismiss: "We must bear the annoyance of the hour. It will pass away. . . . Conscious of high purpose and honorable effort, we cannot yield our posts however the storm may rage."

And so he stayed, but not happily. "We tramp in silence every afternoon an hour," Adams mentioned several days later. "He has nothing to say. I have nothing to ask."

Henceforth Adams began to observe a change in his friend. Hay's anger and frustration over the canal treaty—and over the Senate's chronic meddling with all treaties—were part of a larger dissatisfaction. Reminiscing many years later in his *Education,* Adams described the hardening of Hay's spirit: "Always unselfish, generous, easy, patient and loyal, Hay had treated the world as something to be taken in block without pulling it to pieces to get rid of its defects; he liked it all; he laughed and accepted; he had never known unhappiness. . . . Yet even the gayest of tempers succumbs at last to constant friction. The old friend was rapidly fading," Adams lamented. "The habit remained, but the easy intimacy, the careless gaiety, the casual humor, the equality of indifference were sinking into the routine of office. . . . The wit and humor shrank within the blank walls of politics, and the irritations multiplied."

YET IF HAY SEEMED withdrawn of late, there was one door he always left unfastened. What Adams did not fully realize was that, as harried and embittered as Hay felt, he too had Lizzie Cameron to elevate his mood. The two men, of course, were aware that each was corresponding with Lizzie, and she with them, but they did not share the entirety of their letters or reveal the frequency. "Hay got your letter yesterday, and told me your news," Adams informed her in February. "I rarely mention your letters to me, because it makes people"—Hay, for one—"jealous of me. Too many men still love you."

Hay continued to reach out to Lizzie whenever his wife was away. "I am all alone for weeks to come," he had written the previous November, with Clara in Cleveland. "There is not a living soul in Washington. I wonder if this letter will reach you. If so, send me a line." He signed off: "For your beauty, and your wit, and your brightness, and your sweetness, for all you are and all you have been, active & passive, my deepest gratitude."

A week later, he made a demonstration most daring. "Did you ever get a letter written in a Cabinet meeting," he asked Lizzie, scribbling in pencil on "Executive Mansion" stationery. "I have said all I have to say. Root and Gage [Secretary of War Elihu Root and Secretary of the Treasury Lyman Gage] are good for the next hour and I will talk to you."

While his fellow cabinet members and the president carried on, deliberating the affairs of the nation, Hay, seated within arm's length of McKinley, turned his thoughts to a topic that had absorbed him for the past decade and more. "There is something unreal, something *tant soit peu* divine about all my knowledge of you," he wrote Lizzie. "That you should be the most beautiful and fascinating woman of your generation, the most attractive in wit and grace and charm and yet be so good to me is a thing I never realize and I find it hard to believe when I am away from you. I live over again in memory all the happy hours you have given me, but can hardly believe them real."

The risk of making such a proclamation in such a setting was, to his mind, yet another way of demonstrating the courage of his amorous convictions.

TOO QUICKLY HE WAS tugged back to more earthly concerns. The Danish government had approached him with a proposal to relinquish the West Indian islands of St. Thomas, St. John, and St. Croix. Hay dispatched Henry White to Copenhagen to begin negotiations. He was also obliged to explain and defend American neutrality in the Boer War. American goods—not military matériel per se, but tons of flour and canned food, and horses and mules by the thousand—continued to flow to South Africa; American banks were indirectly helping finance the British campaign.

Hay's own behavior was likewise open to aspersions of favoritism. Before leaving London, he had met cordially with Cecil Rhodes, the diamond magnate and the most prominent champion of British imperialism in southern Africa. After the Boers had expelled British officials from the Transvaal, Hay had offered the services of the American consul to act on behalf of the British government. And when Boer peace envoys came to Washington, he had talked to them for an hour but declined to treat with them in an official capacity, under the technicality that they were not properly credentialed by their government. ("Sicrety Hay meets with them in a coal cellar, wearin' a mask," Mr. Dooley reported.) Gestures like these only fanned rumors of a not so secret Anglo-American alliance, which Hay was obliged to deflect again and again. "As long as I stay here," he assured Henry White, "no action shall be taken contrary to my conviction that the one indispensable feature of our policy should be a friendly understanding with England." But, he reiterated, "an alliance must remain, in the present state of things, an unattainable dream."

As a gesture of equanimity to the Boers, he made a surprising and somewhat controversial decision. In December 1899, he named his son Del as American consul to Pretoria, the capital of Boer-controlled Transvaal. Adelbert Hay was twenty-three, two years out of Yale, and still at loose ends. He had helped out in the American Embassy in London while his father was there and on a lark had gone to the Philippines, as a civilian, to observe the war. This, however, was the extent of his qualifications for the consulship—along with being the son of the secretary of state. "[H]e is naturally lazy and needed something to wake him up," Clara explained to Adams. "He has plenty of courage and capacity but lacks energy." Perhaps Pretoria would prove to be just the tonic. After Del's appointment, Clara remarked with maternal optimism, "He has been on the jump . . . and seems quite a different person."

En route to South Africa, Del passed through London, where he took tea with Lord Salisbury, stirring suspicions that he had been inculcated with a pro-British, anti-Boer bias. "[H]ow could I have paid a greater compliment to the South African Republic [Transvaal] than sending my own son there?" Hay rebutted to a Boer intermediary. Meanwhile, he cautioned Del in the stern voice of the secretary of state: "You will naturally not avow any sympathies at all for either side in the contest, and you will do well not to have any."

Two weeks later, once Del had arrived at Pretoria, Hay wrote again, this time in the voice of a concerned father: "I sometimes feel a twinge of remorse at allowing you at so early an age to go away such a distance and to be loaded with such heavy responsibilities, but I could not resist your earnest desire to go, and I am sure that such a test of character and of endurance, if you come happily out of it, will be of advantage to you all your life." Hay was likely reflecting on his own coming of age thirty-seven years earlier, when he was working in the White House and venturing to the front on orders from President Lincoln.

To his parents' delight and the administration's relief, Del acquitted himself even-handedly and bravely. His greater service was to British prisoners of war in the Transvaal, but he also won the trust of the Boers. "Everyone thought of me as an enemy at first, but I am glad to say that everyone is nice to me now. I had a hard row to hoe," he wrote home from Pretoria.

The celebrated correspondent Richard Harding Davis, who had been with Roosevelt at San Juan Hill and was next assigned to the South African war, provided a colorful glimpse of Del's pluck. The English soldiers, it seemed, were so awed by the deadliness of Boer marksmanship that they believed the grease smeared on the enemies' bullets was poisonous. When Del asked for proof, one of the British complainants produced a bullet covered with a suspicious green compound. "Why, these bullets must have fallen into a pudding by mistake," Del exclaimed. "They're flavored with wintergreen." With that, he licked off the coating with exaggerated enjoyment. "Thus ended the story of Boer barbarism," Davis narrated.

FEW REPUBLICANS DOUBTED THAT McKinley would win his party's nomination in June and the general election in November. Hay, however, had made up his mind that he would not be part of the president's second term. "Nothing—but nothing—would induce me to stay where I am," he proclaimed to Adams, who had deserted him for France to begin work on his next volume of musings on civilization, eventually titled *Mont-Saint-Michel and Chartres*.

Hay's disinterest in serving in the next McKinley administration was more believable than Theodore Roosevelt's insistence that he was not a candidate to succeed Vice President Garret Hobart. Lodge had been working on Roosevelt for months; so, too, had Senator Thomas Platt, the New York Republican boss, who wanted the untamable governor out of his hair. A week before the convention was to begin in Philadelphia,

Roosevelt came to Washington to try out his non-campaign on the White House. "Teddy has been here: have you heard of it?" Hay wrote Adams. "He came down with a sombre resolution throned on his strenuous brow, to let McKinley and Hanna know, once for all, he would not be Vice President, and found to his stupefaction that nobody in Washington, except Platt, had ever dreamed of such a thing. He did not even have a chance to launch his nolo episcopari at the Major. That statesman said he did not want him on the ticket—that he would be far more valuable in New York—and Root said, with his frank and murderous smile, 'Of course you're not—you're not fit for it.' And so he went back, quite eased in his mind but considerably bruised in his amour-propre."

The convention was a different affair. Despite what McKinley had indicated to Hay, Root, Hanna, and other confidants, he never stated publicly that he did not favor Roosevelt; rather, he had merely said that he would let the delegates choose his running mate.

Mark Hanna, now a senator but still chairman of the Republican National Committee, had other ideas. He and Roosevelt had detested each other for years. Hanna had been one of the last holdouts against war with Spain, believing, along with many on Wall Street, that it would be bad for the nation's recently revived economy. Roosevelt, a trustbuster in the making, regarded Hanna as one of those over-grasping plutocrats who believed that because business was good for the country, then business ought to run the government.

Yet there was something more fundamental, almost visceral in their mutual antagonism. The forty-one-year-old Roosevelt was in the peak of health and the prime of life; Hanna, at sixty-two (the same age as Hay), was by now riven by rheumatism. One embodied the past, the other the future—the nineteenth century versus the twentieth. And Hanna, whether he said as much, sensed that Roosevelt had the potential to overwhelm stolid, reserved, moderate McKinley. "Roosevelt burst into that campaign . . . with all the flare of a skyrocket, with the incessant clatter of a riveter; and with a new, gorgeous vocabulary of erudite vituperation," observed the Kansas columnist William Allen White, an early acolyte. "Roosevelt challenged an acclaim which eclipsed Hanna's presidential candidate . . . and elbowed Hanna off the stage as the savior of the nation. . . . Perhaps subconsciously Hanna was jealous of Roosevelt, the pirouetting young dervish of a Teddy who took the spotlight in the drama of the hour."

Hanna did his best to find another vice-presidential candidate—anybody but Teddy. His harangues and arm-twisting had no effect; the delegates would have only Roosevelt, who strode into the convention hall wearing a version of the broad-brimmed hat he had worn as a Rough Rider.

McKinley was nominated unanimously. Then came Roosevelt's turn: he received every vote but one—his own. In his acceptance speech, he struck a posture that surely caught the attention of John Hay, who had remained at his desk at the State Department throughout the convention. "Is America a weakling to shrink from the world work of the great world-powers?" Roosevelt asked in his raptor's falsetto. "No," he answered emphatically. "The young giant of the West stands on a continent and clasps the crest of an ocean in either hand. Our nation, glorious in youth and strength, looks in the future with eager eyes and rejoices as a strong man to run a race."

A week later, an exhausted but unbowed Mark Hanna wrote to McKinley: "Well, it was a nice little scrap at Phila[delphia], not exactly to my liking with my hands tied behind me. However, we got through in good shape and the ticket is all right. Your *duty* to the country is to *live* for *four* years from next March."

WHILE ROOSEVELT WAS STIRRING the pride of the Republican faithful, a crisis was building that would drastically challenge the strength of the giants of the West, and, more particularly, the validity of the Open Door. As it turned out, the Chinese did have something to say about the presence of the powers in their midst.

Two years earlier, in 1898, the reform-minded Chinese emperor, Kuang Hsu, had been deposed and imprisoned by his aunt, Tzu Hsi, an ambitious and superstitious conservative who believed that the empire would be better off with the outsiders gone. The empress dowager and her imperial government realized that they could not achieve this eviction by themselves; the Chinese military, so recently humiliated by Japan, was no match against the muscle of the industrialized powers. Yet in recent months a much larger, potentially more lethal force had awakened in Shantung Province in northern China, unified by hatred of a common enemy.

They called themselves the Fists of Righteous Harmony, after the martial-arts rituals they performed en masse, working themselves into a trancelike fervor that emboldened them to confront "the foreign devils" whom they blamed for all the woes that beleaguered their lives, including a drought that in 1899 inflicted famine across northern China. They believed that, once they drove out the Westerners, the rains would come again. Westerners, slow to grasp the potency of these public theatrics, belittled the movement's adherents as "Boxers."

Missionaries were the first to feel the wrath of the Boxers, who accused the Christians of practicing all manner of demonic acts: incest, mutilation of orphans, drinking of blood. Boxers felt a comparable disgust for Chinese converts to Christianity—"rice Christians," who by 1900, as the famine worsened, numbered nearly a million. To the Boxers, a rice Christian was no longer Chinese at all.

Most of the missions, Protestant and Catholic, were located in far-flung, unprotected districts; as the Boxers' intimidation intensified, some Westerners were prudent enough to get out, but most did not. Before the Boxer Rebellion, as it would soon be known, wound down in August 1900, dozens of missionaries, along with thousands of their followers, would be murdered.

The White House was not alarmed at first. In his annual address to Congress in December 1899, McKinley declared: "The interests of our citizens in that vast Empire have not been neglected during the past year. Adequate protection has been secured for our missionaries." On June 1, 1900, as the cables from China grew more troubling, William Rockhill, regarded as the administration's ablest China hand, jotted a note to Hay: "I return the despatches from [American Minister to China Edwin] Conger which you kindly sent me to read. I cannot believe that the 'Boxer' movement will be very long-lived or cause any serious complications."

Even as Rockhill gave this assurance, Boxers were tearing up the railroad between Peking and Tientsin and burning the stations. Two weeks later, Peking and Tientsin came under full-scale attack.

On June 15, Conger wrote Hay a chilling report from Peking: "I regret to say that since [June 11] we have been completely besieged within our compounds with the entire city in the possession of a rioting, murdering mob, with no visible effort being made by the Government in any way to restrain it. We have cleared and barricaded the streets in the vicinity of the Legation, but they are so scattered and our number of guards so limited that the gravest possible danger is imminent. . . . Since my last despatch, every American mission in the city, except the Methodist, with all their well equipped homes, has been burned, also all the Catholic and English, except one, and many hundreds of native Christians barbarously tortured and murdered. . . . We are simply trying to quietly defend ourselves until re-enforcements arrive, but nearly one hundred 'Boxers' have already been killed by the various Legation guards."

That same day, Hay cabled Conger: "Do you need more force?"

Neither of these messages got through. By then, all communication with the nine hundred foreigners trapped in the Legation Quarter next to the Forbidden Palace was cut off. Making their plight more dire, the empress dowager, despite avowals to the contrary, directed imperial forces to join in the Boxer rampage.

Hay was in the most precarious position of his career thus far, faced with the dilemma of how to relieve the legation without intriguing with other powers or acting the bully in yet another faraway land—all issues that weighed heavily in an election year. The last thing he wanted was for the United States to take part in any action that would lead to a widening of the war, for he grasped that the other powers, particularly Russia, were itching for an excuse to partition all of China. Even within the administration there were some who suggested that the time had come for the United States to grab a port or at the very least a naval station.

Hay proceeded as gingerly as he dared. When Conger, in one of the last cables from Peking, asked if he ought to join the other ministers in demanding that the imperial authorities suppress the Boxers, Hay had advised: "Act independently in protection of American interests where practicable, and concurrently with representative of other powers if necessity arise[s]." Two days later—and a week before the Republican Convention in Philadelphia—Hay cabled Conger even more emphatically: "We have no policy in China except to protect with energy American interests and especially American citizens and the Legation. There must be no alliances."

One hundred American Marines did join a force of two thousand that set out from Tientsin on June 10, heading for Peking; but even after ordering six thousand more troops from the Philippines, the administration was still not eager to enter into a more formal alliance with the powers. Soon, though, the United States would have to commit. Warships of all the powers were anchored off the Taku forts, at the entrance to the Peiho River, preparing an assault that would open the approach to Tientsin, thirty miles upstream, and to Peking, eighty miles farther. As directed by Washington, the U.S. Navy did not participate in the attack on the seventeenth, the only power not to do so. But after the *Monocacy*, a Civil War–era side-wheeler, came under fire from the forts, Admiral Louis Kempff cabled that a "state of war practically exists" and that he was "making common cause with foreign forces for general protection."

It took less than a day to take the Taku forts, but now Tientsin was surrounded. Six hundred foreigners lived along the river in a settlement one mile long and a quarter-mile wide—"not chosen for defense," noted one of the trapped residents, Lou Hoover, wife of an energetic young mining engineer, Herbert Hoover. On the day that Taku fell, thousands of Boxers, now joined by more than ten thousand imperial troops, began firing on the foreigners at Tientsin, whose hasty battlements were manned by two thousand soldiers, three hundred of them American. Enough reinforcements were able to fight their way into the settlement to keep it from being overrun, but the enemy still invested the old part of the city, from which it continued to shell the besieged.

The relief expedition that had left for Peking on the tenth made it barely halfway. It straggled back seventeen days later, reporting three hundred dead and wounded—and still no word from Peking. The sole information that Hay managed to glean on the fate of the legation was a belated dispatch forwarded by the American consul in Shanghai, confirming that the German minister, Baron Clemens von Ketteler, had been murdered by Boxers two weeks earlier. Hay tried not to dwell on what might have happened since then. The only good news came from the viceroys of central and southern China, who assured the State Department that they would do their best to keep the rebellion from spreading to their provinces and would protect the safety of foreigners in their midst.

On July 3, Hay called a meeting of the cabinet. Since the death of Vice President Hobart, and with the president in Canton for the summer, he was now the ranking officer on the bridge. He presented to his fellow secretaries a letter he intended to send to Berlin, Paris, Rome, St. Petersburg, Tokyo, and four other capitals, reiterating his country's position on China. With the death of the German minister, the repulsion of the first relief expedition, and the ongoing assault on the foreign compound in Tientsin, he feared that unless he took a stand diplomatically, the other powers would tear China to shreds. But if the fighting could be contained within the areas where the Boxers were at large, and the imperial government could be assured that the powers desired only the suppression of the Boxers and the relief of their citizens, then perhaps the conflict could be resolved before it escalated into full-scale war. Above all else, he wished to keep the channels of communication open, in the event that the foreigners in the Legation Quarter in Peking were still alive. And so, with the cabinet's blessing, he issued what would thenceforth be known as his Second Open Door note.

He began with a gentle warning intended as a roundabout message to the imperial government. "If wrong be done to our citizens," he stated, "we propose to hold the responsible authors to the uttermost accountability." Then he presented a transparent fiction that would give the Chinese government a chance to save face, and thus save itself from larger reprisal: "So long as [Chinese authorities] are not in overt collusion with rebellion and use their power to protect foreign life and property, we regard them as representing the Chinese people, with whom we seek to remain in peace and friendship."

By now he had to know that the Chinese government was fighting in concert with the Boxers; nevertheless, tactical use of the benefit of the doubt would not hurt his chances of getting Americans out of Peking alive, which was the aim of the next part of his circular. "The purpose of the President," he continued, "is as it has been heretofore, to act concurrently with the other powers, first, in opening communication with Peking and rescuing the American officials, missionaries, and other

Americans who are in danger; secondly, in affording all possible protection everywhere in China to American life and property."

And finally he raised the flag he hoped would rally the powers—and draw the Chinese—to the issue that mattered most. Whatever the outcome of the rebellion might be, regardless of what befell the legations and missions, Hay wanted to make it plain that the United States would "preserve Chinese territorial and administrative entity, protect all rights guaranteed to friendly powers by treaty and international law, and safeguard for the world the principle of equal and impartial trade with all parts of the Chinese Empire."

This time he did not ask for a response from the various powers. Nor did the note solicit their adherence. His letter was more a promise than a plea, a statement of the steadfast intention of the United States to honor the integrity of China—the point Rockhill had wanted to stress in the first Open Door note—with the implied suggestion that it was in the best interests of all the powers to follow the example set by America. It was a long shot, fired at a time when Boxers were hacking Christians to death without mercy and foreign soldiers were cutting down fanatical Boxers by the hundreds. There was not much else Hay could do, short of threatening war against any power that stepped out of line. Yet after the reception of the first Open Door note, as unenthusiastic as some of these responses had been, he had to believe that the example of the United States counted for something.

In the end, the Second Open Door did not "save" China outright, as some have mythologized, but it paid off in several incremental ways that were nonetheless crucial. First, it served to deter one or more of the powers from declaring war on China; and second, none used the Boxer hostilities to seize advantages beyond their existing spheres of influence (although it must be said that Russia's grip on Manchuria and the treaty port of Newchwang grew worrisomely tighter). "The thing to do . . . was to localize the storm if possible, and this we seem to have done," Hay wrote Adams five days after the note was circulated. "All the powers have fallen in with my modus vivendi in the Centro and South."

Hay recognized that his note was little more than a piece of paper, yet he was satisfied to have imposed at least a modicum of good intention and common sense on the chaos of the moment. "I will not tell you the lunatic difficulties under which we labor," he continued to Adams. "The opposition press call[s] for impeachment because we are violating the Constitution [by invading China without a declaration of war] and the pulpit gives us anathema because we are not doing it enough [sending more troops to save missionaries]. . . . If I looked at things as you do in the light of reason . . . I should go off after lunch and die. . . . But I take refuge in a craven opportunism. I do what seems possible every day—not caring a hoot for consistency or the Absolute."

His opportunism—part optimism, part pragmatism—bore more fruit in mid-July, just as all hope seemed to be lost. Over the previous month, attacks on the weary occupants of the Peking legations had been unrelenting. The Boxers had come close to burning them out and breeching their barricades on numerous occasions; food and ammunition were running low. Dozens of foreigners had been wounded or killed, making it even more difficult to defend their half-mile-square perimeter. Three weeks had passed since anyone had heard any news, good or bad. And then on July 16, the *Daily Mail* of London reported that the legations had been overrun and all the inhabitants butchered. A memorial service for "the Europeans Massacred in Peking" was scheduled for St. Paul's Cathedral.

Hay was one of the first with knowledge that the story was cruelly false. Throughout the Boxer ordeal, he had maintained respectful relations with the Chinese minister, Wu T'ing-fang. (The running joke around Washington was that Wu made Hay "woozy" and Hay made Wu "hazy.") On July 11, he delivered a message to Wu, who in turn sent it to trusted contacts in China. No one knows how many hands it passed through from the time it left the State Department until an old man appeared at the legation barricade in Peking five days later, waving a white flag and bearing three words in a code understood only by the American minister, Edwin Conger. Deciphered, it read simply: "Communicate tidings bearer."

Conger wrote back, also in cipher: "For one month we have been besieged in British Legation under continued shot and shell from Chinese troops. Quick relief only can prevent general massacre." The message reached Hay on July 20. There were those who questioned the authenticity of Conger's note, but it was soon verified by another exchange of cables, requesting "bearer" to provide the middle name of Conger's wife. (Answer: Alta.) The memorial service at St. Paul's was canceled.

From here on, the pace quickened. While Hay's and Conger's ciphers were passing between Washington and Peking, an allied force of six thousand drove the Boxers and Chinese soldiers from Tientsin, suffering seven hundred fifty casualties and wantonly looting the city. Preparations began immediately for a march on Peking. A force of nearly twenty thousand—ten thousand Japanese, three thousand Russian, three thousand British, two thousand American, a few French (but no Germans to speak of)—set out before daybreak on August 4, determined to make it the entire way this time.

Hay was too exhausted to wait in Washington for the outcome. The next day, he departed for the Fells. In his absence, he trusted Adee to run the State Department and to keep him informed on the relief expedition via the tiny telegraph office in the nearby village of Newbury.

In New Hampshire, he broke down entirely. "I did not imagine when I left Washington how bad it was," he wrote John George Nicolay, with whom he had shared more than one summer in the capital. "If I had stayed another day I should have not got away at all." His symptoms included backache and an irritable bladder, though at least one newspaper suggested that he was "near the danger point." He was annoyed but also somewhat tickled by the reports of his imminent demise. "I do not care to take the world into my confidence as to the state of my hydraulics. So I must let the story run," he wrote Adee. "But so far as I can learn from my doctor, I am not moribund."

To Nicolay, though, he was more reflective and rather more final. "[T]here is not much more to expect," he confided. "My dreams when I was a little boy at Warsaw and Pittsfield have absolutely and literally been fulfilled. The most important part of my life came late, but it came in precisely the shape I dreamed."

But then he could not close his letter without griping about the Senate and the aggravation of getting treaties ratified. Already he was bracing for the next round of negotiations over the canal and the other pesky chores that stood between him and the end of his term in office.

CHAPTER 16

Rope of Sand

As Hay rested up in New Hampshire, the relief expedition closed in on Peking: Russian Cossacks, English Tommies direct from South Africa, French Indochinese in sun helmets, Japanese in white tunics, and American Marines in khaki stained with the sweat of the Philippines. Maneuvering more as parallel columns than as a unified force, they broke through the gates of the capital on August 14, to the great joy of the legations. Of the nine hundred haggard residents, miraculously only sixty-six had been killed, with another one hundred fifty wounded. During the final days, the Boxers had launched a ferocious attack on the legation defenses but then dissolved into the ravaged countryside once the allies took the city. The empress dowager trimmed her imperial fingernails, donned the coarse clothing of a peasant, and slipped away with her retinue, unrecognized. The rebellion was essentially over, though the ransacking of Peking and the pursuit of remnant bands of hostile Boxers continued for weeks. William Rockhill had left for China as soon as Conger's telegram reached Washington. His mission now would be to help steer the peace negotiations between China and the powers—and of course to ensure that the Open Door did not come off its hinges.

Throughout the siege, Hay's conduct had received widespread acclaim; once word reached the United States that the legations had been saved, the shower became a deluge. "[Y]ou have won for us the greatest diplomatic triumph of our time," cheered Henry Adams's brother Brooks, a champion of American economic supremacy. "I believe you to be one of the two or three Americans living who have measured the present situation, and that your policy will prove to have carried us round one of the great corners of our history."

Others besides Adams recognized that the deeds of the past year could not have been done by any other diplomat. "When all the world was feeding upon manufactured horrors and lashing itself into fury over a crime that had not been committed," *World's Work* observed, "it was the American Secretary of State who succeeded in checking the cry for blood, by securing a message from our Minister in Peking, announcing that he and his colleagues were alive." The Chinese crisis was far from resolved, but Hay's conduct nonetheless stood as a shining example of a new American diplomacy: "To change the map of the world is commonly considered to be a demonstration of great power," *World's Work* concluded, "but it [is] an exhibition of greater strength to prevent it from being changed."

Although Hay was as heartened as anyone by the news from China, his health did not improve commensurably. "I am miserably weak and tottery—in the morning my head swims, in the evening my knees are feeble," he wrote Alvey Adee at the end of August. "I cannot walk half a mile without fatigue and chilliness." He regretted leaving Adee with so much work, yet he did not relish the chores that awaited his return. "I see nothing ahead but ceaseless work and worry," he told Whitelaw Reid in a letter thanking him for the *Tribune*'s sympathetic coverage.

The most pressing question was what to do with a defeated and defenseless China. As united as the powers had been in rescuing their legations, they were now uncertain as to the next step, each eyeing the others, all of them giving the Open Door its due, meanwhile angling to gain advantages of trade, if not territory, much as they had always done.

On August 25, 1900, Russia announced its intention to withdraw its troops from Peking and proposed that the other powers follow suit. McKinley, Secretary of War Elihu Root, and Hay were outwardly gratified that Russia was displaying no desire to conquer any more of China.

Privately, however, the administration saw Russia's withdrawal as a cynical ploy to curry favor with the Chinese and thus to solidify its position in Manchuria—which, as was now quite obvious, Russia regarded as no longer part of China. "Russia has been more outspoken than before in her adhesion to the Open Door," Hay commented to Joseph Choate, "but her vows are false as dicers' oaths."

Russia's announcement put the United States in a cunning bind. McKinley wanted American troops out of China at the earliest possible date, but he preferred not to leave unless all the other powers did so too, and he certainly did not wish to leave in tandem with Russia. The latter option would suggest a compact with Russia that flaunted long-standing American doctrine, devalued the Open Door, insulted the other powers, or, worse, allowed them to have their way with Peking. In the end the White House hedged, advising Russia that it would keep its troops in China as long as "there is a general expression by the powers in favor of a continued occupation." If there were no hue and cry from the powers to stay, then the United States would withdraw its force, although McKinley didn't specify when or under what circumstances this withdrawal might occur.

The yellow press, mostly Democratic, interpreted this wishy-washy response to mean that McKinley had made a pact with Russia after all and that the United States might leave before peace and reparations were fully negotiated. Hay, who favored keeping troops in China for the time being, was said to be sulking in New Hampshire after not getting his way. "I need not say this is stupid lying," he responded, making light of accusations that the administration had been somehow co-opted by Russia. Borrowing an analogy from Adee, he explained, "If you break up a quick whist party by saying [to me], 'Well, I am going to bed, are you?' and I [also] have to go . . . does it follow that I go home with you and get into your bed?"

As for the other powers, he had no great confidence in them, either. Germany, whose force in China was so small it had not participated in the march on Peking, was adamant about staying long enough to inflict a full measure of punishment for the murder of its minister. Even Britain had been standoffish toward the United States in recent months. And so it went, with the future of China as murky as ever and Hay determined "to hold on like grim death to the Open Door."

In mid-September, as he sat gazing upon the turning leaves of the Sunapee hills, he shared his thoughts on the situation with Adee. Even by Hay's standards of exposition, it was an extraordinary demonstration, filling seven pages of stationery in his confident penmanship, nary a word scratched out or a modifier left dangling: a single, uninterrupted, and plainly exasperated précis on the quandary of international diplomacy in the aftermath of the Boxer Rebellion.

"The dilemma is clear enough," he began. "We want to get out at the earliest possible moment. We do not want to have the appearance of being forced out or frightened out, and we must not lose our proper influence in the final arrangement. If we leave Germany and England in Peking, and retire with Russia, who has unquestionably made her bargain already with China, we not only will *seem* to have been beaten, but we run a serious risk of being *really* frozen out. Germany and England will feel resentful and will take no care of our interests, and Russia will sell us out without winking.

"You have, it seems," he continued to Adee, "grave suspicion of the attitude of Japan. There is, therefore, not a single power we can rely on for our policy of abstention from plunder and the Open Door. If we try to deal separately with China, she will say to us, as she said last year, 'We are not free agents. We are not able, without the permission of the other powers, to fulfill any engagements we might make with you.' When I tried to get them to agree not to grant any privileges to other powers which should not be equally granted to us, they said precisely that—'If they use force against us we cannot resist. Will you guarantee us against them?'—a question which I had no authority to answer. The inherent weakness of our position is this: we do not want to rob China ourselves, and our public opinion will not permit us to interfere, with an army, to prevent others from robbing her. . . . The talk of the papers about 'our preeminent moral position giving us the authority to dictate to the world' is mere flap-doodle.

"Anxious, therefore, as I am, to get away from Peking," he wound up at last, "I cannot help fearing that if we retire with Russia, it will end in these unfortunate consequences: Russia will betray us. China will fall back on her *non possumus*, if we try to make separate terms with her. England and Germany being left in Peking, Germany by superior brute selfishness will have her way, and we shall be left out in the cold."

No wonder his convalescence was slow. "I test my strength every day in a little longer walk," he told Adee. "I observe the strictest regimen in eating and drinking. I want to come back and get to work at the earliest possible moment, but it would be worse than useless for me to begin too soon & break down again. I now hope—confidentially—to return on the first of October."

ULTIMATELY, THE UNITED STATES decided against withdrawing its troops from Peking until the powers had finalized a protocol of peace with the representatives of the exiled imperial court. Negotiations among the powers would continue into the following year, hung up mainly on the size of the indemnity the powers demanded from the all but helpless Chinese government. Throughout the talks, Rockhill pushed for moderation but met with only limited success. When he tried to knock the indemnity down to $200 million, he was roundly outvoted; in the end the Chinese were held accountable for $333 million in damages (many billions in today's dollars), of which the United States claimed $25 million, the smallest portion of any of the powers except Italy.

Russia did act on its promise to withdraw from Peking immediately after the siege was relieved, securing from China along the way even greater concessions in Manchuria. Britain and Germany, worried about Russia's go-it-alone impulse, and doubtless impatient with the United States, announced an alliance in October, which, at first blush, seemed a resounding endorsement of the Open Door. Glancing over the document, Hay was flattered to see a renewed commitment to many of the points he had included in his two circulars: a pledge to honor the integrity of China; a promise not to take advantage of the recent turmoil to grab more territory; and an application of Open Door trade guidelines along the coast and rivers of China. Britain and Germany also vowed to stick together if another power secured from China any advantage that compromised their interests. This last was an inoffensive way of agreeing to keep a sharp eye on Russia. On the other hand, to limit the compact to rivers and the coast was a euphemistic way of giving Russia a free pass in Manchuria.

To the extent that the Open Door had any strength, it depended on the unanimous endorsement of all the powers. Yet with Britain and Germany now forging their own offshoot alliance, and with Russia cutting separate deals with China and setting its own course in Manchuria, the Open Door, while not exactly off its hinges, appeared rather battered and flimsy. Still, China, after all its recent violence and vandalism, remained in one piece, not counting Manchuria, of course. Hay had played a crucial role in accomplishing at least that much. "What a business this has been in China!" he exclaimed to Henry Adams. "So far we have got on, by being honest and naïf." How resilient his policy and China's integrity might be he dared not speculate. "I do not clearly see where we are to come the delayed cropper," he added. "But it will come."

Adams reassured his friend that he had done the best he could under such snarled circumstances: "[I]n watching you herd your droves of pigs, I am at times astonished to see how, by hitting one on the snout and by coaxing another with a rotten turnip, you manage to get ahead, or at least not much backward. . . . You have been so right when everybody else was wrong, that I half believe you are too good to drive hogs."

HAY WAS BACK IN Washington by October 1, not exactly reinvigorated but sufficiently fit "to work on my last shift," he told Adee—a shift he expected to end soon after the election. In the closing weeks, McKinley appeared to be a shoo-in. As in 1896, he did not campaign actively, leaving the hard work to Mark Hanna, who raised $2.5 million, so much that he eventually reimbursed his big corporate donors. The peripatetic Theodore Roosevelt more than made up for McKinley's statuary inertia, whistle-stopping twenty thousand miles, delivering six hundred speeches in five hundred towns in twenty-four states.

Roosevelt had his own Hanna in Cabot Lodge, who counseled his protégé after the Republican Convention: "We must not permit the President, or any of his friends, who are, of course, in control of the campaign, to imagine that we want to absorb the leadership and the glory. I want you to appear everywhere as the champion of the party, and above all as the champion of the President. . . . This is going to be of immense importance to us four years hence."

Once again the Democrats nominated William Jennings Bryan, who ran on a pro-silver, anti-trust, anti-imperialist platform. Yet Bryan's charges of imperialism against McKinley did not stick as firmly as he would have liked. Cuba had recently elected delegates to a well-timed constitutional convention. Though insurrection in the Philippines dragged on, McKinley pledged that the islands would be granted self-government (if not independence) once the fighting ended. The relief of the Boxer siege and the evident success of the Open Door put another feather in McKinley's cap—and further served to justify America's presence in the Philippines. Closer to home, opportune settlement of the tense United Mine Workers' strike took some of the wind out of Bryan's anti–big business rhetoric just days before voters went to the polls. The economy was robust; dinner pails were full.

On November 6, 1900, McKinley defeated Bryan by an even wider margin than four years earlier, bettering him by a nearly two-to-one margin in the Electoral College and three quarters of a million popular votes. "We did wallop them proper and I am glad not to live under Bryan and his gang for the next four years—if I am to survive them," Hay wrote Adams. "He would be worse than Teddy; yes, I tell you, worse."

Roosevelt had no idea of the degree to which Hay and Adams mocked him behind his back, just as Cabot Lodge was clueless to the depth of their derision of him. In congratulating the vice president–elect, Hay made sure to address him formally as "Mr. Roosevelt." To which Roosevelt replied: "I wish you would always call me Theodore as you used to."

Roosevelt, meanwhile, addressed Hay as "Mr. Secretary" and flattered him to good effect: "I do not think I am wrong in my historic judgment of contemporary matters," the younger historian wrote the elder, "when I say that President McKinley's administration will rank next to Lincoln's in the whole nineteenth century in point of great work worthily done."

Hay assumed that he and Roosevelt would not be serving in the same administration. But at the first cabinet meeting after the election, McKinley announced that the current membership was irreplaceable, which put his secretary of state, for one, on the spot. "[T]he President made a little speech saying the victory was as much ours as his, saying that he could not afford to part company with us, and asked us all to remain with him for the next four years," Hay wrote to Del, who was still in Pretoria. "It was one of the most touching and dignified things I have ever known him to do." Under the circumstances, Hay did not have the heart to tell McKinley of his intention to leave. Instead, he mustered a lachrymose reply to the president and his fellow cabinet members, assuring them that "the happiest hours I have ever spent are those I have spent in companionship with my colleagues."

He expressed no such satisfaction with the Senate, which on December 20 ratified the Hay-Pauncefote Treaty with three amendments. The first superseded the fifty-year-old Clayton-Bulwer Treaty with Britain; the second stipulated that the United States had the right to defend the canal. And the third deleted the original Hay-Pauncefote language inviting other powers to adhere to the treaty.

Hay was at once aggrieved and ashamed. The amendments, especially the one calling for American defense of the canal, "deform and disfigure" the original treaty, he complained to Joseph Choate, whose job it now was to sell the changes to England. Hay was pessimistic that Choate would succeed. "If Great Britain should now reject the Treaty the general opinion of mankind should justify her in it," he wrote his ambassador. "If our Congress should then go forward and violently abrogate the Clayton-Bulwer Treaty by legislative action, we shall be putting ourselves hopelessly in the wrong. . . . Why should not Lord Salisbury say to us . . . 'Take your Treaty, Brother Jonathan, and God send you better manners.'"

Hay put most of the blame for "the disaster" on Lodge. "The most exasperating thing about it," he confided to Henry White, his trusted embassy secretary in London, "is that a close analysis of the vote convinces me that the treaty could have been ratified without any amendment if our people had any pluck, or if Lodge had acted squarely."

Sensing Hay's ire, Lodge gave an interview extolling the secretary and defending the fairness of the treaty. "Let me say, first, that the amendments were not dictated by hostility for England," the senator asserted, "and still less were they in any degree a reflection on the Secretary of

State, whose patriotism, purity of purpose . . . and high achievement in dealing with our foreign relations, especially in China, are fully and cordially recognized by men of all parties and all shades of opinions in the Senate."

Hay was hardly mollified, and he continued to vent his anger at Lodge and the Senate. "Lodge has now come out in a carefully prepared interview, saying that a treaty when sent to the Senate is not properly speaking a treaty—it is merely a project," he went on to Henry White. "That is to say that if France and the U.S. make a treaty, after careful study and negotiation, it is nothing more, when sent to the Senate, than a petition from the two nations to that body, to make a real treaty for them. The attitude of the Senate towards public affairs makes all serious negotiation impossible. They really seem to think the State Department has no function but to provide their friends with offices."

One way or another, however, the canal was going forward. Its congressional champions—Cabot Lodge, Cushman Davis of Minnesota, William Hepburn of Iowa, and John Tyler Morgan of Alabama—had made it clear that even if the British declined to approve the treaty, they were prepared to abrogate Clayton-Bulwer unilaterally and let the British take their lumps. A month before the vote on Hay-Pauncefote in the Senate, the Isthmian Canal Commission, led by Admiral John Walker, had issued a preliminary report, which concluded that the Panama route was shorter and less costly but that the Nicaraguan route was the "most practicable and feasible." That left only the Hepburn bill, authorizing the United States to build the canal. It had already passed in the House and had preferred status on the Senate calendar.

Even so, the legislation did not sail through the upper chamber as quickly or as smoothly as expected. Forces representing a newly configured Panama canal company—successor to the original French company—went to work on members of the Senate, urging them to give the Panama route more thoughtful consideration and, at the very least, to hold off on their decision until the canal commission had published its final report.

Meanwhile, the administration appealed to the Senate to delay the vote until the treaty with Britain was resolved. "If the stirrers-up of strife would keep still a few minutes, we peacemakers might get a chance," Hay wrote to the newspaper columnist Henry Watterson. "Yet here is our dear old friend Morgan—a heart of gold—saying in the Senate that we are not bound to wait an instant for England to decide a matter which we took a year to discuss, and serving notice on her that . . . we are going to do as we damplease. Of course, that is just what we are going to do—but why say it when we are going through the motions of ordinary civility? A man don't say 'Please pass the butter—[and] if you don't I'll take it anyway and slit your damn weazand [windpipe] if you wink.' Yet Mr. Lodge, bred at Harvard, says this is the proper, honest and honorable way to ask for butter, even when the other side is perfectly willing to pass it along."

In a letter to Andrew Carnegie, Hay used a more elegant metaphor to express his deep and chronic frustration with the state of statesmanship. Although Carnegie had his differences with Hay on America's expansionist foreign policy, he never forsook their friendship. At Christmas he was in the habit of sending Hay a case of whiskey from his beloved Scotland. "I thank you kindly for the 'corpse reviver,'" Hay wrote Carnegie in January 1901 after being bedridden for several days. "[I]f a man could only drink enough of it, he would either never die, or wouldn't care whether he did or not." He then gave his reasons why the latest shipment was especially welcome: "I have had a dismal week of it;—getting well of the grippe is worse than getting sick of anything else. And besides I am tired to the marrow of my bones, twisting the rope of sand which is American Diplomacy."

Hay-Pauncefote, the Open Door, the Alaskan boundary, and every negotiation Hay had conducted with foreign governments—each was a rope of sand, a tangible thread between two points, yet notoriously insubstantial and inherently transitory. Like an hourglass, or like life itself.

BRITAIN MIGHT POSSIBLY HAVE deliberated on the new canal treaty more expeditiously had Queen Victoria not died on January 21. Choate warned Hay not to expect any decisions from the British Foreign Office for quite some time. Hay took the opportunity to remind the new king, Edward VII, of the deep kinship between the two English-speaking nations: "In wishing you, Sir, a beneficent and prosperous reign, I confidently trust that not among the least of Your achievements shall be the corroboration and perfection of those bonds of confidence and esteem between Great Britain and America for which the recent happy years have done so much. . . . The affection we bore the beloved Queen is already Yours. With hearts full of tender memories of the past and high hopes for the future we pray most sincerely, Sir, for your health and prosperity." He signed the letter: "Your Majesty's faithful and obedient Servant, John Hay."

NEITHER HAY'S MORALE NOR health improved as the winter wore on and the inauguration neared. "I am sick to the heart of the whole business, and shall gladly get out at the first opportunity," he told Henry White. "And when I go it will be final. I shall never again accept office, at home or abroad." He had tried to get White promoted to the ambassadorship to Rome, only to be blocked by the "treachery" of Cabot Lodge. "He is equally false about me," Hay commiserated with White. "He is not unfriendly to me personally, in the abstract, nor is he to you. But neither you nor I would weight a feather weight with him, as against any selfish advantage. He would cut my throat or yours for a favorable notice in a newspaper."

Hay grew still more obsessed with the Senate, if that was possible. "When I send a year's job to the Senate," he wrote to Lizzie Cameron in Paris, "they either begin a ghost dance around it with tomahawks drawn, or they pigeonhole it and forget all about it."

Lizzie was another obsession that never waned. His letters to her in the previous year were infrequent—which perhaps only means that many of them are lost—but they were no less tender. "I have seen nobody this winter—and I have the joyful prospect of seeing no one till next winter," he sighed to her with signature self-pity. "Why should I care to see anybody when the only face that is good for tired eyes is that beautiful one that means so much—so rich in beauty, in memory and in suggestion— and is now so far away. I really begin to believe I shall never see you again, you dear sweet woman. If I don't, remember what a blessing you were with your beauty, your wit and your sweetness—one of the great luxuries of my life."

It was true: he hadn't seen much of anybody that winter. Clara's mother had died, and she and Hay were officially in mourning, precluding them from partaking of the "season"—or at least providing an excuse for not accepting invitations.

Beyond that, however, public life had made Hay a more private man. His time was in such great demand that he guarded it like a keepsake. He and Clara hosted fewer of their envied dinner parties, at which they mingled statesmen, diplomats, artists, and authors in their sophisticated salon. And rarely did Hay travel anymore, only to and from the Fells or under official auspices—to confer with the president in Canton, for instance, or to give a speech or accept an honor. (In successive years, he received honorary degrees from Princeton, Yale, and Harvard.) He had not been abroad since leaving London in 1898.

Perhaps he was looking for an excuse not to continue as secretary of state, but by February he truly did not feel up to the job, an opinion seconded by Adams, who was back in Washington for the winter. "I think Hay very far from strong; and doubt his ability to remain in office," he wrote his brother Brooks. Adams's concern increased during the following weeks. "After watching Hay's condition," he wrote Lizzie, "I am regretfully compelled to admit that he must go out or die. His strength is exhausted and his temper too. Whether he will recover must depend, I suppose, on rest and constitution; but for the present he is done. So much of Hay's valetudinarianism has always been nervous that I fully admit that he may live to be ninety; but he is no longer fit to be Secretary."

Hay's doctor diagnosed angina pectoris, a harbinger of worse troubles to come. Adams, though, suspected that his friend might merely have come down with a case of *"angina senatus,"* explaining to Lizzie: "Hay was made to be a first-rate ambassador abroad; he loathes being a third-rate politician at home. He thinks that the proper man for the cabinet is someone . . . with whom the senators can play poker and drink whiskey and hatch jobs in a corner, and so get things done. He feels that he can't do it, and it takes the life out of him. Then comes Cabot, who is more of a bloodsucker than Platt or Quay or Hanna combined, and whose methods exceed the endurance of a coral reef. . . . Hay frets and rages internally, and suffers the more because he keeps, or tries to keep, an external impassivity."

Hay's impassivity was stretched to the breaking point at the end of the month when British newspapers divulged that the Foreign Office had rejected the Hay-Paunceforte Treaty. Hay was not officially notified for several more weeks, but he did not doubt the story's veracity; he had been expecting as much all along.

On March 1, 1901, he submitted his resignation, to take effect on the appointment of his successor. McKinley chose to receive it as an interregnum formality and dismissed it out of hand, not suspecting just how much thought Hay had given to leaving.

The weather was gray and drizzly for McKinley's second inauguration on March 4. This time, Hay did not present the president with a ring with a lock of hair or any other gift, and unlike at Lincoln's second inauguration thirty-five years earlier, sunshine did not break through as the president gave his address. Instead, it poured.

REMARKABLY, AS MCKINLEY'S SECOND term began and Hay found himself still secretary of state, he gained what, for him, constituted a second wind. His aggravation over the rejection of the Senate-amended canal treaty seemed to have fueled his remaining resolve to try again. Exercising greater shrewdness and a degree more of humility, he determined to consult with the Senate as he went along. It went without saying that the greatest hurdle would still be Cabot Lodge.

Lodge was incensed by Britain's rejection of the latest treaty, and he was more impatient than ever to snatch the butter. He assured Hay that if Britain did not replace the old treaty with one "satisfactory to the Senate," then the Senate would "denounce the Clayton-Bulwer Treaty and pass the [Hepburn] canal bill by a majority so large as to fall but little short of unanimity." He defended his brinkmanship by citing a variety of experts on international law who posited that "eternal duration is assured to no treaty between great powers." He even quoted Otto von Bismarck: "International policy is a fluid element which under certain conditions will solidify, but on a change of atmosphere reverts to its original diffuse condition." In other words, a rope of sand.

Hay answered Lodge instantly, straining to contain his temper. "I infer from your letter," he began, "that you think any arrangement we can make with Great Britain will be rejected by the Senate; that Congress will at its next session adopt a resolution abrogating the Clayton-Bulwer treaty, and that this course will have your approval and support." Then, sounding very Lincolnesque, he coolly skewered Lodge's logic: "The fact that you can bring forward many instances of the violation of treaties or their one-sided abrogation, seems to prove hardly more than that wherever there are laws, they are occasionally violated; but this does not necessarily repeal the law."

And he could not close without delivering a final riposte. "I am hardly ready to accept Prince Bismarck as an authority on international morals," he submitted, now rather acidly. "Some of his acts require very ingenious explanation and apology."

In the end, he won by persistence, patience, finesse, and perhaps a little bluff of his own. Because Britain was well aware that the canal would be built, with or without an Anglo-American treaty, Hay sensed that the Foreign Office might come around if he simply refined the language in the next draft. The changes he made, after talking with both the Senate and Pauncefote, were subtle, to the extent that he changed much at all. He removed one or two small legalistic thorns and generally softened the tone throughout, but did not alter the two critical elements of the treaty: Britain's insistence that the canal be neutral and the Senate's sine qua non asserting that the canal be built, maintained, and *defended* by the United States. "I have drawn this up with very great care," he wrote to Choate. "You will see by a careful perusal of it and comparison of it with the extinct treaty, that it contains substantially all that was asked for in the [Senate's] amended treaty, but in a form, which, I hope, will not be objectionable to the British Government."

The new foreign secretary, Lord Lansdowne, was in no hurry to reply, but now at least the process of give-and-take had resumed, and this time Hay was reasonably confident that he and the Senate were on the same page.

ON APRIL 29, 1901, Hay left Washington for a trip with McKinley through the South and West. Seven weeks was a long time to be gone, but he didn't mind getting away from the annoyances of the capital.

During the spring, he and Adams had resumed their afternoon walks, although Hay's stamina was noticeably diminished. "He looks pasty and pale," Adams wrote Lizzie in April. "[H]e can't walk as far as K Street without a duck-fit, at least on a windy day, or at a brisk gait; he gives out, at a pinch, whenever he calls on himself for endurance." All the more reason to escape to a warmer, drier climate.

McKinley intended the trip as a victory lap and a chance to promote his economic agenda for the next term. Initially, he proposed taking along his entire cabinet, but the only members in the party of forty-three passengers aboard the train were Hay and Postmaster General Charles Emory Smith. They made their way through the cotton-producing states of Alabama, Mississippi, and Louisiana, where Hay drew his share of cheers for the Open Door. Then across Texas and onward to Phoenix, Arizona, from which Hay sent Adams a jaded account of the junket thus far—"the getting into hacks and being driven through the principal streets in the broiling sun to the Public Square; then an address of welcome from the Mayor or the Governor. . . . And the long banquets of 22 courses and the drizzle of eloquence to follow. And the peril to my immortal soul when they ask me what I think of their city. I hastily run over all the advantage of London and Paris and Tadmor in the wilderness, and say their town combines all their charms and none of their faults—which is swallowed even as a turkey gobbles a June-bug. It has not yet killed me, and possibly it will not, for after all the racket, it is a sort of rest from the State Department."

In Phoenix, he had hoped to meet up with Clarence King, who was in Arizona for his health. They had seen each other less and less in recent years, as Hay became more absorbed in his public responsibilities and King struggled to make ends meet. Hay and Adams continued to loan King money, collateralized by King's valuable art collection and near-worthless stock certificates. But as creditors they had long since given up on their friend settling his debts—another reason why King had been shy about coming around.

Under the name of James Todd, he had moved his wife and four children to a house in the New York borough of Queens several years earlier, while he continued his peregrinations in quest of windfalls. In the summer of 1900 he had gone to the newly discovered gold strikes in Nome, Alaska, but came away no richer. That fall he was in Prescott, Arizona, inspecting a copper mine, when he came down with whooping cough. By the end of the year, doctors had diagnosed tuberculosis.

Hay had seen King at the end of the previous summer, when he came to the Fells for a day. He was as "delightful as ever," Hay noted, "though hard worked and not too strong." By the following March, when King stopped off in Washington, bound for the Bahamas on doctor's orders, Hay and Adams were shocked by the change. "I have been hit badly by Clarence King," Adams wrote Lizzie. The formerly indefatigable mountaineer was now "broken by pneumonia and gravely threatened by worse." At the time, Hay was doing none too well himself, adding to Adams's anxiety. "So, you see," he continued to Lizzie, "my two friends, and I might say my only two friends, are agitating me by announcing that they don't know whether they are fatally ill or not, but will tell me in a month or two."

One month later, Hay was somewhat better; King was not. "His tuberculosis is now pronounced," Adams wrote again to Lizzie, "and I dread its not confining itself to the lungs. He must go to Arizona at once, and ought to have gone three months ago. He coughs much, with the usual symptoms. . . . Whether we shall ever see him again is a question that one prefers not to ask him."

Before departing the east, King said goodbye to Ada, suspecting that it was the last time they would be together. He gave her money that he said had been given him by two friends and told her to take the children to Toronto to live. Only when he got to Arizona did he confess to her his true identity.

King was in Prescott when Hay stopped in Phoenix, and so they missed each other again. The presidential train continued on to California, where McKinley and his secretary of state saw the Pacific Ocean for the first and only time in their lives.

Yet they had little opportunity to appreciate their vantage point. As the train neared San Francisco, Mrs. McKinley, always frail, developed blood poisoning from an infected finger. For a week she lay near death. While the president remained by his wife's side, Hay served as his surrogate, planting a tree at Stanford and addressing the students and faculty at the University of California. The mayor of San Francisco led him on a tour of the city, including a visit to a gambling den in Chinatown. On May 25, Mrs. McKinley was finally judged well enough to travel. The presidential train arrived back in Washington on the thirty-first, two weeks ahead of schedule. McKinley's speech at the Pan-American Exposition in Buffalo had to be postponed until September.

In the meantime, Hay was sent to stand in for the president at the exposition's opening. As little as he professed to enjoy public speaking, he had been doing a lot of it recently, and he was getting better as he grew older. The Pan-American world's fair was a celebration of the nation's enlarged presence in the hemisphere, from Alaska to the Caribbean and South America, soon to be cinched at the waist by a canal between the oceans. The exposition was also meant to showcase the wonder of electricity; every night the fairgrounds were bejeweled with two hundred thousand lights powered by the turbines of Niagara Falls. In his brief address on June 13, Hay haled the "ideal of the brotherhood of the nations" and saluted "the armies of labor and intelligence in every country of this New World, all working with one mind and one will, not to attain an unhappy pre-eminence in the art of destruction, but to advance in liberal emulation in the arts which tend to make this long-harassed and tormented earth a brighter"—here a salute to the splendid illumination—"and more blest abode for men of good will."

On his next trip to Buffalo, three months later, the atmosphere would be infinitely darker. Had Ida McKinley's finger not become infected, shortening the presidential trip, and had McKinley been able to deliver his world's fair address in June instead of returning in September to fulfill his promise, he might have avoided assassination. But fate had other plans.

HAY BEGAN THE SUMMER in relatively good spirits. The affairs of state were for once free of major crisis. In the Philippines the guerrilla leader, Aguinaldo, had been captured, and the fight appeared to have gone out of the rebels. Hay had still not heard from Foreign Secretary Lansdowne on the canal treaty, but Choate was cautiously optimistic. In China, Rockhill was helping bring negotiations of the Boxer indemnity to a close. Although Russia continued to press its advantage in Manchuria, the rest of China was free of violence, allowing American troops at last to withdraw from Peking. And the dickering over purchase of the Danish West Indies was showing incremental progress.

The Hay household was a happy place. Both Helen and Alice were in love with two of Del's classmates from Yale. Helen's beau was Payne Whitney, heir to a New York street-railway fortune and millions more. Alice had fallen for James Wadsworth, scion of a well-to-do family from western New York; Wadsworth's father, a congressman, was a friend of Hay's, as his grandfather, a Civil War general, had been forty years before. Clarence, not yet seventeen and too frequently lost in the family shuffle, was headed to Harvard in the fall.

The best news of all was Del. The British had taken Pretoria in June 1900, obviating his job as consul to the Boer Republic, but he had stayed on anyway and by all accounts had handled himself well. "You have had a very successful year of it," Hay told his son in a rare expression of approval. "I have not heard a word of criticism of you."

Del finally left South Africa in February 1901, stopping in London for two weeks en route to America. "He is a very dear fellow," Henry White reported to Hay. "I am curious to see whether and how much Mrs. Hay and you find him changed. He talks more than he did—and very well too—and reveals more frequently the possession of that sense of humor which he inherits from you." Clara went to New York to meet the boat and bring him home. He had been gone a year and a half, during which time he had indeed grown up. He was not as polished as his father, but he was nonetheless poised, confident, and, as Clarence King had once remarked, blessed with "disarming bonhomie."

Del was contemplating a career in the diplomatic service, but even his father could not promise him another posting right away. Then something better came up. In June, President McKinley appointed him assistant private secretary, the same position Hay had held in the Lincoln White House. Father insisted he had not helped son "even with a word," though certainly McKinley was astute enough to value the apple of such a trustworthy tree.

Before beginning his new assignment, Del went to New Hampshire with his mother and sisters. Hay remained in Washington until Alvey Adee returned from vacation. He hoped to snatch a day or two at the Fells when he went to Cambridge to receive an honorary degree from Harvard on June 25. He would just miss Del, who was headed to New Haven that same week for the triennial reunion of his Yale class.

At dawn on the morning of the twenty-third, Hay was awakened by McKinley's secretary, George Cortelyou, delivering awful news. Cortelyou had received a telephone call from the proprietor of the New Haven House, informing him that Del had been found dead on the sidewalk in front of the hotel, having fallen from the window of his third-floor room. In a state of shock, Hay packed a bag and hurried to the train station. Arriving in New Haven in mid-afternoon, he went directly to the undertaker's and identified his son, still clad in his pajamas.

Del had been to the theater with friends earlier in the evening and returned to his hotel room at midnight, requesting that he be awakened in the morning at nine. The evidence suggested that he had sat at the window before retiring. His clothes were neatly folded, his bed was turned down, and a half-smoked cigarette was found on the windowsill. Apparently he had dozed off, become dizzy, or lost his balance. At 2:30 am, a city worker saw him plummet sixty feet to the pavement. He died instantly. Neither the doctors, the coroner, the hotel staff, Del's friends, nor certainly his family said anything about drinking—or suicide, a subject that had to have entered the consciousness of his parents at least fleetingly. After all, Clara's father had killed himself, and thirty-five years earlier Hay had published a short story about a young man Del's age who throws himself from the Arc de Triomphe. Adelbert Stone Hay's death, however, was ruled accidental.

Del's final day was the worst of his father's life. Though Hay had been at Lincoln's bedside, had seen the ghastly bullet wound in the president's skull, and had witnessed his last breath, that tragedy, even as it unfolded, was draped in the gauze of history. Hay had been only one of many whose hearts were broken in the boardinghouse across from Ford's Theatre. But in the undertaker's parlor in New Haven, the grief was singular and for that reason incalculably more unbearable.

Helen and Clarence arrived in New Haven later in the day, Clara and Alice soon thereafter. The family gathered at the funeral home for one final glimpse of Del, who was laid out in the blue serge suit he had intended to wear to the Yale-Harvard baseball game later in the week. "He never looked so handsome as in his coffin. His face was not injured. Death had given him a new dignity," Hay wrote to McKinley, who had lost two children of his own—and whose own coffin would be filled soon enough.

The family left by train for Cleveland early in the evening. A modest funeral, attended by thirty friends and family members, was held the following day in a small chapel on the grounds of Lake View Cemetery. Del was buried in a plot next to Clara's father and brother.

The letters of condolence would eventually fill three bound volumes—from Henry James and William Dean Howells, Mark Twain and S. Weir Mitchell, Rudyard Kipling and Bram Stoker, Andrew Carnegie and John D. Rockefeller, seemingly every friend Hay and Clara had ever made, and every public figure, from king to congressman, who cared at all. Scores of newspaper stories celebrated Del's deft service in South Africa and mourned the bright future taken from him. "He had ease and variety; his family idolized him; everybody liked him and sought his company," Hay wrote Clarence King. "He was . . . well known in three continents."

And to John Clark in Scotland, Hay described Del as a young chieftain cut down on the moor: "Twenty-four-years old 6 feet 2 and 15 stone—strong and wise and steady—able to hold his own in fight and council—and of all that brilliant promise nothing but dust and ashes."

Henry Adams, who was traveling in Europe with Cabot and Nannie Lodge, was distressed that he could not be on hand to console his dearest friend. He knew Hay far too well to waste words on treacly platitudes; instead, he offered plainspoken counsel, drawing upon his own painful history. "Fate strikes us at times *too* hard," he wrote the day of Del's funeral. "There is no use struggling. I daren't write to your wife. What could I say? Whatever I should try to say would be wrong, or touch some strong chord. She has got to carry her load. She can't do as I did, sixteen years ago—throw life up, and sit still to wait for its end. I could drop out, and stay out; but she must go on, and carry you all, as before. . . . When one is struck by one of these impossible blows, one either has or has not the strength to go on. If one has it, one picks oneself up, after a time, and limps along, without help, never really oneself again, but able to walk. If one hasn't it, one goes under, and no help serves. Women are better than men, as a rule, in these trials, and react against them with more instinct. . . . Nine times out of ten, it is the man who collapses."

Hay read Adams's note after he returned to Washington. "That was a letter which did its work," he wrote back. "It took my sore mind from my boy and made me think of my wife and the rest. I do not yet know whether I shall get through or not. I am not making any progress. I am waiting to see if the nerves will stand the strain. I have hideous forebodings. I have been extraordinarily happy all my life. Good luck has pursued me like my shadow. Now it is gone—it seems to me forever. I expect, tomorrow, to hear bad news, something insufferable. The bright spot in the gloom is my wife. She has borne the horror wonderfully. For the first twenty-four hours I thought most of her and what could be done to comfort her, but from the hour she arrived at New Haven she took care of me."

Lizzie Cameron wanted to take care of him, too, urging him to come to Donegal, the Cameron estate in Pennsylvania. Reluctantly he declined. "I can not see any friends of Del's at present," he wrote her, his pain compounded. "I can not talk of him nor think of him without breaking down. I thank you with all my heart for your sympathy and for all your goodness to him which he deeply appreciated."

On the same day that he wrote Lizzie, he also wrote to Clara, who had stayed on in Cleveland. He was settling Del's affairs—closing out his bank account, transferring securities. But he could not yet bring himself to open his son's trunks. "[M]y sorrow grips me from time to time so that I can hardly bear it," he told his wife. "Everybody seems to think I will be better at work. I do not know whether they are right or wrong. But I want to get away where I can see nobody but my own."

After a week in Washington, he joined Clara at the Fells, where they kept to themselves until September. "It is a month since our calamity came upon us," Hay wrote Whitelaw Reid at the end of July, "and yet we have not known an hour when we felt that we could talk with you and Mrs. Reid about it. The time will probably never come; we are too old to heal of such a wound. . . . Our loss grows greater as we move away from it."

Del's death had stirred the painful memory of his namesake, Clara's brother Adelbert, who had drowned at Yale. Yet as Adams had forecast, Clara proved to be the brick of the family. She was not only inherently calmer and more nurturing than her husband; she also possessed a greater faith. "[W]e are not in despair," she bravely assured Adams later in the summer. "We cannot understand [Del's death], but we feel it must have been for the best and that he had accomplished in his short life what was intended for him to do. We try to think that he is away on one of his long journeys and that we will meet again someday." In the meantime, she declared, "We have made up our minds that the only way to keep ourselves and our household from going to pieces is to go on just as we did before."

Short of leaving office entirely, Hay had no choice but to resume his participation in the affairs of the world. At the end of August, Britain announced it was ready to put the canal treaty in order. The English ambassador Julian Pauncefote, who knew Hay's mind thoroughly and had his own pride of authorship in the treaty, was home on leave for the summer. Cabot Lodge had passed through London in July and, setting aside his sniping ways, displayed a willingness to hash out the treaty firsthand with Foreign Secretary Lansdowne and the leader of the House of Commons, Arthur Balfour. They seemed to have hit it off, a relieved Joseph Choate informed Hay.

Lodge agreed to stop in London again on his way home from the Continent in September, in order to smooth out any remaining differences in the treaty. Hay was so hopeful that a workable document was near at hand that he made a hasty trip to Canton at the end of August to go over the recent developments with McKinley. "I am profoundly gratified at the way the matter now presents itself," he wrote Choate on September 2, after seeing the president. "If Lord Pauncefote brings [the treaty] back next month in the form we have indicated, I shall be ready to intone my nunc dimittis."

Two days later, on September 4, the president and Mrs. McKinley set out for Buffalo to deliver the address he had intended to give in June, before their western trip was curtailed. The following morning, McKinley gave his speech to a crowd of fifty thousand on the fair's esplanade. The subject was peace and stability through reciprocity. As a politician who had built his reputation as a champion of tariffs, he now proclaimed that America's economy was prosperous enough and its prowess in the world great enough that the time had come to modify its protective posture—high tariffs—and engage in freer trade with overseas markets. "Isolation is no longer possible or desirable," he declared. "Our capacity to produce has developed so enormously and our products have so multiplied that the problem of more markets requires our urgent and immediate attention. Only a broad and enlightened policy will keep what we have. No other policy will get more. . . . We must not repose in fancied security that we can forever sell everything and buy little or nothing. . . . Reciprocity is the natural outcome of our wonderful industrial development."

He knew that lowering the nation's guard in this way would not sit well with cautious conservatives within his party, but he was confident that recent developments, including the Open Door and the prospect of an interoceanic canal, promised a robust future in which the United States could hold its own against its rivals and benefit from more open exchange with its allies. It was arguably the most potent speech of McKinley's career. It was also his last.

The following afternoon, after a visit to Niagara Falls, McKinley held a public reception in the exposition's garish Temple of Music. It was to last for only ten minutes, which would give him enough time to greet several hundred people. Years earlier he had mastered "the McKinley grip," a technique in which he extended his right hand and grasped only the fingers of the person standing before him, while with his left he politely but firmly pulled the fellow past, already grasping the fingers of the next in line. He boasted he could shake fifty hands a minute.

At 4:07 pm, McKinley applied his famous grip yet again. Noticing a bandage or handkerchief over the man's right hand, McKinley reached for the left. At that, Leon Czolgosz, a twenty-eight-year-old half-baked anarchist, thrust a .32-caliber revolver toward McKinley's white-vested midriff and fired two shots before being pummeled to the floor.

One of the bullets glanced off McKinley's breastbone and was of little consequence. The second bullet passed through his stomach and could not be located during exploratory surgery. Initially, the doctors attending the president spoke of a full recovery, basing their optimism on McKinley's stout constitution and the lack of damage to other internal organs. McKinley was taken to the home of the exposition's president, John Milburn, where, over the next few days, he was observed to be slowly improving.

Hay was notified of the shooting via the telegraph office in Newbury. With Vice President Roosevelt and most of the cabinet already en route to Buffalo, Hay prepared to head for Washington, to be in a better position to keep foreign governments and his own ministers and consuls informed on the president's condition. At the suggestion of George Cortelyou, he changed his plans at the last minute and went to Buffalo also, arriving on the tenth.

After visiting McKinley's bedside, Hay assured a newspaperman, "The reports of the doctors are so encouraging that I see no reason for alarm or for fear that the President will not speedily recover." He left for Washington the next day, as did most of the rest of the cabinet. Roosevelt was so unfazed by McKinley's condition that he set off to climb Mount Marcy, the tallest peak in the Adirondacks.

On Friday the thirteenth, McKinley began to sink, as sepsis from his abdominal wound took over. Hay had intended to start for the Fells that morning but then had to wire Clara that he was staying put. "President's condition more serious," he informed her. "The worst is feared." He spent the rest of the day in his office, monitoring the dispatches from Buffalo. An evening paper reported that McKinley looked "worn and nervous and anxious to the last degree." At ten o'clock that night, another bulletin arrived: "The President is pulseless and dying. He may live about an hour."

He lived another four, dying shortly after 2 am on September 14, whispering the words to his favorite hymn, "Nearer, My God, to Thee."

As McKinley was breathing his last, Theodore Roosevelt was racing down the slope of Mount Marcy toward the station at North Creek,

New York. Throughout the previous day, runners had delivered messages advising him that the president's condition was grave and urging him to make haste. When Roosevelt galloped up to the depot shortly after five in the morning, he was handed a telegram bearing the blunt announcement: "The President died at two-fifteen this morning." The sender was John Hay—his first communication to the twenty-sixth president of the United States.

It was agreed among the cabinet that Hay and Treasury Secretary Lyman Gage would remain in the capital. Hay busied himself with the necessary tasks of mourning and transition. He directed that all executive offices be closed. He drafted a letter to be sent to all the ministries abroad, announcing the president's death and the circumstances: "Laid low by the act of an assassin, the week-long struggle to save his life had been watched with keen solicitude, not alone by the people of this country who raised him from their own ranks to the high office he filled, but by the people of all friendly nations, whose messages of sympathy, and of hope while hope was possible, have been most consolatory in this time of sore trial."

Next he issued a memorandum outlining the observances of the days to follow. McKinley would lie in state for a day in the Buffalo City Hall; then to Washington to lie in state in the Capitol, followed by services in the Rotunda; and finally a funeral train to Canton for burial. Recalling the lengthy, overwrought journey of Lincoln's casket from the capital to Springfield, Hay advised, "No ceremonies are expected in the cities and towns along the route of the funeral train beyond the tolling of bells."

Memories of too many assassinations beset him as he struggled through the day. The similarities between Garfield's and McKinley's were especially haunting. Charles Guiteau and Leon Czolgosz were both unhinged loners who had lamely attempted to attach themselves to higher causes—for Guiteau, the Republican Stalwarts; for Czolgosz, the anarchist movement. They had both approached the president in a public place and fired point-blank, fully expecting to be apprehended. Both presidents lingered—though McKinley not nearly as long as Garfield—and then died of infection. (And both Guiteau and Czolgosz were determined by the court not to be insane and were executed promptly: in Czolgosz's case, on October 29, 1901, thirty-three days after his conviction.)

Hay's affinity with the three assassinated leaders—combined with the death of Del—was a crueler coincidence than any nightmare could conjure. "[M]y personal grief is overwhelmed in public sorrow," he wrote to a friend in London. "The President was one of the sweetest and gentlest natures I have ever known among public men. . . . And now he too is gone and left the world far poorer by his absence. I wonder how much grief we can endure. It seems to me I am full to the brim. I see no chance of recovery—no return to the days when there seemed something worth while. . . . What a strange and tragic fate it has been of mine—to stand by the bier of three of my dearest friends, Lincoln, Garfield, and McKinley, three of the gentlest of men, all risen to be head of the State, and all done to death by assassins."

IT HAD BEEN DIFFICULT enough for Hay to adjust to Theodore Roosevelt as vice president; learning to address the man he had once called Teddy and then Theodore as "Mr. President" would take some practice. Roosevelt's rambunctiousness—physical, intellectual, and political—seemed decidedly unpresidential, compared to the decorum of other chief executives Hay had known. There was something unsettling about Roosevelt's push, his certainty—his very inevitability. While McKinley still lay stricken in Buffalo, Adams had written to Hay from Sweden with considerable misgiving: "[B]ehind all, in my mind, in all our minds, silent and awful like the Chicago express, flies the thought of Teddy's luck!" With Roosevelt now president, Hay answered Adams: "I . . . shuddered at the awful clairvoyance of your last phrase from Stockholm about Theodore's luck. Well, he is here in the saddle again."

Whatever uneasiness Hay may have felt, he was too much a gentleman, statesman, and patriot to convey even a shadow of disrespect for Roosevelt. On Roosevelt's second day as president, Hay wrote him a letter of bittersweet affirmation. "My dear Roosevelt," he began, not yet using the formal appellation of office. "If the Presidency had come to you in any other way, no one would have congratulated you with better heart than I. My sincere affection and esteem for you, my old-time love for your father—would he could have lived to see you where you are!—would have been deeply gratified. And even from the depths of the sorrow where I sit, with my grief for the President mingled and confused with that for my boy so that I scarcely know from hour to hour the true source of my tears, I do still congratulate you, not only on the threshold of an official career which I know will be glorious, but on the vast opportunity for useful work which lies before you. With your youth, your ability, your health and strength, the courage God has given you to do right, there are no bounds to the good you can accomplish for your country and the name you will leave in its annals."

Then Hay, the graying chamberlain, presented his seal and sword to the newly crowned king. "My official life is at an end—my natural life will not be long extended," he submitted, "and so, in the dawn of what I am sure will be a great and splendid future, I venture to give you the heartfelt benediction of the past. God bless you." He signed himself "Yours faithfully, John Hay."

Almost before McKinley's corpse was cold, speculation had begun over which cabinet members Roosevelt would keep and which he would replace. At the top of the list of discards was Hay, or so the *New York Herald* reported, recalling how quickly Secretary of State Blaine had departed after Chester Arthur assumed the presidency. Hay's predicted successor was Cabot Lodge, who, like Adams, had been in Europe when McKinley was shot. And if it were not Lodge, then Elihu Root would switch chairs from War to State. Aware of Roosevelt's long-standing disapproval of his handling of the canal treaty, Hay fully anticipated that he would not be asked to stay, and he honestly would not have minded stepping down. He had been talking about leaving at the end of the year, or soon, anyway.

He was at the Washington station on the evening of the sixteenth when the train carrying Roosevelt, the other cabinet members, and McKinley's casket arrived from Buffalo. Before Hay could take the initiative, Roosevelt clasped him vigorously by the hand and, "without waiting an instant, told me I must stay with him—that I could not decline nor even consider," Hay recounted to Adams. "I saw of course it was best for him to start off that way, & so said I would stay, forever, of course, for it would be worse to say I would stay a while than it would be to go out at once."

At Roosevelt's request, Hay remained in Washington while the president and the rest of the cabinet attended McKinley's funeral in Canton. "[A]s I am the next heir to the Presidency," he mentioned darkly, referring to an 1886 law that placed the secretary of state after the vice president in order of succession, "[Roosevelt] did not want too many eggs in the same Pullman car." Once the funeral party had returned and Roosevelt had assured his cabinet of his support and determination to carry forward the policies and ideals of the martyred McKinley, Hay returned to the Fells.

There he received the next sad blow. His oldest friend, fellow presidential secretary, roommate, and co-author, John George Nicolay, had died in Washington on September 26, after a long and gradual decline.

WHILE HAY TALLIED HIS grief and took what comfort he could from the peace and quiet of New Hampshire, Ambassador Choate was making progress in London. There was a brief moment of tension when the British got wind that the canal might be built in Panama instead of Nicaragua, but once Hay assured Choate—who in turn assured the Foreign Office—that the treaty applied to all isthmian routes, no more wrinkles remained to be ironed out. Lodge arrived in London the last week of September and gave his blessing to the last round of revisions. The expectation was that Pauncefote would bring the treaty with him when he sailed for the United States at the end of October, allowing ample time for it to be signed by both countries and presented to the Senate when its session commenced on December 2. Nothing was yet certain, Hay knew, but "it was past the breakers," he told Roosevelt.

These were some of the most buoyant words he had uttered in months. The pleasant air and "tingling silentness" of New Hampshire were doing him good, he acknowledged, quoting the poet Shelley. In a few more weeks he hoped he might be able to resume the rigors of the State Department. He would be sixty-three on October 8, he told Roosevelt, informing him of his intention to stay on at the Fells longer than usual. "On that day I become an old man."

Roosevelt encouraged Hay to take as much time as he needed and chastened him for his dim view of old age. "[Mrs. Roosevelt] is forty, and I do not think I deceive myself when I say she neither looks nor acts nor feels as if she was thirty. As for me, on the whole I have continued all my life to have a better time year after year."

Hay took another step in his climb out of despondency when he went to New Haven on October 23 to accept a degree on the occasion of Yale's bicentennial. His fellow honorees included Roosevelt, Elihu Root, Princeton professor Woodrow Wilson, and Mark Twain. "I wish you might have been at Yale last Wednesday," Hay wrote to Clarence King, an alumnus, who was bedridden in Phoenix, losing his fight with tuberculosis. "It was a splendid and most impressive sight. They were all very good to me, and I had the first day of comfort I have known for ever so long—but always there was the undertone of grief and regret."

He was back in Washington at the end of the month, awaiting word on the canal treaty. At last Choate was able to report from London that "the great job is accomplished." Ambassador Paunceforte was on his way with the final version of the treaty; Choate followed soon thereafter, and all were in Washington at the first of the month. Choate lunched with the president and Hay found them "in the best of spirits."

They had good reason. On November 16, the canal commission issued its final report. The engineering cost of a canal across Nicaragua was estimated at $189 million. Panama, the shorter route, came in lower, at $144 million, but the French canal company had refused to set a firm price on the sale of its concession; estimates ranged from $40 million to perhaps as much as $100 million. In the face of such uncertainty and disparity, the commission unanimously recommended Nicaragua.

Two days later, Hay and Paunceforte signed the treaty that bore their names. Lodge was quick to assure the secretary that this time the Senate would ratify it. Hay was extremely grateful to Choate, not only for his diplomacy toward Foreign Secretary Lansdowne but also for his treatment of Lodge while the senator was in London. "Lodge came home regarding it as his Treaty," Choate told Henry White, adding wickedly, "Never breathe this to a soul."

True to Lodge's word, the Senate ratified the Hay-Paunceforte Treaty, 76–6, on December 6. Four weeks after that, the House of Representatives passed the Hepburn bill, 308–2, appropriating $180 million to construct a canal across Nicaragua. "This has been a year of sorrows—but of great work as well," Hay wrote Clara, who still had not arrived in Washington. "If success could make one happy we ought not to complain."

But the pall of Del's death was still palpable. "Every year of his life comes back to me," Hay admitted to Clara in December. "My sorrow is as keen now, when I suffer my mind to go back to it, as it was last June so that I wonder if I will ever be any better."

Even so, the future did offer a slim hint of sunshine. Helen and Payne Whitney at last announced their engagement and set their wedding for February 1902. "They are old friends and playmates and Payne was Del's most intimate friend," Hay wrote Whitelaw Reid. "Mrs. Hay and I have seen a great deal of him this year and we like him very much."

THAT, HOWEVER, WAS THE last respite from gloom for the year. Clarence King had known for months that he was dying. As the end neared, he told Ada that after his death she might wish to consider changing her and the children's names from Todd to King. He promised a small inheritance. He did not ask that she come see him, and he discouraged other visitors as well. His letters to Hay were full of regret. "In my present condition of uncertainty of folded hands and days of reflection," he wrote in August, "I have been trying to understand why a man as well endowed with intelligence as I should have made such a failure." If he shared with Hay or Adams the details of his double identity, any such letters have been lost, destroyed, or otherwise kept from the eyes of outsiders.

Hay continued to send money, and Adams wrote from Europe, offering to do the same. Hay, meanwhile, kept Adams apprised of King's condition. "He is, I fancy, quite penniless," he reported in November. "Fate has done her worst. I send him a check now and then when I can remember it. . . . If one of us could go out there and kill him, it would be a brotherly act."

No such intervention was necessary. Clarence King died in Phoenix in the early hours of Christmas Eve. Hay's tears, to the extent that he had any left, were those of frustration as well as anguish. For him, and for Adams also, King was their *beau idéal*, "the best and brightest man of his generation," Hay declared, "with talents immeasurably beyond any of his contemporaries, with industry that has often sickened me to witness it." Indeed, King had "everything in his favor but blind luck."

"'*Ca vous amuse, la vie?*'" Hay asked Adams, Heart to Heart.

On hearing of King's death, Theodore Roosevelt took time from his family on Christmas Day to write Hay one more letter of condolence. "Dear John," he began. "I am very, very sorry; I know it is useless for me to say so—but I do feel deeply for you. You have been well within range of the rifle pits this year—so near them that I do not venture to wish you a merry Christmas. But may all good henceforth go with you and yours." He signed his letter: "Your attached friend, Theodore Roosevelt."

In the new year, and during the three and a half years that remained in John Hay's life, this attachment would grow stronger and closer than either man could have foreseen.

CHAPTER 17

A Reasonable Time

When John Hay and Theodore Roosevelt were in each other's company, they got along famously. It was only when they were apart, and after Hay's death, that their differences became more pronounced and tended to overshadow the extraordinary rapport and mutual respect they displayed when they were face to face. Those wishing to stress the distance between Hay and Roosevelt make much of two letters that Roosevelt wrote to Cabot Lodge, the first in July 1905, a few days after Hay's death, and the second in January 1909, shortly after a selection of Hay's correspondence, edited by Clara Hay and Henry Adams, appeared in print.

"Personally," Roosevelt wrote of Hay in the first letter, "his loss is very great to me because I was very fond of him." However, Roosevelt added, "From the standpoint of the public business . . . the case is different. . . . His name, his reputation, his staunch loyalty, all made him a real asset of the administration. But in actual work I had to do the big things myself."

The second letter, while at first offering higher and lengthier praise, was ultimately far more dismissive. "He was a man of remarkable ability," Roosevelt granted Hay after reading through his published correspondence. "I think he was the most delightful man to talk to I ever met, for in his conversation he continually made out of hand those delightful epi-grammatic remarks which we would all like to make. . . . He was more-over, I think without exception, the best letter-writer of his age. . . . His dignity, his remarkable literary ability, his personal charm, and the respect his high character and long service commanded thruout the country, together with his wide acquaintance with foreign statesmen and foreign capitals, made him one of the public servants of real value to the United States."

Then, while laying more garlands, Roosevelt could not resist crimping a few of the leaves: "He was at his best at a dinner table or in a drawing room, and in neither place have I ever seen anyone's best that was bet-ter than his," the president allowed; yet Hay's "easy-loving nature" and "moral timidity" also caused him to "shrink from all that was rough in life, and therefore from practical affairs."

Hay's soigné manner affected his choice of friends, a circle that the hard-nosed Roosevelt found too effeminate. "[H]is temptation," he said of Hay, "was to associate as far as possible only with men of refined and cultivated tastes, who lived apart from the world of affairs, and who, if Americans, were wholly lacking in robustness of fiber. His close intimacy with Henry James and Henry Adams—charming men, but exceedingly undesirable companions for any man of a strong nature—and the tone of satirical cynicism which they admired, and which he always affected in writing them, marked that phase of his character which so impaired his usefulness as a public man."

With characteristic egotism, Roosevelt purported that he had com-pensated for Hay's shortcomings with his own dynamism. "In public life during the time he was Secretary of State under me he accomplished lit-tle," his appraisal continued. "I had a great fascination for his fastidious literary skill, and liked to listen to him; I saw much of him, and found his company a relaxation; but in the Department of State his usefulness to me was almost exclusively the usefulness of a fine figurehead. He never initiated a policy or was of real assistance in carrying thru a policy; but he sometimes phrased what I desired said in a way that was of real service; and the general respect for him was such that his presence in the Cabinet was a strength to the administration."

In summation, Roosevelt asserted to Lodge, Hay "was not a great Secretary of State."

Yet Roosevelt never said any such thing while Hay was alive. Two years into his first term as president, he wrote Hay, "When I came in I thought you a great Secretary of State, but now I have had a chance to know far more fully what a really great Secretary of State you are." And when Hay mentioned that he wanted to leave office, Roosevelt talked him into staying, confessing, "I could not spare you."

Intellectually, the two men were equals—well read, well traveled, multilingual. Roosevelt's knowledge of natural history was as commanding as Hay's appreciation of fine arts and *belles lettres*. Politically, they were likeminded, too—both convinced that American republicanism was the hope and high-water mark of "civilization" and that the world's powers ought to cooperate, however guardedly, to control and uplift "uncivilized" peoples.

Their most obvious difference was physical. Roosevelt was correct in saying that Hay shrank from the rough side of life—his outing to Yellowstone notwithstanding. Hay's habit of an early morning massage and an afternoon walk was tame compared to Roosevelt's rough-riding through Rock Creek Park and a regular White House gymkhana of fighting sticks and fisticuffs. Where Hay was gentle and genteel, soft of hand and voice, Roosevelt was ebullient and relentlessly youthful in his enthusiasms. "You must always remember that the President is about six," observed Cecil Spring-Rice, the British diplomat who was best man at Roosevelt's wedding. Henry James's brother William observed of Roosevelt in 1900 that he was "still mentally in the *Sturm und Drang* period of early adolescence."

One of Roosevelt's sharpest critics was Henry Adams, who recognized in the president a rival for Hay's attentions. (Roosevelt, if he cared to admit it, probably felt the same about Adams.) Adams could not understand what his dear neighbor saw in Roosevelt. He and Hay continued with their afternoon strolls, followed by tea. But beginning in January 1902, Hay and Roosevelt established their own routine: on Sunday mornings, after services at St. John's Church on Lafayette Square, Roosevelt would stop in at Hay's house for an hour or so of talk. Adams, in his letters to Lizzie Cameron, gave no hint of jealousy, but the more he saw of Roosevelt and the more time Hay spent with Roosevelt, the more displeased Adams became. The president, he told Lizzie, was "a stupid, blundering, bolting bull-calf."

Not that Roosevelt did not make at least a token effort to draw Adams into his sphere of influence. "Teddy said the other day," Hay wrote Adams, "'I am not going to be the slave of the tradition that forbids Presidents from seeing their friends. I am going to dine with you & Henry Adams & Cabot whenever I like.'"

In early January 1902, the invitation came and Adams relented, accompanying the Hays to the "slaughter-house," his first visit to the Executive Mansion since he and Clover had dined with Rutherford and Lucy Hayes in 1878. He thoroughly regretted the decision. "[A]s usual Theodore absorbed the conversation," Adams reported to Lizzie, "and if he tired me ten years ago, he crushes me now. To say that I enjoyed it would be, to you, a gratuitous piece of deceit. . . . [W]hat annoys me is his childlike and infantile superficiality with his boyish dogmatism of assertion. He lectures me on history as though he were a high-school pedagogue."

Years later, writing in his *Education*, Adams couched his chronic disdain for Roosevelt in a somewhat more scientific vocabulary, but the message was the same: Roosevelt annoyed him. "Power when wielded by abnormal energy is the most serious of facts," Adams analyzed, "and all Roosevelt's friends know that his restless and combative energy was more than abnormal. Roosevelt, more than any other man living within the range of notoriety, showed the singular primitive quality that belongs to ultimate matter,—the quality that mediaeval theology assigned to God,—he was pure act."

Hay indulged Adams's disparagements and likely joined in with a few blasphemies of his own during their end-of-day constitutionals. Yet he did not let his friend's sour outlook interfere with his own relationship with the president, and gradually he and Roosevelt worked out a modus vivendi that was quite intimate. Hay, who had so recently lost a son, found himself drawn to a vibrant man twenty years his junior. In Hay, Roosevelt realized a palpable link to the generation of his own father, who had died before Roosevelt graduated from Harvard.

While Roosevelt did not always keep Hay abreast of what too often proved to be less than diplomatic decisions, he did not bulldoze his secretary or intend disrespect of any sort. And though Hay was often privately irked by Roosevelt's impetuous outbursts, he did not intrigue against him; nor was he inclined to kowtow in order to get his way. Remarkably they seemed to harbor no sense of rivalry and, while not always complimentary of each other, they were, more often than not, effectively complementary.

Roosevelt was a confronter first, a conciliator second. "I have a horror of bluster which does not result in fight," he told Hay. "[I]t is both weak and undignified." By now, Hay knew by heart the axiom Roosevelt had begun using well before he became president: "Speak softly and carry a big stick; you will go far." In contrast, Hay avoided conflict wherever possible, realizing that a rope of sand was built more on trust than thrust and that the slightest gust of violence could be its ruin. Accordingly, guilelessly, he did his best to balance Roosevelt's strenuosity with subtlety, to forestall and, if need be, repair any damage caused by the president's lunges through the china shop of foreign relations.

Hay's job under Roosevelt was in some ways less complicated, in others far more problematic. McKinley had entrusted the portfolio of foreign relations almost entirely to Hay, allowing his secretary of state to serve as his premier, a term frequently used by the newspapers to describe Hay's Richelieu-like relationship with the White House. That now ended. Roosevelt's appetite for executive control was more voracious than any president so far. Hay, who was more comfortable with the quieter manner of McKinley, was obliged to make the transition from one to the other—an adaptation evidenced in a speech he gave to the chamber of commerce of New York on November 19, two months after McKinley's death.

Hay's audience at Delmonico's that night included senators, generals, the governor of New York State, the mayor-elect of New York City, and "the largest aggregation of plutocrats the world knows," noted the *Evening Star* of Washington. His observations were a model of modesty and discretion and, before this all-male group, they did not lack for drollery. "There are two important lines of human endeavor in which men are forbidden even to allude to their success," he explained, "affairs of the heart and diplomatic affairs. In doing so, one not only commits a vulgarity which transcends all question of taste, but makes all future success impossible." (That Hay possessed considerable expertise in *both* fields was surely not something his audience suspected. This, however, was not the only time he made such categorical comparisons. "There are three species of creatures, that, when seen going, are coming. When they seem coming they go," he would pose to male company. The answer to this mildly risqué riddle was: "Diplomats, women, and crabs.")

When the laughter subsided, he continued to his New York audience: "But if we are not permitted to boast of what we have done, we can at least say a word about what we have tried to do." He alluded to the Open Door, avoidance of entangling alliances, and treaties of reciprocity, summarizing, "The briefest expression of our rule of conduct is, perhaps, the Monroe Doctrine and the Golden Rule. With this simple chart we can hardly go far wrong."

After making a pious bow to the martyred McKinley, he then turned his attention to the future—to the Roosevelt administration—whereupon his rhetoric became more forceful, ever so slightly Rooseveltian. "I can yet assure you," he ventured, "that so long as the administration of your affairs remains in hands as strong and skillful as those to which they have been and are now confided, there will be no more surrender of our rights than there will be violation of the rights of others. The President to whom you have given your valuable trust and confidence . . . feels and knows— for has he not tested it, in the currents of the heady fight, as well as in toilsome work of administration?—that the nation over whose destinies he presides has a giant's strength in the works of war, as in the works of peace."

Winding up, Hay exhorted his listeners, and his countrymen: "Let us be diligent in our business and we shall stand—stand, you see, not crawl, nor swagger—stand as a friend and equal, asking nothing, putting up with nothing but what is right and just, among our peers, in the great democracy of nations."

It was hardly an address he would have given if he had not already attained universal respect as a diplomat and if the United States were not now a world power; in short, not an address he would have given three years earlier. The speech was praised broadly, especially for Hay's coinage of the slogan "the Monroe Doctrine and the Golden Rule." Yet beyond his specific iteration of foreign policy, his remarks also made plain to his listeners, and to millions who read a transcription in the newspapers, that the ship of state would continue to be steered by mature hands—none other than John Hay's. McKinley had been an honorable and decent executive, but the public recognized who had been responsible for engineering the Open Door and saving the Peking legation. And while McKinley's successor was a battle-tested leader, as Hay had proclaimed, there was no question that, at sixty-three, Hay occupied the rightful station of *éminence grise* of the State Department, of the Republican Party, and indeed of the entire government.

It followed, too, that the man who had made McKinley look good was capable of doing the same for Roosevelt. "[Hay] has kept to his great task with as splendid a fortitude, with as exquisite a courage and consecration, as well as with as honorable skill as any man ever showed in a high place," the *Brooklyn Daily Eagle* commented after the New York speech. "The President who appointed him had absolute confidence in him. The President who retained him has an equal confidence in him. The fame of both those Presidents in history will be increased—and that is saying very much—by the vindication which he has given of their confidence in him, and, we may add, by the proofs which he has given of *his* confidence in *them*."

Moreover, for all Roosevelt's later attempts to characterize Hay as a mere amanuensis, incapable of carrying out "big things," the reality was that most of the international challenges Roosevelt now faced as president—the canal, Alaska, China—had already been laid out by John Hay. Roosevelt could assert to Cabot Lodge that Hay had been merely a "figurehead"; but Hay, so long as he was healthy, would continue to lead the State Department and American foreign relations with a sagacity and tact that Roosevelt, try as he may, could not do without.

THE YEAR 1902 GOT off to a promising start, beginning with passage of the Hepburn bill, authorizing construction of the Nicaragua canal, on January 9. A month later, the Senate unanimously ratified a treaty to purchase the Danish West Indies—the Virgin Islands of St. Thomas, St. John's, and St. Croix—for $5 million, a deal negotiated painstakingly by Henry White.*

Hay enjoyed personal satisfactions as well. On February 6, his daughter Helen—who fancied herself a poet and, of Hay's four children, was the one who most took after her father—married Payne Whitney in Washington. Among the six hundred guests able to fit in the Church of the Covenant were President and Mrs. Roosevelt, most of the cabinet and Supreme Court, and a full deployment of senators and foreign diplomats. The officiating minister was Hiram Haydn, who had married Helen's parents and still presided over the Old Stone Presbyterian Church in Cleveland, built by the largesse of Amasa Stone.

Helen Hay was a wealthy young woman before she married; as Helen Whitney, she became immensely more comfortable. The wedding gifts included a solid gold coffee set and, as Henry Adams joked to Lizzie Cameron, "a warming-pan" full of diamonds. Whitney's uncle, Oliver Payne, who had served as the young man's surrogate father and whose portfolio included sizable stakes in Standard Oil, steel, railroads, and tobacco, bestowed upon the newlyweds a steam yacht and a mansion on Fifth Avenue designed by Stanford White that would take the next five years to complete. After a breakfast reception at the Hay house, Payne and Helen departed by private train car for the family plantation in South Carolina, followed by a leisurely tour abroad. Adams, who had elected not to partake of the festivities—blaming "indolence" and "too much family"—nevertheless declared the event "the climax of the season."

And with Helen at last out of the parlor, Alice Hay was free to announce her own engagement to another of Del Hay's Yale chums, Jim Wadsworth. Overwhelmed by the grandiosity of Helen's wedding, she made plans for a smaller, more tranquil ceremony at the Fells at the end of September.

HAY PRESIDED OVER ONE more send-off during the winter. On February 27, he delivered a memorial to William McKinley to a joint session

---

* The Danish parliament later rejected the U.S. offer, not because of any misstep by White or Hay, and the sale was not consummated until 1917—at the inflated price of $25 million.

of Congress, elaborating more formally on his earlier remarks to the New York chamber of commerce. In all his years of service, this was his first time to address Congress, and he rose to the occasion. "The Secretary's figure is slight and his face is usually pale," the *New York Tribune* noted afterward, "but today there was a flush on his cheek. . . . [H]is voice had unusual carrying power, and he was able to make himself heard to the furthest recesses of the hall."

He spoke for more than an hour, and with every flourish of phrase and evocation of patriotic precedent, his audience of congressmen, senators, cabinet, and court—along with a gallery full of wives, daughters, and friends—recognized that the impeccably groomed, consummately poised statesman who rendered the full and fair measure of McKinley did so with unsurpassable authority. "There is not one of us but feels prouder of his native land," Hay offered in closing, "because the august figure of Washington presided over its beginnings; no one but vows it a tenderer love because Lincoln poured out his blood for it; no one but must feel his devotion for his country renewed and kindled when he remembers how McKinley loved, revered, and served it, showed in his life how a citizen should live, and in his last hour taught us how a gentleman could die."

Again the speech was roundly applauded and widely distributed. One of the many readers to be moved by Hay's words was Edith Wharton. "[I]t was oratory in the high sense of the word," she wrote to George Smalley of *The Times*, "[and] I don't know whether to praise it more for its quality of sustained eloquence, or for the way in which idea and expression hold the same high level, & move, all through it, at the same majestic pace. We need so much, in this slip-shod, irreverent, headlong age & country, such object-lessons both in language and thought, that I feel Mr. Hay has done a service to the whole country."

IN THE MONTHS THAT followed, however, Hay's service to his country and his president was fraught with frustration and misdirection, as two familiar bugbears rose up to try his nerves and test his ropemaking skills. One was the Alaska boundary; the other, not surprisingly, was the canal.

The Alaska dispute had lain dormant for the past two years, defused by the interim agreement by which the Canadians and Americans shared access to the Klondike gold fields. The United States had wanted to avoid any disruptions in its negotiations with Britain over the Central American canal, and Britain wished no more friction with the United States while the Boer War dragged on. Four months into his presidency, Roosevelt had far more pressing matters on his plate: an embarrassing report on American brutality in the Philippines, including a torture technique known as the "water cure"; another strike by the United Mine Workers; and an anti-trust suit he had filed against the behemoth Northern Securities, controlled by some of the richest and most powerful men in America. For the moment, Alaska was the least of his worries, and he expressed no eagerness to proceed with a final boundary settlement, preferring, as he said to Joseph Choate, to "let sleeping dogs lie."

But by March 1902, Hay sensed that the time was ripe to resolve the Alaskan business once and for all. The South African war was at last coming to an end, and he had recently heard from both the British ambassador Julian Paunceforte and the Canadian prime minister Wilfred Laurier that they might finally be willing to give way on the disputed coastal territory through arbitration. When Hay presented the case to Roosevelt, the president scoffed at the thought of compromising on a matter in which he was absolutely certain the United States was in the right. Canada and England, he growled, had no more legitimate claim to the stretch of Alaska coastline in question than the United States had to Cornwall or Kent. Having awakened the sleeping dog, he announced that he would send engineers to survey a boundary "as we assert it," adding emphatically, "and I shall send troops to guard and hold it." When George Smalley, who was at the meeting with Roosevelt and Hay, suggested that this action sounded "very drastic," Roosevelt replied bluntly, "I mean it to be drastic." A few days later, he ordered Secretary of War Root to reinforce the garrisons in southeastern Alaska. "Whenever Canada raises a bristle," Henry Adams told Lizzie Cameron, "Theodore roars like a Texas steer, and ramps around the ring, screaming for instant war, and ordering a million men instantly to arms."

Hay had never served a president who was so eager to pick a quarrel, and even as he directed Choate to press ahead with negotiations for a tribunal of arbitration, he feared that Roosevelt might fly off the handle at any moment and send in the gunboats. Later in the summer, Roosevelt still had not cooled off. "It seems to me that the Canadians have no right to make a claim based upon the possible effect of their own wrongdoing," he wrote Hay. "I feel a good deal like telling them that if trouble comes it will be purely because of their own fault; and although it would not be pleasant for us it would be death for them."

WHILE ALASKA SMOLDERED, THE canal caught fire. Admiral Walker's canal commission had chosen the Nicaraguan route because the French canal company had balked at setting a firm price for the sale of its concession in Panama. But in December 1901, after the Hay-Pauncefonte Treaty was signed and with the Hepburn bill heading for a vote in the House, the French awoke to the likelihood that their stock was about to become worthless and announced that they were willing to part with their concession for the bargain price of $40 million—exactly the figure needed to put Panama back in the running against Nicaragua. Informed of the lower, competitive figure, Roosevelt said nothing until the vote on the Hepburn bill on January 9, 1902. Immediately afterward, however, he intervened.

Like the vast majority of Americans and nearly every member of Congress, Roosevelt initially had assumed that Nicaragua was "the American route." Yet he also recognized that, from the standpoint of engineering, Panama had a great deal going for it: the route was shorter, straighter, required fewer locks, and had better harbors at either end. All of these advantages had been underscored in a minority report submitted by a determined engineer named George Morison. Even after being outvoted, Morison did not give up, and on December 10, he had stubbornly restated his pro-Panama argument in a letter to the president. Impressed by Morison's gumption, Roosevelt directed Admiral Walker to reconsider Panama and to take into account the $40 million offer from the French. On January 18, the commission reversed its decision, under Roosevelt's stern gaze, and voted unanimously in favor of Panama.

Although the Hepburn bill, which called for a Nicaraguan canal, had passed easily in the House, it now had to get through the Senate. On January 28, Wisconsin senator John Spooner, a solid Roosevelt man, introduced an amendment to the Senate version of the bill, calling for the government to buy the French concession and secure a six-mile-wide canal zone within the Colombian department of Panama. The amendment also stipulated that if a satisfactory agreement with Colombia could not be struck within "a reasonable time," then America would begin digging in Nicaragua.

GEORGE MORISON'S PLUCK AND Roosevelt's intervention changed the course of history; but they were by no means the Panama route's only friends. Three men—a French engineer, a New York lawyer, and a U.S. senator—had been working for more than a year to turn the tide from Nicaragua to Panama. All knew from the start that the odds were slim, but success promised a terrific payoff—in honor, prestige, and treasure.

Two of the three had direct ties to the French canal company. Philippe Bunau-Varilla had been an engineer under Ferdinand de Lesseps during the first attempt to construct a Panama canal. After the first French company went broke, Bunau-Varilla, along with his brother (and Gustave Eiffel), floated the Compagnie Nouvelle du Canal de Panama ("the new company"), becoming major stockholders. When Bunau-Varilla failed in exhorting his countrymen to finish the canal, he then applied himself to persuading the U.S. government to buy out the French concession and whatever assets were salvageable from the first years of work in Panama. It went without saying that, if the sale could be consummated, his rusty dross would turn to gold.

Yet Bunau-Varilla's impulses were not entirely mercenary. Prim and trim, with a flamboyant red mustache and the bravura of a bantam rooster, he portrayed himself as a high-principled crusader. Panama was his "Great Adventure," his "Great Idea." To have the canal brought to completion, even if not by Frenchmen, would be a tremendous accomplishment that could not be measured in mere dollars or francs.

Bunau-Varilla was unabashed in his proselytizing of the benefits of Panama over Nicaragua. He lavishly entertained members of the American canal commission when they came to Paris in 1899 to examine the French canal records. In 1901, he toured the United States, pitching the Panama route to business groups and politicians. Besides being shorter, straighter, and cheaper, the route was not endangered by a single volcano—something that could not be said for Nicaragua, Bunau-Varilla pointed out. A pamphlet he distributed by the thousand deliberately ignored Panama's malaria, yellow fever, and floods but snidely exploited Nicaragua's national emblem. "Youthful nations like to put on their coats of arms what best symbolises their moral domain or characterises their native soil," he suggested. "What have the Nicaraguans chosen to characterise their country on their coat of arms, on their postage stamps? Volcanoes." Never mind that none of Nicaragua's volcanoes had been judged a threat by the American engineers who examined the Nicaraguan route.

As it turned out, his propaganda had no evident effect on the canal commission's initial decision; after giving Panama a careful look, it chose Nicaragua anyway. Yet Bunau-Varilla did make one crucial acquaintance on his American junket in 1901: Senator Mark Hanna.

Hanna, who had made a fortune in shipping before masterminding the political ascendance of William McKinley, had recognized the virtues of Panama well before the canal commission completed its preliminary report in 1900. Bunau-Varilla told a slightly different story of Hanna's enlightenment, asserting that he had chanced upon the senator outside the Waldorf-Astoria Hotel in New York and not let go until he had transformed him into a zealot for his cause. More likely, Hanna had already been leaning toward Panama, acting as a counterweight to the Nicaraguan route's most fervid advocate, Democratic senator John Tyler Morgan. Regardless, Bunau-Varilla now had his man in Washington.

Hanna was also subject to the persuasions of the New York attorney, William Nelson Cromwell, who had grown very wealthy carrying water for men like Collis Huntington, William Vanderbilt, and J. Pierpont Morgan. Cromwell was silver-haired and silver-tongued, with "a rather theatrical look," according to a profile in the *New York World*. "[B]ut there is nothing theatrical about his methods. He can dig deeper and do big things more quietly than almost anyone downtown." As counsel to the Compagnie Nouvelle since 1894, Cromwell had been charged with the task of finding a buyer for the moribund corporation. Toward this end, he had reincorporated the Compagnie Nouvelle in the United States and done everything he could to derail the pro-Nicaragua Hepburn bill. Unlike Bunau-Varilla, whose avowed client was "Humanity," Cromwell worked for a fee. His final bill to the Compagnie Nouvelle would be $800,000.

Cromwell and Hanna had run in the same circles for years; now their mutual interest in a Panama canal brought them into even closer association. The *World* would later allege that Cromwell had paid for Hanna's favor, although, as a man in possession of a large checkbook himself, Hanna was not so easily bought. Still, it was perhaps not entirely coincidental that after Cromwell sent Hanna's Republican National Committee a $60,000 check for McKinley's reelection, the party platform was edited to call for an "isthmian" canal—not Nicaraguan, as first specified.

In January 1902, when the canal commission changed its endorsement from Nicaragua to Panama, Hanna was still in his first term in the Senate and far from its most loquacious member, preferring to wield his considerable influence behind the scenes. Since the death of McKinley, he and Roosevelt had cobbled a fragile peace. One of their common causes was a canal—across Panama. And so, backed by Roosevelt and the tireless lobbying of Cromwell and Bunau-Varilla, Mark Hanna undertook passage of the Spooner amendment to the Senate canal bill as the hallmark of his public career.

The initial battle took place within the Interoceanic Canals Committee, chaired by Senator Morgan. Hanna, also a member, knew he did not have the votes to keep the committee from reporting the Hepburn bill favorably, but he succeeded in dragging out the hearings by insisting that no report be issued until all the members of the Walker commission had been questioned one more time. On March 13, despite Hanna's obstructionist tactics, the Senate committee rejected the pro-Panama Spooner amendment and gave its blessing to the pro-Nicaragua Hepburn bill. But at least Hanna had bought time in which to prepare the minority report that he would need to turn the vote of the full Senate back toward Panama.

Before he could proceed any further, however, he first needed some assurance that Colombia would sign a treaty allowing the French to sell their concession and permitting the United States to build a canal in Panama.

•   •   •

THERE SEEMS NEVER TO have been a time when Colombia was not struggling to hold itself together. Ever since the 1830s, when Colombia, then known as New Granada, broke off from Venezuela and Ecuador, Conservatives had been at odds with Liberals, the former desiring a stronger nationalist government, the latter more decentralized rule. The Department of Panama, many long days and hundreds of miles by mule and boat from the capital at Bogotá, was frequently either the object or the origin of violent conflict between the two factions. Hardly a year passed without a riot or an insurrection of some sort on the isthmus. Twice Panama had declared independence and formed a provisional government, without success. In October 1899, when Liberals in Santander, northeast of Bogotá, rebelled against the ruling Conservatives and ignited what would be known as the Thousand Days War, Panamanians again talked openly of breaking away or, at the very least, gaining greater autonomy over their own affairs and future—which they surely hoped would include a Panamanian canal.

Conservatives had their own designs on Panama. Virtually bankrupt and struggling to provision their armies, they viewed a canal across Panama not just as an expression of Colombian sovereignty but also as a means to feed their troops and keep their beleaguered government afloat. As one measure of the canal's importance to the regime, in July 1900 Vice President José Manuel Marroquín ousted President Manuel Antonio Sanclemente after the aging Sanclemente committed the egregious gaffe of selling the Compagnie Nouvelle a six-year extension on its concession for 5 million francs—regarded by Marroquín and his adherents to be a fraction of what it was worth.

In early 1901, Marroquín sent Carlos Martínez Silva, an ally in the recent coup, to Washington to strike a harder bargain. In Martínez Silva's first months in the United States, he convinced himself that a canal across Nicaragua was not a serious threat, and accordingly he gave Marroquín the impression that their negotiating position was quite strong. Colombia, he wrote to his superiors, "held the trump cards."

Soon, though, Martínez Silva's certainty eroded. After passage of the Hay-Pauncefote Treaty and the completion of the first canal commission report—the one favoring Nicaragua—the Colombian minister grew nervous, realizing that if he did not make an attractive pitch, and make it promptly, there would be no hope for a Panama canal and no payday for his government. Repeatedly he pressed Marroquín for guidance on the terms of a treaty but heard nothing or, after long silences, received only broad instructions to bide his time and refrain from making firm commitments. Finally, after the canal commission changed its mind, choosing Panama, and the proposed Spooner amendment called for striking a bargain with Colombia within a "reasonable time," Martínez Silva took it upon himself to draft a treaty that he thought would encourage the United States to pass a Panama bill.

His draft treaty granted a one-hundred-year lease on a six-mile-wide canal zone. Colombia would retain sovereignty over the zone and the ports at either end: Colón on the Caribbean and Panama City on the Pacific. Colombia would also take responsibility for defending the zone— although the United States would have the right to intervene at the invitation of Colombia or, in cases of emergency, on its own volition. Last, Colombia would allow the Compagnie Nouvelle to transfer—which was to say, sell—its concession to the United States; for permitting this transfer, Colombia expected the United States to pay an annuity of $600,000.

But then, before Martínez Silva had a chance to present his proposal to Hay, he was called back to Colombia. Fortunately, William Cromwell, seemingly always in the right place at the right time, had a copy of the draft treaty in his possession and was kind enough to forward it to the State Department. Indeed, Cromwell had helped Martínez Silva to write the proposal, which explained why the terms were so accommodating to American interests—and those of the Compagnie Nouvelle as well.

To replace Martínez Silva, Vice President Marroquín sent his tough-minded war secretary, José Vicente Concha, whom he counted on to stand up to the Americans. Concha arrived in the United States prepared to demand $20 million for the rights to build the canal, a drastically steeper fee than what Martínez Silva had proposed to Hay.

Soon enough, with communication from Bogotá as erratic and as vague as ever, Concha too fell into the clutches of William Nelson Cromwell. Unlike his predecessor, Concha had never traveled outside his own country before, and because he spoke no English, he allowed Cromwell to help him write a letter to the Senate canal committee, restating Colombia's desire to allow transfer of the canal concession and construction of the canal through Panama.

The letter did not alter the Interoceanic Canals Committee's March vote on the Hepburn bill and Spooner amendment, but that decision—in favor of Hepburn and Nicaragua—lit a fire under Concha, who wrote to Bogotá warning that, without a firm and reasonable offer by Colombia, the Nicaragua route would win out and, more than likely, a revolution in Panama would follow. "[I]t is not convenient, opportune or practical," the formerly immovable minister advised his government, "to assume . . . an attitude of open resistance to the pretensions of the United States, under penalty of involving the Republic [of Colombia] in a most serious conflict, in which it would certainly not preserve its integrity." Doubtless, Cromwell's fingerprints were on this letter as well.

Concha was assured by his government that new instructions were on the way, but as usual, they were a long time in getting from Bogotá to Washington. In the meantime, he and Cromwell worked up a new treaty, quite similar to Martínez Silva's earlier proposal. Bunau-Varilla was also influential, persuading Concha to reduce his initial demand of $20 million to $7 million. Concha presented the draft to Hay on March 31, and over the next two weeks, with Cromwell serving as intermediary, the Colombian minister and the secretary of state refined the treaty's terms, adding a $100,000 annuity to the $7 million up-front payment.

By mid-April, Concha still had not received his instructions, but quite advantageously, a copy of these instructions came into the possession of the American minister in Bogotá, Charles Hart, who wired a summary to Hay with a promptitude that Colombia's own telegraph agents, for reasons elusive, were unable to match. The most worrisome of the new instructions was a strict order for Concha to hold off negotiating with the United States until *after* Colombia had reached an understanding with the Compagnie Nouvelle on the transfer of the concession.

Knowing what Concha did not yet know, Hay proceeded genially but with as much haste as he dared. Concha signed off on the final draft of the canal treaty on April 18—eight days before he received the belated instructions from Bogotá that probably would have foiled the entire arrangement. By then it was too late to renege. A chagrinned Concha informed Bogotá that to do so would deliver an insult to the Americans that surely would drive them away from Panama.

Hay had been both lucky and more than a little bit shrewd. He chose to treat Charles Hart's summary of Bogotá's instructions as an internal State Department communiqué and, as such, felt under no obligation to share the information with Concha—although he was well aware that Concha was anxiously awaiting his own copy. Hay had not acted deceitfully; nor had he been guilty of peeking at his neighbor's hand; rather, he had merely elected to hold his own cards close to his vest. Besides, from where he sat, he sincerely believed that the deal on the table, bearing the fingerprints of Concha, Cromwell, Bunau-Varilla—and one or two of his own—was plenty fair to all parties.

OF COURSE THE HAY-CONCHA treaty would not be final and official until ratified by the congresses of both countries. In the meantime, Hay endeavored in good faith to negotiate a separate parallel treaty with Nicaragua. Progress was slow on this front as well. "[B]oth in Colombia and in Nicaragua," he explained to Senator Morgan, "great ignorance exists as to the attitude of the United States. In both countries it is believed that their route is the only one possible or practicable, and that the Government of the United States, in the last resort, will accept any terms they choose to demand."

He was careful to maintain a posture of chaste impartiality. His president and his party leader favored Panama; most of Congress still favored Nicaragua. Hay had learned the hard way that to put himself in the middle of a senatorial debate over a treaty brought only damnation for him and too often for the treaty as well. He had already done yeoman's work for the canal by abrogating Clayton-Bulwer and passing Hay-Pauncefote. Now he would let Hanna and Morgan wrestle over the route. "I conceive my duty to be to try to ascertain the exact purposes and intentions of both [Nicaragua and Colombia], and, when I have done so, to inform your Committee of the result of my investigation," he stiffly informed Morgan, who was trying to expose the secretary's bias toward Panama and tip him toward Nicaragua. "I do not consider myself justified in advocating either route, as this matter rests with the discretion of Congress. When Congress has spoken, it will be the duty of the State Department to make the best arrangement possible for whichever route Congress may decide upon."

Although Hay expressed reluctance to help Congress make up its mind, Cromwell and Bunau-Varilla continued to work more energetically than ever on behalf of Panama and the Compagnie Nouvelle. In May, Cromwell drafted a minority report for Hanna, summarizing the technical, geological, economic, legal, and political reasons favoring Panama. He distributed copies to every member of Congress. Bunau-Varilla was equally diligent and in many respects more creative. To enhance Hanna's minority report, he prepared a series of graphs that compared everything from the length of navigation (fifty miles for Panama, three times that for Nicaragua) to the number of locks required (Panama three, Nicaragua eight) and the estimated cost of annual maintenance (Panama $2 million, Nicaragua $3 million). "These simple and lucid diagrams," Bunau-Varilla asserted, "crushingly demonstrated the great superiority of Panama."

Another demonstration helped the Panama cause even more. On May 8, on the Caribbean island of Martinique, Mount Pelée exploded and in less than five minutes wiped out the thirty thousand residents of the town of St. Pierre. Although Martinique was fifteen hundred miles from Nicaragua, Bunau-Varilla's previous warnings about the danger of volcanoes in Nicaragua resonated anew. "What an unexpected turn of the wheel of fortune!" he exclaimed. "If not the strongest of my arguments against Nicaragua, at least the most easily comprehensible of them was made a hundred times more striking owing to the prodigious emotion aroused by the catastrophe."

He dashed off letters to Hanna, Morgan, and the White House, underscoring the terrible object lesson of Pelée. Bunau-Varilla, never shy, also made sure his message reached the newspapers. Quoting the "eminent French engineer"—Bunau-Varilla—the *New York Sun* pointed out that the Nicaragua route was "lined" with volcanoes. The eruption of one of them, Cosequina, in 1835 had been so violent, by Bunau-Varilla's calculation, that in just six minutes of the caldera's forty-four hours of activity, the quantity of stone and ash it belched upon the countryside equaled eight years of canal excavation. "Nothing similar can be feared in Panama," the Frenchman assured.

The bad news on volcanoes got better still. On May 14, a cablegram reached the *Sun*, reporting that another of Nicaragua's volcanoes, Momotombo, had erupted, destroying wharves on Lake Managua, one hundred miles from the canal route. This time the *Sun* made mischievous fun of the event, publishing an editorial in the voice of Momotombo: "My compliments to Senator Morgan," the mountain taunted. "I am not only alive but am capable of sending down, without notice, through Lake Managua and the Tipitapa River in the adjacent Lake Nicaragua, a tidal wave of sufficient volume and malignity to overwhelm any canal that engineering skill can construct through this country, and to wipe out every dollar of the two or three hundred millions which the United States Government may be foolish enough to invest."

The Nicaraguan minister to the United States countered with impassioned denials of any recent emissions from Momotombo (when, in fact, Momotombo had erupted on May 13), and the *Washington Evening Star* published a cartoon of Hanna painting volcanoes on a map of Nicaragua with Bunau-Varilla looking on. Even so, the seed of doubt took hold. And to make sure that it flourished, Bunau-Varilla sent every senator a sheet of paper on which he had affixed a Nicaraguan postage stamp from 1900, showing Momotombo in grand ebullition. Beneath the stamp he captioned: "An official witness of the volcanic activity of Nicaragua."

Senate debate on the Hepburn bill began on June 4. Morgan, the seventy-seven-year-old former Confederate general, carried the banner for Nicaragua. Reiterating his well-worn brief for an American canal, he questioned the legal right of the Compagnie Nouvelle to sell its concession and stressed the uncertainty of negotiating with a country in the throes of civil war. He warned that if the United States were determined to build a canal in Panama, it would inevitably have to annex the isthmus forcibly, which would "poison the minds of people against us in every Spanish-American republic." He blamed the entire thrust toward Panama—the revision of the canal commission report, the Spooner amendment, Hanna's minority report, the volcano scare—on the "direct, constant, and offensive intrusion" of the Compagnie Nouvelle, William Nelson Cromwell in particular.

The following day, Hanna stood up for what was now known among Washington wags as the "Hannama" canal. He came armed with Bunau-Varilla's charts and the briefs prepared by Cromwell—including testimony from eighty-three shipowners, shipmasters, and pilots, stating their preference for Panama. He displayed an enormous map marked with red dots to indicate the location of volcanoes (eight in Nicaragua, none in Panama). Yet instead of unfurling a list of dry facts, he spoke conversationally to the nearly full chamber, as he would to a group of millworkers in Cleveland or to prospective campaign contributors. He was a man of neither elegance nor eloquence, but he was powerful, and many in the room were in his debt. At sixty-four, he was at the height of his career and also, he knew, nearing its end. (He had three years to live.) He spoke for two hours, occasionally referring to a sheet of paper in his hand, on which he had jotted a dozen or so lines. Finally his arthritic knees gave out, and he was obliged to return the following day to conclude his remarks.

Over the next two weeks, with Cromwell and Bunau-Varilla in support, Hanna outgeneraled Morgan, pulling votes, one by one, to his side, including those of half a dozen Democrats. On June 19, the vote was taken on whether to substitute the minority report (Spooner, Panama) for the majority (Hepburn, Nicaragua). Panama won, 42 to 34. Six days later, the House accepted the conference report on the Panama bill nearly unanimously, and on June 28, Theodore Roosevelt signed the Spooner Act authorizing the United States to acquire from Colombia control of a strip of land six miles wide in which to construct a canal and to acquire the rights, privileges, franchises, concessions, and property of the Compagnie Nouvelle for $40 million. As with the original Hepburn bill, the Spooner Act specified that, if these terms were not fulfilled within a "reasonable time," then the president would proceed with a canal across Nicaragua.

Roosevelt was elated. "The great bit of work of my administration, and from the material and constructive standpoint one of the greatest bits of work that the twentieth century will see, is the Isthmian Canal," he wrote Hay after the Spooner Act became law. Contrary to his later claim that he had done Hay's job for him, Roosevelt then left the task of clinching the deal with Colombia squarely in the hands of his secretary of state. "In the negotiations," he exhorted, "I must trust you. . . . I hope you will take personal direction."

Hay, who had stayed clear of the Senate debate, now had his work cut out for him. In the weeks ahead, before heading to New Hampshire for the summer, he ironed out the last details in the treaty, and in early June, Concha sent the document on to Bogotá for the consideration of Marroquín and his government. "I do not imagine we shall get an answer immediately," Hay wrote to Morgan, "but it makes no practical difference whether we get it now or later in the season, so that we have it signed and ready to send to the Senate by the 1st of December."

It would take all of that, and much more.

AT THE END OF June 1902, Hay and Roosevelt traveled to Cambridge to receive honorary degrees from Harvard—Hay having missed his chance a year earlier due to Del's accident. Roosevelt used the occasion to defend the administration's conduct in Cuba and the Philippines. In passing, he also mentioned what "a liberal education in high-minded statesmanship [it was] to sit at the same council table as John Hay."

Hay's address was essentially a fresh invocation of the Monroe Doctrine and the Golden Rule and, as such, provided antidote to Roosevelt's imperial bullishness. "The principles which have governed me are of limpid simplicity," he declared solemnly and soothingly. "We have sought in all things the interest and honor of our own country. We have never found this incompatible with a due regard for the interest and honor of other powers. We have treated all our neighbors with frankness and courtesy; we have received courtesy and frankness in return. We have set no traps; we have wasted no energy in evading the imaginary traps of others. We have sometimes been accused of credulity; but our credulity has not always gone unjustified. . . . There might be worse reputations for a country to acquire than that of always speaking the truth, and always expecting it from others. In bargaining," he concluded reasonably, "we have tried not to get the worst of the deal; remembering, however, that the best bargains are those that satisfy both sides."

After the ceremony, Harvard president Charles Eliot shared with Hay his great admiration for Roosevelt: "'What a man! Genius, force, and courage, and such evident honesty! . . . He is so young and he will be with us for many a day to come.'"

Roosevelt's longevity indeed seemed to be assured—as was his safety, apparently. Earlier in the day, President Eliot was astonished to see Roosevelt wearing a pistol under his coat. Just the same, Hay wanted to be prepared for all contingencies. A few days before the trip to Harvard, he had asked Attorney General Philander Knox for further clarification on the details of succession. The vice-presidential chair would remain empty until 1905, and the void made Hay uneasy. "[T]he President's life is worth twenty of mine in more respects than one," he wrote Knox, "but I suppose as a matter of duty, I ought to know what I should be called on to do as the first executive act in case of the President's death." Soon enough, his inquiry would prove to be anything but academic.

BY THE END OF July, Hay was at the Fells. "I left Washington at 100° and found my family very comfortable about the tea-table with a rousing wood fire in the chimney," he reported contentedly. The president too had departed Washington to pass the summer at Sagamore Hill, his retreat at Oyster Bay, Long Island. During his absence, the White House would undergo a thorough restoration and renovation. The upstairs, where Hay had once lived with Nicolay, was simply not roomy enough to accommodate the Roosevelt family, with six frisky children, and the offices of a no less frisky twentieth-century president. Roosevelt had rejected the suggestion that he forsake the tradition of presidents living and working under the same roof. Charles McKim struck a compromise by designing a new office wing, connected by a portico to the west side of the White House. After the remodeling, the first family would have the run of the entire second floor of the White House, once the sanctum of the Lincoln war cabinet and where McKinley had so recently wrestled with the devil of imperialism. Roosevelt had never liked the term "Executive Mansion," and by executive order he changed the official name to "the White House" because, after all, it was first, foremost, and now forever, a residence.

At Sagamore Hill, the president paid Hay the compliment of devouring all ten volumes of the Lincoln biography and took inspiration from the writing and, above all, from the character of the sixteenth president. "In reading the great work of you and Nicolay this summer," Roosevelt told Hay, "I have not only taken the keenest enjoyment but I really believe I have profited. At any rate, it has made me of set purpose to try to be good-natured and forbearing and to try to free myself from vindictiveness."

In late August, Roosevelt paid Hay the further honor of visiting him in New Hampshire during a speaking tour through New England. "The whole country side is plumb crazy over the President's visit," Hay reported to Alvey Adee the day before Roosevelt's arrival. "I thought it a peaceful and unpeopled wilderness and lo! it is a howling mob."

Roosevelt stopped at the Fells only one night and pronounced his stay delightful, though his sleep was disturbed by the family dogs barking at the Secret Servicemen standing vigil on the veranda. The president's sojourn to the north country was made even more enjoyable by a trip to nearby Corbin Park, a twenty thousand–acre private game preserve created by the founder of the Long Island Railroad. In an afternoon, Roosevelt stalked and killed a 150-pound wild boar. (It was a memorable hunting season; on a similar outing in Mississippi two months later, the president would spare the life of a small bear, triggering the Teddy Bear phenomenon.)

From New Hampshire, Roosevelt continued on to Vermont and then to western Massachusetts, where in Pittsfield on September 3, his open carriage was struck by a motorized trolley. The president and his fellow passengers, Massachusetts governor Winthrop Crane, White House secretary George Cortelyou, and Secret Service agent Bill Craig, were flung from the overturned carriage. Craig was crushed to death beneath the trolley's wheels. Roosevelt, painfully bruised, slightly bloodied, but otherwise unhurt, gathered himself up and furiously charged the trolley operator. It took every bit of the president's meager fund of self-restraint to keep from striking the motorman.

Hay learned of the accident almost immediately by way of a telegram from Adee. While the messenger waited, he scribbled a hasty reply to be forwarded to Roosevelt: "We are greatly concerned to hear of your accident and thank heaven for your escape from serious injury." The next day, Adee reassured Hay that the president was back in Oyster Bay and feeling fine. "What a marvelous escape it was!" Adee exhaled with obvious relief. "The President escaped death by just about two inches."

Hay's relief was greater than almost anyone's. "I had a hideous appreciation for a moment yesterday of how I should feel if the President should be taken away," he wrote Adee. He had served two presidents at the time of their murder, but in neither instance had he been the designated heir to the office. "I could not help asking myself if it is right for me to stay in a place with such possibilities," he reflected morbidly.

When Henry Adams learned of the close call in Pittsfield, he wrote to Clara with caustic cheer, "John seems to have come within just three feet of being President, which caused me to grin at the ways of men and motors and Teddies."

ALICE HAY'S WEDDING WAS small and simple, certainly by the regal standards set by Helen and Payne Whitney seven months earlier. Two private Pullman cars, stocked with Apollinaris and champagne, left Boston's North Station at nine in the morning and arrived at Newbury three hours later; from there the guests were carried by steamer to the dock at the Fells. The New Hampshire hills wore their brightest fall finery. The day had begun cloudy and damp, but "fortunately the sun came out just long enough for our guests from Boston to see us as we ought to be seen," Clara reported to Adams, who once again had sent his regrets.

Hay apologized to the guests for having to come such a long way for just the day, and to Whitelaw Reid he admitted, "It certainly *is* a tax on one's friends to marry two girls in a year." Yet the Reids did make the trip, as did Cabot and Nannie Lodge, Henry White on leave from London, Augustus Saint-Gaudens and his wife, and several dozen more. The younger friends of the bride and groom stayed over, while the rest of the guests departed after a late lunch.

THEODORE ROOSEVELT COULD NOT have attended the wedding even if his schedule had permitted. A bruise on his left shin from the trolley accident had become dangerously swollen and infected, and doctors feared blood poisoning. On September 23, the president underwent emergency surgery. Before the operation, Roosevelt confided to George Cortelyou and Elihu Root, "If John Hay should be President, he would have nervous prostration within six weeks." Roosevelt, who took no anesthetic, survived the procedure and spent the next few weeks in a wheelchair or on crutches, more stationary than he had ever been in his life. "I am thankful that at last he seems to be getting well," Clara wrote Adams. "Everybody who knows the scrofulous nature of the Roosevelt blood has been very anxious as to the outcome of this trouble."

While work on the White House continued, the president, Mrs. Roosevelt, and the children moved into a town house on Lafayette Square once occupied by James Knox Polk's secretary of war, William Marcy, a stone's throw from the Hays' front door. The Roosevelt parlor became the temporary cabinet room and presidential office. For much of October, the president was desperate to resolve the five-month-old coal strike before winter arrived and therefore had little time for Hay, who, as usual, was back in Washington by the first of the month. Finally, on the fifteenth, miners and owners agreed to arbitration, and an ecstatic Roosevelt was able to hobble across the square to a dinner at the Hays' in honor of the new British ambassador, Michael Herbert. "Theodore was in fine form," Hay wrote to Adams in Paris. "He began talking at the oysters, and the chasse-café found him still at it. When he was one of us, we could sit on him—but who, except you, can sit on a Kaiser?"

HAY HAD HIS OWN preoccupation that fall. The Panama treaty had languished in Bogotá while the Colombian civil war wound down. The Liberals had all but surrendered; their last redoubt was Panama, where the fighting had intensified to such a degree that the U.S. Navy had intervened, invoking an 1846 treaty that authorized the United States to protect the transit across the isthmus. Two warships, the *Cincinnati* and *Wisconsin*, anchored conspicuously at Colón and Panama City, and armed Marines and sailors were placed on every train of the American-owned Panama Railroad. The American troops did their best to treat the two sides evenhandedly; yet their presence inevitably benefited the Conservative government more than the Liberal rebels, who, even if they could not prevail in the rest of Colombia, still had hopes of holding on to the isthmus for themselves—and the Panamanians.

Marroquín was not thrilled by the American intervention, but he turned it to his fullest advantage. On September 11, he invited the United States to mediate settlement of the civil war. Roosevelt and Hay willingly accepted, aware that the end of the rebellion would bring welcome stability to the isthmus. Furthermore, Hay recognized that American cooperation would curry favor with Marroquín, who still had shown no inclination to act on the canal treaty forwarded to him by José Concha back in July.

In Washington, Concha chose to view America's expanded intervention in a different light. Unsettled by the events of the previous spring, in which he had been embarrassed and, in hindsight, somewhat bamboozled in the negotiations over the canal treaty, he denounced America's latest meddling in Panama as a threat to Colombian sovereignty. To appease him, Hay directed the navy to allow Colombian troops to make use of the Panama Railroad. By the end of October, six thousand government reinforcements were positioned throughout Panama, and by November 19 the war was over. A peace agreement was negotiated aboard the *Wisconsin*. The American mediators were heartened to hear signatories on both sides avow their sincere desire for an American canal across the isthmus.

Concha, on the other hand, remained agitated. Throughout the fall, he pestered Hay to make various changes to the Hay-Concha draft treaty. Hay listened patiently as Concha's demands grew increasingly irrational. He granted one or two minor adjustments, but in the end, he was firm and clear: unless Colombia agreed to the treaty in time for its consideration by the Senate in December, the United States would be obliged to open negotiations with the Nicaraguans, who, he hastened to add, were now amenable to almost any terms offered them.

Behind Concha's back, Colombian foreign minister Felipe Paúl advised Hay not to take Concha's provocations seriously and then ordered Concha to sign the canal treaty. Concha refused. Distraught and discredited, he sailed for Colombia on December 13, reportedly wrapped in a straitjacket.

Hay, meanwhile, responded to the Concha calamity tactfully yet firmly. He sent a cable to Charles Hart in Bogotá, directing him to congratulate the Marroquín government on resolution of the civil war and to reiterate that the United States had "made all possible concessions to Colombia," and that it was now incumbent on Colombia "to say promptly whether they want a canal or not." For good measure, he added: "Nicaragua offers [a] perfectly satisfactory treaty."

TOMÁS HERRÁN, WHO STEPPED into the post of acting minister with the title of chargé d'affaires, was far more cosmopolitan and reasonable than Concha. He had attended Georgetown University and spent most of his life abroad. He spoke four languages, one of them a fluent English. Serving under Martínez Silva and then Concha, he was familiar with every nuance of the canal negotiations. With the U.S. Congress in session and Senator Morgan insisting that a "reasonable time" had elapsed, the easiest thing would have been for Herrán to exercise his authority as agent for the Colombian government and sign the treaty. Instead, under fresh urging from Bogotá, he jacked up the price again: $10 million up front (instead of $7 million) and $600,000 annuity (instead of $100,000). Hay demurred.

He worried that the Senate might not stand for any more dilly-dallying from Colombia; the Spooner Act had passed by far less than the two-thirds margin that it would take to pass an essential canal treaty. Time was short, Hay warned Herrán. Morgan threatened; Nicaragua beckoned. He let Herrán know that Roosevelt had set January 5, 1903, as the new deadline. All the while, Herrán was hearing rumors that the United States might decide to build the canal even without a signed treaty. On January 3, William Cromwell, who now hovered over Herrán, met with Hay and finagled a few more days. On January 21, Hay made his final bid: $10 million with a $250,000 annuity. This time Herrán took the offer.

At five o'clock the following afternoon, Herrán and Cromwell arrived at Hay's house on Lafayette Square, and with Cromwell as witness, the secretary of state and the Colombian chargé signed what thereafter would be known as the Hay-Herrán Treaty. Hay presented the pen to

Cromwell, whose ink had been all over the document from the beginning. As a fitting endnote to the negotiations, three days after the treaty was completed, Marroquín cabled Herrán not to sign it until he received fresh instructions. But by the perverse chronology of the Panama drama, the cable had not arrived in time.

Three months later, on March 17, 1903, over stubborn objection from Senator Morgan, the Hay-Herrán Treaty was ratified, 73 to 5. It now moved southward for ratification by the Colombian Congress, which had not convened since 1898.

WITH THE COLOMBIANS, HAY's perseverance had taken the trick, but he also had to acknowledge that it was Roosevelt's lurking brinkmanship that had lent decisive gravity to the canal negotiation. There was one thing about the president that Hay was now certain: behind those thick glasses was a man who did not blink.

Back in December, while Hay was absorbed with Herrán, Roosevelt had delivered his own ultimatum, this one to Kaiser Wilhelm II. Either cease the German blockade of Venezuela and withdraw your navy within ten days, Roosevelt had demanded, or face war with the United States. To prove he meant business, Roosevelt had ordered fifty-three warships, the largest concentration of U.S. naval vessels ever assembled, to conduct "exercises" off the coast of Puerto Rico, and he had sent Admiral Dewey, the hero of Manila, to take command. One word from the White House would send the fleet steaming toward South America.

Here at last was one of the "big things" that Roosevelt did on his own. As Henry Adams had observed, there were times when Teddy was pure act.

CHAPTER 18

Fair Warning

Hay and Roosevelt saw much to admire in Germany and much that alarmed. They knew and liked many Germans (with some reservations toward Democratic-voting German-Americans). Hay had been to Germany many times; Roosevelt had spent six months in Dresden as a boy. Both read and spoke German and held German philosophy, arts, science, and industry in high regard. What rankled was Germany's militancy and hunger for expansion. Roosevelt had never forgiven Germany's near interference with Admiral Dewey's fleet at Manila. Hay, from his ambassador's post in London during the Spanish-American War, had relayed warnings of Germany's ongoing ambitions in the Philippines, Hawaii, the Caribbean, and elsewhere. "*Voilà l'ennemi,*" he wrote in July 1898 with his eye on Berlin. Two years later, he was disgusted by Germany's vengefulness after the Boxer Rebellion and ridiculed a medal that Kaiser Wilhelm II had minted of "the German Eagle eviscerating the Black Dragon" of China—the suggestion being, Hay remarked to Roosevelt with acidic sarcasm, "that Germany was It, and the rest of the Universe nowhere."

Like so many rivals, Germany and the United States had a great deal in common, in their pasts and in their prospects. Much has also been made of the similarities between Roosevelt and Wilhelm as exemplars of their respective countries. Both came from mixed lineage: Roosevelt of mostly Dutch and some German ancestry; Wilhelm's grandmother was Queen Victoria. They were born within a hundred days of each other and overcame childhood afflictions—Roosevelt asthma, Wilhelm a withered left arm—and made themselves into scrappy athletes. Both were whip-smart and often hair-triggered. As young men and continuing into their roles as president and kaiser, Roosevelt and Wilhelm possessed a deep fixation on ships and navies—the satisfaction of owning them and the abiding urge to use them. As students of naval strategy and as seekers of greater renown for themselves and their countries, they imagined a day when they would test their might against each other. "Frankly I don't know that I should be sorry to see a bit of a spar with Germany," Roosevelt had written as early as 1889, as if contemplating a round or two of boxing on the foredeck of a man-of-war.

During the years that he served as assistant secretary of the navy and vice president, Roosevelt had called for greater American presence and preparedness on the world's oceans; as president, he was at last in a position to bring his vision of American sea power to fulfillment—especially in the Western Hemisphere. At the same time that he was pushing ahead with legislation and treaties for an American-controlled canal, he was also busy expanding the Caribbean fleet. He established a naval base on Isla de Culebra, off Puerto Rico, "in case of sudden war," and replaced his cautious and aging former boss, Navy Secretary John Long, with the more spry and responsive William Moody.

He also made a show of unfurling the Monroe Doctrine, originally issued in 1823 by President James Monroe's secretary of state, John Quincy Adams. "The Monroe Doctrine is a declaration that there must be no territorial aggrandizement by any non-American power at the expense of any American power on American soil," Roosevelt assured gently but emphatically in his 1901 address to Congress—"American" of course referring to both North and South America.

His words seemed aimed directly at Germany, which for the past several years had shown contempt for the Americans' exclusionary impulse. Otto von Bismarck, the architect of modern Germany, had called the

Monroe Doctrine "insolent dogma," and Wilhelm II, who had been kaiser since 1888, gave it hardly better credence.

By the turn of the century, several hundred thousand Germans were settled in Brazil and throughout Latin America, and German companies were heavily invested in mining, railroads, and trade there. Wilhelm mentioned to his military and ministers that he wished to be "the paramount power" in the Caribbean, and his government was actively looking for a suitable sphere of influence in the basin, similar to its toehold in China, or, at the very least, a naval base. Under consideration were Trinidad, one of the Dutch colonies, or the Jamaican port of Kingston. In the spring of 1901, a German warship was spotted mapping a harbor on Margarita Island, off the Venezuelan coast. From such a base the German admiralty was well within striking distance of both the Isthmus of Panama and the coastline of the United States.

Roosevelt saw the Germans coming from a long way off but chose at first to grant them the benefit of the doubt. He let it be known that he did not construe the Monroe Doctrine to exclude other nations from commercial dealings with Latin America. Nor did it preclude a foreign power from punishing a Latin American country for egregious conduct. "If any South American country misbehaves toward any European country, let the European country spank it," he stated in 1901, while still vice president. But as he emphasized in his congressional address later in the year, such punishment must not take the form of acquisition of territory.

Venezuela, meanwhile, stood by, destitute and disheveled. Since mid-century, it had been invaded by Colombia more than twenty times and had undergone more than two dozen insurrections. In 1899, Cipriano Castro became the latest *caudillo* to seize power. By then the country was already hugely in debt to a phalanx of foreign banks and businesses, including American, Italian, and French, but in arrears to no one more egregiously than Great Britain and Germany. Castro had paid not a single *centimo* in interest, never mind the tens of millions of *bolivars* of principal, figuring that Venezuelan courts and the Monroe Doctrine would shield him from retribution. As a further measure of his malfeasance, he allowed Venezuelan nationals to hijack foreign cargoes and loot foreign-owned farms and businesses with impunity. The German minister to

Caracas called Castro a "megalomaniac." In a letter to Hay, Theodore Roosevelt, who putatively was Castro's backyard protector, sized up the *caudillo* as "an unspeakably villainous little monkey."

By the end of 1901, Germany and Great Britain had exhausted efforts to bring Venezuela to rational arbitration and now looked to military coercion as the last resort. On December 11, the German ambassador in Washington, Theodore von Holleben, alerted Hay that Germany intended to issue an ultimatum for settlement. If the ultimatum were not met, Germany would proceed to blockade the Venezuelan harbors of La Guaira and Puerto Cabello and begin levying duties on imports and exports. Mindful of the Monroe Doctrine, which Roosevelt had brandished in his congressional address only eight days earlier, von Holleben hastened to add that under no circumstances did Germany contemplate "the permanent occupation of Venezuelan territory."

Hay responded promptly and formally, expressing his satisfaction that Germany had "no purpose or intention to make even the smallest acquisition of territory on the South American Continent or the islands adjacent." Wilhelm, however, was not so easily seduced by Hay's attempt at polite persuasion. When von Holleben informed Berlin of Hay and Roosevelt's sentiments against a permanent German occupation, the kaiser was said to have snapped defiantly, "We will do whatever is necessary . . . even if it displeases the Yankees. Never fear!"

Germany waited almost a year to make its move, using the time to work out a plan with Britain to seize Venezuelan gunboats and apply a blockade. Hay never entirely understood why Great Britain decided to gang up with Germany, especially so soon after Britain had shown its respect for the Monroe Doctrine by way of the Hay-Pauncefote Treaty. Out of an underlying faith in their fellow English speakers, he and Roosevelt chose not to regard Britain's pact with Germany and its play in Venezuela as anything more than what Britain purported it to be: a means to collect on a debt.

At the other extreme, Roosevelt and Hay ascribed Germany's posture toward Venezuela to the most nefarious motives. They remained highly skeptical of Germany's avowal that it sought no permanent settlement. Roosevelt would tell a reporter in 1909 that the blockade had been just "the initial step in a plan that had been worked out in Berlin, under the sponsorship of the Kaiser, to seize a Venezuelan port and then coerce the Castro government into leasing it to Germany for ninety-nine years. . . . Once this had been effected, the establishment of a powerful German naval base and the economic penetration of the hinterland would have followed automatically. It would have been only a matter of time before Venezuela became a German colony or protectorate."

At the beginning of November 1902, Ambassador Michael Herbert advised Hay that a joint German and British blockade was imminent. Hay replied that the United States would not object to the two powers "taking steps to obtain redress for injuries suffered by their subjects," provided that—again he underscored the condition on which the United States would not bend—"no acquisition of territory was contemplated." Yet even as Hay was spelling out the ground rules, in hopes that Britain and Germany would comply, Roosevelt, as commander in chief, was putting the navy on high alert, figuring and possibly even hoping that Germany would *not* comply. Hay had pledged in his speech in New York a year earlier that the United States would not be afraid "to insult or defy a great power because it is strong, or even because it is friendly." Roosevelt was now raring to do all of that.

FAIR PLAY CALLED FOR fair warning. On November 24, the president gave a small dinner at the White House, which was still undergoing renovation. His guests were the German diplomat Speck von Sternburg; John St. Loe Strachey, editor of the *Spectator* in London; and Admiral George Dewey, the victor of Manila, already canonized for his war-opening order, "You may fire when you are ready, Gridley." Roosevelt led them through plaster dust and wet paint to the Executive Dining Room in the new West Wing. The point of the gathering was soon obvious to all.

Von Sternburg was not bearing full diplomatic credentials; Roosevelt had summoned him informally to make plain his objections and intentions with respect to the trouble brewing in Venezuela—trusting that "Specky," who was married to an American and had known Roosevelt for fifteen years, would pass the word to the appropriate ministries when he returned home. The same went for Strachey, another old friend, who was similarly well connected in the halls of English government. Dewey, in his braid and medals, was on hand to impress and, ever so implicitly, to intimidate. Roosevelt wanted it known in London and Berlin that the first and only man ever to hold the rank of Admiral of the Navy was soon to command exercises of unprecedented scale within five hundred miles of the Venezuelan coast.

Hay was aware of the dinner and knew both of the European visitors almost as well as Roosevelt did, but he did not attend. To have made the meeting official by including the secretary of state or ambassadors von Holleben and Herbert would have drawn the attention of the press and likely would have escalated the rhetoric of the looming crisis.

On December 1, eight days after von Sternburg and Strachey sailed away, carrying their cautions to Europe, Roosevelt delivered his second annual message to Congress, in which he again let Berlin and London know that his gun was loaded and all but cocked. "There is not a cloud on the horizon," he began. "There seems not the slightest chance of trouble with a foreign power. We most earnestly hope that this state of things may continue." Then he added, his words weighted with both moral and martial gravity, "Fatuous self-complacency or vanity, or short-sightedness in refusing to prepare for danger, is both foolish and wicked in such a nation as ours."

Hay took a more straightforward approach. On December 5, he cabled the American Embassy in Berlin that the president would be grateful if "an arrangement could be made as might obviate the necessity of any exhibition of force on the part of Germany and Great Britain" toward Venezuela. He sent a similar cable to London, where Henry White was talking quietly with Foreign Secretary Lansdowne and still trying to comprehend why England, which still held a grudge against the kaiser for siding with the Boers, would risk harming its relationship with America just to spank Venezuela.

To no avail. On December 7, Germany and Britain told Venezuela that they were closing their consulates in Caracas and soon would begin "measures" to gain recompense for the money owed them. Not entirely by coincidence, on the eighth, Dewey arrived at Culebra to take command of the American fleet. That same afternoon, when von Holleben appeared at the White House in the company of several German businessmen, Roosevelt took the opportunity to pull the ambassador aside and gave him a short course in geography and naval strategy.

The fullest version of their conversation was rendered by Roosevelt in August 1916, in a letter he wrote to John Hay's first biographer, William Roscoe Thayer. Characteristically, Roosevelt cast himself in bronze. "I saw the Ambassador," he recounted, "and explained that in view of the presence of the German Squadron on the Venezuelan coast I could not permit longer delay in answering my request for an arbitration, and that I could not acquiesce in any seizure of Venezuelan territory. The Ambassador responded that his Government could not agree to arbitrate, and that there was no intention to take 'permanent' possession of Venezuelan territory."

This drew a sarcastic scoff from Roosevelt: "I answered that Kiauchau [the German treaty port of Kiaochow in China] was not a 'permanent' possession of Germany's—that I understood that it was merely held by a ninety nine year lease; and that I did not intend to have another Kiauchau, held by similar tenure, on the approach to the Isthmian Canal."

When von Holleben showed no sign of backing down, Roosevelt asked the ambassador "to inform his government that if no notification for arbitration came during the next ten days I would be obliged to order Dewey to take his fleet to the Venezuelan coast and see that the German forces did not take possession of any territory."

Von Holleben was nonplussed by Roosevelt's taunt and replied that the consequences of such a strong reaction by the United States would be "so serious to both countries that he dreaded to give them a name." Roosevelt said he then told von Holleben, "I had thoroughly counted the cost before I decided on the step, and asked him to look at the map, as a glance would show him that there was no spot in the world where Germany in the event of conflict with the United States would be at greater disadvantage than in the Caribbean sea."

(Roosevelt's recollection of this scene, however vivid, may well have been shaded by an entirely different spot on the map. In the summer of 1916, when he put his version of the White House confrontation to paper,

British and German troops were slaughtering each other in the Somme and the United States was on the verge of entering the Great War.)

Whether von Holleben thought Roosevelt was bluffing—never mind whether any such words were actually exchanged—did not alter the course of the British and German navies over the next two days. On December 9, their gunboats captured several Venezuelan ships, with the Germans sinking two. Four days later, a German cruiser bombarded two forts at Puerto Cabello. After a token and hapless flourish of self-defense, Venezuela's Castro appealed to the United States for arbitration with his marauding creditors.

On December 13, Hay's ambassadors in London and Berlin passed along Castro's proposal for arbitration to good effect, if not immediate response. The English public had been outraged and embarrassed to learn that its navy was in league with Germany. Paying Roosevelt back for his recent White House hospitality, John St. Loe Strachey in the *Spectator* condemned the partnership as "one of the most amazingly indiscreet alliances ever made with a foreign power." In Germany the temper for confrontation was tepid at best. Most Germans approved of their navy's chastisement of Venezuela but were unsettled by the intensity of American anger toward them in the days following the Caribbean offensive. Speck von Sternburg made this point even more directly, assuring German chancellor Bernhard von Bülow that Roosevelt's pledge to intervene was made in dead earnest.

Hay may not have known the degree of stridency of Roosevelt's threat to von Holleben, but according to Roosevelt, he did know that Dewey's squadron of fifty or more battleships, cruisers, and torpedo boats was loaded with coal, fully armed, and poised to confront the dozen or so ships of the British and German navies threatening Venezuela. Although there was still no evidence that either of the European powers intended to seize territory other than temporarily, Hay, like von Sternburg, did not doubt for a second that Roosevelt was sincere about siccing Dewey on the perceived flouters of the Monroe Doctrine.

Roosevelt claimed that he held von Holleben's feet to the fire on one more occasion—this time in a conversation that took place six days after their first confrontation. When von Holleben balked at arbitration yet again, Roosevelt countered by advancing his ten-day deadline by twenty-four hours. Again this is Roosevelt's memory against nobody else's.

On December 16, Hay once more presented Castro's proposal for arbitration to Great Britain and Germany. That same day, Foreign Secretary Lansdowne met with Paul Metternich, the German ambassador to London, and told him that, given the "storm of public opinion" coming from America, he would urge the British cabinet to accept Hay's latest offer. Indeed, the cabinet voted to do so a few hours later. The following day, December 17, just hours before Roosevelt's timetable would have sent Dewey's armada southward, the German government agreed to arbitration as well. With that, Dewey concluded his "exercises," and the crisis quieted.

In the end, the question remains: Who had provoked whom? Germany was genuinely shocked by America's disapproval of an action that America had plainly condoned in advance. (Germany was also disappointed by how little blame America placed on Great Britain, not to mention by how quickly Britain had "lost its nerve"—the kaiser's words—under America's glower.) If Roosevelt is to be believed, he threatened von Holleben over his refusal to accept arbitration and not over the blockade itself, which never did involve the seizure of property.

Thus the next question: Would the Germans have planted their flag on Venezuelan soil if Roosevelt had not rattled his saber within earshot of von Holleben and von Sternburg? The best guess is, not likely—not then, anyway. "We are not interested in a couple more palm trees," Metternich insisted. What did matter, however, is that Roosevelt suspected Germany of bad intentions.

And finally: Would Hay have succeeded in leading Germany and Great Britain to arbitration without Roosevelt's private chat with von Holleben and Dewey's presence at Culebra? The most plausible answer to this question is: Of course he would have—sooner or later, by his usual tact and patience, with an additional nudge from an outraged public at home and abroad.

Yet to hear Roosevelt tell it, he had done all the heavy lifting himself. "I succeeded . . . in getting all the parties in interest to submit their cases to the Hague Tribunal," he wrote in his autobiography, referring to the

Permanent Court of Arbitration, where the terms of the Venezuelan debt were eventually sorted out. Here again Roosevelt steals too much of the spotlight, for even if he threatened Germany, as he averred, or simply asked von Holleben in a kindly way to settle its dispute with Venezuela, the real work of defusing the conflict demanded old-school, on-the-carpet diplomacy. Between the time of von Holleben's first visit to the White House and the agreement by Germany and Britain to accept arbitration, Henry White in London and Ambassador Charlemagne Tower, whom Hay had transferred from St. Petersburg to Berlin, were in daily contact with Hay and with the foreign ministers in their respective capitals. It was they, supervised by Hay, who brought the Venezuelan crisis to its adequate conclusion.

But regardless of who did what, and to what degree, Roosevelt wound up a winner. He greatly enhanced the prestige of his navy and added steel to the Monroe Doctrine, effectively fortifying the Panama canal even before it was built. Without letting the world know how near he and Wilhelm had come to war, he convinced himself that he had made the kaiser blink. And shortly after his *têtes-à-têtes* with Roosevelt in the White House, Ambassador von Holleben was recalled because of "illness" and replaced by Speck von Sternburg. It was even said that this was one of Roosevelt's reasons for taunting Germany to begin with. At any rate, the president was delighted.

And ultimately, even though Roosevelt grabbed most of the attention for resolving the Venezuelan affair, Hay received his rightful share of applause. Stuyvesant Fish, whose father had been Grant's secretary of state, recognized that Hay had "kept the President & our Country from falling into a cunningly laid trap."

Andrew Carnegie, who had differed with Hay and the administration over Cuba and the Philippines, now had nothing but praise for Hay's handling of Venezuela and all other aspects of foreign affairs. "I am so happy (& proud, excuse me) that I have known you John Hay," the great tycoon extolled. "You make the Republic what its Founders intended— something higher than the governments that preceded its birth."

Elbert Baldwin, managing editor of the *Outlook* and a friend of Roosevelt's, likewise gave credit where credit was due: "The steadiness with which our present Secretary has adhered to an unselfish policy, the candor, frankness, straightforwardness, above all scrupulous 'squareness' of his methods, are in welcome contrast to the selfishness, secrecy, indirection, delay, and, wherever possible, the harshness of other methods. If America has become a World Power, it is largely because of the success of the new American diplomacy. . . . Humanity in general is freer and finer because such diplomacy exists."

None of Hay's letters reveal his own satisfaction on the resolution of the Venezuela affair or his feelings on Roosevelt's handling of it. But at some point, Hay must have griped to Henry Adams about Roosevelt's conduct, because Adams later mentioned to Lizzie Cameron, "Our Emperor . . . tells his old stories at every cabinet dinner for two hours running . . . describing his preparations for war with Germany. . . . The joke is stale," Adams judged. "We"—he and Hay, presumably—"laugh but shudder."

FOR HAY, ONE GOOD turn led to another. On January 23, 1903, two days after the Hay-Herrán Treaty was signed, he and Ambassador Herbert signed the Alaska boundary treaty. There was no direct connection between the Alaska and Venezuela events, but Herbert, because he was new to his post and eager to get off to a positive start, had an extra motivation for bolstering the Anglo-American alliance, which had been scuffed so unnecessarily of late.

The Alaska treaty was not so much a solution to the boundary dispute as it was an agreement on how to go about a solution. It called for a tribunal of six "impartial jurists of repute"—three from each side—to clarify the old line mapped nearly a century earlier. On the insistence of the United States, the tribunal was not to arbitrate—that is, it would not compromise. Each side would posit a boundary and make its case; a vote would be taken; one side would win, the other lose.

The Senate ratified the tribunal treaty on February 11, and Roosevelt, who was determined to take the match, stacked his team with Senator George Turner of Washington, Secretary of War Elihu Root, and jingo extraordinaire Cabot Lodge. The press guffawed at this roster, suggesting that Roosevelt had found the three *least* impartial men in the country.

Canadian prime minister Wilfred Laurier protested the choice of Lodge in particular, and Hay had to sympathize. "[T]he presence of Lodge on the tribunal is, from many points of view, regrettable," he confided to Henry White later in the spring. Yet he did not do anything to intervene. It didn't really matter who was on the tribunal, anyway. Like Lodge and Roosevelt, Hay was convinced that the American case was unbeatable.

Great Britain played the game rather more fairly. Its jurists were actual jurists: two Canadian judges and the chief justice of England, Lord Alverstone. It was Alverstone who in October, after careful study of the case, cast his vote in favor of the American interpretation of the boundary, thus avoiding a tie.

For once Hay allowed himself to crow a bit, if only to his wife. "[W]e give up 30 square miles of our claim, which we don't want, and the Canadians have to give up 30,000 square miles of their claim, which is of enormous value," he explained to Clara. "I have a right to feel gratified, because at first I was the only one who believed such a result possible. I persuaded McKinley and Paunceforte and Herbert to adopt the plan and then, the hardest task of all, I got Theodore to accede to it. . . . It is one of the most important transactions of my life, and few more important have been accomplished by our State Department."

SUCCESS HAS MANY FRIENDS, and in Hay's case, success made his friendship with Roosevelt that much stronger. In the months following the Venezuela crisis and the signing of the Panama and Alaska treaties, Hay and Roosevelt were effusive in their compliments of each other. One by one, the president had replaced the cabinet members he had inherited from McKinley with younger men, and the press constantly conjectured that Hay would be the next to go. But Roosevelt stood by him, for Hay was pulling his weight.

Roosevelt to Hay: "I wonder if you realize how thankful I am to you for having staid with me. I owe you a great debt, old man."

Hay to Roosevelt: "It is a comfort to work for a President who, besides being a lot of other things, happened to be born a gentleman."

Roosevelt to Hay: "As Secretary of State you stand alone."

Hay to Roosevelt: "It is hard for me to answer your kind letter. I know better than any one how far I am from deserving your okay; but I am nonetheless proud and glad of your confidence."

Invited to address the Ohio Society of New York, Hay used the occasion to deliver a glowing tribute to "the young, gallant, able, brilliant" president:

"From the cloistered life of an American college boy, sheltered from the ruder currents of the world by the ramparts of wealth and gentle nurture, he passed still very young into the wide expanse of the hills and plains. In that environment a man grows to his full stature if the original stuff is good. He came back to the East, bringing with him, as Tennyson sang, 'The wrestling thews that throw the world.' From that time his career has been onward and upward, for that is the law of his being.

"It is no distinction to an American President to be honest, nor to be brave, nor to be intelligent, nor to be patriotic—they have all been all of those," Hay continued. "[B]ut the country is indeed to be congratulated when all these high qualities are heightened and tinged by that ineffable light which for want of a more descriptive term we call genius."

Roosevelt was deeply touched. "Edith and I were saying last night that if I died we could wish that others would put on my tomb the words you spoke; I could not direct them to be put on myself—they describe what I wish I were, not what I am; no one else has ever so spoken of me."

BESIDES THEIR MUTUAL ADMIRATION, Hay and Roosevelt also shared a portrait painter. In mid-February 1903, John Singer Sargent spent a week at the White House, struggling to capture the president on canvas, although it was Sargent who felt like Roosevelt's captive—"a rabbit in the presence of a boa constrictor," the painter confessed after the ordeal. Sargent eventually got the kinetic Roosevelt to pose on the White House stairway, with his meaty right hand grasping the knob of the newel post as if it were the world. Roosevelt's posture and countenance are virile, direct, unflinching. But even while Sargent succeeded in depicting Roosevelt's essential strength and learnedness—necktie slightly askew, pince-nez perched above ruddy cheeks—the painting does not penetrate inward. Roosevelt's portrait, like his psychology, offers very little shadow, as if lit from all sides. When Henry Adams saw the finished picture, he described it to Lizzie Cameron as "Good Sargent and not very bad Roosevelt. It is not Theodore, but a young intellectual idealist with a taste for athletics, which I take to be Theodore's idea of himself. It is for once less brutal than its subject."

Because Roosevelt would not stand still for more than a half-hour at a time, Sargent was able to slip across Lafayette Square and do Hay's portrait in the interims. Hay and Sargent knew each other from England, and their familiarity helped make Hay's picture more intimate than the Roosevelt commission; the latter was intended as the official White House portrait, whereas the piece for Hay was personal.

The painting of Hay is mostly dark. The woodwork of Hay's library is barely discernible, and his black frock coat, vest, and necktie are absorbed in the umber of his chair. Hay appears not too very old but rather as a man who has not been young for quite some time. His hair and brows are sandy-brown, while the sculpted whiskers that soften his jaw and his mustache—splashed across his face like the bow wave of an oncoming yacht—are the color of ashes. His skin too is pale and seems almost brittle. Perhaps as a gesture of kindness, Sargent allows a single youthful stroke of forelock to fall upon Hay's wan brow.

The contrast between the Hay and Roosevelt portraits is in itself a measure of Sargent's extraordinary talents of perception and rendition. Roosevelt basks in a public glow; with Hay, the light is a lamp radiating from within. Roosevelt is fuel; Hay is spark. Roosevelt is knowledge; Hay is wisdom. The potency of Sargent's portrait of Hay comes not only from the intensity of the light but also from its economy, for it spends itself in only two places: Hay's confident, guileless, and persuasive gaze, and his fine-boned right hand—his writing hand—which emerges from the gloom of his tailored sleeve like an Elgin marble.

Hay felt somewhat vain having his portrait done, and at first he tried to keep it secret from Adams and other friends. He already possessed a magnificent art collection: paintings and drawings by John Constable, J. M. W. Turner, Joshua Reynolds, George Du Maurier, Alfred Pinkham Ryder, Raphael, Rubens, Canaletto, and Correggio; works by his friends Edwin Abbey and John La Farge (including a portrait of a young Henry James by the latter); and his crown jewels: a *Madonna* attributed to Botticelli, in the front hall, and a smaller but equally stunning piece believed to be by another master of the Italian Quattrocento, Fra Filippo Lippi. (He also owned a draft of the Gettysburg Address.) But clearly it was posterity and not merely patronage that prompted him to commission the greatest portrait painter of his day. "Mister Sargent finished my portrait yesterday afternoon, signed and dated it. I think it is very good," Hay wrote to his daughter Helen, adding, "It [is] an odd thought that the most of my reputation in after years will depend on this picture."

The painting, which is now in the John Hay Library at Brown University, has done its job ably, for it preserves the likeness of a handsome, luminescent, yet reserved gentleman, whose pen hand is as graceful as Roosevelt's scepter hand is firm.

Hay's legacy was assured in other ways as well. While he was sitting for Sargent, Helen gave birth to his first grandchild, named not John, which must await a son, but Joan—close enough.

KEEPING THE GERMANS OUT of the Caribbean was a simple matter compared with containing the Russians in China. Russia had acknowledged the Open Door with a cynical smirk, making it plain that Manchuria was never part of the deal. Since the Boxer Rebellion, Russia had continued to tighten its grip on the region, particularly along the Russian-built and -controlled Chinese Eastern Railway, which now extended southward from Siberia through the cities of Harbin and Mukden, the length of the Liao-tung Peninsula, to the Yellow Sea ports at Dairen and Port Arthur. Through coercion and bribery, Russia was bent on gaining a monopoly in the region—not only of railroads but also of all commercial concessions, along with telegraph, customs, and tax collection.

In mid-1901, Henry Miller, the American consul in the Manchurian treaty port of Newchwang, a significant point of entry for American cotton, flour, and oil, began warning Hay that, unless Russia was checked by one or more of the powers, it would soon "annihilate" American trade in Manchuria and ultimately annex the region outright. When Hay lodged an official protest, Russia responded with hurt feelings, denying any intention to breech the Open Door or in any way crowd out the interests of its worthy friend, the United States.

Hay had made the Open Door as strong as he could, but he conceded from the start that in order to secure even lukewarm acquiescence from the Russians, the United States had little choice but to allow Russia special standing in Manchuria. "We are not in any attitude of hostility towards Russia in Manchuria," he counseled Roosevelt in May 1902. "On the contrary, we recognized her exceptional position in northern China." America's dispute with Russia had always been strictly over commercial interests; no American lives were at stake in Manchuria. Moreover, the Yellow Sea was not in America's backyard, and the Russian navy was far more formidable than the leaky Spanish flotilla that Dewey had pounced upon at Manila in 1898.

This time, Great Britain and Japan took the initiative. On January 30, 1902, the two powers signed a treaty recognizing, and promising to fight for, each other's Far Eastern interests—Britain's in China and Japan's in both China and Korea. Japan had no particular designs on Manchuria, but it feared that if Russia were allowed to gain sovereignty there, the next target would be Korea, which Japan coveted for its natural resources and as an outlet for exports and emigrants. Nowhere did the Anglo-Japanese treaty single out Russia specifically, but the message was sent—and received—nonetheless. Two months after the alliance was made public, Russia announced that it would withdraw its troops from Manchuria in three stages over the next eighteen months.

Hay was reserved in his approval of the treaty. For one thing, he was opposed to any of the powers cutting side deals over China; for another, he had his doubts that Russia would live up to its pledge to pull its troops. From Newchwang, Consul Miller expressed a similar skepticism. "The alliance between Japan and Great Britain will not seriously alter the intentions of Russia in Manchuria," Miller predicted. "[S]he will be more modest in appearance and more circumspect in methods, but will determine to press all of her enterprises here and nurse her desire to cultivate her determination to become the perfect master of the country."

As promised, the first Russian troops left Manchuria in October 1902, but in all other regards, Russia continued to consolidate its commercial and administrative control, collecting taxes and duties and expanding its railroad and ports. Again, Hay had little diplomatic leverage. Russia's agreements in Manchuria were with China, not with the United States, and until Russia stepped on American toes—for example, by demanding higher tariffs on American goods than those levied at other treaty ports— Hay had no basis for complaint.

The situation grew more frustrating in April 1903, when Russia informed China that it would not honor its second deadline for troop withdrawal from Manchuria—unless the Chinese granted a list of seven concessions that perpetuated Russian authority and severely limited the access and privileges of (non-Russian) foreigners in Manchuria. When Hay asked Russia's ambassador to Washington, his neighbor and not-quite-friend Count Cassini, to explain Russia's latest effrontery, Cassini denied any knowledge of the "convention of seven points" between his country and China. Hay knew Cassini was lying but could only suggest to the president that Russia's demands, if indeed real, were "inadmissible, and in the highest degree disadvantageous."

In a letter to Roosevelt, who was away on another hunting trip, Hay grumbled over his predicament: "I take it for granted that Russia knows as well as we do that we will not fight over Manchuria, for the simple reason that we cannot. . . . If our rights and our interests in opposition to Russia in the far East were as clear as noonday, we could never get a treaty through the Senate the object of which was to check Russian aggression."

Through his minister in Peking, Hay urged the Chinese to resist Russian demands, and since the Russians continued to deny the existence of any such demands, he told them that the United States expected to conduct trade and maintain consuls in Manchuria. The coy game continued throughout the spring. Russia still gave no sign of withdrawing troops from Manchuria; meanwhile it insisted that the Open Door was still wide open, even though the seven-point convention—a verbatim copy of which Hay had on his desk—made a case for near-total exclusion of the other powers. "Dealing with a government with whom mendacity is a science is an extremely difficult and delicate matter," Hay confided to Roosevelt. "It will take a little time for us to ascertain which of two courses the Russian Government is pursuing. We know that they are making these demands of China, and we know they have absolutely denied making them."

Preoccupied with other prey, Roosevelt was content to leave "our Manchurian affair" to Hay's judgment. "[T]here does not seem to be anything for me to say at present, or any need of my saying anything," the normally verbose Roosevelt wrote his secretary of state from California. A week later, he merely echoed what Hay had been saying from the beginning: "The bad feature of the situation from our standpoint is that as yet it seems that we cannot fight to keep Manchuria open. . . . When I get back I shall have to go over the whole China situation with you. That you have handled it in a most masterly manner I need hardly say; now I would like to get some idea what we are to do in the future."

Hay, though, had already seen the future. Although the United States was not willing to go to war with Russia over Manchuria, Japan clearly was. "[I]t would require the very least encouragement on the part of the United States or England to induce Japan to seek a violent solution to the question," Hay advised Roosevelt in April, and a month later he was even more sure of Japan's sanguinity. "[I]f we gave them a wink, [they] would fly at the throat of Russia in a moment."

Hay was not recommending war, but he bore a private desire to see Russia get the thrashing he felt it deserved—and he was gladder still to have someone else do the dirty work. "We are not charged with the cure of the Russian soul," he told Roosevelt. But, he added, "We may let them go to the devil at their own sweet will."

HIS BRIEF AGAINST RUSSIA had been building for some time, and Manchuria was not the only aggravation. On Easter Sunday, April 19, 1903, a Russian mob in the Bessarabian city of Kishinev killed forty-seven Jews, injured hundreds more, and destroyed seven hundred of their houses. Jews in the United States, led by the Independent Order of B'nai B'rith, immediately set about raising a relief fund and beseeching the Roosevelt administration to file a protest with the Russian government. Large rallies took place in major cities across the country; newspapers ran angry editorials.

American Jewry had a proven ally in Hay, who a year earlier had circulated a letter (actually drafted by Alvey Adee) to the European powers, voicing his outrage at the persecution of Jews in Romania and protesting discrimination against American Jews traveling abroad. "[T]he Hebrews—poor dears! all over the country think we are bully boys," Hay congratulated Adee afterward.

As a Gentile, an Anglo-Saxon, and a patrician, Hay was not without prejudice and condescension. He used pejoratives such as "chink," "dago," and "darky" with little compunction, as did most of his friends. Yet he seems seldom to have uttered these slurs in public, and they crop up infrequently in his correspondence. He was even less inclined to disparage Jews categorically—in contrast to Henry Adams, who was rabid and broad-gauged in his disdain. ("I want to put every money-lender to death," Adams once wrote an English friend.) Since Hay's eye-opening foray through the Jewish ghetto of Vienna as a young chargé d'affaires, he had come to know a number of well-to-do Jews in England and the United States, most notably Baron Ferdinand James de Rothschild, the banker Jacob Schiff, and the New York attorney Oscar Straus, who had twice served as ambassador to the Ottoman Empire. While Hay may have still been prone to Semitic stereotyping, he was not anti-Semitic.

Upon receiving word of the Kishinev massacre, and with some coaxing by Simon Wolf of B'nai B'rith, Hay instructed his ambassador in St. Petersburg to inquire whether the Russians would permit aid to reach the victims. Russia responded that there was no need for intervention because no atrocities had been committed at Kishinev. Later, when credible accounts of the attack appeared in newspapers, Czar Nicholas II changed his tune, placing blame for the violence squarely on the Jews. In Washington, Ambassador Cassini backed up his emperor, telling the Associated Press that "Jews continue to do the very things which have been responsible for the troubles which involve them."

Hay was genuinely outraged by the brutality at Kishinev, yet he was worried about jeopardizing his ongoing deliberations with Russia over Manchuria. When Jacob Schiff chastised him for not reacting swiftly or strongly enough to Russia's refutation, Hay wrote back in frustration. "There could be only two motives which would induce this Government to take any positive action in such a case; one is some advantage to itself, and the other is some advantage to the oppressed and persecuted and outraged Jews of Russia," he reasoned with Schiff. "What possible advantage would it be to the United States, and what possible advantage to the Jews of Russia, if we should make a protest against these fiendish cruelties and be told that it was none of our business?"

Keeping in mind that lynchings were still common in America, he asked: "What would we do if the Government of Russia should protest against mob violence in this country, of which you can hardly open a newspaper in this country without seeing examples? I readily admit that nothing so bad as these Kisheneff horrors has ever taken place in America; but the cases would not be unlike in principle."

He was not making excuses; nor was he asking to be let off the hook. "I should have hoped that I would not be required to defend myself against any accusation of neglect of duty in such a matter," he said to Schiff in closing, "but I have no reason to complain. I have received unmerited credit so often that I ought not to object occasionally to unmerited blame." He then wrote a personal check to the Kishinev relief fund for $500.

Hay did not stop there. Recognizing that he had little formal diplomatic recourse—no Americans had been harmed at Kishinev; the incident was entirely internal—he continued to meet with Jewish leaders to come up with a plan that, if nothing else, would demonstrate that America and American Jewry had not turned the other cheek. On June 15, he staged a carefully choreographed and highly publicized meeting at the White House between Roosevelt and a delegation from B'nai B'rith. The Jewish contingent presented a draft of a petition it intended to transmit to the czar, protesting the atrocities at Kishinev and the ongoing acts of prejudice and hostility that had driven tens of thousands of Jews from their homelands in Russia and Eastern Europe.

Hay's remarks to the Jewish delegation that day were also directed at the Russian authorities, however indirectly. "No person of ordinary humanity can have heard without deep emotion the story of the cruel outrages inflicted upon the Jews of Kishineff," he began. "Nobody can ever make the Americans think ill of the Jews as a class or as a race—we know them too well. In the painful crisis through which we are now passing the Jews of the United States have given evidence of the highest qualities—generosity, love of justice, and power of self-restraint."

Roosevelt wrapped up the meeting with a long-winded and considerably clumsier speech, in which he said kind things about various Jews he had served with or appointed and then pledged that his concern for the afflicted Jews of Kishinev was every bit as deep as his sympathy for "any tragedy that had happened to any Christian people."

With that, the delegation departed and began circulating the petition and in no time collected more than twelve thousand signatures. "[T]his is not a Jewish petition, but one emanating from American citizens," Simon Wolf stressed. It bore the names of senators, congressmen, governors, mayors, judges, and members of nearly every profession, including, inevitably, more than a few moneylenders.

By the end of June, two weeks before the petition was completed, newspapers carried reports, uncorroborated, that the Russian government would refuse to receive the document and instead would offer an official explanation or possibly even an apology for Kishinev. Cassini was obliged to issue a statement, again through the press instead of through diplomatic channels, denying the existence of any such apology.

At the time Cassini made his remarks, Hay was away from Washington, visiting Helen and Payne Whitney and his granddaughter Joan in Newport. (Clara, meanwhile, was in Geneseo, New York, awaiting the birth of Alice's first child.) Roosevelt was also out of town, at Oyster Bay. Without Hay on hand to temper his reaction, the president fired off a reply to be released anonymously to the newspapers. "[I]t seemed somewhat strange," an "unnamed" official was quoted, "that the Russian government should choose this particular method of making a statement to the American people [denying apology for Kishinev] at the very time when, by methods which are certainly the reverse of friendly to the United States, it has sought to make China join in breaking the plighted faith of all the powers as to the open door in Manchuria and has endeavored to bar our people from access to the Manchuria trade."

Linking Kishinev to Manchuria was precisely what Hay had been trying to avoid, and now Roosevelt, without checking with him beforehand, had impetuously tied them in a bow and shoved the bundle under the czar's nose.

Hay winced, but he did not fly off the handle, as some newspapers surmised he had done. When it was learned that Hay would stop at Oyster Bay on his way back to Washington, the papers reported "on good authority" that the president's latest outburst had rendered the secretary of state's position in the cabinet untenable and that he intended to resign. Hay denied the rumors vociferously. "There is no reason in the world why people should talk of my resigning," he wrote George Smalley of *The Times*. "My personal relations with the President are still those of friendship which he inherited from his father, and we agree on all points of foreign policy."

But to Clara he confided, "It is a comfort to think I *can* get out whenever I want to."

Though Hay seemed to harbor no hard feelings toward Roosevelt over the Kishinev indiscretion, still he did not look forward to going to Oyster Bay. "When McKinley sent for me he gave me all his time till we got through," he grumbled to Clara, "but I always find T.R. engaged with a dozen other people, and it is an hour's wait and a minute's talk—and a certainty that there was no necessity of my coming at all." Sure enough, when he arrived at Sagamore Hill on July 7—his first visit there—he had to share the president with three senators, a shipping magnate, a promising poet, and the New York socialite Winthrop Chanler.

In the afternoon, Hay bided his time while Roosevelt and Chanler played tennis. A telegram announcing the birth of his second grandchild, Evelyn Wadsworth, lifted his spirits, and he felt guilty for feeling so cross about making the trip. Not until after dinner did he get a chance to talk with Roosevelt at length, and he was obliged to stay the night. Detraining in Washington the following afternoon, he was deluged by reporters eager to learn of his resignation. "I could not resign now if I wanted to," he joked to Clara. "I have denied it so energetically."

In fact, divorce was never discussed. Instead, Roosevelt had regaled Hay with his recent hunting adventures, and in due time they got around to plotting the next chess moves on Kishinev. Rather than send the petition to St. Petersburg without ceremony, as Roosevelt had initially proposed, Hay suggested that they proceed more gingerly—and diplo-matically—by first asking the Russian Foreign Ministry if Czar Nicholas were willing to receive it. "If they answer in the negative—which is virtually certain—we have complied with our engagement to the Jews of this country, and the international incident is thereby closed," he explained to Roosevelt. Roosevelt consented to this tactic, and afterward Hay was able to inform the press that "there was not a shade of difference" between their views on the matter.

Two days later, he notified Roosevelt that Russian authorities were proceeding "with apparent sincerity and certainly with most energetic severity" to punish the perpetrators of the Kishinev violence. "It is evident," he told the president, "that the protests from the United States, even if they never reach the Czar, have had a very great effect on the minds of the bureaucracy, just as we told our Jewish friends a month ago," adding, "The less we do and say now, and the sooner we get through with it, the better." (In the end, however, most charges were dropped.)

Hay and Roosevelt may have gained only symbolic ground on Kishinev, but their approach—and perhaps the president's anonymous scolding of the Russian government—produced a more concrete result on another front. The day the petition was completed, the Russian Embassy in Washington officially notified Hay that it had no objection to American use and development of two key trading cities, Mukden and Ta-tung-kou, in Manchuria. "It seems like a surrender," Hay wrote Roosevelt, "but they are a strange race, and you may expect anything of them except straightforwardness. If we get Mukden and Ta-tung-kou we win a great victory. . . . Perhaps they thought if they shoved in their memorandum today we would drop the [Kishinev] Petition." Hay was highly dubious of Russia's earnestness, especially once he learned that Russia had not yet informed China of its intent to open Mukden and Ta-tung-kou. But he made sure to publicize the offer, anyway.

The Kishinev petition was delivered to Hay the following day. As anticipated, Russia officially informed the State Department that it would not receive the document if presented to St. Petersburg. The B'nai B'rith and other leaders of the protest were already reconciled to this outcome and were highly appreciative of Hay and Roosevelt for going to the lengths they did. "In every part of the world where Jews are to be found," B'nai B'rith president Leo Levi wrote Hay, "there is thanksgiving because the President and you and the entire American people have championed the cause of the oppressed."

By prearrangement, the petition was bound in leather and placed by Hay in the archives of the State Department. "What inept asses they are," Hay said of the Russians in a letter to Roosevelt. "They would have scored by receiving the petition & pigeon-holing it! I think *you* have scored, as it is. You have done the right thing in the right way, and Jewry seems really grateful. As to our 'good relations' with Russia," he continued, "they will soon come around, and lie to us as volubly as ever."

The Kishinev affair was thus closed, but Manchuria was a sore point that would not heal. Roosevelt, who two months earlier had acknowledged that American military action against Russia over Manchuria was unfeasible and insupportable, now entertained second, more Rooseveltian thoughts. "I have not the slightest objection to the Russians knowing that I feel thoroughly aroused and irritated at their conduct in Manchuria," he replied to Hay, "[and] that I don't intend to give way and that I am year by year growing more confident that this country would back me in going to an extreme in the matter."

Hay wrote back with uncharacteristic fierceness: "Four years of constant conflict with [the Russians] have shown me that you cannot let up a moment on them without danger to your midriff. The bear that *talks* like a man is more to be watched than Adam Zad"—a reference to Kipling's Adam-zad, "the bear that walks like a man." Upon reflection, Hay was now glad that Roosevelt had made his aggressive "reverse of friendly" remark about Russia earlier in the summer. "The statement of July 1 was a notice that our patience was becoming exhausted, and, I have no doubt, it hastened their declaration of 'honorable intentions' in Manchuria," he told the president. "Of course I do not wish to exaggerate the value of their professions. There is a lot of pressure and patience needed yet. But I felt that time has come to take them at their word, and to announce to the world their engagements and our belief in their sincerity. Every such incident makes future treachery more difficult for them."

And for once, Hay did not counsel Roosevelt to walk softly. "I am greatly interested in what you say about the country backing you in 'extremes.' I have always regarded it as a handicap to us in our negotiations that the country would *not* stand for an extreme policy. . . . But your judgment in popular currents is better than mine and if you are right, this would be a trump card to play, in some moment of crisis."

They both sensed that war over Manchuria was imminent, as animosity between Russia and Japan escalated. And as their exchange of letters revealed, Russia's fears that the United States might take a stand with Japan were justified. "I am beginning to have scant patience with Adam Zad," Roosevelt again wrote Hay. "I wish, in Manchuria, to go to the very limit I think our people will stand. If only we were sure that neither France nor Germany would join in [with Russia], I should not in the least mind going to 'extremes.'"

ON JULY 17, HAY departed for the Fells. "Everything seems in fair trim," he wrote to Roosevelt, "but I am as stale as a remainder biscuit." As was his habit, he sagged for the first week or so, but gradually the scenery worked its medicine. "This country is surpassingly beautiful just now; a green so deep and yet so brilliant I find nowhere else," he told Roosevelt. Ten days later he wrote Whitelaw Reid, "We are enjoying long tramps by day and birchwood fires by night, and dreading the day of return to Washington."

On August 17, the arcadian tableau was disturbed by a note from Alvey Adee, who was minding the State Department for the summer: The Colombian Senate had rejected the Hay-Herrán Treaty. The Panama canal, which Hay had been digging, diplomatically speaking, for the past three years, now seemed farther away than ever.

The following day, Adee shared with Hay a memorandum submitted to him by a Mr. John Crawford, a man who evidently grasped the situation in Panama better than most. "If report of rejection of the Hay-Herrán Canal Treaty by Colombia's Congress be true," the memo advised, "I believe that State of Panama will secede and declare its independence and offer route to the United States." Thinking ahead, Adee observed: "Such a scheme could, of course, have no countenance from us—our policy before the world should stand, like Mrs. Caesar, without suspicion.

Neither could we undertake to recognize and protect Panama as an independent state, like a second Texas."

Crawford was dead right and Adee only half right. Within three months, Panama would declare its independence, and Hay and Roosevelt, working in concert, would countenance secession every step of the way.

CHAPTER 19

Color of Right

Throughout the spring and summer of 1903, the newly appointed American minister to Bogotá, Arthur Beaupré, had warned Washington that popular sentiment toward the Hay-Herrán Treaty was devolving from approbation to suspicion to opposition and finally to "bitter hostility." On June 20, José Manuel Marroquín, the acting (officially vice) president of Colombia, called a session of congress, after a hiatus of five years, to consider ratification of the treaty. But Marroquín, who had seized power by way of a coup, was now an old man encircled by a spiteful opposition looking for the opportunity to oust him. Originally an advocate of the Panama treaty, he now wavered before the scowls of his detractors.

Colombians, only just recovering from a ruinous civil war, seized upon the canal as a referendum on national honor. Yet few in Colombia had a full appreciation of the resolve of the American government to build a canal—a canal not necessarily in Colombian territory. "It is entirely impossible to convince these people," Beaupré advised Hay in May, "that the Nicaragua route was ever seriously considered by the United States; that the negotiations concerning it had any other motive than the squeezing of an advantageous bargain out of Colombia; nor that any other than the Panama route ever will be selected."

Without question, Colombians badly desired a canal in Panama. They just wanted a better deal—"less scorn for our sovereignty" and "pecuniary advantages much greater than those offered," the waffling Marroquín advised Tomás Herrán. Colombia was now insisting upon a hefty chunk—one quarter or even half—of the $40 million the United States had agreed to pay the Compagnie Nouvelle; it was even considering voiding the French company's concession altogether and taking the entire $40 million for itself. And instead of accepting $10 million from the United States, as stipulated in the treaty, Colombia now wanted $15 million. Nearly every article of Hay-Herrán was challenged anew—from American rights to the Panama Railroad to sanitary regulations in the proposed canal zone.

Hay had stood about enough. On June 9, he cabled a stern message to Beaupré that he wished passed on to Colombia's new minister of foreign affairs, Luis Carlos Rico. If Colombia should reject the treaty or unduly delay its ratification, Hay declared, relations with the United States "would be so seriously compromised that action might be taken by Congress next winter which every friend of Colombia would regret." Beaupré communicated Hay's ultimatum just as the Colombian Congress convened, and when it was read to the Senate, the effect was incendiary. "Construed by many as a threat of direct retaliation," Beaupré wired Washington.

Hay was not the only one who had lost patience with negotiations. On June 13, four days after Hay transmitted his advisory to Bogotá, Philippe Bunau-Varilla sent Marroquín a more reasoned but hardly more subtle warning of his own. "[T]he only party that can now build a Panama Canal is the United States," he wrote from Paris. Failure to ratify the Hay-Herrán Treaty would lead Colombia over one of two precipices: "construction of Nicaragua Canal and absolute loss to Colombia . . . or construction of Panama Canal after secession and declaration of independence of the Isthmus of Panama under protection of the United States." Either one of these choices, Bunau-Varilla admonished Marroquín, "would be equivalent to stabbing your country to the heart."

Meanwhile, William Nelson Cromwell, counsel for the Compagnie Nouvelle, was applying his own influence. He had informants in Bogotá and Panama and ready access to key members of the Senate, including Mark Hanna, John Spooner, and the chairman of the Foreign Relations Committee, Shelby Cullom. He also gained the ear of the State Department. "Secretary Hay honored us with his confidence," was how Cromwell later put it. One of the ways Cromwell won this confidence was by drafting a lengthy memorandum, transmitted under Hay's name, that laid out the legal argument for why Colombia was unjustified in exacting tribute for the transfer of the canal company's concession to the United States. Going further, Cromwell exhorted Hay to keep up the pressure on Marroquín. "*The Marroquín Government has become subdued, non-aggressive and apprehensive of dethronement,*" he advised the secretary in June, with italic emphasis. "I think Marroquín must be *forced* to make a definite stand of *recommendation* in support of the Treaty."

Cromwell also had access to the president. The day before writing to Hay about Marroquín, Cromwell and Roosevelt had talked privately for more than two hours, sharing what proved to be compatible views on Panama. A silky propagandist as well as an adroit attorney, Cromwell left the White House and promptly offered a synopsis of the conversation to a reporter from the *New York World.* The headline in the next morning's paper said plenty: "New Republic May Arise to Grant Canal . . . The State of Panama Ready to Secede If the Treaty Is Rejected by the Colombian Congress . . . Roosevelt Said to Encourage the Idea . . . Bound to Have Panama Route."

Marroquín and the Colombian Congress felt the heat only remotely, thanks to the usual spastic telegraph service between Bogotá and the outside. On July 9, Beaupré informed Hay that Colombia was proposing amendments to the treaty, asking for still more millions. Hay received Beaupré's message three days later and immediately wrote back, rejecting the changes. This cable inexplicably took twenty-five days to reach Bogotá. While he waited for word from Washington, Beaupré, who did not speak Spanish, acted on his own initiative and informed the Colombian foreign minister that any modification of the treaty was tantamount to rejection. To his relief, Hay eventually backed him to the hilt.

Even after the Colombian Senate finally voted down the Hay-Herrán

Treaty on August 12, Beaupré wired that the Colombians might yet come to their senses. By then, however, the administration was already weighing the alternatives, as evidenced by remarks made by Senator Cullom. Following a visit to Oyster Bay on the day Roosevelt learned of the canal treaty's rejection, Cullom divulged to the *New York Herald*: "'Well, we may make another treaty, not with Colombia, but with Panama.'" When pressed further, the senator mentioned that there was "'great discontent on the isthmus over the action of the [Colombian] Congress . . . and Panama might break away and set up a government which we could treat with.'" Would the United States encourage such a schism? "No, I suppose not," Cullom replied. "But this country wants to build that canal and build it now."

Hay was thinking much the same. Although he had never voiced a strong preference for either route, Panama or Nicaragua, he had invested an enormous amount of time and reputation in the Spooner Act and the Hay-Herrán Treaty. Besides which, the president (not to mention Cromwell) was keen for Panama, and so Hay was now on board as well. Yet, while his disgust for the Colombians was as great as Roosevelt's—at one point he called them "greedy little anthropoids"—his nature was to counsel circumspection. "I would come at once to Oyster Bay to get your orders," Hay wrote Roosevelt on the sixteenth, after word of the Colombian Senate's vote had reached New Hampshire, "but I am sure there is nothing to be done for the moment. You will, before our Congress meets [in December], make up your mind which of the two courses you will take, the simple and easy Nicaragua solution, or the far more difficult and multifurcate scheme, of building the Panama Canal *malgré* Bogotá."

Roosevelt wanted to heed Hay's advice. "The one thing evident is to do nothing at present," the president answered from Sagamore Hill. On the other hand, he wondered, "If under the treaty of 1846 we have a color of right to start in and build the canal, my off-hand judgment would favor such proceeding. . . . I do not think that the Bogotá lot of jack rabbits should be allowed permanently to bar one of the future highways of civilization. Of course under the terms of the [Spooner] Act we could now go ahead with Nicaragua and perhaps would technically be required to do so. But what we do now will be of consequence, not merely decades, but centuries hence, and we must be sure we are taking the right step before we act."

Roosevelt's reference to the 1846 treaty and America's "color of right" to build a canal in Panama came from a memorandum prepared for the State Department by Columbia University professor John Bassett Moore, a highly respected scholar of international law. The 1846 treaty between the United States and Colombia (formerly New Granada) guaranteed, among other things, "that the right of way or transit across the Isthmus of Panama upon any modes of communication that now exist, or that may be hereafter constructed, shall be free and open to the Government and citizens of the United States." Moore argued that this clause put the United States "in a position to demand that it shall be allowed to construct the great means of transit which the treaty was chiefly designed to assure." Moore's memo was a purely legal analysis, making no mention of military recourse or resolution. He did, however, preface the memo with a quotation from former Secretary of State Lewis Cass on the subject of a transoceanic canal. "Sovereignty has its duties as well as its rights," Cass had asserted, and no government ought to be permitted "to close these gates of intercourse . . . and justify the act by the pretension that these avenues of trade and travel belong to them."

Roosevelt forwarded Moore's memo to Hay, who recognized its strengths as well as its limitations. "It . . . would be useful in case you should decide to build the canal without Colombian leave," Hay acknowledged. More realistically, "The fact that our position, in that case, would be legal and just, might not greatly impress"—here he borrowed Roosevelt's epithet—"the jack-rabbit mind. I do not believe we could *faire valoir* our rights in that way without war—which would, of course be brief and inexpensive. . . . The Spooner law gives you a 'reasonable time' to make a treaty with Colombia. It is for you to decide what time is reasonable."

Indeed, the United States had not yet received formal notification from the Colombian government that the canal treaty had been rejected. Hay and Roosevelt would wait until then, or until September 22, when the treaty would expire by its own predetermined timetable. "We are in no danger and in no hurry—we can bide our hour," Hay wrote the president.

But he did decide to interrupt his vacation, stopping by Oyster Bay for several hours on his way to Washington on August 28. Afterward, either he or Roosevelt talked to the *Herald*. Under the headline "Canal Troubles May Lead to War," the paper reported that the treaty was "probably dead" and that Colombia's demand for more money was "blackmail." The administration was weighing three options. The first was to invoke the 1846 treaty, "ignore Colombia," and build the Panama canal, even if the United States had to "fight Colombia, if she objects, and create the independent government of Panama." Second choice was Nicaragua. Third was to wait until "something inspired to make Colombia see the light" and then negotiate a new treaty. The article also mentioned that "[p]ersons interested in getting the $40,000,000 for the Panama Canal Company"—presumably Cromwell, et al.—"are of course eager that this government shall go ahead and seize the property, even though it leads to war." The Roosevelt administration, however, pledged to "move with care."

In Panama, news of the treaty's likely demise brought both despair and urgency: despair that the canal would not be built across the isthmus; urgency to set in motion a plan to cast off Colombian rule and sign a Panamanian version of the treaty. The conspiracy was germinated by José Agustín Arango, who was both an attorney for the Panama Railroad and a senator from the Department of Panama. Arango discussed his scheme with a trusted friend, James Beers, a freight agent for the railroad who was also on good terms with William Nelson Cromwell. Whether Beers went to the United States at Arango's behest or was summoned by Cromwell is subject to debate; either way, he arrived in New York in early June and received assurances from Cromwell that he would "go the limit" in support of the Panama revolution. Cromwell sent Beers home to Panama, armed with a codebook to be used in further communications.

Back in Panama, Arango put together a junta that included his sons, sons-in-law, and Manuel Amador, a distinguished physician to the Panama Railroad. Late in July, shortly before Beers's return, Arango arranged a luncheon at which he sounded out a number of Panamanians whose cooperation or, at the very least, acquiescence would be crucial to the success of a revolution. Several Americans were also invited: the assistant superintendent of the Panama Railroad; three officers of the Army Corps of Engineers; the U.S. consul-general for Panama; and, last but not least, J. Gabriel Duque, the influential and mercurial impresario of the Panama *Star and Herald.* When Beers returned from the United States on August 4, he told Arango of Cromwell's vow of support; and when word arrived eight days later of the Colombian Senate's rejection of the treaty, the junta's course was set.

How much Hay and Roosevelt knew of the conspiracy will never be determined absolutely. The extent to which they condoned, encouraged, or abetted the plot is a larger question still. What can be said for certain is that over the next three months—between mid-August, when the treaty with Colombia fell apart, and early November, when the revolution erupted—the affair in Panama turned out rather better than Hay and Roosevelt expected, and not too differently from what they hoped for.

On September 1, Dr. Amador, one of the three leaders of the junta and soon to be the first president of an independent Panama, arrived in the United States to firm up Cromwell's promise to underwrite the revolution and, if possible, to gain firsthand assurance from Hay and Roosevelt that the United States would follow through on pledges intimated in the press and confirmed by Cromwell. For secrecy's sake, Cromwell was given the code name "W"; Hay was "X."

Aboard the same ship with Amador was Gabriel Duque, supposedly on a routine business trip. Amador, for obvious reasons, attempted to keep a low profile in America. Duque, though, had better cover and also better entrée. In New York, he met with Cromwell, who, after discussing ways to finance the junta, placed a long-distance call to Hay to arrange an appointment for Duque. The Panamanian intriguer hurried to the capital and saw Hay on September 3.

For two hours, Duque laid out the plot as it was taking shape in Panama and solicited the support of the administration. According to testimony later given to Congress by a correspondent for the *New York World* (a roundabout corroboration, to be sure), Hay told Duque that the government would not commit to direct assistance but assured him that the United States intended to build the Panama canal and "did not purpose to permit Colombia's standing in the way." Hay is also said to have pledged to Duque that, if the revolutionaries took control of Panama City on the Pacific and Colón on the Atlantic, then the United States would step in to prevent Colombian troops from disturbing the transit across the isthmus.

Three days later, Hay wrote a newsy letter to Roosevelt, who was still at Oyster Bay, bringing him up to date on various foreign matters—a forthcoming treaty with China and a disagreement with the Sultan of Turkey that had put the Mediterranean squadron on alert. The letter also covered Colombia and the canal but said nothing of Hay's meeting with Duque, other than to comment: "Just how much of an attempt at insurrection they will make in Panama can hardly be foreseen at this moment, but some sort of movement is clearly indicated."

Duque was less discreet. Calculating that Hay's promise (if that was what it was) of support for the revolution might persuade Colombia to embrace the canal treaty at last, he blabbed his entire conversation with Hay to Tomás Herrán, the Colombian minister in Washington. The next day, Herrán cabled Bogotá: "Revolutionary agents of Panama here. . . . If treaty is not approved by September 22, it is probable there will be a revolution with American support."

Later that same day, Herrán wrote the Colombian consul in New York: "Yesterday Mr. J. G. Duque, editor and proprietor of the Star and Herald, had a long interview with the Secretary of State, and I understand that the plan for a revolution which he brought with him has been well received by the Government here." Alerted by Duque of Amador's presence in the country, Herrán hired private detectives to track Amador's movements and wrote Cromwell to warn him that Colombia would hold him accountable for his role in any schemes of secession.

Herrán also wanted to be sure that Bogotá understood the increasingly "hostile attitude" that Roosevelt bore toward Colombia. He called attention to "threatening statements which [Roosevelt] has uttered in private conversations, and which by indirect means have come to my knowledge. . . . President Roosevelt is a decided partisan of the Panama route, and hopes to begin excavation of the canal during his administration. Your Excellency [Secretary of Foreign Affairs Rico] already knows the vehement character of the President, and you are aware of the persistence and decision with which he pursues anything to which he may be committed."

EXPOSED BY DUQUE AND with detectives on his tail, Amador had trouble promoting the Panamanian cause. Cromwell welcomed him initially but then shunned him, once Herrán became wise to the doctor's intent. Amador no longer had any chance of gaining an audience with the secretary of state or president.

His prospects brightened, however, when Bunau-Varilla arrived from France on September 22. In Bunau-Varilla's room at the Waldorf-Astoria, Amador filled the Frenchman in on the junta's plan for Panamanian rebellion. He advised him that Panama's new governor, José Domingo de Obaldía, favored secession; he also testified to the weakness of the Colombian garrison on the isthmus. "A revolution would today meet with no obstacle," Amador vouched to Bunau-Varilla—but only if the rebels could keep additional Colombian troops from landing. The ever confident Bunau-Varilla told Amador that it had been a mistake to put his faith in Cromwell but not to despair. Bunau-Varilla, the one true apostle of the Panama canal, would turn their confluent dreams into reality. Amador took heart and sent a one-word telegram to the junta: "Esperanzas"—"Hopes."

Next Bunau-Varilla had a talk with John Bassett Moore in New York. The French engineer and the American professor were in complete agreement on "the right of transit" interpretation of the 1846 treaty. While Moore had been preparing his memorandum for Roosevelt and Hay, Bunau-Varilla had published a remarkably similar article in a newspaper he co-owned with his brother, *Le Matin*, declaring that "nobody could blame President Roosevelt . . . for employing force to obtain what is guaranteed by formal treaty and what he is unable to obtain by good-will." Moore had recently dined with Roosevelt and was able to assure Bunau-Varilla of the president's partiality to their line of reasoning. For Bunau-Varilla, all the pieces were falling into place. A week later he boarded a train for Washington.

Though the deadline for the expiration of the Hay-Herrán Treaty had now come and gone, Hay and Roosevelt were still mulling their options. "It is altogether likely that there will be an insurrection on the Isthmus against that regime of folly and graft that now rules at Bogotá," Hay advised Roosevelt. The choice was whether to wait out the revolution or to "take a hand in rescuing the Isthmus from anarchy." Last, almost as an afterthought, he mentioned the Nicaragua option.

By early October, Roosevelt was close to a decision. "I think it well worth considering whether we had not better warn these cat-rabbits [in Bogotá] that great though our patience has been, it can be exhausted," he confided to Senator Hanna. "I feel we are certainly justified in morals, and therefore justified in law, under the treaty of 1846, in interfering summarily and saying that the canal is to be built and that they must not stop it." Publicly, though, he still hedged. "As yet, the people of the United States are not willing to take the ground of building the canal by force," he told Albert Shaw, editor of the *Review of Reviews*.

On October 10, Bunau-Varilla, through his friendship with one of Hay's assistant secretaries of state, Francis Loomis, gained a brief interview with Roosevelt. Both men recollected the conversation a decade later, with slight variations. Roosevelt had Bunau-Varilla broaching the subject of revolution in Panama; Bunau-Varilla said Roosevelt brought it up first. When Bunau-Varilla asked the president if the United States would prevent Colombian troops from landing, Roosevelt claimed he replied that he could not commit. When Bunau-Varilla pressed Roosevelt further, Roosevelt recalled stating, "All I can say is that Colombia by her action has forfeited any claim upon the U.S. and I have no use for a government that would do what that government has done." According to Bunau-Varilla, Roosevelt then asked his visitor what made him so certain that a revolution was coming. Bunau-Varilla answered enigmatically, "General and special circumstances."

With knowing looks, the conversation concluded. Bunau-Varilla left the White House, believing that "[i]f a revolution were to generate new conditions favourable to the acquisition of the Canal zone by the United States, President Roosevelt would immediately seize the opportunity. I was henceforth certain of this capital point, as certain as if a solemn contract had been signed between us."

Later that same day, Roosevelt wrote again to Shaw of the *Review of Reviews*: "I cast aside the proposition made at this time to foment the secession of Panama. Whatever other governments can do, the United States cannot go into the securing by such underhand means, the secession." Then, with Bunau-Varilla fresh in his mind, he volunteered: "I freely say to you that I should be delighted if Panama were an independent State, or if it made itself so at this moment."

A week later, Bunau-Varilla was introduced to John Hay at the State Department. When their talk was interrupted, Hay invited Bunau-Varilla to stop in at Lafayette Square at the end of the day so that they might discuss Panama more freely. "I had always imagined him as severe and cold, a sort of 'Iron Chancellor' of America," Bunau-Varilla wrote. "How different he was when he doffed his outside armour!"

As they talked over tea, Bunau-Varilla discovered that he had a great deal in common with Hay's "delicate and refined mind." They both believed in the betterment of "the moral and physical condition of man" and, more specifically, "the opening of the Panama Canal [as] the greatest service which could be rendered to the human family." Bunau-Varilla told Hay of the impending revolution and urged the United States to be vigilant. Hay assured Bunau-Varilla, "[W]e shall not be caught napping"— although these are Bunau-Varilla's words, not Hay's. Hay purportedly also informed Bunau-Varilla that orders had already been given for the U.S. Navy to dispatch ships to Panama.

Bunau-Varilla's narrative cannot be substantiated, for Hay made no record of the meeting. At the very least, Bunau-Varilla compressed chronology; for orders directing naval forces to sail for Panama were not issued until several days *after* Bunau-Varilla left Washington. But sail they did.

Yet Bunau-Varilla offered another anecdote from his visit with Hay that has a ring of authenticity, given Hay's literary penchants and the fact that the meeting took place in his well-appointed library. As their conversation took a more general turn, Hay mentioned that he had just finished reading his friend Richard Harding Davis's latest novel, *Captain Macklin*, which, it just so happened, was about an American mercenary who joins up with a French army officer to overthrow a corrupt Central American country—in this case Honduras.

Hay presented the book to Bunau-Varilla. "[I]t will interest you," he said. Bunau-Varilla took the gesture as a signal. "I could not help thinking that Mr. Hay, in giving this volume, had meant to make a subtle allusion in my efforts in the cause of justice and progress."

(Never mind that Davis calls the Honduran revolution a "fake," orchestrated by a New York steamship company, and that during the fighting Macklin comes to learn that "there's very few revolutions down here that haven't got a money-making scheme at the bottom of them.")

"Perhaps he wished to go even further," Bunau-Varilla speculated. "Did he not intend thus to make me understand that he had the presentiment of the personal part I was playing, and which I had not revealed to him? Did he not wish to tell me symbolically that he had understood that the revolution in preparation for the victory of the Idea, was taking shape under my direction?"

Whatever Hay had meant by *Captain Macklin*, Bunau-Varilla left Lafayette Square with all doubts banished. "Notwithstanding Mr. Hay's silence, I knew all," he wrote. "It only remained for me to act. The United States would have a military force in the neighborhood of the Canal if revolution broke out."

Back in New York, Bunau-Varilla called Amador to the Waldorf-Astoria and painstakingly prepped him for the mission ahead. ("Room No. 1162 . . . deserves to be considered as the cradle of the Panama Republic," Bunau-Varilla later declared.) The diligent engineer had thought of everything: he presented Amador with an outline of military operations, a declaration of independence, a constitution, and even a Panamanian flag sewn by Bunau-Varilla's wife. He assured Amador that the United States would intervene within forty-eight hours of the proclamation of a new republic and guaranteed $100,000 for the cause. And finally he drew up a cable for Amador to send once the glorious deed was accomplished, naming Bunau-Varilla minister plenipotentiary "in order to obtain the recognition of the Republic and signature of Canal Treaty." When Amador protested this last detail, suggesting that such an honor ought to be reserved for a Panamanian and not a Frenchman, Bunau-Varilla held firm. "A battle royal will be fought at Washington," he forecast. "Let him wage it who is best equipped to win the victory."

Amador sailed for Panama on October 20, the new flag wrapped around his midriff beneath his shirt. He expected to land at Colón on the twenty-seventh. Bunau-Varilla had given him until November 3 to ignite the revolution.

Just before leaving the United States, Amador mailed a letter to his son, an American army doctor: "The plan seems to me good. A portion of the Isthmus declares itself independent and that portion the United States will not allow any Colombian forces to attack. An assembly is called, and this gives authority to a minister to be appointed by the new Government in order to make a treaty without need of ratification by that assembly. The treaty being approved by both parties, the new Republic remains under the protection of the United States. . . . In 30 days everything will be concluded."

The revolution happened almost exactly this way—except that, instead of thirty days, it took only seventeen.

HAY HAD PLENTY ELSE to think about besides Panama. With the help of his trusted China adviser, William Rockhill, and Edwin Conger in Peking, he was close to completing a commercial treaty with China that would open the Manchurian capital of Mukden and the port of Antung, at the mouth of the Yalu River, to American trade and consulships. The result would give the United States essentially the same privileges in Manchuria held by Russia. The treaty was to be signed on October 8, the day Russia had promised to withdraw its troops.

Rockhill, Conger, the Chinese, the Japanese—all of them doubted that Russia would honor its commitment; but Hay held his tongue. "I agreed, beforehand," he told Adee, "that we can fight Russian aggression in Manchuria better after our treaty is signed than we can now." Conger and Prince Ch'ing of China put their names to the treaty on October 8, on schedule. Russia pronounced the initiative "a Trojan horse," designed to put the United States in position to aid Japan's interests in Korea. Not unexpectedly, Russia did not recall its troops.

Hay fidgeted all day, waiting for the cable from Peking. "This is the day of Fate," he wrote Clara, who was again visiting grandchildren. In the afternoon he took the Brazilian ambassador in to see the president, then went for a carriage ride in Rock Creek Park. Finally a messenger delivered the good news. "Hooray," he wrote Clara, "the treaty is signed." It was his sixty-fifth birthday.

Home alone, Hay did what he had not done in a long while: he wrote to Lizzie Cameron, who for the past two years had been living in Europe. Henry Adams had seen her, but Hay had not. Nor, it seems, had he and Lizzie corresponded. "It has been—as I reckon—fourteen thousand years since I have heard from you," he began. "Other people, happier though no more deserving, see your perfect face and listen to the golden music of your voice, and of course mention it, and fill me with envy." He caught her up with family news and sought her sympathy for his imprisonment in the State Department. "Life has been very dull and gray for the last year or two," he sighed with that mock melodrama he always used with her. "I could never have imagined I would last so long in this place. . . . Now I see no immediate prospect of release." His affection for her was more reserved than in the past, but time and distance had not suppressed it entirely. "[B]itterly as I resent your absence," he declared, "I am sure you have chosen the better part. Every body loves and admires you here—but then that is the habit of people everywhere." And in closing he begged, "Be as good as you are splendid and say Hello."

If she answered, the letter is lost. Three weeks later, he wrote again to express condolences for the death of her nephew: "You will bear it—as you bear everything—with that beautiful strength and fortitude which is peculiar to you; and all we can do is stand by and say we love you and are sorry for you."

HAY HAD TIME FOR another indulgence that October. He wrote to Augustus Saint-Gaudens, asking if the sculptor "could make anything of so philistine and insignificant a head as mine." He apologized for his lack of "profile, size, and every other requisite of sculpture." But, he explained, "I have been an unusual length of time in office and I fear that, after I am dead, if not before, some blacksmith will try to bust me."

Hay well knew that to commission Saint-Gaudens was to enter an august pantheon. The sculptor's catalogue of work had grown to include the magnificent *Standing Lincoln* in Chicago; the heroic *Shaw Memorial* to black soldiers and their white officer in Boston; and the haunting monument to grief that Henry Adams had placed upon his wife's grave in Rock Creek Cemetery. In May, Saint-Gaudens's equestrian statue of Lizzie Cameron's uncle, General William Tecumseh Sherman, had been unveiled in New York. (Family lore holds that the face of Nike, the goddess of victory who leads the general's horse, bears an uncanny resemblance to Sherman's divinely featured niece.)

Saint-Gaudens agreed to try his hand on Hay the following winter. "It is a ruinous expense and folly," Hay wrote to Clara. "It will be ugly but it will be an object of art."

ALL THE WHILE, THOUGH, he kept an eye on Panama. Throughout October, Minister Beaupré did his best to keep the State Department informed on the deliberations, erratic and ineffectual as they were, of the Colombian Congress. On October 19, he cabled Hay that the Colombians were considering sending a special envoy to Washington to renew negotiations on the canal treaty. Hay, plainly exasperated, wired back that if the Colombians believed they could achieve more favorable terms than already agreed upon in the Hay-Herrán Treaty, then Beaupré was to "intimate orally, but not in writing, that it will be useless to send a special envoy."

On October 31, the Colombian Congress adjourned for the year without taking any further action on the canal. Tomás Herrán came to see Hay, looking "most pathetic," Hay told Clara. Herrán mentioned that his predecessor, Carlos Martínez Silva, had died of pneumonia shortly after returning to Colombia. Hay was relieved to hear that Martínez Silva had not been assassinated, as had been rumored. "No," Herrán said to Hay grimly, "but that is what will happen to me when I return."

NEWS FROM PANAMA CAME from several sources, including Gabriel Duque, who was back on the isthmus, eager to share the latest gossip. At the end of September, he informed Hay that Colombian troops were hungry and unpaid. "Now you will see how easy it is to buy these men over."

Roosevelt received higher-grade intelligence from two U.S. Army officers just back from Panama. Captain Chauncey Humphrey and Lieutenant Grayson Murphy, who both understood Spanish, had spent a week on the isthmus, dressed as civilians. On the train from Colón to Panama City, they had overheard Governor Obaldía talking about the coming break with Colombia. They then revealed their identities to members of the junta, who disclosed the extent of their preparations for the overthrow of the Colombian government. Arms were being smuggled into Colón in piano boxes. Señor Duque had formed a "fire brigade" that was really a revolutionary militia. The two officers also took notes that would be useful in the event that the U.S. Army was obliged to occupy the isthmus: details on artillery placement, water supply, locations for camps. All this they reported to a rapt Roosevelt on October 16. Three days later—and three days after Bunau-Varilla's meeting with Hay—the president directed the navy to send warships to within striking distance of Panama, on the Caribbean and Pacific coasts. Roosevelt was in his element—the Philippines and Venezuela reprised.

AMADOR ARRIVED BACK IN Panama on October 27 and was greeted by José Arango and the other members of the junta. Their disappointment was profound and nearly unanimous. They had sent Amador, whom they had already chosen to be the first president of Panama, expecting him to return bearing a firm promise in writing from Hay that the United States would recognize and protect the nascent republic. All Amador brought them was a risky scheme from Bunau-Varilla, a French engineer who owned stock in the Compagnie Nouvelle. Instead of a line of credit for $6 million, which they had hoped for, they got instead Bunau-Varilla's handshake on $100,000, provided the rebellion succeeded. As for the flag that Amador pulled from under his shirt, they hated it—too similar to the Stars and Stripes.

To make matters worse, the following day, Governor Obaldía, who had been living in Amador's house and was now more loyal to the junta than to Bogotá, announced that the Colombian warship *Cartagena*, carrying more than two hundred soldiers, was en route to Colón. Many of the conspirators were ready to call off the revolution.

Amador was not one of them. He took Herbert Prescott, assistant superintendent of the Panama Railroad, into his confidence, and together they sent a desperate telegraph to Bunau-Varilla. The coded message was: "Fate news bad powerful tiger urge vapor Colon," which, using his codebook, Bunau-Varilla ("Fate") translated as Colombian troops arriving ("news") Atlantic side ("bad") in five days ("powerful"); send "vapor" (steamship) to Colón.

With Panama hanging by a thread, Bunau-Varilla raced to Washington and went directly to the house of Assistant Secretary of State Loomis. He told Loomis that a Colombian force was due to land in Panama on November 2 and that he feared a repetition of what had happened in 1885, when a U.S. warship had failed to arrive at Colón in time to prevent Colombian troops from putting down an insurgency and destroying the city.

Loomis gave Bunau-Varilla the time of day but little more. The next morning, Bunau-Varilla, by his "lucky star," encountered Loomis on the street, and this time, so Bunau-Varilla claimed, Loomis told him: "I have thought over what you said to me yesterday. . . . It would be deplorable if the catastrophe of 1885 were to be renewed today." Once again, Bunau-Varilla read between the lines.

He also read the papers. Several days earlier, he had seen in the *New York Sun* that the American cruiser *Dixie*, with four hundred Marines, was en route to Guantánamo, Cuba. Three days later, the *New York Times* mentioned that the *Nashville* had arrived in Kingston, Jamaica, and that, in case of a revolution in Panama, the *Dixie* would be sent to Colón.

On the train north from Washington, Bunau-Varilla made a daring calculation. If Loomis had said what Bunau-Varilla thought he had said, then an American warship was on its way—most likely the *Nashville*; Kingston was only five hundred miles from Colón. Figuring ten knots an hour, plus time to coal and stoke, it would have the *Nashville* arriving in two and a half days. He got off the train in Baltimore and sent Amador a telegram: "All right will reach ton and half"—meaning that the "vapor" would reach Panama in two and a half days.

Bunau-Varilla's hunch had been correct. That same day, Assistant Secretary of the Navy Charles Darling ordered the *Nashville* to proceed at once to Colón and to "telegraph in cipher the situation after consulting the United States Consul. Your destination is a secret." Two days later, Bunau-Varilla was gratified to read in the *New York Times* a dispatch bearing the dateline, Kingston, October 31: "The American cruiser *Nashville* left this morning with sealed orders. Her destination is believed to be Colombia."

Two and a half days: that would be sometime during the evening of November 2. Bunau-Varilla had told Amador to commence the revolution by the third.

THE *NASHVILLE* DROPPED ANCHOR at Colón at 5:30 pm on November 2, almost precisely when Bunau-Varilla had estimated. News of the arrival of the U.S. warship was immediately telegraphed (or possibly telephoned) across the isthmus to Panama City, where the revolution was to begin. The junta and those privy to its intentions drew courage. Amador's trust in Bunau-Varilla had not been misplaced.

But within hours their hopes were dashed. Shortly before midnight, the *Cartagena* arrived in Colón as well, and early the next morning, not two hundred, as had been first reported, but more than four hundred well-drilled Colombian marksmen, led by General Juan Tovar, disembarked at the Panama Railroad wharf and requested immediate transport across the isthmus. They had come to reinforce the garrison at Panama City—which had been diminished a week earlier, when Governor Obaldía deviously dispatched one hundred of its soldiers into the countryside in pursuit of a band of nonexistent insurgents from Nicaragua. Tovar had no way of knowing that General Esteban Huertas, the commander of the remaining Panama garrison, had already agreed not to intervene in the event of organized insurrection. Huertas's price was $50,000, with $40 promised to each of his men.

Upon learning of the *Cartagena's* imminent arrival, the White House ordered Commander John Hubbard of the *Nashville* to "[m]aintain free and uninterrupted transit. . . . Government forces reported approaching the Isthmus in vessels. Prevent their landing if in your judgment this would precipitate a conflict." Under the "color of right," Roosevelt had tipped his hand in favor of the junta. But through a mix-up in the American consulate, the telegram was not given to Hubbard until the Colombian *tiradores* were ashore and forming up at the rail depot. For the moment, the navy's hands were tied.

Into the breech stepped James Shaler, superintendent of the Panama

Railroad. Like all railroad managers in Panama, Shaler answered to New York and was collusively entangled in the junta's plot (which was of course the railroad's and the canal company's plot as well). Before the *Cartagena* appeared at Colón, Shaler had shrewdly sent nearly all the rolling stock across the isthmus, keeping on hand only a special (and intentionally short) train in which he now offered to convey General Tovar and his retinue of aides to Panama City. The soldiers could follow later. (For them to march across fifty miles of jungle was unthinkable.)

Reluctantly, Tovar accepted Shaler's hospitality, and the train left Colón at 9 am, arriving in Panama City shortly before noon. For the rest of the day, Shaler found one reason after another for refusing transport to the rest of the Colombian troops: fares had to be paid in advance; travel on credit required the signature of the governor, who was in Panama City—as were Shaler's trains.

Commander Hubbard, who at last had received and deciphered his orders to maintain free and open transit and to occupy the railroad if need be, anxiously eyed the four hundred Colombian soldiers gathered about the terminal. Dutifully he wired the secretary of the navy—and thus the White House—that the Colombians were already ashore but that there had been no disturbances. "It is possible that movement may be made tonight at Panama [City] to declare independence," he stated. "Situation is most critical if revolutionary leaders act."

FIFTY MILES AWAY, THE revolution came off with hardly a scuffle. Upon arrival in Panama City, General Tovar and his officers were greeted most cordially by the governor and a delegation of leading citizens. The Colombian garrison and a detachment of police—already in the pocket of the junta—stood at attention in the plaza. Also on hand to welcome the general was Felix Ehrman, the American vice consul, who was thoroughly clued in to the charade. Elsewhere in the city, Duque's fire brigade was armed and ready.

It is impossible to say which of the many interested observers in Panama was keeping Washington posted—most likely more than one—but he or they did their job too well, for at 3:45 pm, Assistant Secretary of State Loomis telegraphed the consulate in Panama City: "Uprising at

Isthmus reported. Keep department promptly and fully informed." In the years to come, these ten words would be cited as evidence that the White House was in on the revolution ahead of time; more fairly it serves as an indication of just how leaky the situation was in Panama. Ehrman was not taken aback by Loomis's prematurity but could only reply: "No uprising yet."

Originally, Amador and his co-conspirators had called for the revolution to take place at 8 pm. But by six o'clock, General Huertas's garrison had surrendered and General Tovar and his staff were under arrest, along with Governor Obaldía, the latter as a formality. At 8:17 pm, a telegram arrived at the State Department addressed to "His Excellency Secretary Hay." No longer was there a need for secret code. It read: "Isthmus Independence proclaimed without bloodshed. Canal treaty saved. Amador."

By pre-agreement of the junta, Amador was not named to the council that declared itself the provisional government of the Republic of Panama. That honor went to José Augustín Arango, Federico Boyd, and Tomás Arias. One of the first acts of the council was to telegraph railroad superintendent Shaler in Colón, strongly urging him to continue denying transport for the Colombian soldiers. A public meeting was called for the next day in Panama City to present the declaration of independence. The flag that Bunau-Varilla's wife had made was replaced. Amador's election to the presidency would follow once independence was fully secured.

The day did not end without a few fireworks. Shortly after the telegram was sent to Shaler, the Colombian gunboat *Bogotá* opened fire on Panama City, more in protest than for effect. The bombardment ended after a half-dozen shells fell in the city, and then the *Bogotá* withdrew to an offshore island. The only casualties were a Chinese man and a donkey.

Meanwhile lights burned in the new West Wing, where word of the near-bloodless revolution was met with cautious relief. An hour or so after Amador's telegram was delivered to Hay, another from Vice Consul Ehrman came in, confirming the successful uprising and the establishment of a new government, but also advising that four hundred Colombian troops were still staging at Colón.

President Roosevelt had been in New York to vote in the November 3 election and arrived back at the White House at around 9 pm. Both Secretary of War Root and Navy Secretary Moody were away, but Hay, Loomis, and Assistant Navy Secretary Darling were on hand. After they quickly briefed Roosevelt on the events of the previous twenty-four hours, Darling wrote a telegram to Commander Hubbard of the *Nashville* which he prayed would be delivered on time: "In the interest of peace make every effort to prevent Government troops at Colon from proceeding to Panama [City]. The transit of the Isthmus must be kept open and order maintained." Warships in the Caribbean and Pacific were ordered to make steam toward Panama; the *Dixie* was already on its way.

With that, they all went home to await the next day's developments. Bunau-Varilla grabbed what rest he could on the overnight train to Washington.

A TENSE TWO DAYS followed. While the provisional council was announcing the birth of the Republic of Panama, across the isthmus on the Caribbean, the city of Colón remained under Colombian control. Throughout the day and evening of November 3, Shaler, Hubbard, U.S. Consul Oscar Malmros, and Chief of Police Porfirio Meléndez conspired to keep the increasingly impatient *tiradores* at bay and uninformed. But by the next morning, once Commander Hubbard issued formal orders forbidding transport of troops across the isthmus, the secret could no longer be kept from the Colombians and their commanding officer, Colonel Eliseo Torres.

Torres flew into a rage and declared that if General Tovar and the other Colombians held prisoner in Panama City were not released by 2 pm, he would open fire on Colón and "kill every United States citizen in the place." Any doubts of the Colombians' resolve to hold the city vanished when the *Cartagena* weighed anchor and steamed over the horizon, leaving the soldiers with no immediate way to withdraw.

With a showdown seemingly inevitable, Hubbard held his ground. First, he put American women and children aboard two docked steamers; he had the men barricade themselves in a stone shed belonging to the railroad. At 1:30 pm, a half-hour before the Colombian deadline, he put ashore a landing party of forty-four Marines. The *Nashville* then got under way and steamed back and forth along the waterfront, guns loaded with shrapnel.

Two o'clock came and went, and over the next hour and a half, Americans and Colombians stared down one another's barrels—ten Colombian riflemen for every Marine. At 3:15 pm, Colonel Torres broke the standoff and approached the Americans with a proposition: he would withdraw his troops on orders from General Tovar. Mostly to buy time, Shaler, Police Chief Meléndez, and Consul Malmros consented to send an envoy to Panama City, conveying Torres's request. While they waited, the *Nashville*'s landing party agreed to return to the ship, and the Colombians said they would make camp outside the city.

Early the next morning, Torres and his men were back at the railyard, awaiting orders from Tovar. In Panama City, Amador and the other leaders of the revolution recognized that their republic still hung in the balance. Amador met with Tovar and impressed upon him that the movement had the enthusiastic support of the United States and that no more Colombian troops would ever be allowed to disembark on Panamanian soil. Still, Tovar would not capitulate, and he refused to issue orders for the soldiers in Colón to stand down.

While Amador was working on Tovar, back in Colón, Superintendent Shaler and Chief Meléndez were working on Torres, who had sworn in writing that he would rather "perish in the flames of this city" than withdraw or surrender. With still no directive from his general and presented with Shaler's assurance that five thousand American Marines were on their way to the isthmus, he at last softened. And for $8,000, paid in $20 gold pieces by Shaler from the safe of the Panama Railroad, Torres dissolved entirely.

Shortly after six o'clock in the evening, he and his four hundred fearsome *tiradores* began boarding the Royal Mail Company packet *Orinoco*. At 6:20 pm, the *Dixie*, carrying four hundred Marines, hove into view. An hour later, as the ten-gun American cruiser swung at her anchor abreast the *Nashville*, the *Orinoco* was already steaming toward Colombia. The battle for Panama was over before it began.

•   •   •

Things were not going quite so smoothly for Bunau-Varilla. When he arrived in Washington on the morning of the fourth, Colón was still up for grabs, though the news out of Panama City was encouraging. As far as the Roosevelt administration was concerned, there was yet no Republic of Panama; nor, for that matter, had Amador sent a telegram naming Bunau-Varilla minister plenipotentiary. After a short visit with Loomis (Hay was unavailable), Bunau-Varilla returned to New York, where a telegram awaited him from Amador that still did not mention diplomatic accreditation but urgently requested $100,000. Slightly piqued, Bunau-Varilla decided to send $25,000. That night, a dispatch signed by the Panamanian provisional council of Arango, Boyd, and Arias reached the State Department, announcing the appointment of Bunau-Varilla as "confidential agent" of the republic.

At the cabinet meeting on the morning of November 6, Hay relayed a batch of promising telegrams. Consul Malmros reported the departure of the Colombian troops and the arrival of the *Dixie*. From Panama City, the triumvirate of Arango, Boyd, and Arias proudly announced: "Colon and all the towns of the isthmus have adhered to the declaration of independence proclaimed in this city. The authority of the Republic of Panama is obeyed throughout the territory." Vice Consul Ehrman seconded this assessment: "The situation here is peaceful. Isthmian movement has obtained, so far, success." Ehrman also confirmed that Bunau-Varilla at last had been named envoy extraordinary and minister plenipotentiary.

Roosevelt, Hay, and the rest of the cabinet decided not to wait any longer. When their meeting ended at noon, Hay drafted a telegram to be sent to Malmros and Ehrman: "The people of Panama have, by an apparently unanimous movement, dissolved their political connections with the Republic of Colombia and resumed their independence. When you are satisfied that a de facto government, republican in form and without substantial opposition from its own people, has been established in the State of Panama, you will enter into relations with it as the responsible Government of the territory."

As ever, Bogotá was tardy and out of touch. Ten hours after the administration's hurried recognition of Panama, a telegram arrived from the Marroquín government, beseeching the United States to preserve

Colombian sovereignty in Panama. That the vaunted, oft-cited treaty of 1846, not to mention the signed but unratified Hay-Herrán Treaty, called for the United States to do precisely this seems not to have concerned the secretary of state. No longer Colombia's protector, no longer even neutral, the United States was now the protector of Panama. Elihu Root, returning to Washington a couple of days later, found Hay "as emphatic and free from doubt about our Government's course as our President was." Writing to Clara, Hay was no less resolute. "[T]o make an omelette," he observed, "you must break eggs, and the eggs once broken, they can never be mended again."

Panama was the omelette; Colombia was left with broken eggs. On November 8, a large crowd marched through the streets of Bogotá, shouting for a change of government and throwing stones at Marroquín's house.

THE ULTIMATE OBJECTIVE OF all this nation building and nation breaking was, of course, the construction and control of the Panama Canal. But first Hay's *de facto* recognition of the new republic needed to become *de jure*. Shortly after nine o'clock in the morning on Friday the thirteenth, Bunau-Varilla met Hay at the State Department, where they had their photograph taken. Then, accompanied by Bunau-Varilla's son, they traveled the few short yards to the White House by carriage. In the Blue Room—with its Versailles-inspired mantel and, in deference to the current resident, a bearskin rug on the floor—they were soon joined by Roosevelt. The president and the freshly validated minister exchanged brief but fittingly florid speeches. Bunau-Varilla invoked "the ardent desire to see at last the accomplishment of the heroic enterprise for piercing the mountain barrier of the Andes." Roosevelt, in turn, expressed his hope that Panama would be "the providential instrument of untold benefit to the civilized world, through the opening of a highway of universal commerce."

Afterward, Roosevelt asked Bunau-Varilla what he made of allegations that the two of them had hatched the revolution together. "I think, Mr. President," Bunau-Varilla answered, "that calumny never loses its opportunity even in the New World." Calumny aside, Bunau-Varilla was highly flattered to be regarded as a partner of the American president. And for Roosevelt even to allude to this partnership was to acknowledge something extraordinary—namely, that he had allowed and enabled a foreign agent to shape and guide his policy.

For the time being, however, it wasn't all that important what their relationship had been, or who had manipulated whom. Nor was it an occasion for defensiveness. That would come soon enough. The Republic of Panama was a legal entity in the eyes of the United States, and it could now, Bunau-Varilla hastened to point out, "enter freely into a contract."

Two days later, Hay sent a new treaty to Bunau-Varilla, who was staying around the corner at the New Willard Hotel. Of the twenty-eight articles in the Hay-Herrán Treaty, Hay had significantly altered fifteen. This time around, he was not worried about the approval of Panama, which, after all, was now entirely dependent on the United States for its existence and survival, or of its minister, Bunau-Varilla, who was more closely aligned with American interests than with those of the government to which he was accredited. If there was to be trouble, Hay knew it would likely come from Senator John Tyler Morgan, who still burned a candle for Nicaragua and, despite his lifelong ambition to build a canal *somewhere*, dearly wished to see Roosevelt and the Republicans stumble. And so Hay, instead of dusting off the treaty that had been signed by Tomás Herrán, reached further back to a draft that Morgan had amended in ways so favorable to the United States that Colombia surely would have rejected it—Morgan's cynical ploy to throw the canal to Nicaragua. In this draft, the canal zone was expanded from six miles wide to ten, and Panama City, Colón, and several islands were now added to the zone as well. Instead of sharing legal jurisdiction of the zone, the United States would hold complete authority. The most significant revisions involved sovereignty. The United States did not acknowledge the sovereignty of Panama but claimed for itself absolute sovereignty over the rich corridor of continent it had carved from the new republic.

Hay was satisfied, and he was hopeful that the Senate would be, too. "[Senator Morgan] is as much the author of the present Canal Treaty as I am," he wrote to Henry Pritchett, president of Massachusetts Institute of Technology. "Not only did I embody in it all his amendments to the

Herran treaty, but I went further than he has ever done in getting the proper guaranties for jurisdiction over the Canal."

Bunau-Varilla spent most of the night and all of the next day tinkering with the document with the help of a New York lawyer, Frank Pavey. In the end, he endorsed nearly all of its articles. The biggest favor he did for Panama was to insist on the exclusion of Colón and Panama City from the canal zone. But on the matter of American sovereignty, he stiffened Hay's language even more, granting the United States "all the rights, power and authority . . . which [it] would possess and exercise if it were the sovereign of the territory . . . *to the entire exclusion of the exercise by the Republic of Panama of any such sovereign rights, power or authority*" (italics added).

On the matter of the indemnity—the price to be paid to Panama—Hay was in a quandary and had left a blank to be filled in after further discussion with Bunau-Varilla. To win over those senators who were rankled by the manner in which the United States had jilted Colombia, Hay suggested dividing the $10 million between the old landlord (Colombia) and the new (Panama). Bunau-Varilla objected emphatically, more on principle than as broker for his needy client. "Any man who pays something that he does not owe is immediately thought to be paying under the pressure of blackmail," he told Hay. "Any man who pays under the pressure of blackmail is immediately thought to be paying on account of a concealed crime." Hay gave the point to Bunau-Varilla—and all the money to Panama.

Bunau-Varilla had his own approach to placating the Senate. Beyond offering his blessing to the Morgan bill, he made a show of genuflection. Suppressing his own pride of authorship, as difficult as that was to do, Bunau-Varilla wrote a letter to Morgan that was widely circulated in the press, urging the senator to embrace Panama and "not to throw away the title which the gratitude of humanity owes you, that of Father of the Isthmian Canal." Morgan's Alabama hide was not stroked so easily. When it came time to debate the new treaty in the Senate, he would question the legitimacy of a country, and a canal, wrenched by "caesarian operation . . . from the womb of Colombia."

For reasons obvious to both, Bunau-Varilla and Hay were anxious to have the treaty over and done with. Manuel Amador and Federico Boyd had sailed from Panama on November 10 to ensure that the canal negotiations would be consummated in a manner satisfactory to Panama. They told Bunau-Varilla that they did not intend to usurp his authority, but their distrust of him was implied and not unwarranted. Meanwhile, neither Bunau-Varilla nor Hay wanted any more fingerprints on the treaty, least of all any that might mar their handiwork. Working without letup, Bunau-Varilla put the finishing touches on his revisions and hurried to Lafayette Square at ten o'clock, just as Amador and Boyd were checking in to their hotel in New York. To his dismay, he discovered that Hay had already gone to bed. He left a note in which he fretted that the arrival of the Panamanian delegation would create "a good deal of intrigues" unhelpful to the consummation of their treaty.

Hay read the message in the morning and invited Bunau-Varilla to come to his house after he had finished up at the State Department. At lunchtime, Hay went over the treaty line by line with Secretary of War Root, Attorney General Philander Knox, and Treasury Secretary Leslie Shaw; together they combed out any final snarls. When Bunau-Varilla arrived at Hay's house at six o'clock, they adjusted one more phrase. Hay stipulated that the United States be granted "the use, occupation and control" of the zone in perpetuity. In other words, the treaty was not a lease, as originally proposed; Panama would not be America's landlord after all.

At 6:40 pm, Hay and Bunau-Varilla signed the treaty in Hay's drawing room, using an inkstand that had once been Abraham Lincoln's and a pen belonging to Hay's son Clarence. Neither of them had thought to have an official seal on hand. In its place, Bunau-Varilla used Hay's personal signet ring. Hay chose for himself a memento he had acquired in his travels: a ring worn by the poet Byron at his death in 1824. Hay and Bunau-Varilla were both romantics at heart and worldly enough to know that Lord Byron had died as he was preparing to fight for the independence of Greece from the Ottoman Empire. Hay also recalled that two years before to the very day, he had signed the Hay-Paunceforte Treaty in the same room.

Bunau-Varilla left immediately and hurried to a telegraph office to notify Panama of the momentous news. Two hours later, he was at the station to meet Amador and Boyd, who had lingered a day in New York to meet with Cromwell. When Bunau-Varilla told them what had transpired earlier in the evening, the Panamanians were apoplectic. They produced a letter from the Panamanian junta to Bunau-Varilla, requesting that all the clauses of the treaty be approved by the junta beforehand. When they presented these instructions to Bunau-Varilla, he called them up short. "Cherish no illusion," he pronounced with Gallic seigniory. "[T]he negotiations are closed."

WHEN AMADOR AND BOYD were able to review the Hay–Bunau-Varilla Treaty, their consternation subsided only slightly. Yet they fully recognized that time was of the essence. Colombia was making noises about invading Panama, and Colombian general Rafael Reyes was on his way to Washington to lodge a formal protest against America's role in the insurrection. Amador and Boyd knew that rejection or delay of the treaty would end the dream of a prosperous and independent Panama. To accept the treaty as it stood would immediately gird their tender nation in the armor of the United States. Then, too, there was the $10 million to consider.

On November 24, Amador and Boyd, still chewing on their misgivings, sailed for Panama with the treaty in an envelope, the envelope wrapped in the Panamanian flag, the entire bundle locked inside a strongbox. The next day, Bunau-Varilla met with Hay; immediately afterward, he sent a cable to Panama's new foreign minister, Francisco Vicente de la Espriella, advising him that the chilliness displayed by Amador and Boyd toward a treaty "which the United States justly considered as generous toward Panama" had prompted "surprise in the high spheres which, as hours are passing, degenerates into indignation." Bunau-Varilla warned that if the treaty were not signed promptly, then certain "calamities" would ensue. The members of the junta required no further persuasion; the next day, they cabled back that they would ratify the treaty upon receipt. Bunau-Varilla rushed to Hay's house to share the news, interrupting Thanksgiving dinner. True to their word, the Panamanians ratified the treaty on December 2, 1903, the day after its arrival.

•　　•　　•

MOST AMERICANS AND MOST members of the Senate were pleased by the recent sequence of events in Panama and the prospect, at long last, of a Panama canal. Yet the opposition to ratification—by Democrats, anti-imperialists, portions of the press, and also from the stubborn Colombians—was fierce. They charged that from the start Roosevelt and Hay had been in the thick of the conspiracy to overthrow Colombia; that the revolution was the brainchild of an elaborate "gamblers' syndicate," led by Bunau-Varilla, to make a killing on Compagnie Nouvelle stock; that America's role in the revolution violated the 1846 treaty pledging to preserve and protect Colombian sovereignty in Panama; that the Hay–Bunau-Varilla Treaty violated the Spooner Act; that now more than ever the canal ought to be built in Nicaragua; that the government of Panama (which had yet to hold elections or ratify a constitution) was not legal; and, in general, that Roosevelt had overstepped his authority as chief executive.

Roosevelt did not wait for the blows to land before striking back. On December 7, he devoted a large portion of his annual message to Congress to Panama, providing a thorough tutorial on the history of the canal negotiations and the revolution, stressing the "transcendent importance" to the "whole civilized world" of free and open transit across the isthmus, invoking John Bassett Moore's interpretation of the 1846 treaty, vouching for America's good faith and forbearance toward Colombia, and scolding Colombia for its repudiation of the Hay-Herrán Treaty "in such a manner as to make it evident by the time the Colombian Congress adjourned that not the scantiest hope remained of ever getting a satisfactory treaty from them." Under such circumstances, Roosevelt asserted, "the Government of the United States would have been guilty of folly and weakness, amounting in their sum in a crime against the Nation, had it acted otherwise than it did when the revolution of November 3 took place in Panama."

To dispel suspicions of his active collusion in the conspiracy, Roosevelt released all relevant diplomatic correspondence to the Senate, and in a second address to Congress, he ruled out the "reasonable time" argument for going to Nicaragua and issued an even stronger denial of American participation in the revolution. "No one connected with this government had any part in preparing, inciting, or encouraging the late revolution," he insisted, "[or] any previous knowledge of the revolution except such as was accessible to any person of ordinary intelligence who read the newspapers and kept up a current acquaintance with public affairs."

As for the allegation that he, Hay, or anyone in the administration had been in cahoots with Bunau-Varilla, he declared to John Bigelow that "I have no idea what Bunau-Varilla advised the revolutionists, or what he said in any telegrams to them as to either Hay or myself; but I do know, of course, that he had no assurances in any way, either from Hay or myself. . . . He is a very able fellow, and it was his business to find out what he thought our Government would do. I have no doubt he was able to make an accurate guess. . . . In fact, he would have been a very dull man had he been unable to make such a guess."

On the other hand, out of self-promotion or self-protection, Roosevelt falsely underestimated the part played by Cromwell. "[H]e was merely a stage conspirator," the president was to say of the Compagnie Nouvelle's attorney. "I think that all that Nelson Cromwell did was to walk around New York . . . feeling ecstatic whenever the *World* accused him of being responsible for the 'Panama Infamy.'"

HAY WAS CONTENT TO let Roosevelt (and Bunau-Varilla) take the heat and the credit, for on December 6, the day before the president delivered his annual message, he came down with a fever, and all night he was "plumb crazy." The fever became the grippe, which, he explained to Roosevelt, apologizing for his absence from the State Department, was like "a slatternly house maid . . . leaving more or less rubbish slung in the corners in the shape of neuralgia and other bedevilments." Soon he had bronchitis, and his gout flared up; the doctor put him to bed and forbade him to leave the house for the rest of the month. "I am a prisoner," he wrote Henry Adams, who was in Paris. "I could not walk you or talk you even if you were here." Roosevelt, though, continued to drop by on Sunday mornings after church.

From home, Hay kept apprised of the affairs of the nation and the world. He watched anxiously as Russia and Japan failed to agree upon a buffer zone between Manchuria and Korea and crept closer to war. His only responsibility in the endgame of the canal treaty was to finesse General Reyes, who arrived in Washington at the first of the month and made a polite but tiresome nuisance of himself.

Without consulting Tomás Herrán, who was dispirited and disgraced and would soon retire to a brief and bitter senescence in Bogotá, Reyes announced that Colombia was prepared to cede the canal with no indemnity if the United States would endorse the restoration of Panama to Colombian sovereignty. Reyes's threat that Colombia would soon invade Panama was discounted—especially by Bunau-Varilla, who assured Hay that it was a "mere bugaboo." Even so, the list of grievances Reyes presented to the White House and shared with anti-Panama senators had the potential to tip the outcome of the ratification vote. It was up to Hay to answer and, if possible, hush the irksome general.

Throughout December and January 1904, as the Senate investigated the circumstances surrounding the Panama revolution and marshaled its arguments for and against ratification of the treaty, Hay and Reyes waged their own debate, making their respective cases in long, legalistic letters and repeated face-to-face discussions at Hay's house. Always Hay came back to the same point: the revolution and the recognition of the Republic of Panama were accomplished facts, and though the Hay–Bunau-Varilla Treaty was not yet law, there were already "inchoate rights and duties created by it which place the responsibility of preserving peace and order on the Isthmus in the hands of the Government of the United States."

Hay found that he liked Reyes personally, and once he was confident that Colombia would not or could not invade Panama, he felt slightly sorry for "the fine old soldier." Reyes was widely revered at home, and it was expected that, if he succeeded in gaining at least moderate redress for his grievances, he would become the next president of Colombia. But even with the help of the crafty American lawyer and notorious Mugwump Wayne MacVeagh—whom Hay had known since the Lincoln years and had distrusted since at least the Garfield presidency—Reyes made absolutely no headway against the reasoned yet always cordial adamancy of the secretary of state. When Hay was asked to describe his approach to handling Reyes, he made his answer in a vernacular perhaps borrowed from Pike County. "Kill him," he drawled, "but kill him easy." Like Herrán, Reyes eventually returned home, empty-handed.

Roosevelt, in stark comparison, was nowhere near as sensitive in his regard for the dispossessed Colombians. For him, the case for Panama was day and night, right versus wrong, and, if anything, he wished that he had driven a harder bargain with Bogotá from the beginning. "Colombia has . . . a squalid savagery of its own," Roosevelt wrote Charles Lummis, a western writer who knew a thing or two about America's wild places, "and it has combined with exquisite nicety the worst forms of despotism and of anarchy, of violence and of fatuous weakness, of dismal ignorance, treachery, greed, and utter vanity. I cannot feel much respect for such a country."

A decade later, Roosevelt's antipathy still festered. "To talk of Colombia as a responsible power . . . is a mere absurdity," he wrote to his friend William Roscoe Thayer, who by then was at work on the first biography of Hay. "The analogy is with a group of Sicilian or Calabrian bandits. . . . You could no more make an agreement with them than you could nail currant jelly to a wall."

Roosevelt had scarcely higher regard for those in his own country who were attempting to stymie ratification of the canal treaty. "In this Panama business," Roosevelt ranted to his son Ted, "the entire fool mugwump crowd have fairly suffered from hysterics, and a goodly number of Senators, even of my own party, have shown about as much backbone as so many angleworms."

DOWN THE STRETCH, WHEN Senator Morgan and his fellow Panama detractors realized that they did not have the votes to defeat the Hay–Bunau-Varilla Treaty outright, they attempted to hobble it with trivial amendments, knowing that a revised treaty would have to go back to Panama for re-ratification, and around and around from there. Hay had been the victim of this ploy one too many times already, and he exhorted Senator Shelby Cullom to do everything he could to block the amendments. "I am only speaking of the matter of opportunity and expediency," Hay advised respectfully. "We insisted on an immediate ratification of the treaty by the Panama Government, and they acceded to our wishes. If we now, after a very long delay, send the treaty back to them amended, you can at once imagine the state of things that it will find there. The moment of unanimity and enthusiasm, which only comes once in the life of a revolution, will have passed away and given way to the play of politics and factions. They will have a certain advantage which they have not had before in dealing with the matter."

Hay then made an admission that heretofore he had been careful to keep out of his public statements and correspondence. "We shall have ratified the treaty with amendments," he continued to Spooner, "which gives [the Panamanians] another chance to revise *their perhaps hasty and enthusiastic action.* They will consider themselves as entitled to make amendments as . . . we, and it needs only a glance at the treaty to show what an infinite field of amendments there is from every point of view. The Junta . . . said that, although many of the provisions seemed harsh and hard, yet it was judged for the public good to accept [the treaty] as it was. When they get the amended treaty in their hands again, they will compare it with the treaty we made with Colombia, and see *how vastly more advantageous to us this treaty is than that one was*" (all italics added).

Clearly Hay's sense of fair play nagged at him, but only slightly and not for long. The same day that he wrote Spooner, he offered a stronger rationalization for his actions to the Yale theologian George P. Fisher. He was referring to America's intervention in the revolution, but the same reasoning applied to the treaty as well. "While I agree that no circumstance can ever justify a Government in doing wrong," he allowed, "the question as to whether the Government has acted rightly or wrongly can never be justly judged without the circumstances being considered. I am sure that if the President had acted differently when on the 3d of November he was confronted by a critical situation which might have easily have turned to disaster, the attacks which are now made on him would have been tenfold more virulent. . . . It was a time to act and not to theorize, and my judgment at least is clear that he acted rightly."

Finally it was time for the Senate to act as well. Chaperoned by Spooner, Cullom, and Lodge, the Hay–Bunau-Varilla Treaty was put to a vote on February 23, 1904. Conspicuously absent during the final days of debate was Mark Hanna, the Panama route's greatest champion in Congress. He had been ill for some time and died on February 15, one week before the Senate voted in favor of ratification, 66 to 14.

On February 25, Hay and Bunau-Varilla signed and exchanged treaties. "Two strokes of a pen were sealing forever the Destiny of the Great Thought which had haunted Humanity for four centuries," Bunau-Varilla observed with customary histrionics. Hay in turn told Bunau-Varilla, rather more matter-of-factly, "It seems to me as if we had together made something great."

IN THE MONTHS THAT followed, all parties were paid: $40 million to the Compagnie Nouvelle, of which Bunau-Varilla was a stockholder; $10 million to Panama. Bunau-Varilla resigned as Panamanian minister and returned to France, enjoying his wealth and his laurels, the latter fertilized by an endless stream of self-congratulation. Construction of the canal began in the summer of 1904 and ended ten years later, just as the First World War began.

Bunau-Varilla would later boast that he had written nearly every word in the final treaty, and Roosevelt would assert that he had virtually dug the canal himself. Unlike John Hay, they were not men who kept their lights under a bushel. Moreover, they were allowed many more years to revise and embellish their stories. Hay had only a bit more than a year left, and he was never one to gloat.

But while he was not a braggart, he did not mind compliments. Earlier in the year an editorial had run in the *New York Evening Sun*, which Hay then pasted among the countless other clippings in his scrapbooks. "If wisdom, statesmanship, and good honest service were the factors securing the honor," the *Sun* postulated, "John Hay would be the next Republican candidate for president."

CHAPTER 20

Hayism

Hay had no ambition to be president. He was not even sure he had the strength to remain in office until the election in November, much less until the end of Roosevelt's term the following March. After spending December of 1903 invalided with bronchitis and afflicted by gout, he tried to resume his routine at the State Department. Yet he tired easily. He was up to receiving the diplomatic corps at a New Year's breakfast but too weak to attend a cabinet dinner four days later. On January 15, he canceled a meeting with Roosevelt. "I am very miserable," he apologized, "and have a date with my Doctor."

Hay's tendency toward hypochondria was notorious, but the latest symptoms were real and his overall frailty was indicative of something more chronic than grippe. Since his early years as a wistful poet, he had dwelt on his own mortality, but now, first with the Sargent portrait and then with the Saint-Gaudens commission, he seemed increasingly preoccupied with posterity. In January 1904, he began keeping a diary, something he had not done in forty years. He also prepared a will.

Henry Adams, who had arrived home at the first of the year, was alarmed by his friend's condition. "Hay has not been out of his house since December 1," Adams reported to Lizzie, "and is still too weak to walk round the square. At the same time he is regularly besieged and overrun by diplomats and colleagues. At any other time the Panama business would absorb all our thoughts, but today the Jap-Russian affair dwarfs everything."

Throughout January, Hay conducted a round robin of conversations with Japanese minister Kogoro Takahira and Russian ambassador Cassini, as their countries spiraled toward war. Officially, he professed neutrality; privately, he was thoroughly disgusted by Russia's conduct over Kishinev, its chronic cynicism toward the Open Door, and its cavalier aggression in Manchuria. Japan, by comparison, had been honest in its dealings with America, and Hay and Roosevelt sympathized with Japan's ambition to turn back Russia in Manchuria before it swallowed up Korea, which Japan desired as both outlet and insulation for its island kingdom. The United States was not going to muster a war against Russia over Manchuria; but Japan, with a little encouragement and provocation, could do America's job by proxy.

At this stage, Hay and Roosevelt could only hope for a fair fight and try to keep the conflict from spreading to other parts of China. As it was, the cataclysm would be huge enough. "From dispatches received . . . Russia is clearly determined . . . to crush Japan and to eliminate her from her position of influence in the Far East," Hay recorded in his new diary. Lloyd Griscom, the American minister in Tokyo, was sure that Japan would be no pushover. "The Japanese nation is now worked up to a high pitch of excitement," he wrote Hay, "and it is no exaggeration to say that if there is no war it will be a severe disappointment to the Japanese individual of every walk of life. . . . Nothing but the most complete backdown of the Russian Government will satisfy the public feeling." Japan, Griscom observed, was "pluck personified."

Toward the end of January, with the fuse burning in the East, Hay convalesced at the plantation of Oliver Payne, the wealthy uncle of his son-in-law Payne Whitney, in Thomasville, Georgia, accompanied by his daughter Helen and granddaughter Joan. "I feel better already—morally," he wrote Roosevelt upon his arrival, perhaps making a weak joke about the still-pending and perhaps slightly lopsided Panama treaty. The brief vacation seemed to do the trick. "I have the appetite of an old depraved shark," he told Adams. By the end of the week, he could walk four or five miles in the piney woods.

He returned to Washington on the evening of February 7 and went immediately to see the president. The day before, Japan had severed diplomatic relations with Russia, and Roosevelt and Hay fretted that a general feeding frenzy by the other great powers might ensue. Hay worked late into the night on a circular and passed it by the president the following morning. He thought it best not to delineate a firm boundary for containment of the fighting, outside of which all the powers would be expected to honor Chinese neutrality. He knew that anything so specific would lead to squabbling that would doom the larger aim of the agreement: his old saw, the Open Door and Chinese integrity. All he wanted, he told Joseph Choate, was to "secure the smallest possible area of hostilities and the largest area of neutrality compatible with the military necessities." The circular went out to England, France, and Germany immediately, and to China, Russia, Japan, and the other treaty nations soon thereafter.

Later in the day, Hay received separate visits from Takahira and Cassini. The latter was predictably arrogant. "He spent most of the time in accusing Japan of lightness and vanity; he seemed little affected by the imminence of war, expecting a speedy victory," Hay noted in his diary. Takahira was composed at first, expressing satisfaction in the neutrality circular, but then as he left Hay's office, he broke into tears.

It was Takahira who saw the future more clearly, and it was Cassini who ought to have wept. That evening, February 8, a few minutes before midnight, Japanese destroyers attacked the Russian Pacific Squadron huddled beneath the shore batteries of Port Arthur, Manchuria. In five minutes, Japanese torpedoes disabled three Russian ships, including the *Tsarevich*, the pride of the fleet. Before the Russians could clamber to battle stations, the Japanese had disappeared into the darkness of the Bay of Korea. The next morning, adding insult to injury, they struck again, leaving teeth marks in the Russian flagship *Petropavlosk* and three other warships. The assault accomplished two objectives: first, it pinned back the Russian navy sufficiently to allow Japanese troops to land safely in Korea; second, it sent a resounding message that little Japan was not to

be taken lightly. (Thirty-seven years later, Japan needed to look no farther than Port Arthur for a strategy that would cut another great power
down to size at Pearl Harbor.)

The next day, Hay remarked in his diary that the news of Russia's
comeuppance had arrived "like claps of thunder . . . but as people became used to it, every one said [they] had always expected it." Adams, the
inveterate doomsayer, prophesied that Russia would soon be bankrupt,
the czar would fall, China would go to pieces, leading to the complete
"upset" of Europe and the rest of Asia—"the full maelstrom." Cassini was
more stoic: "He takes the buffet of fortune very gallantly: not too gaily,"
Hay noted, "but seems sure of ultimate victory and a stern reckoning for
Japan."

When Takahira came to Hay's office to deliver his emperor's official
announcement of a declaration of war, "[H]e could hardly prevent his
grim visage from showing some signs of satisfaction," Hay observed, "but
he talked with great dignity and reserve. . . . He also said they did not
intend to make any selfish use of their victory, if Providence continued to
favor them. He said with his strange smile that there need be no fear of
'the Yellow Peril.'"

Within a week of sending out his neutrality circular, Hay received responses from all the powers. Not surprisingly, Russia was the last, and the
least enthusiastic. Hay interpreted the most recent equivocation much as
he had done four years earlier with the first Open Door note: he credited
Russia as "responsive to the proposal of this Government" and immediately forwarded the positive news to China and Japan.

Yet Hay knew that if the Russians ever found a pretext to expand the
war in order to seize more territory, they would not hesitate to do so.
Cassini, who was in Hay's office almost daily, was sure that China was in
league with Japan. At the height of his paranoia, he tried to convince Hay
that the Chinese army was being "organized and drilled with great energy
and assiduity" by the Japanese. A month later, after Cassini for the ump-
teenth time conveyed his government's "terror of some aggression from
the Chinese," Hay wondered "whether their terror is real, or whether they
are simply making up a case against China."

As the author of the neutrality circular, Hay strived to set a good example. He had Roosevelt issue an executive order directing government officials to observe strict impartiality in their public utterances. He took it as a compliment when Cassini told him that in St. Petersburg the secretary of state was referred to as "the Unknown Quantity." Yet for all his efforts at fairness and discretion, he could do little to stifle the favoritism of the president, who admired the fighting spirit of the Japanese and their underdog spunk. Roosevelt had added jujitsu to his White House fitness regimen and enjoyed a rapport with Takahira that Cassini both resented and envied. Japan's other envoy to Washington, Baron Kentaro Kaneko, had been at Harvard with Roosevelt. In a letter to his son Ted, written days after the attack on Port Arthur, the president made his bias plain, if not entirely public: "For several years Russia has behaved very badly in the Far East, her attitude toward all nations, including us, but especially toward Japan, being grossly overbearing. . . . I thought Japan would probably whip her on the sea, but I could not be certain; and between ourselves—for you must not breathe it to anybody—I was thoroughly well pleased with the Japanese victory, for Japan is playing our game."

Nor could Hay muzzle the American press, which, he archly observed, "finds an attractive subject in the Russian misfortunes." Whenever Cassini read of some slight against the czar or of a public toast to Japan, he stormed into Hay's office in high dudgeon. Hay's famous forbearance was not infinite, and finally, after enduring a particularly obnoxious obloquy from the Russian ambassador, he struck back. "I spoke of the daily attacks of the Russian press on the U.S., of the constant ill-will of which we are the object in Russia: and all without cause," he fumed in his diary. "'You have nothing to complain of at our hands,'" he said he told Cassini, who admitted that the administration's neutrality was above reproach. That being so, Hay asked, "'Why do you quarrel with us who do not control our Press, when we make no complaint of you, who do control yours, when they daily insult us?'"

This question quieted Cassini, Hay noted caustically, and he "went away in quite a calm frame of mind." In his diary entry next day, Hay remembered one more thing he had told the ambassador before showing him out: "I said to Cassini . . . that the Russian attitude towards us reminded me of a man who should get into a quarrel on the street and then go home and beat his wife."

During the months that followed, the world looked on in horror and stupefaction as Russia and Japan fought battles bigger and bloodier than Gettysburg and Antietam combined. Outnumbered but better armed and disciplined, Japan won successive victories on land and sea. By late spring of 1904, a confident Takahira approached Hay about acting as mediator in any peace talks, when and if they should be opportune. Hay applauded Takahira's desire for peace but told him that he was reluctant to make "overtures which were likely to be rejected"—by Russia, presumably.

Roosevelt was likewise intrigued by the prospect of playing a part in negotiations to end the war, but he too felt that any sort of involvement by his administration was premature. Yet, he told Hay, "We may be of genuine service, if Japan wins out, in preventing interference to rob her of the fruits of her victory." Accordingly, Hay suggested to Takahira that Roosevelt might be just the mediator Japan was looking for.

In the meantime, Hay continued as the guardian of neutrality and as a leaning post for the ministers of the combatants. "Everything seems to have come out exactly right," he wrote Joseph Choate in London. "The whole world is in line in favor of preserving the neutrality of China, so far as is possible in a state of flagrant war, which must necessarily be fought out, to a great extent, on her own territory. . . . Russia is very cross with us just now," he added, "but our consciences are clear. We have done nothing but observe a strict neutrality between the two parties. Japan is sensible enough to be content with this, and the exasperation of Russia is the natural result of bad luck which has attended her so far."

HAY HAD OTHER ANNOYANCES that spring. His back went out. His gout would not go away. And as Roosevelt prepared to run for election, Hay was called into service in a capacity he did not relish. "In the cabinet meeting today," he wrote on April 12, "the President set forth at great length the difficulties and dangers of the campaign, as a preliminary to the suggestion that the welfare of the Republican party in this trying hour demanded that I should make some speeches. The motion was seconded by [Treasury Secretary] Shaw and [Navy Secretary] Moody with consider-able eloquence. I sat mute—fearing to speak lest I lose my temper."

Roosevelt was hardly in danger of defeat. His most likely opponent was Alton B. Parker, chief justice of the New York Court of Appeals, a decent but hardly charismatic or renowned man—not like the previous Democratic nominee, William Jennings Bryan, and even less like the protean Teddy, who, though he had never actually run for president before, conducted himself as if the office was his for as long as he wanted. Roosevelt was confident of victory but nonetheless refused to take the coming contest lightly. "He sees a good many lions in the path," Hay commented, "but I told him of the far greater beasts . . . in Lincoln's way, which turned out to be only bob-cats after all."

Given Hay's enormous esteem and his long and venerable history as a Republican, Roosevelt was shrewd to want him in a more visible, and more audible, capacity in the campaign. Yet Hay was hardly in a stumping mood. Speechwriting for him was more taxing than any other writing he did. He labored over each address, approaching it more as poetry than prose. "It was simply tortuous [for him] to contemplate a speech," his daughter Helen Whitney would recall. The thought of now having to perform as the president's clarion seemed more like a prank than an honor. "It is intolerable that they should not see how much more advantageous to the administration it is that I should stay at home and do my work than that I should cavort around the country, making lean and jejune orations," he complained to his diary. But in the end he consented.

The first address was scheduled for May at the Louisiana Purchase Exposition in St. Louis. "I can hardly escape it," he lamented, and, as he finished writing, he rated his work "a poor thing." The speech was better than that. Hay used the occasion to celebrate the westward flight of the American eagle and to highlight the nation's great exports of honest dealing and self-restraint. The greatest applause naturally came when he mentioned Roosevelt.

At St. Louis he was appropriately impressed by the exposition's extravaganza of palaces and pavilions; he was driven through the grounds in an automobile and attended the third (modern) Olympic Games. But what moved him even more was the Mississippi River in spring flood. In his speech, he invoked "the amphibious life" of his youth. "It was a land of faëry," he reminisced. "[W]e sang rude songs of the cane-brake and the cornfield; and the happiest days of the year to us who dwelt on the northern bluffs of the river were those that brought us, in the loud puffing and whistling steamers of the olden time, to the Mecca of our rural fancies, the bright and busy metropolis of St. Louis."

The olden time was gone, though. He took a half-day excursion on the river and was made melancholy by the change. "There were only a few boats at the wharves," he noted, "instead of the hundreds that used to be there and the streets near the levee were as desolate as Tadnor in the wilderness." Jim Bludso and the *Prairie Belle* were extinct.

He arrived home on Sunday morning, in time for his customary chat with Roosevelt, who was already looking beyond the election to his new administration. "The President talked a good deal ab[ou]t the next Cabinet," Hay wrote. "He w[oul]d not listen to me when I told him I must be left out. He wants us all to resign—but he wants to reappoint me."

HAY DID NOT PRESS the matter of his retirement, for a new distraction demanded his attention. On May 19, the day he gave his address in St. Louis, the State Department received a telegram from its consul-general in Tangier. "Situation serious," Samuel Gummeré pleaded. "Request man-of-war to enforce demands." The reason soon followed: on the evening of the eighth, Ion Perdicaris, a middle-aged bon vivant who for the past twenty years had been living in affluent idleness in Morocco, was kidnapped, along with his stepson, by the Berber chieftain Muali Ahmed er Raisuli, universally described in the English-speaking press as a "brigand."

Morocco was the nominal suzerainty of a corrupt and ineffectual sultan. Raisuli was the sultan's nemesis, and he had paid a dear price for his hostility. His people had been dragooned into military service and cruelly taxed, their villages had been burned, and he had been imprisoned in chains for four years. In retaliation, Raisuli became a sort of Robin Hood of the Rif. His ransom demand for Perdicaris included not just money— although he wanted a great deal of that: $70,000—but also withdrawal of government troops, release of partisan prisoners, removal of the military governor, and control of the districts surrounding Tangier. It was a stiff order, but Raisuli was both devious and cocksure. He had chosen to kidnap Perdicaris not simply because he knew Perdicaris was wealthy, but because he supposed Perdicaris to be a prominent American. By creating an international incident, Raisuli figured to shame the sultan into meeting all of his demands. Indeed, he did not expect the ransom to be paid by Perdicaris's family or even by the U.S. government. He explicitly demanded that it be extracted from the purse of the local governor. Raisuli was smart enough to know that pressure to comply would be more persuasive if applied by the Americans.

Purely by chance, as the telegram announcing the kidnapping of Perdicaris reached Washington, three naval squadrons were steaming across the Atlantic en route to the Mediterranean, for training but also as a demonstration of American sea power. Never before had the U.S. Navy concentrated so many ships—thirteen in all—in European waters.

Hay and Roosevelt did not receive the ransom terms until May 27, and then only by way of a telegram from Joseph Choate in London; Perdicaris's stepson was a British subject. They agreed that Raisuli's demands were preposterous. Lacking a better remedy, Hay sent orders to the commander of the navy squadrons, Admiral French Chadwick, to show the flag at Tangier.

At first Hay seemed not overly alarmed by the Perdicaris incident. Other Americans had been kidnapped and rescued during his tenure without a multilateral imbroglio. This was not another Boxer Rebellion. He was far more preoccupied, for instance, with his conversation with Takahira that same day, in which the Japanese minister informed him of the horrendous casualties suffered by both sides in the recent battle of Nanshan. "I hope they may not murder Mr. Perdicaris," Hay recorded dismissively in his diary, "but a nation cannot degrade itself to prevent ill-treatment of a citizen."

Rather than be drawn into awkward and potentially demeaning negotiations between the kidnappers and the Moroccans, Hay's inclination was to send a terse telegram to Gummeré, making it plain that the United States would punish Raisuli commensurately for any harm he did to Perdicaris. But before he issued his warning, he heard from Choate that the British were making some headway. So the ultimatum was set aside—for the time being.

Yet negotiations with Raisuli were *not* going well; with each hesitation by the sultan, Raisuli increased his demands and advanced the day of

Perdicaris's execution. The arrival of Admiral Chadwick's South Atlantic Squadron and Admiral Theodore Jewell's European Squadron at Tangier was hardly a deterrent; rather, their presence made Raisuli that much more determined. "Now the Sultan's authorities will be compelled to accede to my demands," Raisuli is said to have told Perdicaris, who by this point, despite the death threats, was being treated more as guest than prisoner in the brigand's mountain hideout.

Hay's distaste for the Moroccan standoff increased on June 1, when he received a letter from A. H. Slocomb, a cotton broker in North Carolina who had met Perdicaris in Athens during the Civil War. "[I]s Perdicaris an American citizen?" Slocomb wanted to know. A good question, it turned out. Perdicaris's father was Greek by birth but naturalized as an American citizen; Ion Perdicaris was born in New Jersey. Slocomb claimed that Perdicaris had come to Greece during the war in order to renounce his American citizenship as a way to keep the Confederates from confiscating property he had inherited from his mother, who was a South Carolinian.

Hay shared Slocomb's query with Roosevelt, and on June 4 he sent a cipher telegram to the American consul in Athens, asking for the facts on Perdicaris. The consul wrote back on June 7 that "one Ionnas Perdicaris" had been made a naturalized Greek citizen on March 19, 1862. Hay did not pass this unsettling intelligence to Gummeré; nor to the British, who now had their own battleship at Tangier; nor to the French Foreign Ministry, whose "good offices" he had also entangled with the diplomatic tar baby of the moment.

Another week went by. Perdicaris remained alive and decently cared for. Raisuli upped the ante once more, requesting that he be given authority over two more Moroccan districts, that more prisoners be released, and that a number of rival sheiks be put in prison. Hay was ready to throw in the towel. "You see there is no end to the insolence of this blackguard," he wrote Roosevelt. "We have done what we could for Perdicaris—I do not think we ought to go any further."

Roosevelt, too, was through negotiating. "Our position must now be to demand the death of those that harm [Perdicaris] if he is harmed," the president declared to Hay. He also broached the notion of a joint military action with England and France. The following day, Admiral Chadwick began working up a plan to put ashore two brigades of Marines and sailors to seize the Tangier waterfront and customshouse. Such emphatic action, the admiral reckoned, ought to cure the sultan's impotence in consummating a deal with Raisuli—which, of course, was what Raisuli had been scheming for all along.

More than ever, Hay wanted the affair behind him. The Republican Convention had begun in Chicago; the campaign would hit full stride after that, and neither Hay nor the president was eager for another war—not over a brigand on horseback and the dubiously credentialed Perdicaris. And so Hay wired Gummeré, repeating a message that he and Roosevelt had drafted at least once already, only this time he put it more bluntly: "We want Perdicaris alive or Raisuli dead."

The telegram included two more sentences that would soon be lost in the smoke and hurrahs of the national convention: "We desire least possible complications with Morocco or other Powers," Hay instructed. "You will not arrange for landing marines or seizing customs house without specific direction from the [State] department." The first line of the telegram—Perdicaris alive, Raisuli dead—had been directed toward the sultan of Morocco, the second part toward the U.S. Navy. Hay had called off the assault on Tangier.

As the cable was being transmitted to Gummeré, a correspondent in Washington got wind of it and forwarded it to Chicago, where it was hurried to Joseph Cannon, Speaker of the House of Representatives and holder of the gavel at the convention. Cannon had to bide his time while Henry Cabot Lodge, never the most electrifying of orators, recited the party's platform to a less than lively hall of party faithful. With Roosevelt a shoo-in, the convention had been short on suspense thus far.

"Uncle Joe" Cannon recognized red meat when he saw it, and when he regained the podium, he fed his listless congregation with good effect. "We want Perdicaris alive or Raisuli dead!" he read aloud, choosing not to complicate the moment by sharing the more temperate sentences of Hay's telegram. The Republicans roared like Romans at the Coliseum. "Fee, Fi, Fo, Fum, give me the blood of the Mussulman [Muslim]," the *New York World* bruited the next morning.

The party nominated Roosevelt by acclamation. (Their choice for vice president was Indiana senator Charles W. Fairbanks.) Most of the delegates had attributed the dead-or-alive ultimatum to bully Teddy, but at least one newspaper praised Hay for a rare display of pugnacity: "In diplomacy Mr. Hay has heretofore stuck to the *suaviter in modo*, rather than the *fortiter in re*. . . . But this Perdicaris outrage seems to have preyed upon his mind until his just wrath could no longer keep within bounds."

A bit surprised at his own virulence, Hay wrote in his diary with wry amusement: "My telegram to Gummeré had an uncalled for success. It is curious how a concise impropriety hits the public."

Yet his telegram had not been necessary at all. By the time Gummeré received Hay's instructions, Raisuli had agreed to release Perdicaris and his stepson, in exchange for the asked-for $70,000 and the freedom of his imprisoned tribesmen. Two days later, Raisuli escorted Perdicaris and his stepson down from the mountains to Tangier. Kidnapper and captives parted as friends, and soon the American warships weighed anchor to resume their summer exercises. The nation, Republicans especially, approved of the administration's tough talk, but Hay exhaled merely a sigh of relief. Several weeks later when it was at last confirmed that Perdicaris had indeed forsaken his American citizenship as a young man, Hay elected to keep the information quiet. He wanted to hear nothing more about "Perigoric," he told Alvey Adee. "Or is it Pericarditis?"

ON JULY 6, HAY delivered the speech of a lifetime. Fifty years earlier, to the day, a group of erstwhile Whigs, Free-Soilers, and Democrats, provoked by the recent Kansas-Nebraska Act, which negated the Missouri Compromise and enabled the spread of slavery west of the Mississippi, had gathered beneath a grove of oak trees in Jackson, Michigan, and held the very first convention under the "Republican" banner. Their movement spread from there, at first strictly anti-expansionist and not anti-slavery outright. Two years later, the Republicans nominated their first presidential candidate; in another two years, Abraham Lincoln ran for Senate against Stephen Douglas and lost, setting the stage for 1860, when Lincoln led the Republican Party to the White House and, ultimately, to war. Since then, Grover Cleveland had been the only Democrat to win the presidency.

Hay was fifteen when the Republican Party was born, and his partisan awakening did not come in full until his arrival in Springfield after college in 1859. Now, in 1904, it was widely accepted that no man alive embodied the half century of Republican tradition, values, and vision more thoroughly and more honorably than the current secretary of state. Hay possessed not only the institutional memory of the party but its conscience as well. There were many who believed John Hay was reason enough to vote for Roosevelt.

Yet he hardly looked like a campaign weapon. "Astute and punctilious" was how one newspaper described him on the morning of his arrival in Michigan. "He has a pleasant manner, like all great men," observed another, "and keeps himself well groomed, which cannot be said of all great men. Natty is the term to apply."

The day was delightfully fair and cool, Hay recorded in his diary. As he mounted the grandstand, he was daunted by the size of the crowd, ten thousand or more, and feared that not even "hardened old spellbinders" could hold the audience. But he did so, for an hour and a half.

He began, appropriately enough, by reflecting upon the early years of Republicanism, and the Lincoln in him found voice: "[T]he whole party stood like a rock for the principle that the damnable institution must be content with what it had already got, and must not be allowed to pollute another inch of free soil," he declared. "On this impregnable ground they made their stand; and the mass convention which assembled here in 1854 . . . gave a nucleus and a name to the new party, destined to a great and beneficent career. Before the month ended, the anti-slavery men of five more states adopted the name"—he was seven pages into his address before he invoked the hallowed word—"'Republican.'"

One listener said Hay wielded the English language like a "musical instrument" and that his diction possessed "singular precision and sibilance." In recapping the Lincoln-Douglas debates, and articulating the difference between the two rivals, Hay observed with lyrical concision, "[Lincoln] was fighting for freedom and could say so; Douglas was fighting for slavery and could not avow it."

And of Lincoln's legacy, Hay claimed rightful ownership for the assembled: "If there is one thing more than another in which we Republicans are entitled to a legitimate pride, it is that Lincoln was our first

President; that we believed in him, loyally supported him while he lived, and that we have never lost the right to call ourselves his followers."

Since this was the campaign season, and the party of Lincoln was now also the party of Roosevelt, Hay set about entwining the two. "I hope I am violating neither the confidence of a friend nor the proprieties of an occasion like this," he ventured with staged etiquette, "when I refer to the ardent and able young statesman who is now, and is to be, our President, to let you know that in times of doubt and difficulty the thought oftenest in his heart is, 'What, in such a case, would Lincoln do?'"

He took considerable care, too, in telling the other story he knew better than anyone else—that of the foreign policy of the McKinley and Roosevelt administrations. In doing so, he also issued a report card on himself, perhaps not applying the most penetrating candor, but nonetheless offering a directness both coherent and persuasive.

"A country growing so fast must have elbowroom—must have its share of the sunshine," he soft-pedaled, making American expansion sound like the most wholesome of impulses. "In the last seven years, without aggression, without undue self-assertion, we have taken the place that belongs to us."

Here, thus, was manifest destiny cast in some of that same benign sunshine: "Adhering with religious care to the precepts of Washington and the traditions of a century, and avoiding all entangling alliances, professing friendship to all nations and partiality to none, McKinley and Roosevelt have gone steadily forward protecting and extending American interests everywhere and gaining, by deserving it, the good will of all the world."

Yet beneath Hay's advocacy, there lay a subtext of defensiveness. He was addressing the choir, meanwhile attempting to quell omniscient doubters—Democrats, anti-imperialists, Mugwumps. "We do not covet the territory, nor the control of any other people," he assured. "We have made, it is true, great acquisitions, but never of set purpose nor from greed of land." He mentioned Hawaii and Samoa with satisfaction. The Panama treaties, the Open Door, and the integrity and neutrality of China were gems in the crowns of McKinley and Roosevelt, "gained by appeals to reason rather than [by] force, without parade or melodrama."

He could just as easily have detoured around the most conspicuous smudge on the escutcheon of the McKinley-Roosevelt era, the Philippines. Instead, he stood guard over it. The spoils of the Spanish-American War had not been his direct responsibility as secretary of state; the United States had no *foreign* policy toward what were now American possessions—until Cuba achieved independence in 1902. Hay had no hand in the suppression of the insurgency in the Philippines, nor in the establishment of a "civil" administration there. (The latter chore was accomplished by William Howard Taft, whose service to America's far-flung "little brown brothers"—Taft's term—had won him promotion to Roosevelt's cabinet as secretary of war, replacing Elihu Root.) Nevertheless, in the oak grove of Jackson, Michigan, Hay stood up for the Philippines and his president without remorse or alibi.

"Some well-meaning people—and others not so well-meaning—are constantly persuading [the Filipinos] that they are oppressed," he told his sympathetic listeners, "and that they will be given their liberty, as they choose to call it, as soon as the Republican party is overthrown in this country. These are the true enemies of the Filipinos, and not the men who are striving with whole-hearted energy and with consummate success to ameliorate their condition and to make them fit for self-government and all its attendant advantages.

"The so-called anti-imperialists," he continued testily, "confound in their daily speeches two absolutely unrelated ideas—the liberty, the civil rights, the self-government which we have given the Filipinos, and the independence which the best of them do not want and know they are unable to maintain. To abandon them now, to cast them adrift at the mercy of accident, would be an act of cowardice and treachery which would gain us the scorn and reproach of civilization."

He did a much better job vouching for Roosevelt, but even then he took the risky tack of acknowledging Roosevelt's principal flaw in order to refute it. "Ask [the Democrats], Has the President been a good citizen, a good soldier, a good man in all personal relations?" Hay urged, commencing a litany of Roosevelt's virtues. "Is he a man of intelligence, of education? Does he know this country well? Does he know the world outside? Has he studied law, history, and politics? . . . Is he sound and strong in mind, body, and soul? Is he accessible and friendly to all sorts and conditions of men? Has he the courage and the candor, the God-given ability to speak to the people and tell them what he thinks? To all these questions they will answer, Yes."

Then Hay asked, and now came the barb at the end of the hook, "What is your objection to him? They"—Roosevelt's opponents—"will either stand speechless or they will answer with the parrot cry we have heard so often: He is unsafe!"

For all Hay's incredulousness that anyone could make such a preposterous charge against Roosevelt, it was in fact something he and Henry Adams had said and thought for years. Roosevelt was a rash cowboy—"pure act," as Adams said. But rather than harbor this heresy, Hay let it run free. "In a certain sense we shall have to admit this to be true," he said of Roosevelt's impulse to brandish a big stick. "To every grade of law-breaker, high or low; to a man who would rob a till or a ballot box; to the sneak or the bully; to the hypocrite and the humbug, Theodore Roosevelt is more than unsafe; he is positively dangerous!" With that the crowd cheered like Rough Riders, which doubtless some of them were.

It was a great day to be a Republican, and it had been a bully half-century. Having fired up his listeners, Hay banked the coals with a benediction: "We who are passing off the stage"—meaning not just from the immediate grandstand but from his own platform of public service as well—"bid you, as the children of Israel encamping by the sea were bidden, to Go Forward; we whose hands can no longer hold the flaming torch pass it on to you that its clear light may show the truth to the ages that are to come."

When he arrived back in Washington, Hay was deluged with congratulations. Strangers declared him the greatest secretary of state in the country's history. Another letter writer announced that he had named a newborn son after him. Yet no praise meant more than that of the president. "It is one of the few speeches which can rightly be called noble," Roosevelt complimented. "I do not feel that it will be merely a good campaign document, though I feel that very strongly too; I feel that it will be one of the speeches dealing with a sufficiently large subject in a sufficiently lofty tone to rank among the few which achieve permanence."

Indeed, Hay had reached a higher plane of distinction. Upon his return from Michigan, he learned that the French government wished to confer upon him the Grand Cross of the National Order of the Legion of Honor—in "appreciation not only of your merits as Statesman and Scholar, but still more of the services rendered by you during your term of office in consecrating your efforts to the maintenance of the peace of the world." He was also named one of the first seven inductees in the newly organized American Academy of Arts and Letters, a class that included Mark Twain, William Dean Howells, and Augustus Saint-Gaudens. And feeding on his fame, Houghton, Mifflin published a new edition of *Castilian Days*.

BY MID-JULY, HE WANTED nothing more than to get away to the Fells. "I have about reached the end of my tether here," he confessed to Roosevelt on July 14, the day he received notice of the French honor. "I had an attack of vertigo and faintness this morning, which keeled me over for about half an hour." He left for New Hampshire the next day.

As usual, the summer was not without its interruptions, but at least one of them was pleasant. At the end of July, Hay made a short trip to Cornish, New Hampshire, where Saint-Gaudens lived and worked. The sculptor had begun Hay's bust in Washington during the spring but was still not quite done. Hay was enchanted by the artist's retreat: an old farmhouse and barn converted into a studio with a Pompeian facade and a frieze like the Parthenon's. He sat for two hours while Saint-Gaudens put the finishing touches on the clay model. Hay was satisfied with the outcome—"a great peril escaped," he joked to his daughter Helen. From the model, Saint-Gaudens then carved a bust in marble and cast another in bronze—for which Hay paid $10,000.

He also commissioned a smaller work: Saint-Gaudens carved and cast a medallion of a winged porcupine, bearing the inscription *Porcupinus Angelicus*, one of Hay's terms of endearment for Henry Adams. When Adams received the medallion by diplomatic pouch in Paris, he wrote the sculptor with prickly delight: "As this is the only way in which the Secretary will ever fulfill his promise of making me Cardinal and Pope I can see why he thinks to satisfy me by giving me medallic rank through you."

• • •

HAY RETURNED TO WASHINGTON in early August. Roosevelt wanted the cabinet back for a midsummer session before the campaign took precedence in the fall. For Hay, there were no pending emergencies—nothing, anyway, on the scale of the Panama tempest of the summer before—but he had more than enough to keep him busy. The Ottoman Empire was not showing American missionaries and schools in Turkey the respect the administration felt they deserved. The disagreement had devolved into pettiness. The sultan refused to give an audience to the American minister in Constantinople; Roosevelt wanted to send the European Squadron to the Turkish coast; Hay suggested withdrawing the minister; the squadron was sent anyway; and in the end the sultan's manners toward the United States improved markedly. Once again, Hay and Roosevelt had worked well as a team, but these foreign fire drills, while winning kudos for the president's measured but unflinching aggressiveness, were becoming all too common, and each was more tiresome to Hay than its predecessor.

Hay fretted, too, over the war in China. Showing a willingness to suffer enormous casualties, the Japanese had driven the Russians from one defensive position to another. Much of the surviving Russian fleet was bottled up at Port Arthur. Increasingly, Hay and Roosevelt worried that Russia would pick a fight with China in order to enlarge the theater of war to a scale more to its advantage. Shortly after Hay arrived in Washington, an incident occurred that nearly gave Russia the excuse it was looking for. A damaged Russian destroyer had sought asylum in the harbor of Chefoo, near Port Arthur, when a Japanese destroyer attacked and forced the enemy ship out of neutral Chinese waters.

Hay did everything he could to keep Chinese neutrality from being shot to pieces, but he got nowhere with his request for Japan to return the Russian vessel. The Japanese insisted that they could not afford to let wounded ships refit in neutral harbors, only to return to battle another day. More Russian ships sought refuge in Shanghai; Japan did not attack them but made no promise not to. In frustration, Hay suggested to Roosevelt: "Might it not be the best solution for China to . . . lie down and say, 'I can't keep the peace between you. Fight it out and be —— with you'? Neither side pays any respect to her rules or her wishes—which she is powerless to enforce. If all her ports were allowed to become 'spheres of hostility' the Russians would stop running there for shelter, and the Japs would have no motive to intrude."

Roosevelt agreed that there was little more that the United States could do and that the navy must not interfere in the event of any further conflict in what, for the time being, were still neutral Chinese ports.

At the end of August, Alvey Adee forwarded to Hay a distressing dispatch from Edwin Conger in Peking: "Russian Minister informed me unofficially that Japanese course warrants extension of hostile zone anywhere in China, and that Russia will no longer consider Chinese Government neutral." The integrity of China, which Hay had toiled so steadfastly to preserve, appeared on the brink of being sundered.

But Hay's worst fears did not materialize. The war was going so badly for Russia and its navy was so diminished that it dared not expose itself as it had done at Chefoo and Shanghai. On September 1, Hay was able to write Joseph Choate, "The bark of both combatants has proved worse than the bite." Neither side renewed its pledge to honor Chinese neutrality, but thereafter neither made any significant demonstrations against it.

Still the fighting raged on in Manchuria. "War grows more and more frightful to me as I grow older," Hay told Choate. "I am more grieved at the slaughter at the Liaoyang"—where nearly ten thousand died and more than thirty thousand were wounded—"than I was at that of Gettysburg, though a lot of my friends fell there."

Two weeks in Washington exhausted him. "I feel good for nothing and tired to death," he told his brother-in-law, Samuel Mather. With Clara in New Hampshire and Adams in Europe, Lafayette Square felt empty. In the afternoons, he took carriage rides by himself, and in the evenings, he read his way through the collected works of Molière. And as he was wont to do when he was alone for more than a few days, he wrote to Lizzie Cameron. He had learned that her brother had died and took the opportunity to renew his affection, although he now girded his heart in the politesse of the first person plural. "What can I say, except that we love you and are sorry for you," he condoled her, extending sympathy by sharing his own suffering. "One of the insoluble mysteries of life is that we should mind about death. As it must come to all why should we fear it and why should the loss of one of our household darken the earth for us forever? Three years ago the death of our boy made my wife and me old, at once and for the rest of our lives. There is no mitigation of grief—it grows worse with the slow exasperation of years."

Looking from his library window, he could see Lizzie's town house, which neither she nor her wearisome husband had occupied since the beginning of the McKinley administration. "When are you coming home?" he asked wistfully. "Your place here has never been filled and can never be but by you. And yet, is there anything to tempt you?"

ON AUGUST 17, TWO days before returning to the Fells, his mood was elevated immensely by a telegram announcing the birth of John Hay Whitney, Helen and Payne's second child.

He spent the rest of that month and all of September in the bosom of his family. Clarence was home from Harvard for the summer. At the first of the month, Alice and Jim Wadsworth paid a visit and then went off to see the world's fair at St. Louis, leaving Evelyn in the care of her grandparents (and nurse). Hay confessed to his old Scottish friend, John Clark, that he and Clara had been reduced to a state of "idiotic adoration." Three weeks later, Helen arrived with one-and-a-half-year-old Joan and the new baby, who would soon be nicknamed "Jock." And for the first time, Hay's younger brother, Charles, who lived in Springfield, came to the Fells.

The autumn was as lovely as any that Hay could remember. "I have never seen such splendor in the woods as today," he wrote in his diary on October 1. "Around the house the maples are blazing in every shade of color from scarlet and orange to pale yellow and delicate pink, while the beeches, birches, ashes, and poplars add their varying shades to the chorus and the evergreens form the grave background of the marvelous picture."

The season ended too soon. Charles fell ill, and Hay, who had nursed his brother back to health in South Carolina during the Civil War, rushed him now to a hospital in Boston. A week later, Hay went to Boston as well, to help the campaign by speaking at the International Congress of Peace at Park Street Church, a forum better suited to him than to the president.

He stressed peace through preparedness, a policy promoted by McKinley and especially by Roosevelt. "It is true that . . . we have had a hundred days of war [Spanish-American]—but they put an end forever to bloodshed which had lasted a generation," he recited. "We landed a few platoons of marines on the Isthmus last year; but that act closed without a shot a sanguinary succession of trivial wars. We marched a little army at Peking; but it was to save not only the beleaguered legations, but a great imperiled civilization. By mingled gentleness and energy . . . we have given to the Philippines, if not peace, at least a nearer approach to it than they have had within the memory of man."

In conclusion, he called for peace through arbitration, an area in which the administration had a somewhat better reputation. In the next Roosevelt term, Hay promised an array of arbitration treaties "with such of the European powers as desire them."

The speech was effective, taking the Roosevelt doctrine to a constituency that otherwise might have drawn different conclusions from recent events. "The great hall was crowded to the roof," Hay noted in his diary. "I was astonished to see how heartily they applauded my report."

HIS TRAIN WAS LATE getting to Washington the next morning and he went directly from the station to the White House. Right off, Roosevelt asked Hay to stay on as secretary of state for another four years. "I did not give him any direct answer," Hay wrote in his diary. He did, however, consent to make one more speech—this one at Carnegie Hall in New York—before election day.

As November neared, Roosevelt's victory was all but assured. Alton Parker and his running mate, eighty-year-old former West Virginia senator Henry G. Davis, had made only the slightest dent in the Republican dreadnought. Their operatives endeavored futilely to prove that Roosevelt was in the pocket of the trusts. To get at Hay, someone in New York put out a pamphlet excerpting his more anti-Catholic comments in *Castilian Days.*

Hay had only one moment of anxiety. On Sunday morning, October 23, Roosevelt dropped by Lafayette Square for their customary talk after church. Hay was taken aback to see the president "badly bunged about the head and face"; his horse had stumbled crossing a bridge and thrown him. When Roosevelt made light of his latest brush with death, Hay changed the subject and brought up the secret pledge Lincoln had made in August 1864, in which he promised to support McClellan in the event that he lost the election. Roosevelt welcomed the history lesson, Hay noted, "and went on, as he often does, to compare Lincoln's great trials with what he calls his little ones."

Not until later did Hay reflect on how near he had come to "a four month troubled term" as president. "Strange that twice I have come so hideously near it—once at Lenox [Pittsfield, actually] and now with a hole-in-a-bridge. The President will of course outlive me, but he will not live to be old."

SIX THOUSAND REPUBLICANS PACKED Carnegie Hall on the evening of October 23. Twice that many were turned away. Hay arrived hoarse from a cold, but once under way, he gained his voice and his nerve. He raised many of the same issues he had covered in Michigan; but with the election less than two weeks away and with Roosevelt so far in front, the moment to engage the national debate had passed. His goal this time was far more straightforward and his rhetoric less decorous. "If you vote the Republican ticket," he declared, "you know what you are doing. The Republican record and the Republican professions are at one. They avow what they have done. They make no apologies, no excuses, for it. They say that under similar circumstances they will do the same again."

On the other hand, to vote for the Democrats was to reap the whirl-wind: "[N]o wizard son of a seventh son can tell what their policy is, what they would do with the Government if they were given it. Their platform is a set of turbid and evasive phrases. The utterances of their public men are shifty and self-contradictory. They talk of a policy of adventure! I have yet to hear of an adventure so reckless and wild as intrusting the fortunes of the Republic to an aggregation like the Democratic party of today."

The partisan crowd loved Hay the ward-warrior, expressing their approbation throughout the hour-long speech. One newspaper reported "outbursts" of applause. In his diary Hay preferred, more modestly, to describe the frequent interruptions as "sighs of adhesion."

• • •

NOVEMBER 8, 1904, WAS anticlimactic. Hay spent the day in his office. "No Sunday is ever so quiet as Election Day at the Department," he remarked. "It was a blessed chance to work and I pretty well cleared off my table." Shortly after nine o'clock, he went over to the White House and found the president standing amid a crowd in the Red Room, his hands full of telegrams. One of them was from Judge Parker, congratulating him on his victory. Roosevelt had won thirty-three of forty-five states, more than twice as many electoral votes as his opponent, and more popular votes than any previous president.

The next morning, an exuberant Roosevelt sent for Hay and showered him with appreciation. "Hayism," the president asserted, had made a difference in the campaign, and he once again beseeched Hay to stay on, stressing that his presence as confidant and foreign minister meant a great deal to his "personal comfort." Before Hay could answer, they were interrupted by a secretary, delivering more letters of congratulation. Two days later, Roosevelt let slip to the newspapers, "Hay Will Stay Four More Years."

Hay felt trapped. "He did it in a moment of emotion," he said of Roosevelt's announcement, "for he has never discussed the matter seriously with me and I have never said I would stay. I have always deprecated the idea, saying there was not four years work in me. Now I will have to go along a while longer, as it would be a scandal to contradict him."

MORTALITY DREW CLOSER STILL. The following day his older brother, Leonard, died in Warsaw. A blizzard had struck Washington, and neither Hay nor his other brother, Charles, who was still in Boston recovering from surgery, could make it to the funeral in time.

Hay shared his grief in a letter to Roosevelt. "I owe him everything. . . . He was always my standard," he said of Leonard, who had made a career of the army. "He was not so quick at his books as I was, but far more sure. He taught me my Latin and Greek. . . . He fought my battles. . . . Once I dreamed we were Christians thrown to the beasts in the Coliseum. He stepped between me and a lion and whipped the great cat with his fists. . . . He was the chief of my tribe, in birth as well as in mind and character. . . . Now he has left us, and I never had a chance to get even with him for all he did for me when we were boys. My uncertain health, the weather, and other futilities have kept me away from his funeral. I feel remorselessly unworthy of him."

Roosevelt responded with a tenderness every bit as fraternal: "[A]ll that you say about not having been able to return the wealth of love and active devotion to your brother would be, in his eyes, were he now alive, a matter for good humored and affectionate laughter. You *have* returned it; all your public acts have been to him, as in a less degree to all your other kinsmen and to all your old friends, a source of keen pride. Think what interest your career has been to him; of the purple threads it continually shot through the woof of his life."

The remainder of the year was consumed with the usual post-election intriguing over appointments. One post that was no longer a matter of conjecture was secretary of state. Hay had agreed to continue. "There is, perhaps, no reason why I should not stay," he wrote his old friend George Smalley, "except weariness of body and spirit, and that seems not to be a sufficient reason. But how long is a question for Providence and the doctors to decide."

He had yet another reason to remain. He learned through Adams that Lizzie Cameron might be coming back. "You, who are always the same, will find a few chill gray relics of the Washington you knew so well," he wrote her. "But I am talking nonsense. You will see no change. Your radiance will, here as elsewhere, light up your environment."

THE NEW YEAR, HOWEVER, brought illness and futility. Winning the election had been a bagatelle compared to the opposition Hay and Roosevelt now faced in the Senate, where treaties were too easily doomed by a minority of one third plus one. "A treaty entering the Senate is like a bull going into the arena," Hay noted in his diary. "[N]o one can tell just how or when the final blow will fall—but one thing is certain: it will never leave the arena alive."

One by one, everything he sent to the Capitol was mutilated or murdered. The first to fall was the Hay-Bond Treaty, a reciprocity agreement between the United States and Newfoundland that exempted certain Canadian exports from tariff in exchange for American access to Canadian fisheries. Its executioner was Cabot Lodge, who used the familiar weapon of amendment. "It was a grotesque sight," Hay wrote bitterly, "seeing Lodge [deal] the treaty its death blow by refusing the Newfoundlanders [duty-]free salt codfish—the only thing they cared about." Lodge's conduct, Hay griped to Joseph Choate, was "as stupid a piece of bad manners as any country has ever been guilty of."

A similar fate awaited arbitration treaties that Hay had signed with nine European countries and Mexico over the previous three months. The treaties were innocuous, singling out no party, people, or industry for favor or offense—no more nor less than straightforward instruments of peace, as Hay had promised in his Boston speech. The signatories agreed simply to take their treaty disputes to the Permanent Court of Arbitration at The Hague. As a deterrent to diplomatic frivolousness, or perhaps as a stage of anger management, there was also a provision stipulating that any dispute had to be spelled out in an "agreement" in advance.

The Senate—Republicans and Democrats united—didn't like the idea of being left out of any phase of the game and changed the word "agreement" to "treaty," thereby creating the absurdity of a treaty requiring a treaty before it could be arbitrated. Such were the principles of the exalted upper house.

Hay and Roosevelt took the rebuke personally. "The President, and in my lesser degree, myself were the subject of a good many venomous speeches," Hay noted bitterly after the Senate voted to change the wording. "There was a loud clamor that the rights of the Senate were invaded, [and that] the President's majority was too big—they wanted to teach him that he wasn't *it*." Roosevelt was indignant and refused to send the treaties abroad for ratification. Hay persuaded him that nothing could be gained by "a battle over the corpse," especially since they had one more treaty pending in the Senate.

This one involved Santo Domingo and a situation similar to the Venezuelan crisis of 1902. After a succession of revolutions, Santo Domingo (today's Dominican Republic) was in a shambles and direly in debt to several European powers, Germany being the most wolfish. In early 1904, so soon after the Panama revolution and the establishment of the canal zone, many pundits wondered if Roosevelt might next set his sights on Santo Domingo. He assured Hay and the rest of the cabinet that he desired another island possession "about as much as a gorged anaconda wants to swallow a porcupine wrong end to."

Roosevelt was more specific and less colloquial in his address to Congress in December 1904. "It is not true that the United States feels any land hunger or entertains any projects as regards the other nations of the Western Hemisphere save such as are for their welfare," he assured his audience. "If a nation shows that it knows how to act with reasonable efficiency and decency in social and political matters, if it keeps order and pays its obligations, it fears no interference from the United States." But on the other hand, he warned, "Chronic wrongdoing, or an impotence which results in a general loosening of the ties of civilized society, may . . . ultimately require intervention."

Roosevelt once more was warning Germany, indirectly, to keep its distance, but he was also thinking specifically of Santo Domingo. Rather than send in gunboats—again—and in order to prevent any other power from doing the same, he had Hay strike a deal with the Dominican government by which the United States would take control of Dominican customshouses and use 55 percent of all revenues to pay down the debt. In exchange, the United States promised to preserve Dominican integrity.

Later on, the president's rationale for intervention in the domestic administration of Santo Domingo—or any other country in the Western Hemisphere—would be recognized and respected as the Roosevelt Corollary to the Monroe Doctrine. But on February 15, 1905, when Hay introduced the Dominican debt plan as a "protocol of an agreement," the Senate saw only a gross violation of the Constitution, an egregious abuse of executive authority. And in the end it was the Senate's authority that prevailed. The Santo Domingo treaty was never given the courtesy of a vote.

HAY MIGHT HAVE BEEN more galled if he'd had more strength. By the end of January, there were days when he could barely make it out of bed, much less to the State Department. "One blessed result of the frame of mind of the Senators towards the State Department is that hardly one of them has come to see me for a fortnight," he joked thinly. "I suppose they mean it as a bitter discipline; if so, I hope it may last for a fortnight longer."

On January 28, he wrote in his diary: "I had last night much pain, feverishness and a horror of dreams. In one I was going to be hanged."

Four days later: "The weather still remains gloomy—*et moi aussi.*"

Yet there were bright spots amid the dreariness. On the diplomatic front, his treaties may have been doomed but three of his friends had at last gained the appointments they longed for. William Rockhill was headed, most deservedly, for China to succeed Edwin Conger. Henry White finally had been promoted from secretary in London to minister in Rome. And for Whitelaw Reid, the wishful thinking and sour grapes were over: Roosevelt had named him the next ambassador to Great Britain. "I cannot help telling you with what long looked for delight I shall counter-sign your commission," Hay wrote to Reid, with only the very slightest vestige of stiffness in his tone.

He was able to reward other friends as well. He went to New York in January for the first meeting of the American Academy of Arts and Letters. Howells and Twain were absent, regrettably, but Hay and the others present voted membership to Henry Adams and Henry James.

In New York, he just missed seeing Lizzie Cameron, who had recently returned from Paris after three years away. Hay's letter to her did not indicate her whereabouts; for a moment he believed there was a chance that they might take the same train to Washington. But he had to leave a day early. "So I must live till Tuesday on the hope of seeing you," he wrote her. "You will shine on us—from all I hear about you—like a beauteous Immortal coming back to earth to find the battered relics of those she used to play with. Every one who sees you sings the sweet and monotonous song, 'She is lovelier than ever,' and I feel like getting smoked glasses for Tuesday. Seeing you again seems too good to be true, and too bright to bear." There is no evidence that she made it to Washington on Tuesday, and no explanation why not. She was never quite as dedicated to Hay as he was to her.

But he did see another dear ex-patriot in Washington. Henry James was back in America, and Hay had lured him to the capital with a promise to introduce him to the president. Roosevelt had always found James's prose too precious for his liking; Hay, however, was a steadfast admirer. He had just read James's recent novel, *The Ambassadors*, which was not actually about ambassadors but a circle of Americans idling abroad. "In its scorn of traditions of all sorts—traditions of style, construction and moral[s]," Hay thought it "wonderful."

James stayed next door, with Adams, and the dinner hosted by Hay and Clara was a great success. Saint-Gaudens, John La Farge, and most of the other members of the American Academy of Arts and Letters were also invited, although, in noting the occasion in his diary, Hay oddly neglected to mention their presence, or even that of James and Adams. The evening evidently belonged to one man. "The President came to dinner," Hay recorded. "It was a very pretty party of 28. The women were good to look at and the men good to talk [to]. The President was in great form." How Theodore Roosevelt got on with Henry James in the Hay salon will never be known. Yet it is safe to say that the Botticelli *Madonna*, beneath which these American immortals conversed, gleamed warmly in their presence.

ON MARCH 3, THE eve of the inauguration, Hay gave Roosevelt a present similar to the one he had given to William McKinley: a gold ring in which was cast a strand of Lincoln's hair. "Please wear it tomorrow; you are one of the men who most thoroughly understand and appreciate Lincoln," Hay wrote. Hay had Lincoln's and Roosevelt's monograms engraved on the ring, along with words from Horace: *Longes, O utinam, bone dux, ferias/Praestes Hesperiae* ("Good Captain, may you grant long periods of peace in Hisperia").

Roosevelt apparently knew nothing about the McKinley ring (or the ring given to Rutherford Hayes) when he thanked Hay for his thoughtfulness. "Surely no other President, on the eve of his inauguration, has ever received such a gift from such a friend," he responded. "I am wearing the ring now; I shall think of it and you as I take the oath tomorrow. I wonder if you have any idea what your strength and wisdom and sympathy, what the guidance you have given me and the mere delight of your companionship, have meant to me in these three and a half years." He signed his letter, "With love and gratitude. Ever yours, Theodore Roosevelt."

Hay sat bundled in heavy topcoat and scarf against a blustery north wind as Roosevelt took the oath of office and delivered his inaugural address—"short and in excellent temper and manner," Hay pronounced it. After lunch at the White House, Hay was joined by Clara and Clarence in the grandstand for the three-hour inaugural parade. The inaugural ball, he tallied wearily, "was a success in numbers if nothing else."

THE CABINET MEETING THE following week was perfunctory. All of the members had submitted their resignations and been promptly reappointed, with the exception of the postmaster general. "I have three Commissions of Secretary of State already and this will be the fourth—all of them countersigned by myself," Hay observed drolly. He was reminded of Mark Twain's quip: "I like to introduce myself because then I can get in all the facts."

Yet he had not been entirely honest with the president. Roosevelt knew that Hay was weak and exhausted, but only Clara and Adams knew just how close he was to complete collapse. Since January, wife and best friend had conspired to pry him from the State Department for an enforced hiatus of rest and treatment in Europe, where the medical expertise and therapeutic baths were esteemed the best in the world. Finally, he felt so awful that he had no choice. Adams booked passage for Hay, Clara, himself, and three servants aboard the *Cretic*, departing New York on March 18, bound for Genoa, Italy. They expected to return at the end of May.

"I tried to walk this afternoon, but it was tough work," Hay wrote on the twelfth. "By going very slowly & stopping often I was able to cover about a mile." His doctor, Surgeon General Presley Rixey, who had been the White House physician since McKinley, suspected "nervous dyspepsia." When Hay complained of "an increasing pain over the heart," Rixey expressed puzzlement.

Even then, he was loath to leave. The situation in China seemed to be reaching a critical juncture. In the five-month-long siege of Port Arthur, Russia and Japan had suffered more than one hundred thousand casualties; in taking a single hill, the Japanese had lost more than ten thousand men. At last Port Arthur surrendered on January 2. Hay broke the news to Cassini at a White House reception.

Things were not going well for Russia at home, either. On January 16, Bloody Sunday, Cossack cavalrymen opened fire on two hundred thousand demonstrators in St. Petersburg, killing and wounding hundreds, perhaps thousands, of citizens. A month later, a socialist blew up the mayor of Moscow, Grand Duke Sergei, the czar's uncle. The revered writer and moral oracle, Leo Tolstoy, was exhorting his countrymen to quit the fight in Manchuria.

On January 26, Hay felt too sick to leave his house but pulled himself together sufficiently to receive Minister Takahira, who was eager to spell out possible conditions for peace.

Meanwhile, Cassini, out of pride and doubtless under orders from St. Petersburg, scoffed at the peace rumors when they appeared in American papers. "I do not know who has set them afloat. They are terms a nation might accept who had only two soldiers left and them in flight," he told Hay with his usual hauteur. "Do not people know we have an army in Manchuria, intact, of 400,000 men and a fine fleet?" He persisted in calling the Japanese successes "*éphémères*." As for the internal disorder in Russia, the ambassador blamed them on "a *nombre infine* of deranged minds."

Cassini was obliged to change his tone, if not his accent, two weeks later when the Russian army was driven from the Manchurian capital of Mukden. In possibly the greatest collision of soldiers in the history of warfare, a Russian force of two hundred ninety thousand was no match for the relentless Japanese, two hundred thousand strong.

On March 10, the day after Russian general Alexei Kuropatkin ordered a retreat, the U.S. minister to Tokyo, Lloyd Griscom, cabled Hay that the Japanese military desired peace and that the Japanese government wanted Roosevelt to mediate it. The precise terms were not yet on the table, nor would the war be over until Russia's Baltic fleet, which was due in Chinese waters any day, was crippled or otherwise brought to heel.

Yet the time was ripe. "If the war stops now," Griscom wrote on March 15, three days before Hay was to depart for Europe, "[the Japanese] will be very little damaged, but within the next few months they see staring them in the face the possibility of acute financial distress and endless suffering. . . . The evident longing for peace is something indescribable, but they are plucky fighters and, like a thorough-bred terrier, they will hold on until they are dead. . . . In a vague sort of way the Japanese undoubtedly look to us for some sort of assistance when the time for negotiating peace comes, although they do not exactly know what form it could take. Possibly they only want that we give the great moral weight of our approval to the peace conditions they would exact."

The great moral weight was at last too much for Hay. Months before, he had recommended the president as the most capable mediator of peace. And now the job would be Roosevelt's alone.

On March 17, Hay, Clara, and Adams took the train to New York, accompanied by Clarence and Jim and Alice Wadsworth. They stayed that night in the apartment Helen kept at the Lorraine Hotel. Roosevelt happened to be in New York also, to attend the wedding of his niece Anna Eleanor Roosevelt to distant cousin Franklin, same last name. Hay was watching from his window as the president's carriage rolled up next door at Delmonico's, escorted by a troop of cavalry.

The next morning, Hay awoke with chest pain. At the White Star pier, he collapsed climbing the stairs to board the *Cretic*; he would have fallen if he had not been caught by Jim Wadsworth and Clarence, who were on hand to see him off. He had to be carried to his cabin in a wheelchair.

From Washington, Dr. Rixey issued a statement that Hay was merely suffering from "overwork." Hay put it differently in a letter to his English friend, the historian George Trevelyan, who was his exact age. "I have great doubts whether this tenement of clay which I inhabit will hold together," he confessed. "Walking with Henry Adams the other day, I expressed my regret that by the time I got out of office, I should have lost the faculty of enjoyment. As you know Adams, you can understand the dry malice with which he replied: 'Make your mind easy on that score, sonny! You've lost it now!'"

CHAPTER 21

All the Great Prizes

Hay spent the first week of the voyage in his cabin. Thankfully, the Atlantic was calm and the *Cretic* "as steady as a church," he reported in his diary. As they reached the Azores, he was able to make turns about the deck. He chose not to go ashore at Gibraltar or Algiers, conserving his energy for lunch and a carriage ride when they put in for a day at Naples. Nearly seven years—seven all-consuming years—had passed since last he set foot in Europe. No man had been more *of* the world than John Hay; ironically, his labors had kept him from living *in* it. Now, by getting away from the State Department and returning to the cosmopolitan comforts of the Continent, he hoped to find the restorative he needed. But on April 1, as they prepared to dock at Genoa, the pain in his chest returned. "We have got to find out what is the matter," Adams wrote to Lizzie Cameron.

At the suggestion of the American consul in Genoa, they drove down the coast to Nervi to consult a German physician. Dr. Stifler examined Hay thoroughly, testing his blood and measuring his pulse and heartbeat. The diagnosis was not simply "nervous" or "dyspeptic," as Dr. Rixey had supposed. Stifler was sure that Hay's heart was enlarged, a condition, he said, "very common among public men." The doctor recommended that

Hay go to Bad Nauheim, near Hamburg, and take a course of therapeutic baths. A railway strike and the dulcet Mediterranean air kept the Hays and Adams in Nervi another two weeks, and they did not arrive at Nauheim until April 22.

Nauheim had been known for its regenerative waters since the Iron Age and probably earlier. In the late nineteenth century, under the direction of Dr. Isidore Groedel, the spa began specializing in the care of cardiac patients. The rich and royal made the pilgrimage from all over Europe, Russia, and America to soak in waters naturally high in salt and carbonic acid. "The baths act like external champagne," Alvey Adee, who knew his way around Europe, wrote to his boss, encouraging him to make the trip. "[T]he carbonic acid bites and tickles the skin as it does the tongue. The circulation is stimulated, the tired nerves wake up, and the whole ganglionic system is put in the way of regaining strength." If Hay needed any further recommendation, he had only to recall that Lizzie Cameron had been to the spa several years earlier after a bout of influenza was feared to have weakened her heart—which, as her admirers well knew, proved to be plenty resilient.

Dr. Groedel confirmed Stifler's diagnosis and prescribed a regimen of twenty baths, four per week. When Hay asked the doctor candidly whether his condition was such that he ought to resign as secretary of state, Groedel pointed out that six years earlier Admiral Alfred von Tirpitz, secretary of the German navy, had come to Nauheim with a similar heart problem and was still at his post. Nonetheless, Hay wrote Roosevelt, telling him that, even though there was "no reason why the malady should be progressive," he would understand entirely if Roosevelt decided to replace him. "I will not go through the form of offering you my commission," he said, "though I often feel I have no right to hold it and not do the work it calls for."

Roosevelt, who was hunting wolves and bears in Oklahoma and Colorado, wrote back to assure Hay that the job was still his. "I want you to rest almost absolutely this summer so as to be ready for the inevitable worries next winter," the president counseled. In the meantime, Adee and his fellow assistant secretary, Francis Loomis, could keep the department running, with Secretary of War Taft "sitting on the lid"—Adee's joke; Taft was obese—while Roosevelt was afield.

Adams went off to Paris, leaving Hay to his treatments. Dr. Groedel put him on a strict diet and forbade him from walking far or fast or up-hill or while talking or after meals. Between baths, that left carriage rides, listening to a regimental band on the terrace, and reading. Clara reported to Adams at the beginning of May that her husband was a star patient. "He certainly does look better this morning," she observed, "having lost that harassed look he had." Groedel confirmed that the hydrotherapy was working and that the enlargement of the heart was diminishing.

Clara was encouraged enough that she too left for Paris; Hay would follow her when he finished his course at the end of the month. With each bath, the carbonation and salinity were increased and the tempera-ture of the water lowered, stimulating the heart in stages. On May 22, Hay immersed himself in a thirty-two-degree bath and pronounced it "warm and comfortable after [the] first minute."

That same day, however, he received a jolt that raised his blood pres-sure considerably. Henry Wilson, the American minister in Brussels, wrote Hay that Leopold II—"King of the Belgians" but also the imperial-ist ravager of the Congo and a "rattlepated old lunatic," in Hay's book—wanted to meet Hay in person. "I do not wish to see Mr. Hay as one of the great men of the world, whose services on behalf of civilization can hardly be overestimated," the king solicited. "I simply want to know him in a democratic every day way, and as one man knows another man."

Three days later, Hay received a telegram from Charlemagne Tower in Berlin that Kaiser Wilhelm II hoped to make his acquaintance as well. Next he heard from Joseph Choate in London that King Edward VII wished Hay could find a moment to call on his way home.

After consulting with Dr. Groedel, who strongly advised against any such royal intercourse, Hay was able to decline the kaiser's invitation and reckoned that he had finessed Leopold as well. But two days before he was to leave Nauheim, he walked into his hotel and found the king seated in an armchair by the elevator. Hay had no choice but to invite His High-ness up to his room, until, pleading fatigue, he was able to send his guest on his way.

The next day, after a final bath, Groedel informed him that his en-largement was gone, and, "although the heart still seemed rather weak and excitable and the sounds not strong, everything was much better than when I came." Groedel then gave Hay a list of prohibitions "as long as a chapter of Deuteronomy": no cabbage, radishes, onions, or anything flatulent; little red meat; no aerated water or champagne; no sweets except the plainest pudding; no public speaking and not much animated conversation, especially after dinner. Groedel also advised him against visiting the foreign offices in Paris and London. He must stay perfectly quiet in the first two weeks after his course of baths—a crucial element of his rehabilitation known as *Nachkur* (aftercare). "On the whole," Hay grumbled, "a very dismal prospect."

He slept well enough that night, but in the morning the chest pain was back. "I seem fated to leave Nauheim as I left New York," he wrote. "Even when the pain would die away the pulse kept racing."

He took an overnight train to Paris, and Adams was there to meet him in a brand-new automobile. They spent the day motoring through the Bois de Boulogne, Saint-Cloud, Versailles, and Marly-le-Roi. It was one of those sublime spring days, the roadsides abloom, and doubtless the memories came flooding back—although this was not how he had observed Paris on his previous visit, on the way back to London from Egypt in 1898. They returned to their hotel by five at "an incredible rate of speed." Over the next two days Hay met with the French foreign minister Théophile Delcassé and took more long outings in Adams's machine. So much for *Nachkur.*

Adams dropped Hay and Clara off at the Gare du Nord on the morning of June 2. "Certainly I have done what little I could," he wrote Lizzie, "and I much doubt its use. Hay has not gained strength yet. Paris pulled him down at once. His nerves are gone. He is in no better physical condition than when we sailed." Adams, ever the cynical outsider, could not comprehend why Hay did not embrace the inevitable and leave office while there was still life and dignity left in him. "Theodore is his own Cabinet, and especially likes to play with foreign kings," Adams continued to Lizzie. "Hay has had no choice but to hold the hats and look on. He had better go out, now that his excuse is good. It is true that I have said so from the first:—Get out before you are kicked out! was my standing proverb. He said he wanted to see himself get kicked out. Instead, he merely stays kicked in."

In London, Hay was even more restive than in Paris; the temptations of his favorite city on earth were too overwhelming. He spent an hour with Foreign Secretary Lansdowne, and the following day, Sunday, he went to Buckingham Palace, where, out of consideration for his health, Edward VII broke with protocol and received him in a small drawing room on the first floor. "He began talking at once with great affability and fluency," Hay wrote, "laying great stress on the agreeable relations between our two countries"—words that may not have mended Hay's heart but surely warmed it, for no one had been more instrumental in nurturing and preserving England's friendship than he.

The pace did not slacken. He and Clara dined with Lord and Lady Algernon Gordon-Lennox and their nephew, who had recently returned from Manchuria. Hay lunched with Whitelaw Reid, who had just begun his ambassadorship. He saw the artist Edwin Abbey and admired his latest sketches. After a morning of shopping, he visited the Royal Academy, where in the past he had spent so many cherished hours, to see John Singer Sargent's latest masterpiece, a portrait of the Duke of Marlborough and family. "An astonishing piece of work," Hay declared, "worthy to rank with the greatest groups of portraits in the history of art."

There just wasn't enough time. On the final evening in London, a parade of devotees dropped by the hotel to say hello and goodbye: the diplomat and international gossip Cecil Spring-Rice, the journalist John St. Loe Strachey, the baronet Sir Robert Cunliffe, and James Bryce, author of *The American Commonwealth*. The attention was touching and bittersweet. Before heading to Liverpool to board the ship for home, Hay wrote a letter to Sir John Clark in Scotland, to whom he had been introduced by Adams twenty years earlier. "When I left Nauheim the German Doctor Groedel told me I must not pass by Paris and London except under bonds to see nobody, and do nothing either sensible or amusing," he explained contritely. "So I go away from these two homes of my heart as if I had passed through them in a nightmare. . . . Farewell, dear and generous friend. We never forget you when we think of this beautiful Elder world, and the happy days we have spent here."

ONE NIGHT DURING THE crossing, he had a dream. "I went to the White House to report to the President who turned out to be Mr. Lincoln," he recorded in his diary. "He was very kind and considerate, and sympathetic about my illness. He said there was little work of importance on hand. He gave me two unimportant letters to answer. I was pleased that this slight order was within my power to obey. I was not in the least surprised at Lincoln's presence in the White House. But the whole impression of the dream was one of overpowering melancholy."

The next morning, as they were approaching New York Harbor, they received a Marconi—a wireless telegram, a first for both of them—announcing the birth of a son to Alice and Jim Wadsworth, named for his father.

Helen and Payne met their ship. They spent the weekend with the Whitneys on Long Island, and on Monday, Hay took the train to Washington, intending to stay long enough to "say Ave Caesar! to the President," he told John Clark, and to straighten his desk if he could. "I owe you a thousand thanks for your generous forbearance in my disablement," he wrote the president from New York. "How far I can continue to accept it is a question we can talk over when we meet."

He dined with the Roosevelts at the White House on Monday night. The president, he was relieved and mildly chagrined to learn, had the nation's foreign affairs well in hand. Roosevelt had gotten around the Senate's rejection of the Dominican debt-collection impasse by implementing it as a modus vivendi, a temporary agreement that the Senate could only derail post hoc.

Roosevelt's much greater achievement was in coaxing Japan and Russia to consider peace. On May 27, the day Hay left Nauheim, the Japanese navy attacked the Russian fleet as it attempted to slip through the Strait of Tsushima, between Korea and Japan, en route to Vladivostok. It was the most decisive naval victory since Trafalgar, exactly a century earlier. When the smoke cleared, thirty-four of thirty-eight Russian ships were sunk, ruined, or captured, and ten thousand Russian sailors were dead or wounded. Japan lost only three torpedo boats and a hundred sailors.

In the days that followed, first Japan and then Russia accepted Roosevelt's offer to mediate a meeting between the two combatants in order "to discuss the whole peace question themselves." Hay had received the happy news when he landed in New York. "It was a great stroke of that good luck which belongs to those who 'know how' and are not afraid," he congratulated Roosevelt. "I need not have worried about my being sick and away. I have evidently not been missed. Reid once told me when I had been running the *Tribune* in his absence that 'the paper has been disgustingly good.' That is what I find your management of the State Department during my truancy."

Neither would have been so ungentlemanly to say so, but it was now quite obvious: the proprietorship of the State Department had changed hands.

HAY HAD NO DESIRE and even less strength to linger in the simmering heat of the capital. But first he had one more call to make before heading to New Hampshire to join Clara. He had heard from Adams that Lizzie Cameron had finally moved back into her house on Lafayette Square. On his first day in Washington, he stepped the short distance to her door, only to find that she had already left for Newport. Greeted by "silence and bitter-sweet memories," he wrote her a letter, full of news about Nauheim and Adams. He signed it gallantly, demurely, wistfully, "Love to Martha" (her daughter) "and things unutterable to you."

Lizzie read his letter and replied immediately. "My Dear and Great Friend," she began. "The sight of your familiar handwriting . . . filled me with joy. . . . [W]hy didn't you come sooner and spend two blissful and hot weeks with me in Washington?" Then, alluding to the mysterious kiss exchanged in Hay's poem "Two on the Terrace," she disclosed, "I drove up to the Capitol one hot moon-filled night, and around the Monument, and thought how very unchanged it all was, and yet how different." She suggested that he join her at Nauheim the following summer. "Do! We can walk around the lake, which is the one thing allowed, and drink black coffee on the terrace like the best of Germans."

She signed off: "Goodbye, dear Mr. Hay. When shall I see you? Could you not come through this way?"

ON FRIDAY, JUNE 23, Hay had a brief interview with Cassini and then saw Dr. Rixey, who listened to his heart with some concern and sent him on his way. He left Washington with Clarence that evening, and they arrived at the Fells the following afternoon. "The night was delightfully cool," he wrote Roosevelt on Sunday, "and the morning air is like that of a new made world."

But he was not long for it. Later in the day, he grew increasingly uncomfortable, unable to urinate, a painful problem that had afflicted him some years earlier. Worried about the strain on his heart, Clara summoned a local doctor and also telegraphed Dr. Charles S. Scudder at Massachusetts General Hospital in Boston. Scudder enlisted a colleague and rushed to Newbury by special train, making the trip in a near-record two hours. He initially diagnosed uremia, an indication of kidney malfunction, but later suspected merely a bladder infection. He inserted a catheter, and within twenty-four hours Hay was reported to be "in no immediate danger" and "doing nicely." Scudder noted that Hay's heart was weak but predicted that he would be up and about in a few days. Clara urged Helen and Payne to go ahead with their trip to Europe; their ship left New York on Tuesday.

In Paris, meanwhile, Henry Adams read of Hay's illness in the *Herald* and wrote to Lizzie Cameron: "Although I could not have prophesied it to a day, I fully expected it this week. . . . The doctors had been all wrong about him. . . . I imagine that Hay's life is as good as ended."

Dr. Scudder returned on Friday evening and was pleased with Hay's progress. He was sitting up in bed, still very weak, but able to sign papers and dictate to Clara a short letter to the State Department. Then he asked for a sheet of stationery, saying he wanted to write a memorandum, Clara recalled, "but he was so tired after he had dictated the letter that I said he better not do it"—the memorandum—"and he said, 'If you promise me I will be better tomorrow I will wait.'" With that he bid her good night and went to sleep.

A few moments after midnight, the nurse noticed him struggling for breath and summoned Scudder and the other doctor, who had remained at the Fells throughout the week. When Clara reached her husband's bedside, she found him groaning as the doctors attempted artificial respiration and injected him with nitroglycerine. "I did not know he was dying till I saw the look of horror on the nurse's face," she later wrote.

"Then the Doctors tried the stethoscope & neither could hear anything and he was gone."

John Milton Hay departed the world at 12:25 am on July 1, 1905.

AFTERWARD, WHEN CLARA OPENED his diary, she discovered that he had made no significant entry since returning to the United States. On June 13, he had recorded his dream of Lincoln in the White House. On June 14, the day before landing in New York, he had jotted these words, surely recognizing that they might be his final testament:

"I say to myself that I should not rebel at the thought of my life ending at this time. I have lived to be old, something I never expected in my youth. I have had many blessings, domestic happiness being the greatest of all. I have lived my life. I have had success beyond all the dreams of my boyhood. My name is printed in the journals of the world without descriptive qualification, which may, I suppose, be called fame. By mere length of service I shall occupy a modest place in the history of my time. If I were to live several years more I should probably add nothing to my existing reputation; while I could not reasonably expect any further enjoyment of life, such as falls to the lot of old men in sound health. I know death is the common lot, and what is universal ought not to be deemed a misfortune; and yet—instead of confronting it with dignity and philosophy, I cling instinctively to life and the things of life, as eagerly as if I had not had my chance at happiness & gained nearly all the great prizes."

CLARA TOOK HER HUSBAND to Cleveland to be buried. "As he had told me once he did not care where I laid him and as our boy was there, it seemed more like home," she reasoned. The flag-draped casket was placed for public viewing in the Chamber of Commerce Auditorium for a day, awaiting the arrival of Roosevelt, the vice president, the cabinet, and the rest of the mourners, a list that included current and former senators, a Supreme Court justice, the governor of Ohio, and a delegation of foreign ministers. Robert Lincoln came; Lizzie Cameron had intended to be there but changed her mind once she learned that the funeral was to be so large and "official."

On the morning of July 5, twenty-four carriages, escorted by an honor guard of cavalry, followed the hearse from Public Square along Euclid Avenue to Lake View Cemetery. After a simple service at the cemetery's chapel, a quartet sang "For All the Saints Who from Their Labors Rest," and Hay was interred beside Del—their graves halfway between the Rockefeller family plot and the massive monument to James Garfield. Services were held the same day at the Church of the Covenant in Washington and at St. Paul's Cathedral in London. Helen and Payne Whitney arrived in England in time to attend the latter.

The headline in the next day's *Cleveland Plain Dealer* read, "Prince of Peace Was Loved by All," and judging by the outpouring of condolences and memorials, it was true.

Most said the same things, in different ways. They touched on the Lincoln years and the Lincoln biography and continued to the Open Door, the Boxer Rebellion, and the Panama Canal. They reprinted and recited "Jim Bludso" and "Little Breeches."

Yet it was not the litany of Hay's deeds that distinguished him as much as the manner in which he had conducted himself while achieving them. "He was not only the foremost statesman of his time; he was the tenderest, dearest, most attractive man of men, and the finest gentleman books make any mention of," James Hoyt of Cleveland attested. "With no thought of self-seeking, simply by . . . the charm of his own personality, he rose step by step until at last he came to be recognized for what he was, the greatest prime minister that this republic has ever had."

One eulogist after another stressed Hay's thoughtfulness—toward subordinates, complete strangers, his peers, and the world. One of the news clippings that Clara added to Hay's scrapbook avowed, "Among his many admirable traits, none was more notable than his deep human sympathy, which leaped the boundaries of home and state and nation and went out to the suffering of all lands."

Above all, they praised his forthrightness. "At first men began to talk about 'shirt sleeve' diplomacy, as if frankness were something brutal," the *Independent* of New York observed. "Mr. Hay believed that simple straightforward directness is good in international as well as personal affairs."

And he was credited with an impeccable sense of timing: "If, as the old Greeks said, Opportunity has only a forelock, so that he cannot be seized after he has passed by," the *Independent* continued, "John Hay was always alert to catch him at the right moment."

Some of the most profound appreciations came from Jews, who regarded the Kishinev petition as a turning point in the government's acknowledgment of anti-Semitism. "[W]e have lost our mightiest friend among the nations; a friend who dared to do in behalf of the Jews that which no man in so high a position has ever dared before," the Tiphereth Zion Society of Pittsburgh proclaimed in an official resolution. Moses Gries of the Central Conference of American Rabbis said in Cleveland on the day of Hay's funeral: "As rabbi, and for the moment as representative of Jews of the land, I honor and revere the name of John Hay. He was clean and pure and belonged to the pure and upright among men."

Hay was not a churchgoer himself; he left that to Clara, a solid Presbyterian. Yet he could quote the Bible with fluency and allowed some of his verse to be turned into hymns. "My faith in Christ is implicit. I am a believer," he had assured Hiram Haydn, pastor of the Old Stone Church in Cleveland, who presided over the wedding of both of Hay's daughters and the funerals of first Del and now his father. The Reverend Teunis Hamlin, pastor of the Church of the Covenant in Washington, said much the same thing of the late secretary of state that had once been said of President Lincoln: "It would be difficult to find in the New Testament a trait of character described as Christian that was not exemplified in Mr. Hay."

More mixed were the expressions of grief from Theodore Roosevelt and Henry Adams. When the president received word at Oyster Bay that Hay had died, he promptly issued a public statement: "His death, a crushing sorrow to his friends, is to the people of this country a national bereavement, and in addition, it is a serious loss to mankind." That same day he wrote to Clara: "I dearly loved him; there is no one who . . . can quite fill the place he held. He was not only my wise and patient advisor in affairs of state; he was the most devoted and at the same time the most charming of friends."

But immediately after returning from Hay's funeral, Roosevelt began putting distance between himself and his former secretary of state, enriching his own esteem by poaching from Hay's. "Hay was a really great man," Roosevelt allowed in a letter to Senator Albert Beveridge, "and the more credit is given him the more I am delighted, while the result of the last election showed how futile it was for the *Evening Post*, the *Sun*, and the rest of my enemies to try to draw the distinction between what Hay did and what I did. Whether I originated the work, or whether he did and merely received my backing and approval, is of no consequence to the party, and what is said of it is of no earthly consequence to me."

Except that it was. "Of course, what I am about to say I can only say to a close friend, for it seems almost ungenerous," Roosevelt confided to Cabot Lodge in the now notorious (and previously quoted) letter of July 11, 1905. "But for two years [Hay's] health had been such that he could do very little work of importance. His name, his reputation, his staunch loyalty, all made him a real asset of the administration. But in actual work I had to do the big things myself, and the other things I always feared would be badly done or not done at all."

Spoken like a son jealous of his father's shadow.

Had Adams known of Roosevelt's letters, he would not have been shocked by their self-serving disrespect. He had been deeply disgusted by the American political system since at least the Grant administration and now blamed it—and the treaty process in particular—for the death of his best friend. "The Senate killed Hay," he wrote bitterly to Lizzie Cameron from Paris. "Our friend Cabot helped to murder him, [as] consciously as possible, precisely as though he put strychnine in his drink."

Writing to Clara Hay, he was not quite so graphic but equally incensed. Adams was convinced that the cause of Hay's physical decline was not his heart. Hay had done well at Nauheim, lost ground in Paris and London, then improved during the voyage home. But the prospect of going to Washington weighed on him, Adams averred. "[I]t was not physical fatigue . . . that caused collapse, but merely the renewed strain of nervous worry. His diplomates tired him out, after his Senators had poisoned him."

Having spilled the cup of bile, Adams let it flow. "I admit that I draw my conclusions largely from myself. Senators poison me, and therefore I avoid them. Diplomates, especially American Ambassadors"—his father had been one of the few good ones—"bore me beyond endurance, and I never go near them. . . . If I had to deal with them, they would kill me, as, in my opinion, they did him."

After the death of his wife twenty years earlier, Adams had gradually pulled himself together, but he was not sure he could do so again. "As for me it is time to bid good-bye," he wrote Clara. "I am tired. My last hold on the world is lost with him. I am too old to make new efforts or care for new interests. I can no longer look a month ahead, or be sure of my hand or mind. I have clung on to his activities till now, because they were his, but except as his they have no concern for me, and I have no more strength for them. He and I began life together. We will stop together."

THERE ARE MANY THINGS Hay was not. He was not so much a striver as he was an inquirer, an insatiable self-improver. He was not a man of the people, like Lincoln, yet if he was guilty of snobbery, he directed it more often toward other snobs than toward the nation's breadwinners.

He was kind and quite generous—giving not just to candidates but also to charities ranging from mission societies to vocational schools for Negroes—but he was not one hundred percent empathetic to the world. One of the reasons he had interceded on behalf of Jews after the Kishinev massacre was out of concern that such pogroms would increase the flow of unwelcome immigrants to the United States. Similarly, it went without saying that the Open Door swung one way only; he did not ask the Chinese for their permission to send out his celebrated notes to the powers; nor was he inclined to open America's door to China's predominant export: its citizens.

It must also be said that on some level—one that will never be fully ascertained—he was not faithful. Then, too, there was one great prize that, as much as he desired it, he never did attain to his satisfaction.

IF ROOSEVELT'S HARSH POSTMORTEM judgment of Hay is valid, why, then, did the president not release him from service on the many occasions that Hay invited him to do so? The answer most often posited is that Roosevelt employed Hay as the venerable, avuncular pilot of the administration's warship as it parted the waves of the world. Still,

Roosevelt's diminishment of Hay did not alter their actual relationship; it only reframed how Roosevelt wanted that relationship perceived in the pages of his own self-inflated record.

In the twentieth century, moderation and neutrality—not merely diplomatic neutrality but also moral evenhandedness—fell into disuse and disfavor. Hay's treaties were said to be soft; they lacked teeth. Perhaps so, but they were not shortsighted. Hay was a romantic but not the sort who clung to rosier yesteryears. He had sought a new and better world since his boyhood in Illinois, since the Kansas-Nebraska Act had brought America to a fork in the road that changed everything. Republicans, to Hay, were futurists, in the United States and in the Spain of *Castilian Days*. He had a notion of what the New World ought to be, but he was never grandiose in his designs; there was no Hay Doctrine per se. Only in hindsight did his footsteps reveal a path and his decisions exceed the sum of their parts.

Did he remake the world, or rather, would the world have been that much different if he had not played his hand so deftly? An isthmian canal would have been built, somewhere. The United States and Great Britain would have bolstered their bond, eventually. But China? China might be a different organism today had it not been for John Hay.

If Hay put any other indelible stamp on the world, perhaps it was that he demonstrated how the United States ought to comport itself. He, not Roosevelt, was the adult in charge when the nation and the State Department attained global maturity. "With Mr. Hay there was not the shade of a shadow of a suspicion of the patriotic gladiator raising his sword to the genius of the Republic with an 'Ave Columbia Imperatrix! moritorus te salutat,'" John St. Loe Strachey eulogized. "All that the world saw was a great gentleman and a great statesman doing his work for the State and for the President with perfect taste, perfect good sense, and perfect good humour."

William Dean Howells admired Hay's universality, but he also cherished Hay as the best sort of native son: "John Hay, whatever he knew of the world elsewhere, or however it had interested his mind or amused his fancy, was very helplessly and inalienably American. He was American and he was Western by virtue of that very fineness of spirit, that delicacy of mind, that gentleness of heart, often imagined incompatible with our conditions. There was never in him any peevish revolt from these; he accepted them, as he accepted our heat and cold; they were the terms of our being worth while.

"Something of this is evident in all he wrote," continued Howells, a westerner himself, who had written the very first biography of Lincoln in 1864 and had been Hay's first real editor. "In the great history which he contributed to our literature; in the admirable study of foreign life which he left; in the striking, if strikingly unequal, poems of which he always thought so modestly, he avouched his ability to have done what he wished in literature, if only he had wished it enough. He showed in these the potentiality of a great popularity, when he turned from them for the other career which was not more than equally open to him. Yet he chose to do his great service to the public independently of the popular choice, and he, the most innately American of our statesmen, came to represent what was most European in the skill of the diplomacy he practised. We shall all of us love always to think that the frankness, the honesty, the brave humanity which characterized it was the heart of Americanism, [and] in any moment of hesitation concerning this or that fact of it, we could say to ourselves that it must be right because Hay did it."

To be more like John Hay was good. To have more of him would have been even better.

THEODORE ROOSEVELT SUCCEEDED IN bringing Russia and Japan together for a peace conference at Portsmouth, New Hampshire, in August 1905, ending the Russo-Japanese War. Russia at last was compelled to withdraw from Manchuria; the integrity of China was preserved; and Roosevelt was awarded the Nobel Peace Prize for his role as mediator.

Roosevelt replaced Hay with former Secretary of War Elihu Root, who served capably and without extraordinary confrontation or crisis. His relationship with Roosevelt was cordial throughout, and he was not reluctant to speak truth to power. For instance, it was Root, commenting on Roosevelt's conduct during the Panama revolution, who famously told the president: "You have shown that you were accused of seduction and you have conclusively proved that you were guilty of rape."

After her husband's death, Clara tried to persuade Henry Adams to write a biography of Hay. Adams resisted but agreed to help her prepare a selection of his letters and diaries. Clara published them in 1908, but in her unwillingness to ruffle feathers, she abbreviated nearly all proper names to first initials, rendering the three-volume collection insipid if not entirely unintelligible to the general public. She kept the house on Lafayette Square but spent little time there, preferring Cleveland, the Fells, and the company of her children and grandchildren. She died in New York at the home of Helen and Payne Whitney in 1914. Both of Helen and Payne's children made considerable names for themselves: Joan Whitney Payson for her art collection and philanthropy and for founding the New York Mets baseball franchise; John "Jock" Whitney for his polo-playing and playboy lifestyle, for starting the first American venture capital firm, and, finally, for following in his grandfather's footsteps: in 1957, President Eisenhower named him ambassador to England.

Alice and Jim Wadsworth took up residence in the Lafayette Square house after Wadsworth was elected to the U.S. Senate the year of Clara's death. The house, along with Adams's, was razed in 1927, and the Hay-Adams Hotel opened on the site a year later. The family political dynasty continued when Alice and Jim's daughter, Evelyn, married Stuart Symington, who served in the Senate and then ran against John F. Kennedy for the Democratic presidential nomination in 1960. In turn, Evelyn and Stuart Symington's son, James, served four terms in the House of Representatives.

After Harvard, Clarence Hay became an archeologist and eventually a curator at the American Museum of Natural History in New York. He loved the Fells more than did anyone else in the family, and over the years he applied his green thumb to converting rugged pastures into terraced lawns and handsome rock gardens. The house and estate are now preserved as a nature sanctuary and historic site with support from the Society for the Protection of New Hampshire Forests and the U.S. Fish & Wildlife Service. The public is welcome.

Henry Adams did not give up the ghost when Hay died, after all. He published a private edition of his autobiographical *Education of Henry Adams* in 1907, with lengthy appreciations of both Hay and Clarence

King. He continued to travel back and forth to Europe, seeing Lizzie Cameron in Paris, until the First World War began. He died in Washington in 1918.

Lizzie Cameron remained in Paris during the war, joining with, among others, Edith Wharton, to care for the refugees who flocked to the city. None of Hay's letters to Lizzie appeared in Clara's collection, and she did not allow William Roscoe Thayer to use any of them in *The Life and Letters of John Hay* (1915). "I am surprised at my forgetfulness when I told you I had letters of Mr. Hay's which you might care to use," she excused herself to Thayer. "On looking them over I find that most of them are what would seem to anyone not well acquainted with Mr. Hay, ardent love letters! You, who must have handled many such, will understand that they merely express his habit of gallantry, and his love of writing pretty phrases." After Lizzie read the completed biography, she wrote Adams: "I think Mr. Thayer makes [Hay] more a decided, vigorous character than he really was—to me he seemed timid, un-self-asserting, and almost feminine in the delicacy of his intuitions & in his quickness." Lizzie's husband, Donald, died in 1918, five months after Adams, and she never remarried. In her final years she lived in England, where she died in 1944, at the age of eighty-three.

As he was dying in 1901, Clarence King disclosed his true identity to his wife, Ada, and explained that he had left behind a trust fund to take care of her and the children. Over the next thirty years, she received monthly checks from an unknown source. Not until 1933, after Ada filed a legal complaint against the trust, was the identity of the source revealed. First John Hay, then, after his death, Clara, and finally Payne and Helen Whitney had been dutifully sending Ada $50 a month—essentially hush money to protect King's name.

Hay's devotion and affection had outlived him. Once a Heart, a Heart forever—the same Heart who, as "J.H.," had written:

> *He seen his duty, a dead-sure thing,—*
>   *And went for it thar and then;*
> *And Christ ain't a-going to be too hard*
>   *On a man that died for men.*

The subject of the rhyme was a Mississippi river man, Jim Bludso, but the benediction might have applied just as easily to another of Hay's heroes, Abraham Lincoln. John Hay would never have volunteered any such words about himself; all the same, the virtues they celebrated—loyalty, humility, grace under pressure, unswerving sacrifice—were his own to the very end.

Acknowledgments

It was serendipity that brought me to John Hay. In reading accounts of Abraham Lincoln's assassination and then of William McKinley's, I was astonished to see that Hay had been at the bedside of both presidents as they lay dying. I soon learned from the seminal biographies of Hay written by William Roscoe Thayer and Tyler Dennett that these events, indelible to be sure, were but two of the benchmarks in Hay's brilliant life. Next I plunged into Hay's Civil War letters and diaries, as transcribed, edited, and annotated by Michael Burlingame. I proudly count myself among the hundreds, more likely thousands, of researchers in Dr. Burlingame's debt. My work would have been exponentially more difficult without the advantage of his painstaking and groundbreaking scholarship on Lincoln's private secretaries, John Hay and John George Nicolay.

Lincoln has had many beneficial biographers over the years, besides Nicolay and Hay. The most valuable—which is to say, the most informative, intelligent, and influential—are Burlingame, David Herbert Donald, and Doris Kearns Goodwin. Theodore Roosevelt has his own cohort of skilled portraitists, the most trenchant, to my eye, being Henry F. Pringle, David McCullough, Howard K. Beale, Kathleen Dalton, and Edmund Morris. And to appreciate the noble and nuanced statuary that is William McKinley, I climbed upon the shoulders of his three keenest observers, Margaret Leech, H. Wayne Morgan, and Lewis L. Gould.

Even the best libraries are only as good as their librarians. For their cooperation, indulgence, and kindness, I whisper my hearty thanks to Ann Sindelar and the staff of the Western Reserve Historical Society Library;

Holly Snyder and the staff of the John Hay Library at Brown University; the staffs of the Massachusetts Historical Society, the Abraham Lincoln Presidential Library, and Houghton Library of Harvard University; and, once again, the conscientious and convivial minders of the Manuscript Division of the Library of Congress.

Likewise I am grateful to John Simpson, director of the Winous Point Marsh Conservancy, who showed me around John Hay's old duck club, where the logs of Hay's shooting days are well cared for, along with a few of his original decoys. Mary Kronenwetter, education director at the Fells, gave me an enlightening tour of the New Hampshire retreat where the spirit of its long-ago resident yet abides in peace and lovingly curated beauty. In Washington, James Symington was equally generous with his time and family lore.

Let me also thank Rebecca Onion, who helped me with early, essential spadework in Austin; the Livingston (Montana) Public Library for allowing me to hog its microfilm reader; Ann Adelman for superb copyediting; Cyndi Hughes for uncrossing my i's; Jane Martin for ferreting photographs; and Jonathan Cox for directing traffic all along the way.

To spend four years in the company of John Hay has been my great prize, and I would not have been able to start or complete my worthwhile endeavor without the advice, consent, and encouragement of my agent, Esther Newberg, and my editor, Alice Mayhew. I trust that I have lived up to their high standards, as I trust that I have done justice to John Hay, a biographer's dream come true.

Notes

Abbreviations used in the Notes:

AA Alvey Adee

AL Abraham Lincoln

ALPLM Abraham Lincoln Presidential Library and Museum

AP Adams Family Papers, Massachusetts Historical Society

B-AL Michael Burlingame, *Abraham Lincoln: A Life*, 2 vols. (2008)

B-CORR Michael Burlingame, ed., *At Lincoln's Side: John Hay's Civil War Correspondence and Selected Writings* (2000)

B&E Michael Burlingame and John R. Turner Ettlinger, eds., *Inside Lincoln's White House: The Civil War Diary of John Hay* (1997)

B-JOUR Michael Burlingame, ed., *Lincoln's Journalist: John Hay's Anonymous Writings for the Press, 1860–1865* (1998)

B-NIC Michael Burlingame, ed., *With Lincoln in the White House: Letters, Memoranda, and Other Writings of John G. Nicolay, 1860–1865* (2000)

B-V Philippe Bunau-Varilla

B-W John Hay, *The Bread-Winners: A Social Study* (1884)

CFW Constance Fenimore Woolson

CK Clarence King

CSH Clara Stone Hay

DEN Tyler Dennett, *John Hay: From Poetry to Politics* (1933)

ESC Elizabeth Sherman Cameron

FR *Papers Relating to the Foreign Relations of the United States*

HA Henry Adams

HAE Henry Adams, *The Education of Henry Adams: An Autobiography* (1918); reprinted as *Novels, Mont Saint Michel, The Education* (Library of America, 1983)

HAL J. C. Levenson, et al., eds., *The Letters of Henry Adams*, 8 vols. (1982–88)

HA-MHS Henry Adams Papers, microfilm, Massachusetts Historical Society

HCL Henry Cabot Lodge

HCL-MHS Henry Cabot Lodge Papers, Massachusetts Historical Society

HJ-JH George Monteiro, *Henry James and John Hay: The Record of a Friendship* (1965)

HW Henry White

HW-LC Henry White Papers, Library of Congress

JC Joseph Choate

JGN John George Nicolay

JGN-LC, John George Nicolay Papers, Library of Congress

JH John Hay

JH-ADD *Addresses of John Hay* (1907)

JH-ALPLM John Hay Papers, Abraham Lincoln Presidential Library and Museum

JH-BU John Hay Papers, John Hay Library, Brown University

JH-CPW *The Complete Poetical Works of John Hay* (1917)

JH-LC John Hay Papers, Library of Congress

JH-LET Clara Hay, ed., *Letters of John Hay and Extracts from Diary*, 3 vols. (1908)

JH-WDH George Monteiro and Brenda Murphy, eds., *John Hay-Howells Letters: The Correspondence of John Milton Hay and William Dean Howells, 1861–1905* (1980)

LC Library of Congress

M-WRHS Mather Family Papers, Western Reserve Historical Society

MCK William McKinley

MCK-LC William McKinley Papers, Library of Congress

MHA Marian Hooper (Clover) Adams

MHS Massachusetts Historical Society

N&H:AL John G. Nicolay and John Hay, *Abraham Lincoln: A History*, 10 vols. (1890)

RTL Robert Todd Lincoln

TR Theodore Roosevelt

TR-LET Elting Morison, et al., eds., *The Letters of Theodore Roosevelt*, 8 vols. (1951–54)

WAD-LC Wadsworth Family Papers, Library of Congress

WDH William Dean Howells

WR Whitelaw Reid

WR-LC Whitelaw Reid Correspondence, Library of Congress

WRHS Western Reserve Historical Society

WRT William Roscoe Thayer

WRT-HU William Roscoe Thayer Papers, Houghton Library, Harvard University

WRT-L&L William Roscoe Thayer, *The Life and Letters of John Hay*, 2 vols. (1908)

WWR William W. Rockhill

WWR-HU William W. Rockhill Papers, Houghton Library, Harvard University

Chapter 1: Oughtnottobiography

page

1 *"ill-kept, inconvenient"*: JGN to Therena Bates, March 26, 1865, B-NIC, 176.

2 *"[S]omething happened"*: Thomas E. Pendel, *Thirty-Six Years in the White House*, 42–44.

2 *"Now he belongs"*: N&H:AL 10:302.

3 *standing amid his father's papers*: Goff, *Robert Todd Lincoln*, 72.

4 *"Words seem so inadequate"*: JGN to Therena Bates, April 24, 1865, B-NIC, 178.

5 *"I found the shadow"*: JH to RTL, August 26, 1865, JH-BU.

5 *"the greatest man of his time"*: N&H:AL 10:295.

5 *"the tall gaunt figure"*: "Abraham Lincoln's Shakespeare," James G. Randall MS, in B&E, 346.

7 *"I'm keeper"*: F. A. Mitchel to JH, February 12, 1905, JH-BU.

8 *"more fun than a goat"*: JH to HA, June 15, 1900, HA-MHS.

8 *"splendid little war"*: JH to TR, July 27, 1898, in WRT-L&L 2:337.

8 *both dog and cat*: White, *Masks in a Pageant*, 285–86.

11 *"You do things so easily"*: JH to ESC, n.d., AP.

11 "embonpoint": Unidentified clipping, n.d., JH scrapbook, JH-LC.

11 *"an oughtnottobiography"*: JH to R. W. Gilder, March 1, 1902, JH-BU.

12 *"He so far overshadows"*: [*New York*] *Evening Sun*, n.d. [1903], clipping, JH scrapbook, JH-LC.

13 *"If a man [were to]"*: "The Great Secretary of State," 6561.

13 *"extreme refinement . . . allege his own merits"*: Address by Elihu Root at the Dedication of the John Hay Library, BU, November 11, 1910, JH-BU.

Chapter 2: Spunky Point

page

14 *a pat on the head*: JH, *Life of Dr. Charles Hay*, 3.

14 *"harsh and arbitrary ideas"*: JH, ibid., 4.

14 *met with "gratifying success"*: *Biographical Review of Hancock County*, 12.

14 *"But he always"*: JH, *Life of Dr. Charles Hay*, 5.

15 *the first man to sign*: JH, ibid., 5–6.

15 *"the rigorous fashion"*: JH, genealogy of David August Leonard, 1896, MS, JH-LC.

16 *"[Y]ou are no doubt . . . Shakespeare expresses it"*: Charles Hay to Elisabeth Hay, July 27, 1829, JH-BU.

16 *"It has made our town"*: Charles Hay to Milton Hay, July 15, 1833, JH-BU.

17 *"the le[a]ven of a better character"*: Charles Hay to "Dear Sister," September 23, 1830, JH-BU.

17 *"light reading . . . favorite reading"*: JH, *Life of Dr. Charles Hay*, 12.

17 *"There are quite as many"*: Charles Hay to Milton Hay, November 3, 1836, Charles Hay Papers, ALPLM.

18 *"[H]e had an inexhaustible"*: Chapman, "The Boyhood of John Hay," 449.

18 *"[S]ome idiots"*: JH to Harriet Loring, June 30, 1870, WRT-L&L 1:7.

18 *"one of the many western"*: [HA], "Biography of John Hay," *The Reserve*, published by the Junior Class of Adelbert College, 1893, 10.

18 *"reposing from its plunge"*: JH, "The Blood Seedling," 281.

18 *"O grandly flowing"*: JH, "On the Bluff," JH-CPW, 171.

18 *"a region whose moral"*: JH to Sarah Whitman, August 30, 1858, JH-BU.

18 *exile from the East*: JH to Sarah Whitman, December 15, 1858, JH-BU.

18 *"The ruling motive"*: N&H:AL 1:16.

19 *reestablishing himself as a physician*: Chapman, "The Boyhood of John Hay," 446.

19 *"They were not especially"*: JH, *Life of Dr. Charles Hay*, 12.

19 *"The rule of the household"*: JH, ibid., 15.

20 *"John was a student"*: Charles E. Hay to WRT, December 22, 1923, WRT-HU.

20 *"It can be proven"*: *Warsaw Signal*, April 24, 1844.

20 *"sitting on his throne . . . iron rod"*: *Warsaw Signal*, February 28, 1844.

21 *"[H]e was everywhere"*: JH, *The Life of Dr. Charles Hay*, 11.

21 *an article to the* Atlantic . . . *"sustain that verdict"*: JH, "The Mormon Prophet's Tragedy," 669–78.

22 *"When we were both"*: Charles E. Hay to WRT, December 22, 1923, WRT-HU.

22 *"[H]e was spoken of"*: Ibid.

23 *"red-cheeked . . . like a professor"*: Chapman, "The Boyhood of John Hay," 449.

23 *"There had been very little"*: N&H:AL 1:154.

23 *"[A]ll the sentimental"*: JH to his sister, March 5, 1854, DEN 18.

24 *"I had a whirling"*: JH to "Dear Friends," September 30, 1855, JH-BU.

24 *"He at once"*: Chapman, "The Boyhood of John Hay," 450.

25 *"[I]f I go through so hurriedly"*: JH to "My Dear friends," November 28, 1955, JH-BU.

25 *"The professors . . . hear him lecture"*: Ibid.

25 *"Hay that is green"*: W. E. Louttit, "John Hay in Theta Delta Chi," typescript, JH-BU.

25 *"Resolved . . . than poets"*: W. E. Louttit, ibid.

25 *"a young Dr. Johnson"*: William Leete Stone, "John Hay, 1858," *Memories of Brown: Traditions and Recollections Gathered from Many Sources* (1909), 154.

25 *"the most felicitous"*: Angell, *Reminiscences*, 109.

26 *"They are our brothers"*: JH, "The Fratricidal Character of War with England," MS, March 1856, JH-ALPLM.

26 *"The first who undertook"*: JH, "Foreign Travel Beneficial to the Man of Letters," MS, n.d., JH-ALPLM.

26 *"Political feeling"*: JH to "My Dear Uncle," March 30, 1856, JH-BU.

27 *Hay and a roommate*: James Angell to William Leete Stone, March 25, 1906, JH-BU.

27 *"To say it was a class poem"*: WDH, "John Hay in Literature," 343.

28 *"When I look . . . upon me now"*: JH to Hannah Angell, August 13 and July 19, 1858, *A College Friendship* 26, 17.

28 *"I am unhappy"*: JH to Hannah Angell, October 20, 1858, ibid., 33.

28 *"The prevailing tendency"*: JH, untitled MS, n.d., JH-ALPLM.

28 *"[N]ow that my journey"*: JH to Nora Perry, August 30, 1858, in Ticknor, ed., *A Poet in Exile*, 13.

28 *"I have been very near"*: JH to Sarah Whitman, December 15, 1858, JH-BU.

28 *"I alternate between"*: JH to Hannah Angell, May 2, 1859, *A College Friendship*, 45–46.

28 *"If you want to see"*: JH to Leander C. Manchester, July 23, 1857, JH-BU.

28 *"How like a fool . . . will be quiet"*: JH to Hannah Angell, October 20 and December 11, 1858, *A College Friendship*, 34, 38.

29 *"I prefer"*: JH to Nora Perry, January 2, 1859, in Ticknor, ed., *A Poet in Exile*, 24.

29 *"Drearily sweeping"*: JH, "In the Mist," ibid., 27–28.

29 *"I believe in the maxim"*: Charles Hay to "My Dear Brother," September 6, 1858, JH-BU.

29 *"I would not do"*: JH to "My Dear Uncle," January 28, 1859, JH-BU.

29 *"In a short while . . . shorter sorrow"*: JH to William Douglas O'Connor, February 6, 1859, JH-BU.

30 *The other attorneys of record*: Miers, ed., *Lincoln Day by Day*, 2:257.

31 *"I am stranded"*: JH to "Dear Friend" [William Leete Stone], May 20, 1859, JH-BU.

31 *"One of his original conundrums"*: Mary Ridgley Hay, "Springfield, Illinois, in 1860, by a Native Springfielder," typescript, n.d., JH-BU.

31 *"a tongue that could"*: Brown, "Springfield Society Before the Civil War," 497–98.

31 *"He was, for those"*: Carr, *The Illini*, 139.

31 *"dark, lustrous . . . in those days"*: Mary Ridgley Hay, "Springfield, Illinois, in 1860."

32 *"the close, methodical"*: John Russell Young, "Lincoln as He Was," *Pittsburgh Dispatch*, August 23, 1891, in Burlingame, ed., *With Lincoln in the White House*, xviii.

32 *"[I]f ever there was"*: Mary Ridgley Hay, "Springfield, Illinois, in 1860."

33 *"My insanity has not"*: JH to Hannah Angell, May 5, 1860, *A College Friendship*, 55.

33 *"When the lightning . . . and jubilant"*: Ecarte, *Providence Journal*, May 26, 1860, B-JOUR 1–3.

34 *"The deluge . . . clamorous plaudits"*: Ecarte, *Missouri Democrat*, August 11, 1860, B-JOUR 3–6.

35 *"It is one of the truest"*: Ecarte, *Providence Journal*, September 19, 1860, B-JOUR 9.

35 *"to symbolize the indissoluble"*: Newton Bateman, *Abraham Lincoln: An Address* (1899), in Holzer, *Lincoln President-Elect*, 21.

35 *"I wish I could find"*: Chapman, "The Boyhood of John Hay," 452.

35 *Nicolay readily took*: B-AL, 651–52.

35 *"great literary talent"*: Weik, *The Real Lincoln: A Portrait*, 321.

36 *"We can't take . . . let Hay come"*: WRT-L&L 1:87.

36 *"a sea of perplexities"*: N&H:AL 1:201.

37 *"In many respects"*: N&H:AL 1:201–02.

Chapter 3: Potomac Fever

page

38 *"It is cowardly"*: JH to Nora Perry, March 4, 1860, in Ticknor, ed., *A Poet in Exile*, 45.

38 *"I never practiced"*: JH to Adelbert Hay, October 20, 1898, JH-LC.

39 *"I shall never enjoy"*: JH to Mrs. A. E. Edwards, November 29, 1860, in B-CORR 3.

39 *"I believe he is strongly"*: Ecarte, *Missouri Democrat*, January 11, 1861, B-JOUR 18.

39 *"Mr. Lincoln will not"*: Ecarte, *Missouri Democrat*, January 29, 1861, B-JOUR 21.

40 *Lincoln would deliver*: Holzer, *Lincoln President-Elect*, 389–90.

40 *"If the reader could"*: "From our correspondent," *New York World*, February 21, 1861, B-JOUR 35.

40 *"as soft and sympathetic . . . captivated and entranced"*: "From Our Special Correspondent," *New York World*, February 25, 1861, B-JOUR 40.

41 *"an organized plan . . . lose them all"*: "From our own correspondent": *New York World*, February 27, 1861, B-JOUR 44.

41 *"Tomorrow we enter"*: JH to Annie E. Johnston, February 22, 1861, JH-BU.

41 *"in broad avenues . . . Appian Way"*: "From Our Special Correspondent," *New York World*, March 4, 1861, B-JOUR 48–49.

41 *"a congerie of hovels . . . from the terrace"*: "From Our Special Correspondent," *New York World*, March 4, 1861, B-JOUR 48–49.

42 *"I waited with boyish"*: JH, "The Heroic Age in Washington," galley proof of lecture, c. 1871, JH-Brown; also B-CORR 119.

43 *"seedy . . . unsuccessful hotel"*: Leech, *Reveille in Washington*, 6; Baker, "The Lincoln White House," 45, 47; Rietveld, "The Lincoln White House Community," 20–21.

43 *"We have very pleasant"*: JGN to Therena Bates, March 7, 1861, B-NIC 29–30.

43 *"the intolerable press"*: JH to William Leete Stone, March 15, 1861, B-CORR 5.

43 *"The President is affable . . . grim Cerberus"*: Noah Brooks, "How They Live in the White House," November 7, 1863, in Burlingame, ed., *Lincoln Observed*, 83.

43 *"sour and crusty" . . . bought him leniency*: Stoddard, *Inside the White House in War Times*, 57.

43 *"[John Hay] might have"*: Nicolay, *Lincoln's Secretary*, 85.

43   *"They don't want much"*: Henry Wilson to William Herndon, May 30, 1867, in Wilson and Davis, eds., *Lincoln's Informants*, 562.

43   *"letting lodgings"*: N&H:AL 4:69.

44   *"The White House is"*: JH diary, April 18, 1861, B&E 1.

44   *"I have seen"*: JH diary, April 24, 1861, B&E 10.

44   *"and pay her"*: JH diary, April 25, 1861, B&E 11.

44   *"He always seemed"*: JH, "Ellsworth," *Atlantic Monthly* 8 (July 1861), 119–25.

44   *"When Ellsworth"*: JH to Mrs. James H. Coggeshall, August 12, 1861, *A College Friendship*, 61.

45   *"[m]iraculous in meanness"*: *Missouri Republican*, n.d., B-JOUR 286.

45   *"blear caravanserai . . . air at once"*: "From Our Special Correspondent," *New York World*, March 4, 1861, B-JOUR 49–50.

45   *"the brains of society"*: JGN to Therena Bates, June 30, 1861, B-NIC 45.

45   *" 'Those light at heart' "*: "From our own correspondent," *New York World*, August 19, 1861, B-JOUR 95.

45   *"O strong, free"*: JH, "Northward," scrapbook of Civil War poems, JH-BU.

45   *"I am getting along"*: JH to JGN, April 9, 1862, B-CORR 20.

46   *"the crumbs of official"*: N&H:AL 4:68.

46   *a letter of introduction*: John W. Starr, "Lincoln and the Office Seekers," typescript, 1936, quoted in B-NIC 231–32.

46   *Letters arrived*: Stoddard, *Inside the White House*, 14.

46   *"the rant and drivel"*: Ibid., 157.

46   *"statuesque"*: Stoddard, "Memoirs," Detroit Public Library, in Burlingame, intro. to Stoddard, *Inside the White House*, xii.

46   *"quick witted," "a born diplomat"*: Stoddard, *Inside the White House*, 57; Stoddard, *Lincoln's Third Secretary*, 91.

46   *"almost boyish . . . far better"*: Stoddard, *Inside the White House*, 151.

47   *"Ah me!"*: "From our own correspondent," *New York World*, August 19, 1861, B-JOUR 97.

47   *"I think the mug"*: JH to Mrs. A. E. Edwards, October 12, 1861, B-COUR 13.

47   *"With the ushering"*: "From our own correspondent," *New York World*, July 24, 1861, B-JOUR 78.

47   *"shipwreck of our"*: *New York Tribune*, July 23, 1861, B-AL 1:185.

47   *"the defeat was not"*: "From our own correspondent," *New York World*, July 24, 1861, B-JOUR 76.

47   *"There is nothing"*: JH, "The Heroic Age in Washington."

48   *also a conservative . . . "might please me"*: Sears, *George B. McClellan*, 58–59, 95.

48   *"The ghosts of twenty"*: JH to JGN, June 20, 1864, B-JOUR 85.

49 *"imperious"*: JH diary, August 28, 1861, B&E 24.

49 *"born leader"*: *Missouri Republican*, October 13, 1861, B-JOUR 101.

49 *"seemed very hopeful . . . no plan"*: JH diary, October 22, 1861, B&E 27–28.

49 *"I can do it all"*: JH diary, November 1, 1861, B&E 30.

49 *"I wish to record"*: JH diary, November 13, 1861, B&E 32.

50 *"[I]t is ill"*: *Missouri Republican*, December 17, 1861, B-JOUR 162–63.

50 *"slows," "idiot," "baboon"*: Sears, *George B. McClellan*, 338, 103, 132.

50 *"weak, vacillating"*: *New York Tribune*, December 23, 1881, in Monteiro, "John Hay and the Union Generals," 51.

50 *"long mismanagement"*: N&H:AL 6:193.

51 *"I went with him"*: JH diary, August 23, 1863, B&E 75–76.

51 *"short shirt hanging"*: JH diary, April 30, 1864, B&E 194.

51 *"What a man"*: JH diary, April 30, 1864, B&E 194.

51 *"He was one"*: JH, "Life in the White House in the Time of Lincoln," 34.

52 *"all one bubble . . . Nobody can tell"*: Stoddard, *Lincoln's Third Secretary*, 166–67.

52 *"laughed through his term"*: JH diary, November 18, 1863, B&E 112; Nicolay, *Lincoln's Secretary*, 85: "It was said that he 'laughed through the war.' But he never laughed *at* it."

53 *"mourning around"*: Stoddard, *Lincoln's Third Secretary*, 153.

53 *"butcher's day"*: Ibid., 170.

53 *"I was amused . . . to shoot them"*: JH diary, July 18, 1863, B&E 64.

53 *"At about 5 o'clock"*: JGN journal, February 20, 1862, B-NIC 71.

54 *"With the fire"*: N&H:AL 10:355.

54 *"the institution of slavery . . . or all the other"*: Foner, *The Fiery Trial*, 25, 99.

55 *"to conserve and protect . . . storm rent republic"*: *Missouri Republican*, May 23, 1862, B-JOUR 264–65.

55 *"There was onset"*: N&H:AL 5:325.

56 *"you must act"*: Sears, *George B. McClellan*, 178.

56 *"[T]he little Napoleon"*: JH to JGN, April 9, 1862, B-CORR 20.

56 *"should not be allowed"*: Guelzo, *Lincoln's Emancipation Proclamation*, 118; Sears, *George B. McClellan*, 227–28.

56 *"God will yet foil"*: Sears, *George B. McClellan*, 236–37.

57 *"will not conserve"*: JH to Mary Jay, July 20, 1862, B-CORR 23.

57 *"Both [extremes are]"*: *Missouri Republican*, July 21, 1862, B-JOUR 284–85.

57 *"that all men could"*: N&H:AL 6:153.

57 *"even when you cease"*: Foner, *The Fiery Trial*, 224.

58 *"general impression . . . of old houses"*: *Missouri Republican*, June 27, 1862, B-JOUR 274.

58 *"seedy gentility"*: Ibid.

59 *Lincoln invited discussion*: Goodwin, *Team of Rivals*, 465–68; Guelzo, *Lincoln's Emancipation Proclamation*, 134–37.

59 *"[A]bout Eight . . . people now"*: JH diary, September 1, 1862, B&E 37–38.

60 *"McClellan's bodyguard"*: N&H:AL 6:175.

60 *"Again I have been"*: Sears, *George B. McClellan*, 263.

60 *"Mr. Lincoln says"*: Stoddard, *Lincoln's Third Secretary*, 169.

61 *"If anyone tried"*: JH, "The Heroic Age in Washington."

61 *"If I could save"*: N&H:AL 6:153.

61 *"What good would"*: Basler et al., eds., *Collected Works of Abraham Lincoln* 5:420.

61 *"commenced fur to pound"*: Artemus Ward, "High-Handed Outrage at Utica," in Ward, *His Works, Complete* (1877), 34.

62 *"a club"*: B-AL 2:409.

62 *an act of national suicide*: B-AL 2:15.

62 *"accursed doctrine"*: Sears, *George B. McClellan*, 324.

62 *"touched neither justice"*: B-AL 2:409.

62 *"There was no doubt"*: *Missouri Republican*, September 29, 1862, B-JOUR 312.

62 *"I shall make no attempt"*: B-AL 2:415.

62 *"the Government [was] done"*: *Missouri Republican*, September 26, 1862, B-JOUR 311.

63 *"They all seemed"*: JH diary, September 24, 1862, B&E 41.

63 *"I have been shaking"*: Carpenter, *Six Months in the White House*, 269–70.

Chapter 4: Bolts of War

page

64 *"a fixed thing"*: Orville Browning diary, January 19, 1863, B-AL 2:478.

65 *"stuck in the mud . . . hope in patience"*: JGN to Therena Bates, February 8 and January 15, 1863, B-NIC 103–04.

65 *"The war seems"*: JH to Adam Badeau, January 9, 1863, B-CORR 29–30.

66 *"I want my abolition"*: JH to JGN, April 8, 1863, B-CORR 33.

66 *"I hope . . . that due honor"*: JH to AL, April 10, 1863, B-CORR 35–36.

67 *"I shall never cease . . . than I do now"*: JH to Mrs. Charles Hay, April 23, 1863, B-CORR 38.

67 *"The air is like June"*: JH to JGN, April 8, 1863, B-CORR 33.

67 *"Linkum" . . . "No man see Linkum"*: JH, "The Heroic Age in Washington," JH-BU.

67 *"It is the only thing"*: JH to JGN, May 1, 1863, B-CORR 39.

67 *"The soil is almost"*: JH to John Hay (grandfather), May 2, 1863, B-CORR 40.

68 *"As we sat"*: JH to JGN, May 1, 1863, B-CORR 40.

68 *So enthralled was he*: Reid, *After the War*, 171–72.

68 *"There is positively"*: JH to JGN, May 24, 1863, B-CORR 42.

69 *"vacillating and purposeless"*: N&H:AL 7:107.

69 *"Had a thunderbolt"*: Burlingame, ed., *Lincoln Observed*, 50.

69 *"the darkest day"*: Stoddard, *Lincoln's Third Secretary*, 173.

69 *"All accounts agree"*: *New York Times*, May 12, 1863, in Goodwin, *Team of Rivals*, 521.

69 *"We need not"*: AL 7:109–10.

69 *"tall, thin, reserved"*: N&H:AL 7:226.

70 *"[T]hese two formidable"*: N&H:AL 7:234.

70 *"No sight so beautiful"*: N&H:AL 7:263.

71 *"gave the last full measure of devotion"*: Basler, et al., eds., *Collected Works of Abraham Lincoln* 7:19.

71 *"There were still"*: N&H:AL 7:309.

71 *"The President seemed"*: JH diary, July 11, 1863, B&E 61.

71 *" 'Our Army held' "*: JH diary, July 19, 1863, B&E 64–65.

71 *"The Tycoon is in fine"*: JH to JGN, August 7, 1863, B-CORR 49.

72 *"Lincoln was, as usual"*: N&H:AL 5:226.

72 *"If I had gone"*: JH diary, July 15, 1863, B&E 63.

72 *"were always clearer"*: N&H:AL 5:402.

72 *"keep his fingers . . . equally firm"*: JH to JGN, September 11, 1863, B-CORR 54.

72 *"I have to a great"*: JH to Charles Halpine, August 14, 1863, B-CORR 51.

73 *"had a fearful orgie"*: JH to JGN, July 18, 1863, B-CORR 45.

73 *"unfit for family"*: JH to Charles Halpine, November 22, 1863, B-CORR 68.

73 *"In eighteen hundred"*: AL, "Lee's Preliminary Report," unidentified clipping, n.d., JH scrapbook of Civil War poems, JH-BU; see also Basler, et al., eds., *Collected Works of Abraham Lincoln*, Supplement 1:194 and B&E 306.

73 *"the Hell-Cat"*: JH to JGN, April 5, 1862, B-CORR 19.

73 *"Madame has mounted"*: JH to JGN, April 4, 1862, B-CORR 19.

73 *"the powers at the other end"*: JGN to JH, January 18, 1864, B-NIC 124.

74 *"domestic troubles"*: Orville H. Browning to JGN, June 17, 1875, in Burlingame, ed., *An Oral History of Abraham Lincoln*, 3.

74 *"The devil is abroad . . . more Hellcatical"*: JH to JGN, April 5 and 9, 1862, B-CORR 19–20.

74 *"some of the best . . . Nico & I"*: JH diary, November 8, 1863, B&E 109.

75 *"J. Wilkes Booth was doing"*: JH diary, November 9, 1863, B&E 110.

75 *"and drank a good deal"*: JH diary, November 11, 1863, B&E 111.

76 *"said half a dozen"* . . . *no one got much rest*: JH diary, November 18, 1863, B&E 112.

76 *"I got a beast"*: JH diary, November 19, 1863, B&E 113.

76 Everett spoke *"perfectly"*: Ibid.

77 *"The world will little"*: Basler, et al., eds., *Collected Works of Abraham Lincoln*, 7:19.

77 *"[T]he President in a firm"*: JH diary, November 19, 1863, B&E 113.

77 *"the rebel power is"*: JH diary, August 9, 1863, B&E 70.

78 *"to inaugurate measures"*: Nulty, *Confederate Florida*, 74.

78 *"pretty warm . . . I made a bad dodge"*: JH diary, February 1 and 2, 1864, B&E 151–52.

79 *"it was not the President's"*: JH diary, January 20, 1864, B&E 145.

80 *"Opened my book"*: JH diary, February 6, 1864, B&E 154.

80 *"I have the best"*: JH to AL, February 8, 1864, B-CORR 76.

80 *"a lot of stragglers"*: Joseph Hawley to Charles Dudley Warner, March 4, 1864, in Arthur L. Shipman, "Letters of Joseph R. Hawley," typescript, 1929, Connecticut Historical Society, in B-CORR 246.

80 *"In [the] middle"*: JH diary, February 18, 1864, B&E 167–68.

81 *"The fighting on both . . . their ranks"*: JH to JGN, February 23, 1864, B-CORR 77.

81 *"unsteady and queer"*: JH diary, February 21, 1864, B&E 169.

81 *"Executive intermeddling . . . one million of dollars"*: *New York Herald*, February 23, 1864.

81 *"brigades of our brave"*: *New York Herald*, March 1, 1864.

82 *"I can't think of leaving"*: JH to JGN, February 23, 1864, B-CORR 78.

82 *"would not give us"*: JH diary, March 3, 1864, B&E 173.

82 disinterested or *"unscrupulous scamps"*: JH diary, March 8, 1864, B&E 177.

82 *"[T]he Tycoon never"*: JH to Charles Halpine, April 13, 1864, B-CORR 80.

83 *"a quiet, self-possessed"*: JH diary, March 27, 1864, B&E 185.

83 *"The primeval forest"*: N&H:AL 10:352.

83 *"Men were killed"*: N&H:AL 8:380–81.

83 *"mutual slaughter"*: N&H:AL 8:360.

84 *"The President thinks very"*: JH diary, May 9, 1864, B&E 195.

84 *"The President is cheerful"*: JGN to Therena Bates, May 15, 1864, B-NIC 141.

84 *"I have never been"*: Basler, et al., eds., *Collected Works of Abraham Lincoln*, 7:395–96.

85 *"He was in the Fort"*: JH diary, July 11, 1864, B&E 221.

85   *"The President is in very"*: Ibid.

85   *"our bleeding, bankrupt"*: Horace Greeley to AL, July 7, 1864, B-AL 2:669.

86   *"yellow hand bag"*: "From our own correspondent," *New York World*, February 19, 1861, B-JOUR 32.

86   *"I do say that a frank"*: Horace Greeley to AL, July 7, 1864, N&H:AL 9:187.

86   *"If you can find"*: N&H:AL 9:187–88.

87   *"abused & blackguarded"*: JH diary, c. July 21, 1864, B&E 224.

87   *"propose terms which"*: Ibid., 224–25.

87   *"To whom it may"*: N&H:AL 9:192.

87   *"tea & toasting"*: JH diary, c. July 21, 1864, B&E 224.

88   *"a seedy looking rebel . . . & false hair"*: Ibid.

88   *"half-witted adventurer"*: Ibid., 229.

88   *"rude withdrawal . . . civilization of the country"*: N&H:AL 9:194.

89   *"Copperheads to get"*: Joseph Medill to JH, August 10, 1864, JH-BU (italics in original).

89   *"The damned scoundrel"*: JH to JGN, August 25, 1864, B-CORR 91.

89   *"half statements"*: N&H:AL 9:199.

90   *"in some respects Mr. Greeley"*: *New York Times*, December 28, 1882, in B-AL 2:671.

90   *"peculiarities of caprice"*: N&H:AL 6:84.

90   *"almost the condition"*: JGN to Therena Bates, August 28, 1864, B-NIC 153.

90   *"I lose my temper"*: JH to JGN, August 25, 1864, B-CORR 92.

90   *"four years of failure"*: B-AL 2:681.

90   *"immediate efforts . . . Federal Union"*: Sears, *George B. McClellan*, 372–73.

91   *"the surrender platform . . . The Lord preserve"*: JGN to Therena Bates, September 4, 1864, B-NIC 157.

91   *"From the moment"*: N&H:AL 9:351.

91   *"I shall fight like"*: JGN to AL, August 30, 1864, B-NIC 155.

92   *"with the steady pace"*: N&H:AL 10:156.

92   "con amore": JH diary, October 11, 1864, B&E 239.

92   *"The night was rainy . . . past against him"*: JH diary, November 8, 1864, B&E 244–45.

93   *"awkwardly and hospitably"*: Ibid., 246.

93   *"rolling himself up"*: Ibid.

94   *"he who is most . . . any man's bosom"*: N&H:AL 9:380–81.

94   *"[n]ot very graceful . . . after the fact"*: JH diary, November 11, 1864, B&E 248.

94   *"At first we tried"*: JH to William Herndon, September 5, 1866, in Wilson and Davis, eds., *Herndon's Informants*, 331.

94 *"Colonel Hay imitated"*: Stoddard, *Inside the White House*, 159.

94 *"the best specimen"*: Burlingame, "The Authorship of the Bixby Letter," B-CORR 171.

95 *"I have been shown"*: Basler, et al., eds., *Collected Works of Abraham Lincoln* 8:116–17.

95 *"a piece of the American"*: Carl Sandburg, *Abraham Lincoln: The War Years*, 4 vols. (1939), 3:669.

96 *In the end . . . seldom in Lincoln's*: Burlingame, "The Authorship of the Bixby Letter," 169–84.

96 *"The more [Lincoln's]"*: N&H:AL 10:352.

96 *"From the hour . . . plainly declining"*: N&H:AL 10:148, 152–53.

96 *"common little wall tent . . . them this winter"*: JH diary, November 16, 1864, B&E 250–51.

97 *"The Anaconda is beginning . . . the great event"*: JGN to Therena Bates, December 16 and 18, 1864, B-NIC, 167–68.

97 *"We are like whalers"*: N&H:AL 10:74.

98 *"a king's cure-all . . . and the whole world"*: N&H:AL 87–88.

99 *"great moral victory"*: Ibid., 88.

99 *"The great job"*: Arnold, *The Life of Abraham Lincoln*, 366.

99 *He had in mind returning*: JGN to Simon Cameron, December 23, 1864, Miles-Cameron Papers, LC.

99 *"About three days"*: JGN to Therena Bates, December 16, 1864, B-NIC 167.

100 *was typeset and printed*: Burlingame, ed., *Lincoln Observed*, 168.

100 *"God . . . speedily pass away"*: Basler, et al., eds., *Collected Works of Abraham Lincoln* 8:333.

100 *"Men are not flattered"*: AL to Thurlow Weed, March 15, 1865, N&H:AL 10:146.

101 *"He bore the sorrows"*: JH, "Life in the White House at the Time of Lincoln," 37.

101 *"entirely unsolicited"*: JH to Charles E. Hay, March 31, 1865, B-CORR 103.

102 *"Mr. Seward, while"*: N&H: AL 6:253.

102 *"The sword is not"*: Paolino, *The Foundations of the American Empire*, 11.

102 *"I think [Paris] will be"*: JH to Manning Leonard, April 13, 1865, B-CORR 104.

103 *"No one, not even . . . on the dead body"*: N&H:AL 10:294–302.

105 *"a great and powerful lover"*: N&H:AL 10:347.

105 *"the greatest character since"*: JH to William Herndon, September 5, 1866, JH-LC.

106 *"Bancroft's address was"*: Ibid.

Chapter 5: Progress of Democracy

page

107   *"I envy you . . . watching us from heaven"*: JH to RTL, August 26, 1865, JH-BU.

108   *"Hay is a bright"*: Thurlow Weed to John Bigelow, April 26, 1865, in Bigelow, *Retrospections* 1:521.

108   *"genial gentleman"*: JH to "My Dear Brother," August 4, 1865, JH-BU.

108   *"In my boyhood"*: JH to Charles Hay, December 15, 1866, JH-BU.

109   *"bright new spick"*: JH to "My Dear Brother," August 4, JH-BU.

109   *"swarming hives . . . new West End"*: Ibid.

110   *"keep from stagnating"*: Ibid.

110   *"[Paris] is so"*: JH to "Miss Wright," n.d., JH-BU.

110   *"Our Countrywomen"*: Bigelow, *Retrospections*, 1:261, 263–65.

110   *"in pursuit of health"*: JH to Richard Parson, April 11, 1866, JH-BU.

110   *"what the newspapers . . . could send out"*: JH, "Shelby Cabell," 607.

111   "I stand at the break": JH, "Sunrise in the Place de la Concorde," JH-CPW 29.

111   *"It never seems to occur"*: JH to "My Dear Father & Mother & Sister," February 2, 1866, JH-BU.

111   *"more gold than broadcloth . . . a light-weight Republican"*: Ibid.

111   *"small clothes . . . fine as her profile"*: Ibid.

111   "I consider Lincoln": JH to William Herndon, September 5, 1866, JH-LC.

112   *"[L]et us look"*: JH diary, n.d., JH-Brown.

112   *"[One] of these days"*: JH to "My Dear Brother," January 16, 1866, JH-BU.

112   *"I will be comfortable"*: Ibid.

113   *"I have money"*: JH to Charles Hay, December 15, 1866, JH-BU.

113   *"the History of Lincoln"*: Ibid.

113   *"the same placid philosophic"*: JH to JGN, February 14, 1867, JH-BU.

113   *"habitual disrespect"*: Nicolay, *Lincoln's Secretary*, 249.

114   *"dessication and fossilizing"*: JH diary, February 4, JH-BU.

114   *"more richly and carefully"*: Ibid.

114   *"[I]f he had done"*: JH diary, n.d., JH-BU.

114   *"I bid farewell"*: JH to JGN, March 5, 1867, JH-BU.

114   *"To own the knowledge"*: JH to William Seward, March 4, 1867, transcript in JH diary, JH-BU.

115   *"[n]obody is keen"*: JH to JGN, March 18, 1867, JH-BU.

115   *"the key to the boxes . . . kicked out"*: Ibid.

115   *"better than usual . . . growing boy"*: Ibid.

115   *"I am doing work"*: JH diary, June 3, 1867, JH-BU.

115   *"I suspect I am"*: JH to John Bigelow, May 18, 1867, JH-BU.

116   *"I have scarcely . . . than anywhere else"*: JH diary, June 3, 1867, JH-BU.

116   *The salary was*: DEN 64.

116   *"directness and simplicity . . . decent stolid fellows"*: JH diary, 1867, JH-BU.

117   *"It is a pleasant"*: JH, "Down the Danube," 625.

117   *"Austria is perhaps"*: JH to "My Dear Young," August 24, 1867, JH-BU.

117   *"The great luxury"*: JH to JGN, September 2, 1867, JH-BU.

117   *"the whole town"*: JH diary, September 8, 1867, JH-BU.

118   *"I have never seen a"*: JH diary, September 9, 1867, JH-BU.

118   *"I have had a pleasant"*: JH to John Bigelow, April 27, 1868, JH-LC.

118   *"The great calamity"*: JH to William Seward, February 5, 1868, WRT-L&L 1:303.

119   *"It is curious"*: JH to John Bigelow, April 27, 1868, JH-LC.

119   *"Wattshisname"*: JH to JGN, July 13, 1868, JH-BU.

119   *"in peaceful pursuit . . . broken down politician"*: JH to JGN, December 8, 1868, JH-BU.

120   *"John Hay"*: Unidentified clipping, n.d., JH scrapbook, BU.

120   *"He is severe upon"*: Unidentified clipping, n.d., JH scrapbook, BU.

120   *"You will find"*: JH to JGN, May 14, 1869, JH-BU.

120   *"He is a bright"*: Unidentified clipping, n.d., JH scrapbook, BU.

121   *"I have determined"*: JH to John Bigelow, July 2, 1869, *Retrospections*, 4:294–95; in *Macbeth*, Act IV, scene i, the hell-broth "boils" rather than seethes.

122   *"cheerless and bare . . . freedom and progress"*: JH, *Castilian Days*, 2, 26, 60.

123   *"I have never imagined"*: JH diary, October 3, 1869, JH-BU.

123   *"blind reverence"*: JH, *Castilian Days*, 56.

123   *"knuckle-bones . . . the lack of modern . . . tender melody"*: Ibid., 57, 371, 12.

123   *"retain the speech"*: JH to John Bigelow, July 21, 1870, JH-BU.

123   *"The longer you look"*: JH, *Castilian Days*, 143–44.

123   *"The Spanish people are too"*: JH to Charles Hay, January 28, 1870, JH-BU.

124   *"If we want the Island"*: JH to John Bigelow, May 9, 1870, JH-BU.

124   *"[A] new and beneficent"*: JH, *Castilian Days*, 369–70.

124   *"Españolismo"*: Ibid., 53.

124   *"You have beauty"*: JH to unidentified woman, n.d., JH-BU.

124   *"built on the old-fashioned . . . of the ologies"*: JH, *Castilian Days*, 18, 33.

124   *"chipper as a mudlark"*: Dennis, *Adventures in American Diplomacy*, 318.

125   *"It seems to be"*: Edward G. Lowry, *Washington Close-ups: Intimate Views of Some Public Figures* (1921), 149.

125   *"I could get along"*: JH to "My Dear Household Circle," August 10, 1870, JH-BU.

127 *"I leave Europe in"*: Ibid.

128 *"The Empire attained . . . 'have been deceived!'"*: [JH], "The Fortunes of the Bonapartes," 16–17.

Chapter 6: Plain Language

page

130 *even tried to have Reid fired*: Duncan, *Whitelaw Reid*, 24.

132 *dinner at the Union League*: WRT-L&L 1:330–31.

132 *"I would rather"*: JH to WR, September 21, 1870, JH-BU.

132 *"I do not find the elements"*: JH to WR, September 7, 1870, WR-LC.

132 *"shy little vineyard . . . easy to take"*: JH to JGN, October 13, 1870, JH-BU.

133 *"au grand sérieux"*: JH to JGN, October 27, 1870, JH-BU.

133 *"I cannot regard it"*: JH to JGN, December 12, 1870, JH-BU.

133 *the most brilliant editorial writer*: WRT-L&L 1:331; DEN 88–89; Bishop, *Notes and Anecdotes*, 45.

133 *"Come as often"*: James T. Fields to JH, December 9, 1870, JH-BU.

134 *"[T]here are many good"*: *New York Tribune*, December 27, 1870.

134 *whose acquaintance Hay and Howells*: Fischer and Franks, eds., *Mark Twain's Letters*, 4:269–71. It is possible that Hay and Twain met in Buffalo as early as 1867, though the evidence is sketchy at best.

136 *"Anglo-Saxon relapsed"*: Bayard Taylor, *At Home and Abroad* (1860), 51, in Pearl, "The Shiftless Belligerent Pike," 114.

137 *"[L]et me thank you"*: James Fields to JH, December 9, 1870, JH-BU.

137 *"That ridiculous rhyme"*: JH to JGN, December 12, 1870, JH-BU.

138 *Twain pointed out*: JH to Joseph Bucklin Bishop, January 11, 1889, JH-BU.

138 *Hay insisted that*: JH to Samuel Clemens, January 11, 1871, in Fischer and Franks, eds., *Mark Twain's Letters*, 4:299.

138 *"a dash of Browning's"*: *Louisville Courier-Journal*, May 9, 1871, clipping, JH scrapbook, JH-BU.

138 *"These specimens"*: *New York Tribune*, clipping, n.d., JH scrapbook, JH-BU.

139 *"Bret Harte and Col. John"*: Unidentified clipping, n.d., JH scrapbook, JH-BU.

139 *"It is poor poetry"*: *Hartford Post*, n.d., JH scrapbook, JH-BU.

139 *"prostitution of the mission"*: Unidentified clipping, n.d., JH scrapbook, JH-BU.

139 *"I am no poet"*: JH to Richard Henry Stoddard, October 4, 1871, JH-LC.

139 *"a temporary disease"*: JH to John Bigelow, March 12, 1871, JH-BU.

139 *"After Bret Harte"*: Unidentified clipping, n.d., JH scrapbook, JH-BU.

140 *"John Hay, Author of"*: JH, "Kane and Abel," 85.

140 *"Reputation is very"*: Unidentified clipping, n.d., JH scrapbook, JH-LC.

140 *The esteemed Boston Lyceum Bureau*: Monteiro, "John Hay's Lyceum Lectures," 48.

140 *"His countenance"*: Unidentified clipping, n.d., JH scrapbook, JH-BU.

141 *"prose epic"*: Unidentified clipping, n.d., JH scrapbook, JH-LC.

141 *"vociferous and prolonged"*: Ibid.

141 *"There was scarcely a desk . . . let me come"*: Bishop, *Notes and Anecdotes*, 8–9.

141 *"I manufacture public"*: JH to John Bigelow, December 23, 1871, JH-BU.

142 *"The leading liberal"*: *New York Tribune*, clipping, n.d., JH scrapbook, JH-LC.

142 *"not only the interests"*: *New York Tribune*, clipping, n.d., JH scrapbook, JH-BU.

143 *"the corrupt cabal"*: *New York Tribune*, clipping, n.d., JH scrapbook, JH-LC.

143 *"[H]e never made the mistake . . . at this moment"*: Bishop, *Notes and Anecdotes*, 51–52.

143 *"I was always fond"*: Isaac Bromley to JH, November 9, 1890, JH-BU.

144 *"Your work thus far"*: WR to JH, December 23, 1870, JH-BU.

144 *"I waste two-thirds"*: JH to John Bigelow, March 12, 1871, JH-BU.

145 *"[Robert Lincoln] entered . . . he was already free from"*: Monteiro, "John Hay as Reporter," 85.

145 *"I have here before me . . . tolerant heavens"*: Ibid., 87–90.

146 *"I have done all"*: JH to WR, October 15, 1871, WR-LC.

146 *"John Hay has, within"*: *Syracuse Standard*, n.d., clipping, JH scrapbook, JH-BU.

147 *"the handsome and popular . . . finical and fine"*: Unidentified clippings, n.d., JH scrapbook, JH-BU.

147 *"He is a delightful"*: JH to John Bigelow, December 23, 1871, JH-BU.

148 *"brilliant and beaming"*: WDH, "Meetings with Clarence King," in Hague, ed., *Clarence King Memoirs*, 139.

148 *"in all its deformity"*: CK, *Mountaineering*, 110.

148 *"Every page sparkles"*: [WDH], "Recent Literature," 637–38.

148 *"so alive that it affects . . . masculine performance"*: Unidentified clippings, JH scrapbook, JH-BU.

149 *"Hay is doing admirably"*: Bigelow, *Retrospections*, 4:572.

149 *"We ought to see"*: JH to WR, "Monday, 1872," WR-LC.

149 *Encountering a line*: Holt, *Garrulities*, 123.

149 *"I cannot get Reid"*: JH to John Bigelow, March 12, 1871, JH-BU.

150 *"I have been brought down"*: JH to Albert Rhodes, August 24, 1873, JH-LC.

Chapter 7: Millionaires' Row

page

152   *"Housekeeping appears"*: Clara Stone, "Literature versus Housekeeping," MS, June 13, 1868, JH-LC.

152   *"She is a very estimable"*: JH to JGN, August 27, 1873, JH-BU.

152   *"Would the music"*: JH to Clara Stone, July 10, 1873, JH-BU.

153   *"Dear Miss Stone"*: JH to Clara Stone, May 9, 1872, JH-BU.

153   *"soldier Dictator"*: *New York Tribune*, n.d., clipping, JH scrapbook, JH-LC.

154   *"discreditable throng"*: *New York Tribune*, n.d., clipping, JH scrapbook, JH-LC.

155   *"present my homage"*: JH to Flora Stone, August 9, 1872, M-WRHS.

155   *"Has Miss Clara"*: JH to Flora Stone, August 29, 1872, M-WRHS.

155   *"I saw you for that short"*: JH to Clara Stone, July 12, 1873, JH-BU.

157   *"finest, most complete"*: *Cleveland Leader*, January 7, 1859.

157   *"which wealth [had] spared"*: *Cleveland Herald*, May 27, 1868, in Dow, "Amasa Stone, Jr.," 28.

158   *danced a quadrille*: Raymond, *Recollections of Euclid Avenue*.

158   *"My house is desolate"*: Horace Greeley to Margaret Allen, November 3, 1872, in Baehr, *The New York Tribune Since the Civil War*, 113.

158   *"house crowded by"*: Unidentified clipping, n.d., accompanying Charles E. Hay to "My Dear Sisters," December 10, 1872, JH-BU.

158   *"I think I will stay"*: JH to Mrs. Charles Hay, December 5, 1872, JH-BU.

159   *Precisely what sympathies . . . Gould's hireling*: Kluger, *The Paper*, 133–35.

159   *"Reid has managed"*: JH to Mrs. Charles Hay, December 5, 1872, JH-BU.

159   *"I didn't try to answer"*: WR to JH, December 24, 1872, JH-BU.

160   *"the utterance of a man"*: *New York Tribune*, n.d., clipping, JH scrapbook, JH-LC.

160   *"I have sometimes gazed"*: JH to Clara Stone, May 4, 1873, JH-BU.

161   *"Ah, think what"*: JH to Clara Stone, May 4, 1873, JH-BU.

161   *"I love you Clärchen . . . but humbly grateful?"*: JH to Clara Stone, May 8, 1873, JH-BU.

162   *"kindest and nicest"*: JH to Clara Stone, n.d., JH-BU.

162   *"I was never a happy"*: JH to Clara Stone, May 15, 1873, JH-BU.

162   *"the dear young saint"*: JH to WR, June 23, 1873, WR-LC.

162   *"I do need somebody"*: JH to Clara Stone, August 3, 1873, JH-BU.

162   *"not very strong . . . you and I?"*: JH to Clara Stone, September 12, 1873, JH-BU.

163   *"I have a letter"*: RTL to JGN, June 19, 1873, JGN-LC.

163   *"He is a man of great"*: JH to WR, October 26, 1873, WR-LC.

164   *"I am making an active"*: JH to WR, October 29, 1873, WR-LC.

164 *"We have more room"*: JH to Flora Stone, February 11, 1874, M-WRHS.

164 *"begin life without"*: Amasa Stone to JH, February 23, 1874, JH-BU.

164 *"Your life and habits"*: Amasa Stone to JH, February 23, 1874, JH-BU.

165 *"affection and esteem"*: Amasa Stone to JH, April 7, 1874, JH-BU.

165 *"[T]he best of all good luck"*: JH to AA, November 28, 1874, JH-BU.

165 *"O you two are"*: Flora Stone to JH, February 13, 1874, JH-BU.

165 *"It does not seem to me"*: JH to CSH, July 11, 1874, JH-BU.

166 *"dazzling of the eyes"*: JH to WR, August 11, 1874, WR-LC.

166 *"I am living a merely"*: JH to WR, August 8, 1874, WR-LC.

166 *"She looked like me"*: JH to Flora Stone, March 19, 1875, M-WRHS.

166 *"[M]y father-in-law wishes"*: JH to AA, November 28, 1874, JH-BU.

167 *"some half hundred"*: JH to WR, June 3, 1875, WR-LC.

167 *"I do nothing but read"*: JH to AA, December 14, 1875, JH-BU.

168 *"There is apparently"*: Henry James to JH, July 21, 1875, HJ-JH 81–82.

168 *"wonderful style"*: JH to WR, July 24, 1875, WR-LC.

168 *"I feel as if my sails"*: Henry James to JH, August 5, 1875, HJ-JH 84.

169 *"The work is a heavy one"*: JH to Schuyler Colfax, July 20, 1875, JH-BU.

169 *"I shall go seriously"*: JH to JGN, December 4, 1875, JH-BU.

169 *"partial blindness"*: JH to JGN, June 23, 1876, JH-LC.

169 *"enfeebled with illness"*: JH to WR, March 27, 1876, WR-LC.

169 *"gilding and black"*: JH to Flora Stone, August 14, 1876, M-WRHS.

169 *"If other people"*: JH to WR, July 29, 1876, WR-LC.

169 *"He is a fine little"*: JH to WR, November 13, 1876, WR-LC.

170 *"a man on one ticket"*: JH to WR, March 16, 1876, WR-LC.

170 *"I shall never"*: JH to AA, February 20, 1877, JH-BU.

171 *"It will be difficult"*: Rutherford B. Hayes to JH, February 27, 1877, JH-BU; a note included in the BU card catalogue citation for this letter mentions that Washington's hair was embedded in the ring.

171 *"like Stentor . . . like Gargantua"*: JH to WR, December 4, 1876, WR-LC.

Chapter 8: Roses in a Glue-Factory

page

173 *"very perfect"*: *Report of the Joint Committee Concerning the Ashtabula Bridge Disaster*, 84–85.

173 *"Mr. Stone had great . . . erected this bridge"*: Peet, *The Ashtabula Disaster*, 207–08.

175 *"the very devil"*: JH to Amasa Stone, August 23, 1877, WAD-LC.

175 *"There is nowhere . . . keep house myself"*: July 24, 1877, WRT-L&L 2:2–3.

175 *"The prospects of labor . . . folly and weakness"*: JH to Amasa Stone, August 23 and September 3, 1877, WAD-LC.

175 *"All your investments"*: JH to Amasa Stone, September 3, 1877, WAD-LC.

176 *"Burn all my letters"*: JH to JGN, February 27, 1878, JH-BU.

177 *"an air of self-contained"*: J. Laurence Laughlin, "Some Recollections of Henry Adams," in Chalfant, *Better in Darkness*, 268.

177 *"outside the social pale"*: HAE 942.

177 *"no* monde . . . *bad judgment"*: HAE, 954, 951, 942.

178 *"We have had a very cheerful"*: HA to Charles Milnes Gaskell, May 30, 1878, HAL 2:338.

178 *"with some force . . . upstairs"*: JH to JGN, February 27, 1878, JH-BU.

178 *"Our city life"*: Mitchell, *Nurse and Patient*, 54.

179 *"moral atmosphere"*: Mitchell, *Fat and Blood*, in Earnest, *S. Weir Mitchell*, 83.

179 *"I have been under"*: JH to RTL, August 25, 1879, WR-LC.

179 *"[s]erene and tranquil"*: JH to Flora Stone, July 10, 1878, M-WRHS.

179 *"I am feeling very well"*: JH to CSH, July 24, 1878, JH-BU.

180 *"scarcely anything"*: JH to Flora Stone, June 27, 1878, M-WRHS.

180 *"I think a man needs"*: JH to Flora Stone, August 11, 1878, M-WRHS.

181 *"the authority of divine"*: Lamon, *Life of Abraham Lincoln*, 157.

181 *"lost all self control . . . crazy as a loon"*: Ibid.

181 *"Mr. Lincoln was a man"*: Ibid., 480–83.

181 *"Notwithstanding his"*: Ibid., 483.

182 *"It is absolutely horrible . . . respectable book"*: RTL to JH, April 7, 1872, JH-BU.

182 *"His heart was"*: N&H:AL 10:354–55.

182 *"We knew Mr. Lincoln"*: N&H:AL 1:xii

183 *"If I could get"*: JH to JGN, March 30, 1879, JH-BU.

183 *"We are having a red hot"*: JH to WR, August 25, 1879, JH-LET 2:43.

183 *"They believed in"*: Cleveland Herald, August 28, 1879.

183 *"I wish you would do"*: WR to JH, April 24, 1879, WR-LC.

183 *"The Congress matter"*: JH to WR, October 21, 1879, WR-LC.

184 *"He had the rare"*: Bishop, *Notes and Anecdotes*, 61.

184 *"Interests which I cannot"*: JH to William Evarts, October 28, 1879, JH-BU.

184 *"I stand like a hydrophobical"*: JH to WDH, November 5, 1879, JH-WDH 40.

185 *"What a pity"*: Plischke, *U.S. Department of State*, 210.

185 *"Today was an important . . . in Lincoln's time"*: JH to CSH, November 25, 1879, JH-BU.

185 *"You don't sufficiently"*: Pennanen, "The Foreign Policy of William Maxwell Evarts," 96.

186   *"more exacting"*: JH to Amasa Stone, December 8, 1879, JH-BU.

186   *"I can hold on"*: JH to CSH, December 7, 1879, JH-BU.

186   *"[H]e and I are such belles"*: JH to CSH, March 2, 1880, JH-BU.

186   *"I had a rather large"*: Holt, *Garrulities*, 136.

187   *"The iron crown"*: Tehan, *Henry Adams in Love*, 28.

188   *"With perfection of grace"*: De Koven, *A Musician and His Wife*, 54.

188   *" 'Mein Gott!' "*: Tehan, *Henry Adams in Love*, 28.

188   *"He is very nice"*: Ibid., 30.

188   *"was looking far more"*: JH to Flora Stone, December 20, 1879, M-WRHS.

189   *"boundless ambition"*: JH to CSH, January 28, 1880, JH-BU.

189   *"The table was absolutely"*: JH to CSH, February 13, 1880, JH-BU.

189   *"[E]very year my"*: JH to CSH, January 19, 1880, JH-BU.

189   *"I cannot believe"*: Ibid.

190   *"He was loyal"*: Wellman, "John Hay: An American Gentleman," 166, 168.

190   *"Hay seemed to me"*: T. C. Evans, "Personal Reminiscences of John Hay: By a Veteran Journalist," *New York Times*, July 16, 1905.

190   *"Everything he undertook"*: "John Hay," *The Nation* 81 (July 6, 1905), 4.

191   *"He is a very agreeable"*: JH to CSH, March 7, 1880, JH-BU.

191   *"The policy of this country"*: Pennanen, "The Foreign Policy of William Maxwell Evarts," 343.

191   *"I work not for"*: Ibid.

191   *"The presence of such"*: Mark Twain to WDH, October 27, 1879, in Smith and Gibson, eds., *Mark Twain–Howells Letters*, 1:277.

192   *"I am doing this"*: JH to CSH, July 23, 1880, JH-BU.

193   *"The Balance Sheet"*: "The Balance Sheet of the Two Parties: A Speech Delivered by John Hay at Cleveland, Ohio, July 31, 1880," pamphlet, 1880, WRHS.

193   *"The Bombardment . . . made havoc . . . The Great Speech"*: Newspaper clippings, n.d., JH-LC.

194   *"We had an excellent"*: JH to WR, August 5, 1880, WR-LC.

194   *" 'Little Breeches' Hay"*: *Cleveland Plain Dealer*, August 2, 1880.

194   *"There was a slight"*: JH to WDH, October 24, 1880, JH-WDH 52.

194   *"head over heels . . . to resist"*: HA to Charles Milnes Gaskell, March 3, 1872, HAL 2:132.

194   *"a perfect Voltaire"*: Edel, *Henry James, The Middle Years*, 29.

194   *"I should say"*: JH to Charles Milnes Gaskell, April 27, 1872, HAL 2:135.

195   *"Mrs. Hay is . . . chats for two"*: Chalfant, *Better in Darkness*, 364.

195   *"mental stimulus"*: Parsons, *Scattered Memories*, 166.

195   *"a serene and classic . . . a climate"*: De Koven, *A Musician and His Wife*, 202–03.

195 *"to learn how the machinery"*: HA, *Democracy*, 12.

196 *"moral lunatic"*: Ibid., 174.

196 *"a third-rate nonentity . . . come in time"*: HA to Charles Milnes Gaskell, June 14, 1876, HAL 2:276.

196 *pronouncing it "coarse"*: Chalfant, *Better in Darkness*, 399.

196 *"given up denying it"*: MHA to Robert Hooper, December 21, 1880, in Thoron, ed., *Letters of Mrs. Henry Adams*, 247.

197 *"chief" of "Clan Ratcliffe"*: HA, *Democracy*, 75.

197 *"At the thought"*: Ibid.

197 *"Beware of your"*: JH to James Garfield, October 18, 1880, JH-LET 2:51–52.

198 *"[A]s you will see"*: JH to WR, October 29, 1880, WR-LC.

198 *"at least to that of"*: James Garfield to JH, December 10, 1880, JH-BU.

198 *"To do a thing"*: JH to James Garfield, December 25, 1880, Garfield Papers, LC.

199 *"trifling" Ohioan*: Ackerman, *Dark Horse*, 253.

200 *"I find myself low"*: JH to WR, March 17, 1881, WR-LC.

200 *"light employment"*: WR to JH, March 18, 1881, JH-BU.

200 *"I write only"*: JH to James Garfield, May 6, 1881, Garfield Papers, LC.

Chapter 9: Scorpions

page

201 *"I wish to say"*: WR to JH, March 27, 1881, in Cortissoz, *Life of Whitelaw Reid*, 2:60.

202 *"Well, which did"*: *New York Tribune*, May 4, 1871.

202 *"Have the people"*: Ibid.

202 *tried to have expunged*: JH to J. Stanley Brown, November 30, 1881, JH-BU.

202 *"Give me a line"*: JH to James Garfield, May 6, 1881, Garfield Papers, LC.

202 *"You are handling"*: James Garfield to JH, May 8, 1881, JH-BU.

202 *"a patriot of the . . . pap and patronage"*: *New York Tribune*, May 14, 1881.

203 *"We found little"*: Young, *Men and Memories*, 460–61.

203 *"There is certainly"*: *New York Tribune*, May 17, 1881.

203 *"Roscoe is finished"*: JH to WR, May 26, 1881, WR-LC.

204 *"You've made a splendid"*: WR to JH, June 21, 1881, JH-BU.

205 *"Never speak to me"*: Ackerman, *Dark Horse*, 338.

205 *"I did it"*: *New York Times*, July 3, 1881; also Ackerman, *Dark Horse*, 379.

205 *"A second President . . . its real character"*: *New York Tribune*, July 3, 1881.

206 *"It is almost impossible"*: JH to WR, July 10, 1881, WR-LC.

206 *"the people's President"*: *New York Tribune*, July 4, 1881.

207 *"It can do no good"*: *New York Tribune*, July 7, 1881.

207   *"It is perfectly amazing"*: JH to WR, August 13, 1881, WR-LC.

207   *"Please send me"*: JH telegram to RTL, July 4, 1881, Garfield Papers, LC.

207   *"I wish I felt better"*: RTL to JH, July 18, 1881, JH-BU.

208   *"I go West tonight"*: JH to J. Stanley Brown, September 17, 1881, JH-BU.

208   *"[S]o brave and good"*: JH to WR, September 4, 1881, WR-LC.

208   *his "interim-ity"*: JH to WR, September 14, 1881, WRT-L&L 1:454.

208   *Hay invested in*: Wilkins, *Clarence King*, 300.

209   *"the official correspondence"*: JH to HA, November 5, 1881, HA-MHS.

210   *"[T]he men worshipped"*: HAE 1005–06.

210   *"He knew more"*: Ibid., 1004.

210   *"It was hard to remember"*: JH, "Clarence King," in Hague, ed., *Clarence King Memoirs*, 125–26.

210   *"I never knew such"*: MHA to Robert Hooper, March 30, 1884, AP.

210   *"contemptible cur"*: Kaplan, *Mr. Clemens and Mr. Twain*, 167.

211   *"dynamitic" biography*: Ibid., 241.

211   *"I took into account"*: JH to WR, September 4, 1881, WR-LC.

211   *"As to Twain"*: WR to JH, September 25, 1881, WR-LC.

211   *The review*: New York Tribune, October 25, 1881.

211   *"no heart"*: Foley, *Criticism in American Periodicals of the Works of Henry James*, 27.

212   *"It is a remarkable book"*: JH to WR, December 16, 1881, WR-LC.

212   *"entirely from . . . moral aspects of our civilization"*: New York Tribune, December 25, 1881.

213   *"at some warm sand . . . in my life"*: JH to WDH, March 26, 1882, JH-WDH 58.

213   *"pounded and sampled"*: JH to HA, April 28, 1882, HA-MHS.

213   *serve as "ballast"*: JH to WDH, March 26, 1882, JH-WDH 58.

213   *"a powerful book"*: R. W. Gilder to JH, June 30, 1882, JH-BU.

214   *"First, if people"*: JH to HA, June 7, 1882, HA-MHS.

214   *"The children have stood"*: CSH to Mrs. Amasa Stone, July 24, 1882, WAD-LC.

214   *"purple glory"*: JH to Samuel Mather, August 31, 1882, M-WRHS.

214   *"I assisted last night"*: JH to Samuel Mather, September 8, 1882, M-WRHS.

215   *"by the thousands"*: JH to HA, August 16, 1882, M-WRHS.

215   *"repudiate for me"*: HA to JH, September 3, 1882, HAL 2:467–68.

215   *"unsight and unseen"*: WDH to JH, September 5, 1882, JH-WDH 61.

215   *"The breads & muffins"*: CSH to Flora Stone Mather, October 18, 1882, M-WRHS.

215   *"Do you think you know"*: JH to HA, October 22, 1882, HA-MHS.

216   *"They wrote it together"*: CFW to CSH, January 8, 1883, JH-BU.

216   *"I never saw a great man"*: JH to HJ, December 9, 1882, HJ-JH 90.

216   *"dizziness, deep"*: JH to S. Weir Mitchell, January 10, 1883, JH-BU.

216 *"Neurasthenia Céphalique"*: Ibid.

217 *"quite reasonable . . . the course of his years"*: JH to Mrs. Amasa Stone, September 2, 1882, WAD-LC.

217 *"suited the hands"*: B-W 5–6.

217 *"His shoes might"*: JH, *The Bread-Winners*, MS, Houghton Library, Harvard University.

217 *"Farnham millions"*: B-W 42.

218 *"rescue the city"*: Ibid., 55.

218 *"a young and thriving . . . velvet lawns"*: Ibid., 7–8.

218 *"marked, like himself"*: Ibid., 6.

218 *"hearty, blowsy"*: Ibid., 22.

218 *"unhealthy sentiment"*: Ibid., 24.

218 *"tell your love"*: Ibid., 113.

218 *"in several capitals"*: Ibid., 121.

218 *"[I]t was a pity"*: Ibid., 12.

218 *"with hearty good-will"*: The kiss was described thus when B-W was serialized in *Century*; in the book version he merely "stooped and kissed her"—Ibid., 133.

218 *"famous bridge-builder . . . bonny face . . . pure and noble"*: Ibid., 40, 42.

219 *"contented industry"*: Ibid., 86.

219 *"oleaginous" Andrew*: Ibid., 74.

219 *"the laziest"*: Ibid., 82.

219 *"what they called socialism"*: Ibid., 215.

219 *"wealth and erristocracy . . . robbers' cave . . . vampire"*: Ibid., 88, 219, 78.

219 *"downfall of the money"*: Ibid., 84.

219 *"reddened by night"*: Ibid., 7.

219 *In his only published commentary*: [JH], "A Letter from the Author," 795.

220 *"[S]hould I be taken away"*: Amasa Stone to JH, January 4, 1883, JH-BU.

220 *"I came abroad hoping"*: JH to Amasa Stone, January 11, 1883, WAD-LC.

221 *"If I am able"*: JH to Amasa Stone, February 9, 1883, WAD-LC.

221 *"I seem to have lost"*: Amasa Stone to JH, March 7, 1883, JH-BU.

221 *"many of the Diplomatic"*: JH to Amasa Stone, April 26, 1883, WAD-LC.

222 *"[E]verything combined"*: Amasa Stone to JH, February 8, 1883, JH-BU.

222 *"You have had a hard"*: JH to Amasa Stone, May 2, 1883, JH-BU.

Chapter 10: Everlasting Angels

page

223 *"I have a long and toilsome"*: JH to HA, May 27, 1883, HA-MHS.

223 *equivalent to more than twenty*: See, e.g., measuringworth.com/uscompare.

224 *"I thought of you"*: Henry James to JH, May 24, 1883, HJ-JH 93.

224 *"the most keenly appreciative"*: *Art Interchange*, n.d., clipping, JH scrapbook, JH-LC.

224 *"bang and crimp . . . do not go together"*: Ibid.

224 *"Everybody is reading it"*: *Critic and Good Literature*, n.d., clipping, JH scrapbook, JH-LC.

225 *"The Sensational Novel"*: Unidentified clipping, n.d., JH scrapbook, JH-LC.

225 *"corresponds almost exactly"*: Advertisement, *Washington Post*, September 20, 1883, in Vandersee, "The Great Literary Mystery of the Gilded Age," 249.

225 *literary Sherlock Holmes*: *Washington Post*, n.d., clipping, JH scrapbook, JH-LC.

225 *"I wish I had"*: Unidentified clipping, n.d., JH scrapbook, JH-LC.

225 *"I long ago forgave"*: JH to HA, August 3, 1883, HA-MHS.

225 *"I am glad you did not"*: HA to JH, September 24, 1883, HAL 2:513.

225 *"I want to roll"*: HA to JH, February 2, 1884, HAL 2:533–34.

225 *The Bread-Winners . . . has*: *Saturday Review* 57 (February 2, 1884), 155.

226 *"touches of Fielding"*: Ibid.

226 *"a novel of action"*: *Critic and Good Literature* 1, new series (January 5, 1884), 7.

226 *"largeness, a force"*: Unidentified clipping, n.d., JH scrapbook, JH-LC.

226 *"How this disagreeable"*: *Literary World* 15 (January 26, 1884), 27.

226 *"no sympathies"*: *Springfield Republic*, n.d., clipping, JH scrapbook, JH-LC.

226 *"A man of his breeding"*: *Boston Evening Transcript*, n.d., clipping, JH scrapbook, JH-LC.

226 *"the anonymous author shows"*: *Cleveland Leader*, n.d., clipping, JH scrapbook, JH-LC.

227 *"conceived from"*: [JH], "A Letter from the Author," 794.

227 *"I hardly know . . . written a novel"*: Ibid., 794–96.

228 *"the ascription of its authorship"*: *Cincinnati News Journal*, January 6, 1884, clipping, JH scrapbook, JH-LC.

228 *new subscribers*: Roswell Smith to JH, November 5, 1883, JH-BU.

229 *"He glanced in the mirror"*: [Keenan], *The Money-Makers*, 49.

229 *"elegant and refined"*: Ibid., 14.

229 *"to shine in the exclusive"*: Ibid., 13.

229 *"solidifying his relations"*: Ibid., 58–59.

229 *"to keep his hand in"*: Ibid., 47.

229 *"If he loved"*: Ibid.

229 *"He still persisted"*: Ibid., 48.

230 *"slatternly hamlet"*: Ibid., 132.

230 *"nothing but business"*: Ibid., 69.

230 *"sharp practices"*: Ibid., 11.

230 *"round his millions"*: Ibid., 112.

230 *"a never-exhausted source"*: Ibid., 136.

230 *"not pretty . . . awkward"*: Ibid., 50.

230 *"He was in no sense"*: Ibid., 168.

230 *"the ideal of her girlish"*: Ibid., 169.

230 " *'That's just what'* ": Ibid., 83.

230 " *'Gad! what beauty'* ": Ibid., 174.

230 " *'Millions may cover'* ": Ibid., 177.

231 *"A robust man"*: Ibid., 272, 280–81.

231 *"as an answer"*: Advertisement for *The Money-Makers*, clipping, n.d., WAD-LC.

231 *"savage libel . . . and her daughters"*: JH to William Appleton, February 3, 1885, WAD-LC.

231 *"a malicious attack"*: William Appleton to JH, January [incorrectly dated; clearly meant as February] 5, 1885, WAD-LC.

231 *"much better in all its parts"*: *Vanity Fair* (Cleveland), "A Weekly Journal of Society, Art, Literature, Music and the Drama," January 31, 1885, clipping, WAD-LC.

232 *"I eat, sleep, and perform"*: JH to S. Weir Mitchell, January 10, 1883, JH-BU.

232 *"I came away from Cleveland"*: JH to WDH, September 9, 1883, JH-WDH 21.

232 *"square brick box"*: MHA to Robert Hooper, December 16, 1883, AP.

233 *"Neo-Agnostic"*: JH to HA, April 27, 1885, HA-MHS.

233 *"God bless you"*: JH to CSH, April 22, 1884, WAD-LC.

234 *"James tells me"*: JH to CSH, May 1, 1884, WAD-LC.

234 *"beautiful, stylish"*: JH to CSH, May 4, 1884, WAD-LC.

234 *"rural sheriff . . . more civilized"*: JH to R. W. Gilder, July 11, 1884, Gilder Papers, New York Public Library.

235 *"He was 83"*: JH to HA, October 2, 1884, HA-MHS.

235 *"The Doctor scared"*: JH to HA, December 20, 1884, HA-MHS.

235 *"I need not tell you"*: JH to RTL, January 27, 1885 (misdated 1884), JH-LET 2:87.

236 *"It is beyond doubt"*: RTL to JH, April 27, 1885, JH-BU.

236 *"The engagement was not"*: N&H:AL 1:186–87.

236 *"[t]his taint of"*: N&H:AL 1:187–88.

236 *"It is as useless"*: N&H:AL 1:201.

237 *"[T]he market is ready"*: JH to JGN, March 2, 1885, JH-BU.

237 *"comprehension and treatment"*: R. W. Gilder to JH, July 29, 1885, JH-BU.

237 *When Gilder offered $50,000*: Thomas, *Portrait for Posterity*, 103; Mearns, *Lincoln Papers*, 79.

238 *"I want you to say"*: JH to JGN, July 27, 1885, JH-BU.

238 *"I think I have left"*: JH to JGN, August 10, 1885, JH-BU.

238 *"We must not show"*: Ibid.

239 *"seize a hill"*: JH to HA, September 13, 1885, HA-MHS.

239 *"our chuckle-headed sovereign . . . [H]e chaws more"*: MHA to Robert Hooper, January 21, 1883, and December 4, 1881, in Thoron, ed., *Letters of Mrs. Henry Adams*, 419, 306.

240 *"wandering soul"*: [HA], *Esther*, 263–64.

240 *"bad figure . . . rough water coming"*: Ibid., 199.

240 *"impalpable tyranny"*: Ibid., 218.

240 *"Once in harness"*: Ibid., 280.

240 *"She is certainly not handsome"*: HA to Charles Milnes Gaskell, March 26, 1872, HAL 2:133.

240 *"Is it not enough"*: [HA], *Esther*, 329.

240 *"a woman's natural tendency"*: [HA], *Democracy*, 90

240 *"How did I ever"*: O'Toole, *Five of Hearts*, 148.

240 *"The business of educating"*: [HA], *Esther*, 317.

241 *"Lot's wife"*: Friedrich, *Clover*, 309.

241 *"As it is now thirteen"*: HA to MHA, March 14, 1885, HAL 2:579.

241 *"Henry is more patient"*: Chalfant, *Better in Darkness*, 503.

241 *"My wife . . . has been"*: HA to Robert Cunliffe, November 29, 1885, HAL 2:639.

241 *"If I had one single"*: Chalfant, *Better in Darkness*, 503.

242 *"I can neither talk"*: JH to HA, December 9, 1885, HAL-MHS.

242 *"Nothing you can do"*: HA to JH, December 8, 1885, HAL 2:640.

242 *"Don is behaving"*: HA to JH, January 7, 1883, HAL 2:487–88.

243 *"I . . . cannot saddle"*: HA to JH, April 8, 1883, HAL 2:497.

243 *"The dogs wept"*: HA to ESC, May 18, 1883, HAL 2:501.

243 *"All I can now ask"*: HA to ESC, December 10, 1885, HAL 2:641.

243 *"Will you keep it"*: HA to ESC, December 25, 1885, HAL 2:645.

243 *"even if it does necessitate"*: H. H. Richardson to JH, December 20, 1885, JH-BU.

244 *"It looks like under the sea"*: ESC to CSH, July 15, 1886, HA-MHS.

244 *"I have forgotten"*: JH to Helen Hay Wadsworth, January 5, 1902, JH-LC.

245 *"Now I am sundered . . . [A]n additional"*: JGN to JH, November 25, 1885, JH-BU.

245 *"I do not know"*: JH to RTL, January 6, 1886, JH-LET 2:101.

Chapter 11: Two on the Terrace

page

247 *"happy village . . . a mere political camp"*: HAE 951, 954.

247 *"all one's acquaintances"*: HAE 951.

248 *"Washington is the place"*: O'Toole, *Five of Hearts*, 94.

249 *"fell daft"*: JH to HA, August 29, 1886, HA-MHS.

249 *"[W]e will give you an acre"*: JH to WDH, September 12, 1886, JH-WDH 90.

250 *"As to Lincoln"*: King, "The Biographers of Lincoln," 862.

250 *"There is every sign"*: *The Nation* 1114 (November 4, 1886), 375.

250 *"Lincoln lives again"*: John Bigelow to JH, January 19, 1887, JH-BU.

250 *"easy, dignified"*: WDH to JH, March 1, 1887, JH-LC.

250 *"astonished at . . . fall still born"*: William Herndon to Jesse Weik, December 5, 1886, William Herndon Papers, LC.

250 *"the Ann Rutledge . . . with an iron pen"*: William Herndon to Jesse Weik, January 2, 1887, William Herndon Papers, LC.

251 *"how damn partisan"*: R. W. Gilder to JGN, April 9, 1887, JGN-LC.

251 *"actors . . . tone & generosity"*: R. W. Gilder to JGN, January 19, 1887, JGN-LC.

251 *"provided we were to do"*: JH to JGN, April 9, 1887, JH-BU.

251 *"I have been passing"*: JH to JGN, August 4, 1887, JH-BU.

252 *"thoroughly fit for power"*: JH to WR, March 16, 1888, WR-LC.

253 *"I little thought"*: ESC to HA, August 16, 1886, HA-MHS.

253 *"Mr. Dobbitt"*: HA to Martha Cameron, February 3, 1888, HAL 3:100.

254 *"I am homesick"*: HA to ESC, September 7, 1887, HAL 3:76.

254 *"I love you very"*: HA to Martha Cameron, September 9, 1888, HAL 3:137.

254 *"Mrs. Cameron"*: JH to HA, June 26, 1889, HA-MHS.

254 *"[W]e bowed"*: HA to ESC, April 28, 1888, HAL 3:109.

255 *"Your invitation is seductive"*: JH to ESC, November 19, 1886, AP.

255 *"I think he must have joined"*: JH to HA, July 12, 1894, HA-MHS.

255 *"Yesterday morning"*: JH to HA, May 19, 1888, HA-MHS.

255 *"To kiss a woman"*: CK to HA, September 27, 1887, HA-MHS.

255 *"If he had a choice"*: HA, "King," in Hague, ed., *Clarence King Memoirs*, 172.

256 *"old-gold" natives*: Wilkins, *Clarence King*, 169.

256 *"studies of the lower"*: Frank Mason to JH, September 1, 1883, in Wilkins, *Clarence King*, 320.

256 *"Man in the process"*: CK to JH, July 28, 1887, JH-BU.

256 *"blithe blue eyes"*: WDH, "Clarence King," in Hague, ed., *Clarence King Memoirs*, 136.

256 *"Miscegenation is"*: Sandweiss, *Passing Strange*, 153.

256 *"I thank God"*: Ibid., 203.

256 *"[N]ow in middle age"*: CK to HA, September 25, 1889, HA-MHS.

257 *"a rough fell land"*: CK to HA, n.d. (August 1886), HA-MHS.

257 *"Buffalo Bill speed"*: JH to HA, July 14, 1888, HA-MHS.

257 *"under par"*: JH to Samuel Mather, August 4, 1888, M-WRHS.

257 *"air, or water"*: JH to HA, July 30, 1888, HA-MHS.

257 *"after the wheat . . . to a smaller scale"*: R. W. Gilder to JGN and JH, July 12, 1888, NIC-LC.

257 *"Leave out anything"*: JH to R. W. Gilder, July 21, 1888, JH-BU.

257 *"I am perfectly"*: JH to JGN, July 22, 1888, JH-BU.

258 *instead, he met with Harrison*: Memorandum attached to JH to WR, October 14, 1889, WR-LC.

259 *"My real trouble"*: Morris, *Rise of Theodore Roosevelt*, 397–98.

260 *"a certain ready-to-fight . . . for possible agreement"*: Chanler, *Roman Spring*, 193.

260 *"He considers himself"*: S. G. Blythe, "The New England Oligarchy," *Saturday Evening Post*, May 7, 1901, in Garraty, *Henry Cabot Lodge*, 126.

261 *"Our little set"*: HA to Lucy Baxter, April 13, 1890, HAL 3:233.

262 *"We shall not have a friend . . . sticking out"*: JH to JGN, October 31, 1889, JH-BU.

262 *"The labor of a generation . . . elbow-room"*: *New York Tribune*, February 9, 1891.

262 *"There is no doubt . . . indistinguishable value"*: R. W. Gilder to "My dear Authors of the 'Life of Lincoln,'" January 2, 1890, JH-BU.

263 *"a work the equal"*: HA to John T. Morse, Jr., July 5, 1890, HAL 3:248–49.

263 *"They were actors"*: Charles Eliot to HA, June 14, 1892, HA-MHS.

263 *"I have . . . the last sheets"*: RTL to JH, January 7, 1890, JH-BU.

263 *"You can never"*: JH to RTL, April 21, 1890, JH-LET 2:189.

263 *"the last kick"*: JH to "Rives," May 13, 1890, JH-BU.

264 *"I have had specially printed"*: JH to HJ, June 5, 1890, HJ-JH, 105.

264 *"In wandering through"*: JH, "Love's Dawn," JH-CPW 240.

264 *"I am rather too old"*: JH to R. W. Gilder, June 3, 1890, JH-LET 2:191.

265 *"fascination possessed"*: Zimmerman, *First Great Triumph*, 183.

265 *"Forget any praises"*: Chanler, *Roman Spring*, 192–93.

265 *"the color of the sky"*: Ibid., 192.

265 *"I had such an unqualified"*: John Singer Sargent to William Endicott, October 28, 1922, in Garraty, *Henry Cabot Lodge*, 31.

265 *"I was drinking tea"*: JH to HJ, June 5, 1890, HJ-JH 105.

266 *"[D]o you remember"*: ESC to HA, April 22, 1891, HA-MHS.

266 *"See the white obelisk"*: JH, "Two on the Terrace," JH-CPW 264–66.

267 *"Great Kung-fu-tse!"*: HA to ESC, August 12, 1891, HAL 3:521.

268 *"John and Nannie"*: ESC to HA, September 2, 1890, HA-MHS.

268 *"Nanny and Cabot"*: ESC to HA, October 29, 1890, HA-MHS.

268 *"a few other quiet"*: ESC to HA, January 27, 1891, HA-MHS.

268 *"I have asked Mrs. Lodge"*: JH to ESC, n.d., AP.

268 *"destroyed all hers"*: ESC to WRT, May 14, 1919, WRT-HU.

268 *"[Hay's] love for"*: ESC to HA, April 22, 1891, HA-MHS.

269 *"He then gave himself"*. B-W 176.

269 *"I do not believe"*: JH to CSH, May 2, 1891, WAD-LC.

269 *"I shall see John"*: ESC to HA, May 12, 1891, HA-MHS.

269 *"I am already looking . . . who cares for me"*: JH to CSH, May 18 and 22, 1879, WAD-LC.

269 *"the Cameron clan"*: JH to CSH, May 15, 1891, WAD-LC.

269 *"John Hay and I"*: ESC to HA, May 26, 1891, HA-MHS.

270 *"Actually I wish"*: HA to ESC, June 3, 1891, HAL 3:482.

270 *"I feel sure now"*: ESC to HA, May 26, 1891, HA-MHS.

270 *and promptly collapsed*: JH to CSH, May 30, 1891, WAD-LC; Smalley, *Anglo-American Memories*, 360–61.

270 *"He told me yesterday"*: ESC to HA, June 7, 1891, HA-MHS.

270 *"When I think"*: ESC to HA, June 9, 1891, HA-MHS.

271 *"I sought her genial presence"*: JH to HA, June 4, 1891, HA-MHS.

271 *"the Cameron party . . . her usual little court"*: JH to CSH, June 9, 13, and 11, 1891, WAD-LC.

271 *"When I think of the seventeen"*: JH to CSH, May 31 (June 1), 1891, WAD-LC.

271 *"London is floating"*: JH to ESC, July 2, 1891, AP.

Chapter 12: Tame Cats

page

272 *"pine shanty"*: JH to ESC, August 28, 1891, AP.

272 *"retire from the world"*: Ibid.

272 *"John Hay writes"*: ESC to HA, September 26, 1891, HA-MHS.

273 *"miserably weak"*: JH to JGN, September 16, 1891, JH-BU.

273 *"a young lady look"*: JH to WR, July 23, 1891, WR-LC.

273 *"He was so tender-hearted"*: Alice Hay Wadsworth to WRT, n.d., JH-BU.

273 *"the jolliest kind of pal"*: Helen Hay Whitney to WRT, n.d., JH-BU.

273 *"The greatest treat"*: Ibid.

273 *" 'If you see a thing' "*: Alice Hay Wadsworth to WRT, n.d., JH-BU.

273 *"fat and dull"*: JH to HA, January 10, 1891, HA-MHS.

273 *"a carload of fishing tackle"*: JH to HA, July 17, 1890, HA-MHS.

274 *"I have no knowledge"*: JH to Samuel Mather, July 15, 1893, M-WRHS.

274 *"To think that you are"*: ESC to HA, August 10, 1891, HA-MHS.

274 *"I am grateful"*: HA to ESC, July 31, 1891, HAL 3:510.

274 *"The more you please"*: Ibid.

274 *"at what hour"*: HA to ESC, October 11, 1891, HAL 3:555.

274 *"Mrs. Cameron is no good"*: HA to Rebecca Dodge Rae, December 5, 1891, HAL 3:582.

275 *"an apocalyptic* Never*"*: HA to ESC, November 5, 1891, HAL 3:556.

275 *"Paris experiment"*: Ibid.

275 *"Thank you a thousand"*: ESC to HA, n.d. [November 1891], HA-MHS.

275 *"[N]o matter how"*: HA to ESC, November 5, 1891, HAL 3:557.

275 *"I would give you"*: Ibid.

275 *"[Y]ou are Beauty"*: HA to ESC, November 10, 1891, HAL 3:510.

275 *"I could find nothing . . . ennui at intervals"*: HA to JH, November 14, 1891, HAL 3:568.

276 *"We all talk"*: ESC to HA, December 6, 1891, HA-MHS.

276 *"the women looked extremely"*: JH to HA, December 17, 1891, HA-MHS.

276 *"I think it was . . . dagoes and dudes"*: JH to HA, January 6, 1892, HA-MHS.

276 *"Good night, my tantalizing . . . to my dying day"*: JH to ESC, n.d., AP. The letter also mentions JH's intention to attend *Julius Caesar*, performed by the Meininger Players, which, according to an advertisement in the *Washington Post*, January 17, 1892, was to open at the New National Theater the following evening.

277 *"I shall remember"*: JH to Donald Cameron, March 1, 1892, AP.

278 *"It is rather funny that"*: ESC to HA, June 6, 1892, HA-MHS.

278 *"This letter ought not"*: JH to ESC, June 5, 1892, AP.

278 *"The first law"*: HA to ESC, June 11, 1892, HAL 4:20.

278 *"I was sorely tempted"*: JH to HA, August 18, 1892, HA-MHS.

278 *"We like the place"*: JH to ESC, August 24, 1892, AP.

279 *"Mrs. Hay is looking"*: ESC to HA, December 2, 1890, HA-MHS.

279 *"I just intimated"*: ESC to HA, January 27, 1891, HA-MHS.

279 *"Our little trip"*: ESC to HA, September 8, 1892, HA-MHS.

279 *"Don was grumpily"*: JH to HA, September 13, 1892, HA-MHS.

279 *"on reasonable terms"*: JH to ESC, September 13, 1892, AP.

280 *"It is the general judgment"*: JH to WR, June 16, 1892, WR-LC.

280 *named the new family member*: WR to JH, September 2, 1892, WR-LC.

280 *"cowardly makeshift . . . Republicans of the East"*: Morgan, *From Hayes to McKinley*, 415, 419.

280 *"[Y]ou will be so"*: JH to HA, June 21, 1892, HA-MHS.

281 *"Woe is me"*: JH to HA, November 9, 1892, HA-MHS.

281 *"I will not waste"*: JH to WR, November 10, 1892, WR-LC.

281 *"But you know"*: Leonard Hay to JH, February 9, 1893, JH-BU.

281 *"[Y]ou must not blame"*: Leonard Hay to JH, February 22, 1893, JH-BU.

281 *While passing through Buffalo*: Mott, *Myron T. Herrick*, 48.

282 *Walker had helped McKinley*: Morgan, "Governor McKinley's Misfortune," 103–20.

282 *"I have no words"*: MCK to JH, February 26, 1893, JH-BU.

283 *"something that the Greeks"*: HA to Franklin MacVeagh, May 26, 1893, HAL 4:103.

283 *"[I]n architectural"*: JH to R. W. Gilder, November 20, 1893, JH-LC.

284 *"Everyone is in"*: HA to ESC, August 8, 1893, HAL 4:117.

284 *"calm as the Lake"*: HA to ESC, July 30, 1893, HAL 4:116.

284 *"I am bored"*: JH to HA, January 1, 1894, HA-MHS.

284 *"Every struggle"*: JH to HA, December 30, 1890, HA-MHS

284 *"A touch of Avarice"*: JH to WDH, January 30, 1890, JH-WDH 97.

284 *"One good Turner"*: Wilkins, *Clarence King*, 331.

285 *"He owes nobody"*: JH to HA, January 6, 1892, HA-MHS.

285 *"[W]henever I think"*: CK to HA, September 25, 1889, HA-MHS.

285 *Ada, had given birth*: Sandweiss, *Passing Strange*, 183.

285 *On Sunday, October 29 . . . wife of his whereabouts*: Ibid., 185–91.

286 *"It would seem incredible"*: JH to HA, January 1, 1894, HA-MHS.

286 *to "jolly" King . . . "bijou of a house"*: JH to HA, January 21, 1894, HA-MHS.

286 *"old-maidish" and "intense"*: Edel, *Henry James, The Conquest of London*, 415.

286 *"tender sentiment . . . feel a real love"*: Edel, *Henry James, The Middle Years*, 88, 205.

286 *"deadly enemy"*: Moore, *Constance Fenimore Woolson*, 36.

287 *"She is worthy"*: JH to Samuel Mather, January 31, 1894, M-WRHS.

287 *"We buried poor Constance"*: JH to HA, February 5, 1894, HA-MHS.

287 *"Miss Woolson was so"*: Henry James to JH, January 28, 1894, HJ-JH 110.

287 *"first great day"*: CSH to Mrs. Amasa Stone, April 27, 1894, WAD-LC.

288 *"My womankind . . . like an ape of Borneo"*: JH to WR, May 4, 1894, WR-LC.

288 *"the goal of every"*: JH to Samuel Mather, June 16, 1894, M-WRHS.

288 *"I never could have"*: JH to JGN, June 3, 1894, JH-BU.

288 *"They are a dear and simple"*: JH to HA, June 9, 1894, HA-MHS.

290 *"absolutely trackless . . . fighting cocks"*: JH to Flora Stone Mather, September 8, 1894, M-WRHS.

290   *"Hay has become"*: HA to ESC, September 1, 1894, HAL 4:206–07.

290   *"We had a pleasant . . . tall as Mont Blanc"*: JH to CSH, August 10, 12, and 19, 1894, WAD-LC.

291   *"Del was a favorite"*: HA to Louisa Hooper, September 29, 1894, HAL 4:217.

291   *"It is a savage irony"*: JH to ESC, n.d. [October 1893], AP.

291   *"Love and Music"*: JH-CPW xii, 243.

292   *"I had a pretty collection"*: ESC to WRT, May 14, 1919, WRT-HU.

292   *"Obedience"*: JH, JH-CPW 244.

292   *"Never was a body"*: JH to ESC, n.d. [c. 1892?], AP.

Chapter 13: The English Mission

page
294   *"I am living in the Place-"*: JH to WR, July 21, 1895, WR-LC.

295   *"How a man can keep"*: JH to HA, September 20, 1895, HA-MHS.

295   in *"relays"*: JH to WR, August 4, 1895, WR-LC.

295   *"rolled and tumbled"*: JH to WR, October 26, 1894, WR-LC.

295   *"I am sure"*: JH to WR, August 4, 1895, WR-LC.

297   *"The summer wanes"*: JH to William Phillips, September 6, 1895, JH-BU.

297   *seeking to cure his chronic bronchitis*: Duncan, *Whitelaw Reid*, 164.

297   *"a fair prospect of"*: WR to JH, November 15, 1895, JH-BU.

297   *"Arizona has to me"*: JH to HA, October 25, 1895, HA-MHS.

298   *"I think you are as good"*: Mark Hanna to JH, December 21, 1895, JH-BU.

299   *"play McKinley"*: Leech, *In the Days of McKinley*, 75.

299   *"somewhat obsequious toward him"*: White, *Autobiography*, 294.

299   *"His attitude was always"*: Kohlsaat, *From McKinley to Harding*, 96.

300   *"Hanna was impulsive"*: White, *Masks in a Pageant*, 157.

300   *"Hanna gave McKinley"*: Ibid., 160.

300   *"until I knew more"*: Mark Hanna to JH, October 7, 1895, JH-LC.

302   *"advertised McKinley"*: Beer, *Hanna*, 165.

302   *"The enemy have begun"*: Mark Hanna to JH, January 7, 1896, JH-BU.

302   *"I never knew him intimately"*: Croly, *Marcus Alonzo Hanna*, 228.

302   *"[Bryan] has succeeded"*: JH to HA, September 8, 1896, HA-MHS.

302   *banks were assessed . . . gave $250,000*: Croly, *Marcus Alonzo Hanna*, 220.

302   *"If Gov. McKinley"*: Mark Hanna to JH, March 4, 1896, JH-BU.

302   *"You can be of great service"*: Mark Hanna to JH, March 24, 1896, JH-BU.

303   *"devotes occasional hours"*: HA to ESC, May 26, 1896, HAL 4:384.

303   *"It is difficult"*: *Daily Chronicle* (London) interview reprinted in the *New York Tribune*, June 15, 1896.

304 *"almost a Republican . . . prospect of it"*: JH to CSH, June 27 and 30, 1896, WAD-LC.

304 *"I inclose a thousand"*: JH to MCK, August 3, 1896, MCK-LC.

305 *"I disclaimed any authority"*: Ibid.

306 *"I might just as well put up"*: Mott, *Myron T. Herrick*, 64.

306 *"Good money . . . good as gold"*: Leech, *In the Days of McKinley*, 90, 91.

306 *"He has asked me to come"*: JH to HA, October 4, 1896, HA-MHS.

306 *"What a strange"*: JH to WR, August 31, 1896, WR-LC.

306 *"half-baked glib"*: Ibid.

306 *"begging for the Presidency"*: JH to WR, September 23, 1896, WR-LC.

306 *"[Bryan] makes only"*: JH to HA, September 8, 1896, HA-MHS.

307 *"the real man back"*: White, *Autobiography*, 332.

307 *"I spent yesterday"*: JH to HA, October 20, 1896, HA-MHS.

307 *"And to think"*: Ibid.

308 *"We are at sea"*: TR to JH, November 16, 1896, JH-BU.

309 *"What you say"*: WR to JH, November 17, 1896, WR-LC.

309 *"I do not see"*: JH to WR, November 18, 1896, WR-LC.

310 *"I told Hanna"*: JH to WR, December 10, 1896, WR-LC.

310 *"How would it answer"*: JH to MCK, telegram, December 26, 1896, MCK-LC; filed erroneously with MCK's 1897 correspondence, although the telegram is clearly marked "Dc 26."

311 *"I send you a ring"*: JH to MCK, December 28, 1896, MCK-LC.

311 *and he began wearing*: MCK to JH, January 1, 1897, JH-BU.

311 *"I shall not question"*: JH to MCK, n.d. [January 1897], JH-BU.

311 *"I do not think it"*: Ibid.

312 *"She said it made"*: WR to JH, January 11, 1897, WR-LC.

312 *"I have so constantly"*: JH to WR, January 22, 1897, WR-LC.

312 *"I think I shall let"*: JH to WR, January 22, 1897, WR-LC.

313 *"Garfield's fatal mistake"*: WR to JH, January 28, 1897, JH-BU.

313 *"You will come back"*: JH to WR, February 2, 1897, JH-BU.

313 *"Repeat in strongest"*: Telegram, WR to JH, February 8, 1897, JH-BU.

313 *"I think you have acted"*: WR to JH, February 8, 1897, JH-BU.

314 *"[I]t would be suicide"*: JH to MCK, February 16, 1897, MCK-LC.

314 *"The President's letter"*: WR to JH, March 27, 1897, WR-LC.

315 *"You are the ideal man"*: George Smalley to JH, February 17, 1897, JH-BU.

315 *"Thucydides . . . was in fine"*: JH to William Phillips, April 20, 1897, JH-BU.

315 *"This is tremendous"*: Henry James to JH, February 22, 1897, HJ-JH 115.

315 *"very plain on the outside"*: CSH to Mrs. Amasa Stone, April 22, 1897, WAD-LC.

315 *"many fine pictures"*: CSH, "Our Life in London," MS, n.d., WAD-LC.

316 *"The scale of expenditure"*: "Mr. Hay's Horses," *New York Journal*, n.d., clipping, M-WRHS.

316 *"The ambassador would"*: Francis Knollys to Henry White, May 8, 1897, JH-BU.

317 *"I had always been"*: JH to MCK, May 9, 1897, MCK-LC.

317 *"[S]he struck me"*: CSH, "Our Life in London."

317 *"I have determined"*: JH to MCK, May 9, 1897, MCK-LC.

318 *"I should have no excuse . . . less noble"*: JH, "Sir Walter Scott," JH-ADD, 54, 57.

319 *"Whitelaw would have gone"*: JH to ESC, May 29, 1897, AP.

319 *"The dark days"*: Chalfant, *Improvement of the World*, 94.

319 *"There is a long history"*: Tehan, *Henry Adams in Love*, 144.

319 *"poorly . . . about the future"*: JH to WR, May 14, 1897, WR-LC.

320 *"It almost consoles"*: JH to ESC, May 29, 1897, AP.

320 *"I have succeeded in effacing"*: JH to MCK, July 16, 1897, MCK-LC.

320 *"they always look alike . . . with Royalties"*: CSH to Mrs. Amasa Stone, n.d. [late June] and July 2, 1897, WAD-LC.

320 *"I have seen my friend Whitelaw"*: JH to HA, July 25, 1897, HA-MHS.

321 *"You dear sweet"*: JH to ESC, August 5 [1897], AP.

321 *"I have a few minutes"*: JH to CSH, August 5, 1897, WAD-LC.

Chapter 14: Setting the Table

page

323 *"we need apprehend"*: JH to MCK, October 6, 1897, MCK-LC.

323 *"that did not differ"*: CSH to Flora Stone Mather, December 10, 1897, WAD-LC.

323 *"Her custom is"*: JH to MCK, December 15, 1897, MCK-LC.

324 *"what a pleasing impression"*: CSH to Mrs. Amasa Stone, December 15, 1897, WAD-LC.

324 *" 'Star Eyed Egyptian' "*: JH to ESC, January 11, 1898, AP.

324 *"lacking in virility"*: Musicant, *Empire by Default*, 115.

324 *"I shall never get"*: Gould, *The Spanish-American War and William McKinley*, 41.

325 *"The Worst Insult"*: Morgan, *William McKinley and His America*, 269.

325 *"Then the Spanish"*: JH to HA, May 9, 1898, HA-MHS.

325 *"We have been much shocked"*: JH to Henry White, February 24, 1898, JH-LC.

325 *"I shall never regret"*: JH to MCK, February 20, 1898, MCK-LC.

326 *"bored into extinction"*: JH to HA, March 11, 1898, HA-MHS.

327 *"We are all very happy"*: JH to Theodore Stanton, May 8, 1898, JH-LC.

328 *"deems it a principal"*: Shippee and Way, "William Rufus Day," in Bemis, ed., *American Secretaries of State*, 99–100.

328 *"The jealousy and animosity"*: JH to HCL, July 27, 1898, HCL-MHS.

328 *"the American-British Society"*: Ginger, *The Age of Excess*, 197.

328 *"The reasons of a good understanding"*: JH, "A Partner of Beneficence," JH-ADD 78–79.

329 *"It is to establish"*: Campbell, *Anglo-American Understanding*, 47.

329 *"partly due"*: JH to HCL, May 25, 1898, HCL-MHS.

329 *"For the first time"*: JH to HCL, April 5, 1898, HCL-MHS.

329 *"The Royal Family"*: JH to HCL, May 25, 1898, HCL-MHS.

329 *"We are glad to think"*: *Daily Chronicle* (London), July 5, 1898, JH scrapbook, JH-LC.

330 *"I am afraid I am the last . . . American character"*: JH to TR, July 27, 1898, WRT-L&L 2:337.

331 *his own inflated exceptionalism*: Thomas, *The War Lovers*, 364–65.

331 *"While we are conducting"*: Olcott, *The Life of William McKinley*, 2:165.

331 *"If old Dewey"*: Kohlsaat, *From McKinley to Harding*, 68.

333 *"Surrender Daring"*: Homans, *Education by Uncles*, 89.

333 *"filled with handsome"*: Ibid., 88.

333 *"two chubby brown"*: Ibid., 89.

333 *"I am a ghastly wreck . . . 'with old Hay?'"*: JH to ESC, n.d. [July 1898], AP.

333 *"Mrs. Don Cameron"*: Homans, *Education by Uncles*, 94–95.

333 *"lighthearted wit . . . nervous tension"*: Ibid., 96.

334 *"utterly depressed"*: Nevins, *Henry White*, 138.

334 *"No serious statesman"*: HAE 1053.

334 *"The place is beyond"*: JH to MCK, August 15, 1898, JH-LC.

334 *"I think it is my duty"*: Telegram, Henry White to William R. Day, August 15, 1898, JH-BU.

335 *"That's what you get"*: JH to CSH, August 29, 1898, JH-LC.

335 *"the most interesting"*: WRT-L&L 2:181.

335 *"the old love . . . now I am old"*: JH to WR, September 14, 1898, WR-LC.

335 *"I am full of hurry"*: JH to William Winter, September 14, 1898, JH-BU.

337 *"I receive twenty"*: JH to CSH, October 12, 1898, JH-LC.

337 *"I feel so dull"*: JH to CSH, October 19, 1898, JH-LC.

337 *"We have never in all our history"*: JH to MCK, July 6, 1898, in Olcott, *Life of William McKinley*, 2:133.

337 *" 'We're a gr-reat people'"*: Dunne, *Mr. Dooley in Peace and War*, 9.

337 *"The President rules"*: JH to ESC, October 27, 1898, AP.

338 *"He scared me"*: JH to CSH, September 29, 1898, JH-LC.

338 *"I do not believe"*: HCL, *Speeches and Addresses*, 372–73.

338 *"to swallow up"*: Beale, *Theodore Roosevelt and the Rise*, 72.

339 *"the greed of conquest . . . criminal aggression"*: Leech, *In the Days of McKinley*, 326.

339 *"new duties"*: Zimmerman, *First Great Triumph*, 317.

339 *"moderation, restraint"*: Ibid.

339 *"the American people would not"*: May, *Imperial Democracy*, 255.

339 *"[O]ne night late"*: Leech, *In the Days of McKinley*, 345.

339 *"It is imperative"*: Millis, *The Martial Spirit*, 385.

340 *an exercise of tyranny*: Beisner, *Twelve Against Empire*, 32.

340 *"vulgar, commonplace"*: Ibid.

340 *"Triumphant Democracy"*: Carnegie, "Distant Possessions—The Parting of the Ways," 239.

340 *"military dictator . . . always your friend"*: Andrew Carnegie to JH, November 29, 1898, JH-LC.

341 *"Hay needs an* alter*"*: HA to Anna (Nannie) Lodge, August 24, 1898, HAL 4:609.

341 *"[W]e tramp"*: HA to ESC, November 21, 1898, HAL 4:621.

341 *"I go to the Department"*: JH to ESC, November 22, 1898, AP.

341 *"I turn green"*: HA to ESC, January 22, 1899, HAL 4:670.

341 *"united in trying"*: HAE 1055.

343 *"[T]he Senator, while agreeing"*: HA to ESC, December 18, 1898, HAL 4:635.

343 *"halfbreed adventurer"*: Miller, *"Benevolent Assimilation,"* 20.

344 *"Our concern was not"*: *Speeches and Addresses of William McKinley*, 188–92.

346 *"Permit me to congratulate"*: JH to John Tyler Morgan, January 21, 1899, Morgan Papers, LC.

347 *"ridiculous and preposterous"*: JH to HW, January 3, 1899, JH-LC.

347 *"The two questions"*: JH to HW, February 14, 1899, JH-LC.

347 *"convinced that the Canadians"*: JH to JC, May 22, 1899, JH-LC.

348 *"quite savage . . . alteration it required"*: HA to ESC, February 5, 1899, HAL 4:679–80.

348 *"[I]t is an evil"*: JH to ESC, February 7, 1899, AP.

348 *"I am horribly rushed"*: JH to HW, March 22, 1899, JH-LC.

349 *"Mrs. Choate's second"*: *New York Times*, May 15, 1917.

349 *only to be blocked by Cabot Lodge*: Varg, *Open Door Diplomat*, 24.

350 *"Poor Hay"*: HA to ESC, December 25, 1898, HAL 4:646.

350 *"I fear he [Reid]"*: JH to Flora Stone Mather, December 25, 1898, M-WRHS.

350 *"I shall continue to hope"*: JH to WR, December 26, 1898, JH-LC.

350 *"[T]he State Department"*: JH to HA, August 5, 1899, HA-MHS.

350 *"Did you ever"*: JH to ESC, June 13, 1899, AP.

351 *"But come and do not"*: JH to ESC, July 18, 1899, AP.

351 *"I am afraid"*: JH to ESC, July 26, 1899, AP.

351 *"It seems so unreal"*: Ibid.

Chapter 15: Spheres of Influence

page

352 *"I am plagued . . . nurseries of woe and worry"*: JH to AA, August 10, 1899, JH-LC.

352 *"the purgatory I have left"*: JH to HA, August 5, 1899, HA-MHS.

353 With that the scramble for larger spheres: Pletcher, *The Diplomacy of Involvement*, 259.

354 *"the extraordinary events"*: FR, 1898, lxxxii.

356 a *"room-for-all" doctrine*: Colquhoun, *China in Transformation*, 368.

356 *"[I]t is imperative"*: Charles Beresford to JH, November 29, 1898, JH-LC.

357 *"absolutely identical"*: Beresford, *The Break-Up of China*, 446.

357 *"The Open Door, or"*: Beresford, "China and the Powers," *North American Review* 510 (May 1899), 535–36.

357 *"It is not very easy to formulate"*: JH to Paul Dana, March 16, 1899, JH-LC.

357 In the early summer yet another China hand: Alfred Hippisley, "The Open Door Notes in Tyler Dennett's 'John Hay,'" August 22, 1935, typescript, Dennett Papers, LC.

358 *"I would like to see"*: WWR to Alfred Hippisley, August 3, 1899, WWR-HU.

358 *"[N]ow that Russia"*: *New York Times*, August 16, 1899; Campbell, *Special Business Interests and the Open Door Policy*, 55.

358 Hippisley prepared . . . *"Of course, if the independence"*: Hippisley, "The Open Door Notes in Tyler Dennett's 'John Hay.'"

359 He promptly asked Rockhill: JH to WWR, August 24, 1899, in Griswold, *Far Eastern Policy of the United States*, 73.

359 *"must be accepted . . . in Peking"*: WWR, memorandum, August 28, 1899, WR-HU.

360 *"As the memo will have"*: WWR to Alfred Hippisley, August 29, 1899, WWR-HU.

360 *"in no way interfere . . . over equal distance"*: FR, 1899, 129–30.

361 *"our relations with England . . . sweat to our brows"*: JH to Charles Dick, September 11, 1899, JH-LC.

361 *"The hills are now wrapped"*: JH to HW, September 24, 1899, JH-LC.

362 *"I hope . . . that England"*: JH to HW, September 24, 1899, JH-LC.

363 *"I get profoundly discouraged"*: JH to HW, December 27, 1899, JH-LC.

363 *"misinterpreted by the people"*: WWR, memorandum, December 19, 1899, JH-LC.

363 *"upon condition that"*: Count Mouravieff to Charlemagne Tower, December 18–30, 1899, FR, 1899, 142.

363 *"We got all that could be"*: JH to HA, June 15, 1900, HA-MHS.

363 *"all the various powers"*: JH circular, March 20, 1900, FR 1899, 142.

364 *Wu T'ing-fang . . . was not aware*: JH to JC, November 13, 1899, JH-LC.

364 *"I sincerely hope"*: JH to Wu T'ing-fang, November 11, 1899, JH-LC.

365 *"If, for example"*: "Secretary Hay and the Open Door," *Independent* 52 (April 5, 1900), 841.

366 *The* Philadelphia Press *predicted*: In "Secretary Hay and the 'Open Door' in China," *Literary Digest* 20 (April 7, 1900), 415.

366 *"is the last Power"*: The *Times* (London), January 4, 1900, clipping, JH scrapbook, JH-LC.

366 *"From the diplomatic"*: *New York Post*, March 28, 1900, clipping, JH scrapbook, JH-LC.

367 *"Nothing in the nature . . . of any complicity"*: JH to JC, January 15, 1900, JC Papers, LC.

367 *"free and open"*: Miner, *Fight for the Panama Route*, 96–97.

367 *"Hay scored"*: HA to ESC, February 6, 1900, HAL 5:86.

367 *"that of a 13-inch shell"*: HA to ESC, February 12, 1900, HAL 5:91.

367 *"What shall be said"*: *New York Sun*, February 7, 1900, clipping, JH scrapbook, JH-LC.

368 *"He is about as furious"*: HA to ESC, February 12, 1900, HAL 5:92.

368 *Roosevelt had issued a statement*: TR-LET 2:1186–87.

368 *"Et tu!"*: JH to TR, February 12, 1900, JH-LC.

368 *"Washington is just at the full"*: HA to ESC, February 19, 1900, HAL 5:94–95.

369 *"You may work"*: JH to HW, August 11, 1899, JH-LC.

369 *"a weak resort"*: JH to HW, March 18, 1900, in Nevins, *Henry White*, 152.

370 *"I have never had yet"*: JH to HW, August 11, 1899, JH-LC.

370 *"[M]y natural pessimism"*: HA to ESC, January 30, 1900, HAL 5:79.

370 *"Curiously enough"*: HA to ESC, March 6, 1900, HAL 5:104.

370 *"The action of the Senate"*: JH to MCK, March 13, 1900, JH-BU.

370 *"Had I known"*: MCK to JH, March 13, 1900, JH-BU.

371 *"We tramp in silence"*: HA to Anne Palmer Fell, March 29, 1900, HAL 5:111.

371 *"Always unselfish"*: HAE 1063.

371 *"Hay got your letter"*: HA to ESC, February 20, 1900, HAL 5:95.

371 *"I am all alone"*: JH to ESC, November 7, 1899, AP.

372 *"Did you ever get . . . believe them real"*: JH to ESC, November 14, 1899, AP.

373 *"Sicrety Hay meets"*: Unidentified clipping, n.d., JH scrapbook, JH-LC.

373 *"As long as I stay"*: JH to HW, September 24, 1899, JH-LC.

373 *"[H]e is naturally lazy"*: CSH to HA, December 10, 1899, HA-MHS.

373 *"[H]ow could I have paid"*: JH to John E. Milholland, January 22, 1900, JH-LC.

373 *"You will naturally not"*: JH to Adelbert Hay, January 17, 1900, JH-LC.

373 *"I sometimes feel a twinge"*: JH to Adelbert Hay, February 6, 1900, JH-LC.

374 *"Everyone thought of me"*: Adelbert Hay to CSH, February 16, 1900, M-WRHS.

374 *"Why, these bullets"*: *New York Times*, June 4, 1901; a slightly different version is in *New York World*, August 5, 1900, clipping, JH scrapbook, JH-LC.

374 *"Nothing—but nothing"*: JH to HA, June 15, 1900, HA-MHS.

375 *"Teddy has been here"*: JH to HA, June 15, 1900, HA-MHS.

375 *"Roosevelt burst into"*: White, *Masks in a Pageant*, 223.

376 *"Is America a weakling"*: Morris, *Theodore Rex*, 8.

376 *"Well, it was a nice"*: Morgan, *William McKinley and His America*, 381.

377 *all manner of demonic acts*: Preston, *Boxer Rebellion*, 28.

377 *"The interests of our citizens"*: FR 1899, xviii.

377 *"I return the despatches"*: WR to JH, June 1, 1900, JH-LC.

377 *"I regret to say"*: Edwin Conger to JH, June 15, 1900, MCK-LC.

378 *"Do you need more"*: JH to Edwin Conger, telegram, June 15, 1900, MCK-LC.

378 *Even within the administration*: John Bassett Moore, memorandum, July 1, 1900, Moore Papers, LC.

378 *"Act independently"*: JH to Edwin Conger, telegram, June 8, 1900, MCK-LC.

378 *"We have no policy"*: JH to Edwin Conger, telegram, June 10, 1900, MCK-LC.

379 *"state of war . . . for general protection"*: Louis Kempff to John Long, telegram, June 19, 1900, MCK-LC.

379 *"not chosen for defense"*: Preston, *Boxer Rebellion*, 114.

380 *"If wrong be done . . . parts of the Chinese Empire"*: JH, "Identic Telegram sent to the United States Embassies in Berlin, Paris, London, Rome, and St. Petersburg, and to the United States Missions in Vienna, Brussels, Madrid, Tokyo, The Hague, and Lisbon," July 3, 1900, JH-LC.

381 *"The thing to do"*: JH to HA, July 8, 1900, HA-MHS.

382 *"the Europeans Massacred"*: In Fleming, *Siege of Peking*, 134–36.

382 *"Communicate tidings . . . general massacre"*: Preston, *Boxer Rebellion*, 172.

383   *"I did not imagine"*: JH to JGN, August 21, 1900, JH-LC.

383   *"near the danger point"*: Unidentified clipping, n.d., JH scrapbook, JH-LC.

383   *"I do not care"*: JH to AA, n.d. (received August 9, 1900), JH-LC.

383   *"But so far as I can learn"*: JH to AA, August 8, 1900, JH-LC.

383   *"[T]here is not much more"*: JH to JGN, August 21, 1900, JH-LC.

Chapter 16: Rope of Sand

page

385   *"[Y]ou have won for us"*: Brooks Adams to JH, August 17, 1900, JH-LC.

385   *"When all the world"*: "Our Place Among the Nations," *World's Work* 1 (November 1900), 54.

385   *"I am miserably weak"*: JH to AA, August 24, 1900, JH-LC.

385   *"I see nothing"*: JH to WR, September 1, 1900, WR-LC.

386   *"Russia has been"*: JH to JC, September 8, 1900, JH-LC.

386   *"there is a general expression"*: Zabriskie, *American-Russian Rivalry in the Far East*, 62.

386   *"I need not say . . . get into your bed?"*: JH to JC, September 8, 1900, JH-LC.

387   *"to hold on like grim death"*: JH to WR, September 1, 1900, WR-LC.

387   *"The dilemma is clear . . . the first of October"*: JH to AA, September 14, 1900, JH-LC.

389   *"What a business"*: JH to HA, November 21, 1900, HA-MHS.

389   *"[I]n watching you herd"*: HA to JH, October 5, 1890, HAL 5:150.

389   *"to work on my last shift"*: JH to AA, September 26, 1900, JH-LC.

389   *"We must not permit"*: HCL to TR, June 29, 1900, *Selections from the Correspondence of Theodore Roosevelt and Henry Cabot Lodge*, 1:467–68.

390   *"We did wallop them proper"*: JH to HA, November 21, 1900, HA-MHS.

390   *"Mr. Roosevelt . . . worthily done"*: TR to JH, November 10, 1900, JH-LC.

391   *"[T]he President made a little"*: JH to Adelbert Hay, November 14, 1900, JH-LC.

391   *"the happiest hours"*: JH, memorandum, November 13, 1900, JH-LC.

391   *"deform and disfigure . . . better manners'"*: JH to JC, December 21, 1900, JH-LC.

391   *"the disaster . . . acted squarely"*: JH to HW, December 23, 1900, JH-LC.

391   *"Let me say, first"*: Clipping, n.d., JH scrapbook, JH-LC.

392   *"Lodge has now"*: JH to HW, December 23, 1900, JH-LC.

392   *"most practicable"*: DuVal, *Cadiz to Cathay*, 148.

392   *"If the stirrers-up"*: JH to Henry Watterson, January 11, 1901, Watterson Papers, LC.

393 *"I thank you kindly"*: JH to Andrew Carnegie, January 12, 1901, JH-LC.

393 *"In wishing you, Sir"*: JH to Edward VII, January 23, 1901, JH-LC.

394 *"I am sick to the heart"*: JH to HW, December 23, 1900, JH-LC.

394 *"treachery . . . in a newspaper"*: JH to HW, February 10, 1901, HW-LC.

394 *"When I send . . . of my life"*: JH to ESC, January 16, 1901, AP.

395 *"I think Hay very far"*: HA to Brooks Adams, February 7, 1901, HAL 5:193.

395 *"After watching Hay's"*: HA to ESC, February 18, 1901, HAL 5:201.

395 "angina senatus . . . *external impassivity*": HA to ESC, February 25, 1901, HAL 5:204.

396 *"satisfactory to the Senate . . . diffuse condition"*: HCL to JH, March 28, 1901, HCL-MHS.

396 *"I infer from your letter"*: JH to HCL, March 30, 1901, JH-LC.

397 *"I have drawn this up"*: JH to JC, April 27, 1901, JH-LC.

398 *"He looks pasty"*: HA to ESC, April 8, 1901, HAL 5:230–31.

398 *"the getting into hacks"*: JH to HA, May 7, 1901, JH-LET 3:206–07; "Tadmor in the wilderness," I Kings 9:18.

399 doctors had diagnosed tuberculosis: Sandweiss, *Passing Strange*, 226.

399 *"delightful as ever"*: JH to John Clark, September 18, 1900, JH-LC.

399 *"I have been hit badly"*: HA to ESC, March 3, 1901, HAL 5:213.

399 *"His tuberculosis"*: HA to ESC, April 22, 1901, HAL 5:237.

400 *"ideal of the brotherhood"*: JH, "A Festival of Peace," JH-ADD 129, 131.

401 *"You have had a very successful"*: JH to Adelbert Hay, September 12, 1900, JH-LC.

401 *"He is a very dear fellow"*: HW to JH, March 9, 1901, HW-LC.

401 *"disarming bonhomie"*: CK to JH, July 27, 1901, JH-BU.

401 *"even with a word"*: JH to HW, June 30, 1901, JH-LC.

403 *"He never looked so handsome"*: JH to MCK, June 29, 1901, JH-LC.

403 *"He had ease and variety . . . in three continents"*: JH to CK, July 14, 1901, JH-LC.

403 *"Twenty-four-years old"*: JH to John Clark, July 13, 1901, JH-LC.

403 *"Fate strikes us"*: HA to JH, June 25, 1901, HAL 5:258–59.

404 *"That was a letter"*: JH to HA, July 11, 1901, HA-MHS.

404 *"I can not see any"*: JH to ESC, July 11, 1901, AP.

404 *"[M]y sorrow grips"*: JH to CSH, July 11, 1901, JH-LC.

404 *"It is a month"*: JH to WR, July 22, 1901, WR-LC.

405 *"[W]e are not in despair"*: CSH to HA, August 5, 1901, HA-MHS.

405 *"I am profoundly gratified at"*: JH to JC, September 2, 1901, JH-LC.

406 *"Isolation is no longer"*: Olcott, *Life of William McKinley*, 2:379–82.

406   *"the McKinley grip"* . . . *fifty hands a minute*: Morgan, *William McKinley and His America*, 124.

407   *"The reports of the doctors"*: Unidentified clipping, n.d., JH scrapbook, JH-LC.

407   *"President's condition"*: JH to CSH, telegram, September 13, 1901, JH-LC.

407   *"worn and nervous"*: Unidentified clipping, n.d., JH scrapbook, JH-LC.

407   *"The President is pulseless"*: Filson telegram, n.d. [September 13, 1901], JH-LC.

408   *"The President died"*: Morris, *Theodore Rex*, 7.

408   *"Laid low by the act"*: JH to Manuel Alvarez Calderon, et al., September 14, 1901, JH-BU.

408   *"No ceremonies"*: JH, "Funeral Announcement to the Public," September 14, 1901, JH-LC.

409   *"[M]y personal grief"*: JH to Lady Jeune, September 14, 1901 [misdated; probably c. September 19], JH-LET 3:229–30.

409   *"[B]ehind all, in my mind"*: HA to JH, September 7, 1901, HAL 5:291.

409   *"I . . . shuddered"*: JH to HA, September 19, 1901, HA-MHS.

409   *"My dear Roosevelt"*: JH to TR, September 15, 1901, JH-LC.

410   *Hay's predicted successor*: *New York Herald*, n.d., clipping, JH scrapbook, JH-LC.

410   *"without waiting"*: JH to HA, September 19, 1901, HA-MHS.

411   *"[A]s I am the next"*: JH to Lady Jeune, September 14 [c. 19], 1901, JH-LET 3:230.

411   *"it was past the breakers"*: Miner, *Fight for the Panama Route*, 117.

411   *"tingling silentness . . . become an old man"*: JH to TR, October 2, 1901, JH-LC.

412   *"[Mrs. Roosevelt] is forty"*: TR to JH, October 5, 1901, TR-LET 3:161.

412   *"I wish you might"*: JH to CK, October 27, 1901, JH-LC.

412   *"the great job is accomplished"*: JC to JH, October 25, 1901, Dennett Papers, LC.

412   *"in the best of spirits"*: JC to HW, November 11, 1901, HW-LC.

412   *"Lodge came home"*: JC to HW, November 11, 1901, HW-LC.

413   *"This has been a year . . . be any better"*: JH to CSH, December 2, 1901, WAD-LC.

413   *"They are old friends and playmates"*: JH to WR, November 18, 1901, WR-LC.

413   *As the end neared*: Sandweiss, *Passing Strange*, 238–40.

413   *"In my present condition"*: CK to JH, August 22, 1901, JH-LC.

413   *"He is, I fancy"*: JH to HA, November 17, 1901, HA-MHS.

413   *"the best and brightest"*: JH to HA, August 9, 1901, HA-MHS.

414   *"I am very, very sorry"*: TR to JH, December 25, 1901, JH-LC.

Chapter 17: A Reasonable Time

page

415 *"Personally . . . his loss is very great"*: TR to HCL, July 11, 1905, TR-LET 4:1270–71.

415 *"He was a man of remarkable . . . was not a great Secretary of State"*: TR to HCL, January 28, 1909, TR-LET 6:1489–90.

417 *"When I came in"*: TR to JH, July 11, 1903, DEN 360.

417 *"I could not spare you"*: TR to JH, July 29, 1903, TR-LET 3:352.

417 *"You must always remember"*: Morris, *Theodore Rex*, 81.

417 *"still mentally in the* Sturm*"*: Beale, *Theodore Roosevelt and the Rise*, 48.

418 *"a stupid, blundering"*: HA to ESC, April 1, 1902, HAL 5:365.

418 *"Teddy said the other day"*: JH to HA, October 13, 1901, HA-MHS.

418 *"slaughter-house . . . high-school pedagogue"*: JH to ESC, January 12, 1902, HAL 5:322–23.

418 *"Power when wielded"*: HAE 1101.

419 *"I have a horror"*: Beale, *Theodore Roosevelt and the Rise*, 51.

419 *"the largest aggregation"*: *Washington Evening Star*, n.d., clipping, JH scrapbook, JH-LC.

419 *"There are two important lines"*: JH, "American Diplomacy," JH-ADD 113–25.

420 *"Diplomats, women, and crabs"*: JH MS, n.d., JH-BU.

421 *"[Hay] has kept"*: *Brooklyn Daily Eagle*, November 20, 1901, clipping, JH scrapbook, JH-LC.

422 *"a warming-pan . . . the climax of the season"*: HA to ESC, February 9, 1902, HAL 5:338–39.

423 *"The Secretary's figure"*: *New York Tribune*, February 28, 1902.

423 *"There is not one"*: JH, "William McKinley," JH-ADD 175.

423 *"[I]t was oratory in the high"*: Edith Wharton to George Smalley, March 2, 1902, JH-BU.

424 *"let sleeping dogs lie"*: Beale, *Theodore Roosevelt and the Rise*, 111.

424 *had to Cornwall or Kent*: Marks, *Velvet on Iron*, 106.

424 *"as we assert it . . . to be drastic"*: Beale, *Theodore Roosevelt and the Rise*, 111.

424 *"Whenever Canada"*: HA to ESC, March 1, 1903, HAL 5:464.

425 *"It seems to me that"*: TR to JH, July 16, 1902, TR-LET 3:294–95.

425 *determined engineer*: McCullough, *Path Between the Seas*, 325–27.

427 *"Youthful nations"*: B-V, *Panama*, 191.

427 *"a rather theatrical look"*: *New York World*, October 4, 1906.

428 *The* World *would later allege*: *New York World*, January 17, 1904.

429 *"held the trump cards"*: Miner, *Fight for the Panama Route*, 111.

431 *"[I]t is not convenient"*: Ibid., 139–40.

432 *"[B]oth in Colombia"*: JH to John Tyler Morgan, April 22, 1902, JH-LC.

432 *"I conceive my duty"*: JH to John Tyler Morgan, April 23, 1902, JH-LC.

433 *"These simple and lucid diagrams"*: B-V, *Panama*, 238.

433 *"What an unexpected"*: Ibid., 228.

433 *"eminent French"*: *New York Sun*, May 12, 1902.

434 *"My compliments"*: *New York Sun*, May 17, 1902, in B-V, *Panama*, 243.

434 *published a cartoon of Hanna*: McCullough, *Path Between the Seas*, 323.

434 *"An official witness"*: B-V, *Panama*, 247.

434 *"poison the minds"*: McCullough, *Path Between the Seas*, 319.

434 *"direct, constant"*: Fry, *John Tyler Morgan and the Search*, 223–24.

435 *the "Hannama" canal*: Croly, *Marcus Alonzo Hanna*, 384.

435 *"The great bit of work"*: TR to JH, July 1, 1902, TR-LET 3:284.

436 *"I do not imagine"*: JH to "Dear Senator" [John Tyler Morgan], July 15, 1902, Dennett Papers, LC.

436 *"a liberal education"*: Bishop, *Theodore Roosevelt and His Time*, 1:195.

436 *"The principles which have governed"*: JH, "At the Universities," JH-ADD 182.

437 *" 'What a man!' "*: JH to TR, June 26, 1902, in Bishop, *Theodore Roosevelt and His Time*, 1:196.

437 *wearing a pistol under his coat*: Morris, *Theodore Rex*, 117.

437 *"[T]he President's life is worth"*: JH to Philander Knox, June 16, 1902, JH-LC.

437 *"I left Washington"*: JH to Babcock, July 20, 1902, JH-BU.

438 *"In reading the great work"*: TR to JH, July 22, 1902, TR-LET 3:300.

438 *"The whole country side"*: JH to AA, August 27, 1902, JH-LC.

438 *a 150-pound wild boar*: " 'Teddy' Roosevelt Hunted Wild Boar in Newport," in Mary and Lawrence Petersen, eds., *A Collection of New Hampshire Stories* (1971), 3–4.

438 *"We are greatly"*: JH to TR, telegram, [September 3, 1902], JH-LC.

439 *"What a marvelous escape"*: AA to JH, September 4, 1902, JH-LC.

439 *"I had a hideous appreciation"*: JH to AA, September 3, 1902, JH-LC.

439 *"John seems to have come"*: HA to CSH, September 21, 1902, HAL 5:407.

439 *"fortunately the sun"*: CSH to HA, October 12, 1902, HA-MHS.

439 *"It certainly is a tax"*: JH to WR, September 13, 1902, WR-LC.

440 *"If John Hay should"*: Morris, *Theodore Rex*, 148.

440 *"I am thankful that"*: CSH to HA, October 12, 1902, HA-MHS.

440 *"Theodore was in fine"*: JH to HA, October 19, 1902, HA-MHS.

441 *In Washington, Concha chose to view*: Collin, *Theodore Roosevelt's Caribbean*, 206–09.

442 *"made all possible"*: Miner, *Fight for the Panama Route*, 187.

Chapter 18: Fair Warning

page

444 "Voilà l'ennemi": JH to HCL, July 27, 1898, HCL-MHS.

444 *"the German Eagle eviscerating"*: JH to TR, November 12, 1901, JH-LC.

445 *"Frankly I don't know"*: Beale, *Theodore Roosevelt and the Rise*, 49.

445 *"in case of sudden war"*: Ibid., 356.

445 *"The Monroe Doctrine is"*: FR 1901 xxxvi.

446 *"insolent dogma"*: Herwig, *Politics of Frustration*, 72.

446 *"the paramount power"*: Ibid., 68–69.

446 *"If any South American"*: JH to Speck von Sternburg, July 12, 1901, in Pringle, *Theodore Roosevelt*, 283.

447 a *"megalomaniac"*: Herwig, *Germany's Vision of Empire*, 86.

447 *"an unspeakably villainous"*: TR to JH, April 2, 1905, TR-LET 4:1156.

447 *"the permanent occupation"*: Hill, *Roosevelt and the Caribbean*, 111.

447 *"no purpose or intention"*: Ibid., 112.

447 *"We will do whatever"*: Herwig, *Politics of Frustration*, 69.

448 *"the initial step"*: Morris, " 'A Few Pregnant Days,' " 4.

448 *"taking steps to obtain"*: Hendrix, *Theodore Roosevelt's Naval Diplomacy*, 39.

448 *"to insult or defy"*: JH, "American Diplomacy," JH-ADD 125.

449 *"There is not a cloud"*: FR 1902, xxvii.

449 if *"an arrangement"*: JH to Percival Dodge, December 5, 1902, FR 1902, 418.

450 *in a letter he wrote to John Hay's first biographer*: TR to WRT, August 21, 1916, TR-LET 8:1102–103.

451 *"one of the most amazingly"*: Morris, *Theodore Rex*, 188.

452 *"storm of public opinion"*: Beale, *Theodore Roosevelt and the Rise*, 355.

452 *"lost its nerve"*: Nevins, *Henry White*, 211.

452 *"We are not interested"*: Mitchell, "The Height of the German Challenge," 203.

452 *"I succeeded . . . in getting"*: TR, *Autobiography*, 526.

453 *"kept the President & our Country"*: Stuyvesant Fish to JH, December 27, 1902, JH-LC.

453 *"I am so happy"*: Andrew Carnegie to JH, December 30, 1902, JH-LC.

453 *"The steadiness with which"*: Elbert Baldwin to JH, January 30, 1903, JH-LC.

454 *"Our Emperor"*: HA to ESC, February 3, 1903, HAL 5:449.

455 *"[T]he presence of Lodge"*: JH to HW, April 10, 1903, HW-LC.

455 *"[W]e give up 30"*: JH to CSH, October 18, 1903, JH-LC.

455 *"I wonder if you realize"*: TR to JH, April 16, 1903, JH-LC.

455 *"It is a comfort"*: JH to TR, July 13, 1903, JH-LC.

455 *"As Secretary of State"*: TR to JH, July 29, 1903, JH-LC.

455 *"It is hard for me to answer"*: JH to TR, August 2, 1903, JH-LC.

456 *"From the cloistered life"*: JH, speech at the Seventeenth Annual Banquet of the Ohio Society of New York, January 17, 1903, transcription, WRHS.

456 *"Edith and I"*: TR to JH, January 21, 1903, JH-LC.

456 *"a rabbit in the presence"*: Mount, *John Singer Sargent*, 206.

457 *"Good Sargent"*: HA to ESC, March 10, 1903, HAL 5:471–72.

458 *"Mister Sargent finished"*: JH to Helen Hay Whitney, February 27, 1903, JH-LC.

458 soon *"annihilate"* American trade: Zabriskie, *American-Russian Rivalry*, 75.

459 *"We are not in any attitude"*: JH to TR, May 1, 1902, in Dennett, *Roosevelt and the Russo-Japanese War*, 135.

459 *"The alliance between Japan"*: Zabriskie, *American-Russian Rivalry*, 82.

460 *"inadmissible . . . Russian aggression"*: JH to TR, April 28, 1903, JH-LC.

460 *"Dealing with a government . . . our Manchurian affair"*: JH to TR, May 12, 1903, JH-LC.

461 *"[T]here does not seem"*: TR to JH, May 13, 1903, TR-LET 3:474.

461 *"The bad feature of the situation"*: TR to JH, May 22, 1903, TR-LET 3:478.

461 *"It would require"*: JH to TR, April 28, 1903, JH-LC.

461 *"[I]f we gave them a wink . . . their own sweet will"*: JH to TR, May 12, 1903, JH-LC.

462 *"[T]he Hebrews"*: JH to AA, August 30, 1902, JH-LC.

462 *"I want to put every money-lender"*: HA to Charles Milnes Gaskell, January 3, 1894, HAL 4:157.

462 *"Jews continue to do"*: Unidentified clipping, n.d., JH scrapbook, JH-LC; Adler, *Voice of America on Kishineff*, xiii.

462 *"There could be only two motives . . . to unmerited blame"*: JH to Jacob Schiff, May 20, 1903, JH-LC.

463 *"No person of ordinary humanity"*: Adler, *Voice of America on Kishineff*, 471.

464 *"any tragedy"*: Ibid., 475.

464 *"[T]his is not a Jewish"*: Schoenberg, "The American Reaction to the Kishinev Pogrom of 1903," 280.

464 *"[I]t seemed somewhat strange"*: Unidentified clipping, n.d., JH scrapbook, JH-LC.

465 *"There is no reason in the world"*: JH to George Smalley, July 9, 1903, JH-LC.

465 *"It is a comfort"*: JH to CSH, July 6, 1903, JH-LC.

465 *"When McKinley sent"*: JH to CSH, July 4, 1903, JH-LC.

465 *"I could not resign"*: JH to CSH, July 8, 1903, JH-LC.

466 *"If they answer"*: JH to TR, July 3, 1903, JH-LC.

466 *"there was not a shade"*: JH to TR, July 9, 1903, JH-LC.

466 *"with apparent sincerity"*: JH to TR, July 11, 1903, JH-LC.

466 *"It seems like a surrender"*: JH to TR, July 14, 1903, JH-LC.

467 *"In every part of the world"*: Leo Levi to JH, October 5, 1903, in Wolf, *Presidents I Have Known*, 213.

467 *"What inept asses"*: JH to TR, July 16, 1903, JH-LC.

467 *"I have not the slightest objection"*: TR to JH, July 18, 1903, TR-LET 3:520.

467 *"Four years of constant . . . some moment of crisis"*: JH to TR, July 22, 1903, JH-LC.

468 *"I am beginning to have"*: TR to JH, July 29, 1903, TR-LET 3:532.

468 *"Everything seems in fair trim"*: JH to TR, July 16, 1903, JH-LC.

468 *"This country is"*: JH to TR, August 2, 1903, JH-LC.

468 *"We are enjoying long tramps"*: JH to WR, August 13, 1903, WR-LC.

468 *"If report of rejection"*: AA to JH, August 18, 1903, JH-LC.

Chapter 19: Color of Right

page

470 *"bitter hostility"*: Arthur Beaupré to JH, April 15, 1903, FR 1903, 134.

470 *"It is entirely impossible"*: Arthur Beaupré to JH, May 4, 1903, FR 1903, 142–43.

471 *"less scorn"*: José Manuel Marroquín to Tomás Herrán, June 24, 1903, in DuVal, *Cadiz to Cathay*, 230–31.

471 *"would be so seriously compromised"*: JH to Arthur Beaupré, June 9, 1903, FR 1903, 146.

471 *"Construed by many"*: Arthur Beaupré to JH, July 6, 1903, FR 1903, 158.

471 *"[T]he only party that can"*: B-V to José Manuel Marroquín, June 13, 1903, in B-V, *Panama*, 267–68.

471 *"would be equivalent to stabbing"*: B-V to José Manuel Marroquín, August 17, 1903, in B-V, *Panama*, 278.

472 *"Secretary Hay honored"*: *Story of Panama*, 279.

472 *"The Marroquín Government"*: William Nelson Cromwell to JH, June 14, 1903, in Dennis, *Adventures in American Diplomacy*, 338–39.

472 *"New Republic May Arise"*: *New York World*, June 14, 1903.

473 *" 'Well, we may make' "*: *New York Herald*, August 15, 1903.

473 *"greedy little anthropoids"*: JH to TR, August 22, 1903, JH-LC.

473 *"I would come at once to"*: JH to TR, August 16, 1903, in Dennis, *Adventures in American Diplomacy*, 342–43.

473 *"The one thing evident"*: TR to JH, August 19, 1903, TR-LET 3:566–67.

474   *"that the right of way . . . belong to them"*: John Bassett Moore, memorandum, August 1903, in Miner, *Fight for the Panama Route*, appendix D, 427–32.

474   *"It . . . would be useful . . . bide our hour"*: JH to TR, August 22, 1903, JH-LC.

475   *"Canal Troubles May Lead"*: *New York Herald*, August 29, 1903.

475   *"go the limit"*: *Story of Panama*, 349.

477   *"did not purpose to permit"*: Ibid., 360.

477   *"Just how much"*: JH to TR, September 7, 1903, JH-LC.

477   *"Revolutionary agents"*: *Story of Panama*, 361.

477   *"Yesterday Mr. J. G. Duque"*: Ibid., 361.

477   *"hostile attitude"*: Ibid., 361–62.

478   *"A revolution would today"*: B-V, *Panama*, 292.

478   *"Esperanzas"*: DuVal, *Cadiz to Cathay*, 292.

478   *"nobody could blame President"*: B-V, *Panama*, 287.

479   *"It is altogether likely"*: JH to TR, September 13, 1902, JH-LC.

479   *"I think it well worth"*: TR to Mark Hanna, October 5, 1903, in DuVal, *Cadiz to Cathay*, 296–97.

479   *"As yet, the people"*: TR to Albert Shaw, October 7, 1903, TR-LET 3:626.

479   *"All I can say is"*: Schoonover, "Max Farrand's Memorandum," 505.

479   *"General and special circumstances . . . between us"*: B-V, *Panama*, 311.

480   *"I cast aside the proposition"*: TR to Albert Shaw, October 10, 1903, TR-LET 3:628.

480   *"I had always imagined . . . caught napping"*: B-V, *Panama*, 317–18.

480   *for orders directing naval forces*: Turk, "The United States Navy and the 'Taking' of Panama," 93.

481   *"[I]t will interest"*: B-V, *Panama*, 318–19.

481   *a "fake"*: Davis, *Captain Macklin*, 75.

481   *"Did he not intend . . . if revolution broke out"*: B-V, *Panama*, 319.

481   *"Room No. 1162"*: Ibid., 320.

481   *"in order to obtain"*: Ibid., 324.

481   *"A battle royal"*: Ibid., 321.

482   *"The plan seems to me good"*: DuVal, *Cadiz to Cathay*, 309.

482   *"I agreed, beforehand"*: JH to AA, September 18, 1903, JH-LC.

482   *"a Trojan horse"*: Zabriskie, *American-Russian Rivalry*, 98.

482   *"This is the day of Fate"*: JH to CSH, October 8, 1903, Dennett Papers, LC.

483   *"It has been—as I reckon"*: JH to ESC, October 10, 1903, AP.

483   *"You will bear it"*: JH to ESC, October 29, 1903, AP.

483   *"could make anything"*: JH to Augustus Saint-Gaudens, September 30, 1903, JH-LC.

484 *bears an uncanny resemblance*: Tehan, *Henry Adams in Love*, 183.

484 *"It is a ruinous expense"*: JH to CSH, October 16, 1903, JH-LC.

484 *"intimate orally"*: JH to Arthur Beaupré, October 22, 1903, FR 1903, 216.

484 *"most pathetic . . . when I return"*: JH to CSH, October 30, 1903, JH-LC.

484 *"Now you will see"*: J. Gabriel Duque to JH, September 21, 1903, JH-LC.

486 *"lucky star . . . renewed today"*: B-V, *Panama*, 331.

486 *"telegraph in cipher"*: Turk, "The United States Navy and the 'Taking' of Panama," 93.

486 *"The American cruiser* Nashville*"*: B-V, *Panama*, 333.

487 *"[m]aintain free and uninterrupted"*: Ibid., 93–94.

488 *"It is possible that"*: Turk, "The United States Navy and the 'Taking' of Panama," 94.

488 *"Uprising at Isthmus . . . No uprising yet"*: Miner, *Fight for the Panama Route*, 363.

489 *"His Excellency"*: Manuel Amador to JH, November 3, 1903, JH-LC.

490 *"In the interest of peace"*: *Diplomatic History of the Panama Canal*, 363.

490 *"kill every United States"*: FR 1903, 268.

491 *"perish in the flames"*: *Story of Panama*, 451.

492 *"confidential agent"*: Ibid., 463.

492 *"Colon and all"*: Ibid.

492 *"The people of Panama"*: Ibid.

493 *"as emphatic and free"*: Elihu Root to Horace Porter, December 15, 1903, in DuVal, *Cadiz to Cathay*, 344.

493 *"[T]o make an omelette"*: JH to CSH, November 30, 1903, WAD-LC.

493 *"the ardent desire"*: B-V, *Panama*, 365.

493 *"the providential instrument"*: Ibid., 366.

493 *"I think, Mr. President"*: Ibid.

494 *"enter freely"*: Ibid., 367.

494 *"[Senator Morgan] is as much"*: JH to Henry Pritchett, December 28, 1903, JH-LC.

495 *"all the rights, power"*: Major, "Who Wrote the Hay-Bunau-Varilla Convention?", 121.

495 *"Any man who pays"*: B-V, *Panama*, 374.

495 *"not to throw away"*: Ibid., 356.

495 *"caesarian operation"*: DuVal, *Cadiz to Cathay*, 402.

496 *"a good deal of intrigues"*: B-V, *Panama*, 373.

496 *"the use, occupation and control"*: Ibid., 376.

497 *"Cherish no illusion"*: Ibid., 378.

497 *"which the United States justly"*: Ibid., 384.

498 *"gamblers' syndicate"*: *New York World*, January 17, 1904.

498 *"transcendent importance"*: FR 1903, xxxix–xl.

498 *"No one connected"*: Collin, *Theodore Roosevelt's Caribbean*, 299.

499 *"I have no idea"*: TR to John Bigelow, January 6, 1904, TR-LET 3:689.

499 *"[H]e was merely a stage"*: TR to WRT, July 2, 1905, TR-LET 8:944.

499 *"plumb crazy"*: JH to TR, December 7, 1903, JH-LC.

499 *"a slatternly house maid"*: JH to TR, December 9, 1903, JH-LC.

499 *"I am a prisoner"*: JH to HA, December 22, 1903, JH-LC.

500 *"mere bugaboo"*: B-V, *Panama*, 419.

500 *"inchoate rights"*: JH to Rafael Reyes, December 11, 1903, JH-LC.

500 *"the fine old soldier"*: JH to CSH, December 4, 1903, JH-LC.

501 *"Kill him"*: Bishop, *Theodore Roosevelt and His Time*, 1:305.

501 *"Colombia has"*: TR to Charles Lummis, January 4, 1904, TR-LET 3:688.

501 *"To talk of Colombia"*: TR to WRT, July 2, 1915, TR-LET 8:944–45.

501 *"In this Panama business"*: TR to Theodore Roosevelt, Jr., November 15, 1903, TR-LET 3:652.

501 *"I am only speaking"*: JH to Shelby Cullom, January 20, 1904, JH-LC.

502 *"While I agree"*: JH to George P. Fisher, January 20, 1904, JH-LC.

503 *"Two strokes of a pen"*: B-V, *Panama*, 429.

503 *"If wisdom, statesmanship"*: *New York Evening Sun*, n.d., clipping, JH scrapbook, JH-LC.

Chapter 20: Hayism

page

504 *"I am very miserable"*: JH to TR, January 15, 1904, JH-LC.

504 *"Hay has not been"*: HA to ESC, January 10, 1904, HAL 5:538.

505 *"From dispatches received"*: JH diary, January 5, 1904, JH-LC.

505 *"The Japanese nation"*: Lloyd Griscom to JH, January 21, 1904, in Esthus, *Theodore Roosevelt and Japan*, 21.

505 *"pluck personified"*: Lloyd Griscom to Rodman E. Griscom, January 29, 1904, in ibid.

505 *"I feel better already"*: JH to TR, January 22, 1904, JH-LC.

505 *"I have the appetite"*: JH to HA, February 1, 1904, HA-MHS.

506 *"secure the smallest"*: JH to Joseph Choate, February 10, 1904, in Esthus, *Theodore Roosevelt and Japan*, 31.

506 *"He spent most"*: JH diary, February 8, 1904, JH-LC.

506 *"he broke into tears"*: Ibid.

507 *"like claps of thunder"*: JH diary, February 10, 1904, JH-LC.

507 *"the full maelstrom"*: HA to ESC, February 7 and 14, 1904, HAL 5:547, 549.

507 *"He takes the buffet"*: JH diary, February 10, 1904, JH-LC.

507 *"[H]e could hardly prevent"*: JH diary, February 11, 1904, JH-LC.

507 *"responsive to the proposal"*: JH to Robert McCormick, February 19, 1904, FR 1904, 725.

507 *"organized and drilled"*: JH diary, March 17, 1904, JH-LC.

507 *"terror of some aggression"*: JH diary, April 29, 1904, JH-LC.

508 *to observe strict impartiality*: JH diary, March 8, 1904, JH-LC.

508 *"the Unknown Quantity"*: JH diary, March 11, 1904, JH-LC.

508 *"For several years"*: TR to Theodore Roosevelt, Jr., February 10, 1904, TR-LET 4:724.

508 *"finds an attractive subject"*: JH to Spencer Eddy, June 7, 1904, JH-LC.

508 *"I spoke of the daily attacks . . . calm frame of mind"*: JH diary, June 2, 1904, JH-LC.

508 *"I said to Cassini"*: JH diary, June 3, 1904, JH-LC.

509 *"overtures which were"*: JH diary, June 7, 1904, JH-LC.

509 *Roosevelt was likewise*: TR to Cecil Spring-Rice, June 13, 1904, in Gwynn, ed., *Letters and Friendships of Cecil Spring-Rice*, 418.

509 *"We may be of genuine"*: TR to JH, July 26, 1904, TR-LET 4:865.

509 *"Everything seems to have"*: JH to Joseph Choate, February 27, 1904, JH-LC.

509 *"In the cabinet meeting"*: JH diary, April 12, 1904, JH-LC.

510 *"He sees a good many"*: JH diary, April 10, 1904, JH-LC.

510 *"It was simply tortuous"*: Helen Hay Whitney to WRT, n.d., JH-BU.

510 *"It is intolerable"*: JH diary, April 12, 1904, JH-LC.

510 *"I can hardly escape"*: JH diary, April 6, 1904, JH-LC.

510 *"a poor thing"*: JH diary, May 1, 1904, JH-LC.

510 *"the amphibious life"*: JH, "The Press and Modern Progress," JH-ADD 244, 245.

511 *"There were only a few"*: JH diary, May 18, 1904, JH-LC.

511 *"The President talked"*: JH diary, May 22, 1904.

511 *"Situation serious"*: Tuchman, "Perdicaris Alive or Raisuli Dead," 19.

512 *Never before had the U.S. Navy*: Hourihan, "Marlinspike Diplomacy," 42.

512 *"I hope they may not"*: JH diary, May 28, 1904, JH-LC.

513 *"Now the Sultan's"*: Perdicaris, "In Raisuli's Hands," 521.

513 *"[I]s Perdicaris"*: A. H. Slocomb to JH, May 30, 1904, in Davis, "The Citizenship of Jon Perdicaris," 521.

513 *"one Ionnas"*: John B. Jackson to JH, June 7, 1904, in ibid., 522.

513 *"You see there is no"*: JH to TR, June 15, 1905, JH-LC.

513 *"Our position must"*: TR to JH, June 15, 1905, JH-LC.

514 *"We want Perdicaris"*: JH to Samuel Gummeré, telegram, June 22, 1904, in Morris, *Theodore Rex*, 335.

514 *"Fee, Fi, Fo, Fum"*: *New York World*, June 23, 1904, in Hourihan, "Roosevelt and the Sultans," 122.

515 *"In diplomacy"*: Unidentified clipping, n.d., accompanying Charles Chaillé-Long to JH, June 24, 1904, JH-LC.

515 *"My telegram to"*: JH diary, June 23, 1904, JH-LC.

515 *"Perigoric"*: JH to AA, September 3, 1904, JH-LC.

516 *"Astute and punctilious . . . pleasant manner"*: Unidentified clippings, n.d., JH scrapbook, JH-LC.

516 *"hardened old spellbinders"*: JH diary, July 6, 1904, JH-LC.

516 *"[T]he whole party stood"*: JH, "Fifty Years of the Republican Party," JH-ADD 269.

516 *"musical instrument"*: Unidentified clipping, n.d., JH scrapbook, JH-LC.

516 *"[Lincoln] was fighting"*: JH, "Fifty Years of the Republican Party," 271.

516 *"If there is one thing"*: Ibid., 272.

517 *"I hope I am violating"*: Ibid., 273.

517 *"A country growing . . . greed of land"*: Ibid., 282.

517 *"gained by appeals"*: Ibid., 284–85.

518 *"Some well-meaning people"*: Ibid., 287–88.

518 *"Ask [the Democrats]"*: Ibid., 293–94.

519 *"In a certain sense"*: Ibid., 294.

519 *"We who are passing . . . are to come"*: Ibid., 301.

519 *"It is one of the few speeches"*: TR to JH, July 9, 1904, JH-LC.

520 *"appreciation not only"*: JH diary, July 14, 1904, JH-LC.

520 *"I have about reached"*: JH to TR, July 14, 1904, JH-LC.

520 *"a great peril escaped"*: JH to Helen Hay Whitney, July 30, 1904, JH-LET 3:302.

520 *"As this is the only way"*: HA to Augustus Saint-Gaudens, September 3, 1904, HAL 5:608.

521 *"Might it not be the best solution"*: JH to TR, August 23, 1904, JH-LC.

522 *Roosevelt agreed that there was little*: TR to JH, August 24, 1904, TR-LET 4:904.

522 *"Russian Minister informed"*: AA to JH, August 25, 1904, JH-LC.

522 *"The bark of both combatants"*: JH to JC, September 1, 1904, Dennett Papers, LC.

522 *"War grows more"*: Ibid.

522 *"I feel good for nothing"*: JH to Samuel Mather, August 19, 1904, JH-LC.

522 *"What can I say . . . to tempt you"*: JH to ESC, August 7, 1904, AP.

523 *"idiotic adoration"*: JH to John Clark, September 7, 1904, JH-LET 3:309.

523 *"I have never seen such"*: JH diary, October 1, 1904, JH-LC.

524 *"It is true that"*: JH, "America's Love of Peace," JH-ADD 309–10.

524 *"with such of the European"*: Ibid., 314.

524 *"The great hall"*: JH diary, October 3, 1904, JH-LC.

524 *"I did not give him"*: JH diary, October 4, 1904, JH-LC.

524 *"badly bunged"*: JH diary, October 23, 1904, JH-LC.

525 *"a four month troubled"*: JH diary, November 3, 1904, JH-LC.

525 *"If you vote the Republican . . . party of today"*: JH, Speech at Carnegie Hall, October 26, 1904, JH-LC.

525 *"outbursts" of applause*: Unidentified clipping, n.d., JH scrapbook, JH-I.C.

525 *"sighs of adhesion"*: JH diary, October 26, 1904, JH-LC.

526 *"No Sunday is ever"*: JH diary, November 8, 1904, JH-LC.

526 *"Hayism"*: JH diary, November 9, 1904, JH-LC.

526 *"Hay Will Stay"*: Unidentified clipping, n.d., JH scrapbook, JH-I.C.

526 *"He did it in a moment"*: JH diary, November 12, 1904, JH-LC.

526 *"I owe him everything"*: JH to TR, November 16, 1904, JH-LET 3:321–23.

527 *"[A]ll that you say"*: TR to JH, November 17, 1904, JH-LC.

527 *"There is, perhaps, no reason"*: JH to George Smalley, November 22, 1904, JH-LC.

527 *"You, who are always"*: JH to ESC, November 28, 1904, AP.

527 *"A treaty entering"*: JH diary, February 13, 1905, JH-LC.

528 *"It was a grotesque sight"*: JH diary, February 10, 1905, JH-LC.

528 *"as stupid a piece"*: JH to JC, February 10, 1905, JH-LC.

528 *"The President, and"*: JH diary, February 12, 1905, JH-LC.

528 *"a battle over the corpse"*: JH diary, February 15, 1905, JH-LC.

529 *"about as much as a gorged anaconda"*: JH diary, March 18, 1904, JH-LC.

529 *"It is not true"*: FR 1904, xli.

529 *"protocol of an agreement"*: Collin, *Theodore Roosevelt's Caribbean*, 424.

529 *"One blessed result"*: JH diary, February 28, 1905, JH-LC.

530 *"I had last night much pain"*: JH diary, January 28, 1905, JH-LC.

530 *"The weather"*: JH diary, February 1, 1905, JH-LC.

530 *"I cannot help telling"*: JH to WR, January 6, 1905, WR-LC.

530 *"So I must live"*: JH to ESC, January 9, 1905, AP.

531 *"In its scorn of traditions"*: JH diary, April 3, 1905, JH-LC.

531 *Saint-Gaudens, John La Farge*: Novick, *Henry James: The Mature Master*, 393.

531 *"The President came to dinner"*: JH diary, January 10, 1905, JH-LC.

531 *"Please wear it"*: JH to TR, March 3, 1905, JH-LET 328.

531   *"Surely no other"*: TR to JH, March 3, 1905, JH-LC.

532   *"short and in excellent temper"*: JH diary, March 4, 1905, JH-LC.

532   *"I have three Commissions"*: JH diary, March 6, 1905, JH-LC.

532   *"I tried to walk"*: JH diary, March 12, 1905, JH-LC.

532   *"nervous dyspepsia"*: JH diary, March 10, 1905, JH-LC.

532   *"an increasing pain"*: JH diary, March 13, 1905, JH-LC.

533   *"I do not know who"*: JH diary, February 23, 1905, JH-LC.

533   *"If the war stops now"*: Lloyd Griscom to JH, March 15, 1905, JH-LC.

534   merely suffering from *"overwork"*: Unidentified clipping, n.d., JH scrapbook, JH-LC.

534   *"I have great doubts"*: JH to George Trevelyan, January 14, 1905, JH-LET 324–25.

Chapter 21: All the Great Prizes

page

535   *"as steady as a church"*: JH diary, March 25, 1905, JH-LC.

535   *"We have got to find out"*: HA to ESC, April 3, 1905, HAL 5:642.

535   *"very common among"*: JH diary, April 8, 1905, JH-LC.

536   *"The baths act"*: AA to JH, April 21, 1905, JH-LC.

536   *"no reason why"*: JH to TR, April 28, 1905, JH-LC.

536   *"I want you to rest"*: TR to JH, May 6, 1905, TR-LET 4:1168.

536   *"sitting on the lid"*: AA to JH, April 21, 1905, JH-LC.

537   *"He certainly does look better"*: CSH to HA, May 3, 1905, HA-MHS.

537   *"warm and comfortable"*: JH diary, May 22, 1905, JH-LC.

537   *"rattlepated old lunatic"*: JH to TR, May 24, 1905, JH-LC.

537   *"I do not wish"*: Henry Wilson to JH, May 20, 1905, JH-LC.

537   seated in an armchair by the elevator: Hammond, *Autobiography* 2:448.

537   *"although the heart still seemed"*: JH diary, May 26, 1905, JH-LC.

538   *"I seem fated to leave"*: JH diary, May 27, 1905, JH-LC.

538   *"an incredible rate of speed"*: JH diary, May 28, 1905, JH-LC.

538   *"Certainly I have done"*: HA to ESC, June 5, 1905, HAL 5:670.

539   *"He began talking at once"*: JH diary, June 4, 1905, JH-LC.

539   *"An astonishing piece"*: JH diary, June 6, 1905, JH-LC.

539   *"When I left Nauheim"*: JH to John Clark, June 6, 1905, JH-LET 3:343–45.

539   *"I went to the White House"*: JH diary, June 13, 1905, JH-LC.

540   *"say Ave Caesar!"*: JH to John Clark, June 6, 1905, JH-LET 3:344.

540   *"I owe you a thousand"*: JH to TR, June 16, 1905, JH-LC.

540   *"to discuss the whole peace"*: Morris, *Theodore Rex*, 390.

541   *"It was a great stroke"*: JH to TR, June 16, 1905, JH-LC.

541 *"silence and bitter-sweet"*: JH to ESC, June 21, 1905, AP.

541 *"My Dear and Great Friend"*: ESC to JH, June 24, 1905, JH-LC.

542 *"The night was delightfully"*: JH to TR, June 25, 1905, JH-LC.

542 *"in no immediate danger . . . doing nicely"*: Unidentified clippings, JH scrapbook, JH-LC.

542 *"Although I could not have"*: HA to ESC, June 27, 1905, HAL 5:680.

542 *"but he was so tired . . . and he was gone"*: CSH, in JH diary, June 25–July 6, 1905, JH-LC.

543 *"I say to myself"*: JH diary, June 14, 1905, JH-LC.

543 *"As he had told me"*: CSH, in JH diary, June 25–July 6, 1905, JH-LC.

543 *so large and "official"*: ESC to HA, July 2, 1905, HA-MHS.

544 *"He was not only"*: James Hoyt, in "Proceedings of the Memorial Meeting of the Citizens of Cleveland Held in the Chamber of Commerce Auditorium, July 5, 1905, in Honor of the Late Secretary of State, John Hay," 7, WRHS.

544 *"Among his many admirable traits"*: Unidentified clipping, n.d., JH scrapbook, JH-LC.

544 *"At first men began"*: *Independent* (New York), July 8, 1905, 45–46, clipping, JH scrapbook, JH-LC.

545 *"[W]e have lost our mightiest"*: Tiphereth Zion Society of Pittsburgh, resolution, July 2, 1905, presented to CSH, JH-BU.

545 *"As rabbi"*: *Cleveland Plain Dealer*, July 6, 1905.

545 *"My faith in Christ"*: Hiram C. Haydn, "The Hon. John Hay, Secretary of State: An Appreciation," pamphlet, July 16, 1905, 14, WRHS.

545 *"It would be difficult to find"*: Teunis S. Hamlin, "John Hay as His Pastor Knew Him," *Congregationalist* 90 (July 8, 1905), 1, in JH scrapbook, JH-LC.

545 *"His death"*: TR public statement, July 1, 1905, unidentified clipping, JH scrapbook, JH-LC.

545 *"I dearly loved him"*: TR to CSH, July 1, 1905, JH-LC.

546 *"Hay was a really great man"*: TR to Albert Beveridge, July 11, 1905, TR-LET 4:1269.

546 *"Of course, what I am about"*: JH to HCL, July 11, 1905, TR-LET 4:1271.

546 *"The Senate killed Hay"*: HA to ESC, July 10, 1905, HAL 5:689.

546 *"[I]t was not physical fatigue"*: HA to CSH, August 10, 1905, HAL 5:700.

547 *"As for me"*: HA to CSH, July 4, 1905, HAL 5:686.

548 *"With Mr. Hay there was not"*: [John St. Loe Strachey], *Spectator* (London), July 8, 1905, clipping, JH scrapbook, JH-LC.

548 *"John Hay, whatever he knew"*: WDH, "John Hay in Literature," 350–51.

549 *"You have shown that"*: McCullough, *Path Between the Seas*, 383.

551 *"I am surprised"*: ESC to WRT, May 14, 1919, WRT-HU.

551 *"I think Mr. Thayer makes"*: Chalfant, *Improvement of the World*, 504.

551 "He seen his duty": JH, "Jim Bludso," *Pike County Ballads*, 20.

Bibliography

Kenneth D. Ackerman, *Dark Horse: The Surprise Election and Political Murder of President James A. Garfield* (2003)

————, *The Gold Ring: Jim Fisk, Jay Gould, and Black Friday, 1869* (1988, reprint with new intro 2005)

Brooks Adams, "John Hay," *McClure's* 19 (June 1902), 173–82

Charles F. Adams, Jr., "The 'Breadwinners' and 'Democracy,'" *The Nation* 38 (February 21, 1884), 165

[Henry Adams], "Biography of John Hay," *The Reserve* (Published by the Junior Class of Adelbert College, Cleveland, Ohio) 13 (1893), 9–14

[————], *Democracy* (1880), in *Novels, Mont Saint Michel, The Education* (Library of America, 1983)

Henry Adams, *The Education of Henry Adams* (1918), in *Novels, Mont Saint Michel, The Education* (Library of America, 1983)

————, "Mountaineering in the Sierra Nevada" (review), *North American Review* 114 (April 1872), 445–48

Jad Adams, *Kipling* (2005)

John E. Adams, *Florida During the Civil War* (1963)

[Alvey Adee], "The Life-Magnet," *Putnam's* 6 (August 1870), 152–62

Cyrus Adler, ed., *The Voice of America on Kishineff* (1904)

Cyrus Adler and Aaron M. Margalith, *With Firmness in the Right: American Diplomatic Action Affecting Jews, 1840–1945* (1946)

Oscar M. Alfonso, *Theodore Roosevelt and the Philippines, 1897–1909* (1970)

H. C. Allen, *Great Britain and the United States; A History of Anglo-American Relations (1783–1952)* (1955)

William H. Allen, "The Election of 1900," *Annals of the American Academy of Political and Social Science* 17 (January 1901–May 1901), 53–73

"The American Ambassador," *Saturday Review* (London) 86 (August 20, 1898), 231–32

C. D. Ameringer, "The Panama Lobby of Philippe Bunau-Varilla," *American Histori-cal Review* 68 (January 1963), 346–63

———, "Philippe Bunau-Varilla: New Light on the Panama Canal Treaty," *Hispanic American Historical Review* 46 (February 1966), 28–52

Stuart Anderson, *Race and Rapprochement: Anglo-Saxonism and Anglo-American Rela-tions, 1895–1904* (1981)

Eugene N. Anderson, *The First Moroccan Crisis, 1904–1906* (1930)

James Burrill Angell, *The Reminiscences of James Burrill Angell* (1912)

Paul M. Angle, *"Here I Have Lived": A History of Lincoln's Springfield, 1821–1865* (1935, rev. ed. 1971)

———, *A Shelf of Lincoln Books: A Critical Bibliography of Lincolniana* (1946)

Gustave Anguizola, *Philippe Bunau-Varilla: The Man Behind the Panama Canal* (1980)

R. Gordon Arneson, "Anchor Man of the Department: Alvey Augustus Adee," *For-eign Service Journal* 48 (August 1971), 26–28

Isaac Newton Arnold, *History of Abraham Lincoln and the Overthrow of American Slavery* (1866)

———, *The Life of Abraham Lincoln* (1884, reprint 1994)

Harry W. Baehr, Jr., *The New York Tribune Since the Civil War* (1936, reprint 1972)

Thomas A. Bailey, *A Diplomatic History of the American People* (1940, reprint 1964)

———, "Theodore Roosevelt and the Alaska Boundary Settlement," *Canadian His-torical Review* 18 (June 1937), 123–30

———, "Was the Presidential Election of 1900 a Mandate on Imperialism?" *Missis-sippi Valley Historical Review* 24 (June 1937), 43–52

David Haward Bain, *Sitting in Darkness: Americans in the Philippines* (1984)

Jean Harvey Baker, *Mary Todd Lincoln: A Biography* (1987)

H. A. Bancroft, *Literary Industries* (1891)

"The Bandits of Morocco," *Outlook* 77 (June 11, 1904), 341

Chester L. Barrows, *William M. Evarts: Lawyer, Diplomat, Statesman* (1941)

William E. Barton, *A Beautiful Blunder: The True Story of Lincoln's Letter to Mrs. Lydia A. Bixby* (1926)

Roy P. Basler et al., eds., *The Collected Works of Abraham Lincoln*, 9 vols. (1953)

David Homer Bates, *Lincoln in the Telegraph Office* (1907, reprint 1995)

Howard K. Beale, *Theodore Roosevelt and the Rise of America to World Power* (1956)

Thomas Beer, *Hanna* (1929)

———, *The Mauve Decade: American Life at the End of the Nineteenth Century* (1926, reprint 1961)

Robert L. Beisner, *From the Old Diplomacy to the New, 1865–1900* (2nd ed. 1986)

———, *Twelve Against Empire: The Anti-Imperialists, 1898–1900* (1968, 2nd ed. 1985)

Michael A. Bellesiles, *1877: America's Year of Living Dangerously* (2010)

Clifford Bender, "Another Forgotten Novel," *Modern Language Notes* 41 (May 1926), 319–22

Clare Benedict, ed., *Constance Fenimore Woolson* (1930)

Charles Beresford, *The Break-Up of China; with an Account of Its Present Commerce, Currency, Waterways, Armies, Railways, Politics and Future Prospects* (1899)

———, "China and the Powers," *North American Review* 510 (May 1899), 53–58

Charles W. Berquist, *Coffee and Conflict in Colombia, 1886–1910* (1978)

Ian J. Bickerton, "John Hay's Open Door Policy: A Re-examination," *Australian Journal of Politics & History* 23 (1977), 54–66

John Bigelow, *Retrospections of an Active Life*, 5 vols. (1909–13)

Biographical Review of Hancock County (1907)

Joseph Bucklin Bishop, "A Friendship with John Hay," *Century* 71 (March 1906), 773–80

———, *John Hay: Scholar, Statesman: An Address Delivered Before the Alumni Association of Brown University, June 19, 1906* (1906)

———, *Notes and Anecdotes of Many Years* (1925)

———, *The Panama Gateway* (1913)

———, *Theodore Roosevelt and His Time Shown in His Letters*, 2 vols. (1920)

Gist Blair, "Lafayette Square," *Records of the Columbia Historical Society* 28 (1926), 133–73

Nelson M. Blake, "Ambassadors to the Court of Theodore Roosevelt," *Mississippi Valley Historical Review* 42 (September 1955), 179–206

Rodney Blake, "How John Hay Suppressed a First Edition," *Biblio* 1 (October 1921), 77–79

Board of Supervisors of Hancock County, *History of Hancock County, Illinois* (1968)

Gabor Boritt, *The Gettysburg Gospel: The Lincoln Speech That Nobody Knows* (2006)

Herbert W. Bowen, *Recollections Diplomatic and Undiplomatic* (1926)

William R. Braisted, "The United States and the American-Chinese Development Company," *Far Eastern Quarterly* 11 (February 1952), 147–65

Fawn W. Brodie, *No Man Knows My Name: The Life of Joseph Smith* (1945, revised 1971)

Noah Brooks, *Washington in Lincoln's Time* (1895, reprint 1971)

Van Wyck Brooks, *Howells: His Life and World* (1959)

Walter C. Bronson, *The History of Brown University, 1764–1914* (1914)

Caroline Owsley Brown, "Springfield Society Before the Civil War," *Journal of the Illinois State Historical Society* 15 (1922), 477–500

Robert V. Bruce, *1877: Year of Violence* (1988)

James Bryce, "The Essential Unity of Britain and America," *Atlantic Monthly* 82 (July 1898), 22–29

F. Lauriston Bullard, *Abraham Lincoln and the Widow Bixby* (1946)

Philippe Bunau-Varilla, *From Panama to Verdun: My Fight for France* (1940)

———, *The Great Adventure of Panama* (1920)

———, *Panama: The Creation, Destruction, and Resurrection* (1913)

———, "Washington and Panama," *Living Age* 332 (March 15, 1927), 484–87

Michael Burlingame, *Abraham Lincoln: A Life*, 2 vols. (2009)

———, "The Authorship of the Bixby Letter," in Burlingame, ed., *At Lincoln's Side: John Hay's Civil War Correspondence and Selected Writings* (2000), 169–84

———, *Honest Abe, Dishonest Mary*, Historical Bulletin 50, Lincoln Fellowship of Wisconsin, 1994

———, *The Inner World of Abraham Lincoln* (1994)

———, "New Light on the Bixby Letter," *Journal of the Abraham Lincoln Association* 16 (Winter 1995), 59–71

———, ed., *At Lincoln's Side: John Hay's Civil War Correspondence and Selected Writings* (2000)

———, ed., *Lincoln Observed: Civil War Dispatches of Noah Brooks* (1998)

———, ed., *Lincoln's Journalist: John Hay's Anonymous Writings for the Press, 1860–1864* (1998)

———, ed., *An Oral History of Abraham Lincoln: John G. Nicolay's Interviews and Essays* (1996)

———, ed., *With Lincoln in the White House: Letters, Memoranda, and Other Writings of John G. Nicolay, 1860–1865* (2000)

——— and John R. Turner Ettlinger, eds., *Inside Lincoln's White House: The Complete Civil War Diary of John Hay* (1997)

David H. Burton, *Cecil Spring-Rice: A Diplomat's Life* (1990)

———, *Theodore Roosevelt: Confident Imperialist* (1968)

William B. Bushong, ed., "The Roosevelt Restoration of 1902," *White House History* 11 (Summer 2002), entire issue

Edwin H. Cady, *The Realist at War; The Mature Years, 1885–1920, of William Dean Howells* (1958)

———, *The Road to Realism; The Early Years, 1837–1885, of William Dean Howells* (1956)

Abraham Cahan, "Jewish Massacres and the Revolutionary Movement in Russia," *North American Review* 560 (July 1903), 49–62

A. E. Campbell, *Great Britain and the United States, 1895–1903* (1960)

Charles S. Campbell, Jr., *Anglo-American Understanding, 1898–1903* (1957)

———, *Special Business Interests and the Open Door Policy* (1951)

———, *The Transformation of American Foreign Relations, 1865–1900* (1976)

Andrew Carnegie, "Americanism versus Imperialism," *North American Review* 506 (January 1899), 1–13

———, *The Autobiography of Andrew Carnegie* (1920)

———, "Distant Possessions—The Parting of the Ways," *North American Review* 501 (August 1898), 239–48

F. B. Carpenter, *Six Months at the White House with Abraham Lincoln* (1866; reprinted as *The Inner Life of Abraham Lincoln: Six Months in the White House*, 1880 and 1995)

Clark E. Carr, *The Illini: A Story of the Prairies* (1904)

Raymond Carr, *Spain: A History* (2000)

C. E. Carrington, *The Life of Rudyard Kipling* (1955)

Sean Dennis Cashman, *America in the Gilded Age: From the Death of Lincoln to the Rise of Theodore Roosevelt* (1984)

Margaret Cassini, *Never a Dull Moment* (1956)

"Castilian Days" [review], *Atlantic Monthly* 28 (November 1871), 636–38

Edward Chalfant, *Better in Darkness: A Biography of Henry Adams: His Second Life, 1862–1891* (1994)

———, *Improvement of the World: A Biography of Henry Adams: His Last Life, 1891–1918* (2001)

Margaret Chanler, *Roman Spring: Memoirs* (1934)

A. S. Chapman, "The Boyhood of John Hay," *Century* 56 (July 1909), 444–54

Jan Cigliano, *Showplace of America: Cleveland's Euclid Avenue, 1850–1910* (1991)

Margaret Clapp, *Forgotten First Citizen: John Bigelow* (1947)

H. Butler Clarke, *Modern Spain 1815–1898* (1906)

Lawrence A. Clayton, "Canal Morgan," *Alabama Heritage* 25 (Summer 1992), 6–19

Samuel L. Clemens, "John Hay and the Ballads," *Harper's Weekly* 49 (October 21, 1905), 1530

———, *Mark Twain's Autobiography*, 2 vols. (1924)

Catherine Clinton, *Mrs. Lincoln: A Life* (2009)

Paul H. Clyde, "The Open-Door Policy of John Hay," *Historical Outlook* 22 (May 1931), 210–14

Kenton J. Clymer, "Anti-Semitism in the Late Nineteenth Century: The Case of John Hay," *American Jewish Historical Quarterly* 60 (June 1971), 344–54

———, "Checking the Sources: John Hay and Spanish Possessions in the Pacific," *Historian* 48 (November 1985), 82–87

————, "John Hay and Mark Twain," *Missouri Historical Review* 67 (April 1973), 397–406

————. *John Hay: The Gentleman as Diplomat* (1975)

William T. Coggeshall, *Lincoln Memorial: The Journeys of Abraham Lincoln: From Springfield to Washington, 1861, as President Elect; and from Washington to Springfield, 1865, as President Martyred* (1865)

A College Friendship: A Series of Letters from John Hay to Hannah Angell (1938)

Paolo E. Coletta, "McKinley, the Peace Negotiations, and the Acquisition of the Philippines," *Pacific Historical Review* 30 (November 1961), 341–50

————, ed., *Threshold to American Internationalism: Essays on the Foreign Policy of William McKinley* (1970)

Richard H. Collin, "The Image of Theodore Roosevelt in American History and Thought, 1885–1965," PhD dissertation, New York University, 1966

————, *Theodore Roosevelt, Culture, Diplomacy, and Expansion: A New View of American Imperialism* (1985)

————, *Theodore Roosevelt's Caribbean: The Panama Canal, the Monroe Doctrine, and the Latin American Context* (1990)

Archibald R. Colquhoun, *China in Transformation* (1899)

Frances Snow Compton [Henry Adams], *Esther* (1884), in *Novels, Mont Saint Michel, The Education* (Library of America, 1983)

Richard Connaughton, *Rising Sun and Tumbling Bear: Russia's War with Japan* (2003)

T. B. Connery, "Secret History of the Garfield-Conkling Tragedy," *Cosmopolitan* 23 (June 1897), 145–62

Royal Cortissoz, *John La Farge: A Memoir and a Study* (1911)

————, *The Life of Whitelaw Reid*, 2 vols. (1921)

Gerald M. Craig, *The United States and Canada* (1968)

Edward Crapol, *James G. Blaine: Architect of Empire* (2000)

Herbert Croly, *Marcus Alonzo Hanna: His Life and Work* (1912)

Shelby Moore Cullom, *Fifty Years of Public Service* (1911)

Caroline Wells Healey Dall, "Pioneering," *Atlantic Monthly* 19 (April 1867), 403–16

Scott Dalrymple, "John Hay's Revenge: Anti-Labor Novels, 1880–1905," *Business and Economic History* 28 (Fall 1999), 133–42

Kathleen Dalton, *Theodore Roosevelt: A Strenuous Life* (2002)

————, "Why Americans Loved Teddy Roosevelt/Or Charisma Is in the Eye of the Beholder," in Robert J. Brugger, ed., *Our Selves/Our Past: Psychological Approaches to American History* (1981), 269–91

J. W. Davidson, *Samoa Mo Samoa: The Emergence of the Independent State of Western Samoa* (1967)

John Paton Davies, "Two Hundred Years of American Foreign Policy: America and East Asia," *Foreign Affairs* 55 (January 1977), 368–94

Harold E. Davis, "The Citizenship of Jon Perdicaris," *Journal of Modern History* 13 (December 1941), 517–26

Richard Harding Davis, *Captain Macklin* (1902)

———, *With Both Armies in South Africa* (1900)

Michael Davitt, *Within the Pale: The True Story of the Anti-Semitic Persecutions in Russia* (1903)

Charles G. Dawes, *A Journal of the McKinley Years* (1950)

Henry L. Dawes, "Garfield and Conkling," *Century* 47 (January 1894), 341–44

Arthur H. Dean, *William Nelson Cromwell, 1854–1948: An American Pioneer* (1937)

Alexander DeConde, ed., *Encyclopedia of American Foreign Policy*, 3 vols. (1978)

———, et al., eds., *Encyclopedia of American Foreign Policy*, 3 vols. (2nd ed. 2002)

Tyler Dennett, *Americans in Eastern Asia: A Critical Study of the Policy of the United States with Reference to China, Japan and Korea in the 19th Century* (1922)

———, *John Hay: From Poetry to Politics* (1933)

———, "The Open Door Policy as Intervention," *Annals of the American Academy of Political and Social Science* 166 (July 1933), 78–83

———, *Roosevelt and the Russo-Japanese War* (1925)

Alfred L. P. Dennis, *Adventures in American Diplomacy* (1927)

———, "John Hay," in Samuel F. Bemis, ed., *The American Secretaries of State and Their Diplomacy*, 9 (1929), 115–89

John A. DeNovo, "The Enigmatic Alvey A. Adee and American Foreign Relations, 1870–1924," *Prologue* 7 (Summer 1975), 68–80

Bernard DeVoto, ed., *Mark Twain in Eruption: Hitherto Unpublished Pages About Men and Events by Mark Twain* (1940)

David H. Dickason, "Henry Adams and Clarence King: The Record of a Friendship," *New England Quarterly* 17 (June 1944), 229–54

———, "Clarence King—Scientist and Art Amateur," *Art in America* 32 (January 1944), 41–51

Diplomatic History of the Panama Canal (1914)

John Dobson, *Reticent Expansionism: The Foreign Policy of William McKinley* (1988)

Justus D. Doenecke, *The Presidencies of James A. Garfield & Chester A. Arthur* (1981)

David Herbert Donald, *Lincoln* (1995)

———, *Lincoln's Herndon* (1948)

Burton Smith Dow III, "Amasa Stone, Jr.: His Triumph and Tragedy," master's thesis, Case Western Reserve University, 1956

John H. Dryfhout, *The Work of Augustus Saint-Gaudens* (1982)

Foster R. Dulles, "John Hay," in Norman Graebner, ed., *An Uncertain Tradition: American Secretaries of State in the Twentieth Century* (1961)

Bingham Duncan, *Whitelaw Reid: Journalist, Politician, Diplomat* (1975)

Finley Peter Dunne, *Mr. Dooley in Peace and War* (1898, reprint 1988)

———, *Mr. Dooley: In the Hearts of His Countrymen* (1898)

Captain Miles P. DuVal, Jr., *Cadiz to Cathay: The Story of the Long Struggle for a Waterway Across the American Isthmus* (1940)

Brainerd Dyer, *The Public Career of William M. Evarts* (1933)

Natalie Dykstra, *Clover Adams: A Gilded and Heartbreaking Life* (2012)

Earnest Penney Earnest, *S. Weir Mitchell, Novelist and Physician* (1950)

Leon Edel, *Henry James*, 5 vols. (1953–72)

———, ed., *Henry James: Letters*, 4 vols. (1974)

Herbert Edwards, "Henry Adams: Politician and Statesman," *New England Quarterly* 22 (March 1949), 49–60

Gerald G. Eggert, *Richard Olney: Evolution of a Statesman* (1974)

David J. Eicher, *The Longest Night: A Military History of the Civil War* (2001)

Jason Emerson, *Giant in the Shadows: The Life of Robert T. Lincoln* (2012)

Charles J. Esdaile, *Spain in the Liberal Age: From Constitution to Civil War, 1809–1939* (2000)

Ovidio Diaz Espino, *How Wall Street Created a Nation: J. P. Morgan, Teddy Roosevelt, and the Panama Canal* (2001)

Raymond Esthus, "The Changing Concept of the Open Door, 1899–1910," *Mississippi Valley Historical Review* 46 (December 1959), 435–54

———, *A Double Eagle and Rising Sun: The Russian and Japanese at Portsmouth in 1905* (1988)

———, *Theodore Roosevelt and Japan* (1966)

———, *Theodore Roosevelt and the International Rivalries* (1970)

Thomas H. Etzold, "Protection or Politics? 'Perdicaris Alive or Raisuli Dead,'" *Historian* 37 (February 1975), 297–305

T. C. Evans, "Personal Reminiscences of John Hay: By a Veteran Journalist," *New York Times,* July 16, 1905

John K. Fairbank, "'American China Policy' to 1898: A Misconception," *Pacific Historical Review* 39 (November 1970), 409–20

Robert H. Ferrell, *American Diplomacy: A History* (1959, rev. ed. 1969)

John H. Ferguson, *American Diplomacy and the Boer War* (1939)

James A. Field, Jr., "American Imperialism: The 'Worst Chapter' in Almost Any Book," *American Historical Review* 83 (June 1978), 644–68

Victor Fischer, et al., *Mark Twain's Letters*, 6 vols. (1988–2002)

Gilbert C. Fite, "Election of 1896," in Arthur M. Schlesinger, Jr., ed., *History of American Presidential Elections, 1789–1968*, Vol. 2: *1787–1873* (1971)

James Kirkpatrick Flack, Jr., "The Formation of the Washington Intellectual Community, 1870–1898," PhD dissertation, Wayne State University, 1968

Robert Bruce Flanders, *Nauvoo: Kingdom of the Mississippi* (1965)

Peter Fleming, *The Siege at Peking* (1959)

William Glover Fletcher, "Canal Site Diplomacy: A Study in American Political Geography," PhD dissertation, Yale University, 1940

Richard Nicholas Foley, *Criticism in American Periodicals of the Works of Henry James from 1866 to 1916* (1944)

Eric Foner, *The Fiery Trial: Abraham Lincoln and American Slavery* (2012)

Philip S. Foner, *The Great Labor Uprising of 1877* (1977)

———, *The Spanish-Cuban-American War and the Birth of American Imperialism*, 2 vols. (1972)

Benjamin T. Ford, "A Duty to Serve: The Governmental Career of George Bruce Cortelyou," PhD dissertation, Columbia University, 1963

Paul R. Fossom, "The Anglo-Venezuelan Boundary Controversy," *Hispanic American Historical Review* 8 (August 1928), 299–329

John W. Foster, *Diplomatic Memoirs*, 2 vols. (1909)

Nicholas Friedlander, "Henry Hobson Richardson, Henry Adams, and John Hay," *Proceedings of the Massachusetts Historical Society* 81 (1969), 137–66

Robert A. Friedlander, "A Reassessment of Roosevelt's Role in the Panamanian Revolution," *Western Political Quarterly* 14 (June 1961), 535–43

Otto Friedrich, *Clover* (1979)

Joseph A. Fry, *John Tyler Morgan and the Search for Southern Autonomy* (1992)

———, "William McKinley and the Coming of the Spanish-American War: A Study of the Besmirching and Redemption of an Historical Image," *Diplomatic History* 3 (Winter 1979), 77–97

Robert Gale, *John Hay* (1978)

John A. Garraty, *Henry Cabot Lodge: A Biography* (1953)

———, "Henry Cabot Lodge and the Alaska Boundary Tribunal," *New England Quarterly* 24 (December 1951), 469–94

Lionel Gelber, *The Rise of Anglo-American Friendship* (1938)

William M. Gibson, "Mark Twain and Howells: Anti-Imperialists," *New England Quarterly* 20 (December 1947), 435–70

———, *Theodore Roosevelt Among the Humorists: W. D. Howells, Mark Twain, and Mr. Dooley* (1980)

Joseph B. Gilder, "John Hay," *Critic* 47 (August 1905), 112–13

J. L. Gilder and J. B. Gilder, *Authors at Home: Personal and Biographical Sketches of Well-Known American Writers* (1888)

Rosamond Gilder, ed., *Letters of Richard Watson Gilder* (1916)

Ray Ginger, *The Age of Excess: The United States from 1877 to 1914* (1965)

John S. Goff, *Robert Todd Lincoln: A Man in His Own Right* (1969)

James M. Goode, *Capital Losses: A Cultural History of Washington's Destroyed Buildings* (1979)

Susan Goodman and Carl Dawson, *William Dean Howells: A Writer's Life* (2005)

Doris Kearns Goodwin, *Team of Rivals: The Political Genius of Abraham Lincoln* (2005)

Harold F. Gosnell, *Boss Platt and His New York Machine: A Study of the Political Leadership of Thomas C. Platt, Theodore Roosevelt, and Others* (1924)

Lewis L. Gould, *The Presidency of Theodore Roosevelt* (1991)

———, *The Presidency of William McKinley* (1980)

———, *The Spanish-American War and President McKinley* (1980)

Douglas R. Gow, "How Did the Roosevelt Corollary Become Linked to the Dominican Republic?" *Mid-America* 58 (October 1976), 159–65

Norman A. Graebner, ed., *Ideas and Diplomacy: Readings in the Intellectual Tradition of American Foreign Policy* (1964)

Henry F. Graff, *Grover Cleveland* (2002)

"The Great Secretary of State," *World's Work* 10 (August 1905), 6561–64

Thomas Gregg, *History of Hancock County, Illinois* (1880)

Constance McLaughlin Green, *Washington: Capital City, 1879–1950* (1963)

———, *Washington: Village and Capital, 1800–1870* (1962)

J. A. S. Grenville, "Great Britain and the Isthmian Canal, 1898–1901," *American Historical Review* 61 (October 1955), 48–69

———, *Lord Salisbury and Foreign Policy: The Close of the Nineteenth Century* (1964)

——— and George Berkeley Young, *Politics, Strategy, and American Diplomacy: Studies in Foreign Policy, 1873–1917* (1966)

Lloyd C. Griscom, *Diplomatically Speaking* (1940)

A. Whitney Griswold, *The Far Eastern Policy of the United States* (1938)

Allen G. Guelzo, *Lincoln and Douglas: The Debates That Defined America* (2008)

———, *Lincoln's Emancipation Proclamation: The End of Slavery in America* (2004)

Stephen Gwynn, ed., *The Letters and Friendships of Sir Cecil Spring-Rice: A Record*, 2 vols. (1929)

James D. Hague, ed., *Clarence King Memoirs: The Helmet of Mambrino* (1904)

Albert Halstead, "The President at Work—A Character Sketch," *Independent* 53 (September 5, 1901), 2080–86

John Hays Hammond, *The Autobiography of John Hays Hammond*, 2 vols. (1935)

Robert E. Hannigan, *The New World Power: American Foreign Policy, 1898–1917* (2002)

Earl Harding, *The Untold Story of Panama* (1959)

Fred H. Harrington, "The Anti-Imperialist Movement in the United States, 1898–1900," *Mississippi Valley Historical Review* 22 (September 1935), 211–30

Robert Harrison, "Blaine and the Camerons: A Study in the Limits of Machine Power," *Pennsylvania History* 49 (July 1982), 157–75

Geoffrey Bret Harte, ed., *The Letters of Bret Harte* (1926)

Alden Hatch, *The Wadsworths of the Genesee* (1959)

Clara S. Hay, ed., *Letters of John Hay and Extracts from Diary*, 3 vols. (1908)

"John Hay," *The Nation* 81 (July 6, 1905), 4

John Hay, *Addresses of John Hay* (1907)

———, *Amasa Stone* (1883)

———, "The Balance Sheet of the Two Parties," pamphlet, Cleveland, 1880

———, "The Blood Seedling," *Lippincott's* 7 (March 1871), 281–93

———, *The Bread-Winners: A Social Study* (1883)

———, *Castilian Days* (1875, reprint 1890)

———, "Colonel Baker," *Harper's Monthly* 24 (December 1861), 103–10

———, *The Complete Poetical Works of John Hay* (1917)

———, "Down the Danube," *Putnam's* 5 (June 1870), 625–35

———, "The Duel of the Spanish Bourbons," *Atlantic Monthly* 25 (May 1870), 626–32

———, "Ellsworth," *Atlantic Monthly* 8 (July 1861), 119–25

[———], "The Fortunes of the Bonapartes," *Harper's New Monthly Magazine* 60 (December 1879), 1–21

———, "The Foster-Brothers," *Harper's New Monthly Magazine* 232 (September 1869), 535–44

———, "Girlhood on the American Plan," *Atlantic Monthly* 43 (March 1879), 399–401

———, "Kane and Abel," *Frank Leslie's Illustrated Newspaper* 32 (April 22, 1871), 85–87

———, "A Letter from the Author," *Century* 27 (March 1884), 794–96

———, "Life in the White House in the Time of Lincoln," *Century* 41 (November 1890), 33–37

———, *The Life of Dr. Charles Hay* (1884, reprint 1929)

———, "The Mormon Prophet's Tragedy," *Atlantic Monthly* 24 (December 1869), 669–78

———, *Pike County Ballads and Other Pieces* (1871)

————, "The Pioneers of Ohio," *Magazine of History*, extra nos. 101–08 (1924–25), 279–90

————, "The Platform of Anarchy: An Address to the Students of Western Reserve University," October 6, 1896, pamphlet, 1896

————, et al., "Reminiscences of Bret Harte," *Overland Monthly* 40 (September 1902), 220–39

Mary Ridgley Hay, "Springfield, Illinois, in 1860, by a Native Springfielder," manuscript, John Hay Papers, Brown University

Hiram C. Haydn, "The Hon. John Hay, Secretary of State: An Appreciation," First Presbyterian Church (Cleveland. Ohio), pamphlet, July 16, 1905

Charles D. Hazen, ed., *The Letters of William Roscoe Thayer* (1926)

David Healy, *Drive to Hegemony: The United States in the Caribbean, 1898–1917* (1988)

————, *U.S. Expansionism: The Imperialist Urge in the 1890s* (1970)

William H. Herndon, "Analysis of the Character of Abraham Lincoln," part 1, *Abraham Lincoln Quarterly* 1 (September 1941), 343–83

————, "Analysis of the Character of Abraham Lincoln," part 2, *Abraham Lincoln Quarterly* 1 (December 1941), 403–41

————, "Facts Illustrative of Mr. Lincoln's Patriotism and Statesmanship," *Abraham Lincoln Quarterly* 3 (December 1944), 178–203

————, *Lincoln and Ann Rutledge and the Pioneers of New Salem* (1945)

———— and Jesse W. Weik, *Herndon's Lincoln* (1889, reprint 2006, Douglas L. Williams and Rodney O. Davis, eds.)

Emanuel Hertz, ed., *The Hidden Lincoln: From the Letters and Papers of William H. Herndon* (1938)

Holger Herwig, *Germany's Vision of Empire in Venezuela* (1986)

————, *Politics of Frustration: The United States in German Naval Planning, 1889–1941* (1976)

Granville Hicks, "The Conversion of John Hay," *New Republic* 67 (June 10, 1931), 100–01

Douglas Warren Hill, ed., *An Idler: John Hay's Social and Aesthetic Commentaries for the Press During the Civil War, 1861–1865* (2006)

Howard C. Hill, *Roosevelt and the Caribbean* (1927)

Mark D. Hirsch, *William C. Whitney: Modern Warwick* (1948)

Henry Russell Hitchcock, *The Architecture of H. H. Richardson and His Times* (1936)

Richard Hofstadter, "Manifest Destiny and the Philippines," in Daniel Aaron, ed., *America in Crisis: Fourteen Crucial Episodes in American History* (1952), 172–200

Paul S. Holbo, "Perilous Obscurity: Public Diplomacy and the Press in the Venezuelan Crisis, 1902–1903," *Historian* 32:2 (May 1970), 428–48

Josiah G. Holland, *Holland's Life of Abraham Lincoln* (1866, reprint 1998)

Henry Holt, *Garrulities of an Octogenarian Editor* (1923)

W. Stull Holt, *Treaties Defeated by the Senate: A Study of the Struggle Between President and Senate over the Conduct of Foreign Relations* (1933)

Harold Holzer, *Lincoln President-Elect: Abraham Lincoln and the Great Secession Winter, 1860–1861* (2008)

————, ed., *Hearts Touched by Fire: The Best of Battles and Leaders of the Civil War* (2011)

Abigail Adams Homans, *Education by Uncles* (1966)

Ari Hoogenboom, *Rutherford B. Hayes; Warrior and President* (1995)

Harlan Hoyt Horner, *Lincoln and Greeley* (1953)

William T. Horner, *Ohio's Kingmaker: Mark Hanna, Man & Myth* (2010)

William J. Hourihan, "Marlinspike Diplomacy," *U.S. Naval Institute Proceedings* 105 (January 1979), 42–51

————, "Roosevelt and the Sultans: The United States Navy in the Mediterranean, 1904," PhD dissertation, Northeastern University, 1975

Albert V. House, Jr., "The Trials of a Ghost-Writer of Lincoln Biography: Chauncey F. Black's Authorship of Lamon's Lincoln," *Journal of the Illinois State Historical Society* 31 (September 1938), 262–96

Mildred Howells, ed., *Life in Letters of William Dean Howells*, 2 vols. (1928)

William Dean Howells, "Editor's Easy Chair," *Harper's Monthly Magazine* 132 (January 1916), 310–13

————, "Editor's Easy Chair," *Harper's New Monthly Magazine* 54 (May 1877), 919

————, "Editor's Easy Chair," *Harper's New Monthly Magazine* 55 (June 1877), 304

————, "Editor's Study," *Harper's* 82 (February 1891), 478–83

————, "John Hay in Literature," *North American Review* 181 (September 1905), 343–51

————, "Recent American Novels: 'The Bread-Winners,'" *Century* 28:1 (May 1884), 153–54

James Floyd Huffman, "John Hay, The Poetic Trumpet: The Rhetoric of 'The Statesman of the Golden Rule,'" PhD dissertation, Michigan State University, 1966

George S. Hunsberger, "The Diplomatic Career of Alvey Augustus Adee with Special Reference to the Boxer Rebellion," master's thesis, American University, 1953

Gaillard Hunt, *The Department of State of the United States: Its History and Functions* (1914)

————, "The Permanent Assistant Secretary of State," *Outlook* 85 (February 23, 1907), 461–64

Michael H. Hunt, "The American Remission of the Boxer Indemnity: A Reappraisal," *Journal of Asian Studies* 31 (May 1972), 539–59

———, "The Forgotten Occupation: Peking, 1900–1901," *Pacific Historical Review* 48 (November 1979), 501–29

———, *Frontier Defense and the Open Door: Manchuria in Chinese-American Relations, 1895–1911* (1973)

———, *The Making of a Special Relationship: The United States and China to 1914* (1983)

Warren Frederick Ilchman, *Professional Diplomacy in the United States, 1779–1939: A Study in Administrative History* (1961)

Akira Iriye, *Pacific Estrangement: Japanese and American Expansion, 1897–1911* (1972)

Kathryn Allamong Jacob, *Captial Elites: High Society in Washington, D.C., After the Civil War* (1995)

Matthew Frye Jacobson, *Barbarian Virtues: The United States Encounters Foreign Peoples at Home and Abroad, 1876–1917* (2000)

Frederic Cople Jaher, "Industrialism and the American Aristocrat: A Social Study of John Hay and His Novel, *The Bread-winners,*" *Journal of the Illinois State Historical Society* 65:1 (Spring 1972), 69–93

Edward T. James, ed., "Constance Fenimore Woolson," in *Notable American Women*, Vol. 3 (1971), 670–72

George Wharton James, "Clarence King," *Overland Monthly and Out West Magazine* 81 (October 1923), 31–36

Philip C. Jessup, *Elihu Root*, 2 vols. (1938)

Eric Johannesen, *Cleveland Architecture, 1876–1976* (1979)

Arthur John, *The Best Years of the Century: Richard Watson Gilder, Scribner's Monthly and the Century Magazine, 1870–1909* (1981)

A. Wesley Johns, *The Man Who Shot McKinley: A New View of the Assassination of the President* (1970)

Robert U. Johnson and Clarence C. Buel, eds., *Battles and Leaders of the Civil War*, 2 vols. (1888)

Stanley L. Jones, *The Presidential Election of 1896* (1964)

David M. Jordan, *Roscoe Conkling of New York: Voice in the Senate* (1971)

E. J. Kahn, *Jock: The Life and Times of John Hay Whitney* (1981)

Eugenia Kaledin, *The Education of Mrs. Henry Adams* (1981)

Justin Kaplan, *Mr. Clemens and Mark Twain: A Biography* (1966)

Michael Kazin, *A Godly Hero: The Life of William Jennings Bryan* (2006)

[Henry Keenan], *The Money-Makers: A Social Parable* (1885)

Thomas Keneally, *American Scoundrel: The Life of the Notorious Civil War General Dan Sickles* (2002)

George F. Kennan, *American Diplomacy, 1900–1950* (1951)

Clarence King, "Artium Magister," *North American Review* 147 (October 1888), 369–84

——, "The Biographers of Lincoln," *Century* 32 (October 1886), 861–69

——, "The Education of the Future," *Forum* 13 (March 1892), 21–33

——, "Fire and Sword in Cuba," *Forum* 22 (September 1896), 31–52

——, "John Hay," *Scribner's Monthly* 7 (April 1874), 736–39

——, *Mountaineering in the Sierra Nevada* (1872)

——, "Shall Cuba Be Free?" *Forum* 20 (September 1895), 50–65

——, "Styles and the Monument," *North American Review* 141 (November 1885), 443–53

Robert Kingsbury, *The Assassination of James A. Garfield* (2002)

Lincoln Kirstein, *Memorial to a Marriage: An Album of the Saint-Gaudens Memorial in Rock Creek Cemetery* (1989)

Maury Klein, *The Life and Legend of Jay Gould* (1986)

Frank L. Klement, *Seven Who Witnessed Lincoln's Gettysburg Address* (1985)

Richard Kluger, *The Paper: The Life and Death of the New York Herald Tribune* (1986)

Stuart E. Knee, "The Diplomacy of Neutrality: Theodore Roosevelt and the Russian Pogroms of 1903–1906," *Presidential Studies Quarterly* 19 (Winter 1989), 71–78

H. H. Kohlsaat, *From McKinley to Harding: Personal Recollections of Our Presidents* (1923)

Harry Lyman Koopman, "Literary Men of Brown," *Brown Alumni Monthly* 9 (April 1909), 206–08

Mrs. Reginald de Koven, *A Musician and His Wife* (1926)

Dorothy Meserve Kunhardt and Philip B. Kunhardt, Jr., *Twenty Days: A Narrative in Text and Pictures of the Assassination of Abraham Lincoln and Twenty Days and Nights That Followed—The Nation in Mourning, The Long Trip Home to Springfield* (1965, reprint 1993)

Howard I. Kushner, "'The Strong God Circumstance': The Political Career of John Hay," *Journal of the Illinois State Historical Society* 67 (September 1974), 362–84

—— and Anne Hummel Sherrill, *John Milton Hay: The Union of Poetry and Politics* (1977)

Gary Laderman, *The Sacred Remains: American Attitudes Toward Death, 1799–1883* (1996)

Richard L. Lael, *Arrogant Diplomacy: U.S. Policy Toward Colombia, 1903–1922* (1987)

Walter LaFeber, *The American Search for Opportunity, 1865–1913,* Vol. 2 of *The Cambridge History of American Foreign Relations* (1993)

——, "Election of 1900," in Arthur Schlesinger, Jr., ed., *History of American Presidential Elections, 1789–1968,* Vol. 3: *1877–1959* (1971)

————, *The New Empire: An Interpretation of American Expansion, 1860–1898* (1963)

Ward H. Lamon, *The Life of Abraham Lincoln: From His Birth to His Inauguration as President* (1872, reprint 1999)

Louis J. Lang, ed., *The Autobiography of Thomas Collier Platt* (1910)

Peter Larsen, "Theodore Roosevelt and the Moroccan Crisis, 1904–1905," PhD dissertation, Princeton University, 1984

"Latest Aspects in the Panama Affair," *Harper's Weekly* 47 (November 28, 1903), 1892–93

J. Laurence Laughlin, "Some Recollections of Henry Adams," *Scribner's Magazine* 69:5 (May 1921), 576–85

Margaret Leech, *In the Days of McKinley* (1959)

————, *Reveille in Washington, 1860–1865* (1941)

———— and Harry J. Brown, *The Garfield Orbit* (1978)

William Leuchtenberg, "The Needless War with Spain," *American Heritage* 8 (February 1957), 32–41, 95

————, "Progressivism and Imperialism: The Progressive Movement and American Foreign Policy, 1898–1916," *Mississippi Valley Historical Review* 39 (December 1952), 483–504

J. C. Levenson, et al., *The Letters of Henry Adams*, 6 vols. (1982–88)

E. H. Lightner, "A Glimpse of Some Washington Homes," *Harper's New Monthly Magazine* 70 (March 1885), 520–33

Seward W. Livermore, "Theodore Roosevelt, the American Navy, and the Venezuelan Crisis of 1902–1903," *American Historical Review* 51 (April 1946), 452–71

Henry Cabot Lodge, "England, Venezuela, and the Monroe Doctrine," *North American Review* 463 (June 1895), 651–58

————, *Early Memories* (1913)

————, "Our Blundering Foreign Policy," *Forum* 19 (March 1895), 8–17

————, *Speeches and Addresses, 1884–1909* (1909)

Mrs. John A. Logan, "A Day of the President's Life," *Frank Leslie's Popular Monthly* 48 (August 1899), 339–43

Edward Longacre, "Damnable Dan Sickles," *Civil War Times Illustrated* 22 (May 1984), 16–25

Joseph P. Lovering, *S. Weir Mitchell* (1971)

Maurice Low, "An Unwritten Chapter in American Diplomacy," *McClure's* 15 (July 1900), 255–61

————, "Washington: City of Leisure," *Atlantic Monthly* 86 (December 1900), 767–78

Sidney Low, "The Change in English Sentiment Toward the United States," *Forum* 26 (October 1898), 364–73

Arthur Lubow, *The Reporter Who Would Be King: A Biography of Richard Harding Davis* (1992)

Tom Lutz, *American Nervousness, 1903: An Anecdotal History* (1991)

John Major, "Who Wrote the Hay-Bunau-Varilla Convention?" *Diplomatic History* 8 (Spring 1984), 115–23

Isaac Marcosson, *Adventures in Interviewing* (1919)

———, *Before I Forget: A Pilgrimage to the Past* (1959)

Orison Swett Marden, ed., *Talks with Great Workers* (1901)

Frederick W. Marks III, *Velvet on Iron: The Diplomacy of Theodore Roosevelt* (1979)

Edward Sanford Martin, *The Life of Joseph Hodges Choate as Gathered Chiefly from His Letters*, 2 vols. (1920)

Joseph J. Mathews, *George W. Smalley: Forty Years a Foreign Correspondent* (1973)

———, "Informal Diplomacy in the Venezuelan Crisis of 1896," *Mississippi Valley Historical Review* 50 (September 1963), 195–212

Henry F. Mattox, *The Twilight of Amateur Diplomacy: The American Foreign Service and Its Senior Officers in the 1890s* (1989)

Ernest R. May, *American Imperialism* (1968)

———, *Imperial Democracy: The Emergence of America as a Great Power* (1961)

——— and John K. Fairbank, eds., *America's China Trade in Historical Perspective* (1986)

——— and James C. Thomson, Jr., eds., *American East-Asian Relations: A Survey* (1972)

Brian S. McBeth, *Gunboats, Corruption, and Claims: Foreign Intervention in Venezuela, 1899–1908* (2001)

Robert McClellan, *The Heathen Chinee. A Study of American Attitudes Toward China, 1890–1905* (1971)

Alexander K. McClure, *Abraham Lincoln and Men of War Time: Some Personal Recollections of War and Politics During the Lincoln Administration* (1892)

———, *Recollections of Half a Century* (1902)

Thomas J. McCormick, *China Market: America's Quest for Informal Empire, 1893–1901* (1967)

———, "Insular Imperialism and the Open Door: The China Market and the Spanish-American War," *Pacific Historical Review* 32 (May 1963), 155–69

David McCullough, *Mornings on Horseback* (1981)

———, *The Path Between the Seas: The Creation of the Panama Canal, 1870–1914* (1977)

Timothy G. McDonald, "McKinley and the Coming War with Spain," *Midwest Quarterly* 7 (April 1966), 225–39

Henry Macfarland, "Secretary John Hay," *Review of Reviews* 21 (January 1900), 33–41

William S. McFeely, *Grant: A Biography* (1981)

Delber L. McKee, *Chinese Exclusion versus the Open Door Policy, 1900–1906: Clashes Over China Policy in the Roosevelt Era* (1977)

William McKinley, *Speeches and Addresses of William McKinley* (1900)

David C. Mearns, *The Lincoln Papers: The Story of the Collection*, Vol. 1 (1948)

Richard Megargee, "The Diplomacy of John Bassett Moore: Realism in American Foreign Policy," PhD dissertation, Northwestern University, 1963

George F. Mellen, "John Hay—Littérateur," *Methodist Review* 101 (July 1918), 547–56

Memorial Addresses Delivered Before the Two Houses of Congress on the Life and Character of Abraham Lincoln, James A. Garfield, William McKinley (1903)

Earl S. Miers, et al., eds., *Lincoln Day by Day: A Chronology 1809–1865* (1960, reprint 1991)

Candace Millard, *Destiny of the Republic: A Tale of Madness, Medicine, and the Murder of a President* (2011)

Hope Ridings Miller, *Embassy Row: The Life and Times of Diplomatic Washington* (1969)

Scott Miller, *The President and the Assassin: McKinley, Terror, and Empire at the Dawn of the American Century* (2011)

Stuart Creighton Miller, *"Benevolent Assimilation": The American Conquest of the Philippines, 1899–1903* (1982)

Walter Millis, *The Martial Spirit: A Study of Our War with Spain* (1931)

Dwight Carroll Miner, *The Fight for the Panama Route* (1940)

Martha Mitchell, *Encyclopedia Brunonia* (1993)

Nancy Mitchell, "The Height of the German Challenge: The Venezuela Blockade, 1902–3," *Diplomatic History* 20 (1996), 185–209

S. Weir Mitchell, *Fat and Blood and How to Make Them* (1885, reprint 2004)

———, *Nurse and Patient, and Camp Cure* (1877)

George Monteiro, *Henry James and John Hay: The Record of a Friendship* (1965)

———, "John Hay as Reporter: Special Correspondence on the Great Chicago Fire," *Books at Brown* 22 (1968), 81–94

———, "John Hay's Short Fiction," *Studies in Short Fiction* 7 (Fall 1971), 543–52

———, "A Note on the Mark Twain–Whitelaw Reid Relationship," *Emerson Society Quarterly* 19 (2nd quarter, 1960), 20–21

———, "William Dean Howells and *The Breadwinners*," *Studies in Bibliography* 15 (1962), 267–68

———, ed., "John Hay and the Union Generals," *Journal of the Illinois State Historical Society* 69 (1976), 46–66

————, ed., "John Hay's Lyceum Lectures," *Western Illinois Regional Studies* 9 (Spring 1986), 48–58

———— and Brenda Murphy, eds., *John Hay–Howells Letters: The Correspondence of John Milton Hay and William Dean Howells, 1861–1905* (1980)

Charles Moore, "The Restoration of the White House," *Century* 65 (April 1903), 807–31

John Bassett Moore, *American Diplomacy: Its Spirit and Achievements* (1905)

————, "The Interoceanic Canal and the Hay-Pauncefote Treaty," *New York Times*, March 4, 1900

————, "John Hay," *Political Science Quarterly* 32 (March 1917), 119–25

————, "Mr. Hay's Work in Diplomacy," *Review of Reviews* 32 (August 1905), 171–76

Joseph West Moore, *Picturesque Washington* (1884)

Rayburn S. Moore, *Constance Fenimore Woolson* (1963)

Charles W. Moores, "John Hay, the Making of a Great Diplomat," *Putnam's* 6 (June 1909), 297–308

H. Wayne Morgan, *America's Road to Empire: The War with Spain and Overseas Expansion* (1965)

————, "The De Lôme Letter: A New Appraisal," *Historian* 26 (November 1963), 36–49

————, *From Hayes to McKinley: National Party Politics, 1877–1896* (1969)

————, "Governor McKinley's Misfortune: The Walker-McKinley Fund of 1893," *Ohio Historical Quarterly* 69 (April 1960), 103–20

————, *William McKinley and His America* (1963, reprint 2003)

————, "William McKinley and the Tariff," *Ohio History* 74 (Autumn 1965), 215–31

Elting E. Morison, et al., eds., *The Letters of Theodore Roosevelt*, 8 vols. (1951–54)

Edmund Morris, "'A Few Pregnant Days': Theodore Roosevelt and the Venezuelan Crisis of 1902," *Theodore Roosevelt Association Journal* 15 (Winter 1989), 2–13

————, "'A Matter of Extreme Urgency': Theodore Roosevelt, Wilhelm II, and the Venezuela Crisis of 1902," *Naval War College Review* 55 (Spring 2002), 73–85

————, *The Rise of Theodore Roosevelt* (1979)

————, *Theodore Rex* (2001)

Roy Morris, Jr., *Fraud of the Century: Rutherford B. Hayes, Samuel Tilden, and the Stolen Election of 1876* (2003)

T. Bentley Mott, *Myron T. Herrick, Friend of France: An Autobiographical Biography* (1929)

Charles Merrill Mount, *John Singer Sargent* (1957)

Robert B. Mowat, *The Diplomatic Relations of Great Britain and the United States* (1925)

————, *The Life of Lord Pauncefote, First Ambassador to the United States* (1929)

Brian Moynahan, *The French Century: An Illustrated History of Modern France* (2007)

"The Muffin-Getters," *Life* 3 (January 10, 1884), 20–21

Richard B. Mulanax, *The Boer War in American Politics and Diplomacy* (1994)

John A. Munro, *The Alaska Boundary Dispute* (1970)

Brenda Murphy and George Monteiro, "The Unpublished Letters of Bret Harte and John Hay," *American Literary Realism* 12, 77–110

Ivan Musicant, *Empire by Default: The Spanish-American War and the Dawn of the American Century* (1998)

David Saville Muzzey, *James G. Blaine: A Political Idol of Other Days* (1934)

David Nasaw, *Andrew Carnegie* (2006)

Mark E. Neely, Jr., *The Abraham Lincoln Encyclopedia* (1982)

————, "John G. Nicolay and John Hay," in *American Historians, 1866–1912, Dictionary of Literary Biography* 47 (1986), 196–202

Allan Nevins, *Grover Cleveland: A Study in Courage* (1932)

————, *Henry White: Thirty Years of American Diplomacy* (1930)

————, *John D. Rockefeller: The Heroic Age of American Enterprise*, 2 vols. (1940)

"The New Life of Abraham Lincoln," *Scribner's Monthly* 4 (August 1872), 506–10

"The New United States Ambassador," *Spectator* (London) 78 (February 27, 1897), 298

Jeannette P. Nichols, "The Monetary Problems of William McKinley," *Ohio History* 72 (October 1963), 263–92

Joe Nickell, "Lincoln's Bixby Letter: A Study in Authenticity," *Lincoln Herald* 91 (Winter 1989), 135–40

Helen Nicolay, "The Education of an Historian," *Abraham Lincoln Quarterly* 3 (September 1944) 107–37

————, *Lincoln's Secretary* (1949)

————, *Our Capital on the Potomac* (1924)

————, *Personal Traits of Abraham Lincoln* (1912, reprint 2006)

John G. Nicolay, "Lincoln's Gettysburg Address," *Century* 47 (February 1894), 596–608

————, *Lincoln's Secretary Goes West: Two Reports by John G. Nicolay on Frontier Indian Troubles, 1862* (1965)

———— and John Hay, *Abraham Lincoln: A History*, 10 vols. (1890)

———— and John Hay, *Abraham Lincoln: Complete Works, Comprising His Speeches, Letters, State Papers, and Miscellaneous Writings*, 2 vols. (1894)

Frank Ninkovich, *The United States and Imperialism* (2001)

Alex Nissen, *Bret Harte: Prince and Pauper* (2000)

Thomas J. Noer, *Briton, Boer, and Yankee: The United States and South Africa, 1870–1914* (1978)

Sheldon Novick, *Henry James: The Mature Master* (2007)

———, *Henry James: The Young Master* (1996)

William H. Nulty, *Confederate Florida: The Road to Olustee* (1990)

Jeffrey Karl Ochsner, *H. H. Richardson: Complete Architectural Works* (1982)

John L. Offner, "President McKinley's Final Attempt to Avoid War with Spain," *Ohio History* 94 (Summer–Autumn 1985), 125–38

———, *An Unwanted War: The Diplomacy of the United States and Spain Over Cuba, 1895–1898* (1992)

Charles S. Olcott, *The Life of William McKinley*, 2 vols. (1916)

Stanley Olson, *John Singer Sargent* (1986)

"The Open Door in China," *Independent* 52 (January 11, 1900), 139–41

Patricia O'Toole, *The Five of Hearts: An Intimate Portrait of Henry Adams and His Friends, 1880–1918* (1990)

"Our New Ambassador to England," *Critic* 30 (March 20, 1897), 197–98

"Our Place Among the Nations," *World's Work* 1:1 (November 1900), 47–54

Walter Hines Paige, "The War with Spain and After," *Atlantic Monthly* 81 (June 1898), 721–27

Albert Bigelow Paine, *Mark Twain: A Biography*, 3 vols. (1912)

Thomas Pakenham, *The Boer War* (1979)

Ernest N. Paolino, *The Foundations of the American Empire: William Henry Seward and U.S. Foreign Policy* (1973)

Vernon Louis Parrington, *An Interpretation of American Literature from the Beginnings to 1920*, 3 vols. (1927), Vol. 3: *The Beginnings of Critical Realism in America, 1860–1920*

Edward B. Parsons, "The German-American Crisis of 1902–1903," *Historian* 33 (May 1971), 436–52

Julia Parsons, *Scattered Memories* (1938)

John Patterson, "Latin-American Reactions to the Panama Revolution of 1903," *Hispanic American Historical Review* 24 (November 1944), 342–51

Roger H. Pearl, "The Shiftless Belligerent Pike: An Early Western Emigrant Type as Described by Clarence King," *California Historical Society Quarterly* 38 (June 1959), 113–29

Stephen D. Peet, *The Ashtabula Disaster* (1877)

Clyde Peirce, *The Roosevelt Panama Libel Cases: A Factual Study of a Controversial Episode in the Career of Teddy Roosevelt, Father of the Panama Canal* (1959)

Norman Pellington, *The Alaska Boundary Dispute: A Critical Reappraisal* (1972)

T. Edgar Pemberton, *The Life of Bret Harte* (1903)

Thomas F. Pendel, *Thirty-Six Years in the White House* (1902)

W. L. Penfield, "Anglo-German Intervention in Venezuela," *North American Review* 177 (July 1903), 86–96

Gary Alvin Pennanen, "The Foreign Policy of William Maxwell Evarts," PhD dissertation, University of Wisconsin, 1969

Ion H. Perdicaris, "In Raisuli's Hands: The Story of My Captivity and Deliverance, May 18 to June 26, 1904," *Leslie's Monthly* 58 (September 1904), 510–22

———, "Morocco, 'The Land of the Extreme West,' and the Story of My Captivity," *National Geographic* 17 (March 1906), 117–57

Bradford Perkins, *The Great Rapprochement: England and the United States, 1895–1914* (1968)

Dexter Perkins, *A History of the Monroe Doctrine* (1941, reprint 1955)

Merrill D. Peterson, *Lincoln in American Memory* (1994)

Kevin Phillips, *William McKinley* (2003)

Peter Pierson, *The History of Spain* (1999)

"The Pike in Literature," *Scribner's Monthly* 2 (August 1871), 430–32

Edgcumb Pinchon, *Dan Sickles: Hero of Gettysburg and "Yankee King of Spain"* (1945)

Matthew Pinsker, *Lincoln's Sanctuary: Abraham Lincoln and the Soldiers' Home* (2003)

D. M. Platt, "The Allied Coercion of Venezuela, 1902–1903: A Reassessment," *Inter-American Economic Affairs* 15 (Spring 1962), 3–28

David M. Pletcher, *The Diplomacy of Involvement: American Economic Expansion Across the Pacific, 1784–1900* (2001)

Alain Plessis, *The Rise and Fall of the Second Empire, 1852–1871* (1985)

Elmer Plischke, *United States Diplomats and Their Missions: A Profile of American Diplomatic Emissaries Since 1778* (1975)

Harry E. Pratt, "Lincoln Literature," *Illinois Libraries* 24 (January 1942), 34–37

——— and Ernest E. East, "Mrs. Lincoln Refurbished the White House," *Lincoln Herald* 47 (February 1945), 13–22

Julius W. Pratt, "American Business and the Spanish-American War," *Hispanic American Historical Review* 14 (1934), 163–201

———, "The 'Large Policy' of 1898," *Mississippi Valley Historical Review* 19 (September 1932), 219–42

Harvey Pressman, "Hay, Rockhill, and China's Integrity: A Reappraisal," *Harvard University Center for East Asian Studies Papers on China* 13 (December 1959), 61–79

Diana Preston, *The Boxer Rebellion: The Dramatic Story of China's War on Foreigners That Shook the World in the Summer of 1900* (2000)

W. W. Price, "President McKinley's Tours," *Cosmopolitan* 34 (February 1903), 383–92

Henry F. Pringle, *Theodore Roosevelt: A Biography* (1931)

Proceedings of the Memorial Meeting of the Citizens of Cleveland Held in the Chamber of Commerce Auditorium, July 5, 1905, in Honor of the Late Secretary of State, John Hay (1905)

John R. Procter, "Isolation or Imperialism," *Forum* 26 (September 1898), 14–26

Stephen J. Randall, *Colombia and the United States: Hegemony and Independence* (1992)

Eric Rauchway, *Murdering McKinley: The Making of Theodore Roosevelt's America* (2003)

Julia Raymond, *Recollections of Euclid Avenue* (1936)

Thomas C. Reeves, *Gentleman Boss: The Life of Chester Alan Arthur* (1975)

Whitelaw Reid, *After the War: A Southern Tour, May 1, 1865 to May 1, 1866* (1866)

Report of the Joint Committee Concerning the Ashtabula Bridge Disaster (1877)

Bertha A. Reuter, *Anglo-American Relations During the Spanish-American War* (1924)

James Ford Rhodes, *The McKinley and Roosevelt Administrations, 1897–1909* (1922)

Serge Ricard, "The Anglo-American Intervention in Venezuela and Theodore Roosevelt's Ultimatum to the Kaiser: Taking a Fresh Look at an Old Regime," in Serge Ricard and Helene Christol, eds., *Anglo-Saxonism in Foreign Policy: The Diplomacy of Imperialism, 1899–1919* (1991)

Anna Ridgley, "A Girl in the Sixties: Excerpts from the Journal of Anna Ridgley," *Journal of the Illinois State Historical Society* 22 (October 1929), 401–46

Ronald D. Rietveld, "The Lincoln White House Community," *Journal of the Abraham Lincoln Association* 20 (Summer 1999), 17–48

Corrine Roosevelt Robinson, *My Brother Theodore Roosevelt* (1921)

William Woodville Rockhill, "The United States and the Future of China," *Forum* 29 (May 1900), 324–31

Theodore Roosevelt, *An Autobiography* (1920)

———, "How the United States Acquired the Right to Dig the Panama Canal," *Outlook* 99 (October 7, 1911), 314–18

———, "What Americanism Means," *Forum* 17 (April 1894), 196–206

———, "W. R. Thayer's 'Life of John Hay,'" *Harvard Graduates' Magazine* 24 (December 1915), 255–58

Elihu Root, "Address by Elihu Root at the Dedication of the John Hay Library, Brown University, November 11, 1910," pamphlet, Brown University, 1910

William Ganson Rose, *Cleveland: The Making of a City* (1950)

Charles E. Rosenberg, *The Trial of the Assassin Guiteau: Psychiatry and Law in the Gilded Age* (1968)

William Howard Russell, *My Diary North and South* (1988)

Ira Rutgow, *James A. Garfield* (2006)

William Ryan and Desmond Guinness, *The White House: An Architectural History* (1980)

George Herbert Ryden, *The Foreign Policy of the United States in Relation to Samoa* (1928)

Homer Saint-Gaudens, ed., *The Reminiscences of Augustus Saint-Gaudens*, 2 vols. (1913)

Lady St. Helier (Mary Jeune), *Memories of Fifty Years* (1909)

Ernest Samuels, *Henry Adams: The Major Phase* (1964)

——, *Henry Adams: The Middle Years* (1958)

——, "Henry Adams and the Gossip Mills," in Max F. Schultz, ed., *Essays in American and English Literature Presented to Bruce McElderry, Jr.* (1968), 59–75

Martha A. Sandweiss, *Passing Strange: A Gilded Age Tale of Love and Deception Across the Color Line* (2009)

"A New American Novelist," *Saturday Review* (London) 57 (February 2, 1884), 154–55

Gary Scharnhorst, *Bret Harte* (1992)

Clara Eve Schieber, *The Transformation of American Sentiment Toward Germany, 1870–1914* (1923, reprint 1973)

Philip E. Schoenberg, "The American Reaction to the Kishinev Pogrom of 1903," *American Jewish Historical Quarterly* 63 (March 1974), 266–83

Thomas Schoonover, "Max Farrand's Memorandum on the U.S. Role in the Panamanian Revolution of 1903," *Diplomatic History* 12 (Fall 1988), 501–06

Thomas F. Schwartz, ed., "'I have never had any doubt of your good intentions': William Henry Herndon and Ward Hill Lamon as Described in Correspondence from the Robert T. Lincoln Letterpress Volumes," *Journal of the Abraham Lincoln Association* 14 (Winter 1993), 35–54

William Seale, "The Design of Lafayette Park," *White House History* 2 (June 1997), 6–19

——, *The President's House: A History*, 2 vols. (1986)

——, *The White House: The History of an American Idea* (1992)

Lorenzo Sears, *John Hay: Author and Statesman* (1914)

Louis Martin Sears, "Bret Harte as Consul," *Mark Twain Journal* 9 (Summer 1954), 17–24

——, "John Hay in London, 1897–1898," *Ohio State Archaeological and Historical Quarterly* 65 (October 1956), 356–75

Stephen W. Sears, *George B. McClellan: The Young Napoleon* (1988)

"Secretary Hay and the Open Door," *Independent* 52 (April 5, 1900), 841–42

"Secretary Hay and the 'Open Door' in China," *Literary Digest* 20 (April 7, 1900), 415–16

Selections from the Correspondence of Theodore Roosevelt and Henry Cabot Lodge, 1884–1918 (1925)

Robert Shackleton, *The Book of Washington* (1922)

Joshua Wolf Shenk, *Lincoln's Melancholy: How Depression Challenged a President and Fueled His Greatness* (2005)

Anne Hummel Sherrill, "John Hay: Shield of Union," PhD dissertation, University of California, Berkeley, 1966

Lester B. Shippee, "Germany and the Spanish-American War," *American Historical Review* 30 (July 1925), 754–77

John Y. Simon, "Abraham Lincoln and Ann Rutledge," *Journal of the Abraham Lincoln Association* 11 (1990), 13–33

Katherine Simonds, "The Tragedy of Mrs. Henry Adams," *New England Quarterly* 9 (December 1936), 564–82

Isidore Singer, *Russia at the Bar of the American People: A Memorial of Kishinev* (1904)

Esther Singleton, *The Story of the White House*, 2 vols. (1907)

"Sketch of the Life of Charles T. Sherman," pamphlet, 1886

Andrew L. Slap, *The Doom of Reconstruction: The Liberal Republicans in the Civil War Era* (2006)

David E. E. Sloane, "Censoring for *The Century Magazine*: R. W. Gilder to John Hay on *The Bread-Winners*, 1882–1884," *American Literary Realism* 4 (Summer 1971), 255–67

———, "John Hay (1838–1905)," *American Literary Realism* 3 (Spring 1970), 178–88

———, "John Hay's *The Bread-Winners* as Literary Realism," *American Literary Realism* 2:3 (Fall 1969), 276–79

George W. Smalley, *Anglo-American Memories* (1911)

Charles Emory Smith, "McKinley in the Cabinet Room," *Saturday Evening Post* 175 (August 30, 1902), 1–2

Hal H. Smith, "Historic Washington Homes," *Records of the Columbian Historical Society* 11 (1908), 243–67

Henry Nash Smith and William M. Gibson, eds., *Mark Twain-Howells Letters: The Correspondence of Samuel L. Clemens and William D. Howells, 1872–1910*, 2 vols. (1960)

Herbert F. Smith, *Richard Watson Gilder* (1970)

Theodore Clarke Smith, *The Life and Letters of James Abram Garfield*, 2 vols. (1925)

Robert Sobel, *Panic on Wall Street: A Classic History of America's Financial Disasters* (1968, rev. 1988)

Walter Stahr, *Seward: Lincoln's Indispensable Man* (2012)

Peter W. Stanley, "The Making of an American Sinologist: William W. Rockhill and the Open Door," *Perspectives in American History* 11 (1977–78), 419–60

Theodore Stanton, "Abraham Lincoln," *Westminster Review* 135:6 (June 1891), 635–47; *Westminster Review* 136:1 (July 1891), 1–13; *Westminster Review* 136:2 (August 1891), 124–31; *Westminster Review* 136:3 (September 1891), 255–67

P. J. Staudenraus, ed., *Mr. Lincoln's Washington: Selections from the Writings of Noah Brooks, Civil War Correspondent* (1967)

Douglas W. Steeples and David O. Whitten, *Democracy in Desperation: The Depression of 1893* (1998)

Zara S. Steiner, *The Foreign Office and Foreign Policy, 1898–1914* (1969)

James D. Stevenson, Jr., and Randehl K. Stevenson, "John Milton Hay's Literary Influence," *Journal of the Illinois State Historical Society* 99 (Spring–Summer 2006), 19–27

David O. Stewart, *Impeached: The Trial of President Andrew Johnson and Fight for Lincoln's Legacy* (2009)

William O. Stoddard, *Abraham Lincoln: The True Story of a Great Life* (1884)

———, *Inside the White House: Memoirs and Reports of Lincoln's Secretary* (Michael Burlingame, ed., 2000)

William O. Stoddard, Jr., *Lincoln's Third Secretary: The Memoirs of William O. Stoddard* (1955)

William L. Stone, "John Hay," *The Shield; A Magazine Published Quarterly in the Interests of Theta Delta Chi* 6 (December 1890), 287–302

———, "John Hay, 1858," in Robert Perkins Brown, et al., eds., *Memories of Brown: Traditions and Recollections Gathered from Many Sources* (1909), 151–55

The Story of Panama: Hearings on the Rainey Resolution Before the Committee on Foreign Affairs of the House of Representatives (1913)

David O. Stowell, *Streets, Railroads, and the Great Strike of 1877* (1999)

John St. Loe Strachey, *The Adventure of Living: A Subjective Autobiography* (1922)

Oscar S. Straus, *The American Spirit* (1913)

———, *Under Four Administrations: From Cleveland to Taft* (1922)

Graham A. Stuart, *The Department of State: A History of Its Organization, Procedures and Personnel* (1949)

Mark Wahlgren Summers, *The Era of Good Stealings* (1993)

———, *Rum, Romanism, and Rebellion: The Making of a President, 1884* (2000)

W. A. Swanberg, *Sickles the Incredible* (1956)

Chester C. Tan, *The Boxer Catastrophe* (1958)

Charles C. Tansill, *Canadian-American Relations, 1875–1911* (1943)

————, *The Purchase of the Danish West Indies* (1932)

Ida Tarbell, "President McKinley in War Times," *McClure's* 11 (July 1898), 208–24

Arlene Boucher Tehan, *Henry Adams in Love: The Pursuit of Elizabeth Sherman Cameron* (1983)

Wayne C. Temple, "Charles Henry Philbrick: Private Secretary to President Lincoln," *Lincoln Herald* 99 (Spring 1997), 6–11

———— and Justin G. Turner, "Lincoln's 'Castine': Noah Brooks," *Lincoln Herald* 72 (Fall 1970), 113–24

Tom E. Terrill, *The Tariff, Politics, and American Foreign Policy, 1874–1901* (1973)

William Roscoe Thayer, "John Hay and the Panama Republic," *Harper's Magazine* 131 (July 1915), 165–75

————, "John Hay's Good Deed in a Naughty World," *Saturday Evening Post* 191 (August 24, 1918), 21–24

————, *The Life and Letters of John Hay*, 2 vols. (1915)

Benjamin F. Thomas, *Portrait for Posterity: Lincoln and His Biographers* (1947)

Evan Thomas, *The War Lovers: Roosevelt, Lodge, Hearst, and the Rush to Empire, 1898* (2010)

James C. Thomson, Peter W. Stanley, and John Curtis Perry, *Sentimental Imperialists: The American Experience in East Asia* (1981)

Ward Thoron, ed., *The Letters of Mrs. Henry Adams* (1936)

Caroline Ticknor, *Poe's Helen* (1916)

————, ed., *A Poet in Exile: Early Letters of John Hay* (1910)

Clint Clay Tilton, "Lincoln and Lamon: Partners and Friends," *Transactions of the Illinois State Historical Society for the Year 1931* (1931), 175–228

E. Berkeley Tompkins, *Anti-Imperialism in the United States: The Great Debate, 1890–1920* (1970)

Eugene P. Trani, *The Treaty of Portsmouth: An Adventure in American Diplomacy* (1969)

David F. Trask, *The War with Spain in 1898* (1981)

Hans L. Trefousse, *Rutherford B. Hayes* (2002)

Barbara Tuchman, " 'Perdicaris Alive or Raisuli Dead,' " *American Heritage* 10 (1959), 18–21, 98–101

Richard W. Turk, "The United States Navy and the 'Taking' of Panama, 1901–1903," *Military Affairs* 38 (October 1974), 92–96

Mark Twain, "My Boyhood Dreams," *McClure's* 14 (January 1900), 286–90

————, "To the Person Sitting in Darkness," *North American Review* 172 (February 1901), 161–76

R. W. Van Alstyne, *The Rising American Empire* (1960)

Mariana Griswold Van Rensselaer, *Henry Hobson Richardson and His Works* (1888, reprint 1969)

David T. Van Tassel, ed., *The Dictionary of Cleveland Biography* (1996)

Charles Vandersee, "The Great Literary Mystery of the Gilded Age," *American Literary Realism* 7 (Summer 1974), 244–72

Paul A. Varg, *The Making of a Myth: The United States and China 1897–1912* (1968)

——, *Missionaries, Chinese, and Diplomats: The American Protestant Missionary Movement in China, 1890–1952* (1958)

——, *Open Door Diplomat: The Life of W. W. Rockhill* (1952)

——, "William Woodville Rockhill and the Open Door Notes," *Journal of Modern History* 24 (December 1952), 375–80

Anne Cipriano Venzon, "Gunboat Diplomacy in the Med," *U.S. Naval Institute Proceedings* 111, supplement (March 1985), 26–31

Harold G. Villard and Oswald Garrison Villard, *Lincoln on the Eve of '61: A Journalist's Story by Henry Villard* (1941)

Henry Villard, *Memoirs of Henry Villard, Journalist and Financier, 1835–1900*, 2 vols. (1904)

James F. Vivian, "The Taking of the Panama Canal Zone: Myth and Reality," *Diplomatic History* 4 (Winter 1980), 95–100

David Walder, *The Short Victorious War: The Russo-Japanese Conflict, 1904–1905* (1973)

Charles Waldstein, "The English-Speaking Brotherhood," *North American Review* 501 (August 1898), 223–38

Richard Walter, *S. Weir Mitchell, M.D.—Neurologist: A Medical Biography* (1970)

John Carl Warnecke and Associates, *Historical Survey of Lafayette Square* (1963)

Dennis Warner and Peggy Warner, *The Tide at Sunrise: A History of the Russo-Japanese War, 1904–1905* (1975)

Charles G. Washburne, ed., "Memoir of Henry Cabot Lodge," *Proceedings of the Massachusetts Historical Society* (April 1925), 324–76

Henry Watterson, "A Live American Poet," *Louisville Courier-Journal*, May 9, 1871

Geoffrey Wawro, *The Franco-Prussian War: The German Conquest of France in 1870–1871* (2003)

Jesse W. Weik, *The Real Lincoln: A Portrait* (1922; reprint 2002, Michael Burlingame, ed.)

Bernard A. Weisberger, "The Strange Affair of the Taking of the Panama Canal," *American Heritage* 27 (October 1976), 6–11, 68–77

Richard E. Welch, Jr., *Response to Imperialism: The United States and the Philippine-American War, 1899–1902* (1979)

William Wellman, "John Hay: An American Gentleman," *Review of Reviews* 32 (August 1905), 166–76

Richard Hume Werking, *The Master Architects: Building the United States Foreign Service, 1890–1913* (1977)

Ernest James Wessen, "Campaign Lives of Abraham Lincoln, 1860: An Annotated Bibliography of the Biographies of Abraham Lincoln Issued During the Campaign Year," *Papers in Illinois History and Transactions for the Year 1937* (1938), 188–220

Henry Litchfield West, "The President's Recent Tour," *Forum* 31 (August 1901), 661–69

John Whitcomb and Claire Whitcomb, *Real Life at the White House: Two Hundred Years of Daily Life in America's Most Famous Residence* (2000)

Ronald C. White, Jr., *Lincoln's Greatest Speech: The Second Inaugural* (2002)

William Allen White, *The Autobiography of William Allen White* (1946)

———, "Hanna," *McClure's* 16 (November 1900), 57–64

———, *Masks in a Pageant* (1928)

William C. Widenor, *Henry Cabot Lodge and the Search for an American Foreign Policy* (1975)

Robert H. Wiebe, *The Search for Order, 1877–1920* (1967)

Thurman Wilkins, *Clarence King: A Biography* (1958, rev. 1988)

Mentor Williams, "Horace Greeley at Niagara Falls," *Inland Seas* 4:2 (1948), 96–100

Robert C. Williams, *Horace Greeley: Champion of American Freedom* (2006)

William Appleman Williams, "The Frontier Thesis and American Foreign Policy," *Pacific Historical Review* 24 (November 1955), 379–95

———, *The Tragedy of American Diplomacy* (1959, rev. 1962)

Garry Wills, *Henry Adams and the Making of America* (2005)

———, *Lincoln at Gettysburg: The Words That Remade America* (1992)

Douglas L. Wilson and Rodney O. Davis, eds., *Herndon's Informants: Letters, Interviews, and Statements About Abraham Lincoln* (1998)

James H. Wilson, "America's Interest in China," *North American Review* 495 (February 1898), 129–41

Robert Wilson, *The Explorer King: Adventure, Science, and the Great Diamond Hoax—Clarence King in the Old West* (2006)

Kenneth Wimmel, *Theodore Roosevelt and the Great White Fleet* (1998)

———, *William Woodville Rockhill: Scholar Diplomat of the Tibetan Highlands* (2003)

Joseph E. Wisan, *The Cuban Crisis as Reflected in the New York Press* (1934, reprint 1965)

Leon Wolf, *Little Brown Brother: How the United States Purchased and Pacified the Philippine Islands at the Century's Turn* (1961)

Simon Wolf, *The Presidents I Have Known from 1860–1918* (1918)

Gordon Wright, *France in Modern Times: From the Enlightenment to the Present* (1981)

John Russell Young, "John Hay, Secretary of State," *Munsey's* 20 (November 1898), 246–50

Marilyn B. Young, *The Rhetoric of Empire: American China Policy, 1895–1901* (1968)

Edward H. Zabriskie, *American-Russian Rivalry in the Far East: A Study in Diplomacy and Power Politics, 1895–1914* (1946)

Warren Zimmerman, *First Great Triumph: How Five Americans Made Their Country a World Power* (2002)

Index

Illustration Credits